This book provides the first rounded account of the new ruling elite of England in the century after 1066. It deals with the revolution in landholding by which the old English aristocracy was swept aside, and with the nature of aristocratic power, as demonstrated by the control of castles and knights, and lordship over men and land.

The book stresses the vitality of aristocratic power throughout the period, particularly during the civil war under King Stephen. The parts played by kinship and family in building up and extending influence are emphasized, and a separate chapter is devoted to the crucial role played by women in the transmission of land. The role of aristocratic benefactors in the wave of generosity which brought great wealth to the church is also examined and, finally, the extent to which the newcomers identified themselves with the country they had conquered.

# The aristocracy of Norman England

# The aristocracy of Norman England

Judith A. Green

*The Queen's University of Belfast*

**CAMBRIDGE**
UNIVERSITY PRESS

PUBLISHED BY THE PRESS SYNDICATE OF THE UNIVERSITY OF CAMBRIDGE
The Pitt Building, Trumpington Street, Cambridge CB2 1RP, United Kingdom

CAMBRIDGE UNIVERSITY PRESS
The Edinburgh Building, Cambridge, CB2 2RU United Kingdom
40 West 20th Street, New York, NY 10011–4211, USA
10 Stamford Road, Oakleigh, Melbourne 3166, Australia

First published 1997

Printed in the United Kingdom at the University Press, Cambridge

Typeset in 9.5/13.5 Swift

*A catalogue record for this book is available from the British Library*

*Library of Congress Cataloguing in Publication data*
Green, Judith A.
The aristocracy of Norman England / Judith A. Green.
    p.    cm.
Includes bibliographical references and index.
ISBN 0 521 33509 4
1. Great Britain – Politics and government – 1066–1154. 2. Aristocracy (Political science) – England – History. 3. Civilization, Medieval – 12th century. 4. Normans – England. 5. Eleventh century. I. Title.
DA195G74 1997
940.1 – dc20    96–43682 CIP
ISBN 0 521 33509 4 hardback

# Contents

# Illustrations

# Preface

When I began the research for this book several years ago, I had in mind the aim of reconstructing the lives of a ruling elite in the round. I had been stimulated by work on continental aristocracies in the high middle ages, and I also had the great pleasure of co-operating with an early modern and a late modern colleague (Martin Ingram and Peter Jupp) in designing and teaching a comparative course on aristocracies which ranged across centuries and across frontiers. Limitations of space and time together with the uneven survival or intractable nature of the sources have conspired to make the end product in front of you somewhat less ambitious in its aims and scope.

So, first of all, here is what this book does *not* try to cover. I have omitted any discussion of the Norman estates of these families which had them, because (as will be argued later) I believe that those with lands in England may be studied as a separate unit, albeit one closely linked in a number of ways both physical and psychological to a much wider diaspora of Normans. Domesday Book may be an invaluable source for the period 1066–86, but much that we should like to know about lands and their management for the later period, and about aristocratic income and expenditure throughout our period, remains obscure. I have also decided not to provide tables of Domesday wealth, because it is quite likely they will be superseded by computer-based analyses. It is also fair to say that, although lesser men and new men are included here, examples tend to be drawn mainly from the greater and middling families simply because of the nature of the surviving evidence. Nor do the great ecclesiastics figure as prominently as they would in an analysis of the whole elite which included both lay and clerical: churchmen figure here chiefly as beneficiaries of the wealth which streamed towards them from laymen. Kinship, marriage, and family are discussed here basically in terms of prudential considerations simply because we lack the private letters, diaries, and other sources which would have thrown more light on personal relationships (and which have so enlivened accounts of aristocracies in later centuries, such as those of Lawrence Stone, J. V. Beckett, and David

Cannadine). And throughout I have concentrated on the documentary rather than the literary evidence.

On the other hand much space has been devoted to what the sources can tell us something about. There is, for example, a very detailed chapter (chapter two) on the land settlement of the Norman conquerors based on the Domesday evidence, and another long chapter (chapter nine) on political relations between crown and aristocracy, since this is what the chronicles, charters, and other sources tell us much about. And where the sources can be squeezed to provide the basis for some reasonably solid hypotheses, something has been said about aristocratic getting and spending, about castles and halls, about the importance of the family and the relationship between the aristocracy and the church, and above all about aristocratic power – what it consisted of, how it was acquired, how it was exercised, and how far it changed in the period 1066–1166. This book may not be the rounded, warts-and-all portrait at first intended, but it *is* an attempt to get beyond the more narrowly based surveys of earlier times, and to integrate, in a way that has not been attempted before, the themes of land, politics, kinship, and religion. The result is a study of the character and power of an elite that will, I hope, compare with similar studies of other periods and other countries, even if the Normans' very success in replacing one landed elite with an almost totally new one was so comprehensive that comparisons with other landed elites is thereby impaired.

Place names are given wherever possible in their modern form and in their own language. As far as personal names are concerned, I have rendered the particle in French for French place names and in English for English or Welsh names; for example: Roger de Beaumont, Roger of Berkeley, Roger of Montgomery. Where there are common usages, however, such as William de Warenne (not Varenne), I have followed the usual form of the name. Domesday entries are to the Record Commission edition unless otherwise stated.

I should like in particular to thank The Queen's University of Belfast for granting me two periods of leave of absence, in 1985–6 and 1993–4, my colleagues in the School of Modern History for helping to provide cover for teaching, and the Inter-Library Loan service at Queen's. I should also like to thank the Leverhulme Foundation which funded leave between January and June 1994 and Dr Mark Philpott, who provided replacement teaching during that period. There are thanks to the children of the late Professor W. L. Warren and to the Administrator of Hedingham Castle for permission to reproduce photographs, and to many friends who have supplied help on specific points or sent me offprints, including James Campbell, David Crouch, Elizabeth Danbury, John Gillingham, Paul Harvey, Sandy Heslop, Katherine Keats-Rohan, Edmund King, Bruce O'Brien, Dorothy Owen, and Kathleen Thompson. William Davies of Cambridge University Press deserves special thanks for his patience in waiting for the book to arrive, and Janet Hall for her speed and efficiency as a copy-editor. To three scholars I owe an extra debt of thanks, David Bates, Marjorie Chibnall, and Jim Holt, who each read an earlier draft and offered extremely helpful and constructive comments: the responsibility for remaining errors is, of course, my own. Above all my greatest debt is to my husband Ian for his unhesitating support, sage counsel, and the unstinting gift of time to read successive drafts. The book is dedicated to my parents. My father took a great interest in the early stages of the project, and it is a particular sadness that he did not live to see the result.

June 1996

# Abbreviations

| | |
|---|---|
| ASC | *The Anglo-Saxon Chronicle, a Revised Translation*, ed. D. Whitelock, D. C. Douglas and S. I. Tucker (London, 1961) |
| CP | *Complete Peerage*, by G. E. C., revised edn. V. Gibbs, H. A. Doubleday, G. H. White, 13 vols. in 12 (London, 1910–59) |
| DB | *Domesday Book*, ed. A. Farley for Record Commission, 4 vols. (London, 1783–1816) |
| Dugdale, Mon. Ang. | W. Dugdale, *Monasticon Anglicanum*, new edn, 6 vols in 8 (London, 1817–30) |
| FW | Florence (John) of Worcester, *Chronicon ex Chronicis*, ed. B. Thorpe, 2 vols. (London, 1848, 1849) |
| Gesta Stephani | *Gesta Stephani*, ed. and trans. by K. R. Potter with a new introduction and notes by R. H. C. Davis (Oxford, 1976) |
| Glanvill | *The Treatise on the Laws and Customs of the Realm of England commonly called Glanvill*, ed. and trans. G. D. G. Hall, Oxford Medieval Texts, reprint (Oxford, 1993) |
| HH | Henry of Huntingdon, *Historia Anglorum*, ed. T. Arnold (RS, 1879) |
| JW | *The Chronicle of John of Worcester*, ed. J. R. H. Weaver, Anecdota Oxoniensia, Mediaeval and Modern Series, XIII (Oxford, 1908) |
| OV | Orderic Vitalis, *The Ecclesiastical History*, ed. M. Chibnall, 6 vols. (Oxford Medieval Texts, Oxford, 1969–80) |
| PR | *Pipe Roll* |
| RADN | *Recueil des actes des ducs de Normandie*, ed. M. Fauroux, Mémoires de la Société des Antiquaires de Normandie, XXXVI (Caen, 1961) |
| RBE | *Red Book of the Exchequer*, ed. H. Hall, 3 vols. RS (London, 1896) |
| RRAN | *Regesta Regum Anglo-Normannorum 1066–1154*, 4 vols., vol. I ed. H. W. C. Davis, vol. II ed. C. Johnson and H. A. Cronne, vols. III and IV ed. H. A. Cronne and R. H. C. Davis (Oxford, 1913–69) |

RS              Rolls Series
Round, *CDF*    *Calendar of Documents preserved in France, illustrative of the*
                *History of Great Britain and Ireland*, Vol. I, A. D. *918–1216*, ed.
                J. H. Round (London, 1899)
SD              Symeon of Durham
*VCH*           *Victoria History of the Counties of England*
WM              William of Malmesbury
WP              William of Poitiers, *Gesta Guillelmi*, ed. R. Foreville (Paris,
                1952)

# Introduction

The introduction of a new aristocracy was one of the most decisive changes arising from the Norman Conquest. Land was transferred on a massive scale to the newcomers, French became the language of the elite, and castles were built which, at the time both instrument and symbol of domination, are enduring reminders in today's landscape. It is also a popular, if usually mistaken, belief, that the ancestors of many English aristocratic families 'came over with the Conqueror'. Despite a plethora of works on the Conquest period, studies of individual families such as the Lacys or the Mowbrays, of particular periods, such as the reign of Henry I or Stephen, and of particular themes, such as the image of aristocracy, there is no single work devoted to the aristocracy of Norman England between 1066 and 1166.[1]

This perhaps surprising omission is partly to be explained by the selective preoccupations of historians during the past century. Much attention has been devoted, for instance, to a debate about feudalism. In this respect an agenda was set more than a century ago by J. H. Round, who argued that the Normans introduced a novel form of military tenure into England. The hypothesis was further developed by F. M. Stenton, whose influential Ford Lectures given in 1929, *The First Century of English Feudalism*, had as their focus feudal lordship, articulated through the lordships or honours of the great men.[2] Much ink has been spilt since over feudalism and military obligation in often arid debates about semantics.[3] In the process, however, much has been learned about the recruitment of

---

[1] W. E. Wightman, *The Lacy Family in England and Normandy 1066–1194* (Oxford, 1966); *Charters of the Honour of Mowbray 1107–1191*, ed. D. E. Greenway (hereafter *Mowbray Charters*), British Academy Records of Social and Economic History, New Series, I (London, 1972); C. A. Newman, *The Anglo-Norman Nobility in the Reign of Henry I. The Second Generation* (Philadelphia, 1988); D. Crouch, *The Image of Aristocracy in Britain 1000–1300* (London, 1992).

[2] J. H. Round, 'The Introduction of Knight Service into England', *English Historical Review*, 6 (1891), 417–23, 625–45; 7 (1892), 11–24, reprinted in *Feudal England*, reset edn (London, 1964), pp. 182–245; for a bibliography of Round's voluminous output see *Family Origins and Other Studies*, ed. W. Page (London, 1930), pp. xlix–lxxiv; F. M. Stenton, *The First Century of English Feudalism*, 2nd edn (Oxford, 1961).

[3] S. Reynolds, *Fiefs and Vassals* (Oxford, 1994), chapter 8 provides a lively recent introduction to the debate.

armies both before and after the Conquest. Among more recent contributors, Richard Abels has provided a realistic reconstruction of military
obligation and has dealt with the knotty problem of how obligation
assessed on land matched up to the need for professional warriors and
armies.[4] One of the key points of Round's argument, that of the novelty of
the Conqueror's quotas of military service, has been subjected to search-
ing reevaluation by John Gillingham and Sir James Holt.[5] More is also
understood about lordship in Normandy and the surrounding regions in
the eleventh century, and any idea that the Conqueror brought with him
to England feudalism of the kind found in twelfth-century England is
untenable.[6] Similarly the belief that enfeoffment on great honours was
undertaken primarily with a view to fulfilling the requirement of a royal
quota of knight service has been reassessed by Richard Mortimer.[7]

There has been a good deal of research, too, into the structure and
history of the great lordships. One invaluable work on the period is *English
Baronies* by I. J. Sanders, which aimed to identify all the major lordships,
and successive holders of them, between 1086 and 1327.[8] William Farrer
had earlier inaugurated a series of *Early Yorkshire Charters*, continued by Sir
Charles Clay, and this has provided a collection of charters with accompa-
nying discussions of the families concerned, as yet unmatched for any
other county.[9] In *Honors and Knights' Fees* Farrer also traced the descent of
the constituent parts of several major lordships and, in *Feudal
Cambridgeshire*, the descent of fees in a single county.[10] In this context the

---

[4] R. Abels, *Lordship and Military Obligation in Anglo-Saxon England* (Berkeley, Los Angeles, and London, 1988).

[5] J. Gillingham, 'The Introduction of Knight Service into England', *Proceedings of the Battle Conference on Anglo-Norman Studies*, 4 (1981), 53–64; J. C. Holt, 'The Introduction of Knight Service into England', *Anglo-Norman Studies*, 6 (1983), 89–106.

[6] D. Bates, *Normandy before 1066* (London, 1982), pp. 99–128; E. Z. Tabuteau, 'Definitions of Feudal Military Obligations in Eleventh-Century Normandy', in *On the Laws and Customs of England. Essays in Honour of S. E. Thorne*, ed. M. S. Arnold, T. A. Green, S. A. Scully, and S. D. White (Chapel Hill, 1981), 18–59; E. Z. Tabuteau, *Transfers of Property in Eleventh Century Norman Law* (Chapel Hill and London, 1988).

[7] R. Mortimer, 'Land and Service: the Tenants of the Honour of Clare', *Anglo-Norman Studies*, 8 (1985), 177–98.      [8] I. J. Sanders, *Feudal Baronies* (Oxford, 1960).

[9] *Early Yorkshire Charters*, I–III, ed. W. Farrer (Edinburgh, 1914–16); IV–XII, ed. C. T. Clay, Yorkshire Archaeological Society, Record Series, Extra Series, I–III, V–X, 1935–65. Extra Series vol. IV is Index to first three vols., C. T. Clay and E. M. Clay (eds.), 1942.

[10] W. Farrer, *Honors and Knights' Fees*, 3 vols. (London and Manchester, 1923–5); and *Feudal Cambridgeshire* (Cambridge, 1920).

work of Stenton and, later, that of D. C. Douglas in publishing charters and texts dealing with the period, must not be forgotten.[11]

Land law and inheritance have also been much discussed. Inspired by Stenton's view that the great honours of Norman England were autonomous, S. F. C. Milsom showed how these could have worked as self-regulating units of jurisdiction. He argued that Henry II's new legal procedures were not intended to undermine honorial justice, only to make it work more effectively, even if the consequences proved to be more far-reaching than was anticipated.[12] He also argued that the right to, as opposed to the expectation of, hereditary succession to land held by knight service took root only slowly. There has been a lively debate on the issue of inheritance, as clearly there was a gradual shift from practice to enforceable rights, and recent writing has tended to emphasize the strength rather than the insecurity of hereditary succession.[13]

The political history of Norman England and thus of its ruling elite has been the subject of a good deal of writing. The motives and identity of those who supported Rufus and Henry I as opposed to those who supported their elder brother Robert has been analysed, as has the manner in which Henry consolidated his hold in England after 1106.[14] Most of all, however, there has been sustained investigation of the complicated politics of King Stephen's reign, when the increasing volume of surviving charters makes it possible to reconstruct aims and alliances in greater detail than before. Round again was a pioneer here with *Geoffrey de Mandeville* (London, 1892), but his attempt to use the career of a single pro-

---

[11] Stenton's work on texts included *Documents Illustrative of the Social and Economic History of the Danelaw* (London, 1920); *Gilbertine Charters: Transcripts of Charters relating to the Gilbertine Houses of Sixle, Ormsby, Catley, Bullington and Alvingham*, Lincoln Record Society, XVIII (1922); *Free Peasants of the Northern Danelaw*; see also *William the Conqueror and the Rule of the Normans* (London, 1908); for Douglas see especially *Feudal Documents from the Abbey of Bury St Edmunds* (London, 1932); Douglas, *The Domesday Monachorum of Christ Church, Canterbury* (London, 1944).

[12] S. F. C. Milsom, *The Legal Framework of English Feudalism* (Cambridge, 1976).

[13] J. C. Holt, 'Politics and Property in Early Medieval England', *Past and Present*, 57 (1972), 3–52; 'Feudal Society and the Family in Early Medieval England', Presidential addresses to the Royal Historical Society, I, 'The Revolution of 1066', *Transactions of the Royal Historical Society*, 5th series, 32 (1982), 193–212; II, 'Notions of Patrimony', *ibid.*, 33 (1983), 193–220; III, 'Notions of Patrimony', *ibid.*, 34 (1984), 1–25; IV, 'The Heiress and the Alien', *ibid.*, 35 (1985), 1–28; J. Hudson, *Land, Law, and Lordship in Norman England* (Oxford, 1994).

[14] C. Warren Hollister, 'Magnates and "Curiales" in Early Norman England', 'The Anglo-Norman Civil War: 1101', 'Henry I and the Anglo-Norman Magnates', reprinted in *Monarchy, Magnates and Institutions in the Anglo-Norman World* (London, 1986).

tagonist as an exemplar of 'feudal anarchy' has not stood the test of time
(see below, pp. 291–2).

Other aspects of the aristocracy's history, however, have been relatively
little studied, especially kinship and the family. It is true that the study of
genealogy has proved attractive – Round, for instance, revelled in the fine
detail of genealogical descents, and the role of family in relation to feudalism has been discussed. An early contribution was made by Sidney
Painter, in a paper called 'The Family and the Feudal System'.[15] Then in a
series of presidential addresses to the Royal Historical Society between
1982 and 1985, Sir James Holt took the theme of feudal society and the
family much further, and discussed points of comparison between
Norman England and the continent.[16] He suggested that the Norman aristocracy was organizing itself into lineages even before 1066, and that the
Normans were already accustomed to the idea of handing on the patrimonial inheritance to one son, while permitting more latitude over the disposition of acquired lands; and he drew attention to the role of heiresses.
Prosopographical research, such as that by K. S. B Keats-Rohan, has also
highlighted the importance of kinship networks, and her studies are
adding to our knowledge of the continental origins of families which
settled in England.[17] There is as yet, however, no broadly conceived study
of aristocratic kinship and family for the whole Norman period.[18]

Kinship and lineage in contrast have been a major concern of historians
of continental aristocracies, and one of the motives for writing this book
was an attempt to provide a survey of Norman England to set alongside
work on the aristocracies of continental Europe.[19] One problem for histo-

---

[15] 'The Family and the Feudal System in Twelfth-Century England', *Speculum*, 35 (1960), 1–16; reprinted
in *Feudalism and Liberty*, ed. F. A. Cazel (Baltimore, 1961), pp. 195–219.

[16] Holt, 'Feudal Society and the Family in Early Medieval England'.

[17] K. S. B. Keats-Rohan, 'The Prosopography of Post-Conquest England', *Medieval Prosopography*, 14 (1993),
1–50; K. S. B. Keats-Rohan and D. E. Thornton, 'COEL (the Continental Origins of English Landholders)
and the Computer: towards a Prosopographical Key to Anglo-Norman documents, 1066–1166',
*Medieval Prosopogaphy*, 17 (1996), 223–62. The standard work on continental places of origin is L. C.
Loyd, *The Origins of Some Anglo-Norman Families*, ed. C. T. Clay and D. C. Douglas, Harleian Society, CIII
(Leeds, 1951).

[18] For the reign of Henry I see, however, Newman, *Anglo-Norman Nobility*, chapter 2.

[19] It is possible to give only a brief indication of a massive bibliography on this subject. On Germany key
figures were G. Tellenbach, *Königtum und Stämme in der Werdezeit des Deutschen Reiches* (Weimar, 1939);
Tellenbach, 'Vom Karolingischen Reichsadel zum Deutschen Reichsfürstenstand', *Adel und Bauern im
Deutschen Staat des Mittelalters*, ed. Theodor Mayer (Leipzig, 1943) (translated in *The Medieval Nobility:
Studies on the Ruling Classes of France and Germany from the Sixth to the Twelfth Century*, ed. T. Reuter

rians of continental aristocracies is how far noble families of the central middle ages were descended from those of the Carolingian era. Another is the timing of the reorganization of noble families into lineages associated with specific lordships and castles. Then there is the role of knights, their relationship with, and particularly their assimilation into, established noble families.[20] The chronological framework for historians of continental aristocracies is, of course, different, in that there is no climactic year of

(Amsterdam, 1978), pp. 39–49; this collection of essays remains an indispensable introduction to the subject); K. F. Werner, 'Bedeutende Adelsfamilien im Reich Karls des Grossen', *Karl der Grosse: Lebenswerk und Nachleben*, ed. H. Beumann, 4 vols. (Düsseldorf, 1965), I, 83–142, translated in *The Medieval Nobility* (ed. Reuter); K. Schmid, 'Zur Problematik von Familie, Sippe und Geschlecht, Haus und Dynastie beim Mittelalterlichen Adel', *Zeitung für die Geschichte des Oberrheins*, 105 (1957), 1–62; Schmid, 'Uber die Struktur des Adels im früheren Mittelalter', *Jahrbuch für fränkische Landesforschung*, 19 (1959), 1–23 (translated in *The Medieval Nobility*, ed. Reuter); and K. Leyser, 'The German Aristocracy from the Ninth to the Early Twelfth Century', *Past and Present*, 41 (1968) reprinted in *Medieval Germany and Its Neighbours, 900–1250* (London, 1982), pp. 161–89; see also J. B. Freed, 'Reflections on the Medieval German Nobility', *American Historical Review*, 91 (1986), 553–75. On France a study which broke new ground was P. Guilhermoz, *Essai sur l'origine de la noblesse en France au moyen age* (Paris, 1902); see also G. Duby, *La société au XIe et XIIe siècles dans la région mâconnaise* (Paris, 1953); Duby, *The Chivalrous Society*; R. Fossier, *La terre et les hommes en Picardie jusqu'au milieu du XIIIe siècle*, 2 vols. (Paris, 1968); O. Guillot, *Le comté d'Anjou et son entourage au XIe siècle* (Paris, 1972); G. Devailly, *Le Berry du Xe siècle au milieu du XIIIe siècle* (Paris, 1973); P. Bonassie, *La Catalogne, du milieu du Xe au fin du XIe siècle* (Paris, 1975); M. Bur, *La formation du comté de Champagne v. 950– v. 1150* (Nancy, 1977); J.-P. Poly, *La Provence et la société féodale (879–1166)* (Paris, 1976); M. Parisse, *Noblesse et chevalerie en Lorraine médiévale* (Nancy, 1982); A. Debord, *La société laïque dans les pays de la Charente Xe–XIe siècles* (Paris, 1984); D. Barthélemy, *Les deux âges de la seigneurie banale. Coucy (XIe–XIIIe siècles)* (Paris, 1984); Barthélemy, *La société dans le comté de Vendôme, de l'an mil au XIVe siècle* (Paris, 1993); L. Génicot, *L'économie namuroise au bas moyen age*. II. *Les hommes, la noblesse* (Louvain, 1960); E. Warlop, *The Flemish Nobility before 1300*, 4 vols. (Kortrijk, 1975–6); for surveys which take account of much of this writing, R. Fossier, *Enfance de l'Europe Xe–XIIe siècles*, 2 vols. (Paris, 1982); J.-P. Poly and E. Bournazel, *La mutation féodale, Xe–XIIe siècles*, translated by C. Higgitt with the title *The Feudal Transformation 900–1200* (New York and London, 1991); J. Martindale, 'The French Aristocracy in the Early Middle Ages: a Reappraisal', *Past and Present*, 75 (1977), 5–45; C. B. Bouchard, 'The Origins of the French Nobility: a Reassessment', *American Historical Review*, 86 (1981), 501–32; Bouchard, 'Family Structure and Family Consciousness among the Aristocracy in the Ninth to Eleventh centuries', *Francia*, 14 (1987), 39–58; for a critique of the view that there was a social revolution see D. Barthélemy, 'La mutation féodale a-t-elle eu lieu?', *Annales*, 47 (1992), 767–75; for a valuable review see T. N. Bisson, 'Nobility and Family in Medieval France: a Review Essay', *French Historical Studies*, 16 (1990), 597–613; for a further important contribution to the debate see Bisson, 'The "Feudal Revolution"', *Past and Present*, 142 (1994), 6–42.

[20] In addition to the works cited in the previous note, see also D. Barthélemy, 'Qu'est-ce que la chevalerie, en France aux Xe et XI siècles?', *Revue historique*, 290 (1993), 15–74; Barthélemy, 'Castles, Barons and Vavassors in the Vendômois and Neighboring Regions in the Eleventh and Twelfth Centuries', *Cultures of Power, Lordship, Status, and Process in Twelfth-Century Europe*, ed. T. N. Bisson (Philadelphia, 1995), pp. 56–68; and for a recent review of the subject see T. Evergates, 'Nobles and Knights in Twelfth-Century France', in the same volume; B. Arnold, *German Knighthood 1050–1300* (Oxford, 1985), pp. 69–75; B. Arnold, *Princes and Territories in Medieval Germany* (Cambridge, 1991); see also works cited below, p. 329n.

1066 to take into account, and the approach adopted has also been regional. Here one thinks of Duby's seminal work on the Mâconnais which prompted a whole series of studies of other French regions.[21]

Yet the studies of French regions provide valuable comparisons, not only between England and France, but also between Normandy and the surrounding regions, as David Bates pointed out in 1982. We need to understand fully the nature of the society from which the conquerors came in order to comprehend their success in England and their impact on social development. Were there special characteristics of Norman society which help to explain their success, as they themselves believed, and if so, what were those characteristics?[22] It used to be thought both that the aristocracy of early eleventh-century Normandy was 'new', in the sense that noble lineages can rarely be traced further back than the millennium, and that that society was permeated by feudalism and thus was especially well organized. However, David Bates in particular has drawn attention to similarities between the society of ducal Normandy and that of surrounding regions.[23]

Another relatively neglected topic is that of aristocratic women in Norman England. There are two recent studies of female religious, but relatively little hitherto has been written about the provision of land for women as wives, widows, and heiresses which makes full use of charter material.[24] Secondly, although much has been written about various aspects of the church in the Norman period, less has been said about the lay aristocracy's role overall as benefactors, despite the wealth of charter material.[25]

Moreover, additional collections of charters of individual magnate families have been published at intervals from the 1970s, and there is a case for attempting a broader survey which can identify common themes and experiences. Collections of the charters of the Mowbrays, the earls of

---

[21] See above, note 19.

[22] See especially R. H. C. Davis, *The Normans and their Myth* (London, 1976); and for a modern view of the Normans which stresses their special characteristics see R. Allen Brown, *The Normans*, 2nd edn (Woodbridge, 1994).

[23] D. C. Douglas, *William the Conqueror* (London, 1964), pp. 83–104; Bates, *Normandy before 1066*, pp. 238–48.

[24] S. K. Elkins, *Holy Women of Twelfth-Century England* (Chapel Hill, 1988); S. Thompson, *Women Religious* (Oxford, 1991).

[25] See however J. Burton, *Monastic and Religious Orders in Britain, 1000–1300* (Cambridge, 1994) which does look at benefactors.

Gloucester, and the Redvers have been published, and there are as yet unpublished theses on the Mandevilles, the Bigods, the Gants, the Ferrers, and on the family of Montgomery-Bellême.[26] Other scholars have produced studies of individual families based on charters, notably Wightman on the Lacy family, Crouch on the Beaumont twins, and English on the lords of Holderness, while Stringer's *Earl David of Huntingdon 1152–1219*, though its subject is somewhat late for this book, provides valuable insights into the different context in which aristocratic lordship operated by the later twelfth century.[27]

In sum, therefore, whole areas of the subject either have been neglected, or have been discussed only in the context of individual families, or for part of the period, not for the century as a whole. Yet the materials for writing the history of the aristocracy of Norman England are plentiful and, in one respect, the evidence of Domesday Book, unique. In Domesday Book we have a snapshot of the ruling elite at a particular moment in time, with an abundance of detail about their rural estates as yet still imperfectly analysed. In addition there are royal and private charters, narrative sources, the records of royal government, statements of law and custom, and the material remains of castles. In the remainder of this introduction a little more will be said by preliminary about the definition of aristocracy adopted, the timescale chosen, and the principal themes discussed.

The title of this book, the 'aristocracy' of Norman England, rather than the nobility, or the baronage, was chosen to reflect the particular combination of birth, wealth, and power found in England after 1066 which other terms fail to convey. Aristocracy was not a term which contemporaries would have used. Chroniclers writing in the period tended to

---

[26] *Mowbray Charters; Earldom of Gloucester Charters*, ed. R. B. Patterson (Oxford, 1973); *Charters of the Redvers Family and the Earldom of Devon 1090–1217*, ed. R. Bearman, Devon and Cornwall Record Society, new series, XXXVII (1994); A. Charlton, 'A Study of the Mandeville Family and its Estates', University of Reading PhD thesis, 1977; S. A. J. Atkin, 'The Bigod Family: an Investigation into their Lands and Activities, 1066-1306', Reading University PhD thesis, 1979; M. Abbott, 'The Gant Family in England, 1066-1191', Cambridge University PhD thesis 1973; P. E. Golob, 'The Ferrers Earls of Derby: A Study of the Honour of Tutbury', Cambridge University PhD thesis 1985; K. Thompson, 'The Cross-Channel Estates of the Montgomery-Bellême Family, c. 1050–1112', University of Wales MA thesis, 1983.

[27] Wightman, *Lacy Family*; D. Crouch, *The Beaumont Twins*, Cambridge Studies in Medieval Life and Thought, 4th series, I (Cambridge, 1986); B. English, *The Lords of Holderness 1086–1260* (Oxford, 1979); K. J. Stringer, *Earl David of Huntingdon 1152–1219* (Edinburgh, 1985).

call leading magnates *nobiles*, *proceres*, or *optimates*. They did not use these
terms in any precise legalistic sense, but as descriptions of men from
leading families. Orderic Vitalis, who of all chroniclers has most to say
about the aristocracy of Normandy and of England, uses the term *nobilis* of
the Grandmesnil family, of the Tosnys, the lords of Maule, and so on.[28]
Like other chroniclers, Orderic uses the term to convey distinction, sometimes as a personal quality, but often in the context of illustrious ancestry.
Although there is some doubt as to how 'old' the aristocracy of Normandy
was in the early eleventh century, clearly the greatest and most illustrious
families were deemed to be noble.

'Noble' is a term, however, that could have been applied to the upper
ranks only of those who form the subject of this book, because the conquest of England gave new opportunities for men of relatively undis-
tinguished origins to acquire great wealth. The term noble was
appropriate for men who were counts or sons of counts, but how appropriate was it for men whose fortunes had been transformed by the Conquest,
like Geoffrey de Mandeville, or Robert d'Oilly (for these men, see below,
pp. 37, 95)? For those with ability and luck, membership of a colonizing
elite obviously threw up opportunities for enrichment beyond their
wildest dreams, as Orderic himself commented: '[King William] made tri-
bunes and centurions from the lowest followers (*clientibus*) of the
Normans.'[29] One of the greatest success stories of the Conquest was that of
Roger Bigod (see below, pp. 84–5). A little can be discovered about his
origins: he came from a family with a certain amount of land in
Normandy, and may have owed his initial advancement to Odo bishop of
Bayeux. He was based in East Anglia, and benefited by being on the spot
during the redistribution of land that followed the revolt of Earl Ralph in
1075. By 1086 he was one of the greatest magnates in Norfolk, and in the
early twelfth century he was sheriff of both Norfolk and Suffolk. He
founded a priory at Thetford, and his son Hugh was later appointed to an
earldom. Even if his family had held more land in Normandy than we
know, clearly the Conquest had made him by modern standards a multi-
millionaire. What is hard to judge is how contemporaries viewed him.
Was he accepted as a social equal by others who had acquired much land
in England, particularly by those who were related to the ducal house of

[28] OV, ii, 74; iii, 126, 178.      [29] OV, ii, 260.

Normandy in some way, or by those whose ancestry was even more illustrious, perhaps as descendants of Charlemagne? We cannot assume, because Norman England was a melting pot of old and new, that social distinctions did not matter: they may indeed have mattered more.

The Conquest itself had thus elevated some men to unaccustomed wealth and power, and in a broader sense too there were growing opportunities for men to rise in the king's service, the powerful royal *ministri*, men 'raised from the dust' to use Orderic Vitalis's phrase.[30] These were the servants of burgeoning monarchical government, men from relatively humble backgrounds who as sheriffs and justices wielded great power and amassed great wealth. As agents of expanding princely governments they were a new phenomenon of the early twelfth century, and not unique to England. Comments were made not just about Henry I's new men, but also about the humble origins of those at the court of King Louis VI of France.[31] In Flanders there were tensions centring on the powerful but baseborn clan, the Erembalds, and these culminated in the murder of Count Charles the Good.[32] What was significant about Henry I's new men was not so much their origins, for these were often respectable if not distinguished: there is no indication that any were of unfree status like the *ministeriales* of Germany.[33] There is no indication that men like Geoffrey de Clinton or William de Pont de l'Arche (see below, pp. 262, 189–90) ever had a military role, and their rise was indicative of their indispensability as royal agents, administering the king's rights and collecting his revenues. The more successful new men were able to rise upwards, and undoubtedly they formed part of the ruling elite of England in the twelfth century.

Upward social mobility, through a career in royal government or by the pursuit of arms, conflicted at least in theory with the idea of an hereditary transmission of wealth and power. In practice, however, the upper

---

[30] OV, vi, 16.

[31] E. Bournazel, *Le gouvernement capétien au XIIe siècle, 1108–1180* (Limoges, 1975), pp. 65–6.

[32] Galbert of Bruges, *The Murder of Charles the Good Count of Flanders*, trs. J. B. Ross, reprint (New York, 1967), pp. 96 ff.

[33] The classic work on the *ministeriales* was that by K. Bosl, *Die Reichsministerialität der Salier und Staufer: Ein Betrag zur Geschichte des Hochsmittelalterlichen Deutschen Volkes, Staates und Reiches*, Schriften der Monumenta Germaniae Historica (Stuttgart, 1950–1); but see also J. B. Freed, 'The Origins of the European Nobility: the Problem of the Ministerials', *Viator*, 7 (1976), 211–41; B. Arnold, 'Instruments of Power: The Profile and Profession of *Ministeriales* within German Aristocratic Society, 1050–1225', *Cultures of Power, Lordship, Status, and Process in Twelfth-Century Europe*, ed. T. N. Bisson (Philadelphia, 1995), pp. 36–55.

echelons of society were less open to complete outsiders than the adverse comments of chroniclers might lead us to suppose. The ruling elite of Norman England established itself by force of arms, and the calibre of their equipment and training must have marked out the elite, those who had fought on horseback at Hastings, from those with more modest equipment. In practice it must have been exceedingly difficult for men not born into aristocratic families to acquire the necessary equipment and training. Yet if by the eleventh century all aristocrats were knights, were all knights aristocrats? In the Mâconnais region Duby found that whereas originally the two were distinct social groups, by about the year 1000 knights had been assimilated into the aristocracy. In other regions the process took longer, however, and in Normandy, the two categories were still perceptibly distinct in the time of Duke William.[34]

In England under William the Conqueror, while it can be assumed that the leading men were equipped and trained to fight on horseback, it is by no means clear that all knights simply by virtue of their skills and equipment were members of the social elite.[35] The word *miles* (strictly speaking the word for 'soldier') occurs not infrequently in Domesday Book, and significantly was applied there to men who held relatively small amounts of land.[36] The prestige of the heavily armed cavalryman was to carry all before him as compared with those who, though possessing horses, fought on foot, with axe and spear like the English at Hastings, or with those who were more modestly armed, about whom less is heard.[37]

---

[34] For a discussion of the literary evidence see T. Hunt, 'The Emergence of the Knight in France and England 1000–1200', *Knighthood in Medieval Literature*, ed. W. H. Jackson (Woodbridge, 1981), pp. 1–22; J. Flori, *L'essor de la chevalerie XIe–XIIe siècles* (Paris, 1986); for a recent review of the subject see T. Evergates, 'Nobles and Knights in Twelfth-Century France', *Cultures of Power* (ed. Bisson), pp. 11–35; Bates, *Normandy before 1066*, pp. 109–10.

[35] For a recent review of the origins and evolution of knighthood in England see P. R. Coss, *The Knight in Medieval England 1000–1400* (Stroud, 1993), chapter 2.

[36] S. Harvey, 'The Knight and the Knight's Fee in England', *Past and Present*, 49 (1970), 1–43; R. Allen Brown, 'The Status of the Norman Knight', *War and Government in the Middle Ages. Essays in Honour of J. O. Prestwich*, ed. J. Gillingham and J. C. Holt (Woodbridge, 1984), pp. 18–32; D. Fleming, 'Landholding by *Milites* in Domesday Book: A Revision', *Anglo-Norman Studies*, 13 (1991), 83–98; J. Scammell, 'The Formation of the English Social Structure: Freedom, Knights, and Gentry, 1066–1300', *Speculum*, 68 (1993), 591–618; J. Gillingham, 'Thegns and Knights in Eleventh-Century England: Who was then the Gentleman?', *Transactions of the Royal Historical Society*, 6th series, 5 (1995), 129–53.

[37] Stenton, *First Century*, pp. 17–23. English warriors before the Conquest obviously had horses, but there have been different opinions as to whether they were used in battle. At Hastings the English were clearly fighting on foot, but it was not unknown in the Norman period (e.g. at Tinchebrai in 1106 and Lincoln in 1141) for knights to dismount and fight on foot. Equally it is not clear precisely when the

Techniques of fighting were adapted to circumstances: it might be the case, as at the battle of Tinchebrai, that knights dismounted and fought on foot.[38] Nevertheless an ability to fight on horseback using the technique of the couched lance, already visible in some of the figures depicted on the Bayeux Tapestry, was to remain the distinguishing characteristic of knights. To the techniques of warfare were married a way of life and values which associated knights with the aristocracy by the later twelfth century in England.[39]

A further cross-current in post-Conquest England was created by the survival of old social ranks: earls, king's thegns and lesser thegns. The old title of earl could be equated with that of count, and the same Latin word, *comes*, was often used for both, even if in practice the powers of the two were not identical. Earldoms had appeared in England in the early eleventh century and, although this was probably not Cnut's original intention, three great earldoms, Wessex, Mercia, and Northumbria, emerged. In Edward the Confessor's reign additional, smaller, earldoms were created, but they were dominated by Earl Godwin of Wessex and his sons.[40] In Normandy the title of *comes* was accorded only to a few men, usually closely tied to the ducal house.[41] After Hastings, Edwin and Morcar retained their earldoms, and King William granted the title, shorn of the great power enjoyed by Godwin and Harold, to a handful of others.[42] Rufus and Henry I added a few earls, with even less power. Only in Stephen's reign did the number of earls increase dramatically, and some of them made themselves in effect independent.

Below earls came those who held their lands directly from the crown. The more important came to be called the king's barons, whose status and

---

new technique of fighting with couched lances was adopted. Again, the Tapestry shows men using lances both as javelins and couched. For recent discussions see j. Flori, 'Encore l'usage de la lance . . . La technique du combat chevaleresque vers l'an 1100', *Cahiers de Civilisation Médiévale*, 31 (1988), 213–40; S. Morillo, *Warfare under the Anglo-Norman Kings 1066–1135* (Woodbridge, 1994).

[38] OV, VI, 86.

[39] For a useful survey of knighthood, and, more generally, of the trappings of aristocracy, see Crouch, *Image of Aristocracy*, chapters 4, 6, 7.

[40] For counts and earls, *ibid.*, chapter 1; M. K. Lawson, *Cnut. The Danes in England in the Early Eleventh Century* (London, 1993), pp. 184–9, where it is pointed out that Cnut probably did not set out to create three great earldoms.

[41] G. Garnett, '"Ducal" Succession in Early Normandy', *Law and Government in the Medieval England and Normandy*, ed. G. Garnett and J. Hudson (Cambridge, 1994), pp. 98–101.

[42] C. P. Lewis, 'The Early Earls of Norman England', *Anglo-Norman Studies*, 13 (1991), 207–23, and see also below, p. 268.

authority were analogous with the king's thegns.[43] The word 'baron' had originally meant 'man'. In England, in the context of the king and his tenants-in-chief, it came to be confined to the major tenants-in-chief, whose lands descended impartibly.[44] Earls and barons in turn had their own barons, their major vassals as distinct from the wider group of those holding smaller amounts of land. The comparable rank in the landed hierarchy of pre-Conquest England was that of middling or median thegns, though the honorial barons appear to have been richer, often had jurisdictional privileges similar to those of king's barons, and their lands too usually descended impartibly. Honorial barons were self-evidently the more important tenants of a lordship, sometimes had castles of their own and, by the twelfth century, might well found religious houses (see below, p. 413).

The dividing line between the aristocracy and rest of society probably came somewhere in the social levels below the honorial barons, but it is not easy to pinpoint exactly where. Landless younger sons of leading families, and those who acquired a fair amount of land to hold by knight service, were doubtless regarded as falling inside, while those who held only small amounts of land by knight service, possibly discharged by cash payments, fell outside. In the later twelfth century knighthood began to emerge more clearly as a criterion of social status. Expanding opportunities in royal government gave knights important responsibilities in the shire as members of grand assize juries, custodians of the peace, and assessors of taxes. The obligations of knighthood were also becoming such that only men who were of substantial means could afford them. This development, however, seems to belong to the later twelfth century, and there is little to suggest that knighthood in itself betokened aristocratic status in the mid-twelfth century.[45]

The aristocracy thus encompassed men of widely different wealth and backgrounds. Honorial barons with substantial estates (sometimes on both sides of the Channel), French toponyms, castles, and their 'own' reli-

---

[43] *Leges Henrici Primi*, ed. L. J. Downer (Oxford, 1972), 14, 2; D. Roffe, 'From Thegnage to Barony: Sake and Soke, Title and Tenants-in-Chief', *Anglo-Norman Studies*, 12 (1990), 158–9.

[44] Sanders, *English Baronies*, pp. v–viii; Stenton, *First Century*, pp. 84–6.

[45] For a discussion of definitions in relation to Yorkshire in the later twelfth century see H. M. Thomas, *Vassals, Heiresses, Crusaders, and Thugs: the Gentry of Angevin Yorkshire, 1154–1216* (Philadelphia, 1993), pp. 7–12.

gious houses, probably had a lifestyle and political perspective not essentially different from that of the great magnates.[46] Priorities and perceptions shifted as one proceeded further down the social hierarchy, and away from the royal court. The likelihood is that lower down the hierarchy there was English blood, and that attitudes towards England and the English differed on this account: men and women who were half-English were less likely to feel that England was a foreign country. Perhaps we should also take into account that 'the English' was only one way of describing the inhabitants of England. In certain regions the impact of Danish settlement or the persistence of Northumbrian tradition may have been a more immediate influence, certainly more immediate than that of Normandy. Another variable was the strength and character of lordship: can we assume that the kind of influence exercised by the king over his tenants-in-chief was comparable with that which the latter exercised over their men? In practice honorial barons who held land of two or more lords may have enjoyed a substantial measure of *de facto* independence, especially in Stephen's reign, since their loyalties did not belong exclusively to any one lord (see further below, p. 318).

One criterion for aristocratic status not so far mentioned is that of language: the new elite spoke a language different from that of the mass of the population.[47] Language alone could clearly be a misleading indicator, for the new lords had brought with them French-speaking servants, craftsmen, and traders; nevertheless a knowledge of French conveyed a social cachet. All the signs are that it continued to do so: it remained the language spoken in the royal court, and in aristocratic households, and it was the medium of a lively written literature. It did not penetrate far into English society, though presumably the servants of the aristocracy had a working knowledge of it. The few snippets of evidence which may be cited to illustrate this point suggest that the ability of Englishmen to speak French was regarded as surprising, and even miraculous.[48] A deaf and dumb youth who gained the power of speech as a result of a miracle in

---

[46] Crouch, *Beaumont Twins*, p. 115.

[47] M. Chibnall, *Anglo-Norman England 1066–1166* (Oxford, 1986), pp. 211–14 provides a brief survey; for the literary language see especially M. D. Legge, *Anglo-Norman Literature and Its Background* (Oxford, 1971).

[48] R. M. Wilson, 'English and French in England, 1100–1300', *History*, 28 (1943), 37–60; I. Short, 'On Bilingualism in Anglo-Norman England', *Romance Philology*, 33 (1980), 467–79.

Beverley Minster in the early years of the twelfth century amazed those
who heard him speak not only in English, but also in French.[49] Two other
pieces of evidence cited in this context relate to hermits. Godric, the
hermit of Finchale who died in 1170, was able to understand Latin and on
one occasion spoke in French, an ability he ascribed to a gift of the Holy
Spirit.[50] Another hermit, Wulfric of Haselbury, was able to confer an
ability to speak French, to the annoyance of his friend Brictric the parish
priest who had not been taught the language and was laughed at in the
presence of his bishop because he could not speak it.[51] Hermits such as
Godric and Wulfric and women like Christina of Markyate had a crucial
role in their localities as counsellors and conciliators, possibly because
local people preferred to turn to them rather than to the clergy.[52] While
those parish priests like Brictric who were of English descent could com-
municate with their flocks, those who were not, including some younger
sons of aristocratic families, may not have known much English.[53]

Many of the newcomers probably acquired some knowledge of English,
possibly from wet-nurses or by marriage. Marriages with English women
occurred soon. They were rare at the top, though King Henry I married a
woman of English descent, educated in an English nunnery. In the middling and lower ranks of the aristocracy, where marriage into native families was more likely, so too was a knowledge of English, though it may
have been fairly basic. One reference cited in this context was the warning
called out in English by Helewise, wife of Hugh de Moreville. Her lover, a
man with the English name of Liulf, was intending to kill Hugh, and had
appeared with a sword: 'Huge de Moreville, ware, ware, ware, Lithulf heth
his sword adrage.'[54] As time went on the form of French spoken in
England began to diverge from that spoken in France, possibly an indication that many of the new elite spent much of their time in England. By
the later twelfth century there are references to the growing difference,

---

[49] Life of John of Beverley, Historians of the Church of York, ed. J. Raine, 3 vols. RS (London, 1879–94), I, lii–lvi.
[50] Reginald of Durham, Libellus de Vita et Miraculis S. Godrici, Heremitae de Finchale, Auctore Reginaldo
Monacho Dunelmensi, ed. J. Stevenson, Surtees Society, xx (1847), pp. 179–80, 203–4.
[51] John of Ford, The Life of Wulfric of Haselbury, ed. M. Bell, Somerset Record Society (1933), pp. 28–9, 30–1.
[52] H. Mayr-Harting, 'The Functions of a Twelfth-Century Recluse', History, 60 (1975), 337–52.
[53] Chibnall, Anglo-Norman England, p. 213.
[54] M. D. Legge, 'Anglo-Norman as a Spoken Language,' Proceedings of the Battle Conference, 2 (1980), 111
pointed out that this episode, usually cited as evidence that Hugh, one of the murderers of Becket,
and Helewise usually spoke in English, has been misinterpreted and that Helewise was indicating to
her lover that she had betrayed him.

and an awareness that those who wished to learn to speak 'correct' French would have to cross the Channel to do so.[55] From being a mark of belonging to the new regime at the start of our period, by the end the French of the aristocracy of England was coming to be seen as rather provincial.

French and English were only two of the languages employed in twelfth-century England: the third was Latin, the language of the church and of the documents employed in royal government. Ian Short has argued that this trilingualism enriched Anglo-Norman literature and helps to explain its precocious development in twelfth-century England.[56] Individual laymen such as royal officials or stewards may have had some knowledge of Latin, sufficient to decipher documents they received, but this fact is not as important as that there were three languages in use in elite circles.

There is, then, no watertight definition for membership of this aristocracy, for criteria of birth, wealth, power, and tenurial status were possessed in differing combinations. Noble birth was important for those who had it, but the enrichment of lesser men with the spoils of English conquest may perhaps have masked its importance for a time. The title of earl was highly prestigious and reserved for a relative minority, and we may speculate that a direct tenurial relationship with the king also conferred prestige. Closeness to the king in another way, being one of his confidential servants, or *familiares*, brought personal influence and, for some, power.

If the definition of the aristocracy within England needs to be explored, so also does its self-perception. Did the newcomers continue to see themselves as Normans, or Flemings, or Bretons, aliens in a conquered country identifying themselves with their continental homelands? At what stage did they begin to put down roots in England? Answers are offered in the conclusion, but these questions have to be raised here because this book rests on the premise that the families settled in England form a feasible unit of study. In 1976 Professor Le Patourel, in *The Norman Empire*, pointed out that the epicentre of that empire was the ruler's court, underpinned by a cross-Channel aristocracy.[57] Great cross-Channel estates came into being after 1066 and, though some disappeared due to the vicissitudes of fortune, new ones then came into being. Only with the more protracted

---

[55] Short, 'On Bilingualism', 468–474.

[56] I. Short, 'Patrons and Polyglots: French Literature in Twelfth-Century England', *Anglo-Norman Studies*, 14 (1992), 229–49.     [57] J. Le Patourel, *The Norman Empire* (Oxford, 1976), *passim*.

separation of England from Normandy under Stephen did the bonds begin to slacken. Le Patourel was at pains to stress that Normandy, which historians of England had previously tended to treat as an offshore continental possession, was just as important to the king/dukes as England. However, it has since been pointed out that although there clearly were some cross-Channel families with major landed interests on both sides of the Channel, there were others whose interests were wholly or mainly on one side or the other, and their concerns did not always match those of the ruling house.[58] It is feasible to concentrate on those who did settle in England, providing the wider context is kept in view. Patterns of religious and literary patronage illuminate the process of settlement and identification with the country of adoption and ties with region of origin.

Estimates of the size of the aristocracy as a percentage of the population as a whole are very difficult to produce, even using the Domesday material for 1086. There were some 283,242 people recorded in Domesday Book by Sir Henry Ellis's calculation, 268,984 (excluding tenants-in-chief and under-tenants) according to H. C. Darby's reckoning.[59] Given that the country was not fully surveyed, that certain classes are underestimated, and that the recorded population was of heads of households, the total population was evidently much higher. Approximately two hundred laymen held land in chief of the crown worth more than thirty pounds a year, and this corresponds to the number of baronies or major lordships which had come into being before 1166 (see below, pp. 127–9). (The number of *families* involved was usually smaller.) Darby further estimated that the total number of tenants-in-chief was about 1,100 and that there were about 6,000 under-tenants in 1086.[60] The completion of a good database for Domesday Book should provide accurate statistics, but there remains the problem of deciding how many lesser landholders should be included in the aristocracy. A criterion based on wealth alone is not sufficient.

This book ends in the mid-twelfth century, when the world inhabited by the aristocracy of Norman England was about to change significantly. The great wave of gifts of land from the aristocracy to the church was just beginning to slacken, not least because families had less to give. Rising

---

[58] J. A. Green, 'Unity and Disunity in the Anglo-Norman State', *Historical Research*, 62 (1989), 114–34; D. Crouch, 'Normans and Anglo-Normans: a Divided Aristocracy?', *Normandy and England in the Middle Ages*, ed. D. Bates and A. Curry (London, 1994), pp. 51–67.

[59] H. Ellis, *An Introduction to Domesday Book*, 2 vols. (London, 1833), II, 514; H. C. Darby, *Domesday England* (Cambridge, 1977), p. 337.    [60] *Ibid.*, p. 89.

population and price inflation meant that leasing out demesne manors was replaced by direct management, capitalizing on the profits that could be made, and imposing a stricter servitude on the peasant workforce.[61] The expansion of royal government in the later twelfth century profoundly affected the aristocracy. The development of common law procedures and their application by a corps of royal justices provided an increasingly effective alternative to honorial justice as well as a point of recourse for lords themselves.[62] Even if honorial courts had never possessed the kind of autonomy which historians such as Stenton and Milsom proposed, the new procedures were bound to diminish their authority in time, and this was part and parcel of a general weakening of honorial authority. However, these new procedures were only available to free men, thus making free status a more critical issue than before. As freemen were dealt with in the royal, public, and ecclesiastical courts, so the unfree were left to the justice of their lords. Legal disability united with the economic interests of the seigneurial class to create classic villeinage, justiciable in manorial courts held by great and petty lords alike.[63]

In this environment the authority of lords over their knightly tenants was also changing. After the initial wave of conquest was complete, most lords had relatively little land to distribute from their own finite resources. They could not therefore rely, as the conquest generation had done, on directly rewarding loyalty with substantial grants of land. Loyalty could be sustained at a personal level while there were only one or two links in the tenurial chain; as this chain became longer it is likely that seigneurial authority was seriously weakened. Even from the outset, however, some tenants had had substantial interests outside the honour, and this tendency too is likely to have increased as time went on, making it difficult for lords to maintain their influence over their tenants. By the later twelfth century the more important tenant families were escaping, as it were, the bonds of honorial lordship. They could look to the king's service for career opportunities, and to the king's courts for justice.[64]

---

[61] For a brief survey see E. Miller and J. Hatcher, *Medieval England, Rural Society and Economic Change 1086–1348* (London, 1978), chapters 5, 7, 8; for the switch to direct management of demesnes, P. D. A. Harvey, 'The Pipe Rolls and the Adoption of Demesne Farming in England', *Economic History Review*, 2nd series, 27 (1974), 345–59.

[62] Hudson, *Land Law, and Lordship*, chapter 9; J. Biancalana, 'For Want of Justice: the Legal Reforms of Henry II', *Columbia Law Review*, 88 (1988), 433–536.

[63] P. R. Hyams, *Kings, Lords, and Peasants in Medieval England* (Oxford, 1980).

[64] P. R. Coss, 'Bastard Feudalism Revised', *Past and Present*, 125 (1989), 27–64.

Great lords still had their retinues, but household knights had to be content with the prospects of small grants of land or the assignment of rents to augment wages and allowances.

By the mid-twelfth century the military context of lordship was changing too. The conquest had been initiated by war, and the protracted disturbances of Stephen's reign reinforced the need for active military service. The wars fought by the Angevin kings, however, were fought mainly outside England. Individual members of the aristocracy still played a leading role, as they did throughout the middle ages; but others acquitted their obligations by financial payments in the form of scutage or aid. Henry II chose to negotiate with the lay and ecclesiastical tenants-in-chief for contributions, and he also turned to other wealthy groups in the community. The levy of a tax on movables, as yet only for a war for religious purposes – the relief of the Holy Land – pointed the way to a lucrative means of tapping the wealth of England which was to be exploited by his successors.[65] In the early days, castles had been built of earth and timber, often hastily erected, and essentially an instrument of subjugation; some, possibly many, similar fortifications were thrown up during the Anarchy. By the mid-twelfth century, however, the king and leading magnates had built large and expensive stone fortresses, symbolic of wealth and status as well as defence, and far removed from the more modest castles and defended manors of the lesser aristocracy. By a programme of building and repair, Henry II made sure that he held a majority of seriously defended castles under his direct control, to prevent a renewal of the challenges to royal authority which had occurred under his predecessor.[66]

Finally, when the link with Normandy was restored under Henry II, it was in the context of a much wider assemblage of territories. There was thus a shift over time, not only in the relationship between the ruling elite and the majority of the population within England, but in the relationship between England and Normandy. England was ruled after 1154 by a king who was only a quarter Norman by descent, whose dynastic interests were much wider than England and Normandy, and who did not

---

[65] S. K. Mitchell, *Taxation in Medieval England* (New Haven, 1951); T. K. Keefe, *Feudal Assessments and the Political Community under Henry II and his Sons* (Berkeley, 1983).

[66] R. Allen Brown, 'Royal Castlebuilding in England, 1154–1216', *English Historical Review*, 70 (1955), 353–98.

try to reestablish any kind of 'special relationship' between the aristocracies of England and Normandy.

The first major theme dealt with in this book is the process of conquest: those involved (chapter one), and the process by which they acquired land (chapter two). The nature of the transfer of land to a new elite is a topic of fundamental importance to our evaluation of the legitimacy of the regime. Was the transfer uncontrolled and unlicensed, an act of land-grabbing, and in this respect to be compared with empire-builders in later periods? Or was it disciplined and organized, the takeover of men who believed they had a legitimate right to succeed to their land (chapter two)? The overall impression gained is of the speed and completeness of the revolution in the midlands and south of England, confirming the achievements of the old English monarchy in creating an integrated political society.

The north (chapter three) was very different; Yorkshire was harried and then carved into great military lordships. Further north and west it was touch and go throughout our period where the boundary between England and Scotland was to be drawn. Here the pace and character of Norman settlement were conditioned by the relations with the kings of the Scots and their ambitions in what was, as events proved, to remain part of England. The themes of immigration and recruitment after 1086 are considered in chapter four. Here it is argued that the influx of Normans and their allies under William the Conqueror was the only major period of migration: there is little evidence of continuing immigration or indeed of much movement in the reverse direction, from England to Normandy, thereafter. Despite an impression of radical social change in the early twelfth century conveyed by chroniclers' comments about the rise of 'new men', access to the top was relatively restricted. There were new faces, certainly, but they tended to be as well born as the old.

The second major theme is wealth and power. In chapter five some of the factors which influenced what men did with the lands they had received from the king are discussed. The pressures on them to give to their own followers, and to make provision for their children, and for pious benefactions, quite apart from any desire to spend on building or luxurious living, are explored. Then the structure of great lordships, and the basic division between the estates kept under direct control by the lords and those granted out by knight service to tenants is discussed. Chapter six deals with castles, and offers a survey of the different types and their development during the century after 1066. We tend to associate the Conquest with a particular type of fortification, the motte (mound) and bailey castle, which came into its own in the context of a military takeover, but archaeologists have drawn attention to fortified enclosures without mottes. As yet we cannot be certain how many grass-covered mounds which still lie unexcavated belong to the years after 1066 and how many, perhaps, to the troubles of Stephen's reign.

Castles were centres of lordship, which is dealt with explicitly in chapters seven and eight. In chapter seven the focus is upon the personal relations between lords and men, their domestic servants, clerks, household knights, and tenants. The cohesiveness of the relationship between the lord and his leading tenants, the community of the honour, is considered. It is suggested that we should be chary about generalizing either about the cohesiveness of all honours in the Norman period, or of their decline starting as early as Stephen's reign: the situation differed from lordship to lordship.

In chapter eight the attributes of power are analysed. The military strength of those who chose to resist the Norman kings is particularly striking, and it is argued here that kings were on the whole careful to negotiate contributions of men and money for their wars. A particular time of tension, however, was in 1084 and 1085 when King William levied the old territorially assessed geld, expected the magnates to billet the troops he had raised and brought to England and, in all probability, was expecting contributions of knights from them as well. The juxtaposition of old and new resulted in crisis, and the Domesday Inquest was ordered as a result. Noble power did not decline under Rufus or Henry I, and under Stephen it clearly grew stronger. It is further argued in chapter eight that although Henry II tackled some of the more obdurate magnates at the start of his reign, he did not seek to 'tame' the aristocracy as a whole.

The third theme is politics (chapter nine). Here the standpoint is not that of the Norman kings, as has often been the case in previous accounts, but that of the lay aristocracy. It is argued that while other magnates, amongst the richest in England and Normandy, had a perspective on the Anglo-Norman realm in line with that of the ruling house, that is, that Normandy and England were better ruled by one person, every family had its own concerns and more often than not these were relatively close to home. When details become available, we can see how alliances and conflicts were often dominated by local rivalries over lands and castles.

The fourth and final theme is entitled 'Aristocratic Society' and here three related aspects are dealt with. First is the role of kinship, particularly in the transmission of land and the formation of alliances (chapter ten). An emphasis on male inheritance, and specifically on primogeniture, had profound consequences for many families by channelling land through the eldest son, but the rigour of primogeniture could be averted by enfeoffing younger sons as tenants. Where male issue failed, as was not uncommon, daughters came to the fore as heiresses. Their importance as heiresses and widows was at a high point in the Norman period, it is suggested, though this did not mean that their status improved. Similarly the increasing provision made for them in religious houses provided additional opportunities for them, but in a controlled environment (chapter eleven). Finally, the foundation of more houses for women was only one manifestation of a proliferation of different types of religious community which was one outcome of profound changes in the western church. Lands, property, and tithes were granted to religious houses by the aristocracy of Norman England in a great tide of giving. In exploring the direction and motives of the givers we thus come closest, in a book devoted mainly to their terrestrial interests, land, power, and politics, to understanding their spiritual and personal concerns as well.

# I Conquest and settlement

# 1   'They came with the Conqueror'

The Conquest of England was the most spectacularly successful of the exploits of the Normans in the eleventh century. Here victory in battle was converted into a lasting and relatively complete conquest. The south, midlands, and much of the north of England and parts of Wales passed into the lands of a new elite. It was hardly surprising, then, that Hastings and the fame of those who had fought there were celebrated by the Normans. The biographer of William the Conqueror, William of Poitiers, wrote within a few years of the battle. He supplied a few names of those who were present, but clearly did not feel impelled to provide a comprehensive list.[1] By the time Orderic Vitalis wrote, in the early twelfth century,[2] the list had expanded, and by the later twelfth century when Wace, a canon of Bayeux cathedral, wrote a verse history of the Normans, the list of combatants had become lengthy.[3] Wace, as an important recent study has argued, was concerned to stress the contribution made by families from the region of Bayeux, and from his account additional names may be culled which often derive from places in lower Normandy.[4] A century after the battle anybody who was anybody wanted to claim an ancestor who had fought at Hastings. Nor did the desire to claim a Norman ancestor wane in later centuries. A list of those who had fought hung in Battle abbey in the nineteenth century, and at Falaise there is a bronze tablet inscribed with 315 names of companions of the Conqueror.[5] A certain readiness to claim that the ancestors of aristocratic families 'came over with the Conqueror' can still be detected in the press and in guidebooks to historic houses. This has not been dampened by scholarly caution. D. C. Douglas pointed out, for instance, how few names of companions of the Conqueror are attested by contemporary or near-con-

---

[1] WP, pp. 194–6.   [2] OV, II, 172–8.

[3] *Roman de Rou de Wace*, ed. A. J. Holden, 3 vols. (Paris, 1970–3), II, 194–210.

[4] E. M. C. Van Houts, 'Wace as Historian and Genealogist', *Family Trees and the Roots of Politics. The Prosopography of Britain and France from the Tenth to the Twelfth Century*, ed. K. S. B. Keats-Rohan (Woodbridge, forthcoming).

[5] M. J. Crispin and L. Macary, *Falaise Roll Recording Prominent Companions of William Duke of Normandy at the Conquest of England* (London, 1938).

1 The memorial plaque to the companions of William the Conqueror at Falaise castle. Photograph: W. L. Warren.

temporary sources, though, since our knowledge of the first invaders is admittedly incomplete, claims that ancestors came over with the Conqueror cannot ultimately be disproved.[6]

What is clear about the men who formed the first wave of the new elite is that the invasion of 1066 had been conceived of as a collective enterprise by Duke William, those closest to him, and his allies, and that they all supplied contingents of kinsmen and followers. When the news reached Normandy of Edward's death and Harold's accession, Duke William called a council attended by the leading men of Normandy at which the possibility of an expedition to England was mooted. Although Normandy's enemies were for the time being quiescent, the enterprise was risky, and not all were in favour. Nevertheless the duke secured the backing of his leading men who promised ships and knights, and, as the news spread, men came from beyond the borders of Normandy to join the

[6] D. C. Douglas, 'Companions of the Conqueror', *History*, 28 (1943), 129–47; J. F. A. Mason, 'The Companions of the Conqueror: an Additional Name', *English Historical Review*, 66 (1956), 61–9.

expedition.[7] A list survives in a twelfth-century manuscript from Battle abbey of names and numbers of those who promised ships.[8] There were evidently negotiations about the numbers of knights, the terms on which they were to be provided, and the scale of rewards. The chief negotiator on the duke's behalf was William FitzOsbern, the duke's steward and head of his military household.[9] In Domesday Book in Essex there is a reference to 'the hundred manors' of Eustace count of Boulogne and this round number might well have been his promised share, possibly a multiple of the number of knights he supplied.[10]

By collating the names of the men said by William of Poitiers to have been in the duke's council in 1066 with those he said were at Hastings, with Orderic's list, the names on the ship list, and those who secured the largest share of lands in Domesday Book, we can identify the leaders of the expedition and those who, if not physically present, gave the greatest material support (see table). The duke's chief lieutenants were his half-brothers, Robert count of Mortain and Odo bishop of Bayeux, who were said to have contributed respectively one hundred and twenty and one hundred ships; they were also among the few individuals named on the Bayeux Tapestry. Odo had been appointed to the bishopric of Bayeux in 1049 or 1050; the date when Robert received Mortain is not clear, but Bates has suggested about 1060.[11] Each had substantial resources at his command, though Robert perhaps had to be cautious in stripping Mortain of knights, for the county was in a frontier region.

Other leading contributors included three men who had long been closely associated with the duke and were related to him by blood: William FitzOsbern, Roger de Beaumont, and Roger of Montgomery.[12] FitzOsbern was William's close friend as well as his steward. He fought at Hastings and was left in charge in England with Odo of Bayeux when

[7] WP, p. 148.

[8] Oxford, Bodleian Library, MS E Museo 93 f. 8v, discussed by E. M. C. Van Houts, 'The Ship List of William the Conqueror', *Anglo-Norman Studies*, 10 (1987), 159–83; see also C. Warren Hollister, 'The Greater Domesday Tenants-in-Chief', *Domesday Studies*, ed. J. C. Holt (Woodbridge, 1987), pp. 219–48.

[9] HH, p. 199; Wace, *Roman de Rou* (ed. Holden), II, 111–12.      [10] *DB*, II, 26b.

[11] D. Bates, 'The Character and Career of Odo, Bishop of Bayeux (1049/50–1097)', *Speculum*, 50 (1975), 1–20; Bates, 'Notes sur l'aristocratie normande. II. Herluin de Conteville et sa famille', *Annales de Normandie*, 23 (1973), 29; B. Golding, 'Robert of Mortain', *Anglo-Norman Studies*, 13 (1991), 119–44.

[12] For the ties of kinship linking these men to William see the discussion by E. M. C. Van Houts, 'Robert of Torigni as Genealogist', *Studies in Medieval History presented to R. Allen Brown*, ed. C. Harper-Bill, C. Holdsworth, and J. L. Nelson (Woodbridge, 1989), pp. 215–33.

Table: *Counsellors, Contributors, and Companions*

| Name | Ducal counsellor | 1066 expedition | Ship List | Lands in 1086 |
|---|---|---|---|---|
| Odo bp of Bayeux | OV, II, 140 | WP, p. 182; BT | yes | class A |
| Robert c. of Mortain | WP, p. 148 | BT | yes | class A |
| Robert c. of Eu | WP, p. 148 | – | yes | class C |
| Hugh bp of Lisieux | WP, p. 148 | – | no | no |
| Richard c. of Evreux | WP, p. 148 | William of Evreux WP, p. 196 | William of Evreux | William of Evreux |
| Roger de Beaumont | WP, p. 148 | Robert de Beaumont WP, p. 192 | yes | Roger plus Robert class C |
| Roger of Montgomery | WP, p. 148 (but cf OV, II, 210) | – | yes | class A |
| William FitzOsbern | WP, p. 148 | WP, p. 196 | yes | yes but died 1071 |
| Hugh de Montfort | – | WP, p. 196 | yes | class C |
| Eustace, c. of Boulogne | – | WP, p. 194 | – | class A |
| Ralph de Tosny | OV, II, 140 | WP, p. 196 | – | class D (and other Tosnys) |
| William de Warenne | OV, II, 140 | WP, p. 196 | – | class A |
| Hugh d'Ivry the butler | OV, II, 140 | – | – | Roger d'Ivry class C |
| Hugh de Grandmesnil | OV, II, 140 | WP, p. 196 | – | class C |
| Roger de Mowbray | OV, II, 140 | – | – | – |
| Richard FitzGilbert | OV, II, 140 | – | – | class A |
| Baldwin FitzGilbert | OV, II, 140 | – | – | class C |

| | | | | |
|---|---|---|---|---|
| Geoffrey son of c. of Mortagne | – | WP, p. 196 | – | – |
| Walter Giffard | – | WP, p. 196 | yes | class A |
| William Malet | – | WP, p. 204 | – | Robert Malet class B |
| Geoffrey bp of Coutances | – | WP, p. 182 | – | class A |
| Turstin FitzRou | – | OV, II, 172 | – | class D |
| Engenulf de Laigle | – | OV, II, 176 killed at Hastings | – | Gilbert de Laigle class E |
| Gilbert d'Auffay | – | OV, III, 254 | – | – |
| Robert de Vitot | – | OV, II, 120 died 1066 | – | – |
| Hugh d'Avranches | – | – | yes | class A |
| Fulk d'Aunou | – | – | yes | – |
| Gerold de Roumare the steward | – | – | yes | Robert FitzGerold class D |
| Nicholas abbot of St Ouen | – | – | yes | – |
| Remigius almoner of Fécamp | – | – | yes | bishop of Lincoln |

*Notes:*

This table is based on a restricted range of sources, and thus most, though probably not all, of the leading men of 1066 appear. The second column refers to the lists in William of Poitiers *Gesta Guillelmi* (p. 148) and *The Ecclesiastical History of Orderic Vitalis* (II, 140) of those who were prominent in ducal councils in 1066. The third column indicates whether the individual concerned is known from either William of Poitiers or the Bayeux Tapestry (BT) to have been on the expedition of 1066. The fourth column refers to contributors on the 'ship-list' of William the Conqueror, Van Houts, 'The Ship List of William the Conqueror', p. 175. The fifth column indicates scale of landed wealth in Domesday Book according to the categories established by W. J. Corbett in 'The Development of the Duchy of Normandy and the Norman Conquest of England', *Cambridge Medieval History*, V (Cambridge, 1926), 505–13: viz. class A lands worth more than £750, class B between £400 and £650, class C £200 to £400, class D £100 to £200, class E £10 to £100.

**2** Odo, William, and Robert. Bayeux Tapestry, eleventh century. By special permission of the city of Bayeux.

William returned to Normandy in 1067, and was then deployed on the Welsh Marches and in the north. Roger de Beaumont and Roger of Montgomery were not on the Hastings campaign. They were left in Normandy in 1066 to defend the duchy. Roger de Beaumont sent along his son Robert, still a very young man (*tiro*), on the campaign.[13] All three men had substantial landed estates in what is today the département of Calvados. Roger de Beaumont had married the heiress to the county of Meulan in the demesne of the Capetian kings of France, and Roger of

[13] WP, p. 192.

Montgomery had married Mabel de Bellême, one of the claimants to this largely autonomous lordship near the southern frontier of Normandy.[14]

Duke William had battled for over twenty years to exert his authority in Normandy. In so doing he had used ties of kinship and service to build up loyalty in the Norman aristocracy. It is thus not surprising to find that those who answered his call to arms are known in some cases to have been related to him: William count of Evreux, Robert count of Eu, Walter Giffard, and Nicholas abbot of Saint-Ouen all figured on the ship list and were his kinsmen. Robert count of Eu and Walter Giffard, lord of Longueville and Montivilliers, had fought for William against the French in 1053 and 1054.[15] Hugh, later earl of Chester, also appears; his father Richard, son of Thurstan Goz, was *vicomte* of the Avranchin, and may have also been related by marriage to the duke.[16] William de Warenne, probably a younger son of Rodulf de Varenne, had also fought for the duke in 1053–4 and had been given land confiscated from one of the defeated rebels of 1054. William in 1066 was thus already a rising man and his involvement in the enterprise of England led to the acquisition of vast estates there.[17] Richard and Baldwin, the sons of Count Gilbert of Brionne, whom Orderic says were at Hastings, were also men with their way to make. Count Gilbert (again related to the ducal house) had been murdered during the troubled early days of William's minority and Richard and Baldwin fled to Flanders. When it was safe to do so they returned, and Richard was granted Bienfaite and Orbec, Baldwin, Le Sap and Meules.[18]

William Malet, who identified Harold's body on the battlefield at Hastings, had slightly different motives for joining the expedition. The headquarters of the Malet family was at Graville near the mouth of the Seine. This William had English blood and may have had land in England before 1066 (see below, pp. 84, 91).[19] From his point of view the invasion of

---

[14] OV, IV, 304; K. Thompson, 'Family and Influence to the South of Normandy in the Eleventh Century: the Lordship of Bellême', *Journal of Medieval History*, 11 (1985), 215–26.    [15] WP, p. 72.

[16] Hollister, 'Greater Domesday Tenants-in-Chief', pp. 223, 231–2; Van Houts, 'Ship List of William the Conqueror', pp. 223–5; for the parentage of Hugh of Chester see E. Searle, *Predatory Kinship and the Creation of Norman Power, 840–1066* (Berkeley, Los Angeles, and London, 1988), p. 202.

[17] L. C. Loyd, 'The Origins of the Family of Warenne', *Yorkshire Archaeological Journal*, 31 (1934), 97–113.

[18] J. C. Ward, 'Royal Service and Reward: the Clare Family and the Crown, 1066–1154', *Anglo-Norman Studies*, 11 (1989), 261–5.

[19] *The Carmen de Hastingae Proelio of Guy bishop of Amiens*, ed. C. Morton and H. Muntz, Oxford Medieval Texts (Oxford, 1972), p. 58.

England offered the prospect of more gain; to Duke William he was a man with connections. Others were powerful lords whose families had already engaged in the quest for land outside Normandy. Ralph de Tosny was lord of Conches. Members of his family had earlier ventured to Italy and to Spain, and no fewer than four Tosnys were to be tenants-in-chief in England by 1086.[20] Ralph had been one of those suspected of disloyalty in about 1060 but was evidently restored to favour.[21]

The involvement of ecclesiastics in the expedition was also striking. The abbot of Saint-Ouen provided ships as did Remigius, almoner of Fécamp. Remigius hoped for preferment in return and was successful, though he found that he had to clear himself of a charge of simony.[22] Odo of Bayeux was probably not the only bishop to have taken part in the expedition, as Geoffrey bishop of Coutances was certainly in England by the time of William's coronation at Christmas 1066. The bishopric to which Geoffrey had been appointed in 1049 was only modestly endowed, and it seems that not long afterwards he visited his kinsman Robert Guiscard in Italy on a fund-raising trip.[23] He doubtless hoped for wealth from England, and by 1086 was one of the richest magnates in the country.

Already a variety of motives amongst the leading participants has become clear. Some probably committed themselves and their men out of loyalty to William, or as an antidote to suspected disloyalty; some fought in the hope of gain; others saw prospects not so much for themselves as for their sons. Richard count of Evreux was mentioned as present at the duke's council in 1066 but it was his son who was at Hastings and who succeeded him in 1067.[24] Gerold de Roumare was a contributor of ships and, though he is not known to have been on the Hastings expedition, his son Robert was a tenant-in-chief in 1086.

What is clearly the case when we turn from consideration of those involved in 1066 to those who by 1086 were major landholders is that by no means all of the Norman aristocracy have acquired land in England. In

---

[20] For this family see L. Musset, 'Aux origines d'une classe dirigeante: les Tosnys, grands barons normands du Xe au XIIIe siècles', *Francia*, 5 (1977), 45–80.     [21] OV, II, 90, 106.

[22] Eadmer, *Historia Novorum*, ed. M. Rule (RS, 1884), pp. 11–12. David Bates has recently drawn attention to an inscription recorded in the seventeenth century by Dugdale, that Remigius was a kinsman of Duke William: Bates, *Bishop Remigius of Lincoln 1067–1092* (Lincoln, 1993), p. 3.

[23] 'De statu hujus ecclesiae ab anno 863 ad 1063', *Gallia Christiania*, XI, Instrumenta, col. 219, cited by J. Le Patourel, 'Geoffrey of Montbray, Bishop of Coutances, 1049–1093', *English Historical Review*, 59 (1944), 137.     [24] WP, pp. 148, 194–6.

some cases this may have been a personal choice. Orderic Vitalis wrote of those who by 1068 had returned to Normandy, threatened by a revolt of their wives.[25] He also mentioned Gilbert d'Auffay as one who, though prepared to fight in England, nevertheless had moral scruples about profiting therefrom.[26] Orderic was making a moralistic point about the spoils of plunder, but it is conceivable that some laymen did have moral if not pragmatic reasons for not accepting land. Certainly if members of the Norman aristocracy are crosschecked with the Domesday hierarchy there are some notable omissions. One of the most striking absentees from the Domesday hierarchy was the lord of Tancarville, one of the greatest lords of upper Normandy. Ralph, lord of Tancarville, was William's chamberlain. He was at William's court in 1066 and Wace included him in his list of those who were at Hastings.[27] If he did participate in the invasion, he did not receive or did not accept land in England. By 1086 he had died and was succeeded by his son William, who supported Robert rather than Rufus in the conflict that followed the Conqueror's death. William the younger made his peace with Henry I in 1106 and thereafter did accept land in England.[28] It is intriguing that the lords of Tancarville themselves were not more directly involved in the Conquest. At least one of their tenants was, however. Urse d'Abetot, who was sheriff of Worcestershire by 1069, was from Abetot which was held of the lord of Tancarville. So far as we know he had not been a member of a contingent supplied by Ralph the chamberlain.[29]

The timing may have been unlucky for some families, faced perhaps with the succession of a minor, or with predatory neighbours. Others were out of favour: the Giroie clan, neighbours and kinsmen of the Grandmesnils, had been brought down by their involvement in the revolt of 1060.[30] Nigel, the powerful lord of Saint-Sauveur in the Cotentin who had earlier been in revolt against the duke, seems to have decided against, or was discouraged from, participation.[31] Ralph II Tesson of Thury Harcourt similarly does not appear to have been involved, though his cousin Robert FitzErneis is mentioned as having been killed at Hastings,

[25] OV, II, 220.    [26] OV, III, 256.    [27] RRAN, I, nos. 3, 4; Wace (ed. Holden), II, 199.

[28] J. A. Green, The Government of England under Henry I, Cambridge Studies in Medieval Life and Thought, 4th series, II (Cambridge, 1986), p. 275.    [29] Loyd, Origins of Some Anglo-Norman Families, pp. 1–2.

[30] J.-M. Maillefer, 'Une famille aristocratique aux confins de la Normandie: les Géré au XIe siècle', Autour de pouvoir ducal normand Xe–XIIe siècles, Cahiers des Annales de Normandie, XVII (Caen, 1985), pp. 175–206.    [31] WP, p. 16.

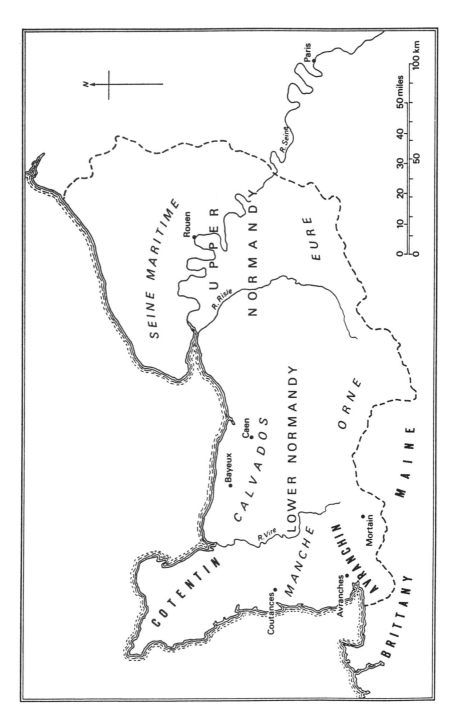

Normandy

and William Tison, said to have been first lord of Alnwick, may have been a kinsman, though there is no proof of this.[32]

One particular concern for Duke William was the security of his frontiers: he could not afford to leave Normandy wide open to attack by stripping frontier lordships of knights. Perhaps this consideration helps to explain why only one of the four principal families of the Norman Vexin was involved in the conquest, the Crispins of Neaufles. Wace included William Crispin amongst those who fought at Hastings, and, though there is no evidence that he was involved, Miles Crispin, who was almost certainly a member of this family, had acquired substantial estates in England by 1086.[33]

In theory it is possible to calculate the numbers of Domesday holders drawn from the different departments of Normandy, as G. Tengvik did in *Old English Bynames*.[34] Tengvik showed that although the duke recruited from all parts of Normandy, the strongest representation was from Seine Maritime (formerly Seine Inférieure) and from Calvados. Fewer came from west Normandy (Manche), Eure, and fewer still from the deep south (Orne) (see map). He reckoned that there were twenty-nine people from nineteen places in Calvados, forty-six from thirty-four places in Eure, thirty-three from twenty-seven places in Manche, twenty-seven from twenty places in Seine Maritime, and five from four places in Orne. A calculation was also included by the editors of Lewis Loyd's 'notebook' on the continental origins of Norman families settled in England. This covered a longer period, 1066 to 1205. It was calculated that ninety-five families came from Calvados, ninety-three from Seine Maritime, fifty from Manche, forty-seven from Eure, and fifteen from Orne.[35]

Straightforward numerical calculations on these lines are, however, seriously misleading. The use of toponyms was spreading by the later eleventh century, but it cannot be assumed it was spreading evenly across

[32] According to Wace, Ralph Tesson was involved in the revolt of 1047 but went over to the duke on the battlefield, *Roman de Rou* (ed. Holden), II, 29; for his son Ralph II see L. Musset, 'Actes inédits du XIe siècle. v. Autour des origines de Saint-Etienne de Fontenay', *Bulletin de la Société des Antiquaires de Normandie*, 56 (1961–2), 11–41; for Robert FitzErneis see Wace, *Roman de Rou*, II, 206 and Douglas, 'Companions of the Conqueror', pp. 142–3; for William Tison see below, p. 114.

[33] Wace, *Roman de Rou* (ed. Holden), II, 199; J. A. Green, 'Lords of the Norman Vexin', *War and Government in the Middle Ages. Essays in Honour of J. O. Prestwich*, ed. J. Gillingham and J. C. Holt (Woodbridge, 1984), p. 49.   [34] G. Tengvik, *Old English Bynames* (Uppsala, 1938), pp. 59–64.

[35] Loyd, *Origins of Some Anglo-Norman Families*, pp. viii–ix.

all regions of Normandy. There are many gaps in the evidence, and these become more numerous lower down the scale of landholding wealth. Tengvik's suggested identifications, likely though they are, have in a number of cases yet to be verified. More seriously, however, the estates of the greatest men were often situated in more than one region of Normandy, and it is not always obvious which had been the original family holdings. It may be that simple statements that X came from Y are too simplistic, as families were only just beginning to use names which identified them with specific places. There is a further related question about the definition of families in this period: are these to be defined in terms of lineage, or more broadly? Different branches might name themselves differently, and by concentrating on a man with a toponym and on his descendants we may miss the presence in England of his kinsmen. It may be, for instance, that detailed work on the families of the lords of Saint Sauveur or the lords of Tancarville will throw up related families in post-Conquest England. A comprehensive study, such as that under way by Dr Keats-Rohan of the continental interests of Domesday families, is badly needed to throw light on these subjects.

It is unlikely, nevertheless, that such detailed investigations will overthrow the correlation clearly perceptible between landed wealth in Domesday and an origin in upper Normandy. Calculations of the wealth of Domesday landholders were made by W. J. Corbett in volume five of the *Cambridge Medieval History*.[36] He graded them into five classes: class A men whose lands (demesne and tenanted) were valued at more than £750 by Domesday values; class B between £400 and £650, class C £200 to £400, class D £100 to £200, and class E £10 to £100. Corbett's categories have been widely used by historians, albeit with some necessary emendations.[37] There were twenty-one individuals who held land in 1086 valued at more than £400. Excluding the duke's two brothers and his niece, and non-Normans such as the Breton Count Alan, Eustace of Boulogne, Gilbert de Gant (Ghent) and Edward of Salisbury (whose ancestry may have been

---

[36] W. J. Corbett, 'The Development of the Duchy of Normandy and the Norman Conquest of England', *Cambridge Medieval History*, v, ed. J. R. Tanner and others (Cambridge, 1926), 507–20.

[37] Corbett included FitzOsbern in his Class A, but the Domesday values of FitzOsbern's lands do not qualify him for inclusion. He excluded Odo of Bayeux and Robert of Mortain whom he put into the same category as the king and queen, rather than that of the lay aristocracy. He included Ivo Taillebois in class B instead of class C where he belongs, but he must have excluded someone else included in his total of eleven, possibly Countess Judith.

at least partly English), there were fifteen men in the top two classes. Of
these William de Warenne, Geoffrey de Mandeville, Robert Malet, Walter
Giffard, and (probably) Ralph Bainard came from upper Normandy, and
William of Eu was the son of the count of Eu.[38]

Of the men from upper Normandy the two dark horses were Geoffrey de
Mandeville, a class A landholder, and Ralph Bainard from class B, neither
of whom is mentioned in any of the lists of those present on the Hastings
expedition. Geoffrey de Mandeville was probably put in charge of the
defences in the south-east corner of the city wall of London (later the
Tower) in the early weeks of 1067, and may well have been granted the
lands of Ansger the Staller at the same time.[39] Ansger had been a wealthy
thegn, a grandson of Tofig the Proud, and he had many men commended
to him. Though a sick man at the time, he was said to have been in charge
of the defence of London when the Normans arrived, and to have been
imprisoned by King William.[40] Geoffrey is mentioned in two documents
before 1066. In one he witnessed the duke's charter for the abbey of Saint-
Ouen, Rouen.[41] On another occasion he acted as proxy for William
FitzOsbern by placing on the altar the symbol of a gift to Saint Amand,
Rouen.[42] The place called Magneville from which Geoffrey came was not
far from Longueville, held by Walter Giffard, and at least two of his
tenants were tenants also of Walter.[43] One of his daughters married a son
of the count of Boulogne; he himself may have married into the family of
the counts of Eu.[44] Although the scale of the rewards he received at first

[38] Robert count of Eu was succeeded by his son William, who is usually identified with the William of Eu
in Domesday Book though there does not seem to be evidence of their relationship from Domesday
itself. The fact that the William of Domesday held land in his own right as a tenant-in-chief in his
father's lifetime can be paralleled by, for instance, Robert de Tosny and Berengar, or Roger of
Montgomery and Roger the Poitevin. The identification was nevertheless rejected by Douglas,
*Domesday Monachorum of Christ Church, Canterbury*, p. 65.

[39] William arranged for the building of fortifications in London in the early weeks of 1067, and his writ
in favour of the Londoners, addressed to the bishop and Geoffrey the port-reeve, is thought to date
from soon after William's coronation: WP, p. 218; BRAN, I, no. 15.

[40] *Carmen*, p. 44; F. E. Harmer, *Anglo-Saxon Writs* (Manchester, 1952, reissued Stamford, 1989), pp. 560–1;
*Liber Eliensis*, ed. E. O. Blake, Camden Society, 3rd series, XCII (1962), p. 165.

[41] RADN, nos. 204, 204 bis.     [42] RADN , no. 182.

[43] Loyd, *Origins of Some Anglo-Norman Families*, p. 57; for the lands of the Giffard family see J. Le Maho,
'L'apparition des seigneuries châtelaines dans le Grand-Caux à l'époque ducale', *Archéologie médiévale*,
6 (1976), 38–46; for the families of Criketot and Guerres, see Loyd, *Origins of Some Anglo-Norman Families*,
pp. 36, 48–9.

[44] DB, I, 36; for the suggestion that Geoffrey may have married into the family of the counts of Eu see
Keats-Rohan, 'The Prosopography of Post-Conquest England: Four Case Studies', pp. 8–12.

sight seems out of proportion to his earlier career, his standing and family connections may have been more elevated than we think. Less is known about Ralph Bainard's origins.[45] He was put in command of the fortification placed within the south-west boundary of the city wall in London, and a substantial and relatively compact lordship was created for him centred on Stansted in Essex where a castle was built. The nucleus were the estates of the family descended from earldorman Beorhtnoth, the hero of the battle of Maldon.[46] It is possible that Ralph married into this family, for his principal predecessor was a woman named Aethelgyth. Both Geoffrey and Ralph had been given command of one of the London castles and a relatively compact and wealthy lordship in Essex.

The places of origin of Roger of Montgomery and Roger Bigod were in the département of Calvados, as were Bienfaite and Orbec, restored by William to Richard FitzGilbert.[47] Henry de Ferrers came from Ferrières-Saint-Hilaire near Orbec in the département of Eure.[48] Miles Crispin was almost certainly a member of the Crispin family of Neaufles; the family also had land in other parts of Normandy which they may have held before William Crispin was posted to Neaufles.[49] Geoffrey bishop of Coutances and Hugh, son of Richard *vicomte* of Avranches, were the only men from western Normandy in this group.[50]

There was only one man in the group from the deep south, William de Briouze from Briouze near Argentan. His most important and valuable lands were in Sussex, where he was granted a compact lordship between about 1068 and 1073, carved out of land previously granted to Roger of Montgomery and William de Warenne (see below, pp. 58–9). The origins of this man, and the reason why he was inserted into the tenurial settlement of Sussex, where land had been distributed in compact lordships not long after Hastings, remain obscure, but there are grounds for thinking that he was an ally of Roger of Montgomery. First, the initial choice of beneficiary for his gift of the church of Saints Gervase and Protase at Briouze was the

---

[45] Douglas, *Domesday Monachorum*, pp. 61–2.

[46] R. Mortimer, 'The Baynards of Baynard's Castle', *Studies in Medieval History presented to R. Allen Brown*, ed. C. Harper-Bill, C. Holdsworth, and J. L. Nelson (Woodbridge, 1989), pp. 241–53.

[47] Loyd, *Origins of Some Anglo-Norman Families*, pp. 68–9, 14–15; OV, IV, 208.

[48] Loyd, *Origins of Some Anglo-Norman Families*, p. 42.     [49] Green, 'Lords of the Norman Vexin', pp. 54–5.

[50] For Geoffrey see Le Patourel, 'Geoffrey of Montbray, Bishop of Coutances, 1049–1093'; for Hugh, L. Musset, 'Les fiefs de deux familles vicomtales de l'Hiémois au XIe siècle, les Goz et les Montgommery', *Revue historique de droit français et étranger*, 48 (1970), 431–3; Keats-Rohan, 'The Prosopography of Post-Conquest England', pp. 23–30.

abbey of Lonlay, a foundation of the lords of Bellême.[51] Secondly, although William de Warenne was compensated for the lands he lost in Sussex to William de Briouze, no such compensation appears to have been granted to Roger, as if, perhaps, Roger was expected to accept his losses on the ground that William de Briouze was his protégé. William de Briouze may have been stationed at Briouze by William the Conqueror at about this time in an attempt to strengthen ducal authority in the region, and perhaps he helped Roger of Montgomery to assert his authority over the lordship of Bellême.[52] At any rate, William de Briouze must have been sufficiently high in the king's favour for the boundaries of lordships in Sussex to be rearranged in this way.

The distribution of Domesday wealth in the upper echelons broadly reflects the geographical distribution of the duke's strength in the duchy. It was crucial for the success of William's enterprise to gain the support of powerful members of the Norman aristocracy with numbers of men at their disposal and the funds to be able to equip them. Ducal authority was strongest in upper Normandy, and it was from this region that he might expect to draw his greatest support. William had himself done a great deal to extend and consolidate ducal influence in the west, though his rule there had met with some resistance in the revolt of 1047. Caen was promoted as a second capital of the duchy, leading members of the aristocracy were granted land in the region, and new religious houses were set up with the backing of houses in upper Normandy. Odo as bishop of Bayeux worked energetically to build up the resources, both material and spiritual, of his see. The Cotentin and Avranchin had been brought under ducal control later than the other regions. Nigel of Saint-Sauveur does not seem to have been directly involved in the enterprise of England, but his kinsman Geoffrey of Coutances was a leading protagonist and evidently hungry for landed wealth in England. Although leading laymen from the Cotentin and Avranchin may not have been conspicuous in the invasion, men of the second rank or lesser ranks were involved, like Nigel d'Aubigny and Peter de Valognes, and in south-west England particularly a number of families with lands in the Cotentin, Avranchin, and north-west Brittany were established by 1086. The southern and south-eastern frontiers of the duchy, abutting Brittany, Maine, Perche, and the Chartrain, were vulner-

---

[51] Round, *CDF*, pp. 397–8.

[52] G. Louise, *La seigneurie de Bellême Xe–XIIe siècles*, Le Pays Bas-Normand, 199 and 200 (1990), I, 379–80.

able. Along the southern border in particular local lords enjoyed a large measure of independence. Families like the lords of Grandmesnil were evidently ready for action in England, but others, like their kinsmen the Giroie, were not involved either through personal choice or through circumstances. They and the duke had to consider not only whether they wanted to be involved but also whether they could spare the necessary time and resources.

The commitment of some families but not others to Norman rule in England had effects on both Normandy and England. The consequences of the conquest of England on Normandy have been discussed far less than the consequences of the Norman conquest on England, but they were nonetheless important.[53] The detachment and perhaps exclusion of some families from England could only lead to detachment and indifference in Normandy about the continuance of the condominium. Henry I faced an uphill task imposing his rule on the duchy after 1106 during the lifetimes of his brother and nephew, and many powerful families had little reason to be grateful to the kings of England.[54] This situation basically did not change after 1135. It meant that when there was a strong challenge to Angevin rule in Normandy in the late twelfth century there was less reason than there might have been for local families to resist a Capetian takeover. It also meant that the costs of defending the duchy in the twelfth century were high and part at least had to be met from England.[55]

The most important groups other than Normans involved in the invasion were from Brittany, Boulogne, and Flanders. These men must have been volunteers, prepared to head contingents in the hope of gaining land. Bretons, like Normans, had already settled in England before 1066. The most prominent was Ralph, the 'staller' of King Edward and possibly the husband of Eadgifu the Fair.[56] He was appointed earl in East Anglia and was succeeded by his son Ralph. Many of the Bretons who settled in the south-west came from north-east Brittany, where Duke William was only too keen to extend his influence, but there were recruits from other regions – the poverty of the region and the cross-currents of local politics

---

[53] D. Bates, 'Normandy and England after 1066', *English Historical Review*, 104 (1989), 851–80.

[54] J. A. Green, 'Henry I and the Aristocracy of Normandy', *La France anglaise au moyen âge, Actes du 111e Congrès National des Sociétés Savantes* (Paris, 1988), 161–73.

[55] J. C. Holt, 'The End of the Anglo-Norman realm', *Proceedings of the British Academy*, 61 (1975), 223–65; Holt, 'The Loss of Normandy and Royal Finance', *War and Government in the Middle Ages* (ed. Gillingham and Holt), pp. 92–105.

[56] P. A. Clarke, *The English Nobility under Edward the Confessor* (Oxford, 1994), p. 57.

made sure of that. Two if not three of the sons of Count Eudo of Penthièvre participated in the Conquest.[57] One of them, Count Brian, one of Eudo's sons, fought in the south-west for a short period, and some of the Bretons who were settled there by 1086 may have arrived either in Brian's company, or with Geoffrey bishop of Coutances, or Robert of Mortain (see below, p. 65). Another son, Count Alan the Red, was one of the richest men in Domesday England. He was granted many of the lands of Earl Ralph and Eadgifu the Fair after 1075; and at some point, possibly as early as 1071, he was given a great northern command in Yorkshire (see below, p. 107).

William also drew considerable support from the regions to the north and north-east of Normandy. Most prominent was Eustace II count of Boulogne, Guînes, and Thérouanne.[58] He is named on the Bayeux Tapestry, and the author of the *Carmen* was particularly keen to emphasize his role at Hastings.[59] According to the *Carmen* it was Eustace who, with Duke William and two others, was responsible for dispatching Harold with sword blows. Although the Bayeux Tapestry indicates that Harold was struck by an arrow through the eye, he is also probably to be identified with the next figure who was being cut down with a sword blow. The prominence given to Eustace in the tapestry has been interpreted as a reminder by Bishop Odo to the king that Eustace, a star in 1066, had fallen from grace but was later reconciled, thus pointing a possible parallel to Odo's own position when the tapestry was created.[60] It is surely simpler to believe, however, that Eustace had played a role more important than was recorded by William of Poitiers or William of Jumièges, who both wished to emphasize Norman achievements.

Eustace, like the Breton count, was faced with powerful neighbours, in his case Baldwin V count of Flanders and Duke William, Baldwin's son-in-law, to the south; an alliance between these two was an obvious threat to Eustace's position.[61] Eustace in turn built up his own alliances, including

---

[57] M. Jones, 'Notes sur quelques familles bretonnes en Angleterre après la conquête normande', *Mémoires de la Société d'Histoire et d'Archéologie de Bretagne*, 58 (1981), 73–97; K. S. B. Keats-Rohan, 'William I and the Breton Contingent in the non-Norman Conquest 1060–1087', *Anglo-Norman Studies*, 13 (1991), 157–72.

[58] WP, pp. 194, 264–8; OV, II, 174, 204–6.   [59] *Carmen*, pp. 34–6, 104, 116–17, 119–20.

[60] S. A. Brown, 'The Bayeux Tapestry: Why Eustace, Odo and William?', *Anglo-Norman Studies*, 12 (1990), 7–28.

[61] H. J. Tanner, 'The Expansion of the Power and Influence of the Counts of Boulogne under Eustace II', *Anglo-Norman Studies*, 14 (1992), 264–5.

his marriage to a sister of King Edward. He had little reason to favour the accession of Harold Godwinson in 1066 and his participation in the expedition may have been motivated partly by the desire for land – possibly, it has been suggested, lands belonging to his wife Goda – and partly to pay off old scores.[62] He probably soon received two valuable manors in Kent, both previously belonging to Earl Godwin. In 1067 he was embroiled in an unsuccessful attempt to take Dover castle, and he was estranged from William for some years.[63] By 1086 his son Eustace III was in the group of very rich class A landholders and had in his turn given lands in England to men from the Boulonnais, such as Arnulf of Ardres, Adelulf of Marck, and Ralph of Marcy.[64]

A number of other tenants-in-chief came from the same region. Drogo de la Beuvrière was given a large compact lordship in the East Riding of Yorkshire. He is said to have been married to a female relative of the Conqueror whom he killed accidentally and gave up his lands, possibly in 1086. It would appear, however, that he left behind several men from his own region, perhaps the best known of whom were the Fauquembergues, kinsmen of the castellans of Saint-Omer.[65] Gilbert de Gant (Ghent) probably received land in Lincolnshire and Yorkshire not long after 1066.[66] Arnulf de Hesdin is presumed to have come from one of the places called Hesdin in the Pas-de-Calais. He acquired substantial estates scattered through a number of counties. Many had been held by Wulfward White, a rich thegn who may have submitted to King William and continued to hold at least some of his lands for a number of years.[67] Sigar and Gunfrid of Chocques came from Chocques west of Béthune. Walter de Douai, presumably came from Douai, and Guy de Raimbeaucourt from Raimbeaucourt near Douai. From the Département of the Somme came Walter of St Valéry and Ansculf de Picquigny, sheriff of Surrey before 1086 and his son William, lord of Dudley. The nucleus of his lands had been held by Earl Edwin, and a date somewhere between 1069 and 1071 seems the likeliest for this castlery (see below, p. 72). Aubrey de Coucy came from

---

[62] Tanner, 'Eustace II', p. 273.

[63] A reconciliation between Eustace and William is referred to by William of Poitiers, and thus must have occurred before William stopped writing, about 1077: *ibid.*, p. 268.

[64] J. H. Round, 'The Counts of Boulogne as English Lords', *Studies in Peerage and Family History* (London, 1901), pp. 156–8.     [65] English, *Lords of Holderness*, pp. 7–8.

[66] SD, 'Historia Regum', *Opera omnia*, ed. T. Arnold, 2 vols. (RS, 1882–5), II, 188.

[67] Clarke, *The English Nobility under Edward the Confessor*, pp. 58–9, 156–7.

Coucy-le-Château in Aisne, and is thought to have been briefly earl of Northumberland before giving up his lands and career in England.[68]

In the early eleventh century relations between the rulers of Normandy and Flanders had not been easy, but they improved when Duke William married a daughter of Count Baldwin V (1035–67). Baldwin like his neighbours had been seeking to expand his territories and influence. Not only had the boundaries of his realms been extended, but he also had links with the family of Earl Godwin. He sheltered Godwin in 1051 and Tostig, Baldwin's son-in-law, took refuge at St Omer in 1065.[69] Many Flemings took service with William in 1066, and it was said that the count himself sent men.[70] Some were of high rank, like Gilbert de Gant, son of the lord of Aalst, and Gherbod, son of the advocate of St Omer.[71] Others were from less distinguished families, known simply as, for instance, Walter the Fleming or Winemar the Fleming. Their estates were scattered throughout England, with particular concentrations in Somerset, Yorkshire, Northamptonshire, and Bedfordshire.[72]

William of Poitiers commented on the fact that some men came from beyond the frontiers of Normandy to answer the duke's call to arms in 1066.[73] Aimary of Thouars in Aquitaine was at Hastings and was prominent amongst those who advised William to proceed to coronation, and Hervey of Bourges and Fulcher of Paris, for instance, are mentioned in Domesday Book.[74] The aristocracy of Norman England was a mixture of men from different regions forming a thin top level over the mass of the population. The dominant strand was, however, Norman, and within the Normans there was a small group of the men closest to Duke William in 1066.

So far the emphasis has been on individuals, the great captains of the

---

[68] Tengvik, *Old English Bynames*, p. 3; Aubrey was called Aubrey de Coucy in Berkshire and Yorkshire, *DB*, I, 58, 329b; Symeon of Durham, 'Historia Regum', *Opera omnia*, II, 199. There was a lord of Coucy named Aubrey at this date: Barthélemy, *Les deux âges de la seigneurie banale. Coucy (XIe–XIIIe siècle)*, p. 67.

[69] D. Nicholas, *Medieval Flanders* (London, 1992), pp. 52–5.     [70] WM, *Gesta Regum*, II, 478.

[71] The origin of Gilbert de Gant was discussed in Abbott, 'The Gant Family in England', pp. 19–21; C. P. Lewis, 'The Formation of the Honor of Chester, 1066–1100', *The Earldom of Chester and Its Charters*, ed. A. T. Thacker, Journal of the Chester Archaeological Society, 71 (1991), p. 38 and references cited therein.

[72] R. H. George, 'The Contribution of Flanders to the Conquest of England, 1065–1086', *Revue Belge de Philologie et d'Histoire*, 5 (1926), 81–99.     [73] WP, p. 150.

[74] J. Martindale, 'Aimeri of Thouars and the Poitevin Connection', *Anglo-Norman Studies*, 7 (1985), 224–45; G. Beech, 'The Participation of Aquitainians in the Conquest of England 1066–1100', *Anglo-Norman Studies*, 9 (1987), 1–24; *DB*, II, 440; I, 211b, 214b, 217b.

conquest, but they of course were accompanied by retinues of knights composed of their kinsmen and vassals. The conquest could not have been achieved without a great co-operative effort in which ties of kinship and lordship were inextricably intermingled in an extension of the techniques which underpinned family strategies. Successful lordship depended on a rolling programme of attracting the service of knights and being able to provide them with wages and land. Men needed sons to carry on their line, but a whole string of sons could only be provided for if the family's stock of land was expanding. If political conditions did not favour such aggressive tactics, younger sons had to be dispatched to seek their fortunes elsewhere. Tancred de Hauteville provides an example of a father with numerous sons whose lands could not provide for them all, so that Robert Guiscard and seven of his brothers went to Italy to win fame and fortune.[75] It also makes the point incidentally about the way men who did travel to Italy, or to England, would be expected to give a start to brothers and cousins who joined them. Information and news were transmitted via family members: the Hautevilles, or the Grandmesnils in Italy could keep their relatives in Normandy informed about what was going on. Similarly the Normans and Bretons in England kept their kinsmen informed about the situation and prospects there.

Several families were represented in Domesday Book by two brothers, like Richard and Baldwin, the sons of Count Gilbert of Brionne. Walter and Ilbert de Lacy came from Lassy in Calvados. Their patrimonial land was later held in fief of the bishop of Bayeux, and they may well have come to England with the bishop. By 1069 Walter was already established on the border with Wales; Ilbert received his opportunity in Yorkshire, probably some time later.[76] Ralph de Pomeroy and William Capra, Walter de Clavile and Gotscelm, Roger de Pîtres and Durand, Arnulf de Hesdin and Ilbod, are all examples of brothers from Domesday Book.[77]

There are other cases of probable kinship. Durand Malet was probably the brother of Robert Malet, lord of Eye.[78] Ralph Taillebois and Ivo Taillebois may well have been kinsmen: Ralph's lands passed by 1086 to Hugh de Beauchamp, who probably came from the vicinity of Tilly-sur-Seulles, and Ivo Taillebois gave a church at Cristot near Tilly to

[75] OV, II, 98–100.    [76] Wightman, *Lacy Family*, pp. 215, 167, 21.

[77] DB Phillimore edition, Devon, notes to ch. 19, 25, Herefordshire 22, 5–6; DB, I, 154.

[78] *Eye Priory Cartulary and Charters*, II, ed. V. Brown, Suffolk Record Society, 13 (1994), p. 6.

Marmoutier.[79] The origins of William Peverel of Nottingham and Ranulf
Peverel of Essex have never been discovered, but it is not impossible that
they were related.[80] Ranulf Peverel may have come from western
Normandy, for one of his tenants was William des Troisgots. William
Peverel of Nottingham's estates were concentrated in the north midlands,
but he had some land in Essex, and his daughter married Richard de
Redvers, who held land in the Cotentin and in lower Normandy.[81]

Detailed study of patterns of landholding in Domesday Book, of their
later history and of the families which held them, strengthens the impression that even where precise evidence of place of origin or family relationship is lacking, allied families pooled their resources. The Bolebecs and
the Giffards were evidently related. Bolebec was the original head of the
Giffard lordship but when Walter Giffard obtained Longueville he moved
his headquarters there and Bolebec became the chief estate of a minor
vassal family.[82] In England Hugh de Bolebec was both an under-tenant of
Walter Giffard and a minor tenant-in-chief. Osbern Giffard, son of Walter,
may be identified with the man who married the widow of Robert
FitzErneis, for in Wiltshire his land included an estate which had been
given to Fontenay, where Robert was buried.[83] Berengar Giffard, another
tenant-in-chief, was also presumably another member of the family.

The great lords also brought with them men from their estates. William
FitzOsbern's career in England proved to be short-lived, for he left in 1070.
Before he did so he held the Isle of Wight, land in Hampshire,
Herefordshire, and several other counties, and men who had probably
arrived in his retinue are found holding land by 1086. Gilbert de
'Bretevile' was a tenant-in-chief in Hampshire, Berkshire, and Wiltshire,
and presumably came from Breteuil, the head of FitzOsbern's Norman
estates. William Alis, a tenant-in-chief in Hampshire, came from a family
which held of the lord of Breteuil.[84] Gozelin de Cormeilles, another
Hampshire tenant-in-chief, came from Cormeilles where FitzOsbern

[79] Loyd, *Origins of Some Anglo-Norman Families*, p. 100.

[80] See the discussion of the background of William Peverel of Nottingham and his relationship to Ranulf Peverel in W. Dugdale, *The Baronage of England*, 3 vols. in one (London, 1675–6), I, 436.

[81] *DB*, II, 89b–90; J. H. Round, 'Tregoz of Tolleshunt Tregoz', *Essex Archaeological Society Transactions*, New Series, 8 (1903), 330–2. For the possible link between William Peverel and Ranulf Peverel, see below, p. 89.     [82] Le Maho, 'L'apparition des seigneuries châtelaines', pp. 37–8.

[83] *DB*, I, 146b, 147, 150b; for Osbern see Musset, 'Actes inédits du XIe siècle. v', pp. 17–18, 40–1; *DB*, I, 72b (Middleton, held by St Stephen of Fontenay).     [84] Crouch, *Beaumont Twins*, p. 106.

founded an abbey. By 1086 the church of the manor of 'Anne' which Gozelin held had been given to Cormeilles.[85] Gozelin was presumably related to Ansfrid de Cormeilles, who had land in Herefordshire. Other Herefordshire landholders who may have owed their start to FitzOsbern were Alfred d'Epaignes, Gilbert FitzTurold, and Hugh Lasne.[86] Roger de Pîtres, the first Norman sheriff of Gloucestershire, received land at Standish from FitzOsbern, and Ralph de Bernai, first post-Conquest sheriff of Herefordshire, received the services of two riding men.[87]

FitzOsbern is a useful example because we know that his career in England lasted only about three years, so we can be virtually certain that he brought these men with him, yet it can be paralleled again and again. Roger of Montgomery, to choose another example, established men from his continental estates in Sussex and Shropshire. Orderic mentioned by name Warin the Bald, William Pantulf, Picot de Sai, Corbet and his sons Roger and Robert, and to these can be added Gerard of Tournai.[88] Families established on the English estates of the counts of Eu whose origins have been traced back to the counts' Norman estates include Bailleul, Cruel, Daivile, Floc, Fraelvilla, Fressenville, St Leger, St Martin, Sept Meules, and Strabo.[89] What the evidence rarely permits us to know is the precise nature of the relationship of the great lords to lesser lineages from their estates, and specifically whether these men were already their vassals when they accompanied their lords to England. In many cases they probably were, but in others it is not inconceivable that men of lower but relatively independent standing in Normandy accepted land in England as tenants from the great lords. The latter also may have been able to use their gains in England to strengthen their lordship in Normandy. The number of fees established on the bishopric of Bayeux was far in excess of those created in other sees as the returns to the inquest of 1172 showed.[90] It is tempting to associate some of them with Bishop Odo, and if he was responsible, did he create them before 1066 to recruit men for the expedition, or afterwards, as his huge resources attracted men to his lordship? In

---

[85] Loyd, *Origins of Some Anglo-Norman Families*, pp. 33–4.

[86] C. P. Lewis, 'The Norman Settlement of Herefordshire under William I', *Anglo-Norman Studies*, 7 (1985), pp. 205–7.     [87] *DB*, I, 164b, 180b.

[88] OV, II, 262; for the origins of Picot de Sai, William Pantulf, Gerard of Tournai, and Rainald de Bailleul who married the niece of Warin the Bald, see Loyd, *Origins of Some Anglo-Norman Families*, pp. 96, 76, 104, 11–12.     [89] Loyd, *Origins of Some Anglo-Norman Families*, pp. 11, 36, 37, 43, 44, 90–1, 97–8, 99.

[90] *RBE*, II, 624–5.

like manner the count of Mortain's vast gains in England may have provided him with resources to establish himself more firmly in Mortain.
Once again we return to the point made above about the importance of
the conquest of England for Normandy, as well as vice versa.

The conquest of England was carried through by a small group of men,
preeminently from William's inner circle. They recruited kinsmen and
followers into contingents which worked closely in co-operation to gain
and secure lands for themselves, and could be reinforced by further
recruits from their lands across the Channel. The dominance of this
group lasted until the death of the Conqueror, after which the contest
over his inheritance divided the aristocracy on both sides of the Channel,
and the separation of England from Normandy was followed by restructuring in the upper ranks of the aristocracy and the recruitment by Rufus
and Henry I of new faces from Normandy. There remained throughout,
however, a section of the Norman aristocracy which stayed aloof from
involvement. Although there were families with major holdings on both
sides of the Channel, there were others whose interests were wholly or
mainly in Normandy, just as there were those whose fortunes were made
in England. The leaders had recruited contingents from their families and
from their estates. Whether the latter were technically feudal vassals or
local lords of lesser standing is not really relevant in this context. What
counted was that they were able to co-operate in the work of conquest and
colonization.

## 2   The revolution

The scale of the transfer of land to a new ruling elite, carried through within twenty years of the battle of Hastings, has rightly been viewed as one of the most dramatic changes wrought by the Norman Conquest. The speed and completeness of the changes in the elite tend to confirm what will be argued here: that where possible the transfer was intended to be both orderly and controlled. The aim at least was that the newcomers stepped into the shoes of one or more predecessors or, as Domesday Book describes them, antecessors (*antecessores*). One of the clearest cases is that of Geoffrey de Mandeville, who succeeded to the lands of Ansger the staller in several counties. Where the needs of the security of the new regime were at stake, however, there were radical changes. In parts of the south-east and along the south coast compact lordships were set up centred on castles. In the south-west also considerations of coastal defence helped to shape lordships. In the west and north midlands more compact lordships were set up as bridgeheads, both as defence and to stake out further advances. In Yorkshire and the surrounding regions at the limits of Norman advance by 1086 there were further great castleries.

Historians have disagreed about the extent both of continuity in patterns of landholding and of control. P. H. Sawyer argued that the new units of lordship in many cases were built upon the old.[1] Robin Fleming, on the other hand, comparing the names of those recorded as pre-Conquest landholders with those holding in 1086, has stressed massive discontinuity, especially in eastern England.[2] F. M. Stenton was impressed by the order and discipline underpinning the presentation of results, and concluded that the Conquest never became a 'scramble for land'.[3] Fleming, in contrast, has argued that many uncontrolled seizures of land occurred, again especially in eastern England. She concluded that the new elite was in effect a kleptocracy.

---

[1] P. H. Sawyer, '1066–1086: a Tenurial Revolution', *Domesday Book. A Reassessment*, ed. Sawyer (London, 1985), pp. 71–85.

[2] R. Fleming, *Kings and Lords in Conquest England*, Cambridge Studies in Medieval Life and Thought, 4th series, xv (Cambridge, 1991), especially chapter 6.

[3] F. M. Stenton, *Anglo-Saxon England*, 3rd edn (Oxford, 1971), p. 626.

It is argued here first, however, that there was a good deal of continuity, more in the east than Fleming allows, since it seems the Domesday record of personal names cannot simply be taken at face value (see below, pp. 78–9). Through a series of regional studies, the prevalence of antecessorial succession is demonstrated, and this, more than anything else, is a testimony of order. If the newcomers had apportioned the land between themselves, a simpler settlement, which took less account of pre-existing units of settlement, would surely have been the result. Again, the idea that King William began by apportioning lands of individual thegns to single Normans but that within a few years the supply of major thegns dried up and so he switched to granting territorial lordships is probably only partly right in the sense that, although many cases of antecessorial succession probably occurred soon after 1066, there are later examples of the same phenomenon, as in the passing of many of the forfeit estates of Earl Ralph of East Anglia to Count Alan after the revolt of 1075. Conversely, some of the more drastic reorganizations into compact lordships, often preserving a nucleus of earlier lordships within them, occurred in the dangerous early years of conquest.

Secondly, there are repeated indications in Domesday Book that the process of transfer was intended to be orderly. Often lands were handed over by men called deliverers in Domesday Book, including Bishops Odo and Geoffrey.[4] Sometimes, perhaps often, the deliverer was the sheriff. Roger Bigod is spoken of as 'such a guarantor as any sheriff might rightly have been in King Edward's time' in Norfolk, and Peter de Valognes delivered land in Hertfordshire where he was sheriff.[5] Not all were sheriffs, however, or at least, not sheriffs of the counties where they were deliverers. Others who are mentioned as deliverers include Humphrey Visdeloup, Hubert de Port, and Ivo Taillebois.[6] Roger d'Ivry is mentioned in Gloucestershire as having put land into royal farms, evidently after the departure of Earl William, and conceivably he had been sent there to take the king's lands in hand, as in this county he had only one estate.[7] In Surrey one hide of land at Malden was held by Robert de 'Wateuile' and was in dispute. The men of the hundred testified that Edward of Salisbury and Robert d'Oilly had adjudged it as belonging to Richard of Tonbridge.[8]

---

[4] *DB*, I, 201b, 151b.    [5] *DB*, II, 290b; I, 141b.

[6] *DB*, I, 50b (Humphrey); II, 377, 450 (Hubert); 290b (Ivo), cf. 150, a reference to Ivo and his colleagues being vouchsafed to warranty by a man named Edric after Earl Ralph had forfeited; I, 151b (bishop of Coutances).    [7] *DB*, I, 162b, 164.    [8] *DB*, I, 35.

On occasion the new lords had royal writs notifying that specific grants had been made. In Berkshire Robert d'Oilly held a hide in Ardington which Azor, King Edward's dispenser, had held. In 1086 Azor was holding from Robert, but the men of the hundred testified that Azor ought to hold it from the king, as King William had restored it and had given Azor his writ for it. Robert therefore held it wrongfully, for none of them had seen the king's writ or a man who put him in possession on the king's behalf.[9] It must have been advantageous for the new lord to be able to produce a writ before a court of shire or hundred, for the members of the court then had a certain responsibility for ensuring that he was fully informed of the whereabouts of his estates; but it was the king's wish that was paramount here, not the written document. Adjustments to the settlement were made by exchanges, and again it would appear that these were at least subject to scrutiny and not completely uncontrolled. In Hampshire a king's thegn called Alwin White held two hides which he said he had held in King Edward's reign under Wigod (of Wallingford); 'now under Miles (Crispin) and it was delivered to Wigod by Humphrey Visdeloup in exchange for Broadwater as he himself states, but the hundred knows nothing of it'.[10]

King William evidently took the major decisions about the land settlement, at least between 1067 and 1072 when he was most actively involved in establishing Norman rule in England. When military considerations came to the forefront, other principles had to be put on one side. After Hastings William wanted to reward the Normans, but he also had to secure the Channel ports and to establish a bridgehead for further advances. In Kent the land distribution took place at an early date, and was shaped in part by security considerations. In this county land was distributed in ways which cut across earlier boundaries. In Surrey, too, the lordship of Richard FitzGilbert was probably created at an early date and without regard to earlier boundaries.[11] It was also presumably William's decision that the Sussex rapes were to be held by Normans. In the south-west considerations of coastal defence were joined with the need to suppress local resistance, and the result here was a series of relatively compact lordships, Hugh FitzGrip based at Wareham, Juhel at Totnes, and Reginald de Vautorte at Trematon, while on the north coast of Devon and

9 *DB*, I, 62.    10 *DB*, I, 50b.

11 *DB*, I, 7b; W. V. Dumbreck, 'The Lowy of Tonbridge', *Archaeologia Cantiana*, 72 (1955), 138–47.

Somerset, the bishop of Coutances held Barnstaple and Bristol, with William de Mohun at Dunster. By contrast the east coast of England was vulnerable to fleets either from Scandinavia or from Scotland, and in Yorkshire Earl Hugh controlled the northern section, and Drogo de la Beuvrière that south of Bridlington. In Lincolnshire there does not seem to have been a conscious policy of concentrating coastal estates in the hands of the Conqueror's most prominent followers, but in Norfolk and Suffolk Roger Bigod held numerous estates in the vicinity of the coast, and held royal manors there in custody. Finally, in Essex a number of key men held important manors on or near the coast. Similarly the king must have taken the decision to grant two whole counties to key men as bastions against the Welsh, and must have created the compact lordships in the midlands and the north from the ruins of Earl Edwin's fortunes. Occasionally there are explicit references in Domesday Book to William's personal involvement in land distribution. The manor of West Ham in Essex was said to have been given by King William to Ranulf Peverel and Robert Gernon.[12] Another entry in Essex stated that the king through Robert d'Oilly commanded that Hugh de Bernières should hold three manors as a tenant of Geoffrey de Mandeville, if Geoffrey could prove that they belonged to his holding (*feudum*), as in fact had happened by 1086.[13]

Yet the king can only have had time to take major decisions, and during his lengthy absences many local matters needed resolution. The individual who stands out as having had most to do with the land settlement apart from the king is his brother, Odo bishop of Bayeux. It is not easy to date his activities from the Domesday evidence, nor is it always easy to distinguish between his activities on behalf of his brother, and those for himself. Odo delivered seisin and decided claims.[14] On one occasion there is a reference to his seal having been used.[15] It is not always easy to ascertain on what basis he acted, though he may have acted as regent on one or more occasions when William was in Normandy, and before his own arrest in 1082.[16] Odo certainly crops up in many different counties in Domesday Book. In Oxfordshire he gave land away belonging to the king.[17] In Cambridgeshire, Hertfordshire, and Lincolnshire he was a deliverer.[18]

---

[12] *DB*, II, 64, 72b.   [13] *DB*, II, 60b–61.

[14] *DB*, I, 202b (deliverer), 175b (a justice at the Bengeworth plea).   [15] *DB*, I, 342.

[16] D. Bates, 'The Origins of the Justiciarship', *Proceedings of the Battle Conference*, 4 (1981), 1–12.

[17] *DB*, I, 154b.   [18] *DB*, I, 202b, 139, 342.

In Bedfordshire, Surrey, Wiltshire, and Worcestershire he took land away.[19] In Hampshire he supervised an exchange, and in Leicestershire he ordered payment from waste land of a royal manor for the service of the Isle of Wight.[20] He is also mentioned in East Anglia: in Norfolk he ordered Roger Bigod to keep land belonging to a freeman 'in the king's hand'.[21] In Suffolk there is a reference to a lawsuit with Robert Malet's mother.[22] Although Odo is not mentioned as intervening actively in the north midlands, he held land in Nottinghamshire and Northamptonshire.[23] In the north he may have been responsible for the establishment of his tenant, Ilbert de Lacy, at Pontefract, though he did not himself hold land in Yorkshire in 1086.[24] The only region where we do not hear about him in an active role is in the south-west. He held one manor each in Dorset and Somerset, previously Earl Leofwin's, and none in Devon and Cornwall.

On occasion Odo's activities were complained of, and perhaps the aggrieved parties felt able to speak at the Domesday Inquest as the bishop was then in prison. In Bedfordshire William the chamberlain claimed two hides which his antecessor had held before 1066, but which the bishop of Bayeux took away by force and gave to his chamberlain Aethelwulf.[25] In Cambridgeshire William de Cahagnes, whose lands were otherwise all held as an under-tenant of Odo in this county, held one estate which had been delivered to him by Odo, but the men of the hundred did not know how.[26] In Worcestershire Odo held two estates. The first had been held by Evesham abbey before 1066; later Urse d'Abetot acquired it from the abbot in exchange for another estate, and in 1086 Urse held it of Odo.[27] The second had also been held 'for many years' until Odo took it from the church and gave it to Urse.[28] The account in Domesday is relatively neutral in tone; less so is the version in 'Evesham D', a record of those Evesham estates obtained by Urse with the connivance of the bishop of Bayeux. Of the first, Acton Beauchamp, 'Evesham D' says that after Abbot Aethelwig's death Urse violently encroached on Acton and also on Bengeworth which he had been given in exchange. The church had lost them entirely unjustly. And of Sheriff's Lench, 'Evesham D' says that after the abbot's death Urse violently seized the land with the support of Bishop Odo, and the church had unjustly lost them. 'There was a larger number of other

[19] *DB*, I, 216, 32, 68, 176; 50b (exchange).     [20] *DB*, I, 50b, 230b.     [21] *DB*, II, 278.     [22] *DB*, II, 447b.
[23] *DB*, I, 284, 220.     [24] Wightman, *Lacy Family*, p. 241.     [25] *DB*, I, 216.     [26] *DB*, I, 201b.
[27] *DB*, I, 176.     [28] *DB*, I, 176.

villages which the church had in the times of Abbot Aethelwig and of the other abbots that preceded him. But the Abbey was wrongfully despoiled through the actions of Bishop Odo. Now very many of the king's barons have them and the church lacks them.'[29]

Odo's activities, arbitrary and unjust as they evidently had been on occasion, nevertheless reinforce the view that the land transfer was subject to overall control, and did not become a free-for-all. The new lords evidently saw themselves not as participating in an act of theft, but as lawful successors by the grant of a king who had lawfully succeeded his kinsman, Edward the Confessor. The picture which is portrayed in the following chapter, therefore, is one which on the whole supports the Stentonian line that the Conquest did not become a 'scramble for land'.

In the first instance Englishmen who lost their lands did so because they had fought in the campaigns of 1066.[30] After the coronation those who fought on were rebels, and again their lands were confiscated (see below, p. 259). Some perhaps did not take arms but simply refused to submit and offer their allegiance. Others may have submitted at first like Edwin and Morcar but, finding life intolerable under the new regime, decided to fight or to flee. Others may have found themselves unable to meet demands for tribute and service, and lost their land on that account. Whether the penalty of confiscation was decided in any kind of formal procedure or if there was any form of appeal is not clear. There were those – and not just the dispossessed and conquered English – who had misgivings about the scale of expropriation. The chronicler Orderic Vitalis put into the mouth of a monk named Guitmond a denunciation of 'the greatest plunder' when Guitmund told King William why he was refusing an offer of preferment in England.[31] Orderic, himself part French and part English and writing long after the years of conquest, was able to weigh the Normans' achievement against its darker side.

Detailed studies throw light on successive phases of the revolution. In 1067 and 1068 the settlement of the south-east was clear in outline; by 1068 the Normans were advancing into the south-west to deal with revolt there; William FitzOsbern was on the Welsh borders by 1068; and castles

---

[29] See translation in Phillimore edition, Worcestershire, appendix IV.
[30] G. Garnett, 'Coronation and Propaganda: some Implications of the Norman Claim to the Throne of England in 1066', *Transactions of the Royal Historical Society*, 5th series, 36 (1986), 91–9.
[31] OV, II, 270–8.

were built at key points in the midlands, and at York. The following year witnessed the beginning of another major rising in the north, followed by the king's infamous harrying, and drastic reorganization in Yorkshire. Two years later occurred the final downfall of Edwin and Morcar. In 1075 the last native earl, Waltheof, allied with the Norman Roger, earl of Hereford, and Ralph, earl of East Anglia. The suppression of their rising was followed by further changes, particularly in East Anglia. Here the transfer had been eased by the fact that Stigand, who held much land in East Anglia, was not deposed straight away, and by the choice as earl of one of King Edward's men, Ralph, a Breton, who was in turn followed by his son Ralph the younger (the rebel of 1075). In the following pages, therefore, counties are grouped into regions which wherever possible reflect both the successive waves of conquest and settlement and the character of landholding. On the whole the county is an appropriate unit for study, in that the new lordships sometimes were based on county boundaries (such as Shropshire and Cheshire), or subdivisions such as hundreds, or the newcomers received the lands of particular individuals within particular counties. Sometimes, however, the county is not as appropriate, as in cases where new lordships straddled boundaries, such as Dudley, spanning Worcestershire, Warwickshire, and Staffordshire. Middlesex and Oxfordshire have been included with the east midland counties, Middlesex because it was surveyed in the same circuit in Domesday Book (circuit III), and Oxfordshire, because the north of the county (together with north Buckinghamshire, also in circuit III) was dominated by the estates held by Odo of Bayeux. Finally, some discussion of the settlement of Yorkshire belongs with the midlands and the south, in that it began early, and the people involved also tended to have land in Lincolnshire. Nevertheless it was decided to deal with Yorkshire in the following chapter, as part of a wider discussion of the Normans in the north.

## I Kent, Surrey, Sussex

William's immediate concerns were with the security of his new realm, and with the need to reward his followers. The battle at Hastings took place on 14 October, after which William moved to Dover and Canterbury, then swept west and north of London, via Wallingford and Berkhamsted,

where he received the submissions of English leaders.[32] The rich thegn
who held Berkhamsted, Edmer Ator, may not have submitted in time, for
all his lands passed to the count of Mortain, who built a strong castle at
Berkhamsted.

William was crowned in London on Christmas day, and moved soon
afterwards to Barking, where he received more submissions and supervised the building of fortifications in London, which were possibly committed around this time to Geoffrey de Mandeville and Ralph Bainard.[33]
William left England for his victory tour of Normandy before Easter 1067,
taking with him hostages including Edwin, Morcar, Edgar, and others,
and leaving in charge William FitzOsbern and Odo of Bayeux, William de
Warenne, Hugh de Montfort, and Hugh de Grandmesnil. He did not
return until December of that year, by which time Eustace II count of
Boulogne had rebelled, probably in the autumn, and tried to seize Dover.[34]
Before his revolt he may have been assigned the two very large and valuable manors of Westerham and Boughton Aluph in Kent, both of which
had belonged to Earl Godwin, but may have felt that he was not getting a
sufficient reward for his efforts.[35] Bishop Odo, soon if not already earl of
Kent, was taking control of the county.[36]

Dover castle was defended against Eustace by Odo of Bayeux and Hugh
de Montfort. Odo was given comital status in Kent in succession to
Leofwin, who had died at Hastings.[37] In 1086 Odo held the vast majority of
the land in that county which did not belong to the church or to the king.
The lay landholders were Count Eustace, Haimo the sheriff, Hugh de
Montfort, and Richard of Tonbridge, whose estates straddled the
Kent–Surrey boundary. With the exception of Haimo the sheriff, these
men may have received their lands in 1067 or thereabouts. Eustace was
said to have been invited to invade by Kentishmen who were oppressed by
the Normans; the latter would not have wished to move too far afield at
this early date and would have needed resources for further conquests.
Much of the available land was held by the archbishop and monks of
Canterbury or by other religious houses. Although Stigand was not for-

---

[32] *ASC* D; cf. WP, p. 216. Williams suggested that most of Odo's activities may have dated from the early
years, partly on the basis that after 1072 his comital powers seem to have been confined to Kent:
Williams, *The English and the Norman Conquest*, p. 14. He may have had more wide-ranging vice-regal
powers, however.     [33] WP, p. 232.     [34] OV, II, 204.     [35] *DB*, I, 14.
[36] Lewis, 'Early Earls of Norman England', 217–18.     [37] WP, p. 240.

mally deposed until 1070, he may have been unwilling or unable to resist the establishment of Normans on Canterbury lands.[38]

Hugh de Montfort held a compact lordship, his *divisio* as Domesday Book called it, of which the main settlement was the borough of Hythe. This had grown up on the archbishop of Canterbury's manor of Saltwood, where Hugh built his castle.[39] The boundaries of the lordship did not exactly follow those of the hundreds or the older units, the lathes, though this may have been the intention. In Kent there were manors with detached pasturelands, or denes, at some distance from the manor to which they belonged.[40] Hugh held the manor of Brabourne himself (that is, in demesne), in the hundred of Bircholt and lathe of Wye. It had been assessed at seven sulungs (ploughlands) in King Edward's day, but in 1086 at only five and a half because the rest was outside Hugh's division and was held by the bishop of Bayeux.[41] In King Edward's day Aldglose in Felborough hundred had been held with Brabourne; in 1086 it belonged to the bishop of Bayeux's fief (*feudum*) and remained outside his division.[42] Hugh is likely to have received these lands at an early date. He was active in Kent as a colleague of Odo's at Dover in 1067,[43] and his command in Kent is likely to have been assigned by King William rather than by Odo, for Hugh was an important Norman lord in his own right, and in England he held his lands in chief not as Odo's tenant. Moreover, the decision to install Hugh on the archiepiscopal manor of Saltwood is likely to have been the king's, with a view to ensuring that the nearby port of Hythe was in safe hands. William of Arques was established at another coastal town, Folkestone. This was the centre of a huge estate, the endowment of an early religious house, and before the Conquest it had been in the hands of Earl Godwin.[44] William came from Arques in upper Normandy, and like Hugh he is not known to have been a follower of Odo. His father was Godfrey, *vicomte* of Arques, who was said to have been a brother of Walter Giffard.[45]

Richard FitzGilbert also could have been an early recipient of land in Kent and neighbouring Surrey.[46] He held a compact lordship, the *lieu* or

---

[38] FW, II, 5.    [39] *DB*, I, 4b.

[40] K. P. Whitney, *The Jutish Forest* (London, 1976), especially chapters 4 and 5.    [41] *DB*, I, 13b.

[42] *DB*, I, 10b.

[43] WP, p. 266. Hugh gave the churches belonging to some of his Kentish estates to Bec. A date of 1067 was suggested by Round for the charter recording the gift, but this is problematic: Round, *CDF*, p. 120.

[44] *DB*, I, 9b.    [45] Douglas, *Domesday Monachorum*, p. 43.

[46] R. Mortimer, 'The Beginnings of the Honour of Clare', *Anglo-Norman Studies*, 3 (1981), 119–41.

lowy of Tonbridge. In Domesday Book the estate seems to have been surveyed under the manor of Hadlow which was held by Odo of Bayeux in
1086.[47] Richard also held many manors in the neighbouring county of
Surrey where he and Odo were the most important tenants-in-chief. Again
one might argue that a compact lordship, guarding a route from the
south coast to London, is likely to have been created early, and on the
king's instructions.

Odo had extensive authority over Surrey, though it was not as comprehensive as in Kent. There were rather more lay tenants-in-chief there and a
number had succeeded to all the manors of Anglo-Saxon predecessors:
Roger of Montgomery to Osmund's land, and William de Briouze to two
manors of Godtovi. Such cases of antecessorial succession could in theory
have occurred at any time after 1066, though it is likely that many
occurred at an early date, especially in south-east England where thegns
are more likely to have been in arms. Moreover the count of Mortain had a
base there as well as Odo, for he held land at Lambeth and Ham, and two
other small estates.[48] Odo's estates included a monastery and waterway at
Southwark, and he had substantial estates including one if not more
which had been held by Aethelnoth *cild* (an important predecessor in
Kent) and two manors which had been held by Earl Leofwin.

Fleming suggested that Surrey was a county where the Conqueror's
original plans for the land settlement had been blurred by extra-legal
seizures, and that the villains of the piece were Odo and Richard
FitzGilbert.[49] Odo, she suggested, may have received his earliest grants in
the county soon after 1066, and continued to build them up, the last as
late as 1081 or 1082. The entry on which Fleming based the later date
derives from an entry for the manor of Farncombe. A royal reeve claimed
it, and the men of the hundred said that he had held it from the king
(unnamed) when the king was in Wales; that he kept it afterwards until
the bishop of Bayeux came to Kent; and that Odo added Farncombe (and
Rodsall) to the farm of Bramley.[50] If the king was William, then the date of
the transfer to Odo was probably 1081 or 1082, for William went to Wales
in 1081 and Odo was arrested in the following year. It is perhaps more

---

[47] *DB*, I, 7b; Tonbridge was later claimed as belonging to the archbishopric of Canterbury, *Radulfi Diceto
Lundoniensis Opera Historica*, ed. W. Stubbs, 2 vols., RS (London, 1876), I, 311; William FitzStephen,
*Materials for the History of Thomas Becket*, 7 vols., I-VI, ed. J. C. Robertson, VII, ed. J. C. Robertson with J. B.
Sheppard, RS (London, 1875–85), III, 43.
[48] *DB*, I, 34.       [49] Fleming, *Kings and Lords*, pp. 188–91.       [50] *DB*, I, 31, 31b.

likely, however, that the king referred to was Edward the Confessor and that the entry was referring to a time before 1066, and thus cannot be used as evidence for Odo's high-handed activities as late as 1081 or 1082. Although there were some seizures by Odo and Richard, they were not particularly significant and the likelihood is that the land settlement here took shape early, and probably at the king's behest.

Sussex was another county in the south-east where the available land was parcelled out early in compact lordships and with military considerations in mind. It was of vital importance that the harbours here, as in Kent, were in safe hands to protect the sea-crossings to Normandy, and to guard them from attacks by Danes or the sons of King Harold. The county was subdivided into six lordships running north–south called rapes, from the Scandinavian word for rope, alluding to the idea that boundaries were sometimes marked out using a rope. Some of the rapes were probably earlier units, though they had not formed the basis of landholding on the eve of the Conquest, when Godwin and Harold had been the dominant landholders. They may have been established in the early tenth century as territories dependent on burhs, in which case they served a function comparable with that of the post-Conquest rapes, or their history may have gone back even further.[51]

If we are to interpret the Bayeux Tapestry literally, a castle was thrown up at Hastings even before the battle. Its first castellan was Humphrey of Tilleul.[52] Humphrey was mentioned as one of those who returned to Normandy in 1068, and it may have been at this stage that Hastings was committed to Robert count of Eu, who held it in 1086. Robert of Mortain may have been stationed at Pevensey in 1066 and William de Warenne may also have been active in the area by 1067, for he is mentioned by Orderic as one of those left in command in 1067.[53] The creation of lordships may have begun a few months later. When William landed in England in December 1067 it was at Winchelsea, and Orderic states that he gave Roger of Montgomery both Arundel and Chichester (i.e. West Sussex). J. F. A. Mason suggested that Robert of Mortain and William de Warenne were given Pevensey and Lewes at the same time, and that Robert of Eu held Hastings by 1070. The last rape, Bramber, was created a little later than the others

---

[51] For a brief history of the Rapes see the notes to the Sussex volume of the Phillimore edition of Domesday Book.     [52] OV, II, 220.     [53] OV, II, 210.

for William de Briouze and involved slicing off the eastern portion of Arundel and the western portion of Lewes.[54] The lords of the Sussex rapes were Normans and men who, with the possible exception of William de Briouze about whom little is known, were close to William.

## II Hampshire, Berkshire, Wiltshire

Whilst Odo had been in charge of Kent, William FitzOsbern was posted to Winchester. He may have soon handed over to Hugh de Grandmesnil, but meanwhile received the Isle of Wight and some, possibly a good deal of, land in Hampshire (see below, p. 127), and several of his followers were also established there. The shape of the land distribution in Hampshire differed from the other counties so far considered. Here, as in Berkshire and Wiltshire, the crown was very rich in land, and there was a very long list of lay tenants-in-chief. They included many of the richest men in Domesday Book whose estates were concentrated elsewhere, but who held one or two manors in Hampshire, such as Robert of Mortain (one), William de Warenne (one) and Count Alan lord of Richmond (three). The most important landholder locally was Hugh de Port, most of whose estates were held of the king, but who also held land of Odo of Bayeux. King Edward had been rich in land in the county as compared with the smaller estates here of the house of Godwin, and it is likely that many of his thegns had fought at Hastings and thus their lands were available for redistribution.

Some of the newcomers had stepped into the shoes of antecessors. Ralph de Mortimer had succeeded to the estates of Chipping of Worthy; two out of three of Count Alan's estates had been held by Wulfward; five out of nine manors of Robert FitzGerold had been held by Tovi. It is likely that some of the early grants of one or two estates to the great men of Domesday Book represent early rewards, perhaps in some cases before major grants elsewhere, or perhaps to ensure that men like Count Alan had a base not far from Winchester and the south coast for transfretation. The Normans were in sufficient control of Winchester by 1069 to raise forces from the city for use in the south-west.

---

[54] J. F. A. Mason, *William I and the Sussex Rapes*, Historical Association 1066 Commemoration Series, Hastings and Bexhill Branch (St Leonard's, 1966), pp. 8–9.

Hugh de Port came from Port-en-Bessin where his son held land of the bishop of Bayeux in 1133.[55] He may have been the first Norman sheriff of Kent, for he succeeded to some at least of the lands of the pre-Conquest sheriff.[56] He soon appeared in Hampshire, however. A royal notification addressed to Bishop Walkelin of Winchester, Hugh de Port, Edward, Oda, Aegelsi, Saulf, and Aelfsi at Haeccan and Cole and Eadric and all the king's thegns of Hampshire and Wiltshire instructed that the bishop and the monastery of St Peter at Winchester were to be worthy of the rights that Bishop Aelfwin had had in King Edward's day, and were not to have any new customs imposed on them.[57] Bishop Walkelin was appointed in 1070 and this notification must have been issued soon afterwards. Hugh was probably sheriff of this county – there are several references to his testimony in disputes mentioned in 1086 – and he was described as vicar of Winchester when he retired to Gloucester abbey to become a monk in 1096.[58] By 1086 he had built up a substantial estate concentrated in Basingstoke hundred, where he acquired almost all the non-royal and non-ecclesiastical land. There were one or possibly two castles at Basing, strategically situated near the junction of Roman roads.[59] In Basingstoke hundred the only non-royal land which was not held by Hugh was Mapledurwell, held by Hubert de Port who was probably a close relation of Hugh, and Eastrop, held by Alfred of Marlborough, whose under-tenant was Hugh, possibly the same Hugh de Port.[60] Again it is possible that Hugh began to acquire land in the county at quite an early date and used his influence to extend it over a period of years. The end result was a lordship formed of the estates of a large number of thegns who had mainly held freely of King Edward. Some perhaps had placed themselves voluntarily under Hugh's lordship, or perhaps he had been allowed to take over their lands because a heavy quota of knight service, possibly fifty-five knights, was imposed.[61] In addition to the lands he held of Odo, he also held of the bishopric of Winchester, the New Minster, Chertsey abbey, and Walter FitzRoger of Pîtres.[62]

There are a few traces of the presence in Berkshire of William FitzOsbern and Odo of Bayeux, but neither William's son Roger nor Odo

[55] Loyd, *Origins of Some Anglo-Norman Families*, p. 79.    [56] *DB*, I, 7b, 8, 9, 9b, 10.    [57] *RRAN*, I, no. 267.
[58] *DB*, I, 48b; see *RRAN*, I, nos. 267, 284, 270, 379.
[59] D. J. Cathcart King, *Castellarium Anglicanum*, 2 vols. (London, 1983), I, 189, 195.    [60] *DB*, I, 46b, 47b.
[61] *RBE*, I, 207–9.    [62] *DB*, I, 46, 40b, 41b, 42, 42b, 43b, 48b.

held land in chief there in 1086.[63] The most important towns were
Wallingford and Windsor, and castles were built at each. At the former
the thegn Wigod was based. His daughter Ealdgyth married Robert
d'Oilly, probably not long after 1066, and his son Toki was killed at the
battle of Gerberoi in 1079 fighting for the Conqueror, but two *nepotes*
(nephews or grandsons) were still holding lands in 1086 (see also below, p.
373).[64] Windsor was kept in the king's hands and became a principal royal
residence. Once again there were cases of antecessorial succession. Henry
de Ferrers, for example, succeeded to the lands of Godric, the last Anglo-
Saxon sheriff, who was said to have died at Hastings.[65]

In the neighbouring county of Wiltshire, again we can see the traces of
William FitzOsbern's presence. He had given land to Amesbury in
exchange for land on the Isle of Wight, he had held two manors in the
king's hands in 1086, and his followers held land here: Gilbert de Breteuil,
Durand of Gloucester, and Hugh the Ass.[66] There were several cases of
antecessorial succession. For instance, Earl Aubrey's manors had previously been held by Harding, and 'Ednod' had held five out of six of Earl
Hugh's manors.

Edward of Salisbury is probably to be identified with the man named
Edward addressed with Hugh de Port in the royal notification mentioned
above; if so, he was probably in Wiltshire not long after 1066. Nothing is
known for certain about the origins of this man, but there are clues to
suggest that his family had English connections. First, there is his English
name: if he was Norman he is the only one known to have been called
Edward. His association with an important centre like Salisbury is also
worth noting. He was probably the man named Edward who in 1086 held
five hides of land at Salisbury from Bishop Herman.[67] In the twelfth
century his lands owed castleguard and muster at Salisbury: perhaps
Edward had custody of the castle at Salisbury.[68] Secondly, there is a reference in the (late) Ramsey chronicle to an Edward of Salisbury who was a

---

[63] *DB*, I, 62b (Earl William), 62, 62b, 63b (the bishop of Bayeux's holding).

[64] *Book of Fees: Liber Feodorum. The Book of Fees commonly called Testa de Nevill, reformed from the earliest MSS, by the Deputy Keeper of the Records*, 3 vols. (London, 1920–31), I, 116; *DB*, I, 166b (Hampton), 160 (Little Stoke and Checkendon, held by Alfred); for other possible references see Williams, 'A Vice-Comital Family in Pre-Conquest Warwickshire', p. 290, n. 48.

[65] *Chronicon Monasterii de Abingdon*, ed. J. Stevenson, 2 vols., RS (London, 1858), I, 485; *DB*, I, 60b. Note the entry for Sparsholt where it is suggested that Godric survived Hastings.

[66] *DB*, I, 64b, 65.      [67] *DB*, I, 66.      [68] *RBE*, I, 239–41.

royal justice in Edward the Confessor's reign.[69] Thirdly, there is the formula used to describe three of his manors in Wiltshire. In this county pre-Conquest landholders are usually named in the description of manors, but the first three manors listed for Edward use the formula 'Edward of Salisbury holds Wilcot of the king'; 'the same Edward holds Alton Barnes'; 'the same Edward holds Etchilhampton.'[70] Wilcot was a valuable manor which had actually increased in value since 1066, as had the other two, and Edward had 'a very good house' there, not a castle. He clearly did not feel the need of a castle at his chief manor. Edward may have been the son of Wulfwynn, his predecessor in many of his estates. One of Wulfwynn's manors was Chitterne, and in this village Edward had also acquired estates held by Kenwin and Azor.[71] Again, Azor's name crops up in this county and elsewhere as an antecessor, and perhaps all the references are to the same man. Wulfwynn was clearly a wealthy woman, and it is at least possible she was related to Kenwin and Azor, in which case we could speculate that the nucleus of Edward's land had come to him from one family, augmented by grants of other thegns' land, notably those of Alfward at North Tidworth, Ludgershall, and Shrewton.[72] It is also worth noting that the son of the Domesday Edward, Edward of Salisbury the younger, witnessed a charter of William de Tancarville in Normandy and held land in upper Normandy at Rogerville and Raimes.[73] There are various possibilities here: the elder Edward could have been an English survivor, or a man of mixed Norman-English descent, and his family could have been based in England under Edward the Confessor. Probably over a period of years, this Edward had acquired a wealthy estate with two concentrations of demesne land, one in Heytesbury hundred and one in Chippenham hundred. Like Hugh de Port's, Edward's lands carried a heavy burden of knight service. In 1166 forty knights' fees were owed for Chitterne and a further twenty were held at that time by Humphrey de Bohun.

If Edward was a survivor, he was not alone in the ranks of Wiltshire tenants-in-chief, for Alured (Alfred or Alvred) of Marlborough was

[69] *Chronicon Abbatiae Ramesiensis*, ed. W. Dunn Macray, RS (London, 1886), pp. 153–4; Patrick Wormald kindly drew my attention to this reference.      [70] *DB*, I, 69.      [71] *DB*, I, 69b.      [72] *DB*, I, 69, 69b.

[73] Le Maho, 'L'apparition des seigneuries châtelaines', p. 21. A late tradition from Lacock abbey founded by Edward's descendants claimed that he was a son of Gerold of Roumare and, although there is no corroborative evidence, this is not impossible, Dugdale, *Mon. Ang.*, VI, 501.

another. He held Ewias in Herefordshire, and there he is described as the nephew of Osbern, probably Osbern Pentecost who was forced to leave when Godwin and Harold returned to power in 1052.[74] Marlborough was a royal borough and if Alured had property there before 1066, it is not mentioned in Domesday Book. The first fifteen manors listed in his return make no references to a pre-Conquest holder, but after the fifteenth entry occurs the sentence 'Karl held all these lands in King Edward's reign'.[75] If this means that Karl had held all fifteen before 1066 then clearly Alured's land had come to him after 1066. He also succeeded to Karl's estates in Surrey, Hampshire, and Somerset.[76] Wiltshire was a county where numerous king's thegns and minor officials were still holding on, and the general picture suggests that the land distribution was driven by the king's concern to use wealthy manors to reward his principal adherents. As sheriff, Edward of Salisbury was able, probably over an extended period, to build up a collection of valuable estates which were not territorially compact.

## III Devon, Dorset, Somerset, Cornwall

Within a short time of his return to England in December 1067 the Conqueror faced a revolt at Exeter headed by Gytha, King Harold's mother, who had very considerable estates in Devonshire. The Conqueror besieged Exeter in 1068, Gytha fled, and the king founded a castle there which he left in the custody of Baldwin of Meules.[77] The sons of Harold made two expeditions from Ireland. In 1069 they were repelled by Count Brian, son of Eudo Penthièvre, and William 'Gualdi', probably from Vauville in western Normandy.[78] This William is mentioned in one source as castellan of Exeter, and he may have been the first Norman sheriff of Devon.[79] In 1069 an attack was also made on Montacute in Somerset, and the bishop of Coutances defeated the rebels with the men of Winchester, London, and Salisbury.[80]

These early revolts and incursions meant that the Normans soon had to

---

[74] Round, *Feudal England*, p. 252.     [75] *DB*, I, 70b.     [76] *DB*, I, 36b, 47b, 97.
[77] *ASC* D 1068.     [78] OV, II, 224.
[79] London, British Library, Cotton MS Vespasian A XVIII, ff. 157r–162v. William's activities in connection with royal manors in Devon are also noteworthy: *DB*, I, 85b, 126b; and see also *RRAN*, I, no. 28 which dealt with royal land in Devon and Oxfordshire and was witnessed by William the sheriff.
[80] OV, II, 228.

establish strongpoints in the south-west, though the distribution of land
doubtless extended over a longer period, for as late as 1086 in Dorset,
Somerset, and Wiltshire there were still king's thegns in possession
whose lands had not been redistributed to Normans. The compact lordships of the south-west probably date from the late 1060s though there is
no firm evidence on this point. The lands transferred by antecessorial
grant may in some cases have been available early. Earl Hugh of Chester
succeeded to the lands of Eadnoth the Staller, for instance, who was killed
in 1068.[81] Hugh may have received his lands soon afterwards, because he
gave Henstridge in Somerset to St Sever, probably soon after its foundation in about 1070.[82] Edmer Ator, whose lands at Berkhamsted probably
soon passed to Robert of Mortain, had also held lands in the south-west;
and accordingly Robert may also soon have moved into this region. A surviving diploma of King William for Bishop Giso of Wells, dated 1068 and
restoring thirty hides in Banwell in Somerset, was attested by several men
already prominent in the south-west, including the count of Mortain,
William de Courseulles, Serlo de Burcy, Roger Arundel, Walter the
Fleming (probably Walter or Walscin of Douai), and William de Vauville.[83]

The fact that several of the locally prominent landholders held little
land outside the south-west might also indicate that some grants at least
occurred as a one-off reward for men who took little further active part in
securing the midlands and the north. Baldwin the sheriff was the brother
of Richard FitzGilbert, and was related by marriage to Robert of Mortain
and thus to the king. Having received land in Devon, Baldwin may not
have wished to receive a further share as the Normans moved into the
midlands and the north. Roger Arundel may have come from the
neighbourhood of Caen: one and a half acres of meadow belonging to him
had been bought by Abbot William of St Stephen's, Caen.[84] Roger also had
a tenant in Dorset called Roger Tilly, who could have come from Tilly-sur-
Seulles not far from Caen.[85] The nucleus of Roger's estates had belonged to
Aelmer and Aethelfrith. Under the manor of Piddletrenthide in Dorset we
are told that this manor, which belonged to St Peter Winchester, had been

---

[81] *ASC* D 1067 (*recte* 1068).     [82] Lewis, 'Formation of the Honor of Chester', pp. 54–5.

[83] *RRAN*, I, no. 23. Walter of Douai was called Walter the Fleming in an entry in the geld roll for
Uffculme: see notes to Phillimore edition, Devon, 23, 9.

[84] *Les actes de Guillaume le Conquérant et de la Reine Mathilde pour les abbayes caennaises*, ed. L. Musset,
Mémoires de la Société des Antiquaires de Normandie, xxxvii (Caen, 1967), no. 14, p. 108.

[85] Note to Phillimore edition, Dorset 47, 104.

held in King Edward's day by Aelmer and Aethelfrith but 'they could not go with this land to whichever lord they would. Later Roger Arundel held it from King William.' Five of Roger's Dorset manors had belonged to Aelmer and four to Aethelfrith, and it is likely that the two were broth-ers.[86] William de Courseulles had held land at Venoix of Bishop Odo of Bayeux which he sold to Lanfranc, then abbot of St Stephen's, Caen. In the Bayeux Inquest of 1133 Walkelin de Courseulles held five knights' fees of the bishopric of Bayeux. It is highly likely that the Somerset family was related to the family which held of the bishop, and may have come to England in the train of Odo of Bayeux.[87]

Bretons and west Normans were numerous in the south-west, possibly as a result of the activities of Count Brian, the bishop of Coutances, and William de Vauville, in 1068 and 1069. Some, such as Ansger the Breton, occur as tenants of the count of Mortain.[88] These may have been men who already held land of the count in Normandy: he could have recruited them into his following after 1066, or he could have found them *in situ* at the time he was given land in the south-west. Amongst the west Norman tenants-in-chief were William de Mohun, Ralph de Pomeroy and his brother William Capra, and Serlo de Burcy.[89] Reginald de Vautorte's place of origin was not far from Mortain, just over the border in Maine.[90] These men were presumably keen to have land and, from the king's point of view, enfeoffing them in England helped to strengthen his hold over both west Normandy and Brittany.

Nevertheless there were men from upper Normandy and from Flanders in the region. Hugh FitzGrip, castellan of Wareham and sheriff of Dorset, came from upper Normandy. He was a brother of Geoffrey and Walter Martel and he married a daughter of Nicholas de Bacqueville (en Caux).[91] Ralph de Limesy, whose lands had passed by 1086 to William of Eu, came from Limésy near Rouen and may have been related to the Robert de Limésy who was appointed bishop of Chester (Coventry and Lichfield) in 1085.[92] Robert FitzGerold was the son of Gerold the steward of Roumare, while Robert of Aumale and Walscin or Walter of Douai presumably came

[86] *DB*, I, 77b; Clarke, *English Nobility*, p. 52.   [87] Loyd, *Origins of Some Anglo-Norman Families*, p. 33.
[88] *DB*, I, 104b, 86b, 91b, 92b.
[89] Loyd, *Origins of Some Anglo-Norman Families*, pp. 66, 78–99; Serlo de Burcy may have come from Burcy, Calvados, arr. Vire, cant. Vassy; Tengvik, *Old English Bynames*, p. 78.
[90] Loyd, *Origins of Some Anglo-Norman Families*, p. 104.   [91] Phillimore edition, note to Dorset 23, 1.
[92] Loyd, *Origins of Some Anglo-Norman Families*, p. 54.

from the places of those names. The latter, called Walter the Fleming in
the geld rolls, married Eddeva, a widow who held the manor of Uffculme
of Glastonbury Abbey at the Conquest, so he may have arrived not long
after 1066.[93] The great majority of his estates were in Somerset and Devon
and had been held by a number of antecessors of whom Alfsi, the holder
of Castle Cary, and Alwaker were the most important.[94] Walscin's most
important manor in Devon, Bampton, had been held by King Edward; on
the whole King William tended to retain these in demesne, so the fact
that he had granted this one out may be indicative of special favour.
Walscin held the manor of Dipford from the queen, so one possibility is
that he had some link with Matilda, who was herself Flemish.[95]

If the framework of land distribution had been envisaged as an orderly
succession, military considerations had nevertheless resulted in the crea-
tion of compact lordships along the coasts of Dorset and Devon at
Wareham, Totnes, and Trematon (straddling the county boundary of
Devon and Cornwall), and inland at Montacute and Okehampton. Hugh
FitzGrip seems to have based himself at Wareham, where there was an
Anglo-Saxon burh, for he is styled as Hugh of Wareham in a charter for
Montivilliers, a Norman nunnery to which he gave land.[96] The distribu-
tion of land in north Somerset was shaped with coastal defence in mind.
In the north-east the bishop of Coutances held several estates, probably
dependent on Bristol, a town not mentioned in Domesday Book but which
may already have been prospering from trade with Ireland.[97] Walscin of
Douai also held a group of manors on the coast, including Worle, Brean,
Burnham, Huish, Alstone, Huntspill, and Stretcholt.[98] Finally, William de
Mohun held a group of estates in the west, and had built a castle at
Dunster by 1086.[99]

By 1086 Robert of Mortain had built a castle at Montacute. We have no
means of knowing whether he was the original grantee, or if he was in
possession when the site was attacked in 1069. Montacute was the place
where Tofig the Proud was said to have found a portion of the True Cross,
and, if the Normans had, as it were, militarized a cult site, this might
explain why the place came under attack.[100] The castle was situated on the

---

93 Phillimore edition, note to Devon 23, 9.    94 *DB*, I, 95, 95b, 111b, 112.    95 *DB*, I, 111b.
96 *Gallia Christiana in Provincias Ecclesiasticas Distributa*, XI, ed. P. Piolin (1874), Appendix, 329e.
97 Viz. Portishead, Easton in Gordano, Weston in Gordano, Clapton in Gordano, *DB*, I, 88.
98 *DB*, I, 95, 95b.    99 *DB*, I, 95.    100 J. H. Bettey, *Wessex from AD 1000* (London, 1986), p. 12.

manor of Bishopstone which before 1066 had belonged to Athelney, and for which the count had compensated the abbey.[101] He had enfeoffed several of his leading followers on the manor: Drogo held nearby Cricket Malherbie; Bretel, North Perrott and Broadway; Robert FitzIvo, Stoke sub Hamdon; Thurstan, East Ham; Mauger of Carteret, Stoke sub Hamdon and Chinnock; and Ansger, Odcombe. The count also kept manors in demesne at Shepton Beauchamp, Chinnock (where his predecessor was Edmer Ator), Bradon, Closworth, Marston Magna, and Tintinhull, which had been held by Glastonbury abbey before 1066.[102]

Baldwin the sheriff's estates were composite in origin. There was a concentration round Exeter and west towards Okehampton and then along the valley of the river Torre towards the north coast. We have no clue when the lordship was put together, but it could be argued that the nucleus was probably early and dictated by the need to hold Exeter and to guard the route west into Cornwall. Baldwin held little land outside the county, and this might be thought to reinforce the notion of a military lordship rather than antecessorial succession. Again, this was a lordship with a heavy assessment to knight service, over ninety fees.[103]

On the north Devon coast the bishop of Coutances held a group of estates round Barnstaple. There were also two relatively compact lordships on the south Devon coast. The first was that of Judhael (Juhel) of Totnes. Totnes itself had been a royal borough in King Edward's day, and was one of the few to be granted to a subject by King William. Judhael's name suggests Breton ancestry. He succeeded to the lands of the pre-Conquest sheriff, Hecha, and this is a possible indication that he stepped into Hecha's office, in which case this is likely to have been soon after 1066.[104] The other compact lordship was the under-tenancy which Reginald de Vautorte held of the count of Mortain. Reginald's estates were intermingled with Judhael's in the east, and they extended west into Cornwall, where Reginald had built a castle at Trematon.[105] Reginald was probably given land when Judhael was already established but that could still have been within a few years of 1066.

It is not clear when Robert of Mortain was granted all the land in Cornwall not held by the church. The Breton Count Brian may briefly have

---

[101] DB, I, 93.    [102] DB, I, 91b, 92, 92b.    [103] RBE, I, 251–4.    [104] DB, I, 109, 109b, 110.
[105] DB, I, 122 where the castle was said to be the count's.

held the county, and was possibly succeeded by Earl Ralph.[106] Tybesta in
Cornwall was described in Domesday Book as having been held by Ralph
the Staller in King Edward's reign; it was his only estate in Cornwall.[107] In
Norfolk we find that Earl Ralph (Ralph the Staller's son) received Caister in
exchange for land in Cornwall, presumably, therefore, for Tybesta, and
presumably before 1075 when he was one of the leaders of revolt.[108] Robert
may thus have stepped into Earl Ralph's shoes in Cornwall, and this would
make sense, given that he already had large estates in the south-west.
Perhaps it was also felt to be appropriate that he, like his brother, should
have comital rights over an English county. Most of the tenanted land in
Cornwall was held by four men: Reginald de Vautorte, Turstin, the sheriff
of Cornwall, Hamelin, and Richard son of Turold. Reginald, as we have
seen, may have been *in situ* when Count Robert arrived; little is known
about the other three men.[109] That their interests were *concentrated* in the
south-west, however, suggests that they were established at a particular
stage of the settlement.

### IV  Gloucestershire, Herefordshire, Worcestershire, Shropshire, Cheshire, Staffordshire

At this point we need to retrace our steps to consider the role of William
FitzOsbern on the Welsh marches, where he went in 1067 with the title of
earl. The scope of his position has been differently assessed. W. E.
Wightman thought that FitzOsbern had powers over Gloucestershire and
Herefordshire like those of Roger of Montgomery in Shropshire and Hugh
in Cheshire, but C. P. Lewis has argued that what the Conqueror was
trying to do in 1067 was to appoint a replacement for Harold Godwinson
as earl of Wessex.[110] It may well be true that William FitzOsbern did not
have such autonomy over Gloucestershire and Herefordshire as Roger and

---

[106] Count Alan's charter for Mont Saint Michel referred to Count Brian as his predecessor: *Cartulary of St Michael's Mount*, ed. P. L. Hull, Devon and Cornwall Record Society, new series, v (1962), no. 5. This, though a late reference, is testimony to a tradition of Count Brian's activity, and he may have been earl.           [107] *DB*, I, 121b.           [108] *DB*, II, 134b.

[109] Turold witnessed a charter of Robert of Mortain for St Michael's Mount and Richard his son was subsequently a benefactor of St Michael's Mount: I. N. Soulsby, 'Richard FitzTurold, lord of Penhallam, Cornwall', *Medieval Archaeology*, 20 (1976), 146–8.

[110] W. E. Wightman, 'The Palatine Earldom of William FitzOsbern in Gloucestershire and Worcestershire (1066–1071)', *English Historical Review*, 77 (1962), 6–17; Lewis, 'Early Earls of Norman England', p. 217.

Hugh were to have over their counties; nevertheless the Domesday accounts of these two counties show him to have had very considerable authority, perhaps all the more striking considering that he left England for the last time in 1070. It is not improbable that the Conqueror established the three border earldoms at the same time as bulwarks against the Welsh, though this assumes that the earldoms of Shropshire and Cheshire were created earlier than has been thought and in particular earlier than the fall of Earl Edwin.

Although Gloucestershire was not far from the border with Wales it was not in the front line of attack as was Herefordshire, nor was the overall distribution of land there dictated by local military considerations. Gloucester was a favoured royal residence both before and after 1066. There were large and valuable royal estates, some of which still rendered their dues in kind. Earl William had perhaps had some authority over King Edward's manors, and certainly the manors he did control were in the king's hands by 1086.[111] Some of his followers had been given land here and in Herefordshire which they held in chief of the crown: Ansfrid de Cormeilles, Roger de Pîtres, his brother Durand the sheriff of Gloucestershire, Gilbert son of Turold, Hugh Lasne, and Alfred d'Epaignes. But what did not happen in this county was a creation of compact lordships dictated by military needs. The number of tenants-in-chief was large; they were drawn from all contingents of the new regime; and in several cases antecessorial succession can be identified. The county with which the comparison is closest is perhaps Berkshire.

The border counties had suffered from Welsh attacks during the Confessor's reign. In Herefordshire Swein, Godwin's son, had been earl, and was succeeded in 1051 by Edward's nephew, Ralph of Mantes, son of his sister Godgifu and Drogo count of the Vexin.[112] Other Frenchmen were established in the shire, and castles were built by Richard son of Scrob and Osbern Pentecost.[113] Robert son of Wymarc was a kinsman of King Edward and of Norman/Breton extraction. Most of his lands were in eastern England but he also had lands on the border with Wales and in Wiltshire

---

[111] *DB*, I, 162b–164.

[112] D. Bates, *Lord Sudeley's Ancestors: the Family of the Counts of Amiens, Valois and the Vexin in France and England during the 11th Century. The Sudeleys – Lords of Toddington*, The Manorial Society of Great Britain (1987), pp. 39–40.

[113] For the suggestion that Osbern's castle was at Hereford see Alecto county edition of Domesday Book, Herefordshire, I, 11; Round thought the castle was at Ewias: *Feudal England*, pp. 249–54.

and Somerset.[114] In 1055 Gruffydd, then effectively ruler of Wales, had defeated Ralph and his Frenchmen outside Hereford, and after this disaster Harold Godwinson was given command and acquired land in the shire.[115] He and Tostig in turn defeated Gruffydd in 1063. In 1065 Harold invaded south Wales, ravaged as far as the river Usk, and began to build at Portskewett not far from Chepstow, where it was reported that his workmen were attacked by the Welsh later that year.[116] Earl William was thus obviously intended to step into Harold's shoes in the front line, for it would not have been obvious that with the death of Gruffydd the threat to the border had for a time at least abated.

In the few short years of his career in England, FitzOsbern left his mark on Herefordshire. He may well have controlled the manors of the royal demesne in this county, and some manors in Worcestershire and Gloucestershire were still accounting at Hereford in 1086.[117] He built castles: Clifford was entrusted to his brother-in-law Ralph de Tosny and Wigmore, in 1086 held by Ralph de Mortimer.[118] Further south he built castles at Chepstow, from which a substantial territory was controlled, and at Monmouth which, according to the Book of Llandaff, he entrusted to three of his barons: Humphrey, Osbern, and William the scribe.[119]

Yet FitzOsbern did not redistribute all the land in Herefordshire. In the first place there were survivors from the previous reign and one of them, Alured of Marlborough, was established at Ewias Harold by Earl William.[120] Secondly, Walter de Lacy was probably sent to the Welsh Marches by the king and so possibly was Turstin FitzRou, as neither man is known to have been a follower of Earl William. Wace described Turstin as the Conqueror's standard-bearer at Hastings. He acquired land in eight counties. His two estates in Herefordshire, three in Berkshire, and one (as an under-tenant) in Herefordshire had all been held by Brictric, and presumably had been granted to him by the king.[121] Ralph de Mortimer could have been another early arrival, for he held a compact lordship straddling the boundaries of Herefordshire, Shropshire, and Worcestershire. He probably acquired his land in Shropshire before the installation of Earl Roger, because he held in chief, not as a tenant of Earl Roger. If Roger of

---

[114] DB, I, 186b, 187, 252b, 74b, 92b, 96b; for Robert see Harmer, Anglo-Saxon Writs, p. 571.

[115] Fleming, Kings and Lords, pp. 98–100.     [116] ASC D 1065.     [117] DB, I, 180b.     [118] DB, I, 183, 183b.

[119] DB, I, 162, 180b; see note to Phillimore edition, Herefordshire, 1, 48.     [120] DB, I, 186.

[121] Wace, Roman de Rou (ed. Holden), II, 208–9; DB, I, ff. 63, 174b. Brictric may perhaps be identified with Brictric son of Aelfgar.

Montgomery had been working with a *tabula rasa* (as far as Normans were concerned), it is unlikely that he would have enfeoffed another tenant-in-chief there rather than one of his own followers.[122] On the other hand, Ralph may not have acquired his estates in Herefordshire until after 1075. He was not the first holder of Wigmore after 1066, and one of his predecessors elsewhere was Queen Edith, who did not die until 1075.[123] The rebellion and forfeiture of FitzOsbern's son Roger in 1075 was followed by adjustments to the tenurial geography of Herefordshire and the surrounding region. Wihenoc the Breton was granted Monmouth, and Normans who held land elsewhere may have been brought in at this time: Robert Gernon (Essex), who held land in the castlery of Richard's castle, William de Scohies (East Anglia), who held land in the castlery of Carleon, and Henry de Ferrers (estates concentrated in Derbyshire), who held land in the castlery of Ewias.[124]

Worcestershire can perhaps be considered briefly at this point, for the distribution of available land – and much was in the hands of the church – was to men whose interests were centred elsewhere. Wulfstan bishop of Worcester, who died in 1095, and Aethelwig abbot of Evesham, who died in 1078, were Englishmen who co-operated with the new regime. There was not the same need to create a powerful military lordship here as there was in some other areas. William FitzOsbern controlled some royal manors, and may also have been responsible for establishing Gilbert FitzTurold and Ralph de Tosny in the county.[125] There were only three other lay tenants-in-chief of any substance. The first, Osbern FitzRichard, was a pre-Conquest survivor. His father had held some of his estates in King Edward's day, but Osbern had since acquired one of Earl Godwin's manors, two of King Edward's, and manors which had belonged to six others.[126] North of Droitwich, and in the north-east of the country, Urse d'Abetot held a small tenancy-in-chief to add to his much more extensive holdings as an under-tenant of the bishop of Worcester, Westminster

[122] *DB*, I, 260b.

[123] *DB*, I, 183b; for a discussion of the suggestion that Ralph may have been Roger's steward in Herefordshire, see J. F. A. Mason, 'The Officers and Clerks of the Norman Earls of Shropshire', *Transactions of the Shropshire Archaeological Society*, 57 (1957–60), 248. On the whole it seems unlikely that an important tenant-in-chief would have been Roger's steward, and the evidence, from a Shropshire jury of 1303, is very late. [124] Lewis, 'Norman Settlement of Herefordshire', p. 209.

[125] Gilbert FitzTurold gave land at Sheriff's Lench for the soul of Earl William, *DB*, I, 176. He has been identified with Gilbert de Bouille, who held a house in Warwick in 1086: Phillimore edition, Warwickshire, note to B2. [126] *DB*, I, 176b.

Abbey, Pershore, Evesham, and Odo of Bayeux. Urse was sheriff by 1069, and he used his local power to assemble a substantial landed estate in the county. He had a bad reputation as one of the villainous sheriffs of the Conquest, but his activities were almost bound to bring him into conflict with powerful vested interests.[127]

In northern Worcestershire the dominant figure was William FitzAnsculf, who held a castlery centred on Dudley. This straddled the boundaries of three counties: Worcestershire, Staffordshire, and Warwickshire. The nucleus was composed of estates listed as having belonged to Earl Edwin (such as Dudley itself, Astley and Erdington in Warwickshire), Earl Aelfgar (Sedgeley and Upper Penn in Staffordshire), and Countess Godiva (Lower Penn, Moseley, and Essington in Staffordshire).[128] William was the son of Ansculf de Picquigny in the département of Somme, sheriff of Surrey, who had died before 1086.[129]

The creation of Dudley cannot be viewed in isolation from the turbulence of the years between 1068 and 1071 in midland England, which came to a head with the fall of Earl Edwin. Dudley, the earldoms granted to Roger of Montgomery and Hugh d'Avranches, Tutbury, Nottingham, and possibly Belvoir and Tickhill, all came into being in these years. The earl and his brother Morcar had not been at Hastings and had submitted, either at Berkhamsted before the coronation, according to the Anglo-Saxon Chronicle, or at Barking afterwards, according to William of Poitiers.[130] They were taken to Normandy in 1067 but presumably returned at the end of the year. We may assume that Normans had begun to acquire lands within the boundaries of the old earldom of Mercia by 1068. If these had belonged to the family of King Harold, or to thegns who had fought for him at Hastings, then perhaps Edwin could not object, but if castles were being built, or if land belonging to Edwin's family or to his earldom was involved, then Edwin had reasons for resentment. The estates which Domesday Book variously records as having belonged to Edwin, Aelfgar, and Godiva which went to form the nucleus of the castlery of Dudley may all have been held by Edwin in 1066.

According to Orderic, who based this section of his work on the lost

---

[127] Urse was in charge of the building of Worcester castle before the death of Archbishop Ealdred who had cursed him in English for the building works: WM, *Gesta Pontificum*, ed. N. E. S. A. Hamilton (RS 1870), p. 253. *The Beauchamp Cartulary Charters 1100–1268*, ed. E. Mason, Pipe Roll Society, New Series, XLIII (1980), xviii–xx.    [128] *DB*, I, 177, 243, 249b, 250.
[129] *DB*, I, 36 (Surrey); 148b (Buckinghamshire).    [130] *ASC* D 1066; WP, p. 236.

ending of William of Poitiers' biography, King William had promised to
subject his brother (unnamed) to Earl Edwin, and to give him his daughter
in marriage, but instead withheld the girl.[131] The brother could be either
Odo or Robert, but of the two the latter is a likelier candidate, given the
location of his estates. In any event it appears that Edwin believed that he
would have a powerful position in the new regime (perhaps Harold
Godwinson had earlier made similar promises) and it was disillusionment
which led him to revolt. He is said to have rebelled in 1068 but was then
reconciled with the Conqueror. By 1071 Edwin was again in revolt and, as
he struggled to find support, he was killed by one of his own men.[132]

The compactness of the castlery of Dudley, the boundaries of which cut
across shires and in some cases earlier patterns of landholding, suggests
that military considerations may have been predominant in its formation
which may in turn point to an early date. The only two clues we have are
inconclusive: Fitz Ansculf's manor of Selly Oak was probably obtained
after the death in 1067 of Wulfwin, who held it from the bishopric of
Worcester to whom the manor should have returned.[133] Secondly, Bell
Hall in Worcestershire was probably not obtained until after 1071, prior to
which it had been held by Ralph FitzHubert.[134]

The troubles besetting the Normans in the midlands formed the back-
drop to the distribution of land in Shropshire and Cheshire. This had
begun as early as 1067 because of the revolt of Eadric the Wild, a leading
thegn in Shropshire who did not submit to William and whose lands were
attacked by Richard FitzScrob and the garrison at Hereford.[135] It may well
have been this revolt which brought William FitzOsbern to the Welsh
border in the first instance, and he came in the company of Walter de Lacy
and Ralph de Mortimer. At some stage – possibly, as we have seen, at the
time FitzOsbern was dispatched to Herefordshire – the decision was taken
to commit the whole of Shropshire, other than church land and that
already granted out to other tenants-in-chief, to Roger of Montgomery. He
thus acquired the lands previously held by King Edward as well as those of
Edwin, Morcar, and Godiva. The earliest indication that Roger was an earl
comes from a royal charter, purporting to have been issued in 1068, and

[131] OV, II, 214–16.    [132] *Ibid.*, II, 256–8; *ASC* D, E, 1072 for 1071; FW, II, 9.

[133] *DB*, I, 177 and see note to Phillimore edition, Worcestershire, 23, 1.

[134] *DB*, I, 177. According to this entry Bell Hall had been held by Ralph for more than five years until it
    was taken away by William FitzOsbern. If correct, this suggests that Ralph obtained the manor very
    soon after Hastings.    [135] FW, II, 1.

confirming the endowments of the collegiate church of St Martin-le-Grand in London, which was witnessed amongst others by 'Earl Roger'.[136] If he was at the same time granted all the king's lands and rights in the county, then this was a challenge to Earl Edwin.

Roger proved to be an energetic lord. By 1086 advances had been made into Welsh territory, for in the far north-west the territory of Ial was held by Earl Hugh as Roger's under-tenant.[137] Roger created three compact lordships in Shropshire, for Warin the Bald, Corbet, and Picot de Sai, all from his patrimonial estates. Castles were built at Montgomery (named after his place of origin in Normandy), Shrewsbury, and Quatford.[138] Roger was a notable patron of religious houses in Normandy and by 1086 was taking an active role in reframing the ecclesiastical organization of his new estates in England. The pre-Conquest foundation at Wenlock had been refounded as a Cluniac priory, and in 1083 the foundations of a Benedictine abbey at Shrewsbury were laid (see below, pp. 399–400). Men who were already tenants-in-chief, Ranulf Peverel, Roger de Courseulles, Odo de Bernières, and William de Warenne, received land here. William was a kinsman of Earl Roger which is one possible explanation of the grant, but it is more likely that he received Whitchurch when he was granted other manors belonging to Harold.[139] Roger de Courseulles also held the only land he held outside the south-west, possibly through a connection with Odo of Bernières.[140] It is difficult to see why Robert de Veci was enfeoffed here. He held three hides of Ralph de Mortimer of a manor previously held by Earl Morcar; all his estates elsewhere had come to him as the successor of Alric son of Meriet.[141]

The county of Cheshire formed the northernmost sector of the frontier with Wales. Chester was important as a port for the Irish Sea, and the Normans, like their predecessors, had to consider the possibility of incursions by the Welsh, or of coastal attack. William was said by Orderic to have ordered castles to be built at Chester and Stafford on his return from harrying the north in 1070.[142] Hugh d'Avranches, who succeeded Gherbod the Fleming at Chester, was a rising man. He may have been moved to Chester from Tutbury, and was probably already in receipt of many of his lands in the midlands and the south, notably those which had belonged to Harold

[136] *RRAN*, I, no. 22.      [137] *DB*, I, 254.

[138] *DB*, I, 254, 252. The Domesday entry described Quatford as a 'new house', but it is likely that the reference is to the motte and bailey castle.      [139] *DB*, I, 257.

[140] Phillimore edition, see note to Shropshire 4, 18.      [141] *DB*, I, 256b.      [142] OV, II, 260.

Godwinson and Eadnoth the Staller. In Cheshire, Hugh on the whole kept Earl Edwin's land in demesne. Unlike Roger of Montgomery, Hugh was not in possession of the family estates in Normandy in 1066 for his father was still living, and his tenants in 1086 were a miscellaneous bunch, presumably recruited as his reputation grew. Only a few of the Cheshire tenants can be identified as having come from the Avranchin. Ilbert was the predecessor, possibly the father, of Richard de Rullos from Roullours, who held Ilbert's lands by the time Chester abbey was founded.[143] Richard held the church of Burcy, whence came, presumably, Nigel de Burcy.[144] Hamon de Massey may have come from Macey near Avranches.[145] Robert of Rhuddlan was Earl Hugh's cousin.[146] Nothing is known about the origins of Robert FitzHugh, though he could have been an illegitimate son of Earl Hugh.[147] Richard and Walter of Vernon presumably came from Vernon on the river Seine. In addition to holding land as an under-tenant of Hugh, Walter also held a small amount of land as a tenant-in-chief in Buckinghamshire and it is not apparent how he came into Hugh's orbit. One possibility is via Richard de Redvers, who was related to the family which held Vernon for the duke, and had land in Calvados and western Normandy.[148] All we know of William FitzNigel is that he was a kinsman of another tenant-in-chief, Gilbert de Gant, and a benefactor of Bridlington priory which Gilbert founded.[149] William Malbank could have been related to Earl Roger's under-tenant Alfred Malbedenc, and Renaud de Bailleul held land in Maelor Cymraeg hundred which was surveyed under Cheshire.[150] Some of the larger lordships were compact. Robert of Rhuddlan held land along both banks of the river Dee. William FitzNigel similarly held lands to the west and east of the river Mersey, with castles at Halton and Widnes. Robert FitzHugh's lordship, centred on Malpas, was also compact.

The neighbouring county of Staffordshire was relatively poor in terms of the values of its manors, and the distribution of land to the newcomers was not complete in 1086. King Edward had held Kingswinford and

---

[143] For Richard's donations to Chester abbey see *Chester Charters*, no. 3; for the family see *Early Yorkshire Charters*, v, 95–9.      [144] *Chester Charters*, no. 6.

[145] Loyd, *Origins of Some Anglo-Norman Families*, pp. 61–2.      [146] *Ibid.*, p. 85.

[147] I owe this suggestion to Dr M. Chibnall.

[148] Richard's name was derived from Reviers in Calvados, and he also held land at Néhou in the Cotentin. In the 1090s he and Earl Hugh supported the future Henry I in the Cotentin, OV, IV, 220. The precise nature of his association with Vernon is not clear. The evidence is discussed in *CP*, IV, 309 and by Bearman in *Charters of the Redvers Family*, pp. 1–2.

[149] Dugdale, *Mon. Ang.*, VI, 285.      [150] *VCH Cheshire*, I, 309; *DB*, I, 276b.

Penkridge, but his lands were outclassed by those of Earl Aelfgar of Mercia, Edwin's father, who had died before 1066. Many of Aelfgar's manors were retained by King William, but three had passed to Earl Roger, a fourth to his son Hugh, and two to William FitzAnsculf.[151] The Normans were in the county by 1068 when, according to Orderic, there had been fighting at Stafford.[152] Henry de Ferrers could have been the first castellan of Stafford, where a castle was built on land belonging to his manor of Chebsey.[153] By 1086 the most important lay tenant-in-chief was Robert of Stafford, who was probably the sheriff.[154] He was a younger son of Roger de Tosny and his lands were concentrated west of Stafford. He may have had a castle at Stafford, where he had half the revenues from the borough.[155] He acquired land from a number of antecessors, the most important of whom was a thegn called Wulfgeat who was still holding three of his manors as a tenant, and Wulfgeat may in turn have been related to men with whom he held estates: Wulfmer, Alfward, and Godric. Robert of Stafford had land in the county before 1072, for he gave land at Wrottesley to Evesham abbey, his charter being witnessed by Urse d'Abetot, Osbern FitzRichard, Aethelwine the sheriff, and Turchil (of Arden) his son.[156] This is an early date to find a Norman giving land to an English Benedictine house in the company of two members of a thegnly family, and one obvious possibility is that he married into the family. He held land at Bobbington which was very close to William FitzAnsculf's castlery, and perhaps he would not have been given this had the latter been in existence.[157] Robert also received three manors which had belonged to Earl Edwin.

### V  Middlesex, Oxfordshire, Buckinghamshire, Bedfordshire, Hertfordshire, Cambridgeshire, Huntingdonshire

The Normans moved early into the counties north of London. In Middlesex the manors tended to be large and valuable and many were in

---

[151] *DB*, I, 248, 248b, 249b.    [152] OV, II, 228, 236.    [153] *DB*, I, 248b.

[154] *RRAN*, I, no. 210, addressed, amongst others, to R. the sheriff and the loyal men of Staffordshire.

[155] Henry I's charter for Conches included confirmation of a charter of Robert of Stafford son of Roger de Tosny: *Gallia Christiana*, XI, instr. 132; Robert possibly had a castle at Castle Church. An entry referred to his land at Monetvile, which may have been at Castle Church: *DB*, I, 249b; *VCH Staffordshire*, V, 84.

[156] R. W. Eyton, *The Staffordshire Cartulary*, Collections for a History of Staffordshire, II (1881), 178.

[157] *DB*, I, 249.

the hands of the church. Some, probably most, of the laymen had succeeded to their lands by antecessorial succession. Three of Roger of
Montgomery's estates had been held by Wigod, two more by men of
Wigod; one of Robert of Mortain's manors had been held by Edmer Ator;
Geoffrey de Mandeville's three demesne manors by Ansger the Staller;
Arnulf de Hesdin's two manors by Wulfward White; Walter de St Valery's
two by Earl Aelfgar; and Walter son of Oter was the successor of Azor and
his men. Even amongst those who held only one estate in the county there
is one case of antecessorial succession, Edward of Salisbury to the manor
of Wulfwynn.

North Oxfordshire and Buckinghamshire were dominated by Odo of
Bayeux, who was probably responsible for the great motte at
Deddington.[158] Odo had succeeded to two estates previously held by
Aethelnoth *cild* of Kent, and to Leofwin's estates. He doubtless received
these with their other estates, an impression reinforced by the way the
names of Kentish tenants recur in Oxfordshire and Buckinghamshire. A
castle was built at Oxford, possibly as early as 1067, and was entrusted to
Robert d'Oilly[159] who probably came from Ouilly-le-Basset west of Falaise
and was a constable in the royal household.[160] As mentioned earlier,
Robert married the daughter of Wigod of Wallingford, and by 1086 had
acquired a substantial lordship. Wigod is stated to have held Goring, but
elsewhere most of Robert's antecessors are not named. Robert's daughter
married Miles Crispin, who also held many lands in Oxfordshire. Robert
was also closely associated with Roger d'Ivry, and according to later tradition the two were blood brothers (see below, p. 331). Roger was a butler in
the royal household, he founded a monastery in the castle at Ivry in 1071,
and was Duke William's castellan at Rouen.[161] Although his predecessors
are not named in Oxfordshire, his estates in other counties came to him
from several predecessors. In Berkshire he held five estates, two of which
were at Harwell. One of these had been held by Wulfric, a free man, and
the other was said to have been of Earl William (FitzOsbern's) fee, while

[158] R. J. Ivens, 'Deddington Castle, Oxfordshire, and the English Honour of Odo of Bayeux', *Oxoniensia*, 49
(1984), 101–19.

[159] *Annales Monastici*, IV, *Annales Monasterii de Oseneia*, ed. H. R. Luard, RS (London, 1869), 9; *Chronicon
Monasterii de Abingdon*, II, 7.

[160] W. T. Reedy, 'The First Two Bassets of Weldon', *Northamptonshire Past and Present*, 4 (1966–72), 243;
Robert was described as constable of Oxford in the Abingdon chronicle, *Chronicon Monasterii de
Abingdon*, II, 12, and attests a royal document as constable, *RRAN*, I, no. 270.

[161] *RRAN*, I, nos. 23, 308; OV, II, 358; *Gallia Christiana*, XI, col. 652.

two others were of the bishop of Bayeux's fee, as was Cubbington in Warwickshire.[162] Three of his Buckinghamshire estates had been held by Azor son of Toti, a housecarl of King Edward;[163] in Gloucestershire one of his estates had been held by Archbishop Ealdred.[164] In Gloucestershire Bishop Odo had taken away the manor of Hazleton from its holder and had given it at farm to Roger.[165]

In Bedfordshire, Hertfordshire, and Cambridgeshire by contrast the pattern of landholding was already complicated in 1066 in that many vills, or units of settlement, were divided between two or more holders. Often Domesday Book does not name them but says only that eight thegns or twelve freemen had held such and such an estate. A great deal of land was held by thegns of modest standing, and by unnamed freemen. A second problem, not unrelated, stems from the fact that these counties, which were all in the same provincial group or circuit for the purposes of the Domesday commissioners (circuit III), provide much the fullest information about pre-Conquest ties of dependence that we have apart from those for circuit VII (Essex, Norfolk, and Suffolk). It appears that in the east midlands particularly the information relating not to demesne manors but to those held by one or other forms of dependent tenure may not have been recorded in quite the same way as elsewhere, and the question therefore arises whether the tenurial status of the man named as the pre-Conquest holder was strictly comparable with that of his successor in 1086.

The Domesday return in these counties may simply record the identity of the person on whom rested the obligation to provide service and geld to the king. He might have been the lord of the land – and if the manor concerned was a demesne manor (that is, managed directly for the lord not let out to tenants) he certainly was – but he could have been a tenant of another unnamed lord.[166] John Palmer pointed out in a computer-assisted analysis of Domesday Book that in Cambridgeshire the scribe consistently distinguished between manors (which were centres for collection of dues such as danegeld) and non-manorial estates.[167] The newcomers took over the demesne manors of their predecessors, and the lands dependent upon

---

[162] *DB*, I, 242b, 62b.    [163] *DB*, I, 151b.    [164] *DB*, I, 168.    [165] *DB*, I, 168.

[166] Roffe, 'From Thegnage to Barony: Sake and Soke, Title and Tenants-in-Chief', pp. 170–6; for a clear explanation of pre-Conquest ties of dependence, Williams, *The English and the Norman Conquest*, pp. 73–6.    [167] J. J. N. Palmer, 'The Domesday Manor', *Domesday Studies* (ed. Holt), pp. 139–53.

them. Sometimes they also took over the lands of men who had simply commended themselves on a personal basis to their predecessors, but usually the bond of soke rather than that of commendation was decisive in determining to whom the land passed. In 1086 what mattered from the point of view of the commissioners was the identity of the tenant-in-chief and any tenant to whom he had granted it and from whom service was owed to the king.[168] In the east midlands circuit it appears that many of the Edwardian landholders listed in 1086 had been tenants not lords. David Roffe has drawn attention to the different formulae used in Domesday Book, and the way in which, in circuit III, dependent tenures are frequently indicated by the formula 'In X, Y holds.'[169] Thus simply to compare, as Fleming did, the names of pre-Conquest landholders with those holding after 1066 in circuit III and argue on that basis that massive discontinuity occurred, is misleading, as it does not take account of unnamed pre-Conquest overlords whose rights over the land in question determined to whom it passed after 1066.[170]

Where manors had been held in demesne before and after 1066, there are numerous instances of antecessorial succession: Odo of Bayeux to Leofwin in Buckinghamshire, the bishop of Coutances to Burgred of Mercia, Geoffrey de Mandeville to Ansger the Staller (in Cambridgeshire and Hertfordshire), Count Eustace of Boulogne to Ingelric's manor of Tring in Hertfordshire and to Alfwold's land in Bedfordshire, Peter de Valognes to Aelmer of Bennington in Hertfordshire, Count Alan to Eadgifu the Fair (Cambridgeshire and Hertfordshire), Earl Roger to Goda, Walter Giffard to Aki, William de Warenne to Toki, and Robert Gernon to Leofsi (all in Cambridgeshire), Lisois de Moutiers to Wulfmaer of Eaton (Cambridgeshire, Bedfordshire, and Essex), Ralph de Limesy to Aelfstan of Boscombe (Bedfordshire and other counties), Picot the sheriff of Cambridgeshire to Blacuin, the sheriff before 1066, Ralph Taillebois to Askil of Ware, Robert de Tosny to Oswulf son of Fran (Bedfordshire, Buckinghamshire, Hertfordshire, and Northamptonshire), Walter the Fleming to Leofnoth, and Osbern FitzRichard to Stori (both Bedfordshire).

Some cases of antecessorial succession in Cambridgeshire were early, such as Geoffrey de Mandeville to Ansger the Staller, and Frederic to Toki's

---

[168] J. C. Holt, '1086', *Domesday Studies* (ed. Holt), p. 54.      [169] Roffe, 'From Thegnage to Barony', p. 162.

[170] R. Fleming, 'Domesday Book and the Tenurial Revolution', *Anglo-Norman Studies*, 9 (1986), 87–102; Fleming, *Kings and Lords*, chapter 4.

land. Aubrey de Vere succeeded to the land of Wulfwine and Gilbert de Gant to that of Ulf Fenisc. By 1086 the most powerful man in the county was Count Alan, by reason of his succession to the lands of Earl Ralph and Eadgifu the Fair. Possibly Count Alan was responsible for the establishment in the county of Hardwin de Scalers from L'Escallerie in Nantes.[171] Picot the sheriff possibly came from Bavent east of Caen, but there is no other indication as to the status or connections of his family.[172] He succeeded to the lands of the Edwardian sheriff, Blacuin. Most of his estates were relatively small, except his chief manor of Bourn, where he built a castle.[173] Like Urse d'Abetot and, as we shall see shortly, Eustace of Huntingdon, he acquired a reputation as a despoiler of church lands.

Cambridgeshire and perhaps Huntingdonshire were part of the earldom held by Earl Waltheof from 1065, and his widow Judith still held land in both counties in 1086. In Cambridgeshire her chief antecessors were Gyrth and Harold, and she also held land previously held by men commended to Waltheof. In Huntingdonshire she had more land, and here Waltheof himself was recorded as one of her predecessors. In both counties there were leading men who were given one or two manors, possibly deliberately to strengthen the Normans' hold in the region. Walter Giffard, for instance, held land in both counties; in Huntingdonshire Count Eustace had two manors; the count of Eu had a single manor which had been Tostig's; Earl Hugh had two manors belonging to Edgar, and William de Warenne was granted a manor of Harold's. The sheriff of Huntingdonshire, Eustace, was a man of obscure origins like Picot. He too picked up bits and pieces of land and acquired an evil reputation for seizing church lands. It is just possible that he had something to do with the count of Eu, for one of Eustace's men was called Ingelram of Eu.[174] Robert count of Eu was involved in the Hastings campaign, but the only reference thereafter to his active involvement in the subjugation of England was his role in 1069, with Robert of Mortain, in helping to keep the Danes penned up in Lindsey. Perhaps it was about this time, and through Robert's influence, that Eustace arrived in the county.[175]

[171] Keats-Rohan, 'William I and the Breton contingent', p. 171.    [172] RRAN, II, no. 685.
[173] DB, I, 200b–201; Liber Memorandum de Bernewelle, ed. J. W. Clark (Cambridge, 1907), p. 40.
[174] VCH Huntingdonshire, I, 334; DB, I, 206; Loyd, Origins of Some Anglo-Norman Families, pp. 55–6.
[175] OV, II, 268.

## VI Essex, Norfolk, Suffolk

Essex by reason of its coastal position and proximity to London was another county which was bound to attract early attention. The list of landholders was long; it included Bretons and Flemings as well as Normans, and there were several locally based lordships as well as men who held some estates here but whose main centre of interest was elsewhere. As usual, examples of antecessorial succession are to be found. Aubrey de Vere, a Breton, succeeded to the lands of Wulfwin, Eudo the steward to Wulfmaer of Eton, Hugh de Montfort to Guthmund, and Henry de Ferrers to Bondi the Staller. Robert son of Wymarc has already been mentioned as a kinsman of King Edward, a 'staller' or royal official, and possibly sheriff of Essex. Domesday Book shows that he had lost some of the estates he had held before 1066 and gained others. Several of his estates were said to have been held 'after the death of King Edward',[176] and others either 'after the arrival of King William',[177] or 'by the gift of the king'.[178] His acquisitions included not only small parcels of land held by freemen but also substantial manors, including Rayleigh, where a castle was built.

The count of Boulogne was the most important lay landholder in Essex, where most of his estates had come to him as successor of Ingelric the clerk or priest, who witnessed royal charters in 1067 and 1069 and founded the church of St Martin-le-Grand in London in 1068.[179] Ingelric's estates must have been granted to the count after the latter's reconciliation with King William, probably in about 1074. Geoffrey de Mandeville succeeded to the Essex lands of Ansger the Staller (and of his commended men) probably in 1067, and Ralph Bainard also received his Essex lands at an early date. The name of Robert Gernon or Greno was a nickname meaning 'moustachioed'; his place of origin has to date proved elusive, but it is likely that he came from the Cotentin. He witnessed three acts issued by William before 1066 relating to the Cotentin, two in the company of William de Vauville.[180] In Essex he held four relatively valuable manors – Stansted, which became the head of his honour, West Ham, East Ham, and (Great) Oakley; the rest, some of which he had received in exchange, had been held by freemen. West Ham had been granted by King

---

[176] e.g. Shoebury, *DB*, II, 44.   [177] e.g. Asheldham, *DB*, II, 46.   [178] e.g. Theydon Mount, *DB*, II, 47b.
[179] *RRAN*, I, nos. 8, 21, 28.   [180] *RADN*, nos. 150, 199, 224.

William to Robert and Ranulf Peverel jointly.[181] There are several other statements to the effect that Robert was claiming land or freemen through the king's gift in Essex.[182] These references, coupled with the way Robert was established in Herefordshire, suggest that he was a man trusted by the king. The wife of Picot the sheriff of Cambridgeshire held her land as an under-tenant of Robert, and was perhaps his daughter.[183] Ranulf Peverel like Robert Gernon probably came from western Normandy. He presumably received his Essex estates relatively early as he received an antecessorial grant, his predecessor being Siward of Maldon. Ranulf's wife was named Ingelrica, and it has been suggested that she was a daughter of Ingelric the clerk.[184] Ranulf like Robert Gernon was also established on the Welsh Marches.

The needs of coastal defence seem to have played a part in shaping the settlement, for the major local landholders held important manors in demesne near the Thames estuary or the coast: West Ham (Robert Gernon and Ranulf Peverel), East Ham (Robert Gernon), West Thurrock (William Peverel), West Tilbury (Suein), Fobbing (Count Eustace), then a group of estates held by Suein; Burnham (Ralph Bainard), Down Hall (Ranulf Peverel), Tolleshunt d'Arcy and East Mersea (Suein), and, at the mouth of the Stour, Foulton (Suein), Michaelstow (Ralph Bainard), and Dovercourt (Aubrey de Vere).

Essex, Norfolk, and Suffolk were surveyed in Domesday Book volume II and in greater detail than the counties in volume I. In all three counties there were many freemen, but in Essex there were more manorial centres with freemen attached, whereas in East Anglia there were also numerous individual entries, 'In X, Y holds; Z freemen at A acres, value B shillings and pence.' Often the Edwardian holder is described as a freeman under the commendation of one man, whilst occasionally the soke is said to have been held by another. For example, in Norfolk amongst the estates of Robert Gernon was Loddon. Before 1066 Wulfric, a free man, had held 'under Gyrth'; in 1086 the land was held by Osbert as Robert's tenant. The manorial assets included one freeman, the value was forty shillings, and Earl Ralph had had the soke.[185] The formulae used show some variation, for sometimes evidently tenants-in-chief had supplied the evidence themselves, but the reason that they take this form is that assessment to geld

[181] *DB*, II, 64, 72b.    [182] e.g. at Wormingford: *DB*, II, 66.    [183] *DB*, I, 197.
[184] Dugdale, *Mon. Ang.*, III, 294.    [185] *DB*, II, 255b.

was not based on manors and hides, but on a financial contribution, usually in shillings and pence, to the levy on each hundred.

In Essex men were usually commended to a single lord, but in Norfolk and Suffolk men could be commended to more than one. Even unimportant men had freemen commended to them, and it has been suggested that some may have been obliged to give their commendation to a particular lord depending on the land they held, and thus have ended up commended to more than one.[186] The numbers of freemen in Norfolk and Suffolk often make it impossible for us to see why particular groups of freemen had ended up with their new lords, and it may be that the newcomers themselves were not altogether clear about the overlapping web of relationships they found, hence the numerous 'annexations' listed at the end of all three counties in little Domesday.[187]

The distribution of land proceeded here step by step. Some Normans were assigned land at an early date: Geoffrey de Mandeville in succession to Ansger in Suffolk, and Ralph Bainard in succession to Aethelgyth in Norfolk, for instance. King William appointed Ralph, son of Ralph the Staller, a Breton, as earl in East Anglia. After his revolt in 1075 some of Earl Ralph's estates and those of Eadgifu the Fair in Suffolk passed to Count Alan of Brittany. Count Brian, Alan's brother, had received land in Suffolk probably not long after 1066, and when he left England these passed to the count of Mortain. Archbishop Stigand was a native of East Anglia and held the East Anglian bishopric until his appointment as bishop of Winchester; then he was succeeded in East Anglia by his brother Aethelmaer. Neither was deposed until 1070, and both were important landholders and had many freemen commended to them. West Suffolk was dominated by the great estates of the abbey of Bury St Edmunds whose abbot was Baldwin, King Edward's doctor, a Frenchman who found it possible to make the transition to the new regime. From William's point of view there was probably less armed resistance to the Normans in East Anglia than in neighbouring regions in the years immediately after 1066, but the coast was vulnerable to landings by Danish fleets. In 1075 when Earl Ralph rebelled he called upon the Danes for assistance, and after his flight more land was granted to men like Roger Bigod and Count Alan.

---

[186] Clarke, *English Nobility*, pp. 94–8.

[187] Cf. Fleming, *Kings and Lords*, pp. 193–4 for the argument that many lands of freemen were simply appropriated by their new lords.

There was still plenty of land available to be granted out, however. Roger the Poitevin, for instance, may have been a relatively late arrival in Suffolk, as he held lands previously held by another post-Conquest holder, plus the lands of many freemen.

In Suffolk the most important lay landholders were Richard FitzGilbert of Clare, Robert Malet of Eye, and Hugh de Montfort of Haughley. Richard FitzGilbert had succeeded to the confiscated lands of Wihtgar and also to those of a lesser thegn called Finn.[188] The only possible clues as to the timing of Richard's establishment in East Anglia are that he was in action at Ely in 1071,[189] and that he was said by Orderic to have been one of the leaders in suppressing the revolt of 1075.[190] William Malet, Robert's father, was part English, and Robert's mother was still living in 1086. Her lands were held of Robert and a few are said to have been 'of the queen's holding'.[191] By 1086 Robert had acquired many estates in Suffolk chiefly as a successor of Eadric of Laxfield, and these were relatively concentrated. Hugh de Montfort succeeded here as elsewhere to the land of Guthmund, brother of Wulfric abbot of Ely. We know from the account preserved at Ely that the abbot had leased land to Guthmund so that he had a sufficiently large estate to be an acceptable bridegroom for a girl of noble birth. Hugh secured not only Guthmund's own land but also those which he had leased, and Ely seems never to have recovered them.[192] Both before and after 1066 there were those whose estates straddled the boundary between Suffolk and Essex: Ansger the Staller and Geoffrey de Mandeville, Aethelgyth and Ralph Bainard, Siward of Maldon and Ranulf Peverel, Wulfwin and Aubrey de Vere, Ingelric and the count of Boulogne, and Robert FitzWymarc.

Roger Bigod acquired his very extensive holdings in East Anglia in stages. His background is obscure: there is a link with Odo of Bayeux, who may have given him his initial start, and he had a connection with Earl Hugh of Chester.[193] Roger arrived in East Anglia probably not long after 1066, for he is said to have acquired one estate in Norfolk in the time of

---

[188] *DB*, II, 448.  [189] *Liber Eliensis*, p. 188.  [190] OV, II, 316–18.  [191] *DB*, II, 310b.

[192] *Liber Eliensis*, p. 167.

[193] Hugh Bigod, Roger's son, was a tenant of the bishopric of Bayeux in 1133 at Les Loges and Savenay: Loyd, *Origins of Some Anglo-Norman Families*, pp. 14–15. One of Earl Hugh's tenants in Cheshire was Bigot de Loges, presumably after Les Loges: *DB*, I, 266b, 268. Roger was an under-tenant of Hugh in East Anglia: *DB*, II, 152b, 153, 299–299b, 302, and from the way the entry for Halesworth is phrased may even have been identical with Bigot of Loges.

Archbishop Stigand, which must have been before 1070 when Stigand was deposed, but it is not clear whether he was similarly quick to acquire land in Suffolk.[194] He is known to have held the shrievalties of both Norfolk and Suffolk at various points in time until his death in 1107; he acquired land after the downfall of Earl Ralph in 1075, and possibly additional estates were committed to him in 1084 or 1085.[195]

Only a very selective account of the land distribution in Suffolk can be attempted here. The list of tenants-in-chief here is very long, and it is not immediately apparent how or why many had acquired land. How, for instance, had Robert de Tosny acquired his four manors, two of which had been held by Ulf and two by Manni, a long way from the rest of his land, or Hugh de Grandmesnil his single estate which had been held by Alnoth, a man of Harold? Some of these great men could have been brought into the county to strengthen royal authority after the revolt. Perhaps this was how William of Arques, who held the great estate of Folkestone in Kent, came to acquire a small tenancy-in-chief and an under-tenancy in Suffolk, or Walter Giffard his small holding.[196]

In Norfolk the pattern is similar: a basic framework of antecessorial succession and changes after the revolt of 1075. Ralph de Tosny's manors had previously been held by Harold, and his freemen had been commended to Harold; Robert Malet had succeeded Eadric of Laxfield, and Hermer de Ferrers, Thorketel. The two most important lay landholders were William de Warenne in the west of the county and Roger Bigod in the east. William's holdings in East Anglia probably originated in the lands his brother-in-law Frederic had acquired as the successor of Toki, and there are numerous references in the description of William's Norfolk estates to his having received land in the exchange or exchanges of Lewes.[197] Roger Bigod's antecessor in Norfolk was Ailwy of Thetford, evidently English and possibly a sheriff who kept his office for a time after 1066.[198] Roger had more manors here than in Suffolk, but in both counties the vast majority of holdings were the lands of freemen. His principal estates were concentrated along the coast and in Norfolk he also had

---

[194] *DB*, II, 173b.

[195] For a brief discussion, J. A. Green, *English Sheriffs to 1154*, Public Record Office Handbooks no. 24 (1990) pp. 60–1, 76–7. Although the evidence is patchy, it looks as though Roger became sheriff of Norfolk not long after 1066, and was also sheriff of Suffolk by 1086. He may well have held both counties until his death, for the other individuals who crop up in royal documents may have been his deputies.

[196] *DB*, II, 431b, 430.      [197] *DB*, II, 157b (Hackford), 167b (Foulden).      [198] *DB*, II, 273, 278.

custody of a number of royal manors on or near the coast, which suggests that he had a special responsibility for coastal defence, not surprisingly in view of its vulnerability to Danish fleets.

## VII  Northamptonshire, Leicestershire, Warwickshire

The distribution of land in Northamptonshire seems to have been both by a combination of antecessorial succession and by the formation of new, territorially compact, lordships. Geoffrey of Coutances succeeded Burgred of Mercia here as elsewhere, Earl Hugh succeeded Askell, and William Peverel, Countess Gytha. Antecessorial succession may be stronger than at first sight appears, because there were territorial sokes, and so unrecorded ties of lordship may have determined some grants. The nucleus of Ghilo de Pinkney's estates had been held by three men: Leofric, Siward, and Saewulf. We discover from the return of Ghilo's lands in Buckinghamshire that Siward and Saewulf were brothers and, as Leofric had held one of the Northamptonshire estates with Siward, it is likely that we have here the lands of one family.[199]

At some stage this county passed to Waltheof son of Siward, possibly when he was appointed earl of Northumbria in 1072.[200] By 1086 however the most important lay landholder in Northamptonshire was Robert of Mortain. Robin Fleming suggested that he received all the available land in some sixteen hundreds, and she pointed out that this seems to have been a grant specifically confined to Northamptonshire.[201] Robert probably already had land there if the man named Edmer who was his antecessor in two estates was Edmer Ator.[202] The fact that the count's estates intermingled with those of William Peverel and Countess Judith in the centre of the county may have been because William and Judith were already in possession. His lordship may have been created in 1070 or 1071, or after the revolt of 1075.

Robert de Tosny, lord of Belvoir, held a group of estates south of Rockingham. Three had been held by Oswulf, whom we may identify as Oswulf son of Fran, Robert's predecessor in Hertfordshire, Bedfordshire, and Buckinghamshire.[203] It is possible that Robert was the first castellan

---

[199] *DB*, II, 227, 152b.     [200] Williams, 'The King's Nephew: Ralph, Earl of Hereford', p. 339.
[201] Fleming, *Kings and Lords*, pp. 149–52.     [202] *DB*, I, 223.
[203] *DB*, I, 138, 149, 215. Robert's other principal predecessor in Gloucestershire, Buckinghamshire, and Cambridgeshire was Ulf.

of Rockingham, where King William had ordered a castle to be built, perhaps at the time of Morcar's revolt.[204] Bottesford in Leicestershire, on which estate the castle of Belvoir was built, consisted of four estates in Domesday Book, three held jointly by four thegns, Oswulf, Osmund, Rolf, and Leofric, and the fourth by Leofric alone. It is possible, therefore, that we are looking at the estates of one family and that Oswulf was Oswulf son of Fran.[205] Robert must have received this land before about 1076 when the priory of Belvoir was founded.[206] Like the honour of Dudley, Belvoir was a compact lordship extending into three counties, Northamptonshire, Leicestershire, and Lincolnshire, and, like Dudley, was probably created at a relatively early date after 1066.

Leicestershire also had some large territorial sokes. That of Barrow-on-Soar, for instance, had been held by Earl Harold and was granted to Earl Hugh. Again our knowledge of the origins of post-conquest lordships is limited by the fact that in this county the identity of Edwardian landholders is not always given. Some lordships can nevertheless be seen to have been based on antecessorial succession. Robert de Veci here as elsewhere succeeded to the land of Alric son of Meriet, and Geoffrey de la Guerche to the land of Leofwin, whose daughter he married. The marriage must have taken place relatively early, as Geoffrey founded a priory at Monks Kirby in 1077.[207]

Hugh de Grandmesnil was the most important lay tenant-in-chief in the county. Orderic Vitalis included Hugh's appointment as castellan of Leicester in his general list of the distribution of rewards. This, though undated, follows his account of the fall of Edwin and Morcar, and it is likely on commonsense grounds that an experienced commander who had been at Hastings would have received land at an early date. It might have been expected that he would have acquired more land than he did. He had been under a cloud a few years previously, and Orderic mentions him amongst those Normans who went home in 1068 to their impatient wives. If he did leave, and Orderic was usually well informed about the affairs of this family, it may only have been on his return to England that he obtained his midland estates.[208] Hugh had received some of his lands in or before 1080 or 1081 when King William confirmed to St Evroul a list of grants from Hugh's Leicestershire lands including the church and two vir-

---

[204] *DB*, I, 220.     [205] *DB*, I, 233b, 234.     [206] Dugdale, *Mon. Ang.*, II, 289.
[207] *VCH Warwickshire*, I, 275–6; Dugdale, *Mon. Ang.*, VI.2, 996.     [208] OV, II, 220.

gates of land at Thurcaston.[209] Some at least of Hugh's lands in Leicestershire and in Warwickshire had come to him as the successor of Baldwin, son of Herluin, a man known to have been established in England by 1036 when he had accompanied the king's daughter Gunnhildr to her wedding to the emperor's son.[210]

Robert de Beaumont had extensive estates in Leicestershire and Warwickshire. Some, perhaps all, of his lands had been held by his father Roger.[211] One of the striking features of Robert's estates in Warwickshire was the survival of Englishmen as tenants, possibly because Roger de Beaumont was not very concerned to oust them, or because of the influence of Turchil of Warwick, also called Turchil of Arden, who survived as a sheriff for some years after 1066.[212] Other local landholders included Geoffrey de la Guerche in succession to Leofwin, Geoffrey de Mandeville to Ansger the Staller, Gilbert FitzTurold as the successor of Cyneweard of Laugherne, and Henry de Ferrers as the successor of Siward Barn. Harold, son of Earl Ralph of Hereford, was still in possession of one manor he had held before 1066, and one belonging to his father.[213] Robert of Stafford held land in the west of the county. His most important predecessor was the thegn Waga, who gave his name to Wootton Wawen.[214] Roger of Montgomery also held land in the county, as he did in Staffordshire; these estates may have been given to him as back-up for his front-line position in Shropshire.

## VIII  Nottinghamshire and Derbyshire

Nottinghamshire and Derbyshire are appropriately considered together, for it is evident that the settlement of both took place during the same period. Ralph FitzHubert succeeded Leofric; Gilbert de Gant, Ulf Fenisc; Roger de Buron, Osmund; Walter of Aincourt, Swain and Thori; and Henry de Ferrers, Siward Barn. Osbern FitzRichard succeeded to Earl Aelfgar's manor of Granby with its soke. Siward Barn's estates extended into eight

---

[209] OV, III, 232–40.    [210] Phillimore edition of *DB*, note to Warwickshire 18,7.

[211] Round, *CDF*, p. 108 and for comment pp. xlix–l. Orderic believed that Robert's brother Henry was given custody of the castle built at Warwick in 1068, but this is unlikely given Henry's youth at that date: OV, II, 218.

[212] Williams, 'A Vice-Comital Family in Pre-Conquest Warwickshire', pp. 279–92.    [213] *DB*, I, 244.

[214] J. E. B. Gover, A. Mawer, F. M. Stenton, and F. T. Houghton, *Warwickshire, English Place-Name Society* (Cambridge, 1936), pp. 242–3.

counties. Most were in Derbyshire, but the most valuable were three in Berkshire and Lechlade in Gloucestershire. As mentioned above, he was involved in the revolt at Ely in 1071, but it is not known when he lost his lands or what his fate was.[215] In the north midlands considerations of defence came to the fore in the setting up of compact lordships centred on Tutbury, Nottingham, Tickhill, and Peak in Derbyshire. According to Orderic, a castle was built at Nottingham and committed to William Peverel in response to the revolt of Edwin and Morcar in 1068.[216]

It has been suggested above (p. 45) that this William, about whose origins little is known, may have been related to Ranulf Peverel of Essex and that both may have come from west Normandy. In 1086 William held a manor just outside Nottingham, which had formerly been held by Countess Gytha and could have been given to him with the castle.[217] Basford in Nottinghamshire had been held by Alwin (Aethelwine) who could have been the man who was William's antecessor in Oxfordshire and all but two of his Buckinghamshire manors, but at some stage William was granted all the available land in Broxtow wapentake.[218] This grant could have occurred when the castle was founded, or at any date between 1069 and 1071 in response to trouble in the north and the north midlands and the revolt of Edwin and Morcar. William's lordship possibly predated Roger de Bully's lordship of Tickhill, with which it interlocked in Broxtow and Rushcliffe wapentakes. It is unlikely that the two relatively compact lordships would have overlapped in this way if they had been granted at the same time.[219] Of the two, given the date of 1068 assigned to the establishment of William at Nottingham, it is more likely that Roger arrived later. His name was derived from Bully near Neufchâtel-en-Bray.[220] A man of this name, either the Domesday Roger or his father, had sold the tithe of Bully to Holy Trinity, Rouen before 1066.[221] Roger dedicated an annual payment to Holy Trinity from the priory he founded at Blyth near his castle at Tickhill in about 1088.[222] Roger's wife was in the queen's favour; perhaps she was a kinswoman or a lady-in-waiting, for the queen (presumably Queen Matilda who died in 1083) gave Roger the manor of

[215] DB, I, 60b, 169; ASC E 1071.     [216] OV, II, 218.     [217] Roffe, 'From Thegnage to Barony', pp. 173–4.
[218] DB, I, 287b, 157b, 148.
[219] Normanton on the Wolds, Stanton on the Wolds, Thrumpton, Costock, and Rempstone, DB, I, 286, 288.     [220] Loyd, Origins of Some Anglo-Norman Families, p. 20.     [221] RADN, no. 200.
[222] The Cartulary of Blyth Priory, ed. R. T. Timson, Historical Manuscripts Commission (London, 1973), no. 325.

Sandford when he married.[223] Beatrix, who was probably Roger's daughter, married William count of Eu.[224]

Henry de Ferrers was the most important lay lord of Derbyshire. His lordship formed a compact bloc in eastern Staffordshire and western Derbyshire with his headquarters at Tutbury, and he probably also had a castle at Burton.[225] By the time he received these lands he had probably been given land in Berkshire, and had a command at Stafford. The creation of the lordship of Tutbury, like that of Nottingham, was linked with the fall of Edwin and Morcar. In Staffordshire Henry's manor of Rolleston had belonged to Earl Morcar, and in Derbyshire his manor of Doveridge had belonged to Earl Edwin.[226] Henry did not totally dominate the county, however, for in the north William Peverel held Peak and, to the south-east, a group of estates, together with some of the manors of the royal demesne. All this suggests that William may have been sheriff of Derbyshire and, if so, of Nottinghamshire too, for the two counties had a single shire court until the thirteenth century.[227]

## IX  Lincolnshire

Neighbouring Lincolnshire was a troubled area in the early years of occupation. A castle was built at Lincoln in 1068, and in the following year a large Danish fleet appeared off the east coast and reached the Humber, where it met up with Edgar Aetheling, Waltheof, Siward (Barn), and other English leaders. Edgar went off on a foraging party and was trounced by William's garrison from Lincoln, and then the English and their allies besieged York.[228] After William had relieved his garrison at York, the Danes took refuge from the Normans in Lincolnshire, and later reemerged when they thought the coast was clear.[229] According to the Anglo-Saxon Chronicle, a Danish fleet appeared in the Humber in 1070 and joined in an attack on Peterborough Abbey.[230] These events showed only too clearly the vulnerability of the regions near the Humber to Danish attack, and the co-operation they were likely to receive from the

[223] DB, I, 113.

[224] M. Chibnall, 'Robert of Bellême and the Castle of Tickhill', Droit privé et institutions régionales. Etudes his-
    toriques offerts à Jean Yver (Paris, 1976), p. 152 and n; CP, v, 151–6 suggests that Beatrix was Roger's sister
    or daughter.        [225] DB, I, 248.        [226] DB, I, 248b, 274.

[227] D. Crook, 'The Establishment of the Derbyshire County Court 1256', Derbyshire Archaeological Journal,
    103 (1983), 98–106.        [228] OV, II, 218, 226.        [229] OV, II, 214–34.        [230] ASC E 1070.

local population, much of which was likely to have been of Anglo-Danish descent.

Identifying the principal elements in the distribution of land in the county is complicated by the number of middling and lesser landholders there on the eve of the Conquest, especially the numerous freemen and sokemen. The list of landholders after 1066 was very long, and included some of the less well-known tenants-in-chief. It would appear that there were men of Breton, or Norman, or perhaps of Anglo-Danish descent already settled in the county who were prepared to ally with the newcomers. Judhael of Lincoln may have been a Breton (see above, p. 67), and a man of this name appears in the (much later) cartulary of Ramsey abbey as the donor of Quarrington.[231] He died in 1051 and there is no reference to him in Domesday Book for Lincolnshire, but a man named Alfred of Lincoln does occur. Alfred of Lincoln was possibly the Alfred *nepos* of Turold mentioned in the description of the city of Lincoln in 1086.[232] Turold was sheriff of Lincolnshire under the Conqueror, and it is possible that he was settled in the county before 1066.[233] By 1086 however Turold's lands had passed to Ivo Taillebois, husband of Lucy, who may well have been Turold's daughter.[234] Ivo is mentioned as present at the siege of Ely in 1071, and as a participant in the pleas by which the abbey of Ely recovered its lands.[235] Colsuein of Lincoln belonged to the same family.[236] He had property in Lincoln and had built thirty-six houses and two churches there on waste land given to him by the king (see also below, p. 98).[237] Finally, William Malet also may have held Alkborough before 1066 and may have been related to Lucy.[238]

Harold Godwinson had held estates here and all but one were granted to Earl Hugh of Chester. These were estates with valuable sokelands and amongst the most valuable held by the earl outside Cheshire. Earl Hugh may have been responsible for the presence in Lincolnshire of Norman d'Arcy, a lesser known tenant-in-chief whose name may have been derived

[231] *Cartularium Monasterii de Ramesia*, ed. W. H. Hart and P. A. Lyons, 3 vols., RS (London, 1884–93), I, 280–1.

[232] *DB*, I, 336b.

[233] *DB*, I, 346b: *RRAN*, I, no. 430 (as T the sheriff); II, 398, no. 288d. Spalding priory, of which Turold was said to have been the founder, was established in 1052: Dugdale, *Mon. Ang.*, II, 119; III, 206–16.

[234] *CP*, VII, appendix J.     [235] *Liber Eliensis*, pp. 182–3, 200.

[236] Robert *nepos* of the countess (Lucy), referred to Ivo (Taillebois) and Colsuein as his *avunculi*: Stenton, *Documents . . . Danelaw*, pp. 268–9.     [237] *DB*, I, 336b.

[238] Robert Malet was described as having been the uncle of Lucy in Henry FitzEmpress's charter for Ranulf II earl of Chester: *RRAN*, III, no. 180.

from Arcy near Avranches.[239] Count Alan of Richmond was also a substantial landholder here, and his presence may in turn help to explain the
presence of other Bretons in the county: Geoffrey de la Guerche, Eudo son
of Spirewic, Oger, and Waldin.

There was only one strikingly compact lordship in the county, the Isle of
Axholme, given at an early date to Geoffrey de la Guerche. Even in this
case there was an antecessorial grant at its heart, for the man named
Leofwin who held some land there was presumably the same Leofwin who
was Geoffrey's father-in-law. The fact that Siward Barn held a manor here
which did not pass to Henry de Ferrers, who succeeded to his other estate
in the country, is an indication that Geoffrey had been established before
the fall of Siward Barn.[240] There were other instances of antecessorial
succession: Gilbert de Gant to Ulf Fenisc and Tonni, Geoffrey Alselin to
Toki son of Auti, Robert de Tosny to Turgot Lag, and Ralph Paynel to
Merlosuein, who had fled to Scotland in 1068 and returned with the Scots
army in the following year.[241]

In general it looks as though the main framework of the settlement
began to take shape early, partly because of the shire's vulnerability to
Danish attack. Odo of Bayeux acquired land, and could have been responsible for the establishment of Erneis de Buron and Ralph de Buron, the
latter a tenant-in-chief in Nottinghamshire and Derbyshire. Little is
known about either of these men. It has been suggested that they came
from Biron in the honour of Evrecy which was an honour held of the
bishop of Bayeux by Ranulf of Bayeux, but in one place Erneis was
described as a man of Earl Hugh.[242]

The great revolution of landholding thus was carried through in the interests of a relatively small cohesive group of Normans and their Breton and
Flemish allies. Over the two decades between 1066 and 1086 there were
inevitably winners and losers. Some received lands but gave them up, like
Gherbod the Fleming, Count Brian, or Aubrey de Coucy. Some may have
been reluctant to take land – perhaps William de Vauville, Count Brian's
colleague in the south-west, came into this category. Others may have
received land at an early date, but were disinclined to commit further

---

[239] Tengvik, *Old English Bynames*, p. 66.     [240] *DB*, I, 369.     [241] *ASC* D, 1067, 1068.
[242] A. S. Ellis, 'Biographical Notes on Yorkshire Tenants named in Domesday Book', *Yorkshire Archaeological
Journal*, 4 (1875–6), 240–1; see Phillimore edition, Yorkshire, biographical notes; *DB*, I, f. 349.

resources to England, perhaps through age, or because they died before they were able to benefit fully. William count of Evreux was mentioned as one of William's allies in 1066, and he received some land, but not much. Robert count of Eu was obviously important in 1066 and for a few years afterwards, but apart from his land in Sussex and Kent he only acquired land in Huntingdonshire and Essex, and he may well have retired to his continental estates in the 1070s.[243] Roger de Beaumont had stayed behind in Normandy in 1066, and his occurrences in later royal documents do not suggest he spent much, if any, time in England.[244]

Most conspicuous amongst the winners were the king's two half-brothers, who are found as landholders in county after county. Odo's lands were worth some £3,000 in 1086 and Robert's £2,100.[245] Both were prepared to commit themselves and their vassals to the enterprise of England, and in several cases their vassals became tenants-in-chief in their own right. For instance, Odo's followers included Walter and Ilbert de Lacy, William de Courseulles, and Hugh and Hubert de Port. Both Odo and Robert inherited land from Anglo-Saxon antecessors, from Aethelnoth *cild* and Edmer Ator respectively, but they acquired much more as the land settlement progressed, and where one did not hold much land the other did.

Comparable in wealth with Robert was Roger of Montgomery. The core here was the rape of Arundel, where the constituent estates were very valuable, and Shropshire. His estates in Surrey, Hampshire, and Wiltshire had come to him principally as the successor of Osmund, and in Cambridgeshire and Hertfordshire from a woman named Goda.[246] In Middlesex two of his manors had been held by Wigod and two by Wigod's men.[247] His estates in Warwickshire, Worcestershire, Gloucestershire, and Staffordshire derived in some way from his earldom.

---

[243] Robert witnessed royal documents drawn up in England in 1068 and 1069. The address clause of *RRAN*, I, no. 50, dealing with the restoration of lands taken by sheriffs, though couched generally, was probably issued in connection with Archbishop Lanfranc's attempt to recover lost Canterbury lands, so Robert may have still been in England after Lanfranc's appointment in 1070. Robert witnessed at Rouen in 1074 and 1080. Other references to him in royal documents cannot be pinpointed in place or time: *ibid.* nos. 22, 26, 50, 75, 123.

[244] Roger witnessed at Le Mans (1073), Troarn (1067/1073), Rouen (1074, 1072/9), Caen (1080), 'Oxcessus' (1082): *RRAN*, I, nos. 69, 72, 75, 118, 125, 146a.

[245] For a table of wealth (demesne and tenanted land) of class A landholders, Warren Hollister, 'Magnates and "Curiales" in Early Norman England', *Monarchy, Magnates and Institutions*, p. 99.

[246] *DB*, I, 34b, 44b, 68b, 193–193b, 137b.    [247] *DB*, I, 129.

The next two greatest landholders were William de Warenne and the Breton Count Alan, each with lands worth more than £1,000. William was granted one of the Sussex rapes; he succeeded to the lands of his brother Frederic, and was also granted manors belonging to King Harold. Count Alan also probably obtained his lands in stages, though the order is hard to determine. His lands around York may have been bestowed at an early date, possibly earlier than the great northern castlery of Richmond, and we know that after 1075 he was given lands belonging to Earl Ralph and Eadgifu the Fair.

The other members of class A (see above, p. 36) held roughly comparable amounts of land and, with the exception of Geoffrey de Mandeville, received land in stages. Eustace count of Boulogne, apart from Count Alan the only other non-Norman at the very peak of the new hierarchy of wealth, probably obtained his land in Kent soon after Hastings. The large estates, chiefly in Essex, of Ingelric the clerk possibly came later, for Ingelric was still living in 1068; conceivably Eustace was granted them after his reconciliation with the king. Richard FitzGilbert's estates can be divided into the later lordships of Tonbridge and Clare. They were received from different antecessors and possibly, therefore, at different times. There were two nuclei to the bishop of Coutances' estates, one in the south-west, where he was engaged in active campaigning by 1069, and the other in the midlands as the successor of Burgred of Mercia. Hugh d'Avranches, earl of Chester, was perhaps one of the greatest success stories in this group because he may well have been relatively young and, as his father was still living, he did not have free access to men recruited from his patrimonial lands, yet he was evidently one of the most committed and effective of the Norman commanders. The greatest wealth was won by those with commitment, resources, and staying power. As resistance flared, as men surrendered the lands they had been granted, or proved disloyal and lost them, those who had been tried and not found wanting were given more land. It has on occasion been suggested that there may have been a shortage of new lords. In absolute terms, this seems unlikely, but it may have been the case that at critical moments the regime had to be shored up, and the way to do this was to assign more to those who knew what they were doing.

It is unnecessary to describe further the gains of individuals, but as the scale of rewards is studied, it is striking how some of the more obvious

winners were a relatively small group whose members soon had their
hands on the levers of power, as sheriffs, as men who held royal manors in
custody, or as deliverers, and whose wealth in England far outstripped
any they had had in Normandy. Sheriffs and deliverers were obviously
well placed to pick up estates both as tenants-in-chief and as under-
tenants. Hugh de Port is one such example, a vassal of Bishop Odo who
was employed in farming royal manors in the midlands.[248] Ivo Taillebois
may have been related to Ralph Taillebois, sheriff of Bedfordshire, as
already noted. Ivo could even have succeeded Ralph for a time as sheriff,
for he is said to have imposed an increment on a royal manor in the
county.[249]

Robert d'Oilly and Roger d'Ivry were exceptionally successful in picking
up land. Robert was a sheriff and constable of Oxford castle; he acted on
one occasion as a justice with Edward of Salisbury, and on another as a
deliverer.[250] His lands had been held by many antecessors and he was also
ready to hold land as an under-tenant.[251] Roger d'Ivry, his sworn companion, also acquired estates from several antecessors, and was prepared to
take on estates as under-tenancies.[252] Slightly lower down the scale of
landed wealth came sheriffs like Picot of Cambridge, Eustace of
Huntingdon, and Urse d'Abetot, notorious despoilers of churches. Only
Urse had a toponym, a possible indication of some social standing in
Normandy; the origins of the other two are veiled in obscurity. Picot succeeded to the lands of a pre-Conquest sheriff, Aluric son of Godric, and he
was sheriff from about 1071. His largest demesne manors were formed by
amalgamating the lands of sokemen – at Bourn, for instance, there were

---

[248] *DB*, I, 219.    [249] *DB*, I, 209b.    [250] *DB*, I, 35; II, 61.

[251] In Oxfordshire he held of the archbishop of Canterbury at Newington, Bishop Odo at Forest Hill and
Barford St John, and Abingdon Abbey at Arncott: *DB*, I, 155, 155b, 156, 156b. Robert also held in pledge
two estates of Sauuold, possibly to be identified with the former sheriff: *DB*, I, 160b. In
Nottinghamshire he was Osbern FitzRichard's tenant at Granby: *DB*, I, 292. In Warwickshire he was
Bishop Odo's tenant at Bidford, and Turchil of Warwick's tenant at Dosthill, Barston Marston,
Lillington and Nuneaton: *DB*, I, 238b, 241, 241b, 248. In Staffordshire he was Earl Roger's tenant at
Shenstone: *DB*, I, 248b.

[252] In Oxfordshire he was named as the bishop of Lincoln's tenant at Yarnton, and co-tenant with Robert
d'Oilly at Arncott and at Blackbourton, the latter from Earl William's (FitzOsbern) holding: *DB*, I,
151b, 156b, 161. He is also to be identified with Roger tenant of Bishop Odo at Yarnton, Forest Hill,
Woodperry, and Cowley: *DB*, I, 156, 155b, *VCH Oxfordshire*, I, 379–81. In Buckinghamshire he and
Robert d'Oilly held Stowe of Odo: *DB*, I, 144b. In Berkshire Roger held part of the bishop of
Winchester's manor of Woolstone and in Gloucestershire he was the tenant of Durand of Gloucester
at Culkerton: *DB*, I, 58b, 168b.

twenty-two. He was also a tenant of the bishop of Lincoln and the abbot of Ely.[253] Eustace, sheriff of neighbouring Huntingdon, also succeeded to Offord, which had been held by a past sheriff, Alwine or Athelwine. He held only one valuable estate in demesne, Staughton, which he held as a tenant of the bishop of Lincoln, and here his tenure was disputed by Ramsey abbey.[254] Urse was sheriff of Worcestershire by 1069 and by 1086 was the most important lay landholder in the county. Only a few of his estates were held in chief, including three which had belonged to Evesham abbey before the Conquest. Most were held of the bishops of Worcester and Hereford, the abbeys of Westminster, Pershore, and Evesham, the bishop of Bayeux, Earl Roger, Ralph de Tosny, and Osbern FitzRichard.[255]

If these were the winners in the land revolution, the losers were predominantly the English.[256] In the top four classes of landholders, those with land worth more than £100, there were only two survivors who were not French, and possibly one or two more of mixed ancestry like Robert Malet and Edward of Salisbury. After the rebellions between 1068 and 1071 it was only by the greatest of good fortune and skill that a few natives not only survived in the upper levels of the aristocracy but also prospered. Anglo-Saxon sheriffs were particularly crucial in the handover of the reins of power. In the short term sheriffs with Anglo-Saxon or Danish names are found. In Somerset Tofi was sheriff; in Oxfordshire Swawold; in Hertfordshire Edmund; in Worcestershire Kineward; and in Lincolnshire the great thegn Merlosuein witnessed a charter of King William as Merlosuein the sheriff. In Warwickshire Alwin or Aethelwine was sheriff and was probably succeeded by his son Turchil of Warwick. 'O' sheriff of Surrey may have been Oswald, the king's thegn of Effingham, and brother of the abbot of Chertsey.[257] Such men had knowledge and contacts vital to the Normans. Godric, the steward of Earl Ralph, in East Anglia, successfully survived the earl's fall, retained his own estates and held some of the earl's in custody.[258] He was possibly sheriff or under-sheriff of Norfolk and Suffolk in Rufus's reign.[259] Godric may nevertheless have been an excep-

---

[253] *DB*, I, 200–201b, 190b, 191.     [254] *DB*, I, 206b, 203b.     [255] *DB*, I, 177b, 172b–176b, *passim*.
[256] For a detailed discussion see Williams, *The English and the Norman Conquest*.
[257] Green, *English Sheriffs*, pp. 73 (Tofi), 69 (Swawold, possibly Sauuold, see above, note 251), 47 (Edmund), 87 (Kineward), 54, and *RRAN*, I, no. 8 (Merlosuein), 83 (Alwin and Turchil), and Williams, 'A Vice-Comital Family in Pre-Conquest Warwickshire'; for 'O', Green, *English Sheriffs*, p. 78, and for Oswald of Effingham, *DB*, I, 32b, 35b, 36b.     [258] *DB*, II, 202–205b, 119–135b; 335b–356, 284b–286b, 7b.
[259] *RRAN*, I, nos. 461, 291, 392.

tional case as an English steward, because as J. F. A. Mason pointed out, contemporary evidence suggests that the new lords recruited their honorial officials from their French followers, not from the English.[260]

Men who submitted early and co-operated with the new regime stood the best chance of survival. One such was Eadnoth the Staller, who was killed resisting an attack by Harold's sons and their allies in 1068. His son Harding still held Merriott and a few other estates in 1086, and the family rose again to prosperity and prominence through its association with Henry FitzEmpress.[261] Harold, son of Earl Ralph of Hereford, a kinsman of King Edward and therefore a possible claimant to the throne, was in the queen's custody in 1066 and was evidently deemed too young or insignificant to pose a threat. Twenty years later he held only Sudeley and Toddington in Gloucestershire, Chilvers Coton and Burton Dassett in Warwickshire, and a small piece of land at Droitwich in Worcestershire. Under Rufus, however, he was granted Ewias Harold, and other possessions of Alured of Marlborough.[262] The chances were better for native families if they were able to marry into the new elite. Recorded examples are few, but probably more numerous than we know.[263] In 1088 William Peche was granted fraternity by Ramsey abbey, and a place of burial in the abbey's cemetery. His wife's name, mentioned in the abbot's confirmation, was Aelfwen.[264] Those English men who were permitted to marry Norman women were few indeed, as Earl Edwin found to his cost. It was easier for natives to retain their lands and status in the far north where the Normans came late and in fewer numbers, and some even prospered, like Ivo son of Forne or Swain son of Ailric.[265]

The two most conspicuously successful survivors south of the Mersey and Humber were Turchil of Warwick and Colsuein of Lincoln. Turchil not only managed to hang on to some of his family's estates but also

[260] J. F. A. Mason, 'Barons and their Officials in the Later Eleventh Century', *Anglo-Norman Studies*, 13 (1991), 256–7.

[261] R. B. Patterson, 'Robert Fitz Harding of Bristol: Profile of an Early Angevin Burgess-Baron Patrician and his Family's Urban Involvement', *Haskins Society Journal*, 1 (1989), 109–10. Note, however, that Lewis has pointed out that the evidence for an identification of Harding of Merriott and Harding son of Eadnoth is not beyond question: 'Formation of the Honor of Chester', p. 67.

[262] Bates, 'Lord Sudeley's Ancestors', p. 44.

[263] E. Searle, 'Women and the Legitimisation of Succession at the Norman Conquest', *Proceedings of the Battle Conference on Anglo-Norman Studies*, 3 (1981), 159–70, 226–9.

[264] *Chronicon Abbatiae Ramesiensis*, p. 233.

[265] For Ivo son of Forne see Sanders, *English Baronies*, p. 50; for Swain, H. M. Thomas, 'A Yorkshire Thegn and his Descendants after the Conquest', *Medieval Prosopography*, 8 (1987), 1–22.

acquired others, possibly as the result of deliberate family decision to channel their wealth through him.[266] In 1088 on the creation of the earldom of Warwick his estates were subordinated to the earldom, and if he lost his status as a tenant-in-chief his family at least kept their land. We can only speculate why he did not suffer the fate of so many others. One possibility is a judicious marriage alliance between his family and the new rulers; another the tardiness of Roger de Beaumont or his son Robert in ousting Englishmen. Colsuein of Lincoln has been described as a quisling, a collaborator prepared to work with the new regime.[267] Certainly his lands are described in such a way as to suggest they all came to him after 1066. We do not know his ethnic origin but he evidently had influential kinsfolk: he was related to Countess Lucy, and conceivably was a brother of Turold of Lincoln, sheriff of the county probably soon after 1066.[268]

There must have been many men of thegnly rank who survived on fractions of their former lands. Some in 1086 were holding land at farm from the king, and it has been pointed out that they were often paying excessive rents.[269] In the longer term some families were able to rebuild their fortunes, as Robert FitzHarding did. The practice of calling sons by Norman names is thought to have spread rapidly, as Robert FitzHarding's own name shows. Colsuein of Lincoln's son was called Picot, and so on. There were after all few advantages to be gained in that brave new world by persisting with names like Aelfric or Wulfstan for those who wished to be upwardly mobile. The adoption of Norman names in the second and third generations after the Conquest means that only rarely is it possible to identify the families of English extraction who may have made up a considerable proportion of knightly families in the early twelfth century. Stenton drew attention to Robert of Astrop, a late twelfth-century Oxfordshire landholder, whose charter endowing Bruern abbey mentions that Milton under Wychwood had belonged to Alewi (Aelfwig) son of Eilsi of Faringdon, who was a king's thegn in Domesday Book.[270]

Even in the euphoria of victory the companions of the Conqueror could hardly have foreseen that they would be able to take over from the old aris-

---

[266] Williams, 'A Vice-Comital Family in pre-Conquest Warwickshire', p. 288.

[267] J. W. F. Hill, *Medieval Lincoln* (Cambridge, 1949), p. 48.

[268] For Turold as sheriff, *DB*, I, 346b; *RRAN*, I, no. 430; ii, 398 (no. 288d). For Lucy, see further below, pp. 369–71 and references there cited.

[269] R. L. Lennard, *Rural England, 1086–1135* (Oxford, 1959), pp. 154–5.          [270] *VCH Oxfordshire*, I, 388.

tocracy so completely. In south Italy, for instance, their compatriots did not completely displace the old aristocracy.[271] Sweeping changes were possible in England mainly because of the relative degree of social and governmental integration in southern England and because of the distortions in English society produced by the previous half-century's upheavals. As Fleming demonstrated, the old English aristocracy had suffered fearful losses in the early eleventh century, and had been subjected to a new Danish dynasty. There had also been a concentration of power in the hands of an overly narrow ruling circle dominated by Godwin and his family.[272] The lack of an adult son to succeed Edward the Confessor provided Duke William with his opportunity and also inhibited the rallying of a coherent opposition to the Normans. Nevertheless the newcomers were ably led, lucky when they needed to be, and tenacious when it counted. Their mastery of the new techniques of fortification gave them protection and bases for further forward advance. Only in the north was their advance checked, and when the region was finally brought under control it was in a later period and in a different context.

[271] For a valuable study of the duchy of Gaeta see P. Skinner, *Family Power in Southern Italy. The Duchy of Gaeta and its neighbours 850–1139*, Cambridge Studies in Medieval Life and Thought, 4th series, xxix (1995).      [272] Fleming, *Kings and Lords*, chapters 1–3.

# 3 The Normans in the north

In the eleventh century 'the north' (in this context a shorthand for describing the whole of England north of the rivers Mersey and Humber) was a patchwork of regions with different histories, ethnic composition, and political alignments. It was only loosely tied in to the kingdom of the southern English, and had recently come under attack from the Scots. In 1055 Edward had appointed as earl Tostig Godwinson, who had lacked any local power base either with the men of York, which had earlier been the centre of an Anglo-Danish kingdom, or with the Northumbrians, whose centre of power was the great coastal stronghold of Bamburgh. Tostig had been appointed earl of Northampton in plurality with Northumbria very probably to boost his resources.[1] In 1061 King Malcolm III Canmore had invaded the north whilst Tostig was out of England; he was probably aiming at plunder rather than annexation. Tostig returned, and four years later he was expelled by a rising which involved both the men of York and the Northumbrians. The northerners advanced south, and demanded that Tostig be replaced by Morcar, brother of Edwin earl of Mercia, whose main claim to the earldom was evidently that he was not a member of the Godwinson family. Edward had had little option but to agree. Tostig returned to England after Edward's death and, having joined forces with Harold Hardrada king of Norway, entered the Humber estuary in 1066. Together they defeated the forces of Edwin and Morcar at Fulford Gate outside York, and Harold had to march north to deal with the situation just at the time he was expecting the landing of William of Normandy in the south. Harold in turn defeated and killed Tostig and Harold Hardrada before returning to face William at Hastings.

The Normans thus faced a different set of problems north of the Humber and Mersey. In the midlands and the south, as the successor to the kings of the English, William could take over a recognised framework of authority and, after the fall of the house of Godwin, remaining opposition to the Normans' takeover was fragmented and uncoordinated. In the

---

[1] Williams, 'The King's Nephew: Ralph Earl of Hereford', pp. 338–9.

north by contrast there were different power groups each with its own interests and all reluctant to be ruled from the south. The fate of Tostig had demonstrated that a southern earl, without a local power base or an entrée by marriage such as Earl Siward (d. 1055) had gained, was in a precarious situation. York was the only major city, and lay at the heart of a region which had been relatively thickly colonized by the Danes. It was hardly surprising that Danish fleets which landed in the Humber were not repulsed but welcomed by the local population. There were far fewer royal estates than in the midlands and the south, and the structure of the church there gave the king few points of entry. The archbishop of York ruled a larger but poorer archbishopric than his counterpart at Canterbury, and Durham was his only suffragan bishopric. Monasticism had been largely swept away during the Viking era so there were few opportunities to strengthen houses by granting them lands and privileges, or by appointing abbots who favoured the new regime. Finally, the north was further away from Normandy and from the regions of England which were wealthiest and most firmly under Norman control. Like the invaders who had preceded them, the Normans' first priority was to gain the valuable arable lands of lowland England; the highland zone held fewer attractions.[2]

Because of Scottish incursions, the Conqueror could not afford to ignore the northern frontier of his realm, but the conquest of the north was not going to be quick and, as the years wore on, his problems in Normandy and the surrounding regions began to occupy more of his time and energies. In the years between 1068 and 1070, moreover, the Norman presence in Yorkshire was challenged and almost overthrown and, as a result, the Normans who took land there went in for radical restructuring of their estates in a way not paralleled further south. By contrast, in what was to become Lancashire, Cumbria, Northumberland, and Durham, the new lordships as far as we can tell (and there are relatively few records for the preceding period) tended to be based on earlier estate units. These were in some cases large, probably very old, estates often called shires.

---

[2] C. Fox, *The Personality of Britain* (Cardiff, 1959) for a discussion of the effect of environment on the distribution and fate of the inhabitants of highland and lowland Britain; see also H. M. Jewell, *The North–South Divide. The Origins of Northern Consciousness in England* (Manchester, 1994); for a recent account of the region in the early Middle Ages see N. J. Higham, *Northumbria A. D. 350–1100* (Stroud, 1993), and more specifically for the eleventh century, W. E. Kapelle, *The Norman Conquest of the North* (London, 1979).

Sometimes they were granted as a whole, or in portions which may have been earlier subdivisions. In terms of numbers Normans were thinner on the ground in the far north throughout our period. The process of colonization began later and was more protracted. It was also different in character in two respects. First, the families which settled in the north tended to have their main bases and thus their main interests there. Secondly, the crucial period in the emergence of a new social and political order coincided with the emergence of new types of religious communities in the early twelfth century, and new houses were founded all over the north. The emergence of a new political order in the twelfth century thus went hand in hand with a great wave of new foundations. Castles and monasteries were and are the visible signs of the Normans' presence in the north. The account which follows here is broadly chronological, and concentrates on the way the political context shaped the timing and character of Norman settlement. The first section deals with the Conqueror's reign and focusses on Yorkshire; thereafter the progress of settlement is viewed within the framework of Anglo–Scottish relations.

Morcar presumably did not lose his lands outright after Hastings, for he had not been present at the battle and had soon offered his submission to the Conqueror.[3] At Barking in the early weeks of 1067, however, William is said to have chosen Copsi as earl of Northumbria, a man about whom nothing is known except that he had governed Yorkshire for Tostig.[4] Morcar, with Edwin and Waltheof, Siward's son, was taken to Normandy in 1067 when William returned there in triumph. Copsi headed north, but within a matter of weeks had been killed by the forces of a man named Osulf, a member of the Northumbrian family based at Bamburgh.[5] William next tried as earl, Gospatric, who was related both to the Scottish kings and to the house of Bamburgh, and therefore had some hope of controlling Northumberland.[6] In 1068 there was a northern revolt, about which few details are recorded. It was evidently serious, however, for William himself marched north, building castles at strategic points, including York. Gospatric fled to Scotland.

By this time Normans had begun to take lands in Yorkshire. William

---

[3]  Morcar witnessed twice as earl: *RRAN*, I, nos. 22, 28 cf. 148. Ulf son of Topi seems to have acquired some of Morcar's land: Clark, *English Nobility*, p. 26.

[4]  WP, pp. 236, 269–71; SD, 'Historia Dunelmensis Ecclesiae', *Opera omnia*, I, 197.

[5]  *Ibid.*, I, 198.      [6]  Kapelle, *Norman Conquest of the North*, p. 18.

Malet was the first Norman sheriff of Yorkshire and, though he was replaced soon after the revolt of 1069, it is clear from Domesday Book that before his fall he held extensive estates in Yorkshire.[7] William de Percy claimed in 1086 that he had held Bolton (Percy) in the time of William Malet, and, in another entry, that at York he had incorporated a house into the castle 'in the first year after the destruction of the castles', that is, in 1069–70.[8] Hugh (Earl Hugh of Chester) may have been assigned the great estate of Whitby at an early date, for William de Percy, who was involved in the attempt to refound the old abbey not long after the harrying of the north, was Hugh's tenant by 1086, which suggests that Hugh was *in situ* by the time William de Percy arrived.[9] Gilbert de Gant was in the county by 1069, and he too may have acquired land at an early date.[10]

When revolt recurred in 1069 it was even more serious than in the preceding year. At the start of the year the Conqueror had appointed a third earl, Robert de Commines, probably from Commines in Picardy. He was the first earl not to be of native extraction but also, equally significantly, not a Norman. He too did not last long: within weeks he and his men were killed at Durham.[11] Gospatric, who by now had returned to northern England from Scotland, joined Edgar Aetheling, grandson of Edmund Ironside, and leading northern thegns such as Merlosuein, Archil, and the sons of Karl. This was a clear attempt to start a second front in the north under the leadership of Edgar. If the rebels had succeeded in establishing a bridgehead in the north, where they could have been reinforced from Scotland, then the prospects for the Normans there would have been much reduced.

Archil killed Robert FitzRichard, the castellan at York, and marooned William Malet in the castle. William sent word to the king who, recognizing the gravity of the situation, travelled north, relieved the siege, and built a second castle at York which was entrusted to William FitzOsbern.[12] However, in the autumn of 1069 the rebels, reinforced by Waltheof son of Siward and a Danish fleet, sacked York again and killed many Normans. Once again the Conqueror marched north. He held his Christmas court in

---

[7] J. A. Green, 'The Sheriffs of William the Conqueror', *Proceedings of the Battle Conference*, 5 (1982), p. 142. It is equally interesting that Robert Malet's title to these estates was challenged.

[8] *DB*, I, 374, 298.     [9] *DB*, I, 305.     [10] SD, 'Historia Regum' in *Opera omnia*, II, 188.

[11] SD, 'Historia Dunelmensis Ecclesiae', *Opera omnia*, I, 199.     [12] OV, II, 220–2.

the ruined city at York, where he wore the regalia as visible symbols of his authority, and proceeded north, harrying as he went. He received the submissions of Gospatric and Waltheof at the river Tees, and marched on to Durham and into Northumberland. The chronicler Symeon of Durham wrote of those who died at the roadside, fled south, or were sold into slavery.[13] A new archbishop, Thomas, was appointed, who was faced with the daunting task of rebuilding his cathedral, and a new sheriff, Hugh FitzBaldric, was also appointed.

It was in the aftermath of the harrying of the north that a new tenurial geography began to take shape. Castles were built and agricultural activity was concentrated in their vicinity in a way that involved the reorganization of previous estate units. The high proportion of manors described as 'waste' in Yorkshire in 1086, and the decline of manorial values by about 68 per cent, have sometimes been interpreted as the effects of the harrying.[14] The word waste suggests physical devastation and some historians have concluded that this was indeed what it meant.[15] Yet others have doubted that there was any direct link between waste and devastation. In the first place, the Yorkshire Domesday presents particular problems of interpretation, because the text was abbreviated and revised as the scribe refined his methodology for dealing with the material.[16] Thus the scribe listed as waste many estates in the king's hands which in other counties were listed as lands of king's thegns.[17] There are other possibilities to explain the frequency of manors reported as waste, including lack of tenants prepared to pay rents, the absence of arable, or lack of information, and, most frequently, reorganization.[18] All that can be safely concluded from the statement that an estate was waste is that, for whatever reason, no geld was forthcoming.

In a recent study of the process of conquest and settlement in Yorkshire,

---

[13] FW, ii, 4; SD, 'Historia Regum', *Opera omnia*, ii, 188.

[14] R. Welldon Finn, *The Norman Conquest and its Effects on the Economy 1066–1086* (London, 1971), p. 198.

[15] See, for example, T. A. M. Bishop, 'The Norman Settlement of Yorkshire', *Studies in Medieval History Presented to Frederick Maurice Powicke*, ed. R. W. Hunt and others (Oxford, 1948), pp. 1–14; Finn, *Norman Conquest and its Effects on the Economy*, p. 199; Kapelle, *Norman Conquest of the North*, pp. 163–7; S. Harvey, 'Domesday England', *The Agrarian History of England and Wales*, ii, ed. H. E. Hallam (Cambridge, 1988), p. 135.

[16] D. Roffe, 'Domesday Book and Northern Society: a Reassessment', *English Historical Review*, 105 (1990), 310–36.    [17] *Ibid.*, p. 324.

[18] W. E. Wightman, 'The Significance of "Waste" in the Yorkshire Domesday', *Northern History*, 10 (1975), 55–71; Wightman, *Lacy Family*, pp. 43–53; D. Palliser, 'Domesday Book and the "Harrying of the North"', *Northern History*, 29 (1993), 1–23.

Paul Dalton has correlated information taken from Domesday (the extent of waste recorded, the decline in values, and number of plough teams) with evidence relating to the physical relief and land quality of an area and to enfeoffment and the construction of castles at an early date. By this method he has constructed a convincing chronology for the creation of lordships in Yorkshire. Lordships which give signs of being relatively well organized, with low levels of waste, seigneurial plough teams, several tenants in place, and evidence of early castles, he points out, are likely to have been in existence for a relatively long time. By this reckoning the great estate of Conisborough which had belonged to Harold was an early grant to William de Warenne.[19] As it had been Harold's it was available for redistribution immediately, and the strategic importance of the site supports an early date for its assignment, though there may have been some delay before William took possession. The lordships of Hugh FitzBaldric and William de Percy were also likely to have come into being at a relatively early date, possibly in the aftermath of the harrying. Both were relatively compact and guarded the approaches to York by road and river, and both show signs of seigneurial activity and had retained much of their pre-1066 value. William de Percy in particular had established a number of tenants.[20] A third relatively compact lordship west of York was that of Osbern de Archis.[21] His background is obscure, though his name suggests that he came from Arques in upper Normandy: perhaps he was a kinsman or associate of Hugh FitzBaldric, whose connections similarly suggest that he came from upper Normandy.[22]

The savagery of William's harrying acted as a deterrence to further revolt by the northerners, but Edgar Aetheling was still at large, and had been joined at Wearmouth by Aethelwine bishop of Durham who had fled to Lindisfarne when King William had approached Durham.[23] Edgar's sister by this time had married King Malcolm, who in 1070 crossed the Pennines via Stainmore and ravaged Teesdale and Cleveland in north Yorkshire. Gospatric, now based at Bamburgh as William's earl of Northumbria (again), launched an attack on Cumberland in reprisal.[24] By

[19] Dalton, *Conquest, Anarchy and Lordship*, pp. 33–4.   [20] *Ibid.*, pp. 34–9.

[21] Fleming, *Kings and Lords*, p. 160.

[22] Charters of Gerold de Roumare: Round, *CDF*, p. 25; King William confirmed a gift of Hugh to the abbey of Préaux: *ibid.*, p. 108. Dalton suggests that Osbern's estates should be classed as an 'embryonic' lordship, because of the decline in manorial values, low number of demesne ploughs, and numerous tenants: Dalton, *Conquest, Anarchy and Lordship*, pp. 58–60.

[23] SD, 'Historia Regum', *Opera omnia*, II, 190.   [24] *Ibid.*, II, 191.

1071 Bishop Aethelwine of Durham had had enough of the Normans and, leaving his see, joined Morcar and Hereward on the Isle of Ely. After William had taken Ely, Aethelwine was sent to Abingdon abbey where he spent the rest of his days. The new bishop, Walcher, was a Lotharingian.[25]

In 1072 William himself marched north. He followed Malcolm as far as Abernethy where he exacted a submission, and on his return march south had a castle constructed at Durham.[26] About this time Gospatric was finally deprived of his earldom, having been accused of complicity in the murder of Robert de Commines at Durham and of the Normans at York.[27] The new earl was Waltheof son of Siward. Waltheof's period as earl, terminated by his revolt and execution in 1076, was too brief to leave much impression on Domesday Book: the only estate he is definitely known to have held in Yorkshire was Hallam (though see also below, p. 108).[28]

The estates formerly belonging to Edwin and Morcar were used as the basis for great castleries, one in the East Riding guarding the coast and the west bank of the Humber estuary, two guarding routes across the Pennines, and Richmond, protecting access from the north-west. Drogo de la Beuvrière, a Fleming, was established in Holderness. Edwin's manors of Gilling in Swaledale, Catterick near the great North Road, and Askham Bryan west of York, were all granted to Count Alan, together with Morcar's manors of Fulford, Clifton, and Foston near York. Kippax and Ledston passed to Ilbert de Lacy, and Laughton en le Morthen to Roger de Bully. We have no way of knowing if these estates belonged to Edwin and Morcar's family or to the earldom of Northumbria. If the latter, it might be regarded as odd that Morcar was not named as the Edwardian holder, but not necessarily so: Earl Siward was the antecessor named in two great coastal estates. Nevertheless the fact that Waltheof is only known to have held one Yorkshire estate, and the possibility that Edwin and Morcar's large and valuable estates passed to Normans, tends to suggest that Waltheof's earldom was not the same as his predecessors'. This could have been one reason why he was tempted to rebel in 1075.

Different views have been expressed about the timing, antecedents, and methods by which the major castleries came into being. The fact that the names Tickhill, Richmond, and Pontefract were not mentioned in Domesday Book led W. E. Wightman to believe that they may only have

[25] Ibid., II, 195.    [26] Ibid., II, 199.    [27] Ibid., II, 196.    [28] DB, I, 320.

come into being in the 1080s, and he also pointed out that Ilbert de Lacy seems only to have received some of his estates shortly before 1086.[29] Yet there is no reason why the grant of Edwin's manor of Laughton en le Morthen, the key manor in the honour of Tickhill, could not have been granted to Roger de Bully soon after Edwin's fall.[30] Count Alan could have been given Edwin's manor of Gilling in the aftermath of the harrying of the north to protect one of the routes into Yorkshire from the north.[31] Ilbert de Lacy possibly received Edwin's manor of Kippax at about the same time, though the boundaries of what became the honour of Pontefract were revised not long before 1086.[32] Cravenshire, which was in the hands of Roger the Poitevin in 1086, was almost certainly a recent grant, and had possibly been bestowed in exchange for Roger's land in Lancashire and Furness.[33]

Little can be deduced from the sketchy information about Craven as to the extent of reorganization there by 1086, if any. On the three other castleries, however, the Domesday information indicates differing situations. On Richmond and Pontefract there were numerous waste entries and declining manorial values. In Richmond many of the waste entries relate to the uplands. In Wensleydale by contrast there were manors with more ploughs reported than ploughlands, that is to say, the manors concerned appear to have been overstocked with ploughs, suggesting that what had happened was that people had moved, either voluntarily or under compulsion, from the uplands to the valley, within easy reach of the earl's chief manor at Gilling. In Pontefract also arable production had been concentrated on three demesne manors: Tanshelf (the chief manor and site of the castle of Pontefract), Leeds, and Kippax.[34] Both honours were conspicuous for the numbers of Anglo-Saxons who were still in possession of their lands according to the Domesday survey.[35] One obvious inference was that the new lords had not had time to dispossess all Englishmen; but it is also possible that there were new under-tenants who had not been listed, or that the new lords had chosen not to enfeoff many of their followers as yet. In Holderness and Tickhill there were fewer waste manors, and in Tickhill manors had retained more of their pre-Conquest

---

[29] Wightman, *Lacy Family*, pp. 21–8, 40–2, 54.     [30] *DB*, I, 319.     [31] *DB*, I, 309.     [32] *DB*, I, 316b, 379b.
[33] K. Thompson, 'Monasteries and Settlement in Norman Lancashire: Unpublished Charters of Roger the Poitevin', *Transactions of the Historic Society of Lancashire and Cheshire*, 140 (1990), p. 202 and n. 4; Dalton, *Conquest, Anarchy and Lordship*, p. 70.     [34] Wightman, *Lacy Family*, pp. 43–53.     [35] *Ibid.*, p. 41.

value, suggesting that in the former at least any disruption had been relatively short-lived.[36]

The Yorkshire lands held by Robert of Mortain were territorially compact, consisting of all the lands in nineteen wapentakes not in the hands of the church or assigned by the principle of succession to an antecessor.[37] There are no very obvious strategic implications and no clues as to the date when they were granted. Where Normans succeeded to antecessors who held land in Count Robert's area, the antecessorial grants were allowed to stand. In theory Robert may have received these estates at any time between about 1069 and 1086. One possible date was in the aftermath of Waltheof's revolt, because the man named Waltheof who was an important predecessor of Robert's in Yorkshire could have been Waltheof Siwardsson. A second possible date is 1080, in the aftermath of the Scots invasion in 1079 and Odo's northern campaign. Many of the estates had been distributed to tenants by 1086, principally Nigel Fossard and Richard de Sourdeval, neither of whom is known to have held of the count elsewhere, and who were evidently expected to take the lead in developing the estates.

One question to which no clear answer can be given is how far the amalgamation of estates and relocation of plough teams was accompanied by changes and increases in peasant obligations. In Yorkshire as elsewhere in the north there were large 'multiple estates' with sokes and berewicks, and demesne cultivation at manorial centres was developed, probably only slowly, with labour services provided by peasants; but the chronology and context of these developments remain obscure. It is not impossible that the opportunity was taken to impose heavier obligations than previously, and in this context it may be noted that the numbers of villagers (*villani*), predecessors of the later villeins, that are recorded in the North and East Ridings are relatively high.[38] The foundation of planned villages in the East Riding could perhaps be associated with such reorganization, though this assumes that the drive towards new settlements and open fields came from the landlords and not the peasants, which may not have been the case.[39]

[36] Dalton, *Conquest, Anarchy and Lordship*, pp. 40–2.     [37] Fleming, *Kings and Lords*, pp. 154–8.

[38] Kapelle, *Norman Conquest of the North*, pp. 174–81.

[39] J. Sheppard, 'Pre-enclosure Field and Settlement Patterns in an English township', *Geografiska Annaler*, 48 ser. B (1966), 59–77; Sheppard, 'Metrological Analysis of Regular Village Plans in Yorkshire', *Agricultural History Review*, 22 (1974), 118–35; M. Harvey, 'The Development of Open Fields in the Central Vale of York: a Reconsideration', *Geografiska Annaler*, 67 ser. B (1985), 35–44.

Despite the distribution of land and the construction of castles, the Normans' situation in Yorkshire in the 1070s remained insecure. The foundation history of Selby abbey alleges that Benedict, a monk of St Germain of Auxerre, ended up in Yorkshire and was taken under the wing of the Norman sheriff there, and that the situation at that time was so dangerous that the sheriff had to travel with an armed escort.[40] Further north, too, the situation of King William's bishop in Durham was hazardous. Bishop Walcher, though not himself a monk, tried to establish a monastery at Durham. He was sympathetic to the aims of the knight Reinfrid and his monk companions who wished to revive the tradition of Northumbrian monasticism, and allowed them to settle first at Jarrow and then at Wearmouth. After Waltheof's downfall the bishop had taken over the earl's authority. To assist him in the temporal affairs of the bishopric he had relied on a man named Leofwin, but Leofwin, in collusion with Gilbert, the bishop's kinsman, had killed Liulf, an important local thegn, whose wife was a granddaughter of Earl Uhtred, and the bishop, Leofwin, and Gilbert, were all killed in retaliation. These murders were a further episode in a protracted and bloody Northumbrian feud in which the hapless Walcher had been caught up.[41]

The king could not afford to let this outrage pass, however, and in 1080 he sent Odo of Bayeux north with a large force to ravage Northumbria. Later in the same year Robert Curthose was sent to Scotland. Robert exacted a renewal of submission from Malcolm but, according to Symeon, he accomplished nothing except the building of a new castle on the river Tyne.[42] Newcastle, however, was of obvious strategic importance in guarding the route north of the Tyne to Durham. At some point Aubrey de Coucy, probably from Coucy in Picardy, was appointed earl of Northumbria, but before the Domesday Survey he had surrendered the lands he had been given in England. A new bishop was appointed to replace Walcher, William of St Calais, who was chosen because of his experience in coping with difficult circumstances: a safe pair of hands, in other words.[43] He may not have visited his new see for some time, partly

[40] *The Coucher Book of Selby*, ed. J. T. Selby, 2 vols., Yorkshire Archaeological Society Record Series (1891–3), XIII, 258, 279.    [41] SD, 'Historia Regum', *Opera omnia*, II, 210.    [42] *Ibid.*, II, 211.

[43] SD, 'Historia Dunelmensis Ecclesiae', *Opera omnia*, I, 119; H. S. Offler, 'William of St Calais, first Norman Bishop of Durham', *Transactions of the Architectural and Archaeological Society of Durham and Northumberland*, 10 (1950), 258–79; W. M. Aird, 'An Absent Friend: The Career of Bishop William of St Calais', *Anglo-Norman Durham*, ed. D. Rollason, M. Harvey, and M. Prestwich (Woodbridge, 1994), pp. 283–97.

because of the dangerous situation there. In 1083, whilst at Rome, he secured the pope's agreement to the setting up of a Benedictine monastery at Durham, an excellent piece of forethought which made resistance to the new foundation by the Durham clerks difficult. Even so they were not enthusiastic: when offered the choice of entering the monastery or of retaining their lands for life, only one of them chose to become a monk.[44]

By 1087 the Norman settlement had made considerable headway in Yorkshire, and there was some Norman presence in Lancashire. The latter had been assigned to Roger the Poitevin, though it was apparently resumed by 1086, possibly in exchange for Craven.[45] The establishment of the new lords in Yorkshire had been pushed through against opposition and in the aftermath of military repression. At York there was a Norman archbishop and steps had already been taken for the foundation of a Benedictine abbey just outside the city walls. At Durham there was a castle and a tough new bishop, who had taken on the project of establishing a cathedral monastery. Nevertheless the Normans' hold on Durham was tenuous, as it probably was also west of the Pennines in Lancashire, while control in Northumberland was minimal, and in Cumbria non-existent. The Conqueror had been defeated by the remoteness of the region from his own centres of strength, the various, often conflicting, interest groups in the north, the lack of points of entry for controlling the north, and the scale of his own problems in his later years, which meant that he did not have the time, the opportunity, or the incentive to devote the sustained commitment needed to push through the conquest of the northernmost counties. He was more successful than his predecessors had been, if the crushing of revolt and the building of a few key castles be rated success, but the real turning point in the government of the north came in the closing years of the eleventh century, for it was William Rufus who laid the foundations of more effective rule in the north and opened up the opportunities for Norman settlement, albeit fragile, in Cumbria and Northumberland.

The great revolt not long after the start of Rufus's reign embroiled several northern lords (see below, pp. 275–7). The bishop of Durham, William of St Calais, was charged with complicity in the revolt which broke out against

[44] SD, 'Historia Dunelmensis Ecclesiae', *Opera omnia*, I, 120–3.
[45] *DB*, I, 269b–270b; 301b–302, 332b.

Rufus in 1088. It is not clear why he became involved, for initially he seems to have been high in Rufus's favour. One possibility is that he followed the lead of Odo of Bayeux, having been a clerk at Bayeux in the early stages of his career.[46] Bishop William disputed the king's attempt to try him in a secular court and eventually negotiated his departure abroad, as we know from a tract composed at Durham about the proceedings against him.[47]

In 1091 Malcolm invaded once again and came perilously close to Durham. Rufus marched north and, with the assistance of his brother Robert, exacted a renewal of the submission Malcolm had made to the Conqueror. Bishop William, who had been restored to his see in the course of 1091, took in hand the building of a great new cathedral. Malcolm laid a foundation stone and his and Margaret's names were probably entered in the cathedral's Book of Life at that time.[48] Bishop William knew that he had to get on with both Scottish and English kings, for the lands and churches which had historically belonged to his see lay on both sides of the Anglo–Scottish border, and St Cuthbert, whose relics were at Durham, was deeply venerated in Lothian. Nevertheless the willingness of the Scottish king and queen to associate themselves with the new cathedral is noteworthy, and is a further indication of their interest in the region.

Rufus meanwhile had evidently decided to take a more aggressive line towards the Scots. In 1092 he marched to Carlisle, drove out the local lord, Dolfin, built a castle and imported peasant families from the south to provide supplies for the new headquarters.[49] It is not clear what arrangements he made for the custody of Carlisle. At some stage the command was given to Ranulf *vicomte* of Bayeux, a cousin of Earl Hugh of Chester.[50] Ivo Taillebois the king's steward was granted Burton in Lonsdale and

---

[46] SD, 'Historia Dunelmensis Ecclesiae', *Opera omnia*, I, 119.

[47] 'De iniusta uexacione Willelmi episcopi primi per Willelmum regem fil(l)ium Willelmi magni regis', *English Lawsuits from William I to Richard I*, I, *William I to Stephen*, ed. R. C. Van Caenegem, Selden Society, CVI (1990), 90–106, discussed H. S. Offler, 'The Tractate *De iniusta uexacione Willelmi episcopi primi*', *English Historical Review*, 66 (1951), 321–41; M. Philpott, 'The *De iniusta uexacione Willelmi episcopi primi* and Canon Law in Anglo-Norman Durham', *Anglo-Norman Durham* (ed. Rollason, Harvey and Prestwich), pp. 125–37.

[48] SD, 'Historia Regum', *Opera omnia*, II, 220; *Liber Vitae*, ed. J. Stevenson, Surtees Society, XIII (1841), 73; G. W. S. Barrow, 'The Kings of Scotland and Durham', *Anglo-Norman Durham* (ed. Rollason, Harvey, and Prestwich), pp. 313–14.     [49] *ASC* 1092.

[50] The date of Ranulf's appointment is discussed by J. A. Green, 'Anglo–Scottish Relations, 1066–1174', *England and Her Neighbours 1066–1453. Essays in Honour of Pierre Chaplais*, ed. M. Jones and M. Vale (London, 1989), p. 57. Ranulf founded Wetheral priory in the time of Abbot Stephen of St Mary's, York (died 1112): *The Register of Wetheral*, ed. J. E. Prescott, Cumberland and Westmorland Antiquarian and Archaeological Society (1897), no. 1.

Kendal, which in effect meant that the route to the north-west was protected.[51] Probably at about the same date, Roger the Poitevin's estates in the north-west were restored to him, and enlarged to include what later became Lancashire, plus part of the Lake District.[52] The new lordship formed another great march to buttress Norman power in the north-west.

Rufus's seizure of Carlisle and Cumbria was probably the reason why Malcolm travelled south in 1093 to meet Rufus. Also at issue, however, was a projected marriage which from Rufus's point of view had obvious dangers (see also below, p. 354). The meeting between the two kings was not amicable, because Rufus wished to treat Malcolm as his vassal rather than as an independent ruler, and to deal with him thus in his court, an ominous precedent for the course of Anglo–Scottish relations. Malcolm returned to Scotland and prepared another invasion force. Both he and his eldest son were killed while crossing the river Aln at the hands of Robert de Mowbray's men.[53]

Malcolm was succeeded first by his brother Donald Bane according to Scottish custom but at the expense of Malcolm's sons by Margaret. They turned for assistance to their powerful southern neighbour and, as Rufus would have seen it, their overlord. Rufus backed the attempt of Duncan, Malcolm's second surviving son, to oust his uncle from the throne in 1094. Duncan had been a hostage at the Conqueror's court; he was married to a daughter of Earl Gospatric and may have been a member of Rufus's military household.[54] Duncan was initially successful in securing the throne, but was then killed by Donald.

Meanwhile Rufus's position in the north was jeopardized by another great baronial revolt in 1095. Robert de Mowbray, a nephew of Bishop Geoffrey of Coutances, had at some stage been appointed earl of Northumbria. Most probably this was in 1094, though it has been suggested he may have been appointed by the Conqueror and, having been unable to secure recognition from Rufus, had rebelled in 1088.[55] Seven years later Robert's revolt was triggered by his refusal to respond to Rufus's summonses to answer charges relating to the cargoes of Norwegian ships seized by him. His protest escalated into a full-blooded

[51] *Records relating to the Barony of Kendale by W. Farrer*, I (Kendal, 1923), 1, 377.
[52] Thompson, 'Monasteries and Settlement in Norman Lancashire'; J. A. Green, 'Earl Ranulf II and Lancashire', *The Earldom of Chester and Its Charters*, Chester Archaeological Society, LXXI (1991), p. 99.
[53] SD, 'Historia Regum', *Opera omnia*, II, 221–2.    [54] FW, II, 21, 32.
[55] F. Barlow, *William Rufus* (London, 1983), pp. 167–8.

coalition of magnates, including William of Eu, Hugh of Montgomery and his brother Philip, Gilbert FitzRichard, Odo count of Champagne, and the latter's nephew Stephen, count of Aumale, and it may have been intended that this Stephen could be king. After his defeat Stephen – perhaps wisely – took the cross and departed from England, as did William de Percy.[56]

In the north of England the sons of Roger of Montgomery went from strength to strength. Holderness was given to Roger the Poitevin's younger brother Arnulf of Montgomery.[57] Robert de Bellême was allowed to succeed to Tickhill (whether to the castle and the honour or just to the castle is not clear), presumably because of suspicions about the loyalty of Roger de Bully.[58] Together, Robert's lands and Roger the Poitevin's lordship of Craven straddled the Pennines. Robert de Rumilly, who may have had some connection with this family, received land in north-west Yorkshire.[59] After the death of Ivo Taillebois, his lordships of Kendal and Burton were probably given to Robert de Stuteville, one of Rufus's new men, who also received a good deal of land in Yorkshire, much of it formerly held by Hugh FitzBaldric.[60] Ivo or Roger FitzGerold (who married Ivo's widow) received land in the East Riding, and Gilbert de Gant's estates there were enlarged.[61] Finally, Geoffrey Bainard, brother of Ralph Bainard, was granted the royal manor of Burton Agnes in the East Riding, possibly at about the time he became sheriff, about 1095.[62]

Rufus thus brought into the north men on whose loyalty he could rely. Like his father, his approach was to create relatively large lordships in Cumbria and Lancashire. What made his policy work, however, was the change in Anglo–Scottish relations after the death of Malcolm Canmore. No longer were the Normans in the north faced by an aggressive and hostile king, but by his sons, who allied first with Rufus and then with Henry, in order to establish and keep themselves on the Scottish throne.

[56] C. W. David, *Robert Curthose* (Cambridge, Mass., 1920), pp. 228–9.

[57] English, *Lords of Holderness*, p. 13.

[58] Chibnall, 'Robert of Bellême and the Castle of Tickhill', pp. 151–5.

[59] Robert was a benefactor of the abbey of Troarn, which had been founded by Roger of Montgomery: R. N. Sauvage, *L'abbaye de Saint-Martin de Troarn au diocèse de Bayeux des origines au seizième siècle*, Mémoires de la Société des Antiquaires de Normandie, 4th series, IV (1911), p. 363; *Early Yorkshire Charters*, VII, 31–5.

[60] Hugh is not to be traced in England after 1087 and possibly joined Robert Curthose: *Mowbray Charters*, pp. xx–xxiv.

[61] Warter was later claimed to have been held by Roger FitzGerold, second husband of Lucy: *Early Yorkshire Charters*, XI, 107–10; see also E. King, 'The Parish of Warter and the Castle of Galchlin', *Yorkshire Archaeological Journal*, 52 (1980), 40–51.      [62] Dalton, *Conquest, Anarchy and Lordship*, p. 86.

They also used their alliance with the Norman kings to recruit Normans into their own realm to provide military muscle.

Normans probably began to establish themselves in Northumberland in the late eleventh century. Even making allowances for the remoteness of the region it is hard to believe that Robert de Mowbray was a solitary figure at Bamburgh at the time of his revolt in 1095, and it is possible Normans had at least fortified key points along the route between Durham and Bamburgh. Families were later to claim that their ancestors had held their lands in Northumberland 'from the Conquest', or from the time of William Rufus.[63] A later tradition that William Tison was the first Norman lord of Alnwick could therefore be true, and, interestingly, a man of this name occurs in the inquest into the archbishop of York's rights in York which was made around the time of Domesday Book.[64] Robert d'Umfraville may have been established at Prudhoe in Rufus's reign, for an early date has been suggested for the castle there.[65] Nothing is known for certain about his background, though Dugdale called him 'lord of Toures and Vian'.[66] Conceivably he was a kinsman of Gilbert d'Umfraville, who went to Glamorgan in the same period and whose family later held land in Devon.[67] Guy de Balliol could have been granted nearby Bywell at about the same time. He came from Bailleul-en-Vimeu and could have arrived in England in the company of Earl Aubrey. In addition to Bywell he also received land at Stokesley in Yorkshire and, at some stage, Gainford in Durham and Barnard Castle in Yorkshire, named after his son Bernard.[68] Nigel d'Aubigny's career in the north may also have begun before 1100, though it was under Henry I that he became really important and received his great estates in Yorkshire.[69] Nigel was a younger brother of William d'Aubigny who is known to have been at Rufus's court, so it would not be surprising if Nigel was also on the lower rungs of the ladder of preferment.[70]

---

[63] e.g. Morpeth, Bolam, and Callerton: *Book of Fees*, I, 220, 397, 202.

[64] D. M. Palliser, *Domesday York*, University of York Borthwick Paper no. 78 (1990), p. 25.

[65] L. Keen, 'The Umfravilles, the Castle, and the Barony of Prudhoe, Northumberland', *Anglo-Norman Studies*, 5 (1982), 170–1.        [66] Dugdale, *Baronage of England*, I, 504.

[67] *Ibid.*, I, 406; a Gilbert d'Umfraville gave the chapel of Down (Umfraville) to Montebourg: *CDF*, p. 318. This suggests Gilbert had ties with the Cotentin peninsula.

[68] G. A. Moriarty, 'The Balliols in Picardy, England and Scotland', *New England Historical and Genealogical Register*, 106 (1952), 273–90; for Guy de Balliol's charter for St Mary's, York mentioning his land at Stokesley and Gainford, see *Early Yorkshire Charters*, I, 436–9.

[69] Barlow, *William Rufus*, p. 291 suggests that the Nigel d'Aubigny in the north was Nigel lord of Cainhoe, but a more likely identification is his nephew Nigel; for the latter's lands see *Mowbray Charters*, pp. xvii–xxv.        [70] William attested a royal diploma issued in 1091: *RRAN*, I, no. 319.

When Henry I seized the throne in 1100, one of his first actions was to imprison Rufus's chief financial minister, Ranulf Flambard, the man perceived as the agent of that king's oppression of the church. Ranulf effected a daring escape from the Tower, however, and made his way to the continent, where he was in due course reconciled with Henry. Henry must have foreseen that the return of his brother Robert from the crusade would be followed by pressure from those who supported his claim to succeed to the whole Anglo-Norman inheritance (see below, pp. 280–1). His opponents included both Robert de Bellême, by now holder of the lands of the Norman lordship of Montgommery, the lordship of Bellême, his father's lands in Shropshire and Sussex, and the honour of Tickhill, and his brothers, Arnulf of Montgomery lord of Holderness, and Roger the Poitevin, lord of the two parts of Lancashire, Craven, and estates elsewhere in England. In 1101 William de Warenne also supported Duke Robert, and by 1106 so did Robert de Stuteville.[71] There was thus a concentration of Henry's enemies in northern England.

For his part Henry was able to rely on the support of Nigel d'Aubigny in Yorkshire and Earl Hugh of Chester.[72] He initially employed as sheriff of Yorkshire another west Norman, Bertram de Verdon, before switching to Osbert the priest, sheriff of Lincolnshire.[73] The choice of Bertram is at first sight odd, because he is not known to have held land in the north. Subsequently, however, Bertram held land in the midlands of the earl of Chester, and it is just possible that he was already the earl's man. Earl Hugh had territorial interests in Yorkshire, though it is doubtful how much he held in demesne by this stage.[74] Robert de Brus acquired some estates that had been held by Earl Hugh in 1086, and King Henry made further grants to Robert probably not long after the start of his reign.[75]

In 1102 Henry banished the sons of Roger of Montgomery. Stephen of Aumale was restored to Holderness, and Roger de Bully the younger seems

---

[71] OV, v, 308; Robert de Stuteville did not attest for Henry I and fought against him at Tinchebrai: *ibid.*, VI, 72, 80–4, 90; see further C. Warren Hollister, 'The Anglo-Norman Civil War: 1101', *English Historical Review*, 88 (1973), 315–74.

[72] Nigel's first datable attestation was in 1101: *RRAN*, II, no. 544 but the delay could have been because he was in the north. Earl Hugh is mentioned as a supporter by OV, v, 298.

[73] *RRAN*, I, no. 427; II, nos. 495, 505.      [74] *DB*, I, 304b–305.

[75] *RRAN*, II, no. 648; G. W. S. Barrow, 'Scotland's "Norman" Families', *The Kingdom of the Scots* (London, 173), p. 322. Robert occurs earlier as a witness to a charter of Earl Hugh, but the authenticity of this text has been doubted: *Chester Charters*, no. 5; for Robert's estates see *Early Yorkshire Charters*, II, 16–19; cf. p. 11 for the suggestion that Earl Hugh may have granted Robert portions of his estate of South Loftus.

to have held part of the honour of Tickhill for a time, though by 1130 the castle and honour were in the king's hands.[76] The honour of Craven was divided between the lord of Skipton and Alan de Percy.[77] William de Warenne made his peace with Henry in 1103.[78] Robert de Lacy of Pontefract was removed by 1114 and his lands granted to Hugh, lord of Laval in Maine.[79] Another new man, Geoffrey FitzPain, was established at Warter in the East Riding.[80] The immediate fate of Roger the Poitevin's lands, the two parts of Lancashire, is not clear: they may have been held for a time by Ranulf Meschin before passing, by 1123, to Stephen of Blois.[81]

After his reconciliation with Henry, Ranulf Flambard devoted his energies to his see. Building work on the cathedral at Durham forged ahead, and the relics of St Cuthbert were moved to their new shrine in 1104. He organized the defence of his duchy, by strengthening the castle at Durham and building a second at Norham on the river Tweed.[82] He proceeded to enfeoff men to hold by knight service in county Durham. Some tenants were recruited from the bishop's estates outside the county, others were members of his family or household. The Amundeville family for instance were the bishop's tenants in Lincolnshire. They had come originally from Mondeville near Caen.[83] The Conyers family may be descended from a man named Robert who was the bishop of Durham's tenant in Allertonshire in Yorkshire.[84] Their continental place of origin is thought to have been Cornières near Caumont (now Anctoville).[85] Walter de Musters who occurred as a witness for Bishop Ranulf is thought to have been a member of the family of that name settled in Yorkshire.[86] Pinceon the bishop's steward was an important tenant in Lincolnshire in the middle of Henry I's reign, and his son Hugh also held Wingate and Thornley in County Durham.[87] William the chamberlain was also granted land to hold by knight service.[88] In some cases an existing tenancy may

---

[76] Chibnall, 'Robert of Bellême and the Castle of Tickhill', pp. 142–4.

[77] Dalton, *Conquest, Anarchy and Lordship*, p. 88.

[78] OV, VI, 14; for Wakefield, which he obtained between 1086 and 1120, see *Early Yorkshire Charters*, III, 178.

[79] Wightman, *Lacy Family*, pp. 66–72.     [80] *Early Yorkshire Charters*, X, 2–5.

[81] Green, 'Earl Ranulf II and Lancashire', p. 104.

[82] H. S. Offler, 'Rannulf Flambard as Bishop of Durham (1099–1128)', *Durham University Journal*, 64 (1971), 20.     [83] *RBE*, I, 417.

[84] *Durham Episcopal Charters 1071–1152*, ed. H. S. Offler, Surtees, Society, CLXXIX (1968), p. 77.

[85] Green, 'Earl Ranulf II and Lancashire', p. 104.

[86] *Durham Episcopal Charters*, pp. 80, 81. Adam de Musters held one knight's fee of the old enfeoffment in 1166: *RBE*, I, 417.     [87] *Durham Episcopal Charters*, p. 97; *RBE*, I, 416.

[88] *Durham Episcopal Charters*, p . 97.

have been converted into an enfeoffment. Thus Papedy the reeve of Norhamshire was enfeoffed by Bishop Ranulf.[89] Dolfin son of Uctred, ancestor of the Nevilles of Raby, was enfeoffed with Staindropshire by the prior and convent of Durham in 1131.[90] The Scolland family may also have been established by Bishop Ranulf. In 1108 Flambard sent a knight named Scolland to Archbishop Anselm, and in 1130 Geoffrey Scolland accounted for the temporalities of Durham after the bishop's death. By 1155 Elias Escolland had succeeded to Geoffrey's lands. These were centred on Seaham and owed two and one-third fees in 1166.[91] Ranulf made provision for members of his family, for three of his nephews seem to have received lands: Richard, Thomas, and Osbert, who was also his sheriff in Durham.[92] Even if some of these enfeoffments predate Ranulf's episcopate, the impression remains strong that Ranulf was essentially responsible for shaping the tenurial geography of the bishopric. The exceptions may have been the enfeoffments of Guy de Balliol at Gainford and Robert de Brus at Hart and Hartness. These men owed their lands in the north respectively to Rufus and to Henry I, and it seems most likely that it was owing to royal influence that they were enfeoffed in County Durham.[93] In some cases enfeoffments may simply have been a conversion of earlier thegnages, and their relation to settlement patterns and episcopal demesnes, together with the building of castles, would repay further investigation.

Henry I continued to pursue a policy of alliance with the Scots.[94] In 1100 he married Edith, daughter of Malcolm and Margaret. He provided his brother-in-law David with a rich heiress to marry and the title of earl, and helped him to extract from his elder brother Alexander the overlordship of Cumbria and Lothian which had possibly been bequeathed to David by their father.[95] Alexander, king between 1107 and 1124, married a daughter of Henry I. Nevertheless Anglo–Scottish relations became tense for a time in 1121 and 1122 for reasons that are not explained. One possible irritant was Flambard's castle at Norham;[96] another was Henry's resumption of

---

[89] Ibid., p. 91.

[90] Feodarium Prioratus Dunelmensis, ed. W. Greenwell, Surtees Society, LVIII (1872), p. 56n; for comment, Durham Episcopal Charters, p. 76.    [91] Ibid., p. 80.    [92] Ibid., pp. 85, 74, 103.

[93] Gainford was mentioned in Guy de Balliol's charter for St Mary's, York: Early Yorkshire Charters, I, 436–9; for Hart and Hartness see ibid., II, 3.

[94] J. A. Green, 'Henry I and David I', Scottish Historical Review, 75 (1996), 1–19.

[95] Ailred of Rievaulx, 'Relatio de Standardo', Chronicles of the Reigns of Stephen, Henry II and Richard I, ed. R. Howlett, 4 vols., RS (London, 1884–9), III, 193.

[96] Walter bestowed the church of Wark on the priory he founded at Kirkham c. 1122: Dugdale, Mon. Ang., VI, 208–9. It is likely that Eustace received Alnwick at roughly the same time as Walter received Wark.

the lordship of Carlisle when he allowed Ranulf Meschin, lord of Carlisle, to succeed to the earldom of Chester. In the case of Carlisle, there are grounds for thinking that David, now heir presumptive to the Scots throne, believed that Cumbria (south as well as north of the border) belonged to the Scots. In 1121 there was a great assembly of northern magnates at Durham, and in the following year Henry himself visited Carlisle and strengthened the fortifications there. Nevertheless relations between Henry and David did not break down, and when David became king in 1124 he was allowed to keep his lands in England. From the time when Henry began to contemplate being succeeded by his daughter the Empress, David assumed a greater importance in Henry's plans. Henry allowed David to retain the earldom of Huntingdon after the latter's stepson came of age, and he persuaded Archbishop Thurstan of York to consecrate a new bishop for St Andrews without a profession of obedience to Thurstan. Good relations with the Scots paid dividends in creating a climate for the consolidation of Norman rule particularly in Cumbria and Northumberland.

Under William the Conqueror, Yorkshire had been the only county north of the Humber and Mersey which was fully incorporated into royal government, with a sheriff, a mint, and two castles at York. The two parts of Lancashire remained a private lordship throughout the period, and County Durham was controlled by its bishop. Carlisle became the headquarters for Cumbria, with a royal castle, a mint, and a royal officer accounting for the king's revenue by 1130.[97] Three years later a bishop was consecrated for Cumbria by Archbishop Thurstan, though he may not have been able to take up residence there.[98] In the first half of Henry's reign there were two royal sheriffs of Northumberland, one, Aluric, based

---

[97] For the castle, Cathcart King, *Castellarium Anglicanum*, I, 83 and references therein cited; H. Summerson, *Medieval Carlisle: the City and the Borders from the Late Eleventh to the Mid-sixteenth centuries*, 2 vols., Cumberland and Westmorland Antiquarian and Archaeological Society, Extra Series, xxv (1993); for the mint, G. C. Brooke, *A Catalogue of English Coins in the British Museum. The Norman Kings*, 2 vols. (London, 1916), I, 302, 377; for Hildret who accounted for the royal revenues, *PR 31 Henry I*, pp. 140–2.

[98] John of Hexham's continuation of SD, 'Historia Regum', *Opera omnia*, 285; A. J. Nicholl, *Archbishop Thurstan* (York, 1964), pp. 146–7; Green, 'Anglo-Scottish Relations', pp. 61–2; J. C. Dickinson, 'The Origins of Carlisle Cathedral', *Cumberland and Westmorland Antiquarian and Archaeological Society*, 45 (1946), 136–46; Dickinson, 'Walter the Priest and St Mary Carlisle', *Cumberland and Westmorland Antiquarian and Archaeological Society*, 69 (1969), 102–14; E. U. Crosby, *Bishop and Chapter in Twelfth-Century England*, Cambridge Studies in Medieval Life and Thought, 4th series, xxiii (Cambridge, 1994), pp. 105–8.

at the old Roman centre at Corbridge, and the other, Odard, at Bamburgh. In the second half of the reign Odard alone was sheriff.[99]

The tenurial geography of Cumbria and Northumberland was gradually sketched in. In Cumbria, Ranulf of Bayeux established his brother William Meschin first at Gilsland on the river Irving protecting the approach to Carlisle from the east and, when he failed to hold it against the Scots, at Egremont, that is, Allerdale above the river Derwent.[100] Allerdale below the Derwent was held by Waltheof son of Gospatric, who was possibly a brother of Dolfin, lord of Carlisle at the time of Rufus's annexation.[101] His brother-in-law Robert de Trevers (from Trevières in Calvados) was based at Burgh by Sands west of Carlisle on the shores of the Solway Firth, and Richer de Boivill at Kirklinton north of Carlisle on the river Lyne.[102] Ranulf may also have been responsible for granting Liddel to Turgis Brundos, a man about whom little is known but who also held Rosedale in Yorkshire.[103] A base as far north of Hadrian's Wall as Liddel prompts the speculation that Ranulf, in an entrepreneurial spirit, would have advanced north if he could. Odard de Logis, who received Wigton, may have been related to Bigot de Logis, a tenant of Earl Hugh in Cheshire.[104] Forne son of Sigulf of Greystoke came from Yorkshire. As his name indicates, he was not a Norman, and his daughter Edith was one of Henry I's mistresses.[105] Kendal guarded the southern entrance to the Lakes. The Furness peninsula was held by the lord of the honour of Lancaster, and much of the peninsula passed into the hands of Furness abbey, founded by Stephen of Blois.[106] Millom, the final piece in the tenurial jigsaw, was held by Godard de Boivill, who was presumably related to Richer.[107] Westmorland was not carved up into lordships at this stage. In much of Cumbria the new lords clearly took over existing, relatively large, units of lordship. Only in the Eden valley near Carlisle were there smaller units of

---

[99] RRAN, II, nos. 640, 641, 955, 993, 1143, 1172, 1124, 1202, 1264, 1279, 1339, 1563; Early Scottish Charters to A. D. 1153, ed. A. C. Lawrie (Glasgow, 1905), no. c; J. H. Round, 'Odard the Sheriff', Genealogist, 5 (1899), 25–8; W. Percy Hedley, Northumberland Families, 2 vols. (Newcastle upon Tyne, 1968, 1970), I, 142.

[100] Sanders, English Baronies, pp. 124, 115.      [101] Ibid., p. 134.      [102] Ibid., pp. 23, 58.

[103] T. H. B. Graham, 'Turgis Brundos', Cumberland and Westmorland Antiquarian and Archaeological Society, new series, 39 (1929), 49–56.

[104] Chester Charters, no. 3. Bigot may have been related to Roger Bigod, the Domesday tenant-in-chief, who held land at Les Loges: Loyd, Origins of Some Anglo-Norman Families, pp. 14–15; see also above, p. 84n.

[105] Sanders, English Baronies, p. 50.      [106] RRAN, II, no. 1545.

[107] The Register of the Priory of St Bees, ed. J. Wilson, Cumberland and Westmorland Antiquarian and Archaeological Society, Chartulary series, no. 3 (Kendal, 1915), pp. 106–7n, 492, 531.

lordship created by the conversion of thegnages into knights' fees.[108] The survival of Waldeve son of Gospatric as lord of Allerdale indicates that here as in County Durham the prospects for native families were brighter than in southern England.

The lordships which came into being in Northumberland tended to be smaller; they were also mainly held by men from less obviously distinguished families and, again, there were men whose names indicate that they were of native stock like Siward of Gosforth and Gospatric, brother of Waldeve of Allerdale.[109] Because so little is known about the preceding period, we cannot judge how far the new lordships replicated or cut across earlier units of lordship, though the likelihood once again is that there were many cases of continuity. Those who were prepared to come so far north were only in a few cases from families of rank. Walter de Bolebec of Styford is known to have been a younger son of the Bolebecs of Buckinghamshire.[110] Ivo de Vesci, lord of Alnwick before Eustace FitzJohn, could have been related to Robert de Veci, a Domesday tenant-in-chief, as both men were benefactors of St Mary's, York.[111] Hubert de Laval of Callerton's name suggests he may have been related to Hugh de Laval lord of Pontefract in Henry I's reign but there is no known connection.[112] William Bertram of Mitford and Nicholas de Grenville of Ellingham bore the name of distinguished Norman families, but again there is no known connection.[113] Only from later statements that these men had been enfeoffed before 1135 do we know when they arrived in the region, and it looks as though they were mainly adventurers and younger sons. Their lordships had relatively small quotas of military service, but they were treated as baronies because of the lords' rights of jurisdiction. The list of baronies which made returns to the Inquest into feudal service in 1166 has the character of a description of the tenancies of a great lordship, however, and one may speculate that these Northumbrian baronies had been established under one or more of the earls of Northumberland, and had then

---

[108] A. J. L. Winchester, *Landscape and Society in Medieval Cumbria* (Edinburgh, 1987), pp. 14–19.

[109] *RBE*, I, 440; Sanders, *English Baronies*, p. 106; R. Reid, 'Barony and Thanage', *English Historical Review*, 35 (1920), 161–99.

[110] Loyd, *Origins of Some Anglo-Norman Families*, p. 17; Walter gave Walton to Ramsey abbey with the services pertaining to two knights' fees, except castleguard at Newcastle: *Cartularium Monasterii de Ramesia*, 3 vols., RS (London, 1884–93), I, 154; J. H. Round demonstrated that Hugh, son of the benefactor of Ramsey abbey, was the holder of Whitchurch and under-tenant of the Giffard honour at his death in 1164 or 1165: *Rotuli de Dominabus et Pueris et Puellis de Donatione Regis in XII Comitatibus 31 Henry II, 1185*, Pipe Roll Society, xxxv (1913), pp. xxxix–xl.    [111] *Early Yorkshire Charters*, I, 273.

[112] Sanders, *English Baronies*, p. 109.    [113] *Ibid.*, pp. 131, 41.

been converted into baronies held in chief of the crown after the resumption of the earldom by Henry II in 1157. As in the case of Durham, there is a need for a detailed study of the aristocracy in this county.

David, first as lord of Cumbria and Lothian and later as king of Scotland, had a range of contacts and friendships with these families. His charter for Selkirk issued about 1120 was witnessed amongst others by Robert de Brus, Robert d'Umfraville, Odard sheriff of Bamburgh, Walter de Bolebec, and Reginald de Muschamp.[114] David's friendship with Robert de Brus went back probably at least as far as 1103 when they were both at Henry I's court, and he granted Robert the whole of Annandale to hold by knight service.[115] Alan de Percy witnessed an inquest of the lands belonging to the bishopric of Glasgow and, with Eustace FitzJohn, the charter by which David granted Annandale to Robert de Brus.[116]

King David was a great benefactor of the church, and maintained links with the religious houses being founded in northern England. In 1124 Robert, prior of the recently founded Augustinian priory of Nostell, was appointed bishop of St Andrews, and it was Nostell which Waldef, David's stepson, chose to enter in about 1130.[117] David issued a number of charters for Durham. These were confirmations rather than new grants, because he seems to have been less sanguine than his predecessors about a close relationship between Durham and the Scottish crown, at least whilst Flambard was bishop.[118] Ailred, a dispenser in King David's court, was paying a visit to the archbishop of York when, visiting Walter Espec, he decided to enter the fledgling Cistercian community at Rievaulx.[119] Ailred's father had been an hereditary priest at Hexham, and arguably therefore part of the old order in the north. It may be significant that Ailred chose to enter the service not of Henry I but of the Scots king, and that when he became a monk he entered a Cistercian house, not a Benedictine one. The Augustinian priory of Merton in Surrey, a house with which David might have been acquainted through his sister Queen Matilda, provided canons for the foundation at Holyrood just outside Edinburgh in 1128.[120]

---

[114] Early Scottish Charters, no. xxxv.     [115] Ibid., no. I.

[116] Ibid., no. LIV. The lord of Topcliffe was either Alan or, more probably, his illegitimate son of the same name who was at the battle of the Standard.

[117] Jocelin of Furness, 'Vita Waldevi', Acta Sanctorum, August, I, 248ff; for the date see The Life of Ailred of Rievaulx by Walter Daniel, ed. F. M. Powicke (Edinburgh, 1950, reprinted Oxford, 1978), p. lxxi.

[118] Early Scottish Charters, nos 32, 33, 34.     [119] Life of Ailred of Rievaulx, pp. 12–16.

[120] G. W. S. Barrow, 'The Royal House and the Religious Orders', Kingdom of the Scots, pp. 178–9.

By 1135, therefore, rule from the south in Cumbria, Northumberland, and Durham was more of a reality than it had ever been. Castles had been built and religious houses were being set up. Much had depended on good relations with the Scots, however, and these only endured during the lifetime of Henry I. King David had committed himself to the claim of his niece the Empress to succeed her father, but as soon as he heard of Henry's death, he invaded the north and seized the key castles of Carlisle, Newcastle, Wark, Alnwick, and Norham.[121] Stephen marched north in 1136 and persuaded David to hand them back, with the exception of Carlisle, and with the addition of Doncaster. The Scots' claim to the earldom of Northumbria was to be considered at some future date.[122] David invaded again in 1137, and twice in 1138, and on the second occasion in 1138 his army was soundly defeated at the battle of the Standard. The battle in prospect posed an acute conflict of loyalties for those northern magnates who were the Scots king's friends, and most of all for Robert de Brus, who alone is known to have had substantial estates on both sides of the border. In the end Robert de Brus the elder fought for Stephen and his son for David. Bernard de Baliol and Walter Espec both fought for Stephen, while Eustace FitzJohn, Alan de Percy, and Edgar son of Gospatric fought for David.[123] Although David's army had been decisively defeated, the peace negotiated at Durham in April 1139 was very favourable to the Scots. David's son Henry did homage to Stephen for the earldom of Northumberland, and was married to Ada de Warenne, daughter of a leading magnate and, through her mother, a descendant of Charlemagne.[124] Thereafter Prince Henry seems to have had full authority over Northumberland, including Bamburgh and Newcastle, though whether this had been Stephen's original intention is not clear.[125] Gilbert d'Umfraville of Prudhoe became Prince Henry's constable, and Ranulf de Merlay witnessed Henry's charters as earl.[126]

David retained Cumbria from 1136, and Carlisle became an important centre of his authority. An important source of silver had been discovered

[121] John of Hexham's continuation of Symeon of Durham's 'Historia Regum', *Opera omnia*, II, 287; Richard of Hexham, *Chronicle*, in *Chronicles of the Reigns of Stephen, Henry II and Richard I*, III, 145.

[122] John of Hexham, SD, *Opera omnia*, II, 287.

[123] Ailred of Rievaulx, 'Relatio de Standardo', *Chronicles*, III, 181–99.

[124] John of Hexham, SD, *Opera omnia*, II, 300.      [125] Dalton, *Conquest, Anarchy and Lordship*, p. 133.

[126] Keen, 'Umfravilles, the Castle and Barony of Prudhoe', p. 171; *Early Scottish Charters*, no. 247; *Regesta Regum Scottorum*, I, nos. 11, 32, 33.

at Alston in 1133, and the mines there could supply the mint at Carlisle, which issued coins in David's name.[127] His nephew, William FitzDuncan, married Alice de Rumilly, the heiress of Egremont and Skipton. William himself inherited Allerdale, and thus acquired a great band of territory running across northern England from Cumbria into Yorkshire.[128] Other Cumbrian lordships were held by men associated with David. Hugh de Moreville, David's constable, took over the two Westmorland lordships of Appleby and Kendal.[129] Ranulf Engaine, who married Ibria, heiress to the lordship of Burgh by Sands, may have been related to the Engaines of Pytchley, tenants of David's honour of Huntingdon.[130] David had moved southwards across the river Duddon into Lancashire probably as early as 1136. He certainly held the north of Lancashire, the 'honour of Lancaster', by 1141, and it is not impossible that he held the south as well, for in 1149 he conceded both parts to Earl Ranulf of Chester.[131] This was the price of an alliance between Ranulf and David, and Ranulf held both regions for the rest of his life.[132]

David also saw an opportunity to intervene in Durham after the death of Bishop Geoffrey Rufus, for the Empress was persuaded to nominate as his successor David's chancellor, William Cumin.[133] Initially Robert de Brus, Eustace FitzJohn, and Bernard de Balliol supported Cumin, but the latter's tactics divided local families and an opposition party formed, headed by Roger de Conyers. As time went on and the difficulties surrounding Cumin's position became clearer, David distanced himself from the struggle. Eventually a rival candidate, William of Ste Barbe, was installed in 1144.

David was also not without ambitions in Yorkshire, as his campaigns of 1138 and 1149 showed. After Archbishop Thurstan died in 1140, David proposed his stepson Waldef as his successor, a candidature not surprisingly vetoed by Stephen, who preferred William FitzHerbert.[134] The election was

---

[127] M. Blackburn, 'Coinage and Currency', *The Anarchy of Stephen's Reign*, ed. E. King (Oxford, 1994), p. 192.

[128] Sanders, *English Baronies*, pp. 115, 142, 134; for a recent reevaluation, Dalton, *Conquest, Anarchy and Lordship*, pp. 211–19.  [129] Barrow, *Anglo-Norman Era*, pp. 71–3.

[130] Sanders, *English Baronies*, p. 23; cf. Barrow, *Anglo-Norman Era*, p. 98, n. 34.

[131] Green, 'Earl Ranulf II and Lancashire', pp. 100–6.

[132] John of Hexham in SD, *Opera omnia*, II, 322–3.

[133] For this episode see A. Young, *William Cumin: Border Politics and the Bishopric of Durham 1141–1144*, University of York, Borthwick Paper no. 54 (1979).

[134] D. Knowles, 'The Case of St William of York', *Cambridge Historical Journal*, 5 (1936), 162–77, reprinted in *The Historian and Character* (Cambridge, 1963).

nevertheless disputed. The rival candidate was Henry Murdac, abbot of Fountains, with whom David was evidently on good terms.[135] David had other friends in Yorkshire, including Robert II de Brus, Walter Espec, and Eustace FitzJohn, and, had the chance arisen, David would doubtless have tried to extend his influence. His authority in northern England was thus a force to be reckoned with. Stephen had to accept the loss of Cumbria and Lancashire, and Northumberland was held in return for homage by David's son. Stephen had more support in Yorkshire, and this in a sense is what we might expect, given that Yorkshire had been colonized by families more closely bound into the kingdom of the English.

For a time, then, there was a real possibility that the border between England and Scotland would be moved further south permanently, but in 1157 Henry II resumed Northumberland, Tynedale, and Cumbria. He spent considerable sums on strengthening the northern castles, and took steps to see that northern lordships were in the hands of men loyal to him.[136] When the Scots tested the strength of his hold over the north in 1173, they were disastrously defeated, but it was by no means certain that the border between England and Scotland would remain at the Solway and Tweed. It had been Stephen's ill fortune, when he had so much else to contend with, that the Scottish throne had been occupied by one of the greatest of her medieval kings.

The tempo and character of Norman colonization of the north thus differed markedly from that of the midlands and the south, and in the early twelfth century it was reinforced by a great wave of religious foundations. Some attracted benefactions from a relatively wide area. St Cuthbert was already widely venerated in northern England and southern Scotland and thus Durham was well placed to attract benefactions. The early benefactors of St Mary's at York included several of the Norman lords in Yorkshire. Furness, founded in 1124 near Preston and then relocated to Furness, became a great power in the north-west. The new orders in particular blossomed in the north (see below, p. 409). The intention of the new communities was to take on the challenge of a spiritual wilderness, but they were so successful in cultivating the wilderness that they became wealthy in the process, the Cistercian abbeys most of all. Lay lords and churchmen

---

[135] Dalton, *Conquest, Anarchy and Lordship*, pp. 225–7.
[136] Green, 'Anglo-Scottish Relations', pp. 68–72.

together provided a framework of authority which tied the north more closely into the kingdom of the English, and in the process the old independent Northumbria was finally destroyed. The new regime was in some respects only a thin veneer, and this factor, plus the special characteristics of the Norman colonization of the north, helped to preserve distinctive features in northern society.

# 4  'An open elite?' The aristocracy after 1086

In the three preceding chapters we have seen how the dominant figures in the first wave of Norman invaders were a relatively small group. Apart from a Breton, Count Alan, and Count Eustace of Boulogne, the most prominent and successful invaders were Normans. The latter were not so much a representative cross-section of the whole aristocracy of Normandy as of the men close to the duke who were prepared to commit themselves and their followers to the enterprise of England. In other words, it was a very particular group who had spearheaded the invasion and conquest. Most had then taken English lands, though they devoted varying degrees of time and resources to them. There were some whose estates and family interests meant that they spent little time in England: Roger de Beaumont and Ralph de Tosny are possible cases in point. Others were more directly and aggressively committed to their new estates, such as Roger de Montgomery in Shropshire or Earl Hugh of Chester. Those who were committed and whose loyalty stood the test of time gained more for themselves or their sons. Already by the time of Domesday in 1086, some had been strikingly successful, whilst others had left for home. The first theme in this chapter is the extent to which the families of the new elite maintained their dominance. A second, related one is the degree of openness to new recruits after 1086: did England continue to be a land of opportunity for landless young men, and if so from where did the new recruits come, and what were the avenues of advancement? In particular, how far was there continuing immigration from across the Channel? Thirdly, the changing composition of, and stratification within, the aristocracy are considered.

At first sight it looks as though there was a contrast between on the one hand the baronies – the basic units of the landed elite – which remained relatively stable, and on the other the composition of the aristocracy which changed dramatically, with many new families appearing as a result of the failure to produce male heirs and the political misfortunes of those already established. Such a sharp dichotomy between structural stability and changing composition is, however, misleading, for as we shall see shortly new lordships continued to come into being and older ones were broken up, and although there was a high turnover in terms of individuals, the newcomers tended to be related to established families.

From Domesday Book we can see how landed wealth was distributed at a particular moment in time, but there is no comparable source for the remainder of the period. Because the greatest lordships in most cases descended as entities, that is, they were baronies, their holders can be and have been traced by I. J. Sanders in *English Baronies*. Our knowledge of the smaller tenants-in-chief (those holding land worth less than about £30 in 1086) is much less complete, however, and the histories of the tenants of only a few lordships have been traced in detail, and not necessarily from an analytical viewpoint: Farrer's work, for instance, was concerned primarily with reconstruction of fees and their histories.[1] One of the few analytical studies which exists, that by Richard Mortimer of the tenants of the honour of Clare, has demonstrated that the larger, older, tenancies were more likely to survive, and that there was more change in the lower ranks.[2]

Although many of the Domesday lordships descended as a whole, several new lordships were created after 1086. Amongst these were a number in the northern regions not surveyed in Domesday Book. In Northumberland in particular a number of relatively small baronies were created.[3] Secondly, five of the Yorkshire honours, Skelton, Skipton, Thirsk, Cottingham, and Warter, together with the honour of Lancaster, were essentially created after 1086, though their constituent estates were surveyed at least notionally in Domesday Book.[4] Elsewhere too there were new creations. Some were based on grants of royal demesne, like the earldom of Surrey created for William de Warenne, Old Buckenham, granted to William d'Aubigny the king's butler, and Erlestoke in Wiltshire granted to Roger de Mandeville.[5] In some cases the manors, though in the king's hands in 1086, had earlier been held by others. Thus many of the manors granted by Henry I to Richard de Redvers in Hampshire, the Isle of Wight, and Berkshire, had been held by William FitzOsbern.[6] The lands of

---

[1] As pointed out by Mortimer, 'Land and Service', p. 181.
[2] Mortimer, 'Land and Service', pp. 181–90.
[3] Roffe, 'From Thegnage to Barony', pp. 158–9; Reid, 'Barony and Thanage', pp. 161–99.
[4] Sanders, *English Baronies*, pp. 126–7, 77, 142, 146, 37, 150 for brief details.
[5] *Liber Monasterii de Hyda*, ed. E. Edwards, RS (London, 1866), p. 298; *Complete Peerage*, XII.I, 494; Sanders, *English Baronies*, pp. 70, 42.     [6] *Charters of the Redvers Family*, p. 22.

Queen Matilda were granted by William Rufus to Robert FitzHaimon.[7] Some of the larger new creations had composite origins – a mix of royal manors, land which had been confiscated, and land previously held in chief but now subordinated. Thus the lands granted to Robert de Stuteville by William Rufus included estates held in 1086 by the king and the count of Mortain, Hugh FitzBaldric, and Geoffrey de la Guerche. When Robert's lands were in turn granted to Nigel d'Aubigny by Henry I further adjustments were made.[8] The honour of Plympton held by Richard de Redvers similarly included royal land plus the lands of several Domesday tenants-in-chief, as did the earldom of Warwick created, probably in 1087 or 1088, for Henry de Beaumont.[9]

Thirdly, some of the great forfeitures which occurred between 1088 and 1104 were not regranted as a whole but were totally or partially broken up. In a number of cases, major tenants were upgraded to tenants-in-chief: this happened to the Kentish tenants of Odo of Bayeux, the Shropshire tenants of Roger of Montgomery, and the west country and Yorkshire tenants of Robert of Mortain.[10] The lands of Geoffrey bishop of Coutances which were said to have passed to his nephew Robert de Mowbray in 1093 were dismembered not long afterwards: many of the Devonshire estates passed to Judhael of Totnes and formed the honour of Barnstaple, while Lavendon in Buckinghamshire became the headquarters of the Bidun family, and Bulwick in Northamptonshire passed to Richard FitzUrse.[11]

Finally, a handful of new lordships came into being by division or accumulation. Into the former category come the lordships of Trowbridge and Chitterne, formed from the estates held in 1086 by Edward of Salisbury, and Keevil and Kempsford, formed from the lands of Arnulf de

---

[7] OV, IV, 220.      [8] *Mowbray Charters*, pp. xx–xxiv.

[9] *Charters of the Redvers Family*, pp. 20–4; for the earldom of Warwick see D. Crouch, 'The Local Influence of the Earls of Warwick, 1088–1242: A Study in Decline and Resourcefulness', *Midland History*, 21 (1996), 4.

[10] For Chatham, Chilham, Folkestone, Patrixsbourne, Port, Ros, Swanscombe, West Greenwich, and Wrinstead see Sanders, *English Baronies*, pp. 31, 111, 45, 135, 105, 144, 97, 151; the barony of Cogges owed castleguard at Dover and it too became a barony: *ibid.*, p. 36; for Castle Holgate, Cause, Pulverbatch, Wem, Clun, and Oswestry, *ibid*, pp. 28, 29, 73, 94, 112, 70; and for Launceston, Cardinham, Trematon, Chiselborough, Hatch Beauchamp, Marshwood, Stoke Trister, Odcombe, Helmsley, Hooton Pagnell, Mulgrave: *ibid*, pp. 60, 110, 90, 34, 51, 64, 84, 132, 52, 55, 66. See also Berkhamsted, *ibid.*, p. 14.      [11] *Ibid.*, pp. 104, 128, 22.

Hesdin (see below, p. 376).[12] The great royal estate of Berkeley was divided at the end of Stephen's reign into two lordships, Berkeley and Dursley, each held by knight service.[13] Finally, the lands held by Eudo the steward in 1086 escheated on his death without heirs in 1120 and formed the basis of two later lordships, Eaton Socon and Walkern.[14]

The rate of turnover in the families that held these lordships is striking. One major reason was lack of male heirs. In all, some fifty-four out of one hundred and eighty-nine English baronies in existence by 1166 and listed by Sanders descended in the female line between 1086 and 1166, six on two occasions. In other words, approximately 29 per cent descended through women.[15] Succession by women provided the king with a powerful point of entry into the succession of the most important lordships, and was of critical importance as a source of patronage for the Norman kings. It may even have been the case that Henry I manipulated the patterns of inheritance in such a way that more land descended through heiresses than might otherwise have been the case, for there were certainly more great heiresses at his disposal than there were at the disposal of his grandson.

Honours escheated for lack of heirs only rarely, because even if the direct line failed there were most likely collateral heirs, or women with hereditary claims. When Eudo the steward died in 1120 there were several potential heirs. He had at least two grandsons, Geoffrey II de Mandeville by his first marriage and William FitzOtuel by his second, plus the descendants of his brother and sister. Henry I however chose not to regrant the estates as a whole, and a substantial part was still in the king's hands in

---

[12] *Ibid.*, pp. 91, 112, 124, 125.     [13] *Ibid.*, pp. 13, 114.     [14] *Ibid.*, pp. 40, 92.

[15] The total of 189 is arrived at by subtracting from Sanders' 206 baronies the following: Ashby, Biset, Blythborough, Braose baronies, Eaton Bray, Flockthorpe, Headington, Knaresborough, Monmouth, Sotby, Writtle, Appleby, Port, Chepstow, Hepple, Langley, and Manchester. Sanders' descents in some cases need correction, and in the following list of honours which passed through the females only variants are mentioned: Aveley, Bampton, Gloucester, Bedford, Belvoir, Blagdon, Bolingbroke, Bourn, Bradninch, Burgh (twice), Castle Combe, Chipping Warden, Ellingham, Field Dalling, Folkestone (twice), Folkingham, Great Bealings, Great Weldon (via his wife, whose father, Geoffrey Ridel, had acquired the land held in 1086 by Robert de Buci), Hanslope, Helmsley, Hockering, Hooton Pagnel (twice), Much Marcle, Nether Stowey, North Cadbury, Okehampton (twice), Oswestry, Pulverbatch, Redbourne, Stainton, Thoresway, Trowbridge, Walkern, Wallingford, Wooler, Alnwick, Barnstaple, Bourne (twice), Brattleby, Clun, Dudley, Egremont, Fotheringay, Haughley, Keevil, Kempsford, Old Warden, Skipton (twice), Stogursey, Swanscombe, Tarrant Keynston (because Ralph de Cahagnes was said to have been granted Tarrant in marriage with his wife, *Book of Fees*, I, 87), Tickhill (via Beatrice de Bully), Wark, and Witham.

1130.[16] Apart from Eudo's lands, there is only one other clear case where an honour escheated in Henry's reign, that of Hatfield Peverel, after the death of William Peverel; this too was accounted for at the exchequer in 1130.[17] The honour of Wrinstead is said to have escheated after the death in 1147 or 1148 of its holder, a second William Peverel, though it is not clear why this should have been so, as William's other honour of Bourn was divided between his sisters.[18] Another William, second son of King Stephen, was munificently provided for by the treaty between Stephen and Henry FitzEmpress, and it was perhaps not surprising that after the deaths of William, in 1159, and his widow, in 1164, his lands were retained by the king.[19] Similarly Henry retained Walter III Giffard's honour of Long Crendon in 1164.[20] It is possible that in such cases the king did not have a predetermined plan to retain the honours, but simply that for the time being he was not prepared to recognize an heir, and that what may have been envisaged as a temporary arrangement became permanent. The king always had the option of recognizing an hereditary claim, as happened in 1189 when the Giffard inheritance was divided between two of Walter Giffard's kinsmen – Richard earl of Clare and William Marshal.

Apart from failure of issue, politics was the main reason for the high turnover in the upper echelons of the aristocracy. The death of the Conqueror and the subsequent contests between his sons for control of his legacy led to waves of forfeitures following rebellions in 1088, in 1095, and in the early years of Henry I's reign. In practice confiscations became less frequent from about 1115 (see further below, p. 262), but the right to confiscate was not abandoned. Moreover, although there was a high rate of turnover in terms of breaks of descent in the male line, the number of complete breaks is far lower when one takes into account collateral succession and descent through heiresses, which at least allowed for the possibility of succession of grandsons. Sometimes when honours were confiscated, another member of the family was allowed to succeed. Thus

---

[16] *PR 31 Henry I*, p. 139; J. H. Round, 'The Counts of Boulogne as English Lords', *Studies in Peerage and Family History*, (London, 1901), pp. 163–5 showed that some of Eudo's manors passed to Count Eustace of Boulogne, presumably between 1120 and 1125.    [17] *PR 31 Henry I*, p. 135.

[18] Sanders, *English Baronies*, pp. 151, 19.

[19] William held the honours of Boulogne, Eye, Lancaster, in addition to the Warenne estates he held through marriage, Sanders, *English Baronies*, pp. 151, 43, 126.    [20] *Ibid.*, p. 62.

when Roger de Lacy lost his Herefordshire lands in 1095 his brother Hugh succeeded.[21] When Roger d'Abetot was exiled in 1110 for the murder of a member of the royal household, his lands passed, possibly by marriage, to Walter de Beauchamp.[22] When Robert de Lacy of Pontefract was exiled, his widow married the grantee of the honour, Hugh de Laval.[23]

Given that there was a relatively high turnover in the upper levels, there were ample opportunities for new recruits, either from the lower ranks of families already settled in England or from men from across the Channel. The Conqueror's successors were all concerned to keep possession of the duchy if they could, and one obvious way of building up support was to use their resources of patronage in England to reward their allies in Normandy, not least those who had hitherto not been involved through either choice or circumstance. In this way the political destinies of England and Normandy could have been drawn ever more closely together. It is clear, however, from studying the descents of the English lordships listed by Sanders, that the number of entirely new recruits (that is, from abroad) was exceeded by men from families settled in England. Indeed, some who look like new recruits may have had kinsmen already in England. Alan FitzFlaad (Oswestry) may have been the first member of his family to hold land in England, but his father Flaad occurred as a witness to the foundation charter of Monmouth priory.[24] The origins of some of the first known holders of Northumberland lordships are particularly obscure, but it is likely that they came from families already in England. One example is Anschatin of Worcester, lord of Hadstone, who presumably came from Worcester. Other examples include Ralph de Gaugy and Hugh de Ellington (Ellingham), William de Merlay (Morpeth), Robert de Muschamp (Wooler), Richard Bertram (Bothal), Hubert de Laval (Callerton), William Bertram (Mitford), and Walter FitzWilliam (Whalton). Naming practices may obscure relationships if, for instance, one branch of a family used toponyms and another patronymics, or each used different toponyms. William Patric, who gave his name to Patrixsbourne, may have been the son of Richard FitzWilliam, who held this manor in 1086.[25] Robert de Beauchamp (Hatch Beauchamp) could

---

[21] OV, IV, 284.     [22] Dugdale, *Baronage*, I, 462.     [23] Wightman, *Lacy Family*, p. 66.
[24] Round, *CDF*, p. 408.     [25] Loyd, *Origins of Some Anglo-Norman Families*, p. 79.

have been related to Robert the constable (of the count of Mortain) who held the manor in 1086.[26] He may also have been related to the Beauchamp family of Bedford or Walter de Beauchamp of Elmley, but there is no evidence in either case. William de Rullos (Bourne) may have been related to the family which held land as under-tenants of the lords of Richmond.[27]

The description 'new recruit' therefore has to be applied carefully. Strictly speaking, collateral succession was a break in the succession of a single lineage, yet collaterals, illegitimate children, or men connected in some way to the king were not strangers to the elite. Ranulf Meschin, earl of Chester, was the first of his line to receive land in England, but he was the cousin of his predecessor, Earl Richard.[28] Odo count of Champagne, who was granted the lordship of Holderness when Drogo de la Beuvrière surrendered it soon after Domesday, was an outsider when viewed from the perspective of families settled in England, but he was married to the Conqueror's sister.[29] Brian FitzCount, who married the heiress to the lordship of Wallingford, was an illegitimate son of Count Alan Fergant of Brittany. Count Alan was related to the lords of Richmond though he did not himself have land in England, and his son Brian was brought up in the household of Henry I.[30] Henry's brother-in-law, David of Scotland, and his own illegitimate son Robert were each provided with heiresses, and his nephew Stephen was given large estates.[31] Two more of Henry's sons, Reginald and Robert FitzRoy, acquired wealth at a later date.[32] Reginald FitzCount, who married the heiress of Much Marcle in Herefordshire, was the son of Earl Roger of Hereford, disinherited in 1075. He obviously was not 'new' in the sense of being an outsider, but he is not known to have held any of his father's land.[33]

Excluding men such as these, there are only some thirty who were, so

---

[26] DB, IV, 271.      [27] Early Yorkshire Charters, V, 95–8.

[28] Ranulf's charter for St Evroul describes Earl Hugh as his uncle: Chester Charters, no. 10.

[29] English, Lords of Holderness, pp. 9–10.

[30] H. W. C. Davis, 'Henry of Blois and Brian FitzCount', English Historical Review, 24 (1910), 297–303.

[31] For David and Matilda de Senlis, ASC H 1114; for Robert, WM, Historia Novella, p. 4, and for a discussion of the date of Robert's tenure of the lands, Gloucester Charters, p. 152; for Stephen, Sanders, English Baronies, pp. 43, 126.

[32] Reginald acquired Launceston, and Robert FitzRoy married the heiress of Okehampton: Sanders, English Baronies, pp. 60, 69.

[33] Sanders, English Baronies, p. 66; OV, II, 318 for the statement that Reginald and his brother Roger were fighting in King Henry's service and were still awaiting the king's pardon for their father's rebellion.

far as is known, new recruits, and, since they include three sets of brothers, the number of new families was even smaller.[34] William Peverel 'of Dover' was the brother of Payn Peverel, to whom Bourn in Lincolnshire was granted; a third brother was Hamo Peverel, who held land in Shropshire.[35] Geoffrey de Mandeville of Marshwood was the brother of Roger de Mandeville of Erlestoke;[36] and Hamelin de Ballon (Much Marcle) was the brother of Wynebald (North Cadbury).[37]

Most of these new arrivals came into the upper ranks of the baronage in the reigns of Rufus and Henry I. Rufus's new recruits came from no single geographical region. Robert de Stuteville came from upper Normandy whilst others came from outside the frontiers of Normandy, like Guy de Balliol (from Somme, see above, p. 114), Simon de Senlis (from the Ile-de-France, see below, p. 217), or Hamelin and Wynebald de Ballon (from Maine, see below, p. 278). Henry's new recruits, however, often came from west Normandy or Brittany, whence he recruited mercenaries.[38] Of men from the west two examples may be cited. Robert de Brus's career in England may have begun before 1100, but it is more likely that he received his Yorkshire lands from Henry I; as we have seen, he had land in Yorkshire by 1103.[39] Rualon d'Avranches was granted the manor of Stanton Harcourt in Oxfordshire which had belonged to Odo of Bayeux.[40]

---

[34] Hasculf de Tani (Aveley), William d'Aubigny the Breton (Belvoir), Payn Peverel (Bourn), brother of William Peverel of Dover, Robert de Trevers, brother-in-law of Ranulf I earl of Chester (Burgh by Sands), Guy de Balliol (Bywell), Robert de Stuteville (Cottingham), Roger de Mandeville (Erlestoke), Hasculf of St James (Field Dalling), Rualon d'Avranches (Folkestone), Geoffrey Ridel (Great Weldon), Geoffrey FitzPain (Hunsingore, Warter), Geoffrey de Mandeville (Marshwood), Hamelin de Ballon (Much Marcle), Wynebald de Ballon (North Cadbury), Robert d'Umfraville (Prudhoe), Walter de Beauchamp (Salwarpe), William de Montfiquet (Stansted), Roger de Nonant (Totnes), William de Lanvalei (Walkern), Henry de Tracy (Barnstaple), Hugh Wake (Bourne), Simon de Senlis (Fotheringay), Simon de Moulins (Haughley), Robert de Vere (Haughley), Patrick de Chaworth (Kempsford), Hugh de Laval (Pontefract), Robert de Rumilly (Skipton), Roger Marmion (Tamworth), William Trussebut (Warter), and William Peverel of Dover (Wrinstead).

[35] *The Cartulary of Shrewsbury Abbey*, ed. U. Rees, 2 vols. (Aberystwyth, 1975), I, 21–2, 34; the origins of this family have not been established. One possibility is that they were related to the Peverels of London, for in 1086 Ranulf Peverel held land in Shropshire: *DB*, I, 256b. Dugdale believed that Hamo Peverel and his brothers were sons of Ranulf Peverel: *Baronage*, I, 437–8.

[36] *Charters of the Redvers Family*, p. 55.     [37] Round, *CDF*, nos. 1045–8, pp. 367–9.

[38] OV, VI, 88; HH, pp. 235, 274; Green, *Government of England*, pp. 146–8; WM, *De Gestis Regum Anglorum*, II, 478.

[39] Robert witnessed a charter of Earl Hugh for Whitby, said to be of dubious authenticity: Farrer, *Early Yorkshire Charters*, II, 193; *Chester Charters*, no. 5. William de Percy, addressed in this charter, died on crusade in 1096. Anschetil de Bulmer, one of the witnesses, was sheriff of Yorkshire in Henry I's reign. Robert had received lands in Yorkshire by 1103: *RRAN*, II, no. 648.     [40] *Ibid.*, nos. 527–8.

Amongst the Bretons was William d'Aubigny the Breton who married Cecily, granddaughter and eventual heiress of Robert de Todeni of Belvoir. He came from Saint-Martin-d'Aubigné (Ile-et-Vilaine), and was said to have fought for Henry on the battlefield at Tinchebrai.[41]

The establishment of men from the west and Brittany, and the advancement of men settled in England whose families were already established in England, did something to redress the earlier preponderance in the higher aristocracy of men from upper Normandy and the Calvados. Yet Henry's new recruits included men from other parts of Normandy. For instance, when Robert de Montfort lost his lands in Kent and in Suffolk in 1107, they passed on marriage to his sister, and to her husbands. The first, Simon de Moulins, was lord of Moulins-la-Marche, on the south-east frontier of the duchy. Simon was one of the king's military commanders, and is mentioned by Orderic as having been put in charge of the garrison of Evreux in 1119.[42] After Simon's death, his widow married Robert de Vere who possibly came from Ver-sur-Mer in Calvados.[43] Henry also looked to Flanders for mercenaries. Some were granted land in England, but it is significant that they became only petty lords: the days had gone when such men might hope for rich spoils. Some time after about 1107 Henry settled Flemings in west Wales, where they established small planned towns along the border between the areas controlled by the Anglo-Normans and those still in Welsh hands. Small groups moved in under leaders who gave their names to planned settlements, such as Wiston (Wizo) and Tancredston (Tancard).[44]

Henry devoted much attention to the southern border of Normandy where ducal authority was less strong and where, until 1112, he was faced by the power of Robert de Bellême. It was essential for him to guard this vulnerable sector of the frontier, which he did by a policy of strong fortification, and by fostering loyalty amongst the local lords, some of whom received land in England. Amongst those who benefited was

---

[41] For a brief outline, Green, *Government of England*, pp. 228–9.

[42] OV, VI, 100, 230–2; for the descent of the Montfort lands in England, see Douglas, *Domesday Monachorum*, pp. 65–70.

[43] *PR 31 Henry I*, p. 64; J. R. Scott, 'Charters of Monks Horton Priory', *Archaeologia Cantiana*, 10 (1876), 269; *RRAN*, II, no. 1898; OV, VI, 450; and see further below, p. 288n.

[44] I. W. Rowlands, 'The Making of the March: Aspects of the Norman Settlement in Dyfed', *Proceedings of the Battle Conference on Anglo-Norman Studies*, 3 (1980), 147–8; SD, 'Historia Regum' in *Opera omnia*, II, 245.

Gilbert de L'Aigle who, like his father, had been a member of the king's military household. He was granted the honour of Pevensey some time after 1106, considerably augmenting the relatively small estates he had held in 1086.[45] Richard de Lucy, later Henry II's chief justiciar, started his career under Henry I. He came from Lucé not far from Domfront, and he, or an earlier namesake, had acquired land in England before 1135.[46] Marriage alliances were used to buttress the loyalty of lords whose lands were just beyond the frontier, hence the marriage of Hugh de Laval from Laval in Maine to the widow of Robert de Lacy of Pontefract.

In Stephen's reign it is evident that in general there were few new arrivals at the top level. Events unravelled too quickly for Stephen to enlarge his base of support south of the Channel by using his resources of patronage to the north of it. One possible new recruit is Henry de Tracy, who was lord of Barnstaple by 1139, but whose family cannot be identified in England before 1135.[47] William of Ypres, Stephen's Flemish commander, was granted large estates in Kent but not, apparently in fief; had his career not been brought to an end by the accession of Henry II, he would perhaps have established a new baronial family, but he departed in 1154.[48] Other Flemings who appear in the reign acquired little or no land. Ralph de Péronne, who joined Stephen in 1138, evidently held some, but probably lost it after the battle of Lincoln.[49] The inner circle on whom Stephen relied after his release from captivity was composed of men who were already in England in 1135: Richard de Lucy, William Martel, William de Chesney, Richard de Camville, Robert de Vere, and Henry of Essex (see below, p. 311).

In his early years Henry FitzEmpress had few resources to attract and reward men, other than the magnates who for a variety of reasons already supported his cause in England. One of those who did enter his service, and was to recover land in England that had been lost by his father in 1106, was Robert de Stuteville.[50] Hubert de Vaux and Manasser Biset also

---

[45] Sanders, *English Baronies*, p. 136.
[46] Loyd, *Origins of Some Anglo-Norman Families*, p. 55; E. M. Amt, 'Richard de Lucy, Henry II's Justiciar', *Medieval Prosopography*, 9 (1988), 62–3, 70.    [47] Loyd, *Origins of Some Anglo-Norman Families*, pp. 104–6.
[48] Amt, *Accession of Henry II in England*, pp. 87–91.
[49] OV, VI, 516; *Chester Charters*, no. 56. The Caldret brothers who established themselves in Gloucestershire for a time were also said to have been Flemings, *Gesta Stephani*, p. 188.
[50] *Mowbray Charters*, p. xxviii.

entered his service before 1154 and were rewarded with land in England.[51] Others, such as Richard de Lucy, Philip of Kyme, or William de Chesney, were already established there. The new political context could have resulted in a new wave of migrants from the continent, from Anjou and Aquitaine as well as Normandy, but this did not happen.

The settlement of much of England, therefore, was essentially the work of the first wave of Normans and their companions; if relatively large numbers followed, they have left no traces in the sources. Of the three kings who followed King William, Henry I, who held the duchy longest, was likeliest to bring over Normans. His promotion of west Normans and Bretons helped to reshape the character of the aristocracy, but few new recruits can be traced after his death. Given contested successions in 1087, 1100, and 1135, it is not surprising that the kings had to woo the powerful families based in England. The Norman conquests in Wales were on the whole the work of men already settled in England, with substantial resources of men and money, like the Clare family. The opening up of the far north provided further opportunities, but the prospect of land there does not seem to have been very enticing. The radical reshaping of tenurial geography in Yorkshire profited men whose families were already settled, like Nigel d'Aubigny, a relative of Nigel d'Aubigny of Cainhoe, Eustace FitzJohn, son of John nephew of Waleran, and Walter Espec, nephew of William Spech, all of whom were Domesday tenants-in-chief. Robert de Brus on the other hand probably was a new arrival from the Cotentin, while nothing is known about the origins of Geoffrey FitzPain.[52]

Yet if new faces are detectable in the upper reaches of the aristocracy, this does not preclude the possibility of continuing migration in the middle and lower ranks. A few examples can be found. Richard de Redvers brought over men from his estates in Normandy in the early twelfth century, for instance.[53] When Robert II earl of Leicester married the

---

[51] Hubert witnessed charters of Baldwin de Redvers, but seems to have left England with Duke Henry in 1149: *Charters of the Redvers Family*, p. 38; *RRAN*, III, nos. 112, 130, 587, 666, 711, 748, 795, 836, 903 (Hubert); Barrow, *Anglo-Norman Era*, p. 196; *RRAN*, III, nos. 49, 61, 64–5, 90, 126–8, 130, 140, 180, 206, 272, 306, 309–10, 339, 363a–365a, 373, 438, 459, 462, 575, 582, 584, 653, 795, 811, 836, 999, 1000 (Manasser); Loyd, *Origins of Some Anglo-Norman Families*, pp. 15–16.

[52] Geoffrey was a frequent witness of Henry I's documents, his earliest attestation being to *RRAN*, II, no. 893, probably issued in 1107 or 1108.

[53] For the Mandeville family of Marshwood, see Loyd, *Origins of Some Anglo-Norman Families*, pp. 57–8; *Charters of the Redvers Family*, p. 38, for this family, Richard de Moreville, and Richard de Lestre.

heiress of the honour of Breteuil he gave lands in England to some of the leading men of the honor, as Crouch has demonstrated.[54] While lord of Carlisle, Ranulf Meschin established in Cumbria his brother, William Meschin, his brother-in-law Robert de Trevers, and Richer de Boivill, probably from his Norman estates (see above, p. 119). Although there were cases of migration in the middle levels, it is unlikely that the numbers involved were large. Those who acquired baronies in the midlands and the south after 1086 often found large tenancies had already been created. Those who settled in the northern counties cannot generally be shown to have created many tenancies in favour of Frenchmen; again perhaps the demand for land was not there. In the late eleventh and early twelfth centuries it might have appeared to younger sons in Normandy, Brittany, or Flanders as though Britain was a land of opportunity, with lands still to conquer in Wales and in the north. Yet those who had settled in the first decades after 1066 proved to be best placed to enrich themselves further.

Moreover, there was little identifiable emigration to Normandy after the death of the Conqueror. Young men may have visited their relatives in Normandy, or, like William Marshal in a later period, have been sent to receive their military training in a great Norman household, but it is hard to find examples of them being established in major Norman lordships.[55] Robert II earl of Leicester, for instance, was granted the lordship of Breteuil by Henry I but although he personally had not inherited the family's Norman estates his elder twin had, so he hardly counts as a new arrival into the Norman aristocracy, and his marriage to the heiress of Breteuil was arranged by Henry I.[56] There is need for more research into the aristocracy of early twelfth-century Normandy, but the impression gained is that the dominant families were just as successful in defending their interests there as were their counterparts in England. There was also movement in ecclesiastical circles across from England to Normandy, particularly in the early twelfth century.[57] But it would appear that cross-Channel migration in the later eleventh and early twelfth centuries was overwhelmingly in the other direction.

[54] Crouch, *Beaumont Twins*, pp. 109–12.
[55] *Histoire de Guillaume le Maréchal*, ed. P. Meyer, 3 vols., Société de l'Histoire de France (Paris, 1891–1901), I, l. 744.
[56] Crouch, *Beaumont Twins*, pp. 8–13 for the division of family lands between the Beaumont twins and their sister.      [57] M. Brett, *The English Church under Henry I* (Oxford, 1975), pp. 9–10.

A further question arises about the social status of the newcomers compared with their predecessors. When the faces at the top did change, were the newcomers men either of humbler status or of a different career pattern? The chief casualties of the disputed successions of Rufus and Henry I had been men from the Conqueror's inner circle, like Odo of Bayeux, the sons of Roger of Montgomery and Robert of Mortain, and the nephew of Geoffrey bishop of Coutances. Duke Robert attracted the support of the sons of his father's companions and kinsmen.[58] When he later came into conflict with his brothers over their father's inheritance, most of the same group supported him and were then by one means or another broken. The removal of some of the greatest magnates of the Conqueror's day provided Rufus and Henry I not only with the opportunity to promote their own men but also with the means to restructure the baronage if they wished, and to create more, but less wealthy, magnates. They did not do so, however.

In terms of social origins no objection could be made to the promotion of men from established noble families. But Henry I was also held to be responsible for inserting new men, 'raised from the dust', into the aristocracy. The promotion of men from lesser families who proved themselves as commanders and castellans was nothing new in itself, but a few of Henry's 'new men' had a different career profile, in that their service to the king had primarily been in the courts, or as sheriffs.[59] The rise of such men predated Henry's reign, but it was in the early twelfth century that their presence was noted by contemporaries. There were never very many new men of this type at any one time, and they were not elevated into the highest levels of the aristocracy in a single generation. The most successful might achieve such promotion for their sons or grandsons. Ralph Basset, the sheriff and justice, held only a modest amount of land in chief despite a lengthy career. His son Richard, himself a sheriff and justice, benefited from his marriage to a daughter of another leading royal justice, but at the time of the marriage her portion was only that of twenty pounds' worth of land from the royal demesne and the service of four knights. It was only as events turned out that he secured all her

---

[58] OV, III, 100–2.

[59] OV, VI, 16; for discussion of the new men see Green, *Government of England*, pp. 139–57 and references therein cited.

[60] *Basset Charters c. 1120–1250*, ed. W. T. Reedy, Pipe Roll Society, new series, I (1995), for 1989–91), no. 47; see also Green, *Government of England*, pp. 231–2.

father's land.[60] Nevertheless the appearance of new men was indicative that the expanding scope of governance – and in this sense we must include the regimes of great magnates, lay and ecclesiastical, as well as of the king – was providing alternative career paths for the upwardly mobile.

We rarely know how such new men gained their entrée into the king's service, and it cannot have been easy. Those already at the top of the greasy pole had every incentive to resist outsiders, and in practice most men looking for advancement must have looked closer to home, to powerful relations or to their lords. In this respect powerful figures in the church, traditionally a means of promotion for the talented but poorly connected, were just as likely as their lay counterparts to work for the promotion of their own kinsfolk. And the careers of the new men of the king, once they became established, remained risky, for they incurred envy for their success. They needed to work to make and keep friends in high places, and they needed money to secure offices or patronage which might in turn lead to permanent gains of land. As royal ministers they exercised great power, but everything depended on keeping the king's favour. The fate of Geoffrey de Clinton, accused of treason in 1130, showed what could happen to those who lost the king's support (see below, p. 289).

Finally, there is the issue of the overall shape and character of the aristocracy. The casualties of politics between 1086 and 1106 included some of the richest of the 'super-magnates', and these were also in most cases men with great estates across the Channel. It is significant, however, that men of comparable wealth were created in the early twelfth century, as Warren Hollister has pointed out, and again the new 'super-magnates' were related to the king. Instead of Odo of Bayeux and Robert of Mortain there were Henry I's nephews, Henry bishop of Winchester and abbot of Glastonbury, and Stephen, count of Mortain, lord of Eye and Lancaster and, by marriage, count of Boulogne, plus Henry's sons and brother-in-law whose advancement has already been noted. In the same way that two bishops, Odo and Geoffrey, had acquired great personal wealth through the Conquest, Roger bishop of Salisbury became vastly wealthy under Henry I. In other words, there was no restructuring of a kind which would have removed the super-magnates and redistributed wealth more widely. We can only speculate about the distribution of wealth in the lower levels, and whether, perhaps, the numbers of lesser but still aristocratic families grew during this period, or whether there was a concentration of wealth in fewer hands.

In one respect there was a significant development in the stratification of the upper aristocracy, and that was by the proliferation of earldoms in the reign of King Stephen. After the old English earldoms were done away with, the title had been used sparingly by Rufus and Henry I. Under the pressure of events Stephen, and, on a smaller scale his rival the Empress, appointed earls in most counties (see below, pp. 298–305). The titles reflected competition for support, but they also recognised the pre-eminence of a single magnate in each county, strengthening a trend towards concentrations of power at the local level. Henry II, however, allowed some of the earldoms to lapse and the title became once again relatively rare.

Lawrence Stone and Jean Fawtier Stone, in a study of social mobility in early modern England *An Open Elite?*, concluded that the new elite did absorb newcomers, but access was relatively restricted.[61] It might be argued that the same is true of Norman England. Political upheavals provided opportunities, but these were exploited by the king. At a secondary level, magnates pursued strategies to further the interests of their families, and of their men. What was to be most significant for the ongoing relationship between England and Normandy was that migration dwindled to a trickle in the twelfth century. A few very important new trans-Channel complexes were created, but these did not compensate for the tendency of other families to divide into Norman and English branches.

[61]  *An Open Elite? England 1540–1680* (Oxford, 1984).

## II  Wealth and power

# 5 The organization of lordships and the management of resources

We have very few details about how the estates of the lay aristocracy were organized and managed during the century following the Norman Conquest. No estate surveys or account rolls survive, and there is little evidence about regional economic trends. Lacking family papers, we do not have evidence about the scale of personal expenditure, whether on residences and castles, military retinues, lavish lifestyle, or pious benefactions. It is especially difficult to discover anything of the fortunes of the middling and lesser aristocracy, particularly in relation to the demands made upon them by their overlords and by the king. Yet although the evidence is patchy, it is possible to identify some of the general considerations involved in the shaping of the great lordships, in particular the crucial distinction between lands which were to be retained in direct control (in demesne) and lands which were granted to tenants. There is a little information too about when and where markets and towns were established and these, though not as lucrative as the revenue arising from land, were nevertheless valuable.

## The context

### Expenditure

As the dust of Conquest began to settle those who had profited most found themselves extremely wealthy, and doubtless were able to reward their followers without difficulty. And they would have wished to be generous, for generosity was a quality intrinsic to good lordship, and, indeed, central to aristocratic power, for lords had not only to win but also to retain the loyalty of their followers: parsimony was essentially counterproductive. Also castles had to be built, and though perhaps the earliest were relatively rudimentary, by the twelfth century the greatest lords were building in stone and at considerable expense. Each generation had to make provision for younger sons, for the honourable marriage of daughters, and for gifts to the church. By the twelfth century benefactors to the church had a variety of options (see below, chapter twelve). Above all there was the chance of founding a new community particularly attached to one's own family, but such foundations were often combined with maintaining established links with other houses or making gifts to other foundations.

Moreover, lords were subject to exactions from the king. 'Speculate to accumulate' is a tag that might well describe the operation of patronage under the Norman kings, in the sense that those who sought to marry heiresses or wealthy widows, or to secure a royal office or the king's intervention in a lawsuit, had to make proffers. In some cases the sums involved were huge, and, although they were paid off in instalments, even the instalments were large. Again, lords doubtless passed as much of the cost as they could onto their tenants by levying aids, though we have no information about this. Geoffrey II de Mandeville accounted for £866 13s. 4d. for his father's lands in 1130, of which he paid into the treasury £133 6s. 8d.[1] William de Pont de l'Arche accounted for one thousand marks for the chamberlainship of Robert Mauduit of which he paid one hundred, and he also accounted for £84 15s. for two offices in the chamber.[2] Aubrey de Vere accounted for £550 and four chargers for allowing a prisoner to escape and for fines from counties (probably in this context Essex and Hertfordshire) where he had been either a sheriff or justice. Of this sum he paid in £34 13s. 4d.[3] Those who were unfortunate enough to incur the king's displeasure could lose their estates and have to find large sums to recover them. This was the fate of Ivo de Grandmesnil who was charged with waging war upon his neighbours. He mortgaged his land to Robert count of Meulan for five hundred marks, and left England for the crusade, never to return.[4] Robert Fossard incurred the king's wrath for some unexplained reason, and in 1130 owed five hundred marks to recover his land, with the exception of Doncaster.[5]

Finally, the costs of personal involvement in war have to be remembered. Those who embarked on the first crusade like Ivo de Grandmesnil had to finance their participation. Duke Robert himself had had to mortgage the duchy of Normandy to his wealthy younger brother. The wars of Stephen's reign, though hostilities were intermittent and localized, bore heavily on individuals. Cash was needed for personal equipment and

[1] PR 31 Henry I, p. 55.   [2] Ibid., p. 37.   [3] Ibid., p. 53.   [4] OV, VI, 18.   [5] PR 31 Henry I, p. 25.

horses, and for paid soldiers, including infantry and archers. In some cases the protagonists may have been able to recoup their costs at the expense of their neighbours or the king, but this was not always possible. Brian FitzCount in a letter to the bishop of Winchester complained of his impoverishment in the Empress's cause.[6]

What we do not know, of course, is how far aristocrats could balance their books, and it is doubtful if they even thought in these terms. Liquidity may well have been a problem for those faced with raising large sums at short notice. There are two references in the 1130 pipe roll, for example, to magnates in debt to the Jews: Ranulf earl of Chester and Richard FitzGilbert (of Clare).[7] In Ranulf's case the Jews owed £60 for the king's help – their original proffer was thus at least this figure, and the earl's debt therefore must have been sufficiently larger to make it worth their while enlisting the king's help. From the fact that this was an old debt we might infer that the debtor was Ranulf I Earl of Chester between 1121 and 1129, and that it related to the huge sum of £1,000 Ranulf II owed in 1130 'for his father's debt for Earl Hugh's land'.[8] This had been an exceptional proffer made to secure Ranulf's succession to the lands and earldom of his cousin Richard who had been drowned in 1120, and he had presumably gone to the Jews to raise a down payment. Richard FitzGilbert had succeeded his father over ten years previously and he also may have needed to raise money for a relief to the king. In a second entry elsewhere in the pipe roll, however, he accounted for his land in Wales, after which a debt for two hundred marks was entered for 'the help the king gave him towards the Jews for his debt'.[9] Here we see both parties looking to the king, and prepared to pay for his intervention. Of the circumstances in which the debt was incurred we are told nothing, but the fact that Richard's debt was entered after the account for his land in Wales arouses the suspicion that the two were not unconnected. Richard and his father were actively engaged in subduing Ceredigion (Cardigan), and the costs of such warfare cannot have been cheap.

The recourse to borrowing may therefore simply have been in order to meet exceptional circumstances, and we cannot assume from two instances that many aristocrats were similarly situated. Nevertheless it has

[6] Davis, 'Henry of Blois and Brian FitzCount', p. 302.     [7] *PR 31 Henry I*, pp. 149, 148.
[8] *Ibid.*, p. 110.     [9] *Ibid.*, p. 53.

to be borne in mind that many families possibly acquired relatively little land after the late eleventh century, and that the pressures to keep giving were recurrent. Beyond a certain point the patrimony had to be preserved for following generations, and any increase in wealth would in the normal course of events have had to be generated by a more intensive exploitation of existing resources or by increasing the land under cultivation.

### The economic context of lordship

The period between the tenth and thirteenth centuries witnessed population growth in England, as elsewhere in western Europe, leading to an extension of cultivation, and providing greater incentives for the cultivation of arable crops. New fields were ploughed from the waste, moorland, or woodland, and new settlements came into being. In the early middle ages land had often been managed in relatively large units described by historians as multiple estates, composed of estate centres with a penumbra of outlying farms or berewicks, and a territorial soke, or district, within which sokemen were responsible for the payment of various dues.[10] Gradually the great estates broke up, sometimes through 'fission from above' as rulers made grants, sometimes by 'fission from below' as peasants established full proprietorial rights, especially on the margins of estates.[11] In the north and parts of the midlands more of the old large lordships had survived, especially when they were in the possession of the king or the church.[12] In eastern England by 1066 lordship was much weaker than in other regions, and the proportion of *liberi homines* or freemen was relatively high. Here too there may have been great estates which had broken up through action from above, or bids for inde-

[10] The extent of large multiple estates in early medieval England has led to some debate. See especially G. R. J. Jones, 'Multiple Estates and Early Settlement', *Medieval Settlement*, ed. P. H. Sawyer (London, 1976), pp. 11–40; N. Gregson, 'The Multiple Estate Model: some Critical Questions', *Journal of Historical Geography*, II (1985), 339–51; G. R. Jones, 'Multiple Estates Perceived', *ibid.*, 352–63; cf. the comments by J. Blair, 'Frithuwold's Kingdom and the Origins of Surrey', *The Origins of Anglo-Saxon Kingdoms*, ed. S. Bassett (Leicester, 1989), p. 105.

[11] T. Williamson, *The Origins of Norfolk* (Manchester, 1993), pp. 94–103, 114–26.

[12] Kapelle, *Norman Conquest of the North*, chapter 3; J. E. A. Jolliffe, 'Northumbrian Institutions', *English Historical Review*, 41 (1926), 1–42; G. W. S. Barrow, 'The Pattern of Lordship and Feudal Settlement in Cumbria', *Journal of Medieval History*, 1 (1975), 117–38; Winchester, *Landscape and Society in Medieval Cumbria*, chapter 3; Kapelle, *Norman Conquest of the North*, chapter 3; M. W. Bishop, 'Multiple Estates in late Anglo-Saxon Nottinghamshire', *Transactions of the Thoroton Society*, 85 (1982 for 1981), 37–47; P. Stafford, *The East Midlands in the Early Middles Ages* (Leicester, 1985), chapter 2.

pendence from below, the latter possibly aided by dislocation during the Viking period.[13]

Quite how far the trend towards extension of arable cultivation had reached by the mid-eleventh century and the extent to which it was disrupted by the Norman conquest is not clear.[14] In the midlands and the south the new lords took over from the old, and it could be argued that their main concern was with cash profit rather than investment in demesne agriculture. If there was little profit to be made from growing surpluses on demesne manors, then perhaps it was better tactics to farm out the manors at relatively high rents, or to increase the dues and services of small producers. In Yorkshire it is clear that there was widespread dislocation and reorganization, as a result of which peasants and their plough teams were concentrated on particular estates, either under compulsion or for their own protection. Planned villages with regular plots in the East Riding may date from this period, possibly founded by the new landlords.[15]

Population growth probably occurred at different dates in different areas.[16] Here and there we can see signs of the extension of the arable in the early twelfth century as, for instance, in the payment for unlicensed cultivation in the forests (assarts), which occur in pipe rolls. The number of such payments in the pipe roll for 1156, when Henry II ordered a visitation of the forests, is particularly striking given the recent civil war.[17] Markets proliferated and some new towns came into being.[18] In some

---

[13] Williamson, *Origins of Norfolk*, pp. 114–26.

[14] For a brief discussion of the various estate structures described in Domesday Book see Lennard, *Rural England, 1086–1135*, chapter 8; Welldon Finn, *The Norman Conquest and its Effects on the Economy 1066–86* was an attempt to assess the impact of the Conquest by using Domesday information on changing land values and the extent and location of manors said to be waste; for a study of Yorkshire which uses the Domesday information in relation to other sources such as land quality and the location of castles see Dalton, *Conquest, Anarchy and Lordship*, chapters 1 and 2; for Surrey see J. Blair, *Early Medieval Surrey. Landholding, Church and Settlement*, Surrey Archaeological Society (1991), chapters 1–3.

[15] Sheppard, 'Pre-enclosure Field and Settlement Patterns in an English Township' and 'Metrological Analysis of Regular Village Plans in Yorkshire', *Agricultural History Review*; M. Harvey, 'Open Field Agriculture and Landholding Arrangements in eastern Yorkshire', *Transactions of the Institute of British Geographers*, new series, 9 (1984), 60–74; Harvey, 'Development of Open Fields in the central Vale of York: a Reconsideration'; B. K. Roberts, 'Norman Village Plantations and Long Strip Fields in Northern England', *Geografiska Annaler*, 70 ser. B (1988), 169–77.

[16] H. E. Hallam, *Rural England 1066–1348* (London, 1981) reviews the evidence; for a discussion of the activities of the lesser aristocracy in Yorkshire see Thomas, *Vassals, Heiresses, Crusaders, and Thugs*, chapter 5.     [17] *RBE*, II, 648–58, discussed by Amt, *Accession of Henry II*, pp. 169–74.

[18] R. H. Britnell, *The Commercialisation of English Society 1100–1500* (Cambridge, 1993), chapter 1.

cases the new lords may simply have been able to attract existing commerce to their markets, as in the case of the market which William Malet established at his chief castle of Eye in Suffolk, to the detriment of a nearby market of the bishop of Thetford at Hoxne.[19] In others, however, new markets and towns evidently capitalized on growing trade, such as Count Alan's port at Boston in Lincolnshire, whose prosperity was founded on the wool trade (see below, p. 158). Rising profits from arable cultivation by the later twelfth century led landlords to switch from leasing manors to direct demesne management.[20] This change in management does not seem to have occurred in our period, so that if profits were already rising they may have benefited lessors rather than the lords of the land.

## Demesne manors

### Numbers and location

The most important criteria for determining which manors were to remain in demesne were as we might expect value and size. Geoffrey I de Mandeville's estates were worth some £791 9s. 10d. in 1086, of which some £540-worth were held in demesne. These included some particularly valuable estates: Great Waltham (£60), Saffron Walden (£50), High Easter (£30) in Essex, Enfield (£50) and Edmonton (£40) in Middlesex, Streatley (£24) in Berkshire, and Long Compton (£30) in Warwickshire.[21] Walter d'Aincourt's estates were worth much less (just over £150) and individually were not particularly valuable, but the two that were, Granby in Nottinghamshire (£20 plus its soke), and Branston in Lincolnshire (two estates, £30 plus the soke), were held in demesne.[22]

A closer look at the organization of the Sussex rapes brings out the way in which value, size, and location determined the choice of demesne manors. By Domesday reckoning some of the most valuable agricultural land in the country lay in Sussex, especially on the coastal plain and the

---

[19] *DB*, ii, 379.

[20] The key article here was that by P. D. A. Harvey, 'The Pipe Rolls and the Adoption of Demesne Farming in England', *Economic History Review*, 27 (1974), 345–59; for a general review of the options open to landlords see Miller and Hatcher, *Medieval England. Rural Society and Economic Change 1086–1348*, chapter 8.

[21] *DB*, ii, 58, 62b, 60b; i, 129b, 243b.       [22] *DB*, i, 289, 361.

South Downs; by contrast, the upland Weald with badly drained clay soil
was much less favourable to settlement. We saw in chapter two how
Sussex was divided into compact lordships, five held by laymen and the
sixth by the bishop of Chichester. In Arundel, Roger of Montgomery had
kept in demesne Earl Godwin's manors of Singleton (paying £126),
Westbourne (paying £50), Stoughton (paying £50), Countess Gytha's
manors of Binderton (£7), Harting and Trotton (paying together £126), and
King Edward's manor of Lyminster (£50). He had granted Godwin's manor
of Climping to the abbey of Almenêches, and that of Sées had received
Tostig's manor of Fishbourne and Harold's manor of Eastergate. In all,
excluding his revenues from Chichester and Arundel, Roger had retained
land worth £409 in Sussex.[23] In neighbouring Bramber to the east,
William de Briouze's demesne manors included Beeding (£40) and
Steyning (£25), both previously held by King Edward, Earl Gyrth's manor
of Washington, of which William's share was worth £50 5s., Harold's
manor of Findon (£28 10s.), and Shoreham, held by Azor of King Edward,
and at farm for £50 'though it could not be borne'. William's demesne in
all totalled £219 15s.[24]

In Lewes, William de Warenne kept only four manors in demesne, but
they were very valuable: Iford, formerly held by Queen Edith, of which his
share was worth £35, Harold's manors of Rodmell and Patching, worth
respectively £37 and £80, and King Edward's Ditchling, where William's
share was worth £60. The value of William's demesne, excluding his revenues from Lewes, was £212, and again the demesne manors had belonged
to King Edward and the house of Godwin.[25] The value of the count of
Mortain's demesne manors in Pevensey (£206 11s. 9d.) was very close to
that of William de Warenne's, and included large and valuable estates
which were situated, with one exception, in a relatively compact group
between Lewes and Pevensey.[26] Only the organization of Hastings rape,
held by the count of Eu, differed. Here relatively few of the valuable
manors are described as being held in demesne by the count and in these
cases small parcels were in the hands of tenants.[27] In addition a number of
small estates, outliers of manors in the rape of Pevensey, were described as
being held by the count. In this part of Sussex, manors were not as valu-

---

[23] *DB*, I, 23, 24, 24b.     [24] *DB*, I, 23.     [25] *DB*, I, 26.     [26] *DB*, I, 20b, 21, 21b, 22, 22b.
[27] e.g. Hooe, *DB*, I, 18.

able as those further west, and had clearly suffered from the invasion of
1066. Filsham and Hollington were both very close to Hastings. Filsham
had been King Edward's manor before 1066 and had then been worth £14;
later it was wasted (*uastata*); in 1086 it was worth £22, of which the count's
share was worth £14.[28] Hollington had been worth 30s., later 20s., and 58s.
in 1086.[29] Also a great deal of land in the rape was by 1086 in the hands of
Battle abbey, or of the count's tenants. His headquarters in the lordship
were presumably at Hastings castle.

The boundaries of the Sussex lordships took shape quite early. The original grants, modified by the insertion into Sussex of William de Briouze,
were made within a few years of the Conquest. As we have just seen, the
lords of four of the rapes chose to keep in demesne the large and valuable
estates on the coast or on the edge of the South Downs, and granted out
either small estates or those situated inland, which were less valuable.
The tenurial organization of post-Conquest Sussex marked a considerable
change from that on the eve of the Conquest. It may have been wholly
novel or was possibly a revival of earlier territorial units, and if the latter,
these had presumably been swept aside by Godwin and his sons.

In Cheshire and Shropshire the Domesday evidence allows us to see how
two great lords organized very large lordships where they acquired almost
all land not held by the church. In Cheshire Earl Hugh retained most of
his predecessor Earl Edwin's demesne manors. Another group of estates
retained in demesne was recorded as waste, including upland regions on
the western flanks of the Pennines.[30] In the case of the upland manors
there are two related points: the fact that the manors were described as
waste, and the fact that they were situated on relatively high land. They
may not have been granted out because in the absence of arable cultivation they would have had little attraction for tenants; but they may well
have been useful as pasture, as hunting reserves, and, in the case of
Macclesfield, for the earl's stud farm.[31] In Yorkshire many upland estates
described as waste may have been in their lords' hands in 1086 for similar
reasons, and in this context it may be noted that when the structure of the
Cumbrian lordships can be traced in the twelfth century their lords often
retained upland pastures in demesne as well as centres of arable cultivation.[32]

---

[28] *DB*, I, 18b.    [29] *Ibid*.    [30] *DB*, I, 263b–264.    [31] *VCH Cheshire*, II, 178–9.
[32] Winchester, *Landscape and Society in Medieval Cumbria*, pp. 19–20.

In Shropshire Earl Roger stepped into the king's shoes. He retained twelve of King Edward's manors with their outlying estates, and eleven other manors.[33] Seven demesne manors had the profits of hundreds attached to them, which gave Roger an added incentive for keeping them.[34] Roger also kept in demesne land at Montgomery: on this large estate of over fifty hides, a castle was built (at Hen Domen), and there was evidently substantial agrarian activity, with three plough teams on the demesne.[35]

In Cheshire and Shropshire the new lords were given their lands all at once, and could take an overview in deciding which estates to keep and which to grant out. Succession to estates held by King Edward or by an earl predisposed the new lord to keep their estates in demesne, in the way King William himself usually retained King Edward's estates. It was more usual, however, to receive grants of land in stages, and geographically dispersed, so that decisions about demesne and enfeoffment might well have been taken before the final shape of the lordship was known. Here again the tendency was to keep very large or valuable estates in demesne and, where there were two or more concentrations of land, to retain at least some demesne in each as a focus of lordship. This was clearly the pattern, for instance, in the formation of the earldom of Chester which has been analysed by C. P. Lewis.[36]

Earl Hugh's grants of lands outside Cheshire stretched over a period of years, and at the time of Domesday Book, when the process was still incomplete, he held lands in chief in twenty counties. Some of his most valuable estates had been held by Earl Harold, most notably in Lincolnshire, Nottinghamshire, Leicestershire, and Yorkshire, and these theoretically could have been assigned not long after Hastings. It seems likely that he was granted three coastal manors attributed to Earl Siward in Yorkshire at an early date, too, for the king would quickly have made arrangements for coastal defence. In four counties, possibly five if the identification of his predecessors Eadnoth and Alnoth is accepted, he succeeded to lands held by Eadnoth the Staller, who was killed fighting the sons of Harold in 1068. The manor of Archbishop Stigand in Oxfordshire

---

[33] *DB*, I, 254.

[34] viz. Wrockwardine, Condover, Baschurch, Hodnet, Morville, Corfham, and Chirbury. Maesbury was also an Edwardian hundredal manor but was held by Reginald (de Bailleul) in 1086.

[35] *DB*, I, 254.     [36] Lewis, 'The Formation of the Honor of Chester, 1066–1100', pp. 37–68.

on the other hand is unlikely to have been granted to Hugh before the archbishop's fall in 1070. Cheshire itself was granted in 1070 or 1071. The grant of East Anglian estates which had belonged to Burgheard postdated the revolt of 1075, for they were held first by Count Alan, who had granted some of them to Walter of Dol. Hugh seems to have been given them, and possibly some of the estates of Burgheard's commended men, in the aftermath of the revolt, perhaps to stiffen the Norman presence there.

Hugh's chief demesne manors outside Cheshire were Greetham, Tathwell, and Waddington in Lincolnshire, Markeaton and Repton in Derbyshire, Barrow on Soar in Leicestershire, Coventry in Warwickshire, and Chipping Campden in Gloucestershire. All his lands in Hampshire, Berkshire, Wiltshire, Dorset, Somerset, Buckinghamshire, Oxfordshire, Huntingdonshire, Northamptonshire, Nottinghamshire, Warwickshire, and Norfolk had passed to tenants by 1086. Some of the larger estates in Suffolk were in the hands of tenants, and two of his four estates in Devon were in the hands of a tenant identified in the geld rolls.[37] These manors were relatively distant from his main centres of power in Cheshire and Lincolnshire. Chipping Campden was probably retained because it was too valuable to grant out: it was used, for instance, as the marriage portion of Earl Ranulf II's daughter.[38]

A second case study is provided by the Lacy honour of Weobley in Herefordshire studied by W. E. Wightman. Walter de Lacy's lands in 1086 were concentrated along the border with Wales in Herefordshire, with another group centred on Ludlow in Shropshire; he also held land in Berkshire, Gloucestershire, Worcestershire, and Oxfordshire. Walter's role was primarily that of defending a sector of the frontier against the Welsh. He kept some estates in demesne because they were near the frontier, such as Weobley itself, Ewyas Lacy, Aldon, Stokesay, Onibury, Stanton Lacy, and Bitterley near Ludlow. A second group centred on Castle Frome may have been retained for a different reason, because they were situated away from the frontier and therefore less vulnerable to attack. Other demesne manors were evidently retained because they were in groups. Painswick, which actually was made up of villages covering some thirty square miles, was not far from Edgeworth and Stratton. Quenington, which had a reeve, may have been managed with Coleshill and Childrey in Berkshire. Temple

---

[37] For the unnamed tenant see note to Phillimore edition, Devon 14, 3–4.　　　[38] *Chester Charters*, no. 59.

Guiting (valuable, Wightman suggested, because of its supplies of salt) with Lower Slaughter and Salford formed another group. Wightman drew attention to the reference to reeves on eight demesne manors, and suggested that in some cases they may have been forerunners of receivers for groups of manors.[39]

A third case study is provided by the Bigod honour in East Anglia. Roger Bigod like Earl Hugh had acquired land in stages (see above, pp. 84–5). He acquired at least one manor before the removal of Archbishop Stigand in 1070, and was a principal beneficiary of the estates confiscated from Earl Ralph in 1075. In Norfolk Roger probably held in demesne Narborough in the west, Hanworth in the north-east, and Sutton in the east, possibly on the principle of keeping some demesne in each of the areas where he held land.[40] Nothing is known of any residential accommodation in these estates, possibly because as sheriff Roger had custody of Norwich castle. In Suffolk, Kelsale, worth £24 with the freemen, was kept in demesne, and was still in demesne in the later thirteenth century.[41] Roger's holdings were thickly concentrated round the mouth of the river Orwell; again most were held by freemen. His chief manor in the district was Walton, where there was a castle in the twelfth century, and which was important because of its proximity to the coast of Flanders. In 1086, however, it was still in the hands of Norman the sheriff, to whose lands Roger had succeeded.[42] Framlingham, which in the twelfth century became the head of the whole Bigod honour and the site of an important castle, was held by Roger in 1086 as an under-tenant of Earl Hugh, and he may have been able to convert it into a tenancy in chief after Hugh's death in 1101.[43] At Bungay, the site of a third Bigod castle, there were two manors in 1086, one belonging to the king, the other to Earl Hugh.[44] The inescapable conclusion is that in 1086 the Bigod honour in Suffolk did not as yet bear much resemblance to its organization in the twelfth century.

Some exceptions to the prevailing rule that large or valuable manors were retained in demesne have already been noted: manors near the

---

[39] Wightman, *Lacy Family*, chapter 4.      [40] *DB*, ii, 178, 179b.

[41] *DB*, ii, 153b, 154; *Calendar of Inquisitions Post Mortem*, i, no. 744.

[42] Cathcart King, *Castellarium Anglicanum*, ii, 460; *DB*, ii, 339b.

[43] *DB*, ii, 302b. A parallel case here may be the manor of Whitby which William de Percy held as a tenant of Earl Hugh in 1086 but where the tenancy subsequently seems to have lapsed: *DB*, i, 305; *Early Yorkshire Charters*, xi, 20 (charter of William de Percy for Whitby Abbey).

[44] *DB*, ii, 288, 288b, 300–300b, 301.

border with Wales, or which were waste in 1086, or remote from the lord's principal estates. Some of those retained probably acted as staging posts between principal castles or en route to the south coast and the Channel ports, or were in proximity to principal royal residences. In Hampshire for instance three great lords had demesne manors near the coast and not far from Winchester. Count Alan had three manors in Titchfield hundred near the coast, Count Robert of Mortain had an unnamed manor in Somborne Hundred, and Count Eustace the valuable manor of Bishops Sutton.[45]

## Management

There were various possible ways to manage demesne manors. These can be divided into three broad categories, but it has to be borne in mind that in practice the categories were not as precisely differentiated as we might think.[46] One option was direct management, using reeves, and producing renders in kind and cash. A second possibility was to let the manors out to farm, again for renders in kind and cash. Little is known about the terms of such arrangements but they could be long-lasting, sometimes became hereditary as fee-farms, and could be combined with military service. A third option was leasing, either for a term of years, or for life or lives.

There were various considerations relating to convenience and profitability to be weighed. So far as convenience was concerned, estates adjacent to principal residences were obvious candidates for direct management. Lay lords, like bishops and kings, travelled round their estates eating the produce. Estates situated near large towns might also be profitable, if surpluses were sold at market. Lords may have preferred to maximize their cash revenues, especially if they spent most of their time at court, or in Normandy. Organizing food renders presupposed that a lord's itinerary was well known and habitual; if not, the food had to be taken to him, and here the story related by the author of the *Dialogue of the Exchequer* about the practical difficulties for farmers who took their renders to Henry I's court could equally well have been applied to great lords.[47]

---

[45] *DB*, I, 44, 44b.

[46] Lennard, *Rural England*, pp. 110–11; see also the comments of S. Harvey, in 'The Extent and Profitability of Demesne Agriculture in England in the later eleventh century', *Social Relations and Ideas. Essays in Honour of R. H. Hilton*, ed. T. H. Aston, P. R. Coss, C. Dyer, J. Thirsk (Cambridge, 1983), pp. 45–52.

[47] *Dialogus de Scaccario*, ed. and trans. C. Johnson with corrections by F. E. L. Carter and D. E. Greenway, Oxford Medieval Texts (Oxford, 1983), p. 41.

So far as profitability was concerned, one question was who was best placed to extract the most: the lord, especially if he was often in residence and could supervise directly, or a middleman. The lord could expect a more assured income from a middleman, but this might have been lower than he could achieve through his own efforts. On the other hand, in King William's England there were some who agreed to pay far more than the value attributed to the estate. As Lennard pointed out, a number had names of native origin, and perhaps their consent to pay such high farms was an indication of their desperation and determination to survive in a hostile new world.[48] Another consideration was the market: could surpluses be sold? By the later twelfth century the trend of rising population was such that landlords generally adopted direct management, but was the profitability of demesne cultivation as general in the preceding century? Thirdly, the profile of the estate has to be taken into account: was the situation different for estates with large demesne sectors as compared with small?

Here at least the Domesday information can help, as Sally Harvey has demonstrated, because the numbers of plough teams recorded give an indication of how much land was cultivated directly for the lord's benefit as a proportion of the whole manor.[49] The mean average ratio of plough teams attached to the lord's sector of the manor (his demesne) to peasant plough teams is often 1:2, so that where the proportion of ploughs involved in demesne cultivation was relatively large in proportion to peasant plough teams, we can see that the demesne must have been substantial. On the basis of her calculation of plough teams, Harvey has shown how few of the new lay lords created large demesnes where none had existed before 1066. The three lay landlords with the largest manorial demesnes were Henry de Ferrers at Tutbury and Rolleston, Roger of Montgomery at Montgomery and Arundel, and Richard FitzGilbert at Clare, Hundon, and Desning. She pointed out that at all of these there were large demesnes before the Conquest and this situation may have encouraged them to retain substantial demesne sectors on their other manors against the prevailing trend. Arnulf de Hesdin was another lord with a relatively high proportion of demesne land and, according to William of Malmesbury, was actively interested in agriculture.[50]

Yet were large manorial demesnes profitable? Here it is possible to

[48] Lennard, *Rural England*, pp. 155-7.      [49] Harvey, 'Demesne Agriculture in England', pp. 52-72.
[50] WM, *De Gestis Pontificum*, pp. 437-8.

compare estate profiles with the valuations assigned to manors, usually given at two dates (*Tempore Regis Edwardi* – in the time of King Edward – and 1086), and sometimes with a third intermediate date. Harvey has pointed out that, in manors with a relatively small demesne sector, much of the revenue came from rights in meadow, pasture, woodland, profits of jurisdiction like those from hundred courts, or the dues of attached freemen.[51] There was little financial incentive to increase the size of manorial demesnes unless lords were likely to live in the vicinity for part of each year, or unless surpluses could be disposed of at market. Increased profits came not from expanding the demesne sector but by exacting more from the small producers, the freemen. The choice of management methods for the lay aristocracy depended thus partly on their patterns of migration and partly on the degree of their commitment to maximizing profits. In most regions of the country there was little financial incentive to restructure manors radically. The exception was Yorkshire, where it is now clear that reorganization during the Conqueror's reign was substantial (see above, pp. 104–8).

## Markets and towns

The new aristocracy was far from being disinterested in the wealth to be gained through commerce or trade, though the evidence is largely indirect and sometimes anecdotal.[52] Weekly markets and annual fairs were established on the demesne manors of many of the greater magnates. Principal demesne manors, especially those where building on castles and religious houses was going on, were likely in any case to attract a variety of craftsmen, tradesmen, and those looking for work in the household of the lord or the religious house. Such settlements might well grow imperceptibly and informally from villages to towns. A lord had everything to gain (literally) by encouraging them, not only as a labour force but also as payers of rents and tolls at markets and fairs and at his mills. The entry for Arundel in Sussex in Domesday Book is illuminating in this respect: before 1066 the dues had been relatively minor, totalling £4; in 1086 £12 was paid for the borough and the ship customs, plus five

---

[51] Harvey, 'Demesne Agriculture in England', p. 65.

[52] For a similar point made in connection with Anglo-Saxon thegns see R. Fleming, 'Rural Elites and Urban Communities in late Saxon England', *Past and Present*, 141 (December 1993), 3–27.

shillings for a fishery and £14 for a mill, in addition to which Earl Roger's Norman followers received rents from burgesses there.[53] Formal grants of markets were made by the crown, though in our period they do not appear to have been a necessary prerequisite.[54] Robert Malet, for instance, was said to be holding his market at Eye in 1086 by the king's gift.[55] Many lords had weekly markets on their demesne manors in the twelfth and thirteenth centuries, and fairs once a year.

Robert of Mortain had what has been described as an active policy of commercial expansion, both on his continental estates and in England.[56] Boussard demonstrated the development of markets and towns in the county of Mortain in the late eleventh century.[57] In England meanwhile the count had increased the number of burgesses at Pevensey from twenty-seven when he received it to sixty, and his dues included payment from rents, toll, a mint, and a mill.[58] There were also trading centres at Berkhamsted and Launceston, where Robert was said to have taken the manor away from the canons of St Stephen's.[59] Robert also took a market away from the bishop of Exeter at Methleigh and he seems to have controlled the market at Trematon, too, though this was in the hands of his tenant.[60]

Some lords went further than this and deliberately founded towns. Le Patourel pointed out how the castle-bourg-monastery complex was used by the Normans both in their homeland and as an instrument of colonization and conquest.[61] Lords were able to offer protection in the shadow of their castles, free status to settlers, low rents, and freedom from toll throughout their lands. The classic study of new towns in medieval England by Maurice Beresford indicated that between 1066 and 1100 a relatively high proportion of new towns were founded adjacent to castles, like Ludlow in Shropshire probably founded in the late eleventh century.[62] On occasion, if the castle was resited, the town followed, as at New Buckenham in Norfolk and Launceston in Cornwall. The protection afforded by castles and the stimulus they provided to local service industries is also seen in the spread of new towns in Cumbria and

---

[53] *DB*, I, 23.    [54] Britnell, *Commercialization of English Society*, p. 17.    [55] *DB*, II, 379.

[56] Golding, 'Robert of Mortain', pp. 133–5.

[57] J. Boussard, 'Le comté de Mortain au XIe siècle', *Le Moyen Age*, 58 (1952), 277–9.    [58] *DB*, I, 20b.

[59] *DB*, I, 136b, 120b.    [60] *DB*, I, 120b, 122.    [61] Le Patourel, *Norman Empire*, pp. 317–18.

[62] M. Beresford, *New Towns of the Middle Ages. Town Plantations in England, Wales, and Gascony* (London, 1967), pp. 334–5.

Northumberland in the twelfth century, such as Egremont in Cumberland, Appleby and Brough in Westmorland, and Alnmouth and Mitford in Northumberland.

Towns, whether close to castles or not, flourished for essentially commercial reasons. Bristol was the headquarters of the twelfth-century earldom of Gloucester. The town is not mentioned in Domesday Book, but may have been in the hands of the bishop of Coutances, who perhaps began the castle. In the reign of Henry I it passed to Robert earl of Gloucester; Bristol castle was the earl's headquarters during the Civil War. The town was ideally placed to profit from trade with Ireland and South Wales, and the income it provided the earl was probably already substantial. In the late twelfth century, when we have figures because the earldom was in the hands of the crown, Bristol provided between 19 per cent and 26 per cent of the earl's revenue.[63]

Towns along the east coast clearly did particularly well, despite their vulnerability to attack, especially from Vikings. One success story was that of Boston in Lincolnshire, whose early growth has been traced by Dorothy Owen. Early traders from across the North Sea were probably attracted at first by the prospect of access to Lincoln. Count Alan of Richmond, one of the lords of Boston, founded a fair on his land there which soon prospered with the growing trade in wool.[64] Nearby Lynn also prospered: here, as Dr Owen has shown, the initiative was taken by the bishop of Norwich who saw the possibilities inherent in the abundant local supplies of salt.[65] Hedon on the banks of the Humber estuary was founded by the count of Aumale, was first mentioned as a town in Stephen's reign, and seems to have traded chiefly in wool and hides.[66] Like Boston and Lynn, Hedon seems to have been conceived as a trading place, not as an adjunct to a castle.

Finally, although impossible to quantify, other sources of revenue must not be forgotten. Many magnates owned properties in towns and cities from which they derived rents. The early twelfth-century surveys of Winchester indicate who held property, and the value of the rents they received; though minor by comparison with the values set on large

---

[63] Painter, *Studies in the History of the English Feudal Barony*, p. 166.

[64] D. Owen, 'The Beginnings of the Port of Boston', *A Prospect of Lincolnshire*, ed. N. Field and A. White (Lincoln, 1984), pp. 42–5. I should like to thank Dr Owen for sending me a copy of her paper.

[65] D. Owen, 'Bishop's Lynn: the First Century of a New Town?', *Anglo-Norman Studies*, 2 (1979), 141–53.

[66] English, *Lords of Holderness*, pp. 214–22.

demesne manors, these rents were not negligible.[67] Some lords were entitled to items of franchisal revenue (see below, p. 250). The possession of
hundreds was profitable both financially and politically.[68] By the time of
the *quo warranto* enquiries in the later thirteenth century, many hundreds
were in private hands, of which some, possibly many, had been acquired
in the Norman period.[69] There were in addition the incidents of lordship:
the reliefs which heirs paid on succeeding to their lands, the unrecorded
payments for privileges made to lords, and the presents made by religious
houses anxious for the confirmation of their endowments.

In the first two decades of Norman rule a vast amount of land was
distributed to a new elite, and clearly there were differences in individuals' approaches and commitment. Looking at the midland estates of
Robert count of Meulan where numerous Englishmen survived as tenants,
it is hard to avoid the feeling that these as yet had attracted little attention from their lord, though to be fair he may not have held them for very
long in 1086. Roger of Montgomery in contrast emerges from the folios of
Domesday Book as a radical reorganizer and colonizer in Shropshire,
where estates were amalgamated into new units, compact lordships set up
for his leading tenants, and new religious houses set up using the endowments of minster churches. In Yorkshire also the new lords took a drastic
approach to their estates, building castles and concentrating crop production in a limited number of centres.

Much research still needs to be done on the organization of the great
estates, to plot demesne manors, castles, and the location of tenancies.
Some, perhaps most of those in the midlands and south, appear to have
taken shape relatively early in terms of the overall balance between
demesne and tenanted land. The stock of demesne land was finite, and
further gains were to be made either by marriage, by serving the king, or
in Wales and Scotland. Existing demesnes could be managed directly, and
perhaps this was already beginning to happen by the end of our period,
and in general the lords of the land were well placed to take advantage of

---

[67] For examples, see F. Barlow, M. Biddle, O von Feilitzen, and D. J. Keene, *Winchester in the Early Middle Ages. Winchester Studies*, I (Oxford, 1976), 387–92.

[68] Painter, *Studies in the History of the English Feudal Barony*, pp. 120–1.

[69] For the situation in Yorkshire and Lincolnshire under Stephen, see P. Dalton, 'William Earl of York and Royal Authority in Yorkshire in the Reign of Stephen', *Haskins Society Journal*, 2 (1990), 155–65; Dalton, 'Aiming at the Impossible: Ranulf II Earl of Chester and Lincolnshire in the Reign of King Stephen', *Earldom of Chester and its Charters*, pp. 109–34.

rising population. Certainly the scale of their building projects and of their benefactions to the church do not suggest impoverishment, rather a lifestyle of conspicuously greater grandeur than their forebears.

## Tenants and tenancies

Just as King William had rewarded his followers with land, so the latter rewarded those who had followed in their train to England. Great lords needed and wanted to give; giving was a sign of power and the means of creating and sustaining a retinue of knights, and what the companions of the Conqueror had above all to give (or at least to grant) was land. Yet the Conquest was a one-off situation, and soon both king and aristocracy had to husband their resources of land, making grants to their followers which were usually relatively modest.

There were different kinds of tenancies. The first and much the most important between members of the aristocracy was tenure by knight service – enfeoffment. It was probably on this basis that the more important tenants of 1086 held land from their lords, though this was not spelled out in Domesday Book.[70] It was only in the twelfth century that charters recording grants of land to be held by knight service began to survive in increasing numbers. Secondly, there were those who held by military service other than knight service, such as the riding men of the Welsh Marches, who were lightly armed cavalry more mobile and thus better suited to the local terrain.[71] Thirdly, there were those who held their land in return for miscellaneous ministerial services, such as hunting staff. Finally, there were tenants by free socage, who paid rent, and they were particularly common in Yorkshire, Lincolnshire, and East Anglia in 1086. Subsequently many socage tenancies were converted into fractional fees, making the point that enfeoffment was sometimes only a thin veneer over older tenurial relationships.[72]

If one considers the reasons which led some lords to grant away a relatively high proportion of the lands they were given, high on the list in the years after Hastings was the need to reward followers who had partici-

---

[70] On this subject the most detailed study is that by J. F. A. Mason, 'Aspects of Subinfeudation on Some Domesday Fiefs', D. Phil. thesis, University of Oxford (1952).

[71] For a study of the organization of the lordship of Clun see F. Suppe, *Military Institutions on the Welsh Marches AD 1066–1300* (Woodbridge, 1994).

[72] For a discussion of such tenancies on the Mowbray honour see *Mowbray Charters*, pp. xxxix–xl.

pated in the military campaigns. Some hailed from the lord's continental estates. For instance, we have seen how Robert, count of Eu, granted out much of his land in the rape of Hastings, and the names of his tenants show that they came from Eu and its neighbourhood (see above, p. 46). The defence of Hastings castle had to be provided for, and the count may soon have preferred to provide for this by enfeoffing knights rather than by paying the wages of a garrison. Some lords probably recruited men into their followings after Hastings, including some who had been perhaps landless knights reluctant to return home. Other lords may have been given land by the king with sitting tenants. Possible examples are the men with Breton names on the fief of Robert of Stafford, a member of the Tosny family from Conches in Normandy (see above, p. 76). When Earl Hugh, for instance, was granted Cheshire, Renaud de Bailleul, Earl Roger's man, may already have been ensconced in Gresford and Erbistock, and William Malbank, Earl Hugh's man, may have held four estates in Shropshire when Earl Roger acquired the county.[73]

Some acquired tenancies from a second or third lord as they built up their estates in a particular area. Ralph de Chesney acquired lands from several lords in Sussex. His name was derived from Le Quesnay near Saint-Saens in upper Normandy, and he had probably come to England with William de Warenne, from whom he held land in Sussex and Norfolk.[74] He also acquired land from Earl Roger and from the archbishop of Canterbury, and held part of Bosham from Bishop Osbern.[75] Even men who held in chief of the crown sometimes accepted tenancies if they were keen to extend or round off their estates in a particular locality. Magnates might well have found it politic, or have been unable to resist, granting land to the sheriff, or to men like Robert d'Oilly and Roger d'Ivry who played a key role in the land settlement. Ecclesiastical tenants-in-chief also needed to make arrangements in order to meet the demands upon them for knight service, and it is not surprising to find that they had granted land to important laymen. Archbishop Lanfranc's knights may be identified from a list almost contemporary with Domesday Book, and they included not only some who were tenants-in-chief elsewhere, but also

---

[73] DB, I, 267b, 257b.

[74] Loyd, *Origins of Some Anglo-Norman Families*, pp. 27–8; J. H. Round, 'Notes on the Sussex Domesday', *Sussex Archaeological Collections*, 44 (1901), 140–3.

[75] DB, I, 23b, 16b, 17. Roger de Chesney was one of those who held Graffham of Earl Roger because he granted tithes there to Lewes Priory, *Ancient Charters*, ed. J. H. Round, Pipe Roll Society, x (1888), p. 12.

several of Odo of Bayeux's men, and Englishmen.[76] In Lanfranc's case, and he may not have been alone in this, some enfeoffments were probably irresistible, in the sense that Normans may have established themselves on Canterbury land before his installation, and their presence was only afterwards regularized.

Domesday Book gives an indication of the proportion of the land of tenants-in-chief in the hands of tenants in 1086, though we have no means of knowing if under-tenants were always recorded. The proportion of land in the hands of tenants varies considerably between tenancies-in-chief, and much must have depended on the date when lands were acquired, the degree of the lord's direct concern with enfeoffment, and the number of his own men to be rewarded. As examples of men who had not made many enfeoffments by 1086 we may cite, first, Geoffrey de Mandeville. He had probably received Ansger the Staller's lands within a few months of Hastings, and we have seen that in terms of value he still held a considerable proportion in demesne in 1086 (some £540), having decided to retain the large and valuable manors of his predecessor. This total compares with that of only about £250 in the hands of tenants. Geoffrey is unlikely to fall into the category of a Norman who received his lands and then returned to Normandy, because he had probably had responsibility for the Tower of London. He may, however, have wanted cash revenues from his estates to pay for the garrison of the Tower, and for this reason made only a limited number of enfeoffments. Secondly, Arnulf de Hesdin held about £223 in demesne whilst land worth only £45 was in the hands of tenants. The knights of Arnulf's *familia* are mentioned in the charter he issued in his house at Chipping Norton, and four *francigenae* are mentioned at Ruislip.[77] Yet clearly he had not passed much of his lands on to his followers, possibly because that interest in agriculture on which William of Malmesbury commented directed him towards the development of demesne agriculture.

Others however had passed on a much higher proportion of their land by 1086. In East Anglia, Roger Bigod as we have already seen had relatively few clearly identifiable demesne manors, and most of his income came from rent-paying peasantry. In the south-west Baldwin FitzGilbert had kept land worth only £127 in demesne, whereas £195 was in the hands of

---

[76] Douglas, *Domesday Monachorum*, pp. 36–63.     [77] Round, *CDF*, pp. 431–2, no. 1326.

tenants. Although the latter figure included lands which he had granted to the church, and two estates held by his wife, the total is still high.[78] A little can be discovered about the tenants' origins. Two came from his Norman lordship of Meules: Roger of Meules and Robert of Pontchardon.[79] Four others had names indicating a Norman origin – Morin de Caen, Robert de Beaumont, Ralph de Bruyère, and Richard de Neville; and at least one came from Brittany – Hugh de Rennes.[80] Baldwin had additionally enfeoffed another tenant-in-chief, Ralph de Pomeroy, and a further three of his tenants were household officials: Rainer the steward, Walter the butler, and Godfrey the chamberlain.[81] Colvin, whose name suggests he was English, was presumably the man who received £12 from Queen Edith's share of Exeter and held at least one of her manors at farm.[82] Apart from Colvin, however, only one man was an Anglo-Saxon: Edwy survived on two estates he had held before 1066.[83] This catalogue thus indicates a variety of explanations for the scale of Baldwin's alienations: gifts to the church, and the enfeoffment of men who had presumably followed him from Normandy and of his household officials. Others could have been recruited, inherited, or even have been foisted upon him as the settlement in the county took shape.

After Domesday Book, the returns to the Inquest into feudal service of 1166 are the next source chronologically which provides an overview of the extent to which tenancies had been created. Tenants-in-chief were asked to supply the following information: the numbers of fees created before 1135 and the names of tenants; fees created since 1135; and the names of those whose service was charged against the demesne.[84] The information provided in the returns varies. Sometimes the amount of land is stated and its location, but usually only a name (in most cases the

[78] DB, I, 107, 107b.

[79] DB, IV, 289, 297, 309 (Roger de Meules); 298, 299 (Robert de Pontchardon); for the latter see Loyd, *Origins of Some Anglo-Norman Families*, p. 83.

[80] DB, I, 108 and see note to Phillimore edition Devon, 16, 173 for the indentification of Morin with Morin de Caen; DB, IV, 298, 308 and see note to Phillimore edition Devon, 16, 65 for the identification of Robert de Beaumont with Robert de Beaumont, count of Meulan; DB, IV, 296, 305.

[81] DB, I, 105b (other tenancies held by Ralph can be identified from Exon DB); DB, IV, 296 (this is the only Exon entry which specifically identifies Rainer as Rainer the steward, but he may have been the Rainer who held other estates of Baldwin in Devon); DB, IV, 306 (for the identification with Walter the steward see Phillimore edition Devon, 16, 123); DB, IV, 296.

[82] DB, I, 100, 100b, 106, 106b.     [83] DB, I, 107b, 108b.

[84] RBE, I, 186–445. Knights were said to be 'in demesne' when their enfeoffments were over and above the quota of knights owing to the crown.

1166 holder) and the amount of service is recorded. The returns show that on most lordships in the midlands and the south, many more fiefs had been created than the quota of service owed to the crown (for quotas see below, pp. 224–5). By contrast in the north the granting of fiefs had been slower, and in many cases the amount of knight service demanded was less.

The size of the tenancies, as reckoned in knights' fees, varied considerably. On many honours the returns can be seen as forming a pyramid with a small number of large tenancies, usually dating from before 1135, and a much larger number of small tenancies. Hugh Bigod's *carta* may be used as an example. In 1166 he owed 125 or 126 knights' fees 'of the old enfeoffment', 25 'of the new enfeoffment', and 10½ belonging to Albreda de Lisle which Hugh had inherited from his mother. (It is not clear if there was an established quota of service for this honour.) At the apex of the pyramid of old fees were seven tenants owing between them fifty-nine fees, of whom one, William de Vaux, owed no fewer than thirty fees, more than many baronies held in chief of the crown. William was presumably descended from Aitard and Robert de Vaux, who both held off Roger in 1086.[85]

Whilst the 1166 returns show the extent to which land had passed into the hands of tenants reckoned in knights' fees, much painstaking research bringing in other sources is needed to throw light on the timing and composition of enfeoffments. On the great honour of Clare in Suffolk, Richard Mortimer has found that there were four families he described as 'division I', owing between nine and fourteen knights' fees, of whom two if not three can be traced back to 1086. In division II there were eleven families owing between three and six knights' fees, in division III eight families owing between 1½ and 2½ fees, twenty in division IV owing one knight's fee, and twenty-three who owed less than one knight. In contrast with the larger tenancies, very few of the smaller can be traced back to 1086.[86] In terms of families, therefore, there was a greater degree of continuity amongst the wealthier families, though, as Mortimer pointed out, they too both gained and lost estates. At a relatively early date there were tenants who held land outside the honour of Clare, and this was a trend which continued. The reasons why the lords of Clare granted lands were as various as the size of the grants they made,

---

[85] *RBE*, I, 395–7.    [86] R. Mortimer, 'Land and Service: the Tenants of the Honour of Clare', pp. 179–83.

but Mortimer concluded that the lord was not primarily making the enfe-offment to provide knights to meet his quota. This quota may have been already agreed and apportioned on the lands of the honour, and when land was granted out the burden of service which already existed was passed on to the tenant.

Mortimer stressed that studies of other honours are needed to see how far the situation on the honour of Clare can be paralleled elsewhere. It may be the case, for instance, that on some honours there was a more pressing need to provide for personal service, particularly in the form of castleguard. A list has survived, evidently relating to the early twelfth century, which shows how castleguard at Richmond in Yorkshire was organized. The total number of knights then owing castleguard was 187¼, whilst the quota of service to the king was probably 50 knights.[87] The knights' fees were arranged in six groups each responsible for a period of two months' guard, with larger groups serving in the summer when the possibility of attack from the Scots was more likely. The potentially com-peting demands for service from the lord and from the king were presum-ably sorted out on a pragmatic basis, and although castleguard was later commuted, there is no reason to doubt that it had originated in personal service.

Details of the various tenancies and the families which held them were traced in *Early Yorkshire Charters* volume v. The lords of Richmond contin-ued to retain substantial demesnes at Gilling, the great estate which had formerly belonged to Earl Edwin, but by 1086 a good deal of land else-where in Richmondshire was in the hands of tenants.[88] Significantly some were survivors from pre-Conquest England, notably Gospatric, son of Arnketil who had been a rebel in 1068 and 1069 but whose son had sur-vived. He held estates as an under-tenant of Count Alan, though not always the same as before 1066, and he also held land outside the honour in chief.[89] As in the case of the honour of Clare, it is the holders of the larger twelfth-century tenancies who can be traced back to the men who held them in 1086: Wimer the steward (fifteen fees), Enisan Musard, prob-ably Count Alan's constable (thirteen), and so on.[90] As already noted, the

---

[87] *Early Yorkshire Charters*, v, 11–12, 4.

[88] For a map of the Richmondshire fees, *ibid.*, between pp. 360 and 361.

[89] DB, I, 309b–310, 310b, 311, 311b–312, 312b, 313 (as a tenant of Count Alan); 330 (in chief).

[90] *Early Yorkshire Charters*, v, 17–79, 81–164 and *passim*.

count enfeoffed two half-brothers, Ribald and Bodin; other tenants had names which betrayed their Breton origins like Robert de Musters, probably from Moutières near la Guerche.[91]

It has been pointed out that on this honour there are indications of antecessorial succession in the ranks of under-tenants. Many of Wimer's estates were held in succession to Gospatric, those of Enisan to Thor, and those of Bodin to Torfin.[92] Such instances remind us that although Richmond is regarded as a creation of the Conquest era, Count Alan had succeeded to the role and estates of Earl Edwin. The count built a castle at Richmond rather than at Gilling, and additional castles were soon built elsewhere in Richmondshire, but the shire itself was probably an old unit of lordship where there were drengs, the old ministerial tenants, as well as knights.[93] The more important tenants held land both in Richmondshire and elsewhere in England. Wimar the steward was a tenant of Count Alan in Cambridgeshire and Norfolk, for instance.[94]

The Mowbray honour had concentrations of land in Yorkshire, Lincolnshire, and the midlands. It had been put together from various sources for Nigel d'Aubigny by Henry I before about 1114. In 1166 it was reported that sixty fees had been in existence when Nigel d'Aubigny had received them.[95] Nigel, who died in 1129, was said to have created another twenty-eight fees, and his son Roger de Mowbray eleven and three-quarters. There was an added complication in that eight fees entered under Roger's lands had been carved off for Robert III de Stuteville, a supporter of Henry II, after 1154. After 1166 only four enfeoffments for knight service were made on the Mowbray honour. Greenway pointed out that the larger tenancies were created relatively early, and on the midland estates; some dated from the time of the first Robert de Stuteville and others from that of Nigel d'Aubigny.[96] In Yorkshire by contrast the creation of fiefs began later, and on the lordships of Burton in Lonsdale and Kirkby Malzeard not until about 1150. Most of the northern tenancies owed one knight's service or less, with the exception of the large tenancies of Arches (probably seven fees) and Tison (probably fifteen) which had been tenancies-in-chief in 1086 and were subordinated to Nigel.[97]

[91] *Ibid.*, p. 246.    [92] *Ibid.*, pp. 17–19, 196–8.
[93] Dalton, *Conquest, Anarchy and Lordship*, p. 132 and references there cited.
[94] *DB*, I, 195b; II, 146b, 147b.    [95] *RBE*, I, 418–21.    [96] *Mowbray Charters*, p. xxxiv.
[97] *Ibid.*, pp. xxxiv–xxxv.

In 1166 Earl William de Ferrers of Tutbury divided the list of his fiefs into enfeoffments dating back to Henry I's reign, those made by his grandfather Robert I who died in 1139, and those of his father Robert II, who died in 1159. In the oldest group the largest tenancy was that held by Henry FitzSewald (five fees) and Fulcher his brother was one of three tenants who each held four fees. Their father was Saswalo the Domesday tenant. There were fifteen tenants holding between two and five fees, of which four had been split up by 1166, and nine owing one fee or less. Robert I, presumably between 1135 and 1139, had created seven fees each owing the service of one knight and six owing the service of half a knight, so although the numbers of enfeoffments in a relatively short period seems high, the amount of service was quite low. Robert II had created only three single fees, plus six at half a knight, two at one quarter and one at one-third.[98]

On the whole, then, larger enfeoffments were usually early, though there were exceptions, such as the provision made on the Mowbray honour for Robert III de Stuteville early in Henry II's reign. Conversely, although most of the returns under the new enfeoffment in 1166 were of tenancies owing small amounts, frequently fractions, of knight service, some fractional fees can be found in the early twelfth century, and the obligations can only have been discharged by money payments.[99] On the Mandeville honour, for instance, new fees (that is, fees created since 1135) had been created owing thirds, quarters, sixths, tenths, and twelfths of knights' fees.[100] Similarly, Hugh de Lacy's list of men enfeoffed since 1135 included eight who held not fractional fees but a hundred shillingsworth of land from the demesne.[101] This pattern, with most of the larger enfeoffments dating from before 1135 and most of the smaller dating from afterwards, reinforces the general impression that from a relatively early stage the tenants-in-chief were husbanding their resources, and that when they did make new enfeoffments they granted only small amounts of land.

Enfeoffments made on some honours during Stephen's reign are likely to have been a product of the civil war, and Dalton has argued that when the tenants-in-chief were asked to report on names and numbers of such enfeoffments in 1166 they not only were (rightly) suspicious that the evidence was to be used against them in the form of increased financial

---

[98] *RBE*, I, 336–40.    [99] Stenton, *First Century*, pp. 188–9.    [100] *RBE*, I, 347.    [101] *Ibid.*, I, 283.

demands, but also were sensitive in cases where new enfeoffments had been made unwillingly.[102] He has drawn attention to enfeoffments made in Cravenshire by three competing families: the Mowbrays, the Percys, and the lords of Skipton.[103] Roger de Mowbray in particular had suffered during the war, having had to enfeoff Eustace FitzJohn, by then constable of the earl of Chester, with fourteen knights' fees for the service of eleven, a grant probably made when Roger was the earl of Chester's captive after the battle of Lincoln.[104] In 1166 Roger only acknowledged that two fees (then held by William de Vescy) had been granted.[105] Similarly he stated that William FitzGilbert of Lancaster held two knights of the new enfeoffment, instead of the four which had been granted, and that Robert III de Stuteville was his tenant, though Robert himself clearly saw himself as a tenant-in-chief.[106]

It would perhaps be unwise to assume that in this instance the experience of the Yorkshire lords was typical of new fees in the country as a whole, and the whole subject of enfeoffment under Stephen, the land settlement at the end of the war, and the situation in 1166, clearly deserves further investigation. It is also worth bearing in mind that even in Yorkshire evidence about the chronology and stability of tenancies is very uneven. In the case of the honour of Warter, the nucleus of which had been held by Erneis de Burun, Sir Charles Clay found it impossible to trace any of the later tenancies back to men mentioned as tenants in 1086.[107]

The internal geography of honours is not a subject which has attracted much attention from historians, and the fact that subinfeudation occurred over a lengthy period makes it difficult to see if there had been an original plan, even if modified by events. The shape of the tenurial geography of Shropshire, however, was clear by 1086. Here, as we have seen already, Earl Roger had retained King Edward's lands plus eleven other manors, and he had created three compact lordships near the Welsh border. In each case the chief manors were evidently substantial, though the number of working ploughs compared with the number of ploughlands shows that they were under-exploited, presumably because of their vulnerability to Welsh attack. Maesbury, a hundredal manor which had

---

[102] Dalton, *Conquest, Anarchy and Lordship*, chap. 6.     [103] *Ibid.*, p. 244.     [104] *Mowbray Charters*, no. 397.
[105] Dalton, *Conquest, Anarchy and Lordship*, pp. 242–3.     [106] *Mowbray Charters*, no. 370; *RBE*, I, 420, 429.
[107] *Early Yorkshire Charters*, x, 62.

belonged to King Edward, became the centre of the lordship of Oswestry, and a castle had been built there by 1086.[108] Worthen, which had belonged to Earl Morcar, became the nucleus of a second lordship, and a castle was built at Cause.[109] A third lordship was based on the great manor of Clun, which had been held by the rebel Eadric the Wild.[110] Here also a castle was built.

On some honours, however, tenancies were composed of lands which were geographically dispersed. On the honour of Warenne, for example, it can be seen from Farrer's table that the larger tenant families held land in both East Anglia and Sussex.[111] Similar examples can be found on the honour of Mowbray. Richard de Moreville, for instance, held five fees in 1166, situated in Leicestershire, Warwickshire, and both the West and East Ridings of Yorkshire.[112] One reason for territorial dispersal is that as the lord received his land in tranches, he distributed it in the same way. Another was the need to provide key men with revenues from wealthier regions with the resources to hold down and develop the regions entrusted to them. We have already noted how some of the major Richmond tenants had estates outside Richmondshire, and in the case of the earldom of Chester, Earl Hugh's leading tenants in Cheshire, Robert FitzHugh of Malpas, Robert of Rhuddlan, William Malbank of Nantwich, and William FitzNigel of Halton, held more valuable estates outside the country.[113] Even in compact lordships, tenancies were not necessarily compact. In Holderness, for instance, Herbert de St Quintin held forty-four ploughlands in eleven different places which in total owed the service of one knight.[114] One possible explanation for such dispersal here is that he had stepped into the shoes of a single Anglo-Saxon thegn.

Knights' fees varied greatly in size and value as well as compactness. In Yorkshire it was not uncommon for fees to be calculated at so many ploughlands. On the honour of Holderness, fees were based on a unit of forty-eight ploughlands; on the neighbouring Gant honour seven plough-lands made a knight's fee, and on the Bulmer estates twelve plough-lands.[115] Fees created on some of the estates of the count of Mortain on the other hand were relatively small, so much that this was taken into account when they were charged scutage in the later twelfth century.[116]

---

[108] *DB*, I, 253b.     [109] *DB*, I, 255b.     [110] *DB*, I, 258.     [111] Farrer, *Honors and Knights' Fees*, III, 296–7.
[112] *Mowbray Charters*, p. 264.     [113] Lewis, 'Formation of the Honor of Chester', pp. 59–60.
[114] English, *Lords of Holderness*, pp. 149–50.     [115] *Ibid.*, p. 142.     [116] *RBE*, II, 498.

Dalton has made a detailed study of the burden of service on another Yorkshire honour, that of the Percys, and has demonstrated how the relatively prosperous estates in the Don valley carried a proportionally heavier burden of service than the central zone of estates; that tenancies were smaller in the more remote outposts; and that in Cravenshire the process of enfeoffment only really got under way in the twelfth century. He also drew a contrast between the tenants who held or built up estates which were dispersed geographically and were of sufficient standing to rate as honorial barons, and those who had only single or fractional fees in perhaps one or two vills.[117]

In the Norman period there was evidently no general consensus about the amount of land to be included in a knight's fee. In the few surviving early charters of enfeoffment it is the knight's service not the knight's fee that is mentioned. The lord often granted land for 'the service of one knight', or the 'service of half a knight' without spelling out either the services to be performed or the land which made up the fee. Charters only gradually came to specify terms and conditions, and there is no reason to disagree with Stenton's magisterial pronouncement that the *feudum militis* 'is a conception which gradually developed as the process of subinfeudation went on'.[118] When Mortimer studied the early constitution of the honour of Clare, he could find no evidence for the service of a knight's fee in the twelfth century: 'We have fees, we have knight service, most of all we have scutage, but not the service of a knight's fee.'[119] In other words, in our period it was the relationship between lords and men that mattered; the idea that a certain *amount* of land should be given in return for a knight's service came later.

As will have become apparent, there have been only a few detailed studies of the process by which lords granted out lands, and the terms on which they gave them. The reason is not hard to find: such studies have to be based on Domesday Book, twelfth-century lists of fees (usually the returns to the Inquest of 1166), and reconstruction of the histories of both fees and tenant families. We are poorly informed about the stability of many tenancies, and the continuity of their composition: there is an obvious bias in the evidence towards the more important families whose histories and estates are more visible in the evidence. Much more work

---

[117] Dalton, *Conquest, Anarchy and Lordship*, pp. 120–9.    [118] Stenton, *First Century*, p. 158.
[119] Mortimer, 'Land and Service', pp. 193–4.

could be done on families which held lands from more than one lord. Some were in this position from the late eleventh century, and were likely to have become more numerous as time went on. Dalton has suggested that in Yorkshire under Stephen the great lords competed for the loyalty and service of lesser men, with the result that not only did such cases of multiple homages increase, but that effectively such men to a large extent were able to exercise a considerable degree of independence.[120]

The organization of great lordships in Norman England took shape at varying speeds which depended to some extent on circumstances and personal commitment. For those who were not lucky enough to acquire large additional grants of land, extra income could only come from a more intensive exploitation of demesne lands, putting more land under the plough, or the foundation of towns. Land, once granted out to tenants by military service, produced revenue only on occasion, such as reliefs. In this sense demesne land and that held by knight service form two distinct categories. From the point of view of lordship, however, both formed a lord's honour, the totality of his wealth and power. The relationship between lords and men has been viewed here primarily in its tenurial aspect, yet lordship was much more than this: it was a concept of personal relations in which a grant of land often played no part. In chapter seven lordship in terms of lords and men is considered further, and the theme of multiple allegiances and the potentially solvent effect of civil war on the coherence of the honour is reviewed. In chapter eight the functional aspects of lordship are discussed, not 'power over whom?', but 'power to do what?' In this chapter the question has already been raised about the rationale behind enfeoffment, and whether lords expected personal service or whether its fiscal commutation came to the forefront. Before tackling these issues, however, we must turn to another subject which arises naturally from considering the organization of lordships: the residences on demesne manors, ranging from stone castles and halls to the more modestly fortified earth-and-timber structures of the lesser aristocracy.

---

[120] Dalton, *Conquest, Anarchy and Lordship*, pp. 185–92.

# 6 Castles, halls, and houses

Castles are the most visible reminder left by the Anglo-Norman aristocracy in the English landscape. They are above all a symbol of the domination of a military class, at once residence and fortification. The English
were overrun so easily, wrote the chronicler Orderic Vitalis with the
wisdom of hindsight, because they had very few castles. In the decades following 1066 many castles were built all over England, and by the end of
our period castles were much more elaborate than the hastily erected
defences put up under the threat of English counter-attack. While many
were still essentially earth-and-timber constructions, the richest lords
now lived in considerably greater splendour in their stone keeps. The
establishment of a strong regime under Henry II might make it appear to
have been less necessary to live in castles, but there was no guarantee that
peace would last, and in any case building or rebuilding castles was an
essential dimension of an aristocratic lifestyle.

Did the new aristocracy introduce castlebuilding into England? The
answer to that question by historians and archaeologists writing between
the late nineteenth and mid-twentieth centuries was a resounding affir-
mative.[1] In the 1960s, however, dissenting voices began to be heard.
Questions were raised about the state of developments in Normandy and
in England in the mid-eleventh century. Part of the problem lay in the
lack of a technical vocabulary in eleventh-century writing for existing
fortifications. What was meant by the word 'castle', *castellum*, or *castel*? The
clear contrast that used to be drawn between England (no castles except
those erected by Edward's Normans) and Normandy (already familiar with
castles, especially the motte and bailey) seemed for a time to be in doubt,
as it was pointed out that relatively few castles in Normandy can be
definitely dated to the period before 1066, that the motte and bailey was
by no means the only or even the chief form of defensive fortification in
the duchy, and that in England not all Norman lords built castles, and
some seem to have moved into late Anglo-Saxon thegnly dwellings. A

---

[1] E. S. Armitage, *Early Norman Castles of the British Isles* (London, 1912) argued that castles were an innovation introduced by the Normans.

castle combined both residence and fortification, but these functions could be very variously combined. Some were obviously much more strongly defended than others, and it is not always easy to decide when a castle was not a castle. After all, few men were going to live in totally unprotected surroundings in the eleventh-century countryside. It is tempting to use the term castle of unexcavated earthwork sites, and, having described them as castles, to assume that they must date from after the Conquest, rather than earlier.

So far as we know to date – and only a minority of relevant sites have been excavated – there were relatively few strongly defended castles in Normandy in 1066. Most of those which did exist belonged to the duke or his kinsmen, and only a handful were held by leading members of the aristocracy. Stone towers, *turres*, which were developed in the Loire valley, were as yet few in number in Normandy. Ringwork or enclosure sites were far more common than mottes and baileys. Lesser members of the aristocracy lived in hall complexes with ditches and banks, but not especially strong fortifications in the early decades of the eleventh century.[2] It may well be, however, that the disturbances of Duke William's minority led to a proliferation of more strongly defended constructions.[3]

The best-known fortifications of late Anglo-Saxon England are the fortified towns, defended settlements dating back to Alfred's reign, located throughout southern and midland England and controlled by the crown. Aristocratic residences, such as Harold's at Bosham depicted on the Bayeux Tapestry, consisted of hall complexes protected by banks and ditches.[4] William of Malmesbury contrasted the modest dwellings of the Anglo-Saxons with the Normans' preference for living in stone buildings.[5] It is not clear, however, that the Norman aristocracy had widely adopted building in stone by 1066, and William may have been projecting back-

---

[2] M. de Boüard, 'Les petites enceintes circulaires d'origine médiévale en Normandie', *Château Gaillard*, 1 (1964), 21–36; E. Zadora-Rio, 'L'enceinte fortifiée du Plessis-Grimoult, résidence seigneuriale de XIe siècle', *Château Gaillard*, 5 (1970), 227–39; J. Le Maho, 'Note sur l'histoire d'un habitat seigneurial des XIe et XIIe siècles en Normandie: Mirville', *Anglo-Norman Studies*, 7 (1984), 214–23.

[3] *The Gesta Normannorum Ducum of William of Jumièges, Orderic Vitalis, and Robert of Torigni*, ed. E. M. C. Van Houts, 2 vols., Oxford Medieval Texts (Oxford, 1992, 1995), II, 92.

[4] On pre-Conquest residences see A. Williams, 'A Bell-house and a Burh-geat: Lordly Residences in England before the Norman Conquest', *Medieval Knighthood*, IV, ed. C. Harper-Bill and R. Harvey (Woodbridge, 1992), pp. 221–40; B. Davison, 'Early Earthwork Castles: a New Model', *Château Gaillard*, 3 (1966), 37–47; Davison, 'The Origins of the Castle in England: the Institute's Research Project', *Archaeological Journal*, 120 (1967), 202–11.   [5] WM, *De Gestis Regum Anglorum*, II, 305–6.

wards a twelfth-century development. Thegnly residences again were defended hall complexes, such as that which has been excavated at Goltho in Lincolnshire.[6] There is no very obvious reason why this site, a few miles east of Lincoln, should have been exceptional, but as yet we do not know how common such buildings were.

It is evident, nevertheless, that the arrival of the Normans was followed by an upsurge in the building of fortifications, and that mottes and baileys came to have pride of place. Strong points were built within the walls of existing burhs, and the countryside was dotted with castles in the hands of William's leading followers. How many castles were there in Norman England? Obviously no precise answer can be given to this question when so many sites remain unexcavated, and when we cannot be sure which castles were actually in use at any one time. Documentary sources only mention a minority: Mrs Armitage calculated there were eighty-four dating from before 1100.[7] Estimates of the numbers of castles in England and Wales in the eleventh and twelfth centuries are in the order of about a thousand but, as Richard Eales has pointed out, it might be wiser not to try for absolute totals. He has suggested that there may have been between 950 and 1,150 castles in England and Wales in the period before 1200. Of these, only about two-thirds or fewer may have been in active use at any one time. In other words, Eales concludes that the earlier estimate by Painter of about 500 to 600 castles in England active at any one time may have been about right.[8] This is still a large number, larger than the number of baronies suggested above – roughly two hundred. Even allowing that the top families might have several castles, it confirms documentary references suggesting that honorial barons and men from the middling ranks of the aristocracy had castles. The castle site at Goltho, for instance, was included in the Domesday description of the manor of Bullington, where there were three landholders in 1086, none very eminent. At some stage, possibly about 1080, one of

---

[6] G. Beresford, *Goltho. The Development of an Early Medieval Manor c. 850–1150* (London, 1987).

[7] Armitage, *Early Norman Castles*, pp. 396–9; for different estimates see J. Beeler, *Warfare in England 1066–1189* (Ithaca, New York, 1966), pp. 427–38; D. J. C. King, 'The Field Archaeology of Mottes: eine Kurze Übersicht', *Château Gaillard*, 5 (1970), 101–12; see also G. Harfield, 'A Handlist of Castles recorded in the Domesday Book', *English Historical Review*, 106 (1991), 371–92.

[8] R. Eales, 'Royal Power and Castles in Norman England', *The Ideals and Practice of Medieval Knighthood*, III, ed. C. Harper-Bill and R. Harvey (Woodbridge, 1990), p. 57; S. Painter, 'English Castles in the Early Middle Ages: their Number, Location and Legal Position', *Speculum*, 10 (1935), 321–32, reprinted in *Feudalism and Liberty* (Baltimore, 1961), pp. 125–43.

them built a motte and bailey on the site of the defended hall of late Anglo-Saxon times.[9]

Peaks and troughs of castlebuilding over the century can only be guessed at. Castles were needed where the Normans met with resistance, most obviously in the counties bordering Wales, and in Welsh territory. Here there were mottes and baileys galore, as any distribution map reveals, plus defended houses, and in the fullness of time castles built in stone.[10] It seems likely that by the late eleventh century, and in Henry I's reign, the need for castles to be built as part of the Conquest process was less pressing; now the impulse towards building may have been more a matter of comfort and prestige. Building in stone began to be more common and used not only by top people but by new men and honorial barons. Stephen's reign was another period when many castles were built, as the Anglo-Saxon Chronicle relates under the year 1137: 'every great man built him castles and held them against the king; and they filled the whole land with these castles. They sorely burdened the unhappy people of the country with forced labour on the castles; and when the castles were built, they filled them with devils and wicked men.' The Chronicler goes on to describe the evils perpetrated by the castlemen. Just how many castles were completely new and how many were old sites reoccupied or residences given serious defences for the first time is not clear.[11] Siege castles were constructed *de novo* at places like Wallingford and Crowmarsh.[12] Other castles are mentioned as having been built during the reign, like that at Cuckney in Nottinghamshire built by Thomas of Cuckney.[13] Much must have depended on the local political situation, and it is not inconceivable that many earth-and-timber fortifications which have been assumed to have belonged to the post-Conquest era were built at this time. The motte and bailey at Goltho could, for instance, have been built in Stephen's reign. Not only that, but strongpoints such as church towers could be, and were, taken over.[14] Many lesser men might well have seen the need in troubled times to protect themselves as best they could.

It was not surprising then that Henry II's rise to power was accompa-

---

[9] Beresford, *Goltho*, pp. 85–110.

[10] For example, E. J. Cathcart King, *The Castle in England and Wales* (London, 1988), pp. 44, 46.

[11] *ASC* 1137; see now C. Coulson, 'The Castles of the Anarchy' in *The Anarchy of King Stephen's Reign* (Oxford, 1994), pp. 67–92.    [12] King, *Castellarium Anglicanum*, II, 566–7.    [13] Dugdale, *Mon. Aug.*, VI, 873a.

[14] *Gesta Stephani*, p. 112.

nied by the takeover or destruction of many unauthorized castles.[15] He retained Wallingford, which had escheated after the death of Brian FitzCount and his wife, Devizes, built by Roger bishop of Salisbury, and the Peak, confiscated from William Peverel. Others were compelled to hand over castles: William count of Aumale, Hugh Bigod, Hugh de Mortimer, Roger earl of Hereford, William son of King Stephen, Geoffrey de Mandeville, and last, but not least, Malcolm IV of Scots in 1158. Such surrenders, accompanied by a policy of strengthening castles in royal control, undoubtedly helped to tip the balance of military power back towards the crown, as Allen Brown demonstrated.[16]

The distribution of castles shows considerable regional variations. So far as the borders are concerned, that with Wales was much more strongly fortified than that with Scotland. Castles were needed in numbers in the west because of the numerous settlements to be defended and the need for forward bases for further advance. In the periods of Scots' raids, under Malcolm Canmore and then again under David, there were fewer bases to defend, mainly key strongpoints defending the border or the routes south. By the time Normans began to settle there, opportunities north of the border were not in the form of conquest as in Wales, but of co-operation with the kings of Scotland. Newcastle was founded in 1080 to protect the route to Durham, where a castle was built next to the cathedral, and by 1095 Robert de Mowbray had taken over the Northumbrian fortress of Bamburgh.[17] In the north-west William Rufus built a castle at Carlisle and established a colony there.[18] Appleby and Brough were the staging posts to Richmond, whilst the western route was defended by Preston and Lancaster.[19] The garrisons were generally small, with the exceptions of Carlisle and Newcastle.[20] It was not until the outbreak of more sustained Anglo–Scottish warfare from the reign of Edward I that the northern border came to bristle with fortifications, both castles and tower houses.

The question of the control of castles in Norman England was sensitive.

---

[15] William of Newburgh, *Chronicles of the Reigns of Stephen, Henry II and Richard I*, I, 1, 94, 102; *The Historical Works of Gervase of Canterbury*, ed. W. Stubbs, 2 vols., RS (London, 1879, 1880), I, 160; Robert of Torigny, *Chronicles*, IV, 177, 193.

[16] Brown, 'Royal Castlebuilding in England, 1154–1216'.       [17] *ASC* 1095.       [18] *ASC* 1092.

[19] Appleby is mentioned in 1130 *PR 31 Henry I*, p. 143; for the site at Brough see Cathcart King, *Castellarium Anglicanum*, II, 491 and references there cited; for a discussion of Preston and Lancaster see Green, 'Earl Ranulf II and Lancashire', pp. 99, 101.

[20] M. Strickland, 'Securing the North: Invasion and the Strategy of Defence in Twelfth-Century Anglo-Scottish Warfare', *Anglo-Norman Studies*, 12 (1989), 182.

Although King William clearly took a close interest in the siting of key fortresses, and in the creation of certain compact lordships on which castles were to be built, he cannot have personally authorized the building of every castle erected during his reign, and we may wonder if contemporaries believed he had ultimate control over all castles.[21] In contemporary statements of custom there are very few references to the crown's rights, and those which there are do not support a theory of complete royal control. First, the question of unlicensed castlebuilding is one of the major preoccupations of the 'Customs and Rights of the Dukes of Normandy', written down in about 1091 and purporting to record the customs of the Conqueror's day. Stipulations were laid down about the nature of defensive fortifications: strong sites such as islands in rivers were not to be fortified without the duke's consent, and castles were to be handed over to the duke at need.[22] Historians have usually assumed that if the Conqueror had enjoyed such power in Normandy he would not have settled for anything less in England. But these claims were recorded in a settlement following recent disturbances in the duchy, and it would be misleading to infer from this text alone either that William had exercised a controlling influence in Normandy or that he followed the same practice in England.[23] Secondly, there are two references in the *Leges Henrici Primi* to castles: *castellatio trium scannorum* occurs in the list of the king's pleas, and *castellatio sine licentia* in a list of pleas which bring a man into the king's mercy.[24] The meaning of the first of these is obscure: Eales offers the plausible suggestion of three-fold defences of ditch, bank, and palisade, which would mean in practice sites which were seriously defended; but the second reference seems clear enough: the king could punish those who built unlicensed castles. Thirdly, an early charter reference to royal permission to fortify a castle is that granted to Geoffrey II de Mandeville in the Empress's second charter: Geoffrey was granted freedom to fortify one castle anywhere on his land,[25] though it would again be unwise to infer from this grant, which occurs in a long list of concessions by the Empress, that any magnate seeking to build a castle had to obtain permission. In the early days after 1066, there can have been no objection and every encouragement to building castles, as the

---

[21] Eales, 'Royal Power and Castles in Norman England', pp. 69–78.

[22] C. H. Haskins, *Norman Institutions* (Cambridge, Mass., 1988), p. 282.

[23] Eales, 'Royal Power and Castles in Norman England', pp. 72–3.

[24] *Leges Henrici Primi*, ed. L. J. Downer (Oxford, 1972), 10,1.      [25] *RRAN*, III, no. 275.

Normans needed all the help they could get to make their rule secure –
and perhaps this always remained the situation in the Norman settlements in Wales in our period. But in subsequent decades it was probably
*wise* to act with the king's approval, even if formal permission did not
have to be sought.

Throughout our period castles were a flashpoint of tension between
crown and rebellious magnates. At the end of the day those who refused
to hand over on request castles they held in custody for the king, or castles
situated on their own lands, faced the prospect of being forcibly dispossessed, as was seen repeatedly in the revolts of the period and most
strikingly in Stephen's reign. The king's usual technique for dealing with
those whose loyalty he suspected was to summon them to court, arrest
them, and demand their castles in return for their liberty.
Contemporaries might cavil at the charges brought against individuals,
but few doubted the king's right to take the castles. Even when Stephen
arrested the three bishops in 1139, Archbishop Hugh of Rouen stated at
the ensuing ecclesiastical council that all castles had to be handed over to
the king in times of necessity.[26]

It is nevertheless true that castles were held on different terms and
conditions which need to be taken into account when considering royal
control. A castle built on the king's demesne land (for example, Windsor)
was not identical with a castle built on the king's orders within a borough
but held for the crown by successive members of the same family (for
example, at Gloucester). In the latter case, custom might well harden into
a belief in the family's right to custody.[27] Hereditary castellanships were
different again from castles built by magnates, at their own expense, on
their demesne manors, in which a sense of proprietorship must have been
even more strongly ingrained.

Moreover, there is the further question of the distinction between
castles held by tenants-in-chief and those of under-tenants. The latter, we
must assume, had come into being with the knowledge and presumably
consent of the overlord, but did the king have to be consulted? In the early
days, it was hardly likely, and perhaps it remained the case that the king
expected his tenants-in-chief to discipline their vassals, but this is a
subject about which we know little. One site of an under-tenant's castle
which has been excavated is Abinger in Surrey. In 1086 the whole of

---

[26] WM, *Historia Novella*, p. 33.     [27] Holt, 'Politics and Property', pp. 25–7.

Abinger was held in demesne by William FitzAnsculf. Soon afterwards, however, the manor was granted out to Robert of Abinger.[28] The castle may have had an unrecorded existence within a few years of the Conquest; alternatively Robert may have built it. If so, the likeliest date was about 1090, and we could further speculate that its building was related to the revolt in 1088 of Gilbert FitzRichard, the most powerful lord in Surrey. Rufus successfully crushed the revolt and established a loyal magnate, William de Warenne, as earl of Surrey, granting him four royal manors in the county. Surrey was not a county with many castles, royal or baronial, which suggests Abinger had been built either in the early days after the Conquest or perhaps as a response to political uncertainty.

In contrast, parts of the midlands were thickly scattered with castles. Why were there so many castles in Northamptonshire, for instance? One possibility is that there were many thegnly residences before 1066 which were taken over and fortified more strongly, as occurred at Sulgrave, a site which has been excavated.[29] This was reported in Domesday Book as having been held by four men before 1066; twenty years later, it was held by three men of Ghilo de Pinkney, tenant-in-chief.[30] It would seem likely that one or more of Ghilo's tenants was established at Sulgrave at quite an early date, and in circumstances where defences were needed.

Bedfordshire, according to Cathcart King's calculation, had the highest density of castles outside the border counties.[31] This was a much contested area during the Danish wars, and it has been suggested that Arlesey, Renhold, and Tempsford were constructed during this period.[32] Another possible explanation is resistance to the incoming Normans. If this occurred there is no record of it in the chronicles, but in neighbouring Buckinghamshire mottes form a significant proportion of the total (seventeen out of twenty-three), and many of these were perhaps thrown up soon after 1066 in the face of resistance to the Normans. Alternatively, many castles could have been built in Stephen's reign. Again there is little evidence of military activity in the county, but Bedford itself passed in and out of Stephen's control, and Meppershall was besieged.[33]

In the early days of the settlement, the siting of castles was dictated by

---

[28] B. Hope Taylor, 'The Excavation of a Motte at Abinger in Surrey', *Archaeological Journal*, 107 (1952), 15–43; J. Blair, 'William FitzAnsculf and the Abinger Motte', *Archaeological Journal*, 138 (1981), 146–8.

[29] B. Davison, 'Sulgrave', *Medieval Archaeology*, 5 (1961), 328; 6–7 (1962–3), 333.

[30] *DB*, I, 227.     [31] King, *Castellarium Anglicanum*, I, 5.     [32] *Ibid.*

[33] For Bedford, *Gesta Stephani*, pp. 46–50, 115, 184, 222, 234; for Meppershall see Crouch, *Beaumont Twins*, p. 80.

strategic considerations. Again and again we find that castles were built within existing fortifications, or close to major roads or river crossings. As time went on the Norman kings must have acquired a deeper and wider knowledge of natural features, routes, and of the local distribution of power, but neither at the outset nor later does it seem likely that the Normans located castles according to a strategic master plan of the kind suggested by Beeler, of the defence in depth of London, and of Coventry as a communication centre.[34]

The manors on which baronial castles were situated were retained in demesne to provide the necessary supplies of food; indeed, there was an obvious case for siting castles on valuable estates, even if the location marked a break with the pre-Conquest settlement. In Sussex, for instance, the castle built at Arundel took over the role previously played by the burh at Burpham.[35] Ilbert de Lacy built his castle at Pontefract, close (though not adjacent) to the point where the Roman Road crossed the river Aire, about a mile from the village of Dadesley where the Anglo-Saxon settlement had been based. Similarly, Roger de Bully chose to build his castle at Tickhill, rather than at the settlement of Tanshelf or at the Roman centre at Doncaster.[36] The Lacy family built a castle at Ludlow, probably situated in the Domesday manor of Stanton (Lacy). Where the castle was, the villagers would follow to provide the service industries, as at Launceston in Cornwall.

In looking at the reasons why lords chose to build castles we also have to bear in mind social prestige. Possession of a castle was the visible manifestation that one had arrived. Orderic Vitalis tells how Richard Basset, the sheriff and justice of Henry I and a man of not particularly distinguished social origins, 'bursting with the wealth of England' built a fortress of ashlar blocks (Orderic is very specific on this point) on his patrimonial fief in West Normandy.[37] It is hard not to hear in the chronicler's choice of words a note of disapproval aimed at a wealthy *arriviste* who had returned to the land of his fathers and built in stone to impress the neighbours. It is perhaps even more interesting that it was in Normandy that Richard built this castle. Great Weldon in Northamptonshire was the

[34] J. Beeler, 'Castles and Strategy in Norman and Early Angevin England', *Speculum*, 31 (1956), 581–601.
[35] A. J. Robertson, *Anglo-Saxon Charters* (Cambridge, 1939), p. 246.
[36] M. S. Parker, 'The Province of Hatfield', *Northern History*, 28 (1992), 42–69 discusses the history of the region.       [37] OV, VI, 466–8.

chief centre of the estates which he acquired by marriage, and if he did have a residence there it was not strongly defended enough to leave substantial earthworks.[38]

William II d'Aubigny married King Henry's widow in 1139, and it looks very much as if he then set out to build castles literally fit for a queen. Adeliza held Arundel in dower, and it is possible that William undertook building work there. His chief work, however, was the magnificent keep at Rising in Norfolk, modelled on that built at Norwich in the reign of Henry I. Both bear comparison with the Warenne residence at Castle Acre, and the keep at Hedingham in Essex built by Aubrey de Vere.[39] The few grand castles in East Anglia in the first half of the twelfth century were evidently conceived in part in competition, and their scale, decoration, and layout indicates that questions of social status as well as defence were involved.

The question of castles and *capita* (the heads of lordships) is worth a closer look. In the first place, a decision about the siting of a castle might well have to be taken before the lord had received all his lands, for essentially military reasons, and before the location of the head of an honour had been established. Even a casual reading of Sanders' *English Baronies* raises doubts about the identity of the heads of some honours.[40] The honorial court of the counts of Boulogne in Essex was held at Witham, but there was a castle at Ongar.[41] Although the count held only a hide at (Chipping) Ongar where the castle was in demesne, he held in demesne the manors Stanford Rivers and Laver.[42] The detailed study of more honours should throw light on the question of the siting of castles in relation to demesne manors.

Secondly, if a lord was castellan of a royal castle, this might have had some bearing on the decision whether to construct a castle on one of his own manors or not. Stenton mentioned the case of Ralph Baynard, castellan of Baynard's in London, whose honour was centred on Little Dunmow where there does not seem to have been a castle.[43] A possible parallel case is that of Edward of Salisbury, Domesday sheriff of Wiltshire and possibly castellan of the castle at Salisbury, who does not appear to have had a

---

[38] Sanders, *English Baronies*, p. 9; *DB*, I, 158b; for Mixbury, where his father may have been responsible for the castle, see *VCH Oxfordshire*, II, 325–6.

[39] R. Allen Brown, *Castles from the Air* (Cambridge, 1989), p. 10.

[40] e.g. Great Bealings and Hunsingore: Sanders, *English Baronies*, pp. 48, 56.

[41] Sanders, *English Baronies*, p. 151; King, *Castellarium Anglicanum*, I, 146; *Early Yorkshire Charters*, VIII, 506.

[42] *DB*, II, 30b, 31.     [43] Stenton, *First Century*, p. 45.

castle on his lands, but whose 'fine house' at Wilcot is mentioned in Domesday Book (see above, p. 62). Robert I d'Oilly was constable, and probably builder for the king, of the castle at Oxford. There is no sign of a castle at his chief manor of Hook Norton, but his brother and successor Nigel d'Oilly, who was living in the early twelfth century, had a house at Stonesfield. Presumably they had lodgings in the royal castle and did not feel the need to build a castle of their own.[44]

Ralph de Tosny's situation was slightly different. The chief manor of his English estates was at Flamstead in Hertfordshire where there was no castle. He came from a distinguished Norman family, and was the brother-in-law of William FitzOsbern, from whom he may have received land in Herefordshire and Gloucestershire.[45] Ralph's involvement in the Conquest may thus have occurred at an early date, and he may not have spent much time in England subsequently, for his two attestations to the Conqueror's acts between 1066 and 1087 were both to documents relating to Normandy and issued in the duchy.[46] Flamstead was near Watling Street, north-west of St Albans, and little more than a mile from Markyate. If we may read into the presence of a large religious community and hermits living in the vicinity that this was a relatively peaceful region, and given that Ralph was probably an absentee landlord, there was probably little need for a castle.

There may be other cases of honours with no castles at their chief manors because their lords were primarily absentees. Take, for instance, the Giffard family. Stenton pointed out that although there was a park at Long Crendon there does not seem to have been a castle.[47] Walter I Giffard died in 1084; his son Walter II was active in England, and is thought to have been created earl of Buckingham. He died in 1102, when his son, Walter III, was almost certainly a minor. Walter III may only have visited England at intervals during Henry I's reign, and rarely if at all after 1135 (see below, p. 431). Nevertheless there were castles, mainly mottes, in Buckinghamshire. Hugh de Bolebec, for instance, both a tenant-in-chief and an under-tenant of Walter, had a castle at Bolebec.[48] It is likely, therefore, that the lack of a Giffard castle reflected the family's own history, not that there were no castles thereabouts.

---

[44] *Chronicon Monasterii de Abindon*, II, 74.
[45] Earl William had built the castle at Clifford which Ralph held in 1086: *DB*, I, 183.
[46] *RRAN*, I, nos. 150, 171.        [47] Stenton, *First Century*, p. 64.
[48] D. Renn, *Norman Castles in Britain* (London, 1968), p. 344.

Clearly some men had houses and hunting lodges as well as or instead of castles. Arnulf de Hesdin, for instance, issued a charter in his *house* at Chipping Norton in Oxfordshire.[49] Robert of Gloucester, who added to the defences of his castle at Bristol, had a house at Tewkesbury, probably near the abbey.[50] Not all houses were in the countryside. William de Pont de l'Arche, for instance, had a stone house at Dowgate in London,[51] and Earl Robert II of Leicester had a large hall at Brackley in Northamptonshire.[52]

The basic elements of a castle were simple, but they could be put together in an infinite variety of forms to take account of the lord's military and domestic needs. In some respects it is more realistic to see a whole range of structures, ranging from the highly fortified military outpost that can only have accommodated a small garrison, to the residences protected by modest defences, as forming the opposing ends of a single spectrum, rather than seeing castle and house as two entirely different structures, for every fort had some accommodation, however primitive, and every country residence would have had some protection at this period.

At one end of the spectrum we could put the structure at Clitheroe in Lancashire, a single, badly lit room with no fireplace, reached by an outside stair, over a basement.[53] The Lacy family, lords of Clitheroe, probably did not spend much time there, and spacious and comfortable residential accommodation was not a priority. Clitheroe can never have housed many men, whereas other castles were evidently designed to accommodate much larger numbers.

At the other end of the spectrum is Castle Acre. Excavations on this site showed that in its earliest phase this was not really a castle at all, but a defended country house. It was only later, probably about 1140, that the house was transformed into a keep and the perimeter defences were strengthened with a flint-faced curtain wall.[54] Castle Acre was the chief East Anglian manor of William de Warenne. In Norfolk he did not have many demesne manors as such; most of his land was held by freemen, and some estates where there was demesne had been granted out to tenants. Acre was one of his more valuable demesne manors (worth £9), and he probably decided to build not long after acquiring his lands, for his wife

---

[49] *CDF*, pp. 481–2.    [50] JW, p. 60; Renn, *Norman Castles*, p. 321.    [51] *RRAN*, III, no. 829.
[52] Crouch, *Beaumont Twins*, p. 27 n.    [53] Cathcart King, *Castle in England and Wales*, p. 70.
[54] J. Coad and A. D. F. Streeten, 'Excavations at Castle Acre Castle, Norfolk', *Archaeological Journal*, 139 (1982), 138–201; J. G. Coad, *Castle Acre Castle*, English Heritage (London, 1984), pp. 19–24.

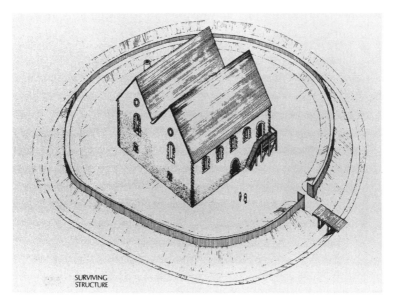

**3** Castle Acre: a defended country house in Norfolk, constructed at the point where a Roman road crossed a navigable river. R. Warmington. Reproduced by permission of the Royal Archaeological Institute.

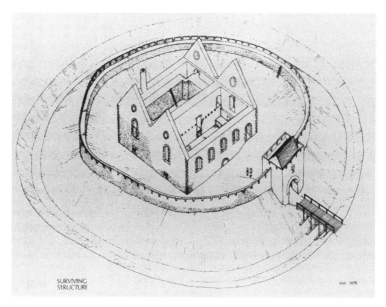

**4** Castle Acre: the defences are strengthened. R. Warmington. Reproduced by permission of the Royal Archaeological Institute.

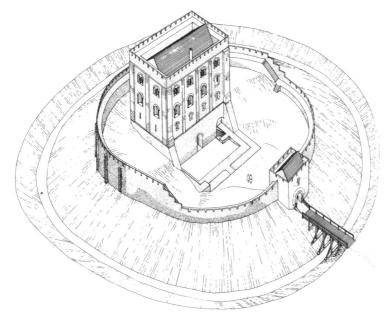

**5** Castle Acre: *c.* 1150. R. Warmington. Reproduced by permission of the Royal Archaeological Institute.

Gundrada died here in childbirth in 1085.[55] The castle was sited at the point where the Peddar's Way crossed the River Nar. A Cluniac priory, originally possibly sited within the castle defences, was founded, but soon moved to a site nearby. The combination of castle and priory was entirely characteristic of the new elite, for the monks could provide spiritual services for the lord's household (see below, p. 392). We have already seen (above, p. 157) how a third element, a town, was not infrequently associated with a castle and priory, as at Castle Acre. The townspeople could provide services needed by the inhabitants of the castle, and, if the urban settlement prospered, rents and tolls to the lord.

In the early days most castles were of earth and timber, and were most commonly of the motte and bailey type. Estimates by Cathcart King and Alcock suggest that mottes and baileys outnumber ringworks in England and Wales by over three to one.[56] It is the motte and bailey castle that we

[55] *The Chartulary of the Priory of St Pancras of Lewes*, ed. L. F. Salzman, 2 vols., Sussex Record Society, XXXVIII, XL (1933–5), II, 18.

[56] D. J. Carthcart King and Leslie Alcock, 'Ringworks of England and Wales', *Château Gaillard*, 3 (1966), 90–127, at p. 98.

associate most of all with the Conquest: after all, the Bayeux Tapestry has a graphic representation of a motte being thrown up at Hastings as soon as the Normans arrived. Mottes vary greatly in both diameter and height: they could be large and high, small and low, or somewhere in between. Cathcart King's attempts to survey surviving mottes led him to the tentative conclusion that larger mottes tended to date from the eleventh century.[57] Certainly on *prima facie* grounds this is not unlikely, given the need for strong defences in the early years, though presumably also to be considered were the workforce available and the numbers of people to be defended.

It used to be thought that the relationship between the motte and any structure upon it was relatively straightforward, that is, that palisades or towers were erected on the top of mottes.[58] This was sometimes the case, as at Abinger in Surrey, where excavation in 1949 revealed a small wooden tower, thought to have been a watchtower, and a surrounding palisade built on top of the motte. Other excavations, however, have revealed that foundations of towers penetrated through the mottes to ground level, as at Farnham, a castle of Henry of Blois, bishop of Winchester, and at South Mimms. Excavations at the latter in 1960 revealed a cylindrical motte revetted in timber which buttressed a wooden tower; in other words, the tower was not built on top of the motte, possibly at a later stage, but was at the heart of the original conception. Entry was by means of a tunnel through the motte into the base of the tower. The castle is thought to have been that built by Geoffrey II de Mandeville as a result of the Empress's grant in 1141.[59]

Many earthworks, however, do not seem to have had a motte. These are the enclosure sites which archaeologists call ringworks. We must be careful to distinguish between different kinds of enclosure site. One type of enclosure was where the main fortified point was at the entrance; another was where the ringwork enclosed a tower or house of some description which fulfilled the same function as a motte. Only excavation can resolve the further question of the intended permanence of a ringwork. Yet there is no doubt that some lords preferred this form. At Richmond, for instance, Count Alan had built a triangular enclosure on a

[57] Cathcart King, 'Field Archaeology of Mottes in England and Wales', pp. 105–6.

[58] Cathcart King, *Castle in England and Wales*, pp. 47–53.

[59] J. P. C. Kent, 'South Mimms, Middlesex', *Medieval Archaeology*, 8 (1964), 255.

**6** Castle Rising: the keep, built by William II d'Aubigny after his marriage to
Queen Adeliza. Photograph: Ian Green.

rocky promontory protected by projecting towers, and with a stone hall. A
keep followed later, in the mid-twelfth century.[60] At Chepstow, high above
the river Wye, William FitzOsbern similarly opted for an enclosure site
with a hall. In each case there was a curtain wall protected by towers. Both
locations were able to take advantage of natural defences, and this may
have tilted the decision towards an enclosure rather than a motte and
bailey.

It was only slowly that the predominantly earth-and-timber castles of
the eleventh century were rebuilt in stone. Stone curtain walls replaced
banks, and were sometimes put on mottes (misleadingly entitled shell
keeps). Stone towers were built, and the largest of these were the keeps.
Keeps were the supreme statement of military power and of wealth, for
only the richest could afford to build them. Although functionally simple,

---

[60] Renn, *Norman Castles in Britain*, pp. 294–5.

**7** Castle Rising: the staircase.
Photograph: Ian Green.

they were sometimes splendidly decorated externally, as at Castle Rising
and Norwich. They were usually entered at first floor level by a staircase
encased in a forebuilding. In England they were divided vertically by a
wall, and the first-floor accommodation thus consisted of two rooms – a
hall and a chamber – over a basement. In the taller keeps like Rochester,
the lord's chamber was over the hall, not adjacent to it. There seems to be
no clear dividing line between keeps and towers other than size: some
castles had small stone towers, sometimes situated on the motte as we
have already seen, and here accommodation was obviously more
restricted. Life in the tower at South Mimms or Ascot d'Oilly would have
been a cramped, uncomfortable affair. Keeps on the other hand presumably held more of the lord's retinue in a protected environment, but the

intended use of a castle would be borne in mind by its lord when deciding what to build or whether to rebuild. A keep would not have been warranted, even if it could have been afforded, on a secondary manor. Nor would it have been justified where there were already adequate halls and chambers, or perhaps a motte which would have had to be cleared before a keep could be built. Thus, only a minority of castles had keeps, and many of these were royal rather than aristocratic.

The starting dates of many stone castles cannot be pinpointed, but it is apparent that some were begun under Henry I. Roger bishop of Salisbury was a great builder. It was he who was responsible for the remarkable constructions at Sherborne and Devizes as well as Malmesbury and possibly the tower at Salisbury, which resembled Sherborne. Both were courtyard complexes more like defended palaces than keeps.[61] Devizes was described by Henry of Huntingdon as the most splendid castle in Europe. A previous castle had burned down in 1113, so presumably Roger began building not long afterwards. Here the decision was to build a keep, eighty or ninety feet high.[62] Bishop Roger was of course exceptionally wealthy, and he was the king's chief minister. Presumably it was with the king's consent, tacit or otherwise, that he was allowed to build on such a scale. Perhaps Henry thought that this was a good way to make wealthy bishops contribute to the costs of defence, for when he granted custody of Rochester to the archbishop of Canterbury in 1127 it was with permission to build a tower there.[63]

Not many lay lords were building stone keeps at such an early date, and it cannot be without significance that amongst those who were were others closely involved with Henry's financial administration. At Portchester, a keep, thought to date from the later years of Henry I's reign, was built in the north-west angle of a Roman fort. The site, overlooking Portsmouth harbour, was convenient for crossings to the Cotentin peninsula, and the landing of Duke Robert at Portsmouth in 1101 may have pointed to the need for greater defences. The site had been held in 1086 by the chamberlain William Mauduit, but under Henry I it passed to his chamberlain and treasurer William de Pont de l'Arche: whether the latter

[61] R. Stalley, 'The Patronage of Roger of Salisbury', unpublished MA Report, Courtauld Institute of Art, 1969.

[62] HH, p. 265; E. J. Kealey, *Roger of Salisbury* (Berkeley, Los Angeles, and London, 1972), pp. 89–90.

[63] *RRAN*, II, no. 1475.

**8** Castle Hedingham, Essex.
Photograph: Ian Green.

was responsible for the keep or whether the king was, is not precisely clear. A priory was established, first within the fort and subsequently moved to Southwick; the land was given by William de Pont de l'Arche, but the foundation was confirmed by the king.[64]

Another early keep was that at Hedingham in Essex built by another chamberlain, Aubrey de Vere. This was modelled on Rochester. In 1133 Aubrey was granted the office of 'master-chamberlain of England and Normandy', and it is possible that his decision to build a splendid keep may have been taken at about the same time.[65] Aubrey was a chamberlain who, like William, had been a sheriff and must have had ample opportunities to enrich himself in royal service. In this context it is also worth

---

[64] E. Mason, 'The King, the Chamberlain and Southwick Priory', *Bulletin of the Institute of Historical Research*, 53 (1980), 1–10.     [65] *RRAN*, II, no. 1777.

**9** Castle Hedingham, internal view of principal chamber in the keep.
Photograph: Ian Green.

pointing out that there is no firm date for the keep at Kenilworth, which could have been started in stone by Geoffrey I de Clinton, another chamberlain.[66] Geoffrey was probably installed in the county by Henry I with a watching brief on Roger earl of Warwick. He built not only a castle but also a priory at Kenilworth and a planned town. If the castle was begun in stone, as is not unlikely, the irritation which the earl must have felt at the new complex, not far from his own headquarters at Warwick, would have been compounded.

Of the other buildings which were part of a castle or residential complex, the most important was the hall. Wooden halls, often aisled and large, had existed in early medieval Europe, and continued to be built in Norman England. They provided accommodation on the ground floor, and an idea of the dimensions can be gained from surviving examples, like that at Leicester castle which measured 76 feet by 51 feet. This dated from about 1150 and therefore was presumably built for Robert II earl of Leicester.[67] Halls built in stone usually had the principal accommodation

[66] R. A. Brown, H. M. Colvin, A. J. Taylor, *History of the King's Works*. II. *The Middle Ages* (London, 1963), 682–3.
[67] M. Wood, *The Medieval English House* (London, 1965), p. 45.

on the first floor, reached by a stairway. The high table was usually at the
far end away from the entrance, and the solar, where this was a section of
the hall partitioned off, lay behind. The dimensions of surviving examples
vary considerably. Substantial ones included Scolland's hall at Richmond,
which was about 56 feet by 26 feet, and that at Framlingham which was
about 64 feet by 25 feet;[68] a smaller one will be mentioned shortly.

Much of the foregoing discussion has centred on the elite, whose castles
and houses have left conspicuous remains in the English countryside.
When we turn from the greatest families to lesser tenants-in-chief and
honorial barons, we find that some built castles, others did not. One who
did was Hugh son of William FitzNorman, the king's forester of Dean. By
1134 Hugh had built in stone at Kilpeck. The shell wall, now ruined, stands
next to a finely decorated church which survives.[69] Abinger in Surrey has
already been mentioned as a castle built by an under-tenant of William
FitzAnsculf, possibly during the troubles at the start of Rufus's reign. This
consisted of a timber tower on the motte. Some of these lesser castles
came into being within a few years of the Conquest as lords and vassals
worked together to impose their authority on a region. Others were a
product of the disturbances of Stephen's reign as honorial barons built or
refortified castles possibly with little reference to overlords.

Other middling and lesser men lived in manorial complexes where
much of the building in our period was in timber rather than in stone. An
interesting early stone hall, however, survives at Hemingford Grey in
Huntingdonshire. This is about 31 feet long and about 18 feet wide.[70] If, as
seems likely, it dates from about 1150, it was built by Payn of Hemingford,
who held two estates at Hemingford, one of Aubrey de Vere and the other
of the abbot of Ramsey. He was sheriff of this and two other counties
under Stephen. This raises two interesting possibilities, one that he may
have acquired the resources to build his hall through his office, and secondly, since the defences of the site do not appear to have been substantial, that the local situation in Stephen's reign was not too
threatening.

It was perhaps about the middle of the twelfth century, or slightly later,
that members of the knightly class seem to have begun to surround their

---

[68] *Ibid.*, p. 32.
[69] *Historia et Cartularium Monasterii Sancti Petri Gloucestriae*, ed. W. H. Hart, 3 vols., RS (London, 1863–7), I,
16.    [70] *VCH Huntingdonshire*, II, 309.

manor-houses with moats. Moated sites are not evenly distributed throughout England, but are very common in lowland areas.[71] It is not exactly certain when the practice of digging moats began, or exactly what their purpose was. They afforded a measure of protection, but not as much as strong banks and ditches; they may have had practical uses such as drainage or fisheries; and, as the practice spread, there was an element of social prestige involved: manorial lords, like their betters, wished to mark out their homes physically from the surrounding countryside.

Castles had come into existence in England as a tool of conquest, the symbols of an alien aristocracy, and it seems likely that this context focussed attention on one particular form of castle, the motte and bailey, which could provide a combination of watchtower and place of last resort with defences for people and animals. Ringworks exhibit greater continuity with the pre-Conquest past, though exactly how much remains to be established. Outside Wales and the borders the possession of castles was confined to the upper levels of aristocracy. The cost of building in stone, plus other competing demands on resources, quite apart from the attitudes of crown and chief lords to proliferation of castles, inhibited their spread. The protracted warfare of Stephen's reign led to an upsurge in fortification and refortification, but after 1154 Henry II fought to recover ground lost by the crown under his predecessor, and it is unlikely that many entirely new private castles were built. By the end of our period, there was a marked contrast between the stone castles of the magnates, which were commodious and embellished with sculptural decoration, and the more rudimentary fortifications thrown up in an era of conquest. Castles remained, however, par excellence the symbol of power and ethos of the military elite.

---

[71] For a brief introduction see D. Wilson, *Moated Sites* (Aylesbury, 1985).

# 7   Lords and men

Lordship was pervasive, a bond which, in a society of orders, ran from top to bottom, and it was ultimately coercive.[1] A lord's ability to command loyalty and obedience, whether from peasants in the fields, from the members of his *familia*, or from his tenants, was the bedrock of his power. In this chapter the focus is on what is in many ways the most characteristic form of medieval lordship: the relationship between lords and men of free birth who offered loyalty and service in return for reward and protection. Within that relationship there was a variety of forms of service, domestic, ministerial, and military, and a variety of rewards, wages, allowances, and land. Above all the grant of land, or fief, in return for military service has come to symbolize lordship in this era.[2]

The nature of feudal lordship at different periods and in different regions has given rise to much debate, nowhere more so than in relation to 1066.[3] The difficulty essentially lies in pinning down, more precisely than the surviving sources permit, the precise nature of lordship in mid-eleventh-century Normandy and England, and thus how much each contributed to lordship in Norman England. Moreover, lordship did not remain static but evolved during the century after 1066. If the followers of the Conqueror gave land in the expectation that their men would rally round at times of emergency, or answer the king's summons to an expedition, was this still the case a century later? As time passed there was the possibility that the tenurial aspect of the relationship would come to the fore, that obligations would be discharged through cash payments, and that tenant families would become entrenched on 'their' lands with a

---

[1] For an important recent survey of the subject see T. N. Bisson, 'Medieval Lordship', *Speculum*, 70 (1995), 743–59.

[2] The classic account is that by M. Bloch, *Feudal Society*, translated by L. A. Manyon (London, 1962).

[3] An extensive bibliography exists on the controversy over the Conquest and the origins of English feudalism. C. Warren Hollister reviewed the debate in '1066: the Feudal Revolution', *American Historical Review* 62 (1968), 708–23, reprinted in *Monarchy, Magnates and Institutions*, pp. 1–16. For a view which saw feudalism essentially as a Norman import, see R. Allen Brown, *The Origins of English Feudalism* (London, 1973), and for a recent restatement of the central issues, and the view that Norman Conquest did not lead to the introduction into England of a novel form of tenure, see S. Reynolds, 'Bookland, Folkland and Fiefs', *Anglo-Norman Studies*, 14 (1992), 211–27, and Reynolds, *Fiefs and Vassals*, chapter 8.

concomitant risk that they would become increasingly independent of their lords. One question tackled here, therefore, is how far lords were still able to discipline their tenants in the mid-twelfth century, given that some, perhaps many, were by this date tenants of more than one lord, and that there were additional avenues for advancement in the king's service. A second question is the extent to which tenant loyalty was sustained over successive generations. Each lord had his own following and would want to reward any 'new men', though his resources, always finite, were often relatively restricted by the end of our period. Other issues include the balance between a lord's 'new men' and his 'old men', the relationship between land and loyalty, and the methods by which loyalty could be sustained.

## Barons and knights

The relationship between lords and their vassals was established by an act of homage or submission and the swearing of an oath of allegiance, followed by solemn investiture with an estate or fief. These procedures were charged with meaning and conceived as essentially personal: one man submitted himself to the power of another and swore fealty to him. Around these ceremonies clustered ideas of service on the one hand and protection and reward on the other, particularly the grant of land.

It is not clear how widespread feudal relationships were in the Normandy of Duke William II's day and, most crucially, how fiefholding fitted into relations between William and the magnates. Did the great families of Normandy hold all their lands 'of' the duke as fiefs? How far did William exercise authority over the vassals of the great men? These are two key questions to which clear answers are not possible. It would appear, however, that in general ducal authority, both over the great men and over *their* men, was growing stronger under Duke William.[4] An analysis of terminology used in eleventh-century Normandy has indicated how the word *feudum* gradually took over from the older word *beneficium* to describe land held conditionally. Secondly, it would appear that the distinction between land which was 'owned' and land which was 'held' was dissolving.[5] At the highest level of Norman society, the authority of the

---

[4] Bates, *Normandy before 1066*, pp. 170–2.
[5] Tabuteau, *Transfers of Property in Eleventh-Century Norman Law*, chapter 5.

duke over the great *families* was increasingly to be reckoned with, as by extension was his authority over their *lands*.

Contemporary sources rarely specify the obligations involved in the granting of fiefs in return for service. In the sense that the whole point of lordship over other warriors was military strength, it may be assumed that lords could summon their vassals to follow them into battle if necessary. Lords who granted fiefs to their men retained certain other rights. In theory at least tenure was for life, and the lord chose whether to renew the tenancy for a second generation. In practice the hereditary tendency was strengthening in early eleventh-century Normandy, and in England after 1066 (see below, p. 337). Tenants paid a succession due, or relief, in recognition of their succession. Lords had a vested interest in securing service, so that if a tenant died leaving children who were minors, or only a daughter or daughters, lords arranged the wardship of the children and marriage of heiresses. Finally the relationship, though subordinating the tenant to the lord, was one predicated on mutual interest. The vassal expected to be consulted from time to time, the lord arbitrated in any disputes between his men, and offered his protection. From the late eleventh century, he might also at certain moments of great expense, ask for pecuniary assistance.[6] These at least were the norms of the relationship between lords and their men, though how they worked in practice varied according to time, place, and circumstance.

In pre-Conquest England thegns held land from lords, and dependent tenure was probably much more widespread than appears in Domesday Book. Some land was held by a privileged tenure called bookland, whose chief characteristics were the right to collect certain dues formerly paid to the king, and which could be bequeathed at will. Other land was held by a precarious tenure, sometimes for money rent, or in return for service. It was evidently possible for men to commend themselves to one lord whilst being in the soke, or jurisdiction, of another.[7] The old English aristocracy was a military elite, so thegns presumably followed their lords into battle if necessary.[8]

---

[6] Reynolds, *Fiefs and Vassals*, p. 154.

[7] *Ibid.*, pp. 338–40; B. Dodwell, 'East Anglian Commendation,' *English Historical Review*, 63 (1948), 289–306; Clarke, *English Nobility*, pp. 61–4, 94–8.

[8] For a survey of military technique in pre-Conquest England see N. Hooper, 'Anglo-Saxon Warfare on the Eve of the Conquest: a Brief Survey', *Proceedings of the Battle Conference*, 1 (1978), 84–93, 211–14.

In England after 1066 the first and most obvious difference was that the terminology of lordship had changed to correspond with the practices to which the newcomers were accustomed. Moreover, lordship and dependent tenure were now universal. The relationship between lordship and land comes into sharper focus, nowhere more so than at the apex of society, in the relationship between the king and his tenants-in-chief. Whether or not the change is to be ascribed to political power or to a set of ideas described as feudalism, the Norman kings intervened in the affairs of their tenants-in-chief in a way not seen before (see below, chapter nine). It can be argued, further, that lords' dealings with their men were in turn influenced by such intervention: the strength of male primogeniture and seigneurial wardship in Norman England, for instance, probably spread downwards from the top. The new lords, though for the most part unable to establish completely autonomous lordships, were nevertheless able over time to impose stricter lordship over unfree peasants and, if they could secure control of hundred courts, they had jurisdiction over freemen in their areas.

The men who received great estates in England after 1066 proceeded to make grants in turn to their followers. Such grants were rarely recorded in writing, for there was no need to do so. Domesday Book usually says only that X held land 'of' or 'under' Y. It is only from later sources that we discover that either from the start or from some date after 1086 the land was held by knight service, and only much later still that something is discovered about the conditions of service. There survives only a handful of early charters of enfeoffment and they were issued by ecclesiastical lords who had a special interest in spelling out terms and conditions. The last thing ecclesiastical lords wanted was to make permanent alienations from the church's lands, though the pressure to make enfeoffments hereditary proved irresistible.[9]

During the century following the Conquest the obligations of tenure by knight service for both parties were slowly defined. The practice of hereditary succession grew stronger, as already mentioned.[10] The relationship between lords and men had to take account of the demands of the king upon his tenants-in-chief for knights, payment in lieu, and for the provi-

[9] For early charters of enfeoffment see *English Historical Documents*, II, *1042–1189*, ed. D. C. Douglas and G. W. Greenway, 2nd edn (London, 1981), nos. 219–21, pp. 960–2.
[10] Hudson, *Land, Law, and Lordship*, and see below, p. 337.

sions of garrison at royal castles. The context of the relationship changed. At the start the new elite was a small minority ruling by military conquest; when the need arose, lords presumably expected their men to turn out for as often and as long as was necessary. A century later, however, the aristocracy's hold over the indigenous population was relatively secure, the state of the country more settled, and the need to summon knights for protection against attack unlikely, except perhaps near the borders with Welsh or Scottish territory.

As mentioned in chapter five, on some of the greatest lordships tenants were divided into a small elite group holding substantial estates and a much larger group holding relatively small amounts of land for knight service. The distinction between these groups corresponds approximately to the two groups who commonly appear in the address clauses of magnates' charters: their barons and knights. The word 'baron' originally meant 'man', but, just as the king's more important tenants-in-chief were described as his barons, so were the leading followers of these magnates. A distinction may also be drawn between those who held all or most of their land from one lord, and those who held land from two or more lords.[11] Honorial barons were themselves aristocrats. In some cases their names were derived from continental places of origin, and possibly they had land there, thus replicating their overlords' cross-Channel interests. They might well have a castle or castles, and although they patronized their overlord's religious foundations in the twelfth century, they also tended to have their own 'family' foundations. Their lands, like those of the king's barons, tended to pass impartibly.[12] They also had certain jurisdictional powers: as Stenton pointed out, these were the kind of men likely to have rights of sake and soke, toll and team, and infangthief.[13]

References to these rights occur chiefly in charters. Sake and soke was the right to hold a court and to summon men to it; team was the right to exact tolls and to supervise sales of cattle, that is, to hold a market; and infangthief was the right to hang thieves caught redhanded. There was obviously a crucial difference between land granted with these rights and that granted without. In the former case the beneficiary had the power to administer justice and to exact financial payments, in the latter he had to accept discipline from another. The rights were obviously not new in

---

[11] Crouch, *Beaumont Twins*, p. 115.    [12] *Ibid.*, chapter 4.    [13] Stenton, *First Century*, pp. 100–12.

1066, and had probably been confined to men and women of high status (see below, p. 246). Amongst them were king's thegns in Anglo-Saxon England, that is, thegns directly commended to the king rather than lesser thegns, and it seems likely that leading tenants-in-chief after 1066, the barons, inherited their powers. Thus although the name changed from king's thegn to baron, there was continuity in rights of jurisdiction and often, too, over the complexes of land over which they were exercised. Barons in turn conveyed these rights when they granted land to their followers, and when charters recording grants become common in the twelfth century, rights of sake and soke were often conveyed. It has been suggested that the assumption by tenants-in-chief of the power to confer these rights on their leading followers or honorial barons was a new development.[14] Through lack of evidence we cannot be sure that rights of sake and soke had been confined to king's thegns, though it is not improbable, and if so, the assumption by tenants-in-chief of the power to grant them out is an indication of their relative independence. It may also provide an insight into the framework of ideas then current: for the newcomers, grants of land at this level were made with such jurisdictional rights as the previous lord had enjoyed. However, if the rights conveyed were substantial at the start of our period, their importance was slowly eroded over time.

The possession of rights of sake and soke is therefore one way of judging which tenants of a tenant-in-chief were honorial barons, though it was not the only criterion. Another was the size and value of the tenancy, though the number of major tenants and the size of their tenancies evidently varied from honour to honour. The return of Aubrey de Vere to the Inquest of 1166, for instance, revealed only two men owing three knights' fees each: Payn of Hemingford, a royal sheriff, and Robert of Cockfield, who also held a knight's fee in Suffolk of Earl Hugh, plus one fee of the new enfeoffment and one and a half knights of the abbey of Bury St Edmunds.[15] By contrast Robert FitzRoy's honour of Okehampton in Devon had nineteen men with two fees or more.[16] Even a simple comparison such

---

[14] Roffe, 'From Thegnage to Barony'.

[15] *RBE*, I, 352, 364, 393, 397; for a discussion of Robert of Cockfield's holding of Bury see Holt, 'Feudal Society and the Family: II Notions of Patrimony', pp. 191–9, and note that Robert's grandfather and great-grandfather had English names, Leofmaer and Wulfric, as Williams has pointed out: *The English and the Norman Conquest*, p. 198.   [16] *Ibid.*, pp. 251–4.

as this raises a question about the qualifications for baronial status. Stenton suggested that an honorial baron should possess land assessed at more than one fee.[17] Questions remain, however: were those who held lands from two or more lords regarded as barons on each of these honours? And what about men of high status who perhaps held only one knight's fee on an honour?

Lords held meetings for their men, the courts of their honour, when matters of mutual concern were discussed, disputes arbitrated, and homage taken. A lord might hold a court when taking up the reins of lordship for the first time, or returning after an absence. Such occasions were appropriate for the recognition of gifts made by a tenant, such as the recognition in the court of Earl Robert of Gloucester of the gifts made by William de Clavile to the abbey of Canonsleigh in Devon.[18] In the Norman period, if a lord wanted to provide for a younger son, he could surrender the land in question to his overlord who would grant it to the son in open court. This meant that the son was not the tenant of the father, and the father had not disqualified himself from inheriting if the son should die without an heir. One such instance of a surrender and regrant is mentioned in a charter of William d'Anisy, a royal dispenser, which describes the procedure as having taken place in the court of Henry de Port held at Basing.[19] Another family arrangement formed the subject of a concord drawn up in the court of Earl William de Ferrers, by which an elder brother Henry allowed his younger brother Sewall to succeed to the lands of their uncle. The reason behind the arrangement may have been to provide for Sewall on his marriage to Maud Ridel, for it was stipulated that if the marriage produced no children, the inheritance was to revert to Henry and his heirs. In return Sewall had made certain gifts to Henry. The concord provided that if either should not stand by the agreement, the earl was to take seisin of the fee until the injury was made good. 'Of this deed and agreement Earl William is both judge and witness, and these are the witnesses, Robert the earl's brother and William Pantulf.'[20]

Disputes about land or services lay behind other proceedings in the lord's court. Where disputes were between tenants, the honorial court was an appropriate forum for their resolution, as Henry I's writ for the

---

[17] Stenton, *First Century*, p. 98.     [18] *Gloucester Charters*, no. 44.

[19] *Sir Christopher Hatton's Book of Seals*, ed. L. C. Loyd and F. M. Stenton (Northamptonshire Record Society and Oxford, 1950), no. 301; the case is discussed by Stenton, *First Century*, p. 55.     [20] *Ibid.*, pp. 51–4.

shire and hundred courts had recognized.[21] Who better to adjudicate than
the peers of the honour? Sometimes the outcome was recorded in the
form of a concord promulgated in the lord's court. One often-cited case is
the settlement, probably dating from the closing years of Stephen's reign,
arranged in the court of Earl William de Roumare at Bolingbroke in
Lincolnshire. The parties were Roger of Benniworth and Peter of Goxhill
who were in dispute over the land of Gervase of Halton and the inheritance of Odo of Benniworth (Roger's grandfather). The text carefully
spelled out the terms and conditions of the agreement reached, and each
of the principals and one other pledged to keep the agreement.[22] It was
this case which drew Stenton to comment that 'the honour of Bolingbroke
was a feudal state in miniature', 'independent of the king's direction or
control'.[23] Crouch has pointed out that Robert II earl of Leicester's court
evidently had a high reputation, to judge from the number of surviving
concords drawn up there.[24] In the circumstances of Stephen's reign, Earl
Robert's authority may have been the most effective locally in ensuring a
judgement was carried out, and when he became chief justiciar under
Henry II it was obviously convenient for his tenants to attend his court in
the midlands.

It is virtually impossible to reconstruct the range of options open to liti-
gants in a given set of circumstances. Certainly there were alternatives to
the honorial court. One possibility was to remove actions to the shire
court by a procedure known as *tolt*.[25] Another was for a litigant to obtain a
royal writ, often a writ of right. Although this did not in itself mean that
the action was removed to the king's court, contempt of the writ was a
royal plea and so justiciable in the king's court. The writ was thus a useful
means of putting pressure on one's opponent, and the sums accounted for
such writs in 1130 suggest that they were not difficult to obtain.[26]

It is particularly difficult to assess how effective lords were in disciplin-
ing their tenants. If a tenant refused or disputed service, or made an
unauthorized grant of land, what options were open to the lord? S. F. C.
Milsom argued that tenants by knight service were tenants for life

[21] Stubbs, *Select Charters*, p. 122.     [22] Stenton, *First Century*, pp. 47–51.
[23] *Ibid.*, p. 51; further light on the context is shed by Dalton, 'Aiming at the Impossible', pp. 115–17.
[24] Crouch, *Beaumont Twins*, pp. 159–62.     [25] Hudson, *Land, Law, and Lordship*, pp. 136–7.
[26] Green, *Government of England*, pp. 103–5. The going rate for a writ of right at that time seems to have
been ten marks (£6 13s. 4d.).

without security or rights of ownership, and that it was the introduction of new legal processes under Henry II which helped to strengthen the position of tenants, and then unintentionally. Henry did not set out to reduce honorial autonomy but to make seigneurial jurisdiction work. The new procedures, however, came to be used in such a way as to diminish lords' ability to discipline tenants and to choose successors.[27]

In practice, however, lords were not as free to discipline unsatisfactory tenants, to prevent their tenants from making alienations (thus adding another link in the tenurial chain), or to choose their tenants' successors as Milsom has suggested. Nor were lords able to secure performance of services or revoke unauthorized grants in all cases. Disputes figure in the sources, though all too often we do not know the outcome.[28] Much doubtless depended on the status of the lord and his tenant and the circumstances of the case. Not infrequently the king was called upon to intervene. Often this intervention took the form of a writ of right addressed to the court holder and instructing him 'to do right'. As noted above, failure to obey the king's writ constituted a royal plea, and the action could then be raised in the king's court. The number of payments on the 1130 pipe roll *pro recto* tends to suggest that such intervention was by no means unusual.[29] Lords' powers to take action against unsatisfactory tenants were also limited in practice by norms about what was considered to be reasonable. A lord was not expected to take the extreme action of dispossessing a tenant of his land without a judicial hearing.[30]

It has also been argued persuasively that hereditary succession was relatively strong in Norman England, and that a tenant who fulfilled his obligations and died leaving an adult son could reasonably expect that son to be recognized as his successor. Where succession was less straightforward there was more scope for lords to intervene, but the presumption nevertheless was in favour of inheritance.[31] If hereditary succession was already strong by 1135, then the lord's power over the choice of a successor to a fief was relatively restricted. Tenants who defaulted on their service were at risk of disseisin, but here too it was thought appropriate that disseisin should not be purely arbitrary, but should be preceded by a

[27] Milsom, *Legal Framework of English Feudalism*, pp. 179–86.
[28] *Ibid.*, chapter 4; Hudson, *Land, Law, and Lordship*, chapters 5–8.
[29] Green, *Government of England*, pp. 102–3.
[30] Hudson, *Land, Law, and Lordship*, pp. 22–51.     [31] *Ibid.*, chapters 3–4.

judicial hearing. The protracted uncertainties of Stephen's reign may have made it more difficult for some lords, perhaps especially those in regions of divided loyalties, to secure the performance of services (see below, p. 318). In this context the development of the action of novel disseisin helped lords against recalcitrant tenants as it did tenants against arbitrary lords.

Moreover, there is evidence that during the civil war some lords had tenants foisted upon them. Roger de Mowbray, for instance, was forced to allow Robert III de Stuteville to have a share in the Mowbray lands after 1154, thus reversing the confiscation of the lands of Robert I de Stuteville in 1106 (see above, p. 166). Roger also had to accept the presence of William of Lancaster at Burton in Lonsdale, and this was converted into a tenancy of two knights' fees.[32] Finally, Roger was compelled to grant Eustace FitzJohn land on terms disadvantageous to himself whereby Eustace owed only eleven knights' fees instead of the fourteen expected by the king. The grant probably occurred when Roger was the prisoner of Ranulf of Chester in 1141.[33] Yet such pressures had probably been there from the start in 1066. No lord was immune to the pressure of powerful neighbours, or from the king. A few tenants-in-chief found that their service was assigned by the king to new lords, an act which demonstrated strikingly the royal power to intervene in the hierarchy of service. The difference under Stephen may have been that the king ceased to be able to act in this way, and his power passed to others, not that the abilities to alter the terms of service or to insert mesne tenants were in themselves novel.

All this having been said, it may be that recent writers such as Dalton and Hudson have taken an overly pessimistic view of the effectiveness of the honorial court and the related issue of the lord's discipline over his tenants. Honorial jurisdiction did not exist in a vacuum, but honorial courts were not necessarily less effective than the alternatives. Lords could offer an arbitration service, publicity and ratification for family arrangements, and a regional forum for the expression of solidarity. Such solidarity might be strengthened during a minority, when honorial

---

[32] *Mowbray Charters*, no. 370, where it is suggested that Roger de Mowbray recovered Burton in 1149. In fact it seems more likely that William of Lancaster had simply taken these estates at an earlier date and that Roger now had to accept him as tenant. William was the chief lord of north Lancashire which was in Scots control by 1141.      [33] *Ibid.*, pp. xxvii–xxviii.

barons might have a specially important role to play. On a lordship where there was a distinct group of tenants who were wholly or primarily of that lordship, intra-honorial loyalty might be relatively strong, perhaps less so where tenancies were smaller, or shared with neighbouring lordships; but until there are more studies of honorial communities it would be premature to write off the honour.

One way of assessing the strength of continuing links between lords and tenant families is by their presence in the witness lists of surviving documents issued in the name of lords. This evidence must be used with caution.[34] As in the case of royal acts, far more survive for ecclesiastical beneficiaries than for laymen, and the possibility that different kinds of witnesses would be used for different beneficiaries has to be borne in mind. Secondly, we have to consider not only the differing character of the documents concerned, but also the peripatetic nature of the baronial lifestyle. How did the composition of retinues of lords with large estates on both sides of the Channel differ from that of lords whose estates were situated in England? How effectively did lords who had estates in England but chose to live in Normandy, such as Walter III Giffard, maintain contact with their tenants in England? Moreover, the great increase in survival of such documents towards the end of our period has to be borne in mind: there are very few documents, relatively speaking, for the first generation of the new elite, and one has to consider the possibility that the context which prompted the issuing of documents changed during the course of a century. The documents issued by some great lords in Stephen's reign were attested by middling and lesser lords who were not their tenants. Was their presence recorded because beneficiaries were worried about the possibility of a challenge to gifts in uncertain times, or should it be interpreted as a reflection of local or regional affinities, that is, of changes in the character of lordship?

The number of surviving acts for individuals who were contemporaries varies considerably. At one end of the spectrum was someone like Roger de Mowbray, a great lord who was a prolific benefactor of religious houses which preserved his acts carefully. There are almost three hundred surviving in the edition by Diana Greenway, dating between 1138 and 1186, when Roger took the cross, an average of approximately seven a year.

---

[34] On this subject see D. Postles, 'Choosing Witnesses in Twelfth-Century England', *Irish Jurist*, new series, 23 (1988), 330–46.

There are some eighty known for his contemporary Ranulf II earl of Chester dating between 1129 and 1153, an average of fewer than four a year. For Baldwin de Redvers between about 1110 and 1155 there are only twenty-five, less than one a year. For Robert earl of Gloucester, between about 1126 and 1147 there are only seventeen surviving, particularly disappointing in view of his political importance. Moreover not all surviving texts have full witness lists.

As yet there are only a handful of published editions of acts of particular lordships in the relevant period, and even fewer analyses of the witness lists. The studies by Keith Stringer of the acts of Earl David of Huntingdon and by Grant Simpson of Roger de Quincy earl of Winchester supply models which could be used for further studies.[35] So far as the Anglo-Norman era is concerned, Robert Bearman has studied the acts of Baldwin de Redvers, who died in 1155, and other historians such as David Crouch and Hugh Thomas have used charter evidence to study the composition of individual magnates' retinues.[36] More studies are needed, however, particularly of different kinds of lordships, cross-Channel as compared with England or Normandy, lordships where there was much sharing of tenants with neighbours compared with those lords whose tenants held primarily of them, and, most crucially of all, of small lordships (if particularly well-documented instances could be found) to compare with large.

The first question which arises, therefore, is whether the acts indicate continuing links between overlords and their tenants: did these remain relatively strong throughout our period, particularly in the case of the more important families who were themselves aristocrats, the honorial barons? Did a change of dynasty have any effect on relations with tenants? The Warenne earls of Surrey, whose charters were collected by Sir Charles Clay, were a family of the first importance with large estates in Normandy and England.[37] In England most of the tenancies which were created were in Sussex (the rape of Lewes) and East Anglia; Wakefield and Conisborough

[35] K. J. Stringer, *Earl David of Huntingdon 1152–1219* (Edinburgh, 1985); G. Simpson, 'The Familia of Roger de Quincy Earl of Winchester and Constable of Scotland', *Studies in the Nobility of Medieval Scotland*, ed. K. J. Stringer (Edinburgh, 1985), pp. 102–30.

[36] R. Bearman, 'Baldwin de Redvers', *Anglo-Norman Studies*, xviii (1995), 19–46; D. Crouch, 'Debate. Bastard Feudalism Revised', *Past and Present*, 131 (May 1991), p. 173 (Earl Roger of Hereford); Crouch, *William Marshal* (London, 1990); Thomas, *Vassals, Heiresses, Crusaders, and Thugs*, chapter 1.

[37] *Early Yorkshire Charters*, VIII.

in Yorkshire were probably held for the service of only two knights; no
return was made to the Inquest of 1166. Sixteen documents[38] survive
issued by William II de Warenne (1088–1138), and there are sixteen individuals whose names indicate an origin from Warenne estates: Robert de
Beuzeville,[39] Osbern de Cailly,[40] Ralph and John de Chesney,[41] Robert
d'Esneval,[42] Hugh de Grigneuseville and Walter,[43] Robert de Mortemer
(presumably from Mortemer, the ducal castle entrusted to William I de
Warenne), Geoffrey de Pierrepont, William his son, Nigel his son-in-law,
and Robert de Pierrepont,[44] Waukelin de Rosay,[45] Hugh de Wanci,[46]
Drohard of Wakefield, and Ralph of (Castle) Acre. Ralph de Chesney,
Geoffrey de Pierrepont, and Hugh de Wanci came from leading tenant
families.[47] Given that the number of surviving texts is small, it is not surprising that most of these witnessed only once or twice. For William II's
son, William III, who died in 1148, there are eighteen documents, sixteen
of which have witness lists.[48] The witnesses include Osbert and Simon de
Cailly, Ralph, John, and Philip de Chesney, Robert de Frievill (six times),
Robert, Hugh, and William de Pierrepont, and Robert d'Esneval (five
times). Guy de Mencecourt sheriff of Lewes occurs three times and
William his son, also probably sheriff, three times.[49] Adam de Poynings
occurs three times, and John once.[50] This suggests that in certain tenant
families links remained strong until the mid-twelfth century.

Fifteen of Robert of Gloucester's acts have witness lists, though three of
these have only one witness.[51] Like William II de Warenne, Robert had
estates in Normandy, the honours of Evrecy and Saint-Scholasse-sur-

---

[38] *Ibid.*, VIII, nos. 10–13, 15–21, 23, 25–8. No. 10 was witnessed only by the archbishop of Canterbury and
no. 21 only by Countess Isabel.        [39] *Ibid.*, VIII, 70–1; Loyd, *Origins of Some Anglo-Norman Families*, p. 19.

[40] *Early Yorkshire Charters*, VIII, 78; Loyd, *Origins of Some Anglo-Norman Families*, p. 22.

[41] *Early Yorkshire Charters*, VIII, 58–9, 63, 70–2; Loyd, *Origins of Some Anglo-Norman Families*, pp. 27–8; J. H.
Round, 'Notes on the Sussex Domesday', *Sussex Archaeological Collections* (1901), 140–3.

[42] *Early Yorkshire Charters*, VIII, 2, 75; in the list of knights of Bellencombre drawn up for Philip Augustus,
Robert de Wesnevalle held half a knight's fee: *Receuil des historiens des Gaules et de la France*, ed. M.
Bouquet and others, 24 vols. (Paris, 1869–1904), XXIII, 708.

[43] *Early Yorkshire Charters*, VIII, 70, 75, 81; Loyd, *Origins of Some Anglo-Norman Families*, p. 48.

[44] *Early Yorkshire Charters*, VIII, 58–9, 65, 70, 71, 72, 73; Loyd, *Origins of Some Anglo-Norman Families*, p. 78.

[45] *Early Yorkshire Charters*, VIII, 77; Loyd, *Origins of Some Anglo-Norman Families*, pp. 86–7.

[46] *Early Yorkshire Charters*, VIII, 58–9, 77; Loyd, *Origins of Some Anglo-Norman Families*, p. 111.

[47] Farrer, *Honors and Knights' Fees*, III, 305–6, 313–22, 331–3, 380–2.

[48] *Early Yorkshire Charters*, VIII, nos. 30, 32, 33, 34, 35, 36, 37, 38, 39, 41, 42, 43, 44, 45, 46, 47.

[49] *Ibid.*, VIII, 76, 85–7, 241–2.

[50] *Ibid.*, VIII, nos. 32–4, 43; Farrer, *Honors and Knights' Fees*, III, 327 ff; Loyd, *Origins of Some Anglo-Norman
Families*, pp. 82–3.

[51] *Gloucester Charters*, nos. 1, 2, 68, 70, 83, 84, 85, 95, 109, 110, 119, 152, 156, 157, 166, 283.

Sarthe, and also held for a time other temporalities belonging to the bishopric of Bayeux; and in Wales he held Glamorgan. In 1166 a return was made by his son William to the Inquest into feudal service.[52] One tenant, Jordan Sor, held fifteen fees; six tenants – Robert de la Mare, Walter de Clavile, William son of Robert son of Roger, Elias *aureis testiculis*, William FitzJohn, and Richard of St Quentin – held ten knights' fees; four – Gilbert d'Umfraville, Robert de Gournay (at an earlier date), the son of William FitzBaldwin, and Robert de Maisi – held nine fees; Poyns son of Simon held eight; the fief which had previously belonged to Richard de Grainville owed seven fees, as did that of Adam de Sumeri, and so on. Amongst the witnesses to Robert's acts were Robert FitzRoger, Robert de Clavile, William FitzJohn, Richard and Robert de Grainville (Richard was the earl's constable), Geoffrey de Maisi, Richard de St Quentin, Odo and Robert Sor, and Gilbert d'Umfraville. In other words, given the small number of surviving documents to work from, there is a reasonable correlation between the most important tenants and the witness lists. There is no sign of Robert de la Mare, Robert de Gournay, the unnamed son of William FitzBaldwin, or Adam de Sumeri. Robert de Gournay, however, appears in a charter of Earl William, as does Symon Poinz.[53] Other lesser tenants appear in the witness lists: Gregory, who may have been the man of that name who held one knight's fee, Osbert Huitdeniers the sheriff of London who held a knight's fee in Kent, Fulk FitzWarin (one knight's fee of the new enfeoffment), and Robert Norensis the sheriff of Glamorgan (two fees). Maurice of London was the father of William of London who held four fees in 1166.[54] Hugh de Guminvilla the constable is perhaps to be identified with Hugh de Gundeville who held a knight's fee of the new enfeoffment.

Among those who tended to witness often were household officials, and some tenant families developed particular traditions of service to their lords by providing such officials over several generations. Ranulf II's steward Robert was the son of an earlier steward, and head of one of the leading families of Cheshire, the Montalt family, with a castle at Mold.[55] The lords of Holderness in the early twelfth century recruited two

---

[52] *RBE*, I, 288–92.     [53] *Gloucester Charters*, nos. 5, 189.
[54] Maurice was the founder of Ewenny Priory, *Gloucester Charters*, no. 68; *Historia et Cartularium Monasterii Sancti Petri Gloucestriae*, I, 284.
[55] English, *Lords of Holderness*, p. 67; C. Clay and D. Greenway, *Early Yorkshire Families*, Yorkshire Archaeological Society (Wakefield, 1973), p. 78.

stewards, Peter and Everard de Ros, from a leading tenant family in Holderness. Ralph, the butler of Robert count of Meulan and of his son Robert II of Leicester, was a major tenant of theirs.[56] Great lords were free to take on new men as household officials – in this sense magnate households developed on similar lines to the king's household – but traditions of service in particular families helped to keep the bonds with their lords vital.

The witness lists of surviving documents may not be a wholly accurate picture of the lord's entourage, and in particular may give undue prominence to tenants, in that most related to land transactions and were settled in full meetings of the lord's court which tenants probably took care to attend. Documents which were of only ephemeral importance and possibly witnessed by household officers are less likely to have survived. A comparison between lay lords' documents and those issued in the king's name is useful here, in that executive orders had shorter witness lists than formal diplomas, which were much more fully attested. Nevertheless the impression gained from reading witness lists is that honorial barons (or most of them) continued to put in an appearance at lords' courts from time to time, and therefore that the bonds between lords and their honorial barons continued to be of some importance down to the end of our period.

## Members of the household and following

On most honours the steward was the most important official. Whereas the king had several stewards, most lords only had one at any given time, although Crouch has shown in the case of the Beaumont twins that Waleran count of Meulan had a steward who travelled in his household, and two others, one for Meulan, and one for the Gournay estates. His twin, Robert II earl of Leicester, also had two stewards.[57] As in the royal household, some stewardships became hereditary whereas others were held at pleasure. Three members of the d'Amory family are found attesting as stewards of the honour of Gloucester, first, Gilbert, in the time of Robert FitzHaimon, followed in Earl Robert's lifetime by Hubert, who also served Earl William, and then Robert. For a time Hubert and Robert evidently served together. Only one reference (no. 16) connects the family with land,

---

[56] Crouch, *Beaumont Twins*, p. 40 n.    [57] *Ibid.*, pp. 139–42.

and this was in Glamorgan, which suggests that they were not honorial barons.[58] Two other stewards are mentioned in Robert's *acta*. One was known only as William the steward.[59] The other, Geoffrey de Waterville, was a younger son of a family holding as under-tenants of Peterborough Abbey.[60] This is an interesting case where a great magnate recruited a key official from outside his own estates. Robert had land in Northamptonshire as did Geoffrey, and it was presumably this connection which brought the latter to the earl's attention.[61]

There were exceptions to the custom that the steward was a lord's chief officer, and these probably arose, as Crouch has suggested, because of the influence of individual officials early in an honour's history.[62] The constable's duties encompassed both command of the knights of the household and the garrisoning of castles, and this must have brought him into a close relationship with his lord. The constable and not the steward was the principal officer on the northern honours of Mowbray, Chester, and in the household of the king of Scots, at least until 1162. Roger de Mowbray's constable from about 1154 to about 1186, Robert de Daiville, was evidently his lord's constant companion, and Greenway has pointed out that he was the first lay witness in fifty charters. He also held five knights' fees in 1166.[63]

In the case of the earldom of Leicester under Robert II it was the butler who seems to have been the principal official in charge of the honour.[64] The butler's office usually carried less prestige than the stewardship or the constableship, but Ralph the butler seems to have been pre-eminent in the earl's household until his retirement to the abbey he had founded at Alcester in about 1140. Robert, the butler of Ranulf II of Chester, was the most frequent witness of that earl's *acta* (32 occurrences), and, we must assume, his constant companion.[65] He was not Ranulf's only butler, however; a William the butler also appeared as a witness to a charter

---

[58] *Chronicon Monasterii de Abingdon*, II, 96, a charter of Robert FitzHaimon confirming a grant of Gilbert his steward; Gilbert, *Gloucester Charters*, nos. 166, 283; Hubert, nos. 84, 95, 119, and cf. no. 12 where he was addressed in a charter of Earl William; nos. 5, 71, 124, 280 with Robert d'Amory; both were witnesses and pledges of no. 96, the treaty between Earl William of Gloucester and Earl Roger of Hereford; Robert, nos. 7, 34, 35, 36, 43, 69, 98, 168, 192. William d'Amory witnessed two charters of Earl William, nos. 77, 115.     [59] *Gloucester Charters*, no. 157.

[60] E. King, 'Dispute Settlement in Norman England', *Anglo-Norman Studies*, 14 (1992), 115.

[61] *PR 31 Henry I*, p. 86.     [62] Crouch, 'Administration of the Norman Earldom of Chester', pp. 74–5.

[63] *Mowbray Charters*, p. lx; *RBE*, I, 419.     [64] Crouch, *Beaumont Twins*, p. 175.

[65] *Chester Charters*, nos. 22, 24, 26, 3–7, 45–6, 55, 59, 66–7, 69, 73, 77, 80–2, 84–5, 88, 90, 98–9, 101, 107–9, 113, 115, 118.

granted by Ranulf 'in his house at Lincoln in the presence of his barons', and in addition there were Reginald and Robert Fumichon, to whom Ranulf granted land in Thorley, Lincolnshire.[66]

Stewards and constables each had subordinates, dispensers in the case of stewards and marshals in the case of constables. Dispensers were in charge of household supplies, while marshals were responsible for the stables and horses. Two dispensers occur among the witnesses to the charters of Ranulf II of Chester, who presumably had one of the largest baronial entourages: Geoffrey, who occurs several times and was the brother of Ranulf's constable of Coventry, and a man named Warin.[67] Marshals occur still less frequently. In Earl Ranulf's charters, Blund the marshal witnessed the grant of the constableship to Eustace FitzJohn.[68]

The chamberlains' duties were to provide their masters with personal service, and also to take care of their personal possessions and ready money. It is likely that already on the greater honours there were two chamberlains in service at any one time. This cannot be demonstrated from all available collections of *acta*, but this may have been because their offices and standing were not as prestigious as the stewards' and constables'. On the Mowbray honour, for instance, Greenway pointed out that there were no knights' fees attached to chamberlainships, and there is no information about their duties.[69] In addition to the lay officers of the domestic household, clerks and chaplains also witnessed their lords' charters. Clerks who had attended cathedral schools were distinguished by the title *magistri*. These were the high-flyers of their day, the best-educated entrants into the clerical profession, seeking preferment via the households of bishops, the king, or great magnates. Of the households studied here, *magistri* are only to be found, as expected at this early date, in the households of the very great – the earls of Chester and Gloucester. One of Earl Ranulf's clerks was John *magister*.[70] Five or six of Earl William's clerks attest at some point as *magistri*, including one, Hervey, whom Patterson has identified as one of the scribes who drew up documents

---

[66] *Ibid.*, nos. 35, 105, 122, 45, 55, 80, 92–3, 126.

[67] *Ibid.*, nos. 64, 82, 85, 89 (Geoffrey); 101 (Warin); Crouch, 'Administration of the Norman Earldom', p. 78.

[68] *Chester Charters*, no. 67. On the earldom of Gloucester a marshal does not occur until the time of Earl William, though it is likely that his father, as the principal magnate fighting on the Empress's side in the Civil War, also had a marshal. Crouch has identified marshals in the households of each of the Beaumont twins: *Beaumont Twins*, p. 146.      [69] *Mowbray Charters*, p. lxv.

[70] *Chester Charters*, nos. 37, 41, 59. He may be identical with John the chaplain, a frequent witness.

issued in the king's name. Three, Henry Tusard, Hervey, and Picard, held
benefices of Tewkesbury Abbey; Picard also held livings in Cornwall and
Normandy; a fourth, Samson, held a benefice in Hampshire; and a fifth,
Ernesius, held a fractional knight's fee, for which he must have paid a
money rent.[71]

*Medici* or physicians were a specialized group, and only rarely is anything known about them other than their names. One exception is a
physician named Paulinus, who witnessed a charter of Gundrada de
Gournay, widow of Nigel d'Aubigny, who seems to have been based at York
in the mid-twelfth century.[72] It is perhaps not surprising to find physicians in attendance in periods of severe illness. Two physicians who witnessed a charter of Geoffrey II de Mandeville for the priory of Holy Trinity,
Aldgate, may well have been in attendance during the earl's final illness.[73]

Hunting officials were a second specialized group of officials. Hunting
was the chief sport and leisure activity of the aristocracy, and the very best
hunting staff were highly prized. Although hunting within the king's
forests was a royal monopoly and restricted to the king's friends, great
lords made parks on their own estates, and only needed permission if
these were within the bounds of the forest. A few of the greatest magnates
had private forests. In Cheshire, for instance, the earl had four forests and
it has been pointed out that falconers, hawkers, and hunters are to be
found as witnesses to the charters of Earl Ranulf II, more so than in the
charters of any of his contemporaries. Serlo the huntsman witnessed
Ranulf's documents no fewer than ten times, and Hugh the hawker
sixteen times.[74] Ranulf enfeoffed Alan Silvester with Storeton and
Puddington in Wirral, and it is known from later evidence that the office
alluded to in the charter was that of chief forester of Wirral.[75] In a second
charter Ranulf granted land at Gawsworth in the forest of Macclesfield,
where the earls later had their stud farms, so the reference to Hugh's
payment of a valuable horse 'at my treasury at Chester', and the fact that
the witnesses included Serlo and Ranulf the hunters and Geoffrey the
hawker, are both significant.[76]

[71] *Gloucester Charters*, pp. 10–14, 17, 25–9.
[72] E. J. Kealey, *Medieval Medicus* (Baltimore and London, 1981), pp. 138–9.
[73] J. H. Round, *Commune of London* (London, 1899), p. 101.
[74] Crouch, 'Administration of the Norman Earldom', p. 79.      [75] *Chester Charters*, no. 35.
[76] *Ibid.*, no. 43.

The functions of the lay and clerical members of the household were at once domestic and more broadly administrative. The stewards of the great lords, for instance, may have performed their customary duties in the lord's hall on occasion, but they were also usually the head of his finances and, often, lords in their own right. The local reeves handed over the rents and dues they collected and, on two honours at least, their performance was subjected to an audit described as an exchequer.[77] The clerks' functions of drawing up documents has obvious parallels to the growth of documentation in royal government. Indeed, there was a certain amount of transfer of personnel between lay households and royal government. Lords' stewards had experience that made them suitable candidates for shrievalties, as both Henry I and Henry II found. Clerks also made the transfer, most conspicuously from the household of William earl of Gloucester to that of Henry II.[78]

Witness lists are most informative about those who attended formal meetings of the lord's court, and about the officers of his *domus* or household. Yet we also need to know about household knights who were not honorial barons but who must have formed an essential part of a lord's retinue, especially in the early days after 1066 and during the reign of Stephen. What we may describe as rank and file household knights are mentioned only occasionally in the sources. One of Hugh de Lacy's household knights retired to the wilderness, and his retreat led to the foundation of Llanthony priory.[79] Knights of Roger de Mowbray's household entered the fledgling Cistercian house at Hood in Yorkshire. The three named in the foundation narrative were Landric de Agys, Henry de Wasprey, and Henry Bugge. The first two were described as men of great reputation and discretion, the third as a man of equal discretion, and it is interesting to note that although the first two can be identified as witnesses to Mowbray charters, the third, evidently a man of lesser status, cannot.[80] Household knights were recompensed by wages and allowances, or the assignment of rents.[81] Hence it is not often that they can be identified in the documents issued by their lords.

[77] Stenton, *First Century*, pp. 69–70.
[78] *Gloucester Charters*, pp. 12 (Adam of Ely), 13 (Herbert, Richard of Ilchester).
[79] Dugdale, *Mon. Ang.*, VI, 129, cited Stenton, *First Century*, p. 140.    [80] *Mowbray Charters*, p. lxi and n.
[81] Stringer, *Earl David*, pp. 166–76, discusses the prospects for household knights in the later twelfth century.

## New men

Great lords needed to keep the loyalty and service of tenant families, but they also recruited new men into their service, and, like the king, their retinues reflected a balance between 'old' men and 'new'. In most cases there is not enough evidence for the early part of our period to shed light on this subject. One significant exception, however, is Ranulf II earl of Chester, whose surviving acts are sufficiently numerous to enable his new men to be identified. Some were genuinely new, in that little is known for certain about their origins, whilst others were lesser local men who clearly attached themselves to the fortunes of the powerful earl.

Robert Basset witnessed nine times for Ranulf II, but not for his predecessors.[82] He may well have been a kinsman of Richard Basset of Weldon as a Robert Basset witnessed his marriage settlement.[83] Robert held land at Cawkwell, and Goulceby which he gave to the Templars, and the overlord of the former was the earl of Chester.[84] He seems to have established himself on part of the honour of Belvoir, at Redmile, the church of which he bestowed on Pipewell Abbey.[85]

William de Colleville witnessed eight times. Given that Ranulf of Chester was *vicomte* of Bayeux, it is likely that William's name derived from one of the two places called Colleville near Bayeux, Colleville-sur-Orne and Colleville-sur-Mer, where in 1133 a man named William de Colleville held land of the bishop of Bayeux. If so, William was a member of the Colleville family found in Yorkshire, Lincolnshire, and Scotland.[86] Another, less likely, possibility is Colleville near Valmont in upper Normandy, whence came the family who were tenants of the honour of Eye.[87] In 1166 William de Colleville, so far as may be seen the same man who witnessed for Earl Ranulf II, held two knights' fees of the honour of Bourne in Lincolnshire (then held by Hugh Wake, himself a man who had been in Ranulf II's sphere of influence), and also held one fee of Walter

---

[82] *Chester Charters*, nos. 40, 45, 64, 68, 73, 92, 93, 104, 114.     [83] *RRAN*, II, no. 1389.

[84] *Records of the Templars in England in the Twelfth Century*, ed. B. A. Lees, British Academy Records of Social and Economic History (London, 1935), pp. 107, 108.

[85] *Chester Charters*, no. 52; for discussion see E. King, 'The Foundation of Pipewell Abbey', *Haskins Society Journal*, 2 (1990), 170, n. 18.

[86] G. W. S. Barrow, *The Anglo-Norman Era in Scottish History* (Oxford, 1980), p. 177; H. Navel, 'L'enquête de 1133 sur les fiefs de l'évêché de Bayeux', *Bulletin de la Société des Antiquaires de Normandie*, 42 (1934), 21 and no. 181.     [87] Loyd, *Origins of Some Anglo-Norman Families*, p. 30.

d'Aincourt, and one of Robert de Gant.[88] Like Robert Basset, William may have acquired a foothold on the honour of Belvoir, for at some stage the Colleville family acquired land at Muston.[89] He may also have acquired land on the earl's manor of Waddington, for in the survey of the Templars' lands in 1185 it was recorded that land there was given by William de Coleville.[90]

Hugh Bardulf witnessed four times for Earl Ranulf. His family is thought to have come from the neighbourhood of Cherbourg, and to have been connected with the family of de la Haye, constables of Lincoln castle.[91] In 1166 Hugh held two fees of the new enfeoffment and his brother Doun one of Richard de la Haye.[92] Ranulf granted Hugh most of his demesne manor of Waddington near Lincoln, and he married a woman named Isabel, thought to have been a member of the Condet family and thus a kinswoman of the earl.[93]

Fulk de Bricessart, who witnessed three times, presumably came from the earl's castle at Briquessart in Normandy.[94] Finally, Robert Grevesac witnessed seven times for Ranulf II.[95] He figures in the 1130 pipe roll as holding Buscot in Berkshire, as paying for land which he acquired with his wife, and for a plea between himself and Robert Girbert.[96] It is possible that Robert had been recruited by Ranulf I towards the end of his life, but despite the references to his land, he does not appear to have established himself permanently in the honour.

The information about these men is admittedly incomplete, but they did not witness for Ranulf's predecessors, and it would appear that they were recruited by him. Yet Ranulf's documents were also witnessed by men who were already lesser landholders elsewhere and chose to associate themselves with him. Simon FitzWilliam, who witnessed thirteen times, came from a Lincolnshire family which by the mid-twelfth century had accumulated, probably by a mixture of inheritance and acquisition, substantial estates as under-tenants of a number of honours.[97] Simon's

---

[88] RBE, I, 379, 380, 434.

[89] Historical Manuscripts Commission, Rutland, IV, 11–12, 115, 141; A. C. E. Welby, 'Bytham Castle and Coleville Family', Lincolnshire Notes and Queries, 15 (1919), 18–26.

[90] Lees, Templars, pp. cxcv, 67, 68.

[91] C. T. Clay, 'Hugh Bardolf the Justice and his Family', Lincolnshire History and Archaeology, 50 (1966), 5–28.

[92] RBE, I, 391.    [93] Chester Charters, no. 66.    [94] Ibid., nos. 42, 88, 98.

[95] Ibid., nos. 15, 35, 55, 56, 59, 66, 70.    [96] PR 31 Henry I, p. 123.

[97] Farrer, Honors and Knights' Fees, II, 117–27; B. Golding, 'Simon of Kyme: the Making of a Rebel', Nottingham Medieval Studies, 27 (1983), 23–36.

chief residence was at Bullington, where a Gilbertine priory was founded (see below, p. 389). In 1166 Philip of Kyme, Simon's son, held thirty fees of various lordships, viz. the earldom of Chester, the bishoprics of Durham and Lincoln, and the honours of Aincourt, Gant, de la Haye, Brus, Curci, Percy, Roumare, Peverel, and Senlis. As Dalton has demonstrated, Ranulf and his brother William de Roumare were keen to extend and consolidate their influence over lesser Lincolnshire families, who appear from time to time as witnesses to their acts, such as William FitzHacon the sheriff,[98] Gilbert Neville,[99] and William and Walter de Amundeville.[100] Hugh Wake, who witnessed five times, has been plausibly suggested as someone who may have come to England with Ranulf II of Chester and was inserted into Lincolnshire society by his marriage to Emma, daughter of Baldwin FitzGilbert, lord of Bourne, who also witnessed for Ranulf.[101]

The most assiduous witness amongst Ranulf's new men was Norman de Verdon, who occurs sixteen times. He was the son of Bertram, a minor tenant-in-chief and sheriff of Yorkshire in 1100 (see above, p. 115). The family held land in Bouillon and Chavoy near Avranches.[102] Norman had acquired land in Staffordshire and Leicestershire by 1130, and he married Lesceline, daughter of Geoffrey de Clinton.[103] Their son Bertram married Matilda, a daughter of Earl Robert II de Ferrers and, perhaps through marriage, acquired a tenancy of the Ferrers family.[104] The family also at some stage became tenants of the earls of Chester in Staffordshire.[105] Norman de Verdon was almost certainly a tenant of both Ferrers and the earl of Chester, yet he clearly attached himself to the following of Ranulf II and it was not surprising that in 1153 his whole fee was granted by Duke Henry to the earl of Chester.[106]

Thus Ranulf's retinue was made up of a mix of new men, household

[98] Dalton, 'Aiming at the Impossible', pp. 126–30; Chester Charters, nos. 69, 77, 111; RRAN, II, no. 1784; possibly sheriff later: London, British Library Cotton Vespasian E xviii, f. 73 (William the sheriff).

[99] Chester Charters, nos. 66, 80, 111; CP, IX, 491 ff.

[100] Chester Charters, nos. 21, 93; C. T. Clay, 'The Family of Amundeville', Lincolnshire Architectural and Archaeological Society Reports and Papers, new series, 3 (1949), 109–36.

[101] E. King, 'The Origins of the Wake Family. The Early History of the Barony of Bourne in Lincolnshire', Northamptonshire Past and Present, 5 (1975), 167–73.

[102] Loyd, Origins of Some Anglo-Norman Families, p. 109.

[103] Curia Regis Rolls, v (1207–9), 54, where Lesceline is identified as the grandmother of Nicholas de Verdon; PR 31 Henry I, pp. 76, 87.

[104] M. Jones, 'The Charters of Robert II de Ferrers, earl of Nottingham. Derby and Ferrers', Nottingham Medieval Studies, 24 (1980), no. 23, p. 26.    [105] Farrer, Honors and Knights' Fees, II, 255–6.

[106] RRAN, III, no. 180.

officials, honorial barons, kinsmen, allies, and other aristocrats. In order of frequency of attestation came Richard his butler (thirty-two times), William and John his chaplains (respectively nineteen and thirteen times), Geoffrey the dispenser (sixteen times), and Hugh the falconer (sixteen times). William the constable (possibly William FitzNigel) witnessed four times, and his successor, Eustace FitzJohn, a magnate in his own right, six times.[107] Robert FitzHugh, the seneschal and lord of Mold in Cheshire, witnessed at least six times.[108] Apart from Robert, the Cheshire tenants tend to appear chiefly when the beneficiaries of the charters were situated in Cheshire. Adam de Praers witnessed a confirmation charter for St Werburgh's and the charter to Alan Silvester, both issued at Chester.[109] Others who witnessed only once and for documents issued for Cheshire include Oliver de Manners, his son Hugh, Richard de Vernon, Alured de Combrai, William Malbank, and Simon Tuschet.[110] By contrast Turstin Banastre witnessed eight times and Robert three times.[111]

Given the wide range of Ranulf's territorial interests it is not surprising to find that other local magnates appeared at his court and witnessed his documents. In the late 1140s he began to assume a leading role in support of the Angevin cause. Cadwaladr, brother of the king of Gwynedd, and his brother-in-law Gilbert FitzRichard, earl of Hertford, each witnessed, as did William FitzAlan, lord of Oswestry, at Chester.[112] A grant at Wenlock to the monks of Wenlock, probably in 1153, was witnessed by Walter brother of the earl of Hereford, Richard of Clare the younger brother of Earl Gilbert, Gilbert FitzBaderon (of Monmouth), and William FitzOtuel the half-brother of Earl Richard of Chester (d. 1120).[113] Yet the significance of such attestations is that the men concerned were not his tenants, but his kinsmen and allies, and in this respect Ranulf's documents do not stand alone. It has been suggested by David Crouch that in Stephen's reign magnates were constructing affinities, coalitions including tenants and magnates bound by mutual interests closer akin to those of fourteenth- and fifteenth-century England, in other words alliances which seem not to have been based only or primarily on tenurial relationships.[114]

[107] *Chester Charters*, nos. 34, 103, 115, 118, 81, 90.     [108] *Ibid.*, nos, 34, 40, 55, 71, 103, 118.
[109] *Ibid.*, nos. 27, 35.     [110] *Ibid.*, nos. 74, 38, 73, 25, 40, 73.
[111] *Ibid.*, nos. 36, 61, 67, 68, 69, 72, 73, 82, 40, 88, 114.     [112] *Ibid.*, nos. 64, 84, 85.     [113] *Ibid.*, no. 109.
[114] Crouch, 'Bastard Feudalism Revised', pp. 173–6, and for a recent discussion of the subject see M. Hicks, *Bastard Feudalism* (London, 1995).

## From honour to affinity?

Robert of Gloucester's documents, like those issued by Ranulf II of Chester, were also witnessed on occasion by allies not known to have held land from him, such as Humphrey de Bohun (the son-in-law of Miles of Gloucester), Earl Reginald (Robert's half-brother), Richard du Hommet (perhaps the man of this name who was Henry FitzEmpress's constable), and Stephen de Mandeville and William of Montfiquet, identifiable respectively as lords of Marshwood and Stansted.[115] Crouch has drawn attention to the alliances built up by Roger earl of Hereford in the later years of Stephen's reign. His documents were witnessed by the lords of Clifford, Ewyas, and Monmouth, William de Beauchamp and his brother Walter, Robert de Candos, Richard de Cormeilles (and his brother), Oliver de Merlimont, and William de Briouze.[116]

We are faced with the difficulty of determining whether such alliances were new, or were being recorded in writing for the first time. If the latter, the reason may have been because the grantors were aware that their decisions might well be challenged and were eager to have on record the attestation of allies as well as tenants. But it is unlikely that such groupings were entirely novel. Men often made alliances cemented by oaths of allegiance which did not involve the creation of a tenurial bond. The treaty between Henry I and the count of Flanders, for instance, was made in order that the count would supply five hundred knights to the king, but although he swore allegiance, provisions were made for the possibility that the count's lord might be at war with Henry, and there was, of course, no idea that the county of Flanders was to be subject to Henry.[117]

Moreover, not all allies occur as witnesses to charters. The second charter of the Empress for Geoffrey de Mandeville makes grants to men who, we must presume, were his allies, but who do not occur as witnesses to his charters: William FitzOtuel, William de Say, William Capra, William FitzWalter constable of Windsor, and Matthew de Rumilly.[118] Another ally was Aubrey de Vere, the earl's brother-in-law, who received his own charter.[119] Hugh Bigod, who married Juliana de Vere, also collaborated with Geoffrey in his revolt of 1143–4, and he does not attest

---

[115] *Gloucester Charters*, nos. 83, 6, 70, 283.   [116] Crouch, 'Bastard Feudalism Revised', p. 173.
[117] *Diplomatic Documents preserved in the Public Record Office*, ed. P. Chaplais (London, 1964), no. 1.
[118] Round, *Geoffrey de Mandeville*, pp. 169–70.   [119] *RRAN*, III, no. 634.

Geoffrey's documents.[120] Clearly we need more work on charters issued by leading protagonists in the war to see how widespread such practices were, or whether perhaps they were confined to particular regions or individuals, and how much significance should be read into them.

Land was one element in creating or sustaining loyalties, but it was not the only one, and it may be that historians have concentrated too much on it, and have as a result neglected those who associated themselves with lords of whom they held little or nothing. It has also perhaps been too readily assumed that commendation which did not involve the subordination of land disappeared at the Conquest. It is more likely that men retained the freedom to attach themselves to a new lord providing any prior tenurial obligations were met. There was as we have seen a whole spectrum of relationships between lords and men involving land and a varying degree of subordination.

If we suppose that alliances based on personal rather than tenurial allegiances *did* become more important under Stephen, how are we to interpret this development? The most obvious and likeliest explanation is that they were a response to political disturbances at that time. The appearance of affinities did not mean the decline of the honour, however.[121] It is likely that the bonds between many lords and an inner nucleus of tenant families remained strong until the end of our period. If some factors diluted loyalty, others reinforced it: the ceremonies attached to fealty and homage, shared experiences on campaigns, marriage into other tenant families or even into the lord's family (see chapter ten), endowment of a religious house (chapter twelve), and a *tradition* of loyalty. Multiple homages did not prevent men from attaching themselves to one liege lord. Although honorial courts may not have been all powerful, neither were other formal judicial processes at this date, and it is easy to see that where honorial courts were providing fora for agreed settlements, they could work more speedily and effectively than royal justice.

---

[120] *Gesta Stephani*, p. 166.

[121] For discussion about the decline of the honour and the rise of bastard feudalism see Crouch, *William Marshal*, pp. 4, 157–68; P. R. Coss, 'Bastard Feudalism Revisited', *Past and Present*, 125 (November, 1989), 43–5; Crouch, 'Debate. Bastard and Feudalism Revisited', pp. 172–7.

# III  The aristocracy and the crown

# 8   Collaborators and competitors
   in the pursuit of power

In the preceding chapter the focus was on the different categories of men over whom lordship was exercised; here it is on the nature of power. As a military elite, the aristocracy had the power to enforce obedience, constrained ultimately only by their obligations to God and the king, though in practice power was rarely exercised without reference to social and familial constraints. In a small, relatively centralized kingdom like Anglo-Norman England, it is the power of the king about which most is heard in the sources, so that although this chapter is concerned primarily with characteristics of aristocratic power, it is inevitable that these have to be described in relation to the king's power. It would be misleading, however, to see aristocratic power as fitting into a framework of royal government, as has too commonly been the case in the past. Military power has too often been described in terms of obligations owed to kings in the form of quotas of knight service, whereas in reality the political history of the Anglo-Norman period was characterized by frequent rebellions where the military muscle of the aristocracy was turned *against* the king. The history of financial exactions in our period *has* to be written largely in terms of geld and scutage because virtually nothing is said in the sources about exactions by the aristocracy, yet clearly knights, freemen, and peasants were all expected to contribute to their lords' coffers in the form of aid or tallage. Finally, relatively little has been written about aristocratic powers of justice and jurisdiction because so little is recorded in writing, as compared with royal rights. Here, too, however, it is a mistake to see aristocratic powers of justice and jurisdiction as delegated by the king, even if it suited kings at the time or later to claim that their ancestors had been granting franchises: in many areas, whether defined in terms of geography or issues, it must have been the authority of the great lord that was decisive, not the power of the king.

Aristocrats – in this context both lay and ecclesiastical – and kings were at once collaborators and competitors in the pursuit of power. By the end of our period their collective authority over the mass of the people was measurably greater than it had been a century earlier, and for this reason aristocrats and kings were not competing for shares of a cake which remained the same size. Moreover, because successive kings needed the co-operation of their magnates, and because from 1087 each succession to the throne was disputed, kings could not 'tame' the magnates in any real sense, as we shall see.

## Military obligations and financial payments

The whole rationale of the aristocracy was that of a military elite, and when the chips were down lords expected their men to follow them into battle. The fact that we rarely hear about this dimension of lordship in any detail does not obscure its importance, particularly in the years after 1066 and again in Stephen's reign. There may have been conventions about the terms on which service was provided. The greatest loyalty (and presumably therefore personal service) was to a man's liege lord, but where there was a second or a third lord to take into account, the greatest obligation was to the lord from whom most land was held. If two lords were at war, then a potential conflict of loyalty could be avoided by the concept of a paramount or liege homage to the chief lord and a limited liability to a second. An obligation which recurred regularly was castle-guard and, as we have seen (see above, p. 166), garrison duties at a major castle such as Richmond were organized and assessed against land by the early twelfth century. Whether the expectation was that castleguard was discharged in person or commuted may have depended on personal inclination or circumstances such as the likelihood of attack or competing demands for service from other lords or from the king.

The king's position in pre-Conquest England was in brief as follows: there was a general obligation to serve in the king's host, and to provide for the defence and repair of burhs and bridges, and these obligations had come to be assessed on land.[1] Much of southern England was assessed in hides, with the exception of Kent where the unit of assessment was the sulung or ploughland. In the east midlands and northern England the unit was also the ploughland, here called carucate; in east Anglia hundreds were the unit of assessment. These units of assessment could be used for service in the army, work on burhs or bridges, or for levying geld,

---

[1] Abels, *Lordship and Military Obligation in Anglo-Saxon England*, especially chapter 2.

or tribute. Gelds were levied to buy off Danish attack, and between 1012 and 1051 an annual heregeld was taken in addition for the upkeep of the army.[2] The relationship between obligation to army service and armies fielded in the late Anglo-Saxon period is not spelled out, but the nucleus of major armies was evidently formed by the retinues of the king, including the housecarls, and those of earls and leading thegns, supplemented by shire levies which were perhaps recruited from a wider social base.[3]

King William did not intend to lose these rights, nor did he wish to see them taken over by his followers. Bridgework and burh work were obviously vital for the internal defences of the country. The value of military obligations was equally so, but what kind of service was to be provided, and how was it to be recruited, given the differences between Anglo-Saxon and Norman military techniques? Moreover, were contributions in lieu to be taken on the basis of the old geld obligations assessed by counties, or by negotiation with tenants-in-chief and, if the latter, were those who served to pay as well, and how much?

There is in Domesday Book a particular passage on the king's customs in Berkshire in the Confessor's day which has long attracted attention because of its information about military obligation. When the king called an army anywhere, one man went from every five hides. He who failed to go when summoned forfeited all his land to the king; if he promised to send a substitute and the substitute did not go, his lord was fined fifty shillings.[4] The way this was expressed is rather odd but a distinction was clearly being made between those who were personally summoned and those who were summoned through their lords. The term of service was two months, though nothing was said about its type or frequency. The amount of land involved suggests, though this has been disputed, that the soldier involved was not a member of the rank and file but a thegn.[5] The Berkshire customs are the most detailed in Domesday Book on the question of military service. In the customs of Oxfordshire it was

---

[2] M. K. Lawson, 'The Collection of Danegeld and Heregeld in the Reigns of Aethelred II and Cnut', *English Historical Review*, 99 (1984), 721–38; J. Gillingham, '"The Most Precious Jewel in the English Crown": Levels of Danegeld and Heregeld in the Early Eleventh Century', *English Historical Review*, 104 (1989), 373–84; M. K. Lawson, '"Those Stories Look True": Levels of Taxation in the Reigns of Aethelred II and Cnut', *ibid.*, 385–406.    [3] Abels, *Lordship and Military Obligation in Anglo-Saxon England*, chapter 8.

[4] *DB*, I, 56b.

[5] Abels, *Lordship and Military Obligation*, pp. 142–5; cf. Stenton, *First Century*, pp. 117–18 who argued that the five-hide warrior was a ceorl.

stated that when the king went on an expedition twenty burgesses of Oxford went 'for all the others', or they acquitted themselves by paying twenty pounds.[6] Here the number of men was not assessed against hides, but chosen from the men of the borough; once again fiscal commutation is mentioned. The customs of Worcestershire were concerned not with who went, and on what basis they were chosen, but with the penalties for non-compliance with a summons. A distinction was drawn between the man with sake and soke, who was to be in the king's mercy for his land if he did not attend, and the free man of another lord, who was fined forty shillings.[7] These passages are concerned with service in the army, but ships could also be supplied by levies upon the hide.[8] There is an obvious problem in deciding the extent to which military obligations corresponded to the armies fielded in the early eleventh century. What kings, like all military leaders, wanted was experienced and well-equipped fighting men, and they may well have turned in the first instance to their own followings. We can only speculate how often and in what circumstances orders for a general levy were sent out before 1066 and the importance of obligations on the hide or ploughland in providing service or money in lieu.

The Norman kings retained the old obligations and on occasion used them. The chronicler John (Florence) of Worcester recorded how in 1094 footsoldiers were summoned but, when they had congregated at Hastings, their support money was taken from them by Ranulf Flambard and they were sent home.[9] From their tenants-in-chief the Norman kings expected men who were fully equipped and, it is to be presumed, trained in the latest techniques of cavalry fighting. Some doubtless answered summonses with all their available manpower, and all probably struck bargains about the number of knights they could supply. Similar negotiations between William and the leading Normans for men and ships had preceded the invasion of 1066.[10]

Bishoprics and abbeys remained in possession of the lands they had held before 1066, and, probably prior to William's expedition to Scotland in 1072, quotas of service calculated in round numbers were imposed.[11]

---

[6] *DB*, I, 154.    [7] *DB*, I, 172; for sake and soke see further below, p. 246.

[8] N. A. Hooper, 'Some Observations on the Navy in Late Anglo-Saxon England', *Studies in Medieval History presented to R. Allen Brown*, ed. C. Harper-Bill, C. Holdsworth, and J. L. Nelson (Woodbridge, 1989), pp. 201–13.    [9] FW, II, 35.    [10] Van Houts, 'The Ship List of William the Conqueror', pp. 161–74.

[11] Round, *Feudal England*, p. 234.

Quotas may not have been novel: there may well have been similar bargains between kings and leading laymen and ecclesiastics about the numbers of men to be provided before 1066.[12] There is also the possibility that the bargains which were struck were thought to relate only to this campaign. Nor did they render the king's right to service from all free men otiose, though the latter may have been used mainly at times of severe emergency.

Insights into the different kinds of contributions demanded from the church may be gained from Eadmer's account of the tensions between William Rufus, who exploited his power over the church to finance his wars, and his archbishop of Canterbury, Anselm. In 1094 Rufus asked for financial contributions for his expedition to Normandy. Anselm offered five hundred pounds, but annoyed the king by preaching that it was better to have offerings made freely than under pressure.[13] Rufus was asking, however, not only for cash but also for men (though possibly not both from Anselm), for footsoldiers were raised for the same expedition. Three years later, Anselm sent men for the army which Rufus took to Wales, but the king complained that they were badly trained and unsuitable for war.[14] The insights provided by Eadmer reveal that a mix of men and money was asked for, and the sum of five hundred pounds, which the king's advisers thought should be raised to one or two thousand, was evidently a subject for negotiation, not assessed against a set quota.

The great lay lordships also came to be assessed in quotas, but probably not all at once, because, unlike the ecclesiastical lordships, the lay lordships in the main took shape over a period of years. Some of the older quotas have been shown to have been decimal and they dated back to within a few years of the Conquest. Random quotas came into being in at least four ways: through conversion of under-tenancies into tenancies-in-chief, assessments on lordships near the borders of Wales and Scotland, escheat to the crown, and reorganization.[15] Quotas however were only one way of reckoning contributions to the king's army. When Henry II held an inquiry into the subject in 1166, some tenants-in-chief were evidently hazy about their quotas, and it is not impossible that the last time they

---

[12] Gillingham, 'The Introduction of Knight Service into England', pp. 53–64.

[13] Eadmer, *Historia Novorum*, pp. 43–5; *Vita Anselmi*, pp. 67–9.

[14] Eadmer, *Historia Novorum*, p. 78; *Vita Anselmi*, p. 88.

[15] Gillingham, 'The Introduction of Knight Service into England', pp. 89–106.

had been used for a general levy was under Henry I.[16] The sources also do not reveal whether any distinction was made between an expedition, let us say, against the Welsh or the Scots, when the king might have issued a general summons, and the frequent royal campaigns in Normandy. In the late twelfth century 'foreign service' became a contentious political issue, but so far as we know in the earlier period no stipulations were made about the theatres of war for which military service was due or towards which contributions were demanded.

Tenants-in-chief had to find men or money to meet their obligations. Once again we have no information about how this worked in practice. Lords distributed land to their followers, and charters of enfeoffment surviving from the twelfth century specify that land was being granted in return for so much knight's service. On many honours more knights were enfeoffed than the quota, and we do not know how the tenant-in-chief chose whom to send to the king. There were various possibilities: the obligation could be set against specific fees, or the knights could elect some of their number, or their lord could choose for them. The tenant-in-chief clearly was expected to provide for his personal service. If the obligation was to be discharged by money, it appears that the cost was passed on to his tenants. This could have been by individually negotiated contributions, like the aids which the lord agreed with the king, and assessed either on the quota or on the number of knights enfeoffed.

The assignment of castleguard for the custody of key royal castles seems to have occurred not long after 1066. The assignment of Abingdon abbey's knights to castleguard at Windsor was attributed by the abbey's chronicler to King William.[17] Baronies were grouped to provide garrisons in rotation. Windsor was garrisoned by Abingdon abbey (thirty knights), Pinkney barony (fifteen), Windsor (fifteen), an Essex barony (ten), and three single fees.[18] The obligation potentially conflicted both with that of service in the king's host and with obligations to the lord. Only one obligation could be provided personally, so again it must be assumed that the respective elements of cash and service must have been sorted out on a pragmatic basis.

---

[16] For examples of uncertainty as to the quotas see Round, *Feudal England*, pp. 195–6.

[17] *Chronicon Monasterii de Abingdon*, II, 3.

[18] J. H. Round, 'Castleguard', *Archaeological Journal*, 59 (1902), 144–59; S. Painter, 'Castleguard', *Feudalism and Liberty* (ed. Cazel), pp. 144–56.

The maintenance of military obligation to the crown was a distinguishing feature of Anglo-Norman kingship, and its origins lay far back in the past. Exactly which features were traditional and which innovatory has been one of the most hard-fought battles between historians arguing for continuity or change after 1066. If at present there is a temporary lull it will doubtless not last long, and the arguments will resume. Heavily armed cavalry, castles, vassalage, and quotas have all been detected in England before as well as after the Conquest. In this context, however, less important than innovations in warfare are obligations and the way they developed during the century following the Conquest. As we saw in chapter five, the aristocracy of Norman England made their own arrangements for settling their followers on land and exacting military service, whilst at the same time recognizing obligations to the king. They may have bargained with the king about the size of their contribution, and the number of soldiers or size of payment may not have been fixed once for all, but it was in the interests of all the newcomers to stick together and fight as long and as hard as necessary. However, as they became more settled on the land and the atmosphere became more peaceful, financial contributions may have come to the fore. Instead of providing personal service, scutage – shield money – could be exacted instead. The practice of commuting service was not novel, but there may have been some shift in emphasis in the late eleventh century. The crown may have varied its demands according to the campaign. When Rufus and Henry I were campaigning in Normandy, they probably used household knights, mercenaries, and the retinues of their close associates. If a major expedition against the Scots or Welsh was envisaged, writs may have been issued of the kind sent to Aethelwig abbot of Evesham, ordering him to produce the five knights due for his abbey and all those in his bailiwick.[19] Rufus was said to have summoned the 'service owed', the *servitium debitum* or quota of knight service, to repress revolt at the start of his reign.[20] In 1101 Henry I, anticipating his brother's invasion, summoned 'an army of his whole realm'.[21] In Yorkshire in 1138 locally recruited levies as well as the retinues of the great magnates faced the Scots at the battle of the Standard.[22] If heavy cavalry was the *crème de la crème*, the crown was nevertheless not

---

[19] Round, *Feudal England*, p. 238.    [20] *Liber Eliensis*, p. 218.    [21] *Chronicon Monasterii de Abingdon*, ii, 121.
[22] Richard of Hexham, *Chronicles*, iii, 161; Ailred, 'Relatio de Standardo', *Chronicles*, iii, 191–2.

going to abandon a more broadly based military obligation, either for providing service or for money in lieu.

The capacity to take national taxes was one of the most potent features of Anglo-Saxon monarchy. Those who held hides of land were responsible for the obligations which lay upon them, including geld. It appears that under Swein and Cnut, and possibly under Aethelred, those who could not meet their obligations were liable to forfeit their estates to the king, who might allow them to be redeemed, or might grant them to whoever could pay the geld due. Heming, writing in Worcester in the late eleventh century, said that those who in Cnut's day had not paid their tax by the appointed time, lost their land to whoever gave the money due to the shire-reeve.[23]

At some stage King William revived the practice of taking geld. The earliest explicit reference occurs in the Anglo-Saxon Chronicle for 1084.[24] This was, if not the first, then probably the heaviest geld taken since 1066. A reference in Domesday Book suggests that geld was taken by the Conqueror every year, but this comes from an account of the customs of Stafford: 'All these [viz. those who have houses in Stafford] have sake and soke. The king has from all geld each year.'[25] While this could be a reference to rent or *gafol*, many boroughs did pay geld, though it would be unsafe to infer from levies taken from boroughs that William had been taking regular annual geld levies throughout the realm.[26] The rate, six shillings per hide, was extremely high, and the intention may have been to levy two shillings a year for three years. Geld rolls for the south-western counties, which have been shown to date from 1086, may refer not to a new levy but to a further visitation for the first levy.[27] The geld was probably ordered in the awareness that Cnut king of Denmark was planning to invade England. In the following year the Chronicle reported that William returned from Normandy with a massive force of horse and foot from France and Brittany, 'greater than any that had ever come to this

---

[23] *Hemingi Chartularium Ecclesiae Wigorniensis*, 2 vols., ed. T. Hearne (Oxford, 1723), I, 278, cited by Lawson, 'The Collection of Danegeld and Heregeld in the reigns of Aethelred II and Cnut', p. 724, who cites other references pointing to the conclusion that failure to pay geld might be followed by loss of land.

[24] William evidently exacted money from his new dominion. See for instance, FW, II, 2 for a reference to *tributum* levied in 1068; what is not clear is whether there were levies of geld or, if there were, whether they were taken at such a high rate.       [25] *DB*, I, 246.

[26] S. Harvey, 'Taxation and the Economy', in *Domesday Studies* (ed. Holt), p. 249.

[27] J. F. A. Mason, 'The Date of the Geld Rolls', *English Historical Review*, 69 (1954), 283–6.

country'. The men were distributed throughout England and billeted on the king's vassals according to their wealth. The king also ordered the coastal districts to be wasted, to inhibit the progress of an invasion force.

In 1084 and 1085 William evidently believed that Norman rule in England was facing its severest challenge. Cnut was a great-nephew of King Cnut; he had at least as valid a claim to the English throne as William, and was likely to meet with support from the Anglo-Danish population in eastern and northern England. Cnut was also married to the daughter of the count of Flanders, and it was rumoured the latter would assist an invasion, thus bringing to an end an era when relations between Normandy and Flanders had been relatively amicable. William must also have been concerned about the numbers and loyalty of his forces in England. In 1082 he had thrown his brother Odo into prison on suspicion of wishing to remove numbers of knights from England for his own purposes, an expedition to Italy according to Orderic Vitalis.[28] In 1084 William began to raise funds to augment his forces in England, and spent the following year recruiting an unprecedentedly large army serving for wages.

The year 1085 was when the strains imposed by taxation and by the military emergency were at their height, and they fell on the aristocracy as well as the population at large. It is not difficult to see that the former may have felt concerned about both the scale and the distribution of the burden.[29] The Normans in England had to be prepared to defend their lands against invasion and to provide billets for troops. The geld lists bound up with the Domesday Survey for the south-west counties and the fragments of a geld roll for Northamptonshire dating from earlier in the Conqueror's reign indicate that manorial demesnes of manors held in chief were exempt from geld, some recognition for the service they provided.[30] Such exemption went some way to recognizing the service provided by tenants-in-chief, but manorial demesne of the demesne manors of their under-tenants was presumably still liable.[31]

---

[28] OV, IV, 40–2.

[29] The ideas expressed above were formulated before the publication of N. Higham, 'The Domesday Survey: Context and Purpose', *History*, 78 (1993), 7–21. Whilst there is a large measure of agreement between us about the context of Domesday Book, it will be evident that I place rather less emphasis on billeting as the primary cause of the Inquest.

[30] On this issue, see the discussion by R. S. Hoyt, *The Royal Demesne in English Constitutional History* (Cornell, 1950), pp. 52–8.    [31] Higham, 'Domesday Survey', p. 15.

Moreover, officials in 1085 had to work with the situation as it was, and there may well have been considerable disputes about assessment. The assessment of Northamptonshire in the Confessor's day and in the 1070s, for instance, has been calculated as 2,663½ hides, compared with some 1,244 in 1086.[32] In the south-eastern counties there had been sweeping reductions of assessments under King William which were particularly generous on demesne manors, as opposed to *manorial* demesne of demesne manors, which meant that the burden of geld was increasingly being shifted onto peasants, both free and unfree, and away from demesne. There is some indication also that those with exempt but hidated manors could collect and keep the geld for themselves.[33] These reductions could have been made some time before 1086, or shortly before, perhaps because many troops were billeted in the south-east. They may be indicative of a feeling in the aristocracy that if they provided military service, then geld was to be exacted from the subject English. By Christmas 1085 when the king was at Gloucester there may well have been a recognition on all sides that more accurate information was needed.

The king ordered an inquest into his own resources, and into those of his leading subjects, both lay and ecclesiastical. The detail provided about manorial assets is astonishing, as the Anglo-Saxon Chronicler commented, and went far beyond what was needed for a straightforward levy of geld. Not only were hides listed, and the number of ploughs on the demesne as opposed to those held by peasants (which would not have been needed if manorial demesnes were to be exempt), but a rating was given of arable capacity (there is land for X ploughs), estate assets such as wood and pasture were listed, and values were given for two, or sometimes three, dates. The detail for lay and ecclesiastical tenants-in-chief, though checked by a second team of investigators, must in the first instance have been provided by the landholders.[34] There is evidence that this was so, and this further suggests that they actively co-operated in the aims of the survey.

It has been suggested that they co-operated basically because Domesday

---

[32] C. Hart, *The Hidation of Northamptonshire*, Department of English Local History Occasional Papers, second series no. 3 (Leicester, 1970), summary table at p. 38.

[33] Harvey, 'Taxation and the Economy', pp. 257–9.

[34] Addition by Robert of Hereford to the chronicle of Marianus Scotus, translated in *English Historical Documents*, II, 912.

Book provided them, in effect, with written title to their lands. Maitland discounted the idea that it was a 'register of title', and he had good reason, in the sense that title to land did not depend on possession of a written record.[35] Nor was settling disputes a principal purpose of the survey, another theory sometimes advanced for the ordering of the Inquest, although some settlements may have been reached during the inquiry. Disputes, annexations, and *clamores* were recorded in some counties, probably until the decision was taken not to record any more.[36]

Maitland, like Round, preferred the explanation that Domesday Book was an investigation into geld. Round believed that the record of the Inquest into the County of Cambridgeshire, arranged geographically hundred by hundred rather than tenurially by landholder like the returns for that county in Domesday Book volume one, were the 'original returns' to the inquiry and their form proved that the intention had been an investigation into geld. V. H. Galbraith countered by pointing out that Round's theory had ignored the Exon Domesday, where the results were arranged tenurially and subsequently revised in Domesday Book volume one.[37] Galbraith's hypothesis has in turn been subject to criticism, for not having made sufficient allowance for the importance of hundredally arranged information within the returns for tenants-in-chief, and because he did not tackle the question of the ploughland formula.

There have been different views about the meaning of this set of data in Domesday Book. Sally Harvey suggested that the ploughland formula (there is land for X ploughs) represented an attempt to assess arable capacity. It was thus a different way of calculating assessments, and a more accurate one, since it reflected productive capacity more closely than the old hides and ploughlands. She argued further that the details about manorial assets and values were collected with the aim of reassessing geld. In the south-east of England, where assessments had been reduced before 1086, ploughlands were higher than the old hides and, here at

---

[35] F. W. Maitland, *Domesday Book and Beyond*, (Cambridge, 1987 edition), p. 3.

[36] viz. Hunts., Yorks., and Lincs. in the north; Cornwall, Devon, and Somerset in the south-west; and Essex, Norfolk, and Suffolk; for comment see P. Hyams, '"No Register of Title": the Domesday Inquest and Land Adjudication', *Anglo-Norman Studies*, 9 (1986), 127–41; P. Wormald, 'Domesday Lawsuits: a Provisional List and Preliminary Comment', *England in the Eleventh Century. Proceedings of the 1990 Harlaxton Symposium*, ed. C. Hicks (Stamford, 1992), pp. 61–102.

[37] V. H. Galbraith, *The Making of Domesday Book* (Oxford, 1961), pp. 28–9 and see also *Domesday Book: its Place in Administrative History* (Oxford, 1974).

least, a reassessment occurred. At some stage the idea of reassessment was abandoned, and, although the 'land for X ploughs' formula continued to be recorded in most, though not all, counties, it often simply reproduced the hidage or a total of working ploughs.[38]

It is not impossible that royal officials had had a reassessment in mind: Harvey drew attention to the story related by Orderic Vitalis that Ranulf Flambard, already influential and later Rufus's chief financial minister, had some idea of remeasuring assessments.[39] Yet not all historians agree that the ploughland figures were new assessments.[40] Moreover any such planned reassessment would have been bitterly opposed if an *increase* in liability was the result, and why would the aristocracy have supplied information about assets and values which could have been used against them? Even if envisaged, such a scheme was not carried through, for twelfth-century assessments were based on Edwardian data.

Although historians will continue to debate the various possibilities, we should perhaps take literally the statement in the Anglo-Saxon Chronicle that a primary reason for the inquest was an investigation into royal resources, both by way of land, and the annual dues from each county. The fact that everyone else's lands were investigated as thoroughly, and with information provided by them, is best explained in terms of an inquiry into the status quo, even if for a time there may have been a more radical proposal of reassessment. The general aim was to provide information from which demands for service, for the incidents of feudal lordship, or for money, could be calculated carefully.

The inquiry was followed on 1 August 1086 by a great oath-swearing at Salisbury, where 'all the landholding men of any account bowed down to him and became his men'. The oath, so closely following the Inquest, cannot be disassociated from it, as Holt has pointed out.[41] It was a means of establishing and renewing loyalties not just with tenants-in-chief but with under-tenants. King William may even have made a concession to the latter by allowing them freedom from geld for manorial demesnes. In

[38] S. Harvey, 'Domesday Book and Anglo-Norman Governance', *Transactions of the Royal Historical Society*, 5th series, 25 (1974), pp. 186–8; Harvey, 'Taxation and the Economy'.     [39] OV, IV, 172.

[40] See the comments of W. E. Kapelle, 'Domesday Book: F. W. Maitland and His Successors', *Speculum*, 64 (1989), 633–5; among scholars who have suggested that the ploughland formulae were not a new assessment in 1086 is J. S. Moore, 'The Domesday Teamland: A Reconsideration', *Transactions of the Royal Historical Society*, 5th series, 14 (1964), 109–30.

[41] Holt, '1086', in *Domesday Studies* (ed. Holt), pp. 41–64.

1100 his son seems to have granted this: it may have been a new concession, but equally he may have been restoring a grant made by his father.[42]
In general William may have been in a conciliatory mood, for the crisis
had been eased by the death of Cnut, and William was intending to travel
to France and to wage war there.

It has been argued that the strains imposed by billeting a large army in
1085 fell particularly heavily on under-tenants who also carried a dispro-
portionate share of geld, and that their resulting discontent prompted
the ordering of the Survey.[43] Billeting should not be taken out of the wider
context of the crisis of 1084–5, however, for it was only one element of the
demands made on the aristocracy at that time. Billeting was likely to have
been only a short-term problem. As serious if not more so for the aristocracy as a whole was the prospect of further heavy gelds taken from those
who were also expected to provide military service.

The question that remains is when and why the results were written up
in the form of a book.[44] William saw 'writings' in 1086 according to the
Anglo-Saxon Chronicle, but these need not have been the two volumes of
Domesday Book as they now exist. It has been demonstrated that the pro-
cessing of results continued into the reign of William Rufus, and this
perhaps militates against the candidature of Bishop William of St Calais
as the mastermind of the whole survey, as he fell from grace in 1088.[45]
Domesday Book volume one covers all the counties surveyed except Essex,
Norfolk, and Suffolk where the volume of detail was particularly large.
Although there were precedents for inquests of this kind, if not on this
scale, the incorporation of the results in book form, rather than rolls,
made Domesday unique.[46] It indicates the intention to provide a lasting
work of reference, not to be superseded as lands passed to other lords, or
as the amount of land under cultivation and manorial assets changed. It
is known that the book had come into existence by about 1110, for there
are references to the 'book of the treasury' and the 'book of
Winchester'.[47]

---

[42] Stubbs, *Select Charters*, p. 119.     [43] Higham, 'Domesday Survey', pp. 15–16.

[44] For a recent discussion see Roffe, 'Making of Domesday Book Reconsidered', 152–66.

[45] C. P. Lewis, 'The Earldom of Surrey and the Date of Domesday Book', *Historical Research*, 63 (1990),
329–36; D. Bates, 'Two Ramsey Writs and the Domesday Survey', *ibid.*, 337–9.

[46] J. Percival, 'The Precursors of Domesday Book', *Domesday Book: a reassessment* (London, 1985), pp. 5–27;
R. H. C. Davis, 'Domesday Book: Continental Parallels', *Domesday Studies* (ed. Holt), pp. 15–39.

[47] *RRAN*, II, no. 1000; cf. nos, 976, 1488, 1515, 1887 which refer to a *carta* rather than a codex.

Was William following in the footsteps of Augustus or Diocletian in ordering a general review of taxation? Although the Domesday Inquest was not strictly comparable with these earlier measures, there are interesting points of comparison.[48] It is arguable that the use of arable land as a unit of assessment was more realistic and up to date as a measure of wealth than the old customary units of hides and carucates. There is also a case for saying that where land had dropped out of cultivation but was still assessed for taxation, accurate assessments could be in the interests of taxpayers as well as the king, which might go some way to explaining the co-operation of the aristocracy.

The concentration of military and fiscal pressures on the regime in the last years of the Conqueror's life had thus led to an immensely detailed review of resources, followed by a general oath-taking at Salisbury, by which time, we must assume, King William had come to an agreement with the leading landholders. Domesday Book stands alone in terms of its conception and execution, yet 1086 did not witness the supercession of one method of assessment, by hides and carucates, in favour of another, by bargains based on the number of knights that could be provided. Instead a variety of methods continued to be employed, in different combinations, throughout and beyond our period.

The next exceptional financial effort was needed to meet the costs of Robert's participation in the first crusade. It is not quite clear from contemporary accounts how the money was raised. Rufus is said to have levied geld at four shillings a hide and not to have allowed earlier exemptions of manorial demesne to apply, according to the (later) text known as the *Leges Edwardi Confessoris*.[49] Eadmer describes an aid of two hundred pounds which Anselm offered, in addition to money he had been able to raise from his vassals.[50] Florence of Worcester states that Rufus ordered that each of the nobles should lend him money according to their means. Ecclesiastics broke up the gold and silver ornaments of their churches while the lay magnates exacted money from their knights and peasants.[51] The unpopularity of these measures, even in a good cause, may explain Henry's concession in 1100 that 'the demesne ploughs of those who served

---

[48] Percival, 'Precursors of Domesday Book', pp. 6–13.

[49] *Leges Edwardi Confessoris*, c. 11, 2: F. Liebermann, *Die Gesetze der Angelsachsen*, 3 vols. (Halle, 1903–16), I, 636.    [50] Eadmer, *Historia Novorum*, pp. 74–5.    [51] Gervase of Canterbury, *Historical Works*, I, 198.

with their shields' should be exempt, which could be interpreted as a return to practices before 1096.[52]

Geld returned its usefulness as a levy which reached out to a wide community directly, and substantial sums were still raised. In 1110 when Henry took an aid for the marriage of his daughter, he did so in the form of a three-shilling geld.[53] The rate recorded in the *Leges Henrici Primi* was one shilling a hide, but by the late 1120s it had evidently been doubled.[54] Twelfth-century evidence indicates that it was on the Edwardian hidages that danegeld was charged, not the ploughland figures, perhaps because a radical reassessment had proved impractical, and it proved to be more politically expedient to work on the old assessments. It also has to be remembered that it was in relation to the Edwardian hidages that a record had been made of demesne and tenant ploughs.[55]

In the 1130 pipe roll danegeld, as it is specifically called, appears as a levy that had been taken in 1128–9 and 1129–30, and at two shillings a hide.[56] The term danegeld, which is used in the three twelfth-century levies, was used only once in Domesday Book, the term geld being used elsewhere.[57] In the account of the Isle of Wight a debt is also recorded for 'earlier danegelds of the island for five years in the time of Hugh Gernon', which is suggestive, though not conclusive, evidence that geld had become an annual levy.[58] The point here is that at the time Hugh may have been acting on behalf of Baldwin de Redvers, lord of the Isle, not the king. What is most striking about the danegeld accounts in 1130 is the long lists of exemptions. These include royal servants, presumably those exempted because they sat at the exchequer as mentioned in the *Dialogue of the Exchequer*, and the sheriffs on their demesne land.[59] There does not seem to have been a customary exemption of manorial demesne for tenants-in-chief. For instance, William Peverel of Nottingham, Henry de Port, and Walter Giffard do not appear in the exemptions for the counties in which they held demesne land, namely, Nottinghamshire, Hampshire, and

---

[52] Stubbs, *Select Charters*, p. 119.     [53] HH, p. 237.
[54] *Leges Henrici Primi*, 15,1; the same rate is cited in *Leges Edwardi Confessoris c.* 11a: Liebermann, *Die Gesetze der Angelsachsen*, i, 634.
[55] J. A. Green, 'The Last Century of Danegeld', *English Historical Review*, 96 (1981), 243.
[56] e.g. *PR 31 Henry I*, pp. 5, 11.
[57] 'The king's borough of Stamford gave geld in the reign of King Edward for 12½ hundreds. In the army and in ship service and in danegeld': *DB*, i, 336b.     [58] *PR 31 Henry I*, p. 41.
[59] *Dialogus de Scaccario*, p. 56; for examples of sheriffs' pardons see *PR 31 Henry I*, pp. 12, 49.

Buckinghamshire. Whilst exemptions may have secured enough co-operation for the tax to be levied successfully, there was evidently a division between those who were liable and those who were not; and for those who were both liable and had large estates, the burden was considerable.

The year 1130 may have been the last year when Henry took danegeld, for he was said to have promised in the following year not to collect it for seven years in thanksgiving for an escape from shipwreck.[60] Whether or not the king's decision was a thank offering, he may well have considered it politic to ease off financial demands at a time when he needed magnate support for his plans for the succession. Henry of Huntingdon claimed that Stephen promised to abolish the tax, but failed to keep his promise.[61] If danegeld continued to be collected, we may doubt how much reached the king. In those counties where powerful earls established control over sheriffs, it is more likely that they kept the proceeds.[62]

When Henry II became king, there was a major risk of financial reconstruction to be undertaken. In 1156 danegeld was levied at two shillings, plus one pound per fee calculated on the quotas of tenants-in-chief. The former is noteworthy for the proportion of the amount demanded that was written off in waste. This had almost wholly disappeared in the next levy, that of 1163–4, and historians have been much exercised as to the reason, and specifically whether waste reflected war damage.[63] The two levies have to be considered together, because whereas there were relatively few pardons in 1156, there were many more in 1163–4. One partial explanation of the contrast between the two accounts is that there were many disputes over liability in 1156 subsumed in the waste totals, which in many cases were subsequently resolved in favour of the claimant, so that waste was reduced and pardons were recorded instead. There can be no doubt that there were such disputes, for it is significant that amongst those pardoned for the first time in 1163–4 were religious houses founded since 1135. These had been granted land in free alms, and were presumably arguing that this freed them not just from services to the donors but also from obligations like geld.[64] Emilie Amt has

[60] JW, pp. 33–4.     [61] HH, p. 258.

[62] J. A. Green, 'Financing Stephen's War', *Anglo-Norman Studies*, 14 (1992), 104.

[63] H. W. C. Davis, 'The Anarchy of Stephen's Reign', *English Historical Review*, 8 (1903), 630–41; Green, 'Last Century of Danegeld', pp. 251–2; G. White, 'Were the Midlands "Wasted" during Stephen's Reign?', *Midland History*, 10 (1985), 26–46; E. M. Amt, 'The Meaning of Waste in the Early Pipe Rolls of Henry II', *Economic History Review*, 44 (1991), 240–8.     [64] Green, 'Last Century of Danegeld', p. 252.

recently reviewed the whole knotty problem, arguing persuasively that much of the waste reflected war damage; also that the officials might have been using out-of-date geld lists in 1156.[65] Another possibility is that earls collected geld in their counties, and had been more generous with exemptions than the exchequer was prepared to allow.

In January 1163 Henry returned to England after a lengthy absence to deal with a revolt in Wales, and at Woodstock in July he announced that he wished to assign to the fisc a customary annual payment to the sheriffs of two shillings a hide.[66] He was frustrated by the objection of Becket that such a sum was being paid to the sheriffs voluntarily, whereas the king wished it to be given as rent and written down in the royal records. There are references to a levy called sheriffs' aid collected locally through the hundreds and forming part of the sheriffs' farms. The contributors must have realised that if the king took over the aid, then payments would still have to be made for the sheriffs' goodwill. From the king's point of view, taking two shillings a hide in the form of sheriffs' aid may have been more productive and collectable than danegeld. Becket's resistance deterred the king, however. Writs were sent out one more time for a levy of danegeld in 1175, but the plan was called off. Instead Henry preferred to negotiate with his tenants-in-chief and other wealthy groups for aids, gifts, and scutage.

In the 1130 pipe roll there are references to a whole range of levies called aids or gifts.[67] Several were to an aid of, or for, knights. This was evidently not an annual levy, since it was paid by at least one religious house, Crowland, which did not hold its land by military service, and the sums may have been round figures rather than a calculation based on the quota or number of enfeoffed knights.[68] In the case of Crowland, therefore, the aid was a means of raising cash from a community which was not liable to knight service. The same consideration may explain the debt from the knights of Carmarthen. This works out at one mark per fee.[69] Moreover, in one instance, the aid paid by the knights of the bishopric of Durham, the

---

[65] Amt, 'Meaning of Waste'.

[66] Edward Grim, 'Life of St Thomas', *Materials for the History of Thomas Becket*, ed. J. C. Robertson and J. B. Sheppard, RS (London, 1875–85), II, 373–4; Garnier de Pont Saint-Maxence, *La Vie de Thomas Becket*, ed. E. Walberg (Lund, 1922), pp. 27–8; for a discussion of the confrontation, Green, 'Last Century of Danegeld', pp. 255–8.     [67] Green, *Government of England*, pp. 76–8.     [68] *PR 31 Henry I*, p. 84.

[69] *Ibid.*, p. 89; T. K. Keefe, *Feudal Assessments and the Political Community under Henry II and his sons* (Berkeley, Los Angeles, and London, 1983), p. 37.

bishop had died and so the payment was like the aid taken by Rufus from the knights of the bishopric of Worcester in 1095. This time the aid works out at a rate of one pound per knight enfeoffed.[70] In 1130 two lay magnates, Baldwin de Redvers and Robert of Bampton, had debts for an old aid of knights.[71] There is no reason to indicate how or why the debts had been incurred.[72] Henry was also taking an annual aid from the boroughs, an occasional aid from the counties, and gifts from soke tenants of Grantham in Lincolnshire, which belonged to the royal demesne. Although 1130 was evidently not a year of exceptionally heavy taxation since most of the aids were arrears, the pipe roll shows a variety of methods of assessment – on the hide, on the individual, and on the community. The word *not* used in the pipe roll is scutage, or shield money. According to the *Dialogue* scutage was taken in lieu of knight service at a rate of one pound or one mark per fee.[73] Explicit references to this levy are rare in the first half of the twelfth century, and it would appear that it was another means of assessing a financial contribution in lieu of knight service.[74] When all these references are put together, it seems that aid was a generic description for a variety of different levies.

Henry II revived both the pre-Conquest method of taxation on the hide and the post-Conquest concept of aids or gifts. In 1156 danegeld was levied in conjunction with an aid or gift from the counties, cities, boroughs, and Jews, and a levy called scutage and assessed on knights' fees by the quota was imposed on ecclesiastical tenants-in-chief. In 1159 there were many more exactions called 'gifts' to fund Henry's Toulouse campaign. Two marks per fee on the quota was raised from lay and church fees, and in addition ecclesiastical tenants-in-chief were asked for a gift, as were religious houses which did not owe knight service, the towns, the sheriffs, the Jews, and the moneyers. In the following years a variety of levies was taken, including danegeld in 1162.[75]

Henry's defeat over his plan to revive an annual levy of two shillings on the hide meant that he had to depend on negotiations with the tenants-in-chief. In 1165 a marriage between his eldest daughter Matilda and

---

[70] *PR 31 Henry I*, p. 132; Keefe, *Feudal Assessments*, pp. 36–7.    [71] *PR 31 Henry I*, pp. 153, 154.
[72] There was no return for Plympton in 1166, so perhaps there was no agreed quota, but the son-in-law of Robert of Bampton did make a return, *RBE*, I, 256–7.    [73] *Dialogus de Scaccario*, p. 52.
[74] Hollister, *Military Organization*, chapter 7; Keefe, *Feudal Assessments*, chapter 2.
[75] Round, *Feudal England*, pp. 209–25.

Henry the Lion was proposed, and Henry II needed to raise the money for her marriage portion. He may well have considered taking an aid on the hide, as his grandfather had done in 1110, but the objections raised to sheriffs' aid may have warned him off. Instead he turned to a levy based on the knight's fee, and set in hand an inquest into knight service in 1166.[76] Tenants-in-chief had to provide the names and amounts of service, first, of all those enfeoffed before 1135 (the old enfeoffment), and secondly, of all those enfeoffed since 1135 (the new enfeoffment), and also how many knights, if any, were charged against the demesne. When in 1168 an aid was taken for the marriage of Henry's eldest daughter, it was taken as a levy on the number of knights enfeoffed.

The century following the Conquest was the last in which levies on the hide played a major part in royal finance. Despite, or perhaps because of, light assessments and exemptions, the Norman kings had been able to use the system successfully whilst relying on contributions assessed in other ways from their tenants-in-chief, and from other wealthy groups in the community. There was slippage in royal control in Stephen's reign; at all events, however enraged Henry II was at Becket's opposition to the revival of annual two-shilling levies, he was not prepared to push the issue further. In that respect the Council of Woodstock marked a retreat from this particular method of taxation, towards a greater reliance on contributions negotiated with tenants-in-chief for knights or scutage which were in theory freewill offerings, not imposts.

Like the king, tenants-in-chief could also raise money from their vassals, from tenants by free socage, and from the unfree peasants of their demesne manors, but only scraps of evidence on this subject survive for our period. According to Glanvill, aids were taken from knightly vassals in times of need, to meet extraordinary expenses such as the knighting of an eldest son, the first marriage of his eldest daughter, or the ransoming of the lord's body. Although Glanvill queried whether an aid could be taken to meet the lord's military expenses, he answered that it could, but was not to be exacted unwillingly.[77] Evidently lords did take such aids, and it should not be concluded that they all coincided with royal demands.

Levies were also taken from the peasantry, and again there was probably little fixity about occasions and rates during the century after the

---

[76] Keefe, *Feudal Assessments*, pp. 13–14.     [77] *Glanvill*, IX, 8.

Conquest. Domesday Book records substantial sums levied from many Lincolnshire manors in the form of *tailla*, with single references to the same impost in Nottinghamshire and Yorkshire, in addition to the values set on the manors.[78] The word *tailla* simply means a levy, with no clue as to those liable, but in the Domesday context sokemen renders appear to be meant.[79] Such renders were almost certainly more common than appeared in 1086, probably because they were seigneurial not royal dues.

In eleventh-century France the term 'taille' was used of the levies taken by lords from the free and unfree peasants of their demesne manors. Seigneurial tallage in twelfth-century England was similarly an impost on peasants of demesne manors, but when it began is not clear. During the civil war of Stephen's reign there was evidently an extension of such imposts. Laymen were not restricting themselves to taxing their own peasants, which was bad enough, but extended their activities to peasants living on lands belonging to the church.[80] The word most commonly used for such levies was *tenserie* but in the ecclesiastical council of 1151 where such levies were condemned the word tallage was used.[81] Slowly the terminology began to settle. 'Aid' came to be used of the contributions of knightly vassals to their lords; this was taken at irregular intervals and was negotiable. 'Tallage' came to be applied to an annual tax on a lord's unfree peasants; only on royal demesne manors were free peasants tallaged. The profitability of tallage to lords may be gauged from incidental references in the pipe rolls to tallages levied when barons died and their lands came into the king's hands. These were collected by Painter, who showed that in 1200 tallage on the honour of Richmond was worth about 66 per cent of its annual revenue without Boston fair. In 1209 the bishop of Winchester collected £580 in tallage from his demesnes, equivalent to 50 per cent of their annual value.[82]

We are so used to thinking of this society as organized round the provi-

---

[78] *DB*, I, 321 (Conisborough), 285b (Gunthorpe).

[79] See note to Phillimore edition, Nottinghamshire, 9, 74; C. Stephenson, 'The Origin and Nature of the Taille', *Revue Belge de Philologie et d'Histoire*, 5 (1926), 801–70; Stephenson, 'The Seignorial Tallage in England', *Mélanges d'histoire offerts à Henri Pirenne par ses anciens élèves et ses amis*, 2 vols. (Brussels, 1926), II, 465–74.

[80] E. King. 'The Anarchy of King Stephen's Reign,' *Transactions of the Royal Historical Society*, 5th ser. 34 (1984), 137.

[81] *Councils and Synods, with Other Documents Relating to the English Church*, ed. D. Whitelock and others (Oxford, 1981), I.II, 823, discussed by King, 'Anarchy of Stephen's Reign', pp. 141–2.

[82] Painter, *Studies in the History of the English Feudal Barony*, pp. 168–9.

sion of services that it is easy to underestimate the significance of cash payments. Yet in twelfth-century England a whole range of demands for money was made on men of differing status, assessed in various ways, collected by different agencies, and for different ends. Some were fixed by custom whilst those called aids or gifts were negotiable. Some were collected by the crown, or by sheriffs for their own ends (sheriffs' aid), or by the church (tithe), or by lay and ecclesiastical lords (aids and tallages). In this complicated picture there was an element of overlap and competition between king, church, and lay aristocracy for revenue. The comprehensiveness of geld may have been a sore point for the aristocracy at the end of the Conqueror's reign; promises made by Henry I in 1100 and 1130 and by Stephen on his accession suggest that it continued to be a sensitive issue, and Henry II was compelled by Becket's stance to put the tax on the back burner, relying instead on aids and gifts. Although there were later levies based on land, the future of taxation lay with the concept underlying tithe, which covered revenues and moveable property as well as land. Louis VII levied a tax to raise money for the relief of the Holy Land, and this served as a precedent for Henry II's similar tax in 1166.[83] In Richard I's reign a levy on moveables was included in measures to raise money for the king's ransom, and in 1207 was applied for the first time directly to the costs of the king's campaigning.[84]

## Justice and jurisdiction

Sources relating to the judicial powers of the lay aristocracy in this period are fragmentary and difficult to interpret. We know virtually nothing about the jurisdictional powers of the old English aristocracy and thus how much may have been passed on to their successors, and the few surviving references have been subjected to very different interpretations. Two themes strongly pursued in historical writing have been royal power and the strength of the courts of shire and hundred in the later Anglo-Saxon period. Those scholars who have emphasized both have tended to play down the possibility that laymen and ecclesiastics might have exercised powers over serious criminal jurisdiction in their areas before 1066. There is little concrete evidence, moreover, that the crown made many

---

[83] Robert of Torigny, *Chronicles*, IV, 227.    [84] For the writ see Stubbs, *Select Charters*, pp. 278–9.

major jurisdictional grants in the Norman period.[85] Moreover, the century from 1066 to 1166 has often been treated in terms of the pre-history of the common law, and specifically how far Henry II's actions were novel. But the period has to be assessed in its own terms, and it will be suggested here that so far as the aristocracy is concerned, generalizations may be misleading, and what mattered was the particular concentration of powers in the hands of individuals and families. To make this point we need first to understand the context in which that power was exercised.

In the eleventh and twelfth centuries, judicial process was only one option for the punishment of wrongs and the resolution of disputes, and, by its nature, not necessarily the most appropriate. Injuries inflicted by the powerful on the weak were rarely going to come to a court of law. A large variety of injuries were regarded as matters to be sorted out between individuals, and once again they rarely surface in the written records. The king concerned himself principally with offences against his own authority and officials, plus a narrow range of the most serious offences such as murder and robbery. Some of these were regarded as his alone, whereas jurisdiction over other offences might be shared. Courts often provided appropriate fora for dealing with concrete matters of rights to property, land, and services, and their resolution is what chiefly crops up in the sources. When matters were raised in courts, personal status often decided where and how a resolution was to be reached. An important method of proof was by using oaths backed by oath helpers, and the ability to recruit oath helpers was a reflection of a man's standing in his community. Juries of local men were used to deliver verdicts on disputes over land and property. Where proof was less cut-and-dried, the judgement of God might be invoked by the use of an ordeal, either by iron or by water. Finally, the compensatory principle was strong in early English law in cases of homicide or personal injury, though fines (*wites*) were also levied and the most serious offences were regarded as unemendable, or bootless.

Exactly how much this pattern changed in the period after 1066 is diffi-

---

[85] See most recently two important papers by P. Wormald, 'Oswaldslow: an "Immunity"?', *St Oswald of Worcester. Life and Influence*, ed. N. Brooks and C. Cubitt (Leicester, 1996), pp. 116–28; and Wormald, 'Lordship and Justice in the Early English Kingdom: Oswaldslow Revisited', *Property and Power in the Early Middle Ages*, ed. W. Davies and P. Fouracre (Cambridge, 1995), pp. 114–36.

cult to assess, partly because of the lack of direct evidence about lords' courts, and partly because of the changing context. One variable was royal power. A case has been made that in the early Norman period the kings developed their jurisdiction over serious crime by a strict control of procedure and the application of discretionary penalties rather than fixed fines.[86] This is debatable, though a general proposition that the Norman kings tended to a strict law-and-order policy is more credible (see below, p. 252). Royal power certainly waxed between 1120 and 1135, waned under Stephen, and was reinvigorated and taken to new heights under Henry II. Another variable was the rise of ecclesiastical courts. These claimed jurisdiction not only over personnel, property, and land belonging to, or claimed by, the church, but also over a range of other issues such as legitimacy and marriage. From Stephen's reign, appeals were increasingly being made to Rome, and Henry II had only limited success in trying to turn the clock back.

One very significant extension of royal authority was over homicide, but this probably occurred at the expense of the kin rather than the lord. In 1066 it would appear that homicide could still be compensated for, but probably by the end of Henry I's reign the crown had taken cognisance of homicide.[87] It is not clear why this had happened, but one possible explanation is the effects of the operation of the murder fine. William the Conqueror, following Cnut, had protected his Norman followers by prescribing that if any corpse was found and was not proved to have been an Englishman, the lord of the murdered man (replaced by the men of the hundred in the twelfth century) had to produce the murderer within seven days or face a hefty fine.[88] It is possible that as a result of this enact-

---

[86] J. Goebel, *Felony and Misdemeanour* (New York, 1937), chapter 6 provides the most detailed discussion, but the argument offered here differs in some important respects. Also useful in tracing the history of trespass is J. S. Beckerman, 'Adding Insult to *Iniuria*: Affronts to Honor and the Origins of Trespass', *On the Laws and Customs of England. Essays in Honor of Samuel E. Thorne*, eds. M. S. Arnold, T. A. Green, S. A. Scully, and S. D. White (Chapel Hill, 1981), pp. 159–81.

[87] N. D. Hurnard, *The King's Pardon for Homicide before AD 1307* (Oxford, 1969), pp. 1–30; T. A. Green, 'Societal Concepts of Criminal Liability for Homicide in Medieval England', *Speculum*, 47 (1972), 669–74.

[88] *Willelmi Articuli*, 3,1; 3,2: Liebermann, *Die Gesetze der Angelsachsen*, I, 487; *Leis Willelme* 22: *ibid*., 511; *Leges Henrici Primi*, 13,2; 75,6; 76,6a; 75,6b; 91;92. For the suggestion that the murder fine had pre-Conquest antecedents, G. Garnett, '"Franci et Angli": the Legal Distinctions between Peoples after the Conquest', *Anglo-Norman Studies*, 8 (1985), 116–28; and see now B. R. O'Brien, 'From *Mordor* to *Murdrum*: the Preconquest Origin and Norman Revival of the Murder Fine', *Speculum*, 71 (1996), 74–110. I should like to thank Professor O'Brien for sending me a copy of his article in advance of publication.

ment it proved to be less than straightforward to secure compensation for 'ordinary' homicides. The distinction between murder and homicide may have been difficult to prove in the early twelfth century. Perhaps those kin who did bring charges were too frequently falling foul of royal justices, or the likelihood of fines to the king being imposed as a result of legal process meant that in practice there was little left over for the kin.

A second extension of royal authority which did very directly affect the aristocracy was forest law. In Normandy the duke had great forests, and so did some of his more important lords. In England, however, forests were much more exclusively royal. The restrictions imposed on access and usage of forests were from the first politically sensitive. The Conqueror's love of hunting and the laws he imposed to protect game attracted comment from the Anglo-Saxon Chronicler.[89] In 1088 Rufus tried to win the support of the English when faced with revolt by promising them free hunting, but later he is said to have so restricted hunting that it became a capital offence to take a stag.[90] William of Malmesbury commented on the unpopularity with the aristocracy of William's monopoly of hunting and specifically linked this to noble plots against him.[91] Henry I said at his coronation that he proposed to retain the forests as his father had held them with the consent of his barons.[92] Only a very few of the magnates were allowed to have their own forests; permission was needed for creating parks and warrens, and hunting within the royal forests also in theory required the royal assent.[93] By the end of the reign the forest may have covered as much as a third of the country, and even great magnates like Baldwin de Redvers found themselves heavily indebted at the exchequer for forest offences.[94] As early as 1155 Henry II ordered a forest eyre, and imposed fines for unlicensed ploughing within forest bounds (assarting).[95] It is easy to underestimate the nuisance of the forest laws to the aristocracy. Hunting provided exercise and recreation as well as food, and any restriction for those who lived within forest bounds was irksome if the law was rigorously applied. It may be a mistake to assume the full panoply of forest law was in force during the first century after the

---

[89] *ASC* 1087.     [90] *ASC* 1088.     [91] WM, *De Gestis Regum Anglorum*, II, 372.

[92] Stubbs, *Select Charters*, p. 119.     [93] OV, VI, 100; Green, *Government of England*, pp. 124–30.

[94] *PR 31 Henry I*, p. 153. It is not clear whether Baldwin himself had incurred the fine or was accounting for the proceeds of a forest eyre, but in either case he was held responsible.

[95] E. M. Amt, 'The Forest Regard of 1155', *Haskins Society Journal*, 2 (1990), 189–95; Amt, *Accession of Henry II*, pp. 168–73.

Conquest, but when an eyre did take place it must have been all the more bitterly resented.

A third development was the prescription by the Conqueror of procedures in cases where Frenchmen accused Englishmen of serious offences, or vice versa.[96] The Englishman was to defend himself by ordeal or battle; the Frenchman, however, had the option of compurgation. These regulations had at least three important aspects. One is the reference to trial by battle, thought to have been unknown in pre-Conquest England. A second was the restriction of the Englishman's ability to clear himself of serious charges by oathswearing, in a situation where his fellow Englishmen might have been very ready to help. Third, as Barlow pointed out, the use of the ordeal took less account of a man's social status than oathswearing.[97]

How did these regulations affect the position of the lay aristocracy, however? Goebel thought that the ordeal was strictly controlled by the king, though he was aware that there is no direct information about what was going on in lords' courts.[98] Barlow stressed the role ascribed to the clergy, suggesting that the ordeal, or at least that of hot iron, was exclusively under the control of the bishop, on the basis of the Conqueror's writ dealing with ecclesiastical pleas in the hundred courts.[99] Yet lords' courts evidently did use trial by battle, for this was laid down by Henry I as the procedure for dealing with disputes over land between tenants of the same lord.[100] Some lords may have had pits, in which ordeals by water could have been carried out.[101]

There is an almost total lack of evidence about the role of magnates before and after the Conquest in the maintenance of law and order as it related to matters other than disputes over land and services. In Cnut's second lawcode certain offences were said to belong to the king unless he chose to grant them away, such as housebreaking, the fine for fighting, and breach of the peace.[102] Maitland thought that the offences mentioned were serious, and that pre-Conquest kings granted away not only the profits but also the right to try them. Naomi D. Hurnard subsequently

---

[96] For the relevant texts, see Liebermann, *Die Gesetze der Angelsachsen*, I, 486–8; 492–520.

[97] Barlow, *English Church 1066–1154*, p. 159.    [98] Goebel, *Felony and Misdemeanour*, p. 417.

[99] Barlow, *English Church 1066–1154*, p. 159.    [100] Stubbs, *Select Charters*, p. 100.

[101] A grant to Battle abbey of the ordeal by water was confirmed by the bishop of Chichester: *Acta of the Bishops of Chichester*, ed. H. Mayr-Harting no. 5, as cited by Barlow, *English Church*, p. 159, n. 45.

[102] II Cnut 12, cf. 14, 15.

demonstrated, however, that these were not the gravest offences, and Patrick Wormald has strongly reinforced the view that in this respect Maitland was wrong, and that pre-Conquest kings were not granting away their criminal jurisdiction.[103] The question of when and where offences other than those reserved to the king were ordinarily dealt with, both before and after the Conquest, remains to be answered.

One particular problem is that of deciding the significance during the century after the Norman Conquest of rights of sake and soke, often combined with toll and team, and sometimes with infangthief. In general terms the right of sake and soke meant the power to exercise justice (see above, p. 198). Such rights may have been coterminous with a hundred. In 1253 William Mauduit IV defended his right to Wrangdike hundred on the basis of early twelfth-century grants, but the relevant texts do not specifically refer to the grant of the hundred, only to the grant of the lands of Michael of Hanslope with rights and liberties including sake, soke, toll, team, and infangthief.[104] In other cases, rights of sake and soke were held over particular estates, and probably conferred upon the holder permission to deal with matters which otherwise would have been heard in the hundred court. David Roffe has suggested that before the Conquest such rights were confined to those closest to the king, earls and king's thegns; that after the Conquest they were taken over by those who came to be called the king's barons; and that they in turn – a novel development – passed them on to *their* barons when they granted them manors.[105] If this was novel, then the aristocracy had increased its power to act independently at the expense of the crown.

There are two imponderables here, however. The first is the significance of the lack of pre-Conquest documentation of such grants by earls or king's thegns to their men, given that charters recording land grants from layman to layman only become common in the twelfth century. Could it be that in the early eleventh century powerful lords did convey these rights when they granted land, but that they were not recorded in

---

[103] Pollock and Maitland, *History of English Law*, 2, 453–8; N. D. Hurnard, 'The Anglo-Norman Franchises', *English Historical Review*, 64 (1949), 289–327, 433–60; Wormald, 'Lordship and Legislation in the Early Kingdom'. The documentary evidence for alienation of powers over serious crime is thin, but the point made in the text above is that some laymen either *de facto* had such power themselves, or were perhaps royal justices, or had influence over the local sheriff.

[104] *The Beauchamp Cartulary*, ed. E. Mason, Pipe Roll Society, new series, XLIII (1971–3), p. xxxv.

[105] Roffe, 'From Thegnage to Barony', pp. 175–6.

writing? Secondly, there is the question of the importance of the powers being conferred. Evidence in the form of court rolls held by lords with powers of sake, soke, toll, team, and infangthief survive only from the thirteenth century. One example is provided by the court rolls of the great Yorkshire manor of Wakefield, where the Warennes claimed to hold these rights. The rolls reveal a relatively extensive jurisdiction over matters such as slander, burglary, and larceny, and the right to a private gallows was exercised, remarkably, until 1850.[106] If the lords of Wakefield still had extensive powers over relatively serious offences in the late thirteenth century when royal justice over crime had expanded considerably, this argues that they probably had at least as much in the Norman period.

So far as disputes about land were concerned, matters within estates were dealt with in manorial courts, which were descended from the hall-moots mentioned in Domesday Book.[107] Disputes between under-tenants, or vavassors as they were described in Henry I's writ concerning the holding of the shire and hundred courts, were dealt with in the lord's court, the place and time of meetings being fixed by custom. In many cases the location was the lord's principal castle, his *caput honoris*. In theory at least lords could summon tenants thither from their remotest estates.[108] In practice lords seem to have held courts in more than one location: the Redvers family, for instance, held courts at Carisbrooke on the Isle of Wight, at Plympton in Devon, and possibly at Christchurch in Hampshire.[109] The Mowbrays held courts at Masham and Malzeard in Yorkshire, and at Crowle in Lincolnshire.[110]

Issues dealt with in honorial courts arose from the terms and conditions of tenure by knight service. Sometimes the disputes were between lords and tenants, such as a denial of homage and service, or perhaps they were between different tenants. Sometimes the lord's court was simply the forum in which an exchange or surrender was agreed, with the authority of the lord and the memory of those present to support the transaction. Memory and oral testimony were of course vital, given that the proceedings were not, as far as we know, recorded in writing. Oaths,

---

[106] *Court Rolls of the Manor of Wakefield* I, *1274–1297*, II, *1297–1309*, ed. W. Paley Baildon, III *1297–1309*, IV, *1315–1317* ed. John Lister, V, *1322–1331*, ed. J. W. Walker, Yorkshire Archaeological Society Record Series, XXIX, XXXVI, LVII, LXXVIII, CIX (1900, 1906, 1917, 1930, 1945).

[107] Stenton, *First Century*, pp. 43–4.     [108] *Leges Henrici Primi*, 55, 1a.

[109] *Charters of the Redvers Family*, pp. 29, 31–3. There is relatively little evidence for an honorial court at Christchurch: *ibid.*, pp. 30–1.     [110] *Mowbray Charters*, pp. lvi–lix.

quitclaims, and perambulations of boundaries were all made with the testimony of the court, and occasionally there are references to trial by
battle.

What powers did members of the new aristocracy have in practice?
Already in 1066 it appears that the archbishops of Canterbury and York
had very considerable jurisdictional privileges. Archbishop Lanfranc
reasserted his privileges in the legal proceedings at Penenden, and it has
been demonstrated how in later versions of the record the claims were
enlarged and made more precise.[111] The king was said to have only three
customs in the lands of the church of Canterbury relating to offences
committed on or near the king's road; for his part the archbishop claimed
other customs in the lands of King William and Earl Odo, and in addition
made a general claim to rights of sake, soke, toll, team, and infangthief for
the lands of Canterbury.[112] Henry I confirmed to Archbishop Gerard in the
archbishopric of York all his customs including pleas of moneyers and
robbers.[113] The great abbeys of Ely, Ramsey, Bury, and Glastonbury had
important judicial privileges; again, the basis of their privileged position
went back to before the Conquest.[114]

There was much less continuity in terms of both land and privileges in
the case of the lay aristocracy. Only the earl of Chester and bishop of
Durham held lordships which comprised whole counties and they eventually established quasi-regalian rights over them. In Cheshire the earl
appointed the sheriff, and so far as we know the shire court had a full
range of judicial powers. The bishop of Durham came to have comparable
powers over Durham though his authority can only have been imposed
gradually and in the early years must have been nominal given the difficulty of imposing his authority.

It seems likely, however, that a few laymen at least had comparable privileges, especially those with compact lordships. Earl Reginald probably
had powers over Cornwall between 1141 and 1175 comparable with those
of the earl of Chester over Cheshire, for like Cheshire no account was
presented for Cornwall at the exchequer during the earl's lifetime.
Geoffrey de Mandeville for a brief period controlled the shrievalties and
justiciarships of three counties: London and Middlesex, Essex, and

---

[111] D. Bates, 'The Land Pleas of William I's Reign: Penenden Health Revisited', *Bulletin of the Institute of Historical Research*, 51 (1978), 1–19.   [112] Van Caenegem, *English Lawsuits*, I, no. 5.   [113] *RRAN*, ii, no. 518.
[114] See especially H. Cam, 'The Evolution of the Medieval English Franchise', *Speculum*, 32 (1957), 427–42.

Hertfordshire.[115] William Peverel was a very powerful figure in the north midlands in the early years of Henry I's reign. He seems to have acted as justiciar for Henry I in Nottinghamshire, and Helgot, sheriff by 1105, was his under-tenant, as was his successor, Robert de Heriz.[116] William probably had forest rights over the Peak; he may have been given Glossop in Longdendale, and lands in Lancashire; and Robert de Pavilly, sheriff of Northamptonshire at some point between 1103 and 1106, was his tenant.[117] William I Peverel died in 1114; his son William II did not witness a royal document until 1121.[118] He may not have enjoyed the same influence as his father, for his next appearance in a royal document was at the council of Northampton in 1131, or he may simply have stayed away from court.[119] King Henry nevertheless had employed him as a justice to effect an agreement between the abbot of Burton-on-Trent and Robert de Ferrers concerning disputed woods, a concord which was agreed at Tutbury castle at some date between about 1121 and 1127.[120] Although William may initially have prospered under Stephen, he was not created earl. He was captured at Lincoln and his son-in-law Robert de Ferrers, earl of Derbyshire, extended his authority over Nottinghamshire as well.[121] Robert de Ferrers may have controlled the shrievalties of the two counties, for his steward, Robert de Perers, was sheriff at the start of the following reign.[122]

The earls of Leicester, Robert I and Robert II, were also very powerful within their county. There was a royal sheriff there, but in Stephen's reign the office probably came under the earl's influence; in 1154-5 the county was accounted for at the exchequer by a man who was or had been the earl's steward.[123] The county was also subject to the visitation of royal justices, at least during the 1120s. It was at 'Hundehoge' (probably Huncote) in Leicestershire that Ralph Basset hanged forty-four thieves in 1124, and Richard Basset, Ralph's son, held pleas in the county in 1129-30.[124] Again, it is likely that Robert II administered such justice as there was in Stephen's reign. He also had his own forest – 'Hereswoode'.[125]

---

[115] *RRAN*, III, nos. 275, 276.     [116] *Ibid.*, II, nos. 870, 704-5, 1355; Farrer, *Honors and Knights' Fees*, I, 211, 154.

[117] Green, 'Earl Ranulf II and Lancashire', p. 105; *RRAN*, II, nos. 879, 704-5, 1355; Farrer, *Honors and Knights' Fees*, I, 188.     [118] *RRAN*, II, no. 1285.     [119] *Ibid.*, no. 1715.

[120] Van Caenegem, *English Lawsuits* I no. 252.

[121] Jones, 'Charters of Robert II de Ferrers', pp. 9-10.     [122] *RBE*, II, 653.

[123] *Ibid.*, II, 655; Stenton, *Documents . . . Danelaw*, pp. 248-9.     [124] *ASC* 1124; *PR 31 Henry I*, p. 88.

[125] Crouch, *Beaumont Twins*, p. 191.

Some lords after 1066 had the privilege of holding private hundred courts, dependent on their principal demesne manors, and this gave them rights not only over the inhabitants of the demesne manors but also over other inhabitants of the hundred. Some hundreds were already in private hands before 1066. It is not certain whether this meant that lords simply received the profits or that they held the courts as well: the latter may have been the case if the lord owned all the land there.[126] In the Norman period further hundreds were granted out to, or simply slipped into, private hands, as noted in an earlier chapter (see above, p. 159).[127] Such jurisdiction may have been particularly desirable in counties where there were still considerable numbers of freemen, but elsewhere too hundreds slipped into private hands.

Since the original powers of hundred and wapentake courts are not clear, it is hard to gauge the effects of the coming of the Normans on them. Much depends on our view of tenth-century government and society. It has been suggested that from their inception hundred courts had important powers in the pursuit and capture of criminals.[128] If hundred and wapentake courts had been very powerful, were they then sidelined by the administration of royal justice, or the development of honorial courts? Whether they had declined from an earlier, more powerful role or not, by the twelfth century hundred courts dealt only with relatively local land cases and minor affrays.[129] Whether in private or royal hands, however, it is likely that hundred courts were influenced by local great lords. As Robin Fleming has pointed out in a recent study of oral testimony and the Domesday Inquest, jurors could be overawed. In a dispute between the bishop of Rochester and the sheriff of Cambridgeshire, a jury meeting in the shire court in the presence of sheriff Picot gave a verdict in favour of the king. Odo bishop of Bayeux demanded that a freshly sworn jury confirm the verdict of the first, which they did, but subsequently one

---

[126] For a recent restatement of this view, Wormald, 'Lordship and Justice in the Early English Kingdom', p. 120.

[127] P. Dalton, 'William Earl of York and Royal Authority in Yorkshire in the Reign of Stephen', *Haskins Society Journal*, 2 (1990), 155–65; Dalton, 'Aiming at the Impossible: Ranulf Earl of Chester and Lincolnshire in the Reign of King Stephen', *Earldom of Chester and its Charters*, pp. 109–34.

[128] H. R. Loyn, 'The Hundred in England in the Tenth and Early Eleventh Centuries', *British Government and Administration*, ed. H. Hearder and H. R. Loyn (Cardiff, 1974), pp. 1–15; P. Wormald, 'In Pursuit of Crime: the Early English Approach', unpublished paper, British Legal History Conference, Oxford 1991. I am grateful to the author for sending me a copy of the text in advance of publication.

[129] *Leges Edwardi Confessoris*, 28, 1.

of the original twelve confessed to perjury. All were summoned to London; the first jury was found guilty of perjury and the second failed the ordeal of hot iron.[130] On this occasion the jury was overawed by the king's sheriff, but there must have been other occasions when the presence of local magnates had a decisive influence over verdicts. Writing of the affairs of the abbey of Bury St Edmunds at the end of the twelfth century, Jocelin of Brakelond made a revealing comment about the summons of a hundred court to deal with a claim made by the earl of Clare about a payment of five shillings a year. The earl, we are told, not only appeared in person, but was attended by Aubrey de Vere, earl of Oxford, and was surrounded by barons and knights.[131]

A related issue is the development of frankpledge, and the power of lords to police the activities of their men. How could men be persuaded not to offend, or be brought to justice if they did so? A man's kindred was expected to make formal accusations in cases of death or injury, and the notion of compensation gave them a financial incentive to do so. The concept of pledging, or 'borh', was a way of establishing an individual's lawworthiness, in that he looked to others to reinforce his word. Yet these two concepts could only work within limits: there might be very good reasons, as we have already seen, why kinsmen were reluctant to make appeals. Equally, the man who had no kin, or was untrustworthy, 'tyht-bysig', was difficult to deal with. By the reign of Cnut the king was insisting that all free men had to be in a tithing or in pledge.[132] By the twelfth century tithings were either groups of ten men or a territorial unit, the township. In other words, pledging came to be organized using hundreds and their subdivisions, and could date back at least to Cnut's reign if not before. Already it would appear that frankpledge was compulsory, though it was probably not universal. In the twelfth century there were areas where frankpledge did not apply, in the counties bordering Wales and in the north, and if frankpledge had been a Norman innovation then it would probably have been set up in these regions. By the twelfth century many free men were also falling outside the scope of the frankpledge system, and it became a way of policing the lower orders.[133]

Many unanswered questions therefore remain about the scope of aristo-

---

[130] R. Fleming, 'Oral Testimony and the Domesday Inquest', *Anglo-Norman Studies*, 17 (1995), 101–22.
[131] *The Chronicle of Jocelin of Brakelond*, p. 57.  [132] II Cnut, 20.
[133] W. A. Morris, *The Frankpledge System* (Cambridge, Mass., 1910).

cratic justice and policing during the century following the Conquest, because there is so little surviving strictly contemporary evidence. One problem lies in assessing the starting point: how vigorous was royal justice in the late Anglo-Saxon period, how important were aristocratic powers then, and how much lay totally outside the legal process? A second problem lies in evaluating developments in the Norman period. Norman sheriffs were not infrequently local magnates themselves. They could have used their influence to buttress the king's authority locally, or have used their power for their own ends. The king for his part intervened more rigorously in the local courts after 1066; as Fleming has pointed out, the Domesday assemblies indicate 'the rapid and immediate expansion of royal power in regional assemblies after the Norman Conquest'.[134] Some great magnates clearly had important rights of justice under the Norman kings, and those whose estates were in the far north had peacekeeping duties as a matter of course.

There is little sign that the aristocracy's power to command armed men had been eroded by the end of our period. Indeed, the protracted civil war of Stephen's reign argues the reverse: it was the great men who provided much of the military muscle and it was they who in effect brought the war to an end by forcing the leading protagonists to negotiate. The Anglo-Norman kings inherited an impressive governmental legacy, but disputes surrounding each change of ruler and the costs of their continental wars necessitated a *laissez-faire* attitude to loyal nobles. A firm, even brutal, regime of peacekeeping was imposed, but the only evidence we have of a policy which seriously impinged on magnate powers of justice comes in the 1130 pipe roll. From this it is evident that where royal officials had intervened, the king tended to be lenient to those closely associated with him. Such a degree of judicial intervention must perforce have ended, at least in some regions of the country, under Stephen. Henry II's accession brought to the throne a ruler whose title was undisputed, and he set out to recover lost lands and rights, yet he had to tread warily and to compromise in individual cases. In one area it proved politically impossible to turn the clock back, and this was over taxation on hides, and here he backed down in the face of Becket's objection. His vigorous administration of justice, particularly in land law, was to have profound conse-

---

[134] Fleming, 'Oral Testimony and the Domesday Inquest', p. 119.

quences for seigneurial courts, but the full implications were not immediately obvious.

Finally, although the crown and magnates, both lay and ecclesiastical, were in some respects in competition, they were also each increasing their power base. Royal taxation did not increase at the expense of aristocratic taxation; each increased in parallel and was ultimately sustainable by economic growth. Hapless peasants somehow had to find the resources to pay tallage, tithe, and a multiplicity of other levies. Government generally grew in power, scope, and professionalism in this period. Most is known about the rise of professionals in the king's service: the clerks and laymen who were able to make careers for themselves. The laymen are especially significant as, enriched with lands, they moved up the social ladder. But the servants of great magnates shared to some extent in this development; magnates too needed clerks to draw up their documents and at a minimum they needed stewards to manage their estates. By the mid-twelfth century the state and society within which aristocratic power was exercised had changed radically.

# 9   The political world of the aristocracy

## The role of the court

At the court of the Norman kings the members of the lay aristocracy formed but one element. The royal entourage included, in varying numbers according to circumstances, ecclesiastics, servants, women of all ranks, and visitors. Access to the king was crucial to personal advancement and for involvement in decision making. Yet there are no political diaries or personal papers to throw light on the workings of court politics, on who was closest to the king at any one time, and who – if anyone other than the king himself – shaped major decisions. Narrative sources comment only occasionally on the role of individuals, and the use of witness lists to assess attendance at court has limitations. In any case, assiduity of attendance is not an infallible guide to the degree of influence, particularly where great magnates, who had their own affairs to look after, were concerned.

Yet the court was the centre of the political world, and the tempo of politics was set by the power struggles within the ruling dynasty. Issues such as war with neighbouring powers, relations with the papacy in general and investitures in particular, the relations between the two archbishops of Canterbury and York, the suppression of revolt, and the disposal of patronage, formed the warp and weft of politics. So far as we can see there were no clear lines of division between lay and clerical matters: ecclesiastical councils sometimes followed on great courts. Lay magnates might be involved in ecclesiastical matters: the role of the count of Meulan in Rufus's and Henry I's dealings with Anselm is the most conspicuous example in the Norman period.[1] Conversely curial bishops were key figures in the governments of the Norman kings until the fall of Roger of Salisbury and his nephews in 1139. Ranulf Flambard, Robert Bloet bishop of Lincoln, and Roger of Salisbury were all deeply involved in administering the king's rights, and they may have been consulted about the waging

---

[1] S. Vaughn, *Anselm of Bec and Robert of Meulan. The Innocence of the Dove and the Wisdom of the Serpent* (Berkeley, Los Angeles, and London, 1987).

of war. The point is that there were no hard-and-fast rules about who was to be consulted on what issues; the court was a small, competitive, and highly personal world. In Rufus's day it was full of men of fashion with long hair and pointed-toed shoes; in Henry I's there is said to have been an atmosphere of suspicion, so much so that the king changed the position of his bed each night. Attendance by the great men from time to time was a duty and was politic; it may or may not have been enjoyable, and we can only guess whether individuals were trusted, or liked, or both. We can see, for instance, that there was a small group close to William the Conqueror made up of William FitzOsbern, Roger of Montgomery, and Roger de Beaumont who had fought by his side in Normandy before 1066. Rufus's intimates included William d'Aubigny, son of a lesser lord from the Cotentin, and Robert son of Haimo the steward. Henry I relied on Robert of Meulan and his brother Henry earl of Warwick in the first half of his reign, but they were probably some years older than he was. He was also attached to Robert FitzHaimon, and wept when he heard of his death. Stephen seems to have started off being everyone's friend, but it is hard to see who were his personal friends as opposed to the members of his house-hold and loyalist magnates like the Clares.

This world could only hold together, however, if kings could command sufficient support and loyalty from the great men. Loyalty to the king in theory overrode all other loyalties except that to God. It was given and renewed on a personal basis and this, as well as the small size of the elite, gave a personal edge to political relationships. The death and succession of a king were thus moments of great political tension. All the successions until that of 1154 in our period were contested, and created a critical dilemma for the magnates of England and Normandy as to whom they should support. The claimants made promises, both general and individ-ual, and partly on that basis loyalty was given. Understanding the implica-tions of loyalty, and the nature of rewards, is therefore a starting point of this chapter.

For the magnates the factor which in a sense complicated their rela-tions with the king was that he was their lord as well as their king. He took their homage and in return they offered service and counsel. Notions of 'good lordship' informed political relationships at the highest level, with the result that those who felt that the king had not behaved to them as a good lord should, could withhold service and in the last resort break off relations. Much of the sub-text of these relationships is concealed from us in the sources. Orderic tells us that William de Roumare rebelled against Henry I because the king held William's mother's lands, which had been handed over by William's stepfather Ranulf earl of Chester as part of a deal. The background was that his stepfather had held William's lands during his minority, and had surrendered them to Henry when he succeeded to the earldom of Chester. William in effect went to war to recover his inheritance, of which he felt he was being deprived. The end of the story was that William did receive at least two-thirds of his mother's lands, her dower lands passing to a younger son. Viewed from one angle, therefore, William was a rebel against the king/duke; from his point of view he was using pressure to persuade his lord to accept his homage for his mother's lands.[2]

Often in the Norman period a flashpoint was custody of a castle. Some castles, though royal, were held for several generations in the same family, yet they were supposed to be handed over if the king demanded them. Such was Bedford castle, held by the Beauchamps since the Conquest. Stephen demanded it from Miles de Beauchamp in 1138; the latter replied that he feared to lose his entire inheritance – correctly, for Stephen planned to bestow the marriage of Miles's niece, with the Beauchamp lands and Bedford, on Hugh de Beaumont. Miles clearly felt that Stephen's attitude was unjust; hence his response was to fortify the castle against the king (see below, pp. 297–8). Castles were often the crux, because handing them over to the king or his men was a palpable indication of loyalty; refusal was followed by military action. Another test was a refusal to answer three royal summonses to court. From the lord's point of view it was both dangerous to attend and dangerous not to do so. Those who did might be arrested, as was Robert de Bellême who attended Henry I's court in Normandy under safe conduct, or so he believed. Stephen used similar tactics against Geoffrey de Mandeville and Ranulf earl of Chester. Those who stayed away, however, like Robert de Mowbray in 1095, had to be prepared to fight it out. It was not surprising that the bishop of Durham, who was summoned to court by Rufus in 1088, after his loyalty and commitment had been found wanting during the recent rebellion, spent a good deal of time negotiating the terms and pledges for his

---

[2] OV, VI, 332–4.

journey. The political history of Anglo-Norman England was therefore turbulent, and armed force was used frequently. But force was only one, the
most extreme, weapon in an armoury of methods used by the king and
the aristocracy, and has to be seen in a context where the magnates
expected to be treated by the king, their lord, as they treated their men.

A central issue was how far loyalties could be strained without being
breached, given that there was a grey area between actions such as a
refusal of service or surrender of a castle, or withdrawal from the king's
court, and actions which might more clearly have been perceived as a
direct attack on the king. Historians have perhaps sometimes used the
term 'rebellion' to describe actions which contemporaries might have
regarded as the application of pressure rather than a breach of loyalties. It
has been pointed out that when Robert of Gloucester famously renounced
his fealty to Stephen in 1138, the statement by William of Malmesbury
that this was according to custom may have been misleading, in the sense
that a formal renunciation of this kind is not known to have occurred
before in Norman England.[3] It has also been argued that the behaviour of
Ranulf II earl of Chester in Stephen's reign also needs to be interpreted
with caution. His actions in 1141 suggest that he saw himself as a man
with a grievance, treated unjustly by the king, not as an opportunist or a
committed Angevin supporter. Until his arrest in 1146 he may never have
broken formally with Stephen, and even after 1146 he was not whole-
heartedly an adherent of the Angevin cause.[4] We must attempt to see how
Ranulf saw his own situation at each stage, as well as how his actions may
have been viewed by the king and by the Angevins.

The word most commonly used in narrative sources after 1066 to
describe treachery, is *proditio*. In the *Leges Henrici Primi*, *infidelitas* (breach of
fealty) and *proditio* are both listed with the other rights of jurisdiction
which the king had over all men.[5] It is not clear how the two were distinguished: presumably the act of betrayal in itself constituted a breach of
an oath of fealty. How were these offences defined? Orderic Vitalis
includes in his account of the involvement of Earl Waltheof in the revolt
of 1075 an imagined reply made by Waltheof to the other earls who

---

[3] J. Gillingham, '1066 and the Introduction of Chivalry', *Law and Government in the Middle Ages. Essays in honour of Sir James Holt*, ed. G. Garnett and J. Hudson (Cambridge, 1994), p. 48.

[4] P. Dalton, '*In Neutro Latere*: The Armed Neutrality of Ranulf II Earl of Chester in King Stephen's Reign', *Anglo-Norman Studies*, 14 (1992), 48–9, 52.     [5] *Leges Henrici Primi*, 10.

invited him to join them, and from this account valuable insights may be gained into the situation as it was in the early twelfth century when Orderic was writing. In this reply Waltheof said that he owed faith to his lord and that King William had received his fealty as a greater from a lesser man. How was he therefore to be unfaithful, *infidus*? He would be publicly proclaimed as a sacrilegious traitor, *proditor sacrilegus*. The law of England punished the traitor by beheading and removed from his whole progeny their natural inheritance. Orderic continued by describing how, when Earl Roger was subsequently summoned before the king's court, he was unable to deny his treachery, *proditionem*, and was condemned by the laws of the Normans to perpetual imprisonment after forfeiting all his earthly inheritance, *haereditate terrena*. Waltheof's defence was that although he knew of the treachery, he had not consented to it; the judges were divided, but Waltheof remained in prison and was executed after a year.[6] Yet Waltheof did not attack William personally, and he had disengaged himself from the conspiracy at a very early stage. He had rebelled before and had been forgiven, and it was remarkable that the king had him executed whereas another leading rebel, Morcar, was simply kept in prison until William's death.[7] Waltheof was thus the only leading Englishman known to have suffered the death penalty in this way.

If we look to earlier practices for guidance, we find that Alfred's laws had prescribed the death penalty and loss of all possessions for any man who plotted the king's death.[8] A direct attack on the person of the king had obviously been a heinous offence worthy of the severest punishment; the difficulty is to know how widely the offence was defined. There were men who had lost their lands and their lives in the tenth and eleventh centuries; the last years of Aethelred's reign and the early years of Cnut's were notably bloodthirsty. The problem is again that we have no information about contemporary justification for the way the king's enemies were treated.[9] Desertion of the king's army was also severely punished in pre-Conquest England. In Cnut's lawcode he who deserted an expedition by land or sea was to lose his life and all he had; if he had bookland, it was to pass to the king.[10]

The Norman dukes, so far as is known, had tended to use the weapons of

---

[6] OV, II, 310–22.    [7] OV, II, 258; IV, 98.    [8] Alfred, 4: Liebermann, *Die Gesetze der Angelsachsen*, I, 50–1.
[9] e.g. ASC 1002, 1015, 1016.    [10] II Cnut 77: Liebermann, *Die Gesetze der Angelsachsen*, I, 364–5.

loss of lands and exile against their enemies. Desertion of the duke's army was evidently regarded as a serious offence. William of Poitiers gives as the reason for the breach between William and William count of Arques the latter's unauthorized departure from the siege of Domfront. Most of Count William's estates were confiscated.[11] In 1054 Roger de Mortemer, commander of Duke William's army, offered shelter to Count Ralph of Amiens-Valois-Vexin, one of the leaders of the army opposing William, because he had done homage to Ralph. The duke exiled Roger who, though subsequently reconciled and restored to his lands, did not recover the castle of Mortemer, which was entrusted instead to Roger's kinsman, William de Warenne.[12] Another case of temporary exile described by Orderic was that of Arnold of Echauffour, who was banished for a time in the early 1060s, spending part of his exile only twenty-five miles beyond the frontier of Normandy.[13] Deaths did take place, notably in the power struggles of the Conqueror's minority, but it does not appear that the dukes themselves imposed the death penalty against rebels.

In England as we have seen Waltheof was the only Englishman of rank to be put to death, and in the speech attributed to the dying Conqueror by Orderic, William said that he had kept Morcar in prison for many years not for any just cause but because he feared that if he were released he would stir up rebellion, and that it was a king's duty to restrain evildoers. Nevertheless he proposed to set all prisoners free, except his brother Odo, if they took an oath to public officials to keep the peace in England and Normandy. Rufus did not exact death penalties after the rebellion of 1088, and Henry I also imprisoned his enemies: he kept his brother Robert and cousin William in custody from 1106 until their deaths.[14] Robert de Bellême too did not regain his freedom after his arrest in 1112.[15]

The second revolt against Rufus, however, that of 1095, was followed by impressive trials. William of Eu was appealed of treason and, having failed in trial by battle, was blinded and castrated, whilst his cousin and steward, William of Alderi, was hanged.[16] Rufus may have been influenced to act harshly because of the rumour that the rebels plotted his death.[17] Henry was notably severe in dealing with rebels in Normandy in 1124. Two were blinded and castrated on the grounds that they had become his

[11] WP, p. 52.   [12] OV, III, 88.   [13] Bates, *Normandy before 1066*, pp. 166–7; OV, II, 92–4, 106.
[14] For William see C. Warren Hollister, 'Royal Acts of Mutilation', *Monarchy, Magnates and Institutions*, p. 298.   [15] WM, *De Gestis Regum*, II, 372–3.   [16] FW, II, 39.   [17] FW, II, 38.

men freely and yet had broken their fealty by following their lords. A third, Luc de la Barre, was similarly punished though he was not the king's man because, having been allowed to leave the castle of Pont-Audemer, he had continued to aid Henry's enemies and had lampooned the king. Orderic's account of this episode clearly has an element of special pleading. Henry perhaps was justified in acting so severely as king of England, but not in Normandy; in any case the tide of opinion was flowing away from such severe punishment of aristocratic rebels. Orderic relates how the count of Flanders had challenged Henry's actions, especially in the case of Geoffrey de Tourville and Odard of Le Pin, who had been following their lords.[18] It is significant that Henry mutilated his captives rather than put them to death.

Stephen is known to have hanged members of the rebel garrison at Shrewsbury in 1138, including Arnulf de Hesdin. Again it is Orderic who explains that the king was angered by their refusal to accept honourable surrender: in other words, by their refusal they had sacrificed their right to life.[19] There is an interesting account of a case in 1149 when two men in the king's army at Bedford were accused of plotting the king's death. Both were the men of the abbot of Bury, who successfully claimed that the case belonged to the liberty of St Edmunds. The king's response was to go to Bury where he was reconciled with the two men.[20] If we are to take the account at face value, the accused men had plotted the death of the king, yet Stephen was prepared to allow the case to be heard at Bury. It was not quite clear whether the abbot had presided over the trial, and why the king was reconciled with the men rather than punishing them, but by Henry I's standards it was a remarkable act of clemency.

There was a range of options other than corporal punishment of traitors. Land could be confiscated and then restored, or a punitive fine could be imposed. Both of these methods offered at least some prospect of rehabilitation and stopped short of permanent disseisin. Thus William de Warenne was able to recover his English estates which he had lost by supporting Robert in 1101, and thereafter remained loyal to Henry I.[21] William de Mandeville was subjected to a huge fine of more than £2,000, probably for allowing Ranulf Flambard to escape from the Tower in 1100.

---

[18] OV, VI, 352–6.   [19] OV, VI, 520–2.   [20] Van Caenegem, *English Lawsuits*, I, no. 331.
[21] C. Warren Hollister, 'The Taming of a Turbulent Earl: Henry I and William de Warenne', *Monarchy, Magnates and Institutions*, pp. 137–44.

The fine was raised by mortgaging three demesne manors to Eudo *dapifer*, though Geoffrey II de Mandeville was able eventually to recover them.[22] Ivo de Grandmesnil was not so fortunate. Accused of waging war by burning his neighbours' crops, he was heavily fined. He mortgaged his land to Robert of Meulan to meet the fine, and left on a pilgrimage from which he did not return.[23]

Another possibility was confiscation of castles rather than land. Stephen used this manoeuvre against the bishops in 1139, Geoffrey II de Mandeville in 1143, and Ranulf II earl of Chester in 1146. On each occasion the charge was different. The bishops were held to be responsible for a brawl in the king's court involving their men.[24] Geoffrey de Mandeville was accused of appropriating royal prerogatives and of planning to bestow the country on Matilda. This is more obviously a case of treason, and the author of the *Gesta* uses the word *proditio*, but Geoffrey was released after surrendering his castles.[25] Ranulf of Chester came under suspicion from the king's advisers because he retained royal lands and castles and had not given pledges or hostages as proof of his loyalty. When he came to court to solicit Stephen's aid against the Welsh, the king's advisers were even more suspicious that Stephen would be put in danger, and suggested that Ranulf should first make satisfaction about lands, castles, pledges, and hostages.[26]

Nevertheless the Norman kings did confiscate lands permanently. Odo of Bayeux was the chief casualty of the revolt of 1088, and in 1095 Stephen of Aumale lost Holderness, William of Eu the estates he held in chief, and Robert de Mowbray the earldom of Northumberland. Sometimes the chronicle accounts make it clear that forfeiture followed a trial, and in this respect we can compare the king's actions with those of a lord whose right to confiscate his tenant's land was supposed to be exercised circumspectly and after legal process.[27] William of Eu, as already mentioned, was formally appealed of treason in 1095 by Geoffrey Baynard. Robert de Mowbray's lands were confiscated after he had failed to answer three summonses to court. In 1102 Henry I took away all the English and Welsh lands of Robert de Bellême, Roger the Poitevin, and Arnulf of Montgomery. Robert had been watched by the king for more than a year,

---

[22] Hollister, 'The Misfortunes of the Mandevilles', *Monarchy, Magnates and Institutions*, pp. 18–20.
[23] OV, VI, 18.      [24] WM, *Historia Novella*, p. 27.      [25] *Gesta Stephani*, p. 163.      [26] Ibid., pp. 184, 194–6.
[27] Hudson, *Land, Law, and Lordship*, p. 34.

was summoned to answer forty-five charges and, when he failed to attend, suffered forfeiture. Orderic imagines a discussion in the king's forces outside Bridgnorth, in which the leading men argued for a reconciliation between Henry and Robert on the ground that Henry, if successful in this instance, would proceed to trample on them like helpless slave girls, whereas the rank-and-file knights urged the king not to make peace but to capture Robert alive or dead.[28] In 1104 William count of Mortain lost his English estates, as did Robert de Stuteville in 1106 and Robert de Montfort in 1107. In 1110 William Malet and William Bainard lost their lands as did, at least for a time, Philip de Briouze, and at some stage before 1114 Robert de Lacy and Robert son of Picot also lost their lands.

There were few if any major permanent confiscations of estates in England after about 1120, as Henry became increasingly dominant. The Norman lands of Waleran of Meulan were confiscated in 1124 but restored in 1129.[29] A striking trial occurred in 1130, when Geoffrey de Clinton the king's chamberlain and treasurer was accused of treason, *proditio*.[30] The case was heard before Henry I and King David of Scotland at Woodstock. It has been suggested that it might well have been engineered by Roger earl of Warwick, who had little reason to relish the appearance in Warwickshire of such a powerful *curialis*.[31] The basis of the charge may well have been some kind of financial maladministration, as there was obviously concern in 1129–30 about the receipts from royal revenues. In the 1130 pipe roll Geoffrey was still sheriff of Warwickshire, rendering account for lands and offices, and in possession of vast estates. He disappears from view soon afterwards, however, and his lands and chamberlainship passed to his son Geoffrey.[32]

Stephen and Matilda had by no means abandoned the right of confiscation; their difficulty rather proved to be that of enforcement. Baldwin de Redvers, who was amongst the first to rebel against Stephen, was said to have lost his lands when he fled, but the king did not regrant them and

---

[28] OV, vi, 26.     [29] *ASC* 1129; OV, vi, 356.     [30] HH, p. 252; OV, iv, 276.

[31] D. Crouch, 'Geoffrey de Clinton and Roger Earl of Warwick: New Men and Magnates in the Reign of Henry I', *Bulletin of the Institute of Historical Research*, 55 (1982), 120.

[32] Green, *Government of England*, pp. 239–42; on p. 93 there the suggestion was made that Geoffrey may have gone to Jerusalem, but Emma Mason has pointed out that the relevant reference, which occurs in the cartulary of Rochester cathedral priory, is more likely to have been to Geoffrey II: 'Fact and Fiction in the English Crusading Tradition: the earls of Warwick in the Twelfth Century', *Journal of Medieval History*, 14 (1988), 94.

Baldwin seems to have recovered control over some of them in the 1140s.[33] Robert of Bampton's lands were also confiscated, as we know from the fact that Stephen regranted his estates in Essex.[34] Stephen also tried to take over Robert of Gloucester's lands when the latter renounced his homage, but seems to have secured only the royal castle of Dover, and that after Queen Matilda blockaded Walkelin Maminot there.[35] Quite what happened to the lands of the midland earldom of Northampton–Huntingdon after 1141 is not clear. Stephen was not prepared to tolerate Prince Henry of Scots as earl, and it seems likely that Simon de Senlis retained possession at least of the estates in Northamptonshire.[36] Matilda in 1141 began to cancel grants made by Stephen, and, according to the *Gesta Stephani*, a hostile witness, 'she arbitrarily annulled any grant fixed by the king's royal decree, [and] she hastily snatched away and conferred on her own followers anything he had given in unshakeable perpetuity to churches or to his comrades in arms'.[37] Both the Empress and her son were prepared to make promises to win support, but at the end of the war it was clear that the only realistic basis for a peaceful settlement of disputes over land was to turn the clock back to the situation at the death of Henry I, modified as and when political needs dictated. But there was to be no return to the practices of Henry I: pragmatism accorded here with strengthening rights of inheritance. Henry II was well aware that it would no longer have been considered acceptable to remove lands from a family permanently except for the most grave reasons, and armed rebellion against the king was no longer among them. When Henry of Essex was appealed of treason in 1163 it was on a charge of deserting the king's standard on campaign, an offence severely punished already in Cnut's laws, as we have seen.[38]

The removal of rebellion from the definition of treasonable offences has recently been associated with the rise of chivalric values, by which it ceased to be regarded as decent to kill or to mutilate aristocratic enemies.[39] It can also be seen as a victory for the aristocratic view of rebellion. Men incurred no dishonour by remaining loyal to lords to whom they had pledged homage and fealty. Moreover, the crown's right to dis-

---

[33] *Gesta Stephani*, p. 44; *Charters of the Redvers Family*, p. 8; Green, 'Financing Stephen's War', p. 95.
[34] *RRAN*, III, no. 276.    [35] OV, VI, 520.    [36] Farrer, *Honors and Knights' Fees*, II, 297–8.
[37] *Gesta Stephani*, p. 121.
[38] Gervase of Canterbury, I, 165; Jocelin of Brakelond, *Chronica*, ed. H. E. Butler (London, 1964), pp. 68–71.
[39] Gillingham, '1066 and the Introduction of Chivalry into England', pp. 44–55.

seise, which had been such a powerful weapon in the hands of the first
three Norman kings, was arguably coming to be regarded as unacceptable
as the practice of hereditary succession grew stronger. The removal of
land not just from a rebel but also from his progeny, the disinheritance of
a whole family, was an extreme measure. Yet the most powerful influence
on the lenient treatment of rebellion at a practical level was the defective
titles of Rufus, Henry I, and Stephen, for in each reign their opponents
could use the same argument employed by the Conqueror against Harold:
that in taking the throne they had perjured themselves. It was a case of
the biter bit. Had the Anglo-Norman monarchs been all powerful, they
clearly would have continued to punish rebellion harshly. There does not
seem to have been any rejection by them of their right to do so, only of its
expediency.

In this world those who served their lords faithfully hoped for reward, and
the king, as the greatest of earthly lords, had most to give. The Conqueror
was in a situation totally different from that of his successors in having so
much land with which to reward his followers. The boundaries of Norman
settlement in England and Wales continued to expand under Rufus and
Henry I, and these kings had confiscated lands as well as a still considerable stock of royal land with which to reward their men. But over time the
balance of patronage perforce had to shift away from land to other
sources of patronage.

   Without doubt the most lucrative of these for the Norman kings was
the right to dispose of heiresses in marriage, most conspicuously exercised by Henry I. The whole issue of female inheritance, and the amount
of a family's land which could be passed to one woman, was a major political issue. It cropped up in the Charter of Liberties which Henry issued in
1100, when he promised that if any of his men died leaving a woman as
heiress, he would dispose of her with the consent of his barons; yet, as we
shall see in chapter eleven, there was still scope for deciding in what circumstances women could inherit, and how much land.[40] Wealthy widows
were also plum objects of royal patronage, for they had marriage portions
bestowed on them by their fathers plus dower, a share in their former husbands' lands. The subject of their remarriage was raised in 1100. Henry

---

[40] Stubbs, *Select Charters*, p. 118.

promised that widows were to be allowed to have their marriage portions and dower on the deaths of their husbands; custody of any children left under age was to be given either to the next of kin or to another as seemed most suitable.

It was not only the marriage of heiresses that was controlled by the crown, however. The marriage of any female relatives of his tenants-in-chief had to be regulated for fear they might result in alliances with the king's enemies. In 1100 Henry laid down that his consent was required for all such marriages, and he added that he would make no charge for granting permission, nor prohibit them unless they were to one of his enemies. Henry was perhaps thinking in 1100 of the possibility, even likelihood, that men might be tempted to form alliances with Duke Robert's men, or with families living outside the borders of Normandy.[41] Certainly marriage as well as kinship was to be a crucial factor in the formation of an Angevin party in south-west England in the 1130s.[42]

The crown's control of the marriage market clearly had run into difficulties by Stephen's reign. Stephen did not have the power to control all marriages, and some which occurred were self-evidently against his interests. Moreover the number of instances of sole heiresses tapered off. The cause is hardly likely to have been biological: rather, it is more likely that fewer situations of female inheritance were allowed to arise. The number of great heiresses of whose marriage Henry II was able to dispose was certainly fewer than had been available to his grandfather (see below, pp. 381–2).

Wardships also were highly sought after, as guardians were not only able to exploit the lands of the heir (though they were not supposed to), but could also arrange the marriage of the heir and his or her siblings. The Norman kings disposed of wardships to their own men, but clearly there was already disquiet in 1100 about the way the wind was blowing, for Henry promised that guardianship was to be given to either a relative 'or another, as was most appropriate', a concession which did not fetter his power at all. One view of guardianship was that the widow was the most appropriate choice. Another was that as she was bound to remarry, her children's welfare was at risk from their stepfather and it was wiser to

[41] Holt, 'Politics and Property', p. 22.
[42] Green, 'Family Matters: Family and the Formation of the Empress's Party in South-West England', forthcoming.

commit guardianship to the lord, and if the lord was also the king he could sell on the guardianship.

The crown had a great deal of latitude in the exploitation of the 'feudal incidents', more in this period than later, and the use of this power was acceptable in the sense that the king's tenants-in-chief had similar powers over their men. Yet there were practical constraints. The very prominence of these issues in 1100 indicates that kings were not to operate in an arbitrary way without taking advice and, as in the area of confiscation of land, the views of the aristocracy, or the weakness of Stephen's position, had the effect of imposing limits. Henry II was chary of pushing his rights too far, and it was not until the reign of King John that they became a major political issue once more.[43]

Moreover, we can see when we look at the recipients of different kinds of patronage under Henry I that there was some awareness of sensitivities on these issues. Although Henry was criticized for raising men 'as it were from the dust, above earls and illustrious castellans', he rarely in fact did this.[44] Those who received the greatest lands either from the royal demesne or from the richest heiresses were usually well born, either members of his family or men to whom he had a special debt, like Richard de Redvers. Some of the 'new men' did marry heiresses, but more commonly they were eased into the middling ranks of the aristocracy, rather than its topmost layer.[45] Contemporaries were aware of social distinctions and men like the Beaumont twins who could claim descent from Charlemagne saw themselves as a different breed from the Ralph Bassets and Geoffrey de Clintons of their day. The marriage of highly born women to lower-born men happened frequently in this political world; all accepted its inevitability as a mechanism of upward social mobility. But the crown in turn had to recognize that there were constraints upon its freedom to bestow heiresses at will.

One of the features of royal patronage which comes more clearly into view under Henry I was the way 'new men' in particular were established as mesne tenants (middle men). Geoffrey de Clinton and William de Pont de l'Arche, the two treasury chamberlains in the second half of the reign, picked up large amounts of land in this way (see above, pp. 189–91). Some

---

[43] J. C. Holt, *Magna Carta*, 2nd edn (Cambridge, 1992) pp. 50–5.     [44] OV, VI, 16.

[45] R. W. Southern, 'The Place of Henry I in English History', first published *Proceedings of the British Academy*, 47 (1962), 127–70, reprinted in *Medieval Humanism and Other Studies* (Oxford, 1970), pp. 206–33.

tenancies may well have been granted under pressure from the king (in this case, Henry I), such as the grant by the earl of Warwick of seventeen knights' fees to Geoffrey de Clinton. If such tenancies were to last longer than the lifetime of the beneficiary, pressure from the king might have to be renewed. There are possibly two cases in the 1130 pipe roll where a man's heirs were fining to recover portions of their predecessor's lands, and in one of these there is independent testimony to the difficulty they experienced. According to the chronicle of Meaux abbey, Osbert the priest's sons, William and Richard, found that their father's overlords wished to take back estates, using the grounds that they were a priest's sons and might not inherit, and this is borne out by proffers made by their overlords in 1130 to recover land.[46] On the other hand, when the heir of the beneficiary had influential support, a lord might have little option but to renew the tenancy. Geoffrey Ridel secured a grant of the manor of Pytchley in Northamptonshire from his brother the abbot. When this brother died, the next abbot tried to recover the estate but Geoffrey refused to surrender it, though he did agree to pay rent. After Geoffrey's death the custody of his lands passed to Richard Basset, who was dispatched to Peterborough in 1125 to take charge of the abbey's revenues for the crown during a vacancy. Not surprisingly Richard also was able to renew the tenancy.[47]

One of the most lucrative objects in the crown's portfolio of patronage was the grant of a shrievalty. The office was highly profitable, as sheriffs paid a fixed farm for most of the king's rights in the shire. Sheriffs also enjoyed the privilege of exemption of their demesne lands from danegeld, and sometimes had custody of the castle in the principal royal borough. In the heady days following Hastings, the first Norman sheriffs were well placed to enrich themselves, and it was no coincidence that several acquired very large estates. From the late eleventh century, however, these opportunities were largely sealed off. The sheriffs were no longer the only representatives of royal authority in the shires, for there were in addition local justiciars and itinerant justices. Nevertheless the shrievalty remained highly desirable as a means of profit and also of political influence. For the great magnates, effective control of the shrievalty set a seal

---

[46] PR 31 Henry I, pp. 25, 112.

[47] The Peterborough Chronicle of Hugh Candidus, ed. W. T. Mellows (Oxford, 1949), pp. 88–9, 98–9; for enfeoffments on the land of Roger de Mowbray, see above, p. 168.

on their local influence, and whilst great lords did not wish to spend their time counting revenue, sheriffs who were closely tied to them as their tenants gave them an edge in their counties. The persistence of magnate influence in several counties under Henry I is noteworthy, and it was to become ubiquitous in the reign that followed. Here the critical factor was the escalation in the numbers of earls appointed, chiefly by Stephen.

The title of earl, or *comes*, was the most prestigious a king of England could bestow. It carried with it military responsibilities and authority in the public courts of shire and hundred. The first three Norman kings had been sparing in creating earls: the Conqueror had created Odo of Bayeux earl of Kent and William FitzOsbern earl in Herefordshire; then Roger of Montgomery and Hugh d'Avranches were given comital status in Shropshire and Cheshire respectively, the bishop of Durham in Durham, and (possibly) Robert of Mortain in Cornwall.[48] Apart from Odo's earldom of Kent, the others were on the frontiers of the realm and, insofar as we can judge, the earls probably controlled the sheriffs.[49] Rufus created two earls in 1088 (Warwick and Surrey) and possibly a third for Walter Giffard.[50] Henry I created earldoms for Robert count of Meulan, his brother-in-law David, and his son Robert. In the last three cases at least, it seems that the new earls did not take over the shrievalties.[51] In Stephen's reign, however, far more earldoms were created, and a number of them were able effectively to take charge of the shrievalties (see below, p. 304). Henry II reversed the trend by allowing many of the earldoms to lapse, by replacing sheriffs, and by enforcing accountability at the exchequer for all counties except Cornwall, held by his uncle.[52]

The king also had a range of privileges at his disposal, and was prepared to lend either his support or his protection for those who were prepared to pay, and those who were in his service were well placed to have their proffers accepted. The king could intervene in lawsuits on behalf of one of the parties, and concords or settlements could be agreed in his count; conversely, legal proceedings could be postponed. He could also turn a blind

[48] Green, *Government of England*, pp. 118–19; Lewis, 'Early Earls of Norman England'.

[49] Green, *English Sheriffs to 1154*, pp. 45, 71, 32, 38, 33.

[50] The evidence for Walter is inconclusive: Barlow, *William Rufus*, p. 93 n.

[51] In all three counties the sheriffs accounted for their farms at the exchequer in 1130: *PR 31 Henry I*, pp. 81, 43–4, 76–7. Gilbert the knight (Hunts.) and Walter of Gloucester (Gloucs.) were in office before earls were appointed: Green, *English Sheriffs to 1154*, pp. 53, 48, 43.

[52] Amt, *Accession of Henry II in England*, pp. 118–19.

eye when his men engaged in somewhat dubious practices. It seems likely that it was with the king's acquiescence that Robert of Meulan took outright control of the royal borough of Leicester, where he had been only one of four landlords in 1086, and the gloss put by Orderic on the process does not disguise the reality of what had happened.[53] By the closing years of the reign, Simon II de Senlis must have been old enough to inherit his father's lands (the earldom of Huntingdon), yet Henry preferred to allow these to remain in the hands of King David because he needed David's support for his plans for the succession (see below, p. 290).

Financial penalties could also be pardoned 'for the love' that the king felt for one of the great magnates, as the 1130 pipe roll shows.[54] Such references do not occur on the pipe rolls of Henry II's reign. The largest proffers in the 1130 roll relate to the succession to honours, to offices, and to the marriage of women. That the king was prepared to accept them at all was a sign of his favour and, in some cases at least, an indication that the issues involved were not entirely straightforward, as for instance in the cases of the agreements made by Countess Lucy and one of her sons, Ranulf II earl of Chester, to put her affairs in order, to ensure that her family lands would pass to Ranulf and his half-brother after her death and to avoid a (fourth) marriage (see below, p. 370), or the restoration of his father's lands to Geoffrey II de Mandeville.[55] Yet the acceptance of proffers did not mean that regular instalments would be exacted; in the case of some of the largest, only a fraction had been paid off. They remained on the roll as a lien which could be used as security for good behaviour, in contrast with the schedule of payments laid down by an increasingly desperate King John.[56] Here is another contrast in Henry I's reign between on the one hand the theoretically arbitrary power of the crown and on the other a realistic assessment as to how far the king's rights could be pressed against his nobles.

The rigour of forest laws, which must have greatly irritated magnates whose lands lay within the forest bounds, could be alleviated for the favoured few (as we have seen) by allowing subjects to have private forests or by the grant of privileges in royal forests. Some were granted judicial

---

[53] OV, vi, 18–20.

[54] For example, *PR 31 Henry I*, p. 123 (William de Pont de l'Arche); these payments are discussed by S. L. Mooers, in 'Patronage in the Pipe Roll of 1130', *Speculum*, 59 (1984), 298–9.

[55] *PR 31 Henry I*, pp. 110, 55.    [56] Holt, *Magna Carta*, pp. 190–2.

privileges over their own lands. Those who sat at the exchequer were exempt from danegeld and murder fines. Thus as the administration of the king's rights became more vigorous, their impact for those in favour was mitigated.

Finally, the king could make sure that progress up the ladder of promotion was eased not just for individuals but for their families, especially for sons making their way in the church, in the royal household, or in the shires. The king had a range of ecclesiastical preferment at his disposal, and, at least until 1135, had a decisive say in the choice of bishops and abbots.[57] He could arrange advantageous marriages for the sons of his servants, as for instance the marriages of Miles of Gloucester to the daughter of Bernard de Neufmarché (see below, pp. 373–4), William Mauduit to the daughter of Michael of Hanslope, or Payn of Houghton to the widow of Edward of Salisbury.[58]

Great nobles had what were in many respects comparable rights of patronage: they had offices and privileges to bestow, and the right to dispose of heiresses, widows, and wardships of their men, plus presentations to ecclesiastical benefices. Under Stephen some great lords began to move in on royal rights. A conspicuous example is provided by the operations of Earl Ranulf II in the marriage market (see below). By the time Henry II came to the throne, there were more constraints on royal power over the king's feudal rights. In other respects, however, the renewed expansion of royal government in the later twelfth century opened up a whole new range of possible opportunities in the form of offices such as coronerships, offices in the central administration or courts of justice, or in the forest hierarchy; and as royal government became more pervasive and powerful, exemption from or mitigation of its activities became increasingly valuable.

## Political perspectives

The aim of the ruling dynasty was to keep Normandy and England together, and in this they were supported by the wealthiest section of the

---

[57] For Rufus's appointments to bishoprics and abbacies, see Barlow, *William Rufus*, pp. 179–85; for a brief survey of ecclesiastical preferment granted by Henry I, Green, *Government of England*, pp. 174–6; for Stephen and appointments, see F. Barlow, *English Church 1066–1154* (London, 1979), pp. 92–103, and K. Stringer, *The Reign of Stephen* (London, 1993), pp. 61–72.    [58] *RRAN*, II, no. 1719; *PR 31 Henry I*, p. 81.

aristocracy of Norman England. These families had extensive estates on both sides of the Channel; their marriage alliances often looked outwards (see below, pp. 351–4); and above all most of them were committed to keeping Normandy and England in a condominium. The decision of a number of key families to support Robert between 1088 and 1106 led in most cases to their removal from England, and the tendency to divide estates at the Channel between sons meant that most of the original trans-Channel complexes were broken up by the early twelfth century. Others however took their place, and it was necessary for Henry I that they should do so, because he needed support and ruling Normandy was an uphill struggle. For over a decade after 1141 Normandy and England went different ways, and although they were politically reunited under Henry II, only a few trans-Channel complexes survived into the later twelfth century.

The horizons of most families in Norman England were necessarily fixed on more localized objectives: consolidation and extension of their estates and the pursuit of advantageous marriage alliances. They could not afford to ignore court politics and the possibility that, if they opted out, their lands might be subject to predation; but their immediate concerns were likely to be rooted in family and neighbourhood, and it is this, what might be described as the local or regional dimension of politics in Norman England, which has begun to attract historians' attention. A court-centred analysis of the political world of the Anglo-Norman state has led in the past to a neglect of a different set of priorities which were rooted in family and neighbourhood.

That different perspective is most obvious on the margins of England. For families who settled in the far north in the early twelfth century, the power of the king of Scots was as close as, if not closer than, that of the king of the English. The organization of rural society, the lack of towns and monasteries, all meant that the new lords, thinner on the ground than in the south, operated in a different context. Many in Cumbria, Northumberland, and Durham had little known land elsewhere. For allies they looked to neighbouring families and, as they began to endow religious houses, these too helped to root them in their locality. Those who settled on the Welsh borders or in Wales itself looked west as well as east and south. They had to consider the defence of their lands and the prospect of further gains. The marriage of Arnulf of Montgomery, lord of Pembroke, to the daughter of an Irish king was not exotic but prudent in the context of politics in the region bordering the Irish Sea.[59] The strength of Welsh resistance in the early twelfth century led Henry I to plant his own men with powerful resources in Welsh lordships, and they had a window on the wider political world. To take just one example, Roger bishop of Salisbury was made lord of Kidwelly. Henry's men were there for a reason: they had to commit men and resources to defence and knew that the king/duke could only devote short bursts of attention to affairs in Wales.

If such local considerations are most obvious at the margins, they were not absent elsewhere. They come most sharply into view under Stephen both because of the protracted nature of local struggles and because of the sudden growth in surviving evidence. The roots went back well before 1135, however, and they were in a sense part and parcel of the aristocratic world, and as more individual families are studied in detail the more we understand their strategies and how these fitted into the larger political picture. In Leicestershire, for instance, Earl Robert I and his son Robert II grew stronger by degrees. In the vicinity of Leicester this brought them into conflict with the bishop of Lincoln, and in the north-west of the county at Mountsorrel with the earl of Chester.[60] In Devon we can see how rivalry developed between two families for control of the shrievalty. Baldwin FitzGilbert as we have seen held a large honour and was sheriff and castellan of Exeter. Soon after the accession of Henry I, Richard de Redvers was given large estates in Devon and the shrievalty passed to an associate of his, Geoffrey de Mandeville (not to be confused with the Essex tenant-in-chief). The shrievalty subsequently passed to Richard, a son of Baldwin FitzGilbert, until about 1128. He was replaced by Geoffrey de Furneaux, a Redvers tenant. In 1136 Baldwin de Redvers seized Exeter castle and held it against Stephen, and at this point we find that Richard FitzBaldwin was once again sheriff.[61]

The political world of the aristocracy of Norman England was less centrally focussed than has often been portrayed. One of the most urgent tasks for historians is the reconstruction of tenurial geography within this political world by the collection and analysis of family charters. Only then will a comprehensive political history which takes account of the

---

[59] OV, VI, 30.

[60] D. Crouch, 'Earls and Bishops in Twelfth-century Leicestershire', *Nottingham Medieval Studies*, 37 (1993), 9–20; E. King, 'Mountsorrel and its Region in King Stephen's Reign', *Huntington Library Quarterly*, 64 (1980), 1–10.     [61] Green, 'Family Matters', p. 158.

interplay of family strategy with the wider political history of the Anglo-Norman monarchy be possible.

There were four main phases in the history of the upper aristocracy. The first is roughly coterminous with the Conqueror's reign. The second, lasting until about 1106, was dominated by the struggle of Rufus and Henry I against Robert to unite the two portions of the Conqueror's legacy in one pair of hands, a contest which divided the aristocracy. The third was a period of relative peace, and the fourth the protracted conflict under Stephen.

## A political history

### Keeping a united front

Conflict within and between powerful aristocratic families had been frequent in early eleventh-century Normandy as elsewhere. Duke William had imposed his authority within the duchy ruthlessly and by force of arms when needed. He and his companions, Normans and non-Normans, were well aware that to turn their victory at Hastings into a permanent occupation their unanimity of purpose had to be sustained. The first revolt against the Conqueror came within months of Hastings and involved Count Eustace of Boulogne, who was clearly disenchanted with his share of the spoils of victory and tried to seize Dover. Eustace had been a key player in the political revolution of 1051 and it may be that King Edward had intended to grant him Dover at that time. Eustace had made a significant contribution to William's invasion force in 1066 and at the battle of Hastings. Although he was granted two large and valuable estates in Kent, he may well have been antagonized by Odo's authority in the county. Eustace perhaps had good reasons for revolt, therefore, but his attempt to seize Dover failed and he left England. Within a decade he had decided, probably because of the shifting pattern of power in northern France, that a rapprochement with King William was desirable, and by 1086 his son was one of the greatest tenants-in-chief.[62]

The most serious breach in the unanimity of purpose of the new regime came in 1075 when Roger earl of Hereford, William FitzOsbern's son,

[62] Tanner, 'Expansion of the Power and Influence of the Counts of Boulogne', 275–6; according to William of Poitiers the rapprochement between Eustace and the king had occurred before William broke off his biography, in about 1077: see *ibid.*, p. 268.

allied with Ralph of Gael, earl of East Anglia, and, at least until he repented of his complicity, Waltheof, earl of Northumbria. The aim of the rebels was a tripartite division of England with one of the three chosen as king.[63] Waltheof, son of Siward, had rebelled before but had been reconciled with the king, and may have been hoping for more land in the north. Roger was evidently resentful that his lands and authority did not match those granted to Roger of Montgomery and Hugh of Chester. A letter of Lanfranc urging him to return to the fold referred to the activities of sheriffs in a way that suggests Roger was objecting to their intrusions on his lands.[64] Ralph was the son of a Breton lord favoured by Edward the Confessor; he was appointed earl of East Anglia by William, but he too may have been disappointed in the shareout of land once Normans were being installed in East Anglia. The flashpoint of trouble was a wedding between Roger and Ralph's sister which was said to have been forbidden by the Conqueror. Waltheof was executed, Roger was imprisoned and lost his lands, and Ralph fled to his Breton estates where with Breton and Angevin help he continued his resistance based at the castle of Dol, whither William pursued him in 1076. The revolt had occurred at a dangerous moment when William was out of England, but it was suppressed by Normans loyal to the king, and in the west by the staunch support of Bishop Wulfstan.

As the years wore on new names occur in witness lists. Robert de Mowbray, Bishop Geoffrey's nephew, began to appear in royal documents from 1080.[65] William of Eu, son of Robert count of Eu, Robert FitzHaimon, son of Haimo the steward, and Miles Crispin, probably a younger son of William Crispin, first appear in the later years.[66] William of Eu and Miles Crispin had already been rewarded with lands by 1086; more problematic was the position of those who reached adulthood without having acquired or inherited land.

## The struggle for the succession, 1087–1106

Tension between fathers and heirs, such as was at the root of the estrangement between the Conqueror and his eldest son Robert, was not uncom-

---

[63] FW, II, 10–12; and OV, II, 310–322.
[64] *Letters of Lanfranc*, ed. H. Clover and M. Gibson (Oxford, 1979), no. 31.
[65] RRAN, I, nos. 125, 170. 171.     [66] *Ibid.*, I, nos. 154, 202, 232.

mon, for adult heirs were impatient for land and power. The last years of William's life must have been an anxious time for magnates on both sides of the Channel, because the king's quarrel with his eldest son, earlier acknowledged as his successor in Normandy, had thrown the succession to England and Normandy into uncertainty. The accession of a new ruler was always a difficult and tense time, and a lack of clear and publicly understood arrangements in this case were to lead to war. William was persuaded on his deathbed to acknowledge Robert as his heir for Normandy, and he either left the question of the succession to England open, or, more probably, expressed a wish that William Rufus was to succeed him.[67] In the event, the accession of Robert to Normandy and Rufus to England divided the aristocracies of England and Normandy.

In 1087 and 1088 the claim of Robert to succeed to the whole Anglo-Norman inheritance was backed by a powerful group of magnates.[68] Robert's earlier companions had been sons of his father's friends; now his cause was backed by a weighty coalition of some of the greatest of the Anglo-Norman magnates. They were led by Odo of Bayeux, who may have been influential in drawing in Roger Bigod and Roger de Lacy, both of whom held land from the bishopric of Bayeux, and William of St Calais, bishop of Durham, whose career had begun in the chapter of Bayeux.[69] Bishop Odo may also have recruited Gilbert FitzRichard, heir of Richard, lord of Tonbridge, as Tonbridge was situated on land held by Odo in 1086. Robert of Mortain, Eustace III count of Boulogne, William of Eu, and Roger of Montgomery and his sons were also involved (the latter evidently not for long), as was the bishop of Coutances, or at least so the king believed. Geoffrey de Mandeville may also have been implicated.[70] Odo was actually in prison at the time of his brother's death, and was only released on the urgent entreaty of some of the magnates. The rebels evidently felt loyalty to Duke Robert, and they wished to see him rule in England to ensure continued security in the estates which they had acquired there. There may have been additional personal reasons, too, in the form of unsatisfied demands for patronage. Robert de Mowbray, for instance, may have been

[67] The subject has been discussed most recently by B. English, 'William the Conqueror and the Anglo-Norman Succession', *Historical Research*, 64 (1991), 221–36, and E. Z. Tabuteau, 'The Role of Law in the Succession to Normandy and England, 1087', *Haskins Society Journal*, 3 (1991), 141–69.

[68] Barlow, *William Rufus*, pp. 70–98.     [69] For the connections of the two laymen, see above, pp. 84, 441.

[70] For a reference to trouble in London see SD, 'De injusta uexacione', *Opera omnia*, I, 189. A son of Geoffrey was married to a daughter of Count Eustace of Boulogne: *DB*, I, 36.

appointed earl of Northumberland by the Conqueror, only to find that Rufus was not prepared to recognize the appointment (see above, p. 112).[71]

Rufus persuaded Archbishop Lanfranc to crown him, and he was then accepted by most of the leading officers of the royal household and the sheriffs, though one or two, like Roger Bigod, seem to have flirted with the idea of revolt. He managed to win over Roger of Montgomery and Earl Hugh, and William de Warenne and Henry de Beaumont were both created earls.[72] Odo fortified Rochester castle, Gilbert FitzRichard, Tonbridge castle, and Robert of Mortain, Pevensey. Rufus took personal command in the south-east, and successfully besieged Tonbridge and Rochester. In the west two more rebels, the bishop of Coutances and his nephew Robert de Mowbray, based themselves at Bristol. Robert attacked Bath and the surrounding region. In the Marches, Osbern FitzRichard, Roger de Lacy, Ralph de Mortimer, and Bernard de Neufmarché took Hereford, burned Gloucester, and marched on Worcester, where they were repulsed by Bishop Wulfstan.[73] There was also trouble in Norfolk. The Anglo-Saxon Chronicle states that Roger Bigod behaved very badly, and scuttled off to Norwich castle. Perhaps he thought about rebellion, then saw which way the wind was blowing, and retreated. He evidently did not lose Rufus's favour, so any question about his loyalty must have been short-lived. The author of the Anglo-Saxon Chronicle identified another whose loyalty was suspect: 'Hugh [de Grandmesnil] was another who did nothing to improve matters, neither in Leicestershire nor in Northampton.'[74] The bishop of Durham retreated to his castle at Durham, whither the king sent an army led by Roger the Poitevin (whose disloyalty had also been short-lived), Count Alan, and Odo of Champagne. They entered the city but not the castle, and negotiated an agreement with the bishop for a safe conduct to and from the king's court (see above, pp. 110–11). The bishop was finally persuaded to hand over Durham castle and was allowed to leave England for Normandy.[75]

The chief casualty of this revolt was Odo of Bayeux who lost his English lands. Robert of Mortain seems to have retired to Normandy, and his son

[71] Barlow, *William Rufus*, pp. 167–8.
[72] WM, *Gesta Regum*, II, 361–2; OV, IV, 128 mentions as supporters of Rufus Hugh, William de Warenne, Robert FitzHaimon, and Robert de Mowbray – the last was obviously a mistake. Henry de Beaumont's loyalty is to be inferred from the creation of an earldom.     [73] FW, II, 25–6.
[74] ASC 1086.     [75] 'De injusta unexacione', SD, *Opera omnia*, I, 171–95.

William does not attest Rufus's documents, from which we may deduce he remained estranged from the king.[76] William of St Calais was exiled from his see until 1091, but was then restored, probably because his presence in Durham was needed as a rallying point against the Scots. Roger of Montgomery and his sons made their peace with the king and prospered in his service.[77] The eldest, Hugh, succeeded his father in Shropshire and Sussex. Robert, the second son, succeeded to Bellême and (by marriage) to the county of Ponthieu. He persuaded Rufus to allow him to succeed to Tickhill after the death of Roger de Bully; Roger the Poitevin's estates were enlarged; and Arnulf of Montgomery, yet another son, was granted the honour of Holderness after the departure of Stephen of Aumale in 1096 (see above, p. 124).

The sons of Roger of Beaumont also survived and prospered. Robert count of Meulan seems to have been accepted at the courts of both Robert and Rufus. Henry (of Beaumont), who had evidently spent most or all of his time in Normandy before 1086, was at Rufus's court in 1088, was created earl, and was provided with land in Warwickshire.[78] An earldom was created for William de Warenne in Surrey, in all probability to counterbalance the power there of Gilbert FitzRichard.[79] It was probably around this time too that Hugh d'Avranches was given more land in Staffordshire and Leicestershire.[80]

In the west Queen Matilda's lands were bestowed not on Prince Henry, who had petitioned for them, but on Robert FitzHaimon, one of only a handful of men who owed the acquisition of large estates in England to Rufus.[81] One reason why Robert received such a generous grant of lands concentrated in Gloucestershire was the conquest of Glamorgan which was under way at this time. In the far north-west, Rufus's annexation of Cumbria in 1092 created opportunities for Ranulf vicomte of Bayeux, and Ivo Taillebois the steward (see above, pp. 111–12).[82] In Yorkshire, too, there were changes, as we have seen (above, p. 113). Another new recruit was Simon de Senlis who married Waltheof's daughter Matilda. Simon presumably came from Senlis in the Ile-de-France. He may have been a

---

[76] Golding, 'Robert of Mortain', p. 122.

[77] J. F. A. Mason, 'Roger of Montgomery and his Sons', *Transactions of the Royal Historical Society*, 5th series, 13 (1963), 16–20.    [78] *RRAN*, I, no. 302; Barlow, *William Rufus*, p. 266, n. 12.

[79] J. A. Green, 'William Rufus, Henry I and the Royal Demesne', *History*, 64 (1979), 345–6.

[80] Farrer, *Honors and Knights' Fees*, II, 6.    [81] OV, IV, 220.    [82] For Ivo and Warter, see above, p. 113.

member of the Le Riche family, but nothing is known about when and how he entered Rufus's service.[83] His marriage occurred in or about 1090, by which time he must have been high in Rufus's favour.[84] Walter Tirel, who was accused of shooting the arrow which killed the king in 1100, was lord of Poix in the Beauvaisis. Rufus did not bestow estates on him in England, but he held Langham in Essex from Richard FitzGilbert, his father-in-law.[85]

The other region whence several of Rufus's 'new men' were recruited was Maine, where Rufus had inherited the difficult task of trying to assert Norman overlordship against local nobles and the rival ambitions of the count of Anjou.[86] In 1098 Rufus's commander Robert de Bellême had captured Count Helias de la Flèche, a local lord who claimed the county. The count of Anjou invaded and occupied Le Mans; Rufus retaliated by himself invading and, having captured some of Count Fulk's knights, forced the count to hand over Le Mans. The Manceaux who first appear in England in Rufus's reign were presumably men who favoured the Norman cause. Wynebald de Ballon was given lands in Somerset and the lordship of Caerleon; he was a benefactor of the recently founded priory of Bermondsey.[87] His brother Hamelin was lord of Much Marcle in Herefordshire by the early years of the twelfth century.[88] The brothers came from Ballon, which was besieged by Rufus's forces in 1098. Patrick de Chaworth came from Sourches near Le Mans. Although Patrick does not occur as a witness to any document issued by Rufus, he was established in England before 1096, for in that year Rufus confirmed gifts to Gloucester Abbey including that of Patrick, who married the daughter of Arnulf de Hesdin.[89]

The group of magnates so promoted overlapped but were not identical with the *curiales* on whom Rufus relied as an executive group. The latter included Ranulf Flambard, royal chaplain and bishop, William Giffard the chancellor, Robert Bloet, chancellor and bishop, the stewards, Eudo, Haimo, and Roger Bigod, and the constable, Urse d'Abetot.[90] The laymen

[83] 'Vita et Passio Waldevi comitis', *Vitae Quorundum Anglo-Saxonum*, ed. J. A. Giles, Caxton Society (1854), p. 18. Warner of Senlis was a benefactor of Saint Martin de Pontoise: *Cartulaire de Saint-Martin de Pontoise*, ed. J. Depoin (Pontoise, 1899), Appendix, pp. 278–9.

[84] P. Feuchère, 'Une tentative manquée de concentration territoriale entre Somme et Seine: la principauté d'Amiens-Valois au XIe siècle', *Moyen Age*, 60 (1954), 14.

[85] J. H. Round, 'Walter Tirel and his Wife', *Feudal England*, pp. 355–63.

[86] For the background see Barlow, *William Rufus*, pp. 37–9, 270, 381–8, 390–2, 402–6.

[87] Sanders, *English Baronies*, p. 68.     [88] *Ibid.*, p. 66.     [89] *Ibid.*, p. 125.

[90] Barlow, *William Rufus*, pp. 191–213.

were in varying degrees magnates in their own right, though their wealth
did not compare with that of the sons of Roger of Montgomery or William
de Warenne.

The identification of an inner group at court rests on the witness lists of
documents issued in the king's name, though, as Professor Bates has
reminded us, it is dangerous to attach much weight to witness lists which
may well be composed of interested parties, and these were not necessarily physically present.[91] All we may conclude is that those who appear frequently were evidently regarded as men whose attestation was important
to the matter in hand, whilst absence did not necessarily mean alienation
or estrangement. The principal officers of the household were magnates
in their own right, albeit not perhaps of the first rank, with affairs of their
own to deal with, though some perhaps had more inclination than others
to spend time at court. Hence the view, based partly on attestations, that a
gulf had opened up between magnates and *curiales* in Rufus's reign and
was only healed by Henry I, is untenable.[92]

It is certainly true that some individuals and families, whilst escaping
the confiscation of their English lands, were evidently not happy about
the division of the Conqueror's inheritance, and in 1095 there was a
second revolt (see above, pp. 112–13). The trigger was the refusal by Robert
de Mowbray to attend the king's court to explain why he had failed to
make restitution to Norwegian merchants whose ships he had seized.
Robert was supported by some of the other conspirators of 1088, but Rufus
marched north and captured Robert and the castle of Bamburgh where he
had taken refuge.[93] The proclamation of the first crusade provided an
opportunity for some of those implicated to absent themselves. Duke
Robert himself answered the call, and his companions included Odo of
Bayeux, Eustace III of Boulogne, and Ivo de Grandmesnil and two of his
brothers, plus Arnulf de Hesdin, and William de Percy. In general,
however, the leading lords of Norman England did not join the crusade,
and it has been suggested that they may have been discouraged by the
king on the grounds that those who had been granted land in England

[91] D. Bates, 'The Prosopographical Study of Anglo-Norman Royal Charters: Some Problems and
Perspectives', *Family Trees and the Roots of Politics. The Prosopography of Britain and France from the Tenth to
the Twelfth Century*, ed. K. S. B. Keats-Rohan (Woodbridge, forthcoming).

[92] Hollister, 'Magnates and Curiales', *Monarchy, Magnates and Institutions*, pp. 97–115.

[93] Barlow, *William Rufus*, pp. 346–59.

were expected to stay and defend them. Breach of this principle had led the Conqueror to arrest Odo in 1082.[94]

Duke Robert was still absent when Rufus died unexpectedly in the New Forest. The strange nature of his death has prompted speculation that it may have been the result of a noble conspiracy in favour of Henry I, engineered by Walter Tirel, Walter Giffard, Gilbert FitzRichard, and other members of the Clare family, but there is no evidence that the king's death was anything but an accident.[95] Henry made himself master of the treasury at Winchester and persuaded the bishop of London to crown him. Among the aristocracy he was supported by Earl Hugh, who with Richard de Redvers had been Henry's ally in western Normandy.[96] Other west Normans who supported him from an early date included the brothers William and Nigel d'Aubigny, and Rualon d'Avranches.[97] The Bretons Hasculf of St James and Alan FitzFlaad were also early recruits.[98] Robert count of Meulan, Henry de Beaumont, Walter Giffard, and Simon de Senlis threw in their lot with him, as did the leading members of the royal household.[99] It was only going to be a matter of months, however, before his brother Robert returned from the crusade, anxious to redeem Normandy and to claim the kingdom of England as the eldest surviving son of William the Conqueror.

When he did return, Robert began to amass formidable support, including Robert de Bellême and his brothers Arnulf and Roger, William count of Mortain, William de Warenne, Walter Giffard, Ivo de Grandmesnil, Eustace of Boulogne, and Robert de Lacy of Pontefract.[100] The overlap between 1088 and 1101 is clear: the families which had most to lose by the separation of England and Normandy and had a tradition of allegiance to Robert were not prepared to see his claim to be king of England ignored.

---

[94] C. Tyerman, *England and the Crusades* (Chicago and London, 1988), p. 18.

[95] C. Warren Hollister, 'The Strange Death of William Rufus', *Monarchy, Magnates and Institutions*, pp. 59–77 discusses the evidence and earlier interpretations.     [96] OV, IV, 220.

[97] William was at court by October 1100, and Nigel by September of the following year: *RRAN*, II, nos. 497, 544. By Michaelmas 1102 at the latest Rualon d'Avranches had been granted the manor of Stanton Harcourt in Oxfordshire: *RRAN*, II, no. 528.

[98] Hasculf of St James witnessed a charter issued in 1100 or 1101: *RRAN*, II, no. 533; and Alan FitzFlaad by September 1101: no. 547.

[99] Henry, Simon, and Walter witnessed the Charter of Liberties, as did Robert de Montfort (constable), Roger Bigod and Eudo (stewards), Robert FitzHaimon, and Robert Malet (chamberlain): *RRAN*, II, no. 488. Robert of Meulan was at court by Christmas: no. 501.

[100] Hollister, 'The Anglo-Norman Civil War: 1101'.

Some may have been prepared to be won over: William count of Mortain was said to have asked for the county of Kent, but Henry refused and offered him instead marriage to his sister-in-law, Mary of Scotland, a proposal which William in turn rejected.[101]

Robert crossed to England in 1101. His army included Ranulf Flambard who had escaped from the Tower in the previous year, possibly, though the chroniclers remain silent on this point, with the assistance of the constable, William de Mandeville.[102] Robert and Henry met not far from Winchester. A peace was hammered out by baronial intermediaries and subsequently sworn to by twelve men from each side. Robert accepted Henry as king, freed him from the homage he had performed, and accepted a pension; if either died without a male heir the other was to inherit the whole, and those who had been disseised for supporting either side in 1101 were to have their lands restored. William de Warenne, however, lost his English estates.[103] As noted earlier, William de Mandeville had to mortgage his three most valuable demesne manors to Eudo the steward, probably because he was held responsible for Flambard's escape.[104] Ivo de Grandmesnil was charged with waging war in England; he mortgaged his estates to Robert of Meulan and left for Jerusalem.[105] Henry managed to win over Eustace of Boulogne, whose lands in England may have been restored at this time, and Eustace also married Mary of Scotland.[106] Robert de Bellême and his brothers, however, were not as fortunate and lost all their lands.[107]

The fate of this most powerful family served as a warning to others who were tempted to resist Henry further. William de Warenne decided to petition for the recovery of his estates and was reinstated in 1103; thereafter he remained loyal to Henry I, and after 1107 began to appear at court frequently.[108] In 1104 William count of Mortain lost his English estates because, according to the Anglo-Saxon Chronicle, he refused to obey the

---

[101] WM, *De Gestis Regum*, II, 473; the proposed marriage is discussed by Hollister, 'The Anglo-Norman Civil War: 1101', p. 78 and n.

[102] Hollister, 'Misfortunes of the Mandevilles', *Monarchy, Magnates and Institutions*, pp. 118–19.

[103] OV, v, 320.        [104] Hollister, 'Misfortunes of the Mandevilles', pp. 118–19.

[105] OV, vi, 18.        [106] FW, II, 51.

[107] C. Warren Hollister, 'The Campaign of 1102 against Robert of Bellême', *Studies in Medieval History presented to R. Allen Brown*, ed. C. Harper-Bill, C. Holdsworth, and J. L. Nelson (Woodbridge, 1989), pp. 193–202.

[108] Hollister, 'The Taming of a Turbulent Earl: Henry I and William de Warenne', *Monarchy, Magnates and Institutions*, pp. 142–4.

king and went to Normandy.[109] By this stage Henry may already have been working towards taking Normandy from his brother, because Orderic reports a visit to the duchy in that year.[110] In the following year Henry nailed his colours to the mast; he burned Bayeux, thereby persuading the townsmen of Caen of the wisdom of making their peace with him.[111] Yet Duke Robert's supporters, headed by William of Mortain and Robert de Bellême, held firm, and it was Henry's good fortune that he was able to force the issue by bringing his brother to the battlefield at Tinchebrai, where he defeated and captured him together with Count William, Robert de Stuteville, and William de Ferrers.[112] Henry was now master of the duchy, of the person of his brother and, initially, of his nephew William. William escaped from custody, however, and remained at large to provide a focus for rebels who allied with other enemies of Henry I, in particular Fulk count of Anjou and Louis VI, king of France.

Further disseisins followed. Some were of known supporters of the duke's cause who presumably were not prepared to accept Henry's rule in Normandy. Robert de Montfort was accused in 1107 of breach of fealty, and, says Orderic, knowing himself to be guilty he gave up his lands and went to Jerusalem.[113] William II Malet's forfeiture is dated by the Anglo-Saxon Chronicle to 1110 together with those of William Bainard and Philip de Briouze.[114] The context for these forfeitures is not explained.[115] William II Malet was the brother of Robert, Curthose's supporter in 1101, and it has been suggested that the Malets lost the honour of Eye for their support of the duke.[116] William, however, continued to hold the Norman lands of the family.[117] William Bainard was lord of Little Dunmow and of Baynard's castle in London. We can only speculate about the reason for his forfeiture: perhaps his loyalty as keeper of one of the castles in London had been found wanting. Nothing is known either about the circumstances in which Philip de Briouze lost his lands, but the loss can only have been temporary.[118] Roger d'Abetot lost his lands for killing a member

---

[109] *ASC* 1104.    [110] OV, VI, 56–60.    [111] *Ibid.*, 60–8; 78.    [112] *Ibid.*, 84–90.    [113] *Ibid.*, 100.    [114] *ASC* 1110.

[115] For the suggestion that the confiscations may have been related to Henry I's differences with Louis VI of France see C. Warren Hollister, 'Henry I and Robert Malet', *Monarchy, Magnates and Institutions*, p. 133, citing Suger, *Vie de Louis VI le Gros*, ed. H. Waquet (Paris, 1929), pp. 104–10 (pp. 69–75 in translation by R. C. Cusimano and J. Moorhead, Washington, 1992).

[116] Hollister, 'Henry I and Robert Malet', p. 133.    [117] *Ibid.*, p. 132.

[118] Philip occurs as a witness to one document, *RRAN*, II, no. 1896 (1130/5), and occurs in the 1130 pipe roll: *PR 31 Henry I*, pp. 72, 103, 126, 157. It is not impossible that these references are to a younger Philip.

of the royal household not long after this.[119] Robert de Lacy of Pontefract may have survived even longer, but by 1114 his lands had been granted to Hugh lord of Laval in Maine, whose support Henry was keen to have.[120] It thus took two decades for the division arising from the succession crisis of 1087 to work its way out finally, and the greatest families of the Norman settlement were in the main expelled from England for supporting the cause of Duke Robert.

### Checks and balances

After 1106 Henry was able to establish a remarkable degree of influence over the aristocracy of England, essentially by making sure the major lordships were held by men loyal to him. Of the powerful families at the start of the reign, he showed himself particularly generous to the Clares and the Beaumonts. It was his generosity to the former that has aroused suspicions amongst some historians that they may have been involved in arranging an accident for William Rufus.[121] In fact, one of the Clares, Gilbert FitzRichard of Tonbridge, had been involved in both of the revolts against Rufus, from which we may suspect that if anything he had a preference for the cause of Robert, and the bestowal of the abbey of Ely on his younger brother Richard may, as Ward has suggested, have been to gain Clare support rather than to reward it.[122] Gilbert FitzRichard established close relations with the king, but after he was granted Ceredigion (Cardigan) in Wales in 1110, he did not appear often at court. William Baynard's lands were granted to Gilbert's brother Robert FitzRichard soon after 1110, and Netherwent (Chepstow) to a third brother Walter FitzRichard before 1119. Roger FitzRichard, who had inherited the Norman lordships of Orbec and Bienfaite, received most of the land held in 1086 by Rannulf brother of Ilger.[123]

Of the Beaumont brothers, Robert of Meulan, who was evidently Henry I's leading lay counsellor, spent much more time at court than Henry earl of Warwick. Robert's reward was the title of earl of Leicester (probably in 1107), and the enlargement of his estates in the county, mainly at the

---

[119] WM, *Gesta Pontificum*, p. 253.   [120] Wightman, *Lacy Family*, p. 66.
[121] See especially Hollister, 'Strange Death of William Rufus', pp. 59–75; and E. Mason, 'William Rufus and the Historians', *Medieval History*, 1 no. 1 (1991), 6–22.
[122] J. Ward, 'Royal Service and Reward: the Clare Family and the Crown 1066–1154', *Anglo-Norman Studies*, 11 (1988), 268.   [123] For these details, *ibid.*, pp. 267–73.

expense of the exiled Ivo de Grandmesnil.[124] Robert, one of the last of the conquest generation, did not die until 1118. He left three sons, all under age, of whom the eldest two were twins. The elder twin, Waleran count of Meulan, rebelled in 1123. He was imprisoned until 1129 but the king then released him and restored his lands, a remarkably restrained reaction given the severe punishment meted out to other captives. The younger twin, Robert earl of Leicester, for whom the king had provided a splendid marriage to Amice, the heiress of Breteuil, remained loyal to Henry I.[125] The third brother, Hugh, inherited relatively little and remains a shadowy figure until Stephen's reign.[126] Henry earl of Warwick died in 1119. His heir Roger does not appear to have enjoyed the king's confidence to the same extent as his father had done, and it may have been for this reason that Geoffrey de Clinton was given the shrievalty of Warwickshire soon after 1120, and was established as the earl's under-tenant.[127]

Henry I showed particular favour to his illegitimate son Robert, who was married to a daughter of Robert FitzHaimon and succeeded to the latter's lands. He also granted the Malet honour of Eye to his nephew Stephen probably in 1113, and at about the same time, and allegedly at Queen Matilda's request, allowed his brother-in-law David to marry the heiress to Huntingdon. In the west, several new faces appeared in the middle of the reign. At Worcester, Walter de Beauchamp succeeded to the d'Abetot lands.[128] Walter of Gloucester, castellan of Gloucester, began to witness royal documents in 1114 and was probably appointed to a constableship of the court.[129]

Some of the new faces appear in the sources by ones and twos, the timing reflecting the accidents of mortality. It is evident, however, that a number of decisions about patronage were taken at one time, probably at an assembly of tenants-in-chief whose advice and agreement were necessary. In 1113, at the successful conclusion of his campaign on the continent, Henry gave land to Stephen and David. Several changes also had to be made perforce after the deaths of two of the king's children and of many members of his court in the wreck of the White Ship in November

---

[124] C. F. Slade, *The Leicestershire Survey*, University of Leicester Department of English Local History Occasional Papers no. 7 (Welwyn, 1956), pp. 85–7.

[125] Crouch, *Beaumont Twins*, chapter one.    [126] *Ibid.*, p. 9.

[127] Crouch, 'Geoffrey de Clinton and Roger, Earl of Warwick', pp. 116–18.    [128] *RRAN*, II, no. 1062.

[129] *Ibid.*, XVI; G. H. White, 'Constables under the Norman Kings', *Genealogist*, new series, 38 (1922), 120–1.

1120, after which the sorrowful king returned to England. The Christmas feast of 1120 must have been a gloomy occasion, but it was well attended by all the leading magnates including Earl David, Stephen of Blois and his brother Count Theobald, and Robert, the king's eldest illegitimate son.[130] Henry, a widower since 1118, married Adeliza of Louvain in January 1121, for it was of the utmost urgency to have a male heir. In political as well as personal terms the death of his heir Prince William could not have come at a worse moment. In the autumn of 1120 Henry had seemingly triumphed over all his enemies, and King Louis of France, defeated in battle at Brémule, had been persuaded to accept Prince William's homage for Normandy, thus overriding the undoubtedly superior claims of Duke Robert's son, also William. Now all was uncertain once again, until Henry's second marriage produced a male child.

Meanwhile Henry took steps to strengthen his position in England. In 1121 and 1122 he showed particular concern about his western and northern borders (for the latter see above, pp. 117–18). Before this time he had granted to Brian FitzCount the lordship of Abergavenny, and his chamberlain Payn FitzJohn was posted to Herefordshire, probably by 1115 which is when he made his first appearance in a royal document relating to that county.[131] At some stage Payn married a daughter of Hugh de Lacy, and came to control Ewias Lacy and Archenfield. In 1121 Henry created an earldom of Gloucester for his son Robert who was also lord of Glamorgan, and about the same time a prestigious marriage was arranged for Miles son of Walter, castellan of Gloucester, to the daughter of Bernard of Neufmarché. The career prospects of Miles were dramatically transformed by this marriage, for his father's lands were relatively modest and the presence in Gloucestershire of an earl who was the king's son restricted the possibilities for further gains in this county, whereas Bernard's lands lay to the west, in Brecknock.[132]

Henry's marriage was still childless when the surviving child of his first marriage, Matilda, was unexpectedly widowed. Her potential as a successor in her own right, or, if remarried, at least as the mother of a grandson of Henry I, acquired added significance.[133] In about 1125 Henry allowed his nephew Stephen of Blois to marry the daughter and heiress of Eustace

[130] *RRAN*, II, nos. 1241, 1243, 1244.     [131] *Ibid.*, II, no. 1101.     [132] Round, *Ancient Charters*, p. 9.
[133] K. Leyser, 'The Anglo-Norman Succession 1120–1125', *Anglo-Norman Studies*, 13 (1990), 225–41.

III count of Boulogne who retired into a monastery. Matilda of Boulogne was the biggest catch on the marriage market as heiress to Boulogne and large estates in England. Her wealth made Stephen the richest magnate in England. Why did Henry shower yet more wealth on his already richly endowed nephew? The king needed the support of the house of Blois to counteract the hostility of King Louis of France and Anjou. There were other considerations. If Henry was already thinking of Matilda as a potential successor, and possibly of her remarriage to the heir of the count of Anjou, then he may already have been trying to buy support for a marriage that was bound to be unpopular. However, we cannot be sure that this is what the king *did* have in mind, not least because the precise timing of the marriage in relation to the death of the Emperor is unclear. It could simply be argued that Henry wanted to make sure Boulogne was in safe hands. What he achieved, as events turned out, was to make Stephen rich enough to provide him with the wherewithal for his coup in 1135.

The king brought his daughter to England and in 1127 David, her uncle and now king of Scotland, Stephen of Blois, Robert of Gloucester, and the other magnates, swore to accept her as his successor in default of a son.[134] Henry relied on the support of a few men to carry through this new plan for the succession. Earl Robert and Brian FitzCount escorted the Empress to Normandy for her wedding to Geoffrey of Anjou, and were in charge of an audit of the treasury in 1128–9 which may well have been held as part of the fund-raising for Matilda's lavish wedding.[135] David of Scotland was also evidently part of the inner group. He spent the whole of 1126 in England and took the oath to his niece. The archbishop of Canterbury may have been persuaded to concur with the king's plan for the succession by a well-timed grant of the custody of Rochester castle.[136] Duke Robert was removed from the custody of Roger bishop of Salisbury and committed instead to Robert of Gloucester, and the still imprisoned Waleran of Meulan was transferred from Payn FitzJohn's custody at Bridgnorth to that of Brian FitzCount at Wallingford.[137]

---

[134] WM, *Historia Novella*, pp. 3–5.

[135] *ASC* 1127 (*recte* 1126); the audit is discussed by Green, *Government of England*, p. 47.

[136] C. Warren Hollister, 'The Anglo-Norman Succession Debate of 1126', *Monarchy, Magnates and Institutions*, pp. 159–60.    [137] *ASC* 1126.

There may have been question marks over the loyalty of Bishop Roger and Payn over the succession, as Hollister has suggested.[138] The bishop later was to claim that he was not bound by his oath because the king had promised not to arrange a marriage for his daughter outside the kingdom.[139] Hollister has suggested that there were two factions over the succession in 1126, one of which fell in with Henry's plans and an opposing faction which preferred William Clito.[140] Whilst the former group may be identified, as indicated above, it is by no means as certain that there was a coherent opposition. Nor is it clear that Stephen at this stage entertained any great hopes of succeeding his uncle. When Stephen's eldest son was born, probably in 1130 or 1131, he was named Eustace after his maternal grandfather, and he may well have believed that any family claim to succeed Henry I rested with his elder brother Theobald. Theobald himself, who visited England in 1129, probably thought so too.[141] It is almost certain that his trip was related to Matilda's marriage. Presumably Theobald acquiesced in Henry's plans, and the nomination of his younger brother Henry to the see of Winchester was perhaps another element in a political deal. There is also a reference in the form of London of 1130 of Theobald's quittance from the toll of merchants. His steward Andrew of Baudemont secured a pardon for Ralph Villanus in the account of London, and Andrew himself was pardoned forest fines in Devon, which suggests he may have been given land there.[142] In 1136 it was Theobald, not Stephen, whom an assembly of Norman magnates initially chose as their duke.[143]

Henry took other steps to ensure his daughter's succession in the event of his death. Robert of Gloucester was probably given custody of Dover castle, which he held by 1138, at this time, and may have taken overall charge of Kent.[144] The honour of Haughley passed to Robert de Vere (see above, p. 134), a man about whose origins little is known but who was pos-

---

[138] Hollister, 'Anglo-Norman Succession Debate', pp. 153–4.     [139] WM, *Historia Novella*, p. 5.
[140] Hollister, 'Anglo-Norman Succession Debate', pp. 145–69.     [141] *RRAN*, II, no. 1607.
[142] *PR 31 Henry I*, pp. 144, 155; Suger, *The Deeds of Louis the Fat* (translated by Cusimano and Moorehead), p. 90.     [143] OV, VI, 42, 454.
[144] OV, VI, 518–20; in 1135 the men of Dover refused Stephen entry on his return to England from Normandy: *Historical Works of Gervase of Canterbury*, I, 94. The sheriff of Kent in 1130 was a man named Rualon. In Green, *Government of England* it was suggested (p. 271) that this was Rualon d'Avranches. I now think it more likely that the sheriff was Rualon de Valognes as W. A. Morris suggested, *The Mediaeval English Sheriff to 1300* (Manchester, 1927), p. 85, n. 94.

sibly a tenant of Robert's in Normandy.[145] The shrievalty of Devon and Cornwall was transferred to a tenant of Baldwin de Redvers, and by 1133 the reeve of Southampton was Payn Trenchard, another Redvers tenant.[146] Robert II d'Oilly, who married Edith, one of the king's mistresses, was appointed to the shrievalty of Oxfordshire in 1129 and was possibly given custody of Oxford castle.[147] Whilst it could be argued that some of these changes might have occurred anyway, cumulatively they convey a clear impression that Henry was taking steps to ensure that key castles and ports were in the hands of men whom he could trust to back Matilda. The concession to the Londoners in 1130 of the right to elect their own sheriffs, and the possible subsequent lowering of the farm, may come under the same heading.[148] In addition Henry gave to Payn of Clairvaux, a follower of Fulk and Geoffrey of Anjou, the manor of Harting in Sussex. Payn accompanied Geoffrey to Rouen for his marriage to Matilda.[149] Although Payn held Harting at farm in 1130, he had not in fact paid any money over at the exchequer and his debt was pardoned.

The problem for Henry was that whatever plans he made were still threatened by his nephew William Clito. In 1123 he had been able to scotch a proposed marriage between William and a daughter of the count of Anjou, but William's undoubtedly just claim to his father's duchy still had much support within Normandy, and from the count of Anjou and the king of France. In 1127 King Louis arranged a marriage for William,

---

[145] Robert's father was named Bernard, and it seems likely that the family came from Ver-sur-Mer rather than Vern-sur-Seiche in Brittany whence came Aubrey de Vere. The reason is that a writ of Henry I issued between 1133 and 1135, of which the sole witness was the earl of Gloucester and which was addressed to the king's justices and the custodians of the see of Bayeux, ordered them to cause Reginald son of Robert Nep to have the tithe which Ralph de Rais detained out of the fee of Hugh de Crevecoeur and Robert de Vere: *RRAN*, II, no. 1898. Earl Robert supervised the inquest held into the fiefs of the bishopric held in 1133. His son Richard was consecrated as the next bishop in 1135, and the earl is said to have taken charge of many of the temporalities of the see during his son's episcopate: Haskins, *Norman Institutions*, p. 203.

[146] For Geoffrey de Furneaux, see Green, *Government of England*, p. 255; for Payn Trenchard, *RRAN*, II, nos. 1796–7; *Charters of the Redvers Family*, appendix I no. 8.

[147] While it is not certain that Robert is to be identified with the man who became sheriff in 1129, this is the likeliest identification: *PR 31 Henry I*, pp. 1–2; Green, *Government of England*, pp. 264–5.

[148] *PR 31 Henry I*, p. 148; *RRAN*, II, no. 1645; the dating and authenticity of this charter have been much discussed. The more noteworthy recent contributions include C. N. L. Brooke, G. Keir, and S. Reynolds, 'Henry I's Charter for the City of London', *Journal of the Society of Archivists*, 4 (1972), 558–78, and C. Warren Hollister, 'London's First Charter of Liberties: Is it Genuine?', *Monarchy, Magnates and Institutions*, pp. 191–208.

[149] *PR 31 Henry I*, p. 42; *Chroniques des comtes d'Anjou et des seigneurs d'Amboise*, ed. L. Halphen and R. Poupardin (Paris, 1913), p. 178.

and chose him to succeed the murdered count of Flanders. William there-
upon went to Flanders to make good the grant and, had he succeeded,
would have gained ample resources to attack Normandy and then
England. Henry distributed bribes in Flanders via Stephen, but the threat
to Henry was only removed by William's death from wounds in 1128.[150]

Following his daughter's remarriage, Henry seems to have been building bridges with alienated aristocrats. In 1129 he released Waleran of
Meulan and restored his lands, though not his castles.[151] Waleran's earliest attestation was in the company of Theobald of Blois. The document
concerned recorded the demise of land and forest in Leicestershire from
Ranulf of Chester to the king, who regranted it to Waleran's twin brother,
Robert earl of Leicester.[152] One uncertainty in the situation, apart from
the obvious one that Matilda had to produce a male child, was the position of Bishop Roger. His term as vice-regent had ended when Henry had
returned to England in September 1126, and there is no evidence to show
whether or not he was left in charge during the king's subsequent
absences, though he evidently remained head of the royal administration.[153] Roger may have been under a cloud in the late 1120s. He made his
only known visit to Normandy in 1129 after the audit of the treasury. In
the following year there were sweeping changes in the ranks of the sheriffs and Geoffrey de Clinton, one of the two treasury chamberlains, was
charged with treason and removed from office. Henry was evidently dis-
satisfied with the management of his revenues, and as the king's chief
minister Roger was clearly vulnerable, as also were Geoffrey and the other
treasury chamberlain, William de Pont de l'Arche. Roger and William survived, but Geoffrey was probably a victim. The accusation of treason
against him may have been engineered by Roger earl of Warwick, but
close examination of the king's revenues could have revealed a shortfall
which lent colour to any such accusation. In 1131, however, Bishop Roger
was given a fresh mark of royal favour when he received a royal charter
'restoring' the custody of Malmesbury abbey to Salisbury and its bishop,

---

[150] S. B. Hicks, 'The Impact of William Clito on the Continental Policies of Henry I of England', *Viator*, 10
(1979), 1–21; Hicks, 'England's Henry I and the Flemish Succession Crisis of 1127–1128', *Journal of the
Rocky Mountain Medieval and Renaissance Association*, 2 (1981), 41–9.      [151] *ASC* 1129.

[152] *RRAN*, II, no. 1607; for this episode see below, p. 313; King, 'Mountsorrel and its Region'.

[153] For a different view, see C. Warren Hollister, 'The Vice-Regal Court of Henry I', *Law, Custom, and the
Social Fabric. Essays in Honour of Bryce Lyon*, ed. B. S. Bachrach and D. Nicholas (Kalamazoo, 1990),
pp. 131–44.

and two years later his nephew Nigel was appointed to the bishopric of Ely.[154] Others received marks of the king's favour at about this time. King David, as already mentioned, was allowed to retain the earldom of Huntingdon, and Aubrey de Vere was granted an office called the master chamberlainship of England and Normandy in 1133.[155] Moreover, Geoffrey de Mandeville, who had not hitherto witnessed royal documents, appeared at Henry's court in Normandy in 1135.[156]

The growing use of inheritance language in royal charters to the aristocracy has been plausibly interpreted as yet another indication that the king was trying to be conciliatory.[157] A possible royal decree prescribing partition of lands between heiresses has been similarly interpreted as bowing to the wishes of the aristocracy (see below, p. 379). It would be a mistake to assume that his own imminent death preoccupied Henry to the exclusion of all else in the last years of his reign, but it may well have been the case that his wish to pave the way for Matilda and her children did lead him to be as conciliatory as possible. When his grandson was born in 1133, his joy was evident, and he must have believed that he had created enough goodwill to carry the succession through. How wrong he was!

Over more than three decades Henry imposed his authority over the aristocracy by a mixture of carrot and stick. He was ruthless when he felt he had to be, as in the case of Robert de Bellême and his brothers, but he was loyal and even generous to those who were loyal to him. He knew the value of information: Orderic Vitalis noted that no revolt against him ever succeeded because he was always forewarned.[158] His rule in England to no small extent depended on the calibre of those who administered his rights: the constables of his castles, the sheriffs and the justices, and, above all, his chief minister, Roger of Salisbury.

By 1135 the political scene had changed considerably. Where, as Orderic said, was William FitzOsbern, the flower of Normandy? His sons held no land in England in the reign of Henry I, when Orderic was writing.[159] Nor did the sons of Roger of Montgomery, ruined by their loyalty to Duke

---

[154] *RRAN*, II, no. 1715; *Liber Eliensis*, pp. 283–4.     [155] *RRAN*, II, no. 1777.     [156] *Ibid.*, nos. 1915–1917.

[157] Holt, 'Feudal Society and the Family in Early Medieval England: IV. The Heiress and the Alien', p. 9.

[158] OV, VI, 100; see further J. O. Prestwich, 'Military Intelligence under the Norman and Angevin Kings', *Law and Government in England and Normandy*, ed. G. Garnett and J. Hudson (Cambridge, 1994), pp. 1–30.

[159] OV, II, 318–20.

Robert. Of the three men closest to Duke William, only Roger of Beaumont's sons and grandsons had prospered, and one of them, Waleran of Meulan, had been in disgrace between 1124 and 1129. The reign of Henry I had seen the rise to greater prominence of men from west and lower Normandy, and of Bretons, than had been the case in his father's day. It had also witnessed the rise of men through new channels, of administrative service, as well as valour in battle. Not only had the faces changed, therefore, but so had the rules of the game.

Henry's regime had inevitably favoured some at the expense of others, and it is legitimate to ask, therefore, if he had so stoked up the fires of baronial discontent that they inevitably burst into flames after his death. In the narrower context, Henry could not overcome the problem that by rewarding some, he disappointed others: each family had its own ambitions. And in the broader context, certainly, his decisions had created a potential contest between the counts of Blois and Anjou for the control of Normandy and England. The civil war of Stephen's reign was thus not only a dispute confined to the Anglo-Norman realm but became part of a struggle between the rulers of different regions of France. In other respects, however, it could be argued that in the closing years of his reign Henry was conciliatory rather than confrontational to the aristocracy in general. Henry was a king who, with all the problems besetting him, had by a mixture of guile and ruthlessness discouraged magnates from resorting to force of arms to achieve their objectives for a longer period than any other Norman king.

## Civil war

When J. H. Round published his book *Geoffrey de Mandeville* he believed that after a period of strong rule the aristocracy simply reverted to type under King Stephen's weak rule. Feudal anarchy was a reaction to weak kingship. Geoffrey was a man whom Round described as the 'most perfect and typical presentment of the feudal and anarchic spirit that stamps the reign of Stephen', an opportunist who sold his support to the highest bidder.[160] Round believed in the importance of using record evidence and especially charters in his reconstruction of the career of Geoffrey de

---

[160] Round, *Geoffrey de Mandeville*, p. v.

Mandeville. R. H. C. Davis in a celebrated redating of the charters issued by Stephen and the Empress demonstrated to the satisfaction of most historians, though not all, that Round's dating was wrong. According to this view Geoffrey was a loyal supporter of Stephen except for a few months in 1141, when many others also defected, and he was no more and no less cynical than most of his contemporaries.[161] The extent of the aristocracy's responsibility for causing the war has been a subject of much comment since, both from those who have attempted general assessments and from those who have studied individuals. Davis argued that the lay magnates, far from being selfish opportunists, were in fact trying to secure rights of inheritance over their land because they were tired of holding their land at the king's will, as they had been under Henry I.[162] Although Davis may have underestimated the relative security of inheritance by 1135, his view that the magnates were not intent on destroying the fabric of government has been supported by Edmund King and, more recently, Warren Hollister, who have each argued that the magnates were not on the whole aggressive opportunists but reacted defensively to protect their lands in uncertain times.[163]

Study of individual careers in recent years has indicated that there was a whole range of motives amongst the lay magnates either for getting involved or for avoiding involvement or trying to be neutral. At one end of the spectrum was Ranulf II earl of Chester, one of the most aggressive and opportunist of all magnates.[164] William count of Aumale was similarly acquisitive.[165] The Beaumont twins, whose careers have been reconstructed by David Crouch, began the reign well, for they and their allies were high in Stephen's favour, and for a time they went from strength to strength. Waleran count of Meulan, however, faced with the loss of his

---

[161] R. H. C. Davis, 'Geoffrey de Mandeville Reconsidered', *English Historical Review*, 79 (1964), 299–37; cf. J. O. Prestwich, 'The Treason of Geoffrey de Mandeville', *English Historical Review*, 103 (1988), 283–312; for the subsequent debate between Prestwich and Davis, *ibid.*, 960–6 and 105 (1990), 670–2.

[162] R. H. C. Davis, 'What happened in Stephen's Reign', *History*, 49 (1964), 1–12.

[163] E. King, 'King Stephen and the Anglo-Norman Aristocracy', *History*, 59 (1974), 180–94; C. Warren Hollister, 'The Aristocracy', *The Anarchy of Stephen's Reign*, ed. E. King (Oxford, 1994), pp. 37–66.

[164] H. A. Cronne, 'Ranulf de Gernons, Earl of Chester', *Transactions of the Royal Historical Society*, 4th series, 20 (1937), 103–34; R. H. C. Davis, 'King Stephen and the Earl of Chester Revised', *English Historical Review*, 75 (1960), 654–60; G. White, 'King Stephen, Duke Henry and Ranulf de Gernons Earl of Chester', *English Historical Review*, 91 (1976), 555–65; King, 'Mountsorrel and its Region', pp. 1–10; King, 'Foundation of Pipewell Abbey, Northamptonshire'; J. A. Green, 'Earl Ranulf II and Lancashire', *Earldom of Chester and Its Charters*, pp. 97–108; Dalton, 'Aiming at the Impossible', *ibid.*, pp. 109–54.

[165] Dalton, 'William Earl of York'; see also *Conquest, Anarchy and Lordship*, chapter four.

Norman estates by 1141, eventually had to come to terms with the Angevins. His twin, Robert earl of Leicester, by contrast, remained loyal to Stephen until 1153, suffering the loss of his Norman estates for a time.

The role of the lay magnates has to be seen in context, however. Did the magnates act as they did because of King Stephen's weakness? Davis was in little doubt about the responsibility of Stephen's weak rule in leading to the outbreak of the war, but in recent years there has been a reassessment both of the contribution of Henry I's policies to Stephen's difficulties, and of the extent to which Stephen's actions provoked the war.[166] We also now have a clearer picture of the Empress's role, thanks to a fine biography by Marjorie Chibnall.[167] The publication by R. H. C. Davis and H. A. Cronne of the acts of Stephen, Matilda, Henry, and Geoffrey provided a necessary footing; there have been studies of the war and of its effects on specific aspects of royal government – the exchequer, revenue collection, and coinage – and on different geographical areas.[168] Finally, much more is known about the church in this period than a century ago.[169] People and land belonging to the church were the victims of violence or of novel demands for service or money, but this was also a time when religious houses continued to be founded. Towards the end of the reign ecclesiastics led by Archbishop Theobald worked towards a peaceful resolution of the question of Stephen's successor, which had become the critical issue.

The analysis offered here is concerned first and foremost with the lay aristocracy, however. It considers, first, the importance of their role in

---

[166] See especially J. Bradbury, 'The Early Years of Stephen', *England in the Twelfth Century*, ed. D. Williams (Woodbridge, 1990), pp. 17–30; Stringer, *Reign of Stephen*, pp. 8–13.

[167] *The Empress Matilda* (Oxford, 1991).

[168] *RRAN*, III, IV; of the many works dealing with the impact of the war on government and society only the more important are mentioned here: J. Bradbury, *Stephen and Matilda. The Civil War of 1139–1153* (Stroud, 1996); H. A. Cronne, *The Reign of Stephen. Anarchy in England* (London, 1970); E. King, 'The Anarchy of Stephen's Reign', *Transactions of the Royal Historical Society*, 5th series, 34 (1984), 133–153; *The Anarchy of Stephen's Reign*, ed. E. King (Oxford, 1994); K. Yoshitake, 'The Arrest of the Bishops in 1139 and its Consequences', *Journal of Medieval History*, 14 (1988), 97–114; Green, 'Financing Stephen's War', pp. 102–4; W. L. Warren, 'The Myth of Norman Administrative Efficiency', *Transactions of the Royal Historical Society*, 5th series, 34 (1984), 113–32; Warren, *The Governance of Norman and Angevin England* (London, 1987), pp. 89–95; for comment see Dalton, *Conquest, Anarchy and Lordship*, pp. 177–8; G. C. Boon, *Coins of the Anarchy 1135–54*, National Museum of Wales (Cardiff, 1988); M. Blackburn, 'Coinage and Currency', *Anarchy of Stephen's Reign* (ed. King), pp. 145–206; R. Eales, 'Local Loyalties in Norman England: Kent in Stephen's Reign', *Anglo-Norman Studies*, 7 (1985), 88–108; Amt, *Accession of Henry II*, chaps. 2–4; White, 'Were the Midlands "Wasted" during Stephen's Reign?', and see also White's paper 'Continuity in Government' in *Anarchy of Stephen's Reign* (ed. King), pp. 117–43.

[169] For a recent survey see C. Holdsworth, 'The Church', *Anarchy of Stephen's Reign* (ed. King), pp. 207–30.

causing the war until 1138; secondly the phase between 1138, when the Empress decided to fight for her cause in England, and the end of the climactic year of 1141; thirdly, the stalemate of the 1140s and the effects of the war; and, fourthly, the search for peace.

The first question that arises is how deep rooted were the origins of the war? On the governmental side, it has been argued, most recently by Keith Stringer, that the reign of Henry I was one of imperial overstretch, in that the costs of sustaining the empire were overtaxing the resources of England.[170] There is no doubt that Henry's determination to keep Normandy at all costs did lead to pressure on English sources of revenue because, as I have argued elsewhere, this aim could only be achieved by mercenaries and castles rather than the committed support of the aristocracy of Normandy.[171] The 1130 pipe roll indicates how such monies were raised from royal lands, from danegeld, but, most of all, from magnates prepared to pay for royal intervention on their behalf. Did these demands place intolerable strains on the administration and bequeath an impossible legacy to Stephen? In financial terms the answer has to be 'no', for at Henry's death there were large amounts of treasure both at Winchester, which Stephen seized, and at Falaise, taken by Robert of Gloucester.[172] It could be argued that these reserves had been accumulated at a high *political* price in imposing strains on those committed to pay large sums or on those whose bids for royal patronage had been rejected. On the other hand, as we have seen, there are signs that Henry was conciliatory towards the aristocracy in the final years of the reign. There were the 'disinherited', men like Ilbert de Lacy of Pontefract or Gilbert de Lacy of Weobley, but these were relatively few in number. There were also those who might be described as the 'discontented', men who had unsatisfied claims to castles, lands, or office, such as Hugh Bigod, who was keen to hold Norwich castle and probably also the shrievalty of Norfolk and Suffolk. Another was Simon II de Senlis, who had attained his majority some years before 1135 but whose stepfather continued to hold his patrimonial lands. Geoffrey de Mandeville has been suggested as another possibility, though he may have recovered his demesne manors before Henry's death (see above, p. 290). However, there were always men waiting to press their

---

[170] Stringer, *Reign of Stephen*, p. 10.     [171] Green, 'Henry I and the Aristocracy of Normandy'.
[172] *Gesta Stephani*, p. 8; OV, VI, 448.

claims on the king, and it is hard to see that their number was unusually large in 1135.

There is no doubt that the Welsh and Scots were going to cause major problems for Stephen to a degree his uncle had not experienced. Henry knew that there was trouble brewing in Wales, and at the end of his life had been preparing to cross from Normandy to deal with it. His approach to the Welsh frontier had been to commit the Anglo-Norman lordships to trusted adherents with ample resources to hold the Welsh in check. This had worked until just before his death, but the scale of the subsequent revolt pushed back the Anglo-Norman lords. So far as the Scots were concerned, Stephen's accession gave David the opportunity he needed to advance his own ambitions whilst supporting the Empress's cause. Equally the cost of securing and holding Normandy was likely to be high for the ruler of England. The defence of Normandy had cost Henry much in terms of castles and garrisons, especially on the frontiers. He had had to deal with the hostility of Louis VI of France and that of Fulk count of Anjou. The Norman magnates, faced with the prospect of the succession of Matilda married to the count of Anjou, might well look to the old king's nephews as alternatives, but their first thought was that Theobald should succeed, not Stephen, and it was only when they found out that Stephen had been crowned king in England that they transferred their support to him.[173]

Stephen had a difficult inheritance as there was pressure on all the frontiers of the Anglo-Norman realm, plus magnates in England who had their own goals. It is not clear whether he had given any indication beforehand that he was intending to make a bid. What made his accession possible was that at the moment her father died, Matilda had quarrelled with her father and was outmanoeuvred by the speed of Stephen's actions in securing the throne and the homage of most of the leading laymen and ecclesiastics. By the time she had sent envoys to Rome, she found that Stephen had beaten her there too and had secured a recognition from the pope. The Empress was not entirely without support. Her uncle King David had invaded Cumbria and Northumberland and was preparing to attack Durham, but Stephen marched north and concluded a truce by the terms of which David's son Henry did homage at York for Huntingdon, Carlisle, and Doncaster, and Stephen promised not to grant the earldom

[173] OV, VI, 454.

of Northumberland to anyone without hearing Henry's claim in his court.[174] This was not good news for the Empress, for it suggested that David would allow his support for her claim to be bought off by territorial concessions.

Furthermore Stephen secured the support of Miles of Gloucester, and probably his colleague Payn FitzJohn, in the early days of January 1136. Stephen granted Miles in inheritance the shrievalty of Gloucester and custody of the royal castle at Gloucester.[175] This was an astute move, for it helped to increase the pressure on Robert of Gloucester to do homage. Robert's own position at this time was acutely difficult. Realistically Robert had little choice but to accept Stephen, especially by Easter 1136, and he therefore made his way to England.[176] The trouble for Stephen with making such concessions, however, was that they stimulated rather than satisfied demand. In 1136 Hugh Bigod took over the royal castle at Norwich having heard a rumour that the king was dead. He may have been hoping for a grant like that of Gloucester castle to Miles, but if so he was disappointed.[177]

In the west Baldwin de Redvers took over the royal castle at Exeter and put it onto a war footing. Baldwin has usually been portrayed as a rebel on a point of principle, but he probably had a specific grievance and wanted custody of Exeter castle and control of the shrievalty.[178] Baldwin may have thought his revolt would lead to a general uprising against the king, and he did have allies, namely Alfred FitzJudhael, lord of Barnstaple, who had a claim to the lordship of Totnes, and Robert of Bampton, who had lost the manor of Uffculme, which had been restored by Stephen to the abbey of Glastonbury.[179] The revolt was initially unsuccessful. The garrison at Exeter castle surrendered and Baldwin was disinherited and exiled. He retired to the Cotentin peninsula where he continued the struggle in the company of Reginald, another of the illegitimate sons of Henry I.[180] Robert

---

[174] Richard of Hexham, 'De Gestis Regis Stephani et de Bello Standardii', Chronicles, III, 145–6.

[175] RRAN, III, no. 386.

[176] J. W. Leedom, 'William of Malmesbury and Robert of Gloucester Reconsidered', Albion, 6 (1974), 251–63; for a different assessment see R. B. Patterson, 'William of Malmesbury's Robert of Gloucester: a Re-Evaluation of the Historia Novella', American Historical Review, 70 (1965), 983–97; WM, Historia Novella, p. 17.     [177] HH, p. 259.

[178] Richard of Hexham, 'De Gestis Regis Stephani et de Bello Standardii', Chronicles, III, 143. Baldwin's ambitions are discussed in Green, 'Family Matters', forthcoming.

[179] Gesta Stephani, pp. 36–8, 28–30; H. P. R. Finberg, 'Uffculme', in Lucerna (London, 1964), pp. 204–21.

[180] OV, VI, 510, 514.

of Bampton fled and his son took refuge at the court of King David.[181] If the point at issue in Baldwin's revolt was the shrievalty of Devon and custody of Exeter castle, Stephen was within his rights to besiege Baldwin, and he successfully ejected him from what was a royal castle.[182] Where Stephen arguably did err was in underestimating the ramifications of the revolt. Many of the families in the south-western counties had little land outside the region and chose their marriage partners from neighbouring families. It was a closely knit society, hence the lead given by Baldwin was consolidated and built on to produce a power base for the Empress.[183]

In 1137 Stephen had to turn his attention to Normandy. The Angevins had overrun the southern marches and there were localized outbreaks of fighting. Stephen's arrival in person in 1137 won him some support and, most significantly, King Louis accepted the homage of Stephen's son Eustace for Normandy – a blow for the Empress and her sons. Stephen intended to carry the war into southern Normandy against Geoffrey of Anjou, but an outbreak of fighting between the followers of Robert of Gloucester and those of William of Ypres resulted in the breakup of his army. He was forced to return to England, but he nevertheless negotiated a truce with the Angevins.[184] Davis suggested that 'it was a mistake to abandon the struggle so easily', but it is hard to see what more Stephen could have achieved.[185] The comparison with his uncle's similarly inconclusive campaigns in 1105 and the early months of 1106 is worth remembering in this context. Had Stephen been able to suppress revolt in England, he could have returned to Normandy later.[186]

A contest developed next over the succession to Simon de Beauchamp's honour and custody of Bedford castle. Simon had died at some point between Easter 1136 and the end of 1137, leaving a daughter whom Stephen planned to marry to Hugh de Beaumont, younger brother of the Beaumont twins. The Beaumonts were Stephen's leading advisers in the early years, and with their relations and clients formed a very powerful political coalition. They were cousins of Roger earl of Warwick, and related by marriage to William de Warenne and Simon II de Senlis.

[181] *Gesta Stephani*, pp. 46–7.

[182] Bradbury, 'Early Years of the Reign of Stephen's Reign', p. 28; cf. R. H. C. Davis, *King Stephen*, 3rd edn (London, 1990), pp. 22–4.     [183] Green, 'Family Matters', pp. 158–64.

[184] OV, vi, 486; Robert of Torigny, *Chronicles*, iv, 132.     [185] Davis, *King Stephen*, p. 26.

[186] R. Helmerichs, 'King Stephen's Norman Itinerary, 1137', *Haskins Society Journal*, 5 (1993), 89–97 offers a favourable verdict on the Norman campaign.

Moreover in 1136 when the see of Canterbury fell vacant, Stephen chose to back Theobald abbot of Bec, not his own brother, Henry bishop of Winchester. Although Bec had close ties to the Beaumont family, Stephen was doubtless influenced by the appropriateness of another archbishop (the third) from Bec and by the knowledge that if he had supported his brother's candidature he would have been creating a huge headache for himself.

By Christmas 1137 Stephen was besieging Bedford castle, which Miles de Beauchamp had fortified against him, but this was a localized revolt and Stephen may well have been feeling relatively cheerful, having secured and kept the allegiance of most of the aristocracy.[187] The year 1138, however, was when his problems multiplied, and when the war in England really began. The key factor was the decision of the Empress and her half-brother Robert of Gloucester to make a fight of it, and it was this, combined with renewed attacks from Scotland and the precarious situation along the Welsh March, that led to an escalation of the conflict. Robert by 1138 had evidently had enough of Stephen. He had left Stephen's camp in Normandy in the previous year because he feared for his life, and he cannot have relished the influence of the Beaumont twins over the king.[188] It was some months between his leaving Stephen's camp and formally issuing his defiance in Whitsuntide 1138, and the likelihood is that he was negotiating with potential allies during this period. Stephen reacted to the threat by appointing a number of earls; Matilda landed in England and was able to attract a nucleus of support. At this stage Stephen had shown that he was able to deal with isolated revolts; what the Angevins needed to be able to do was to start a fire which could not be put out.

Davis calculated that between 1136 and 1140 Stephen created earls in fourteen English counties, the Empress created several more, and there were possibly one or two later additions, so that there were only five counties with no known earl at some stage of the reign.[189] (The exceptions were as follows: Shropshire, held in dower by Queen Adeliza; Kent, where the

---

[187] OV, VI, 510.

[188] Patterson, 'William of Malmesbury's Robert of Gloucester', pp. 990–1; D. Crouch, 'Robert, Earl of Gloucester, and the Daughter of Zelophehad', *Journal of Medieval History*, 11 (1985), 227–43.

[189] Davis, *King Stephen*, pp. 90–1, 125–41.

*powers* of earl were held either by Robert earl of Gloucester or by the archbishop of Canterbury – see above, p. 287; Middlesex, which was dominated
by the city of London; Hampshire; and Berkshire.) The title of earl was the
most prestigious the king could bestow. Earls were in some cases entitled
to the third penny of the shire and borough courts, but as the title was
given to men who had substantial estates in the areas concerned this may
not have been much of a consideration.[190] In 1136 Stephen had recognized
Henry of Scotland's claim to his father's midland earldom of Huntingdon,
and either about the same time or in 1138 when the Scots attacked again,
the claim of Henry's half-brother Simon II de Senlis to the earldom of
Northampton.[191] The creation of an earldom of Bedford for Hugh de
Beaumont may also have occurred in 1138. Miles de Beauchamp may not
have held the family estates before he defied Stephen, but his loyalty may
already have been in doubt. In this context it may be significant that
Beatrix de Beauchamp, probably Miles's sister, was married to Hugh de
Moreville, King David's constable.[192] Also possibly in 1138 the earldom
of Cambridgeshire was granted to William de Roumare, brother of
Earl Ranulf and one of Stephen's commanders in Normandy.[193]
Huntingdonshire was the only county from the old midland earldom of
Waltheof which remained to the Scots, and it is conceivable that Stephen
deliberately made earls in Northampton, Cambridge, and Bedford to
make sure that these counties at least were in reliable hands.

The creation of at least two northern earldoms was also in response to
the Scots threat: the creation of William of Aumale as earl of Yorkshire,
and of Robert de Ferrers as earl of Derby, followed the battle of the
Standard in 1138. In the following year after the treaty of Durham,
Stephen recognized Prince Henry as earl of Northumberland.[194] Alan, son
of Count Stephen of Brittany and lord of Richmond, was styled Count Alan
from 1136, though it is not apparent whether Alan was simply calling
himself count or was actually created an earl by the king. Stephen also
had reason to be concerned about his western frontier, and about the
Norman lordships in south Wales. He betrothed his infant daughter to
Waleran of Meulan, and created him earl of Worcester with grants of

[190] Round, *Geoffrey de Mandeville*, Appendix D.
[191] Richard of Hexham, *Chronicles*, III, 146; John of Hexham, SD, *Opera omnia*, II, 287; Davis, *King Stephen*,
p. 131.          [192] Barrow, *Anglo-Norman Era*, p. 71.          [193] Davis, *King Stephen*, p. 135.
[194] Richard of Hexham, *Chronicles*, III, 177.

Worcester, Droitwich, and other lands and rights.[195] In this way Waleran became the overlord of William de Beauchamp, a royal constable and hereditary constable of Worcester and sheriff. If, as is likely, Stephen was concerned about William's loyalty, he had subjected him to one of his own close allies. In Wales itself, Gilbert FitzGilbert was created earl of Pembroke.[196] He was the brother of Richard FitzGilbert who had been killed by the Welsh in 1136, and, as Davis suggested, the new earl was probably intended to take command in West Wales.

To this point, therefore, Stephen's creation of earldoms was defensive, especially against the Scots. There was no wholesale distribution of titles in regions where he was strong. The creation in or before 1139 of an earldom of Lincoln for William d'Aubigny the butler, who had married King Henry's widow, was different, however. This title was presumably granted at the time of his marriage and was a mark of distinction. His marriage had presumably been arranged by the king and this, together with the creation of an earldom, is indicative of Stephen's favour – and it worked, in the sense that d'Aubigny remained consistently loyal.[197] His estates were in Norfolk, where he and William de Warenne acted as counterweights to Hugh Bigod, and, as Adeliza's husband, d'Aubigny held Arundel castle. The choice of Lincoln for d'Aubigny's county is hard to explain, though Davis pointed out that William's mother was a grand-daughter of Robert de Todeni and thus William had a claim to the honour of Belvoir.[198] The choice proved to be a mistake, however, for it was an affront to the power in Lincolnshire of Ranulf of Chester and his brother William de Roumare. William de Roumare possibly lost Cambridgeshire when peace was made with the Scots in 1139, and he may have been transferred to Lincolnshire at Christmas 1140, whilst William d'Aubigny transferred in turn to Sussex.[199] This was possibly the deal which was arranged between Stephen, William de Roumare, and Ranulf of Chester, of which Stephen soon seems to have repented.[200]

In 1140 more earldoms were created. When Reginald, the illegitimate son of Henry I, established himself in Cornwall, Stephen created Count Alan earl there. This is an example of a second kind of earldom, where Stephen had his back to the wall and had nothing to lose in granting the

---

[195] Crouch, *Beaumont Twins*, p. 30.     [196] Davis, *King Stephen*, p. 133; Crouch, *Beaumont Twins*, p. 39.
[197] Davis, *King Stephen*, p. 134.     [198] *Ibid.*     [199] *Ibid.*, pp. 134, 135.
[200] *Gesta Stephani*, p. 110; WM, *Historia Novella*, pp. 46–7.

title to one who might have been able to establish himself in the shire. A possible parallel here was Stephen's grant of comital rights in Herefordshire to Robert earl of Leicester. The grant cannot be precisely dated but was clearly made in the context of the Empress's creation of an earldom of Hereford for Miles of Gloucester.[201] It also meant that one of the Beaumont twins held Worcestershire and the other Herefordshire. Although Alan prevailed for a time in Cornwall, Reginald made a comeback, and it was probably at this stage that he was created earl either by Robert of Gloucester or by the Empress.[202] In 1140 Stephen made his son-in-law Hervey the Breton earl of Wiltshire and commander of Devizes castle; this was presumably in an attempt to counteract the power of Walter of Salisbury.[203]

The last of Stephen's earldoms to be considered are Essex and Hertfordshire. Stephen created Geoffrey de Mandeville earl of Essex, probably around Whitsuntide 1140. Geoffrey was the most powerful magnate in Essex apart from Stephen himself. The king may well have felt that generosity would serve him well and, because the royal demesne was substantial and because he also had the lands of the count of Boulogne in Essex, his own authority would not be eroded too far. The terms of Stephen's first charter say only that the earldom was granted hereditarily.[204] By this stage Geoffrey had evidently recovered those demesne manors which his father had lost, if indeed these had not been restored by Henry I. It is possible that Geoffrey was intended to fulfil the same role as had Eudo *dapifer* in 1101, though there is no indication that Stephen granted Geoffrey Colchester, which Eudo had received.[205]

The title of earl of Hertford was conferred on Gilbert FitzRichard of Clare. Suffolk seems the more obvious choice as Clare was in Suffolk, but Stephen seems to have been reluctant to create an East Anglian earldom.

---

[201] *RRAN*, III, no. 437 discussed by Davis, *King Stephen*, 137. Davis suggested that this grant and two others which granted *comitatus* were using formulae appropriate to the situation where a man who was already an earl was granted a second county. For a different view see P. Latimer, 'Grants of "Totus Comitatus" in Twelfth-Century England: their Origins and Meaning', *Bulletin of the Institute of Historical Research*, 59 (1986), 137–45.

[202] According to William of Malmesbury, Earl Robert made Reginald an earl: *Historia Novella*, p. 42. For Alan see *Gesta Stephani*, pp. 102, 116. Although the phrasing of the latter could be interpreted as a gift of the county rather than the earldom, Alan issued a charter for St Michael's Mount in which he styled himself Count of Brittany, Cornwall, and Richmond: see Davis, *King Stephen*, p. 136.

[203] *Gesta Stephani*, pp. 108, 116.     [204] *RRAN*, III, no. 273.

[205] For the grant of Colchester by the Empress to Aubrey de Vere, see *RRAN*, III, no. 634.

He was himself rich in estates in Suffolk as lord of the honour of Eye, and probably did not want to see a rival earl in the county. The earldoms of Essex and Hertford are clearly not to be explained either in terms of defence of a frontier region or in reaction to a challenge to his authority, and probably the likeliest explanation is Stephen's deteriorating position politically and financially, and the need to strengthen his own support.

It is clear that Stephen in making so many earls was not simply granting honorific titles as Round believed. The evident reluctance of both king and Empress to duplicate earls in the same counties is one indication. Most of the Empress's earldoms were created after the battle of Lincoln in 1141 when she believed she would be able to take the throne. The Empress, as Dr Chibnall has shown, tended to be cautious in the way she made ecclesiastical appointments, and on the whole she created earls only when she believed she had the power to do so: a possible exception here was Earl Reginald's earldom.[206] She created Miles of Gloucester earl of Hereford, Aubrey de Vere earl of Oxford, William de Mohun earl of Somerset, and Baldwin de Redvers earl of Devon.[207] Her first charter for Geoffrey de Mandeville used the terminology of donation ('do et concedo').[208] Patrick of Salisbury's earldom of Wiltshire probably post-dated the departure of Stephen's earl, Hervey (for whom see above, p. 301).[209] If the titles had been purely honorific, there was little reason for Matilda to desist from creating rival earldoms in counties where there were Stephanic earls.

The above reconstruction is only tentative because in many cases the timing of an earldom is not precise, but it is hard to avoid the conclusion that most of Stephen's earldoms were created for defence in border counties, and the rest either to put in a local supremo over a sheriff or castellan of dubious loyalty, or, in one or two cases, as straightforward recognitions of loyalty. Most of the grants of title were clustered between 1138 and 1140. 1138 was the year of two invasions by the Scots and Robert earl of Gloucester's public renunciation of homage, and William of Malmesbury attributed many of the earldoms to the autumn of 1138.[210] The beneficiaries, as Davis pointed out, were men of standing, and they were in effect the 'military governors' of their shires.[211] Davis believed that one

[206] M. Chibnall, 'The Empress Matilda and Church Reform', *Transactions of the Royal Historical Society*, 5th series, 38 (1988), 107–33.       [207] Davis, *King Stephen*, pp. 137, 138, 139.       [208] *RRAN*, III, no. 273.
[209] Davis, *King Stephen*, pp. 136–7.       [210] WM, *Historia Novella*, p. 23.       [211] Davis, *King Stephen*, pp. 30–1.

motive was to slot in a new layer of men over the sheriffs, many of whom had been appointed by Roger of Salisbury and whose loyalty might have been suspect. In fact it is hard to associate any of the sheriffs specifically with the bishop, though that does not necessarily mean that such a link did not exist or, just as important, that Stephen did not believe that it existed.

Charters survive in connection with only three of the new earldoms. First there is that of Stephen creating Geoffrey de Mandeville earl of Essex, which says only that he was to hold hereditarily as other earls held.[212] Secondly there is the Empress's charter creating Miles earl of Hereford. The Empress granted him the motte and castle of Hereford, and also the third penny of the borough and county, three royal manors, the hays of Hereford and the forest of 'Trivela', and the service of three named individuals.[213] The problem is to know how many of the concessions to Miles were regarded as appurtenances of the earldom and how many were personal grants. Thirdly, the charter in which she created Aubrey de Vere earl simply said that he was to be earl of Cambridge or one of four other counties, and was to have the third penny.[214] Stephen's charter to Earl Robert of Leicester granted him the borough, castle, and county of Hereford, except those lands belonging to the church which were held in chief, and the service of four named individuals, but the title of earl was not explicitly granted in the charter.[215]

Two other specific references to grants of the 'whole county' are known in addition to Hereford: the grant of the county of Staffordshire to Ranulf of Chester in 1153, and that of Norfolk to Stephen's son William, notwithstanding Hugh Bigod's third penny.[216] The former was one of a long series of grants in the charter Henry FitzEmpress issued in favour of Ranulf of Chester, probably in the early months of 1153. This was at a time when Henry was desperate to consolidate and extend his power base and was negotiating for the allegiance of key men. The Staffordshire grant did not represent a major loss to the crown as the royal lands were not particularly valuable, and the leading tenant-in-chief (and possibly sheriff) Robert of Stafford was already Ranulf's ally. The grant of Norfolk to Stephen's son William was made in an agreement between Henry FitzEmpress and Stephen later in 1153. William had succeeded to the

[212] RRAN, III, no. 273.   [213] Ibid., no. 393.   [214] Ibid., no. 634.   [215] Ibid., no. 437.
[216] Ibid., nos. 180, 272.

great Warenne lands centred on Castle Acre in Norfolk by his marriage to William III de Warenne's daughter and heiress. Although Stephen had not been prepared to concede the earldom of Norfolk to Hugh Bigod, the Empress had allowed Hugh the title in 1141.[217] The agreement of 1153 conceded to William castles and vills to the value of £700, though the lands and rights which belonged to the bishops, abbots, and earls, and Hugh Bigod's third penny were protected. In other words, it would appear that comital *rights* were held by William, but the agreement tacitly recognized Hugh Bigod's *title*.

It is not easy to be precise about the nature of an earl's powers, but certain features recur in the relevant texts. The earl might well hold the principal castle plus the king's rights in the town, together with some of the royal manors in the county. It would appear that he could command the service of some laymen in the country. The lands of the church were specifically exempted as was the service of named laymen, but the fact that others were subordinated to the earls has perhaps not been given enough attention, for it strengthens the impression that the earls were intended to command the forces levied locally. It may well explain also why some earls seem to have taken over the collection of geld, if geld was collected from land which was not providing military service.[218]

Some earls acquired even greater powers than this over the government of their shires. A number evidently controlled the sheriffs. At the start of the following reign the revenues of almost half of the counties of England were channelled through earls or sheriffs who were earls' men.[219] As in the case of William of Aumale's power in Yorkshire, it is difficult to know whether this situation had been intended from the start, as some historians have suggested, or whether it had developed from a progressive loss of control.[220] What may have begun in a small way, with the grant of titles and in some instances substantive powers, may have escalated with the pressure from others for equivalent titles, with additional titles being granted by the Angevins, and with the struggle dragging on and on. Perhaps Stephen, facing the prospect of further invasions by the Scots and the Empress's arrival, envisaged the appointment of earls as a short-term measure in 1138. He may have thought that he would be able to defeat her forces or buy her off, as his uncle had done with his brother in 1101, and

[217] Davis, *King Stephen*, pp. 138–9.    [218] Green, 'Financing Stephen's War', p. 104.    [219] *Ibid.*, pp. 93–4.
[220] Warren, *Governance of Norman and Angevin England*, pp. 93–4; Stringer, *Reign of Stephen*, pp. 53–5; Dalton, 'William Earl of York', p. 165.

as he himself was trying to do with the Scots. The further creations of 1140 may have been a more desperate attempt to revive his flagging fortunes. After the crisis was over, he probably intended that the earls would keep their titles and be subject to royal authority in the way the earls created by Rufus and Henry I had been. But from the start the creation of so many earls was a risky policy as there was an alternative model for the power of an earl in the shape of Ranulf's earldom of Chester, and it was a distinct possibility that other earls would seek to invest their titles with as much power as possible.

In 1139 Stephen made a pre-emptive strike against Bishop Roger of Salisbury and his two nephews, Alexander of Lincoln and Nigel of Ely. A brawl at court was manufactured so that Stephen had a pretext for arresting the bishops. He captured two, but Nigel escaped to Ely.[221] At issue was the surrender of the bishops' castles. Alexander had built a castle at Newark, Roger held Sherborne, Devizes, Malmesbury, and the royal castle of Salisbury, and Nigel held Ely. If Stephen believed that they were likely to go over to the Empress and hand their castles over to her, then his actions were justifiable. Nevertheless they outraged his brother, Henry bishop of Winchester, who called a legatine council in response. The bishop's criticism of the arrests was countered by the argument put forward by the archbishop of Rouen that bishops ought to surrender their castles to the king on demand. Davis suggested that Stephen was also or even primarily concerned with the power of the bishops over the sheriffs, many of whom had been appointed before 1135 and owed their careers to Bishop Roger.[222] By removing the bishops and by appointing earls, Stephen could ensure that the shires were in the hands of men loyal to him. On the debit side, he lost Bishop Roger's financial expertise, and the fact that at the time of his arrest Roger was in the *camera curie*, the financial office of the court, shows that he was still active. Few can have known more about ways and means of raising funds and running the administration than the bishop. By this stage Stephen may well have been running short of funds and he may have seen Bishop Roger as part of the problem, rather than as providing a solution. As events were to prove the removal of the bishops does not seem to have had any materially damaging effects on the conduct of government.[223]

---

[221] WM, *Historia Novella*, pp. 25–8.     [222] Davis, *King Stephen*, pp. 29–31.
[223] Yoshitake, 'Arrest of the Bishops in 1139'.

The other development which followed the Empress's arrival in England was the emergence and consolidation of her party, and in the making of this party ties of kinship, marriage, and loyalty to her father all played their part. As well as her brother, Robert, she was able to count on another half-brother, Reginald, who had been with her at Argentan and had aided Baldwin de Redvers in the Cotentin, plus Baldwin himself who landed at Corfe in 1138.[224] By 1141 a third half-brother had joined her, Robert FitzRoy.[225] Brian FitzCount, who with Robert of Gloucester had escorted her to her marriage in 1128, also went over immediately, and Miles of Gloucester admitted her to the royal castle at Gloucester.[226] The crucial question, however, was how much more support could be mustered.

We saw how in 1136 Baldwin had had the support of Alfred FitzJudhael and Robert of Bampton; neither of the latter is mentioned amongst the rebels of 1138 but others were: Ralph Lovel at Castle Cary, William FitzJohn at Harptree, William de Mohun at Dunster, and Robert of Lincoln at Wareham.[227] William FitzJohn was a major tenant of Robert of Gloucester, and married Denise, daughter and heiress of Ralph de Mandeville of Marshwood.[228] William FitzOdo and Henry de Pomeroy, both royal constables at the end of Henry I's reign, joined the revolt. FitzOdo was lord of Great Torrington in Devon, and that his loyalty was suspect is suggested by the attack on him by Henry de Tracy, Stephen's commander in Devon.[229] Henry de Pomeroy did not witness royal acts, but he married a sister of Earl Reginald. By 1139 Humphrey de Bohun, lord of Trowbridge in Wiltshire, a royal steward and kinsman of Alexander de Bohun who served the Empress in Normandy, had transferred his allegiance; his wife was a daughter of Miles of Gloucester.[230] At some point in the course of 1139 John FitzGilbert the Marshal who held a castle at Ludgershall also changed sides. John married a daughter of Walter of Salisbury, and his mother-in-law was a daughter of Patrick de Chaworth

[224] *RRAN*, III, no. 567, as redated by M. Chibnall, 'The Charters of the Empress Matilda', *Law and Government in the Middle Ages*, p. 295; OV, VI, 510; *Gesta Stephani*, p. 84.

[225] *RRAN*, III, no. 393. Robert's mother was married to Robert II d'Oilly, castellan of Oxford, who had transferred his allegiance to the Empress in 1141: *Gesta Stephani*, p. 116. Robert died in 1142 and his son Henry (the half-brother of Robert FitzRoy), appeared before the Empress on at least one occasion, but did not attest for her. He witnessed for Henry in 1153 or 1154, which suggests that he was not prepared to come out openly on the Angevin side until it was safe to do so: *RRAN*, III, nos. 632, 306, 1000.

[226] *Gesta Stephani*, p. 90.    [227] *Ibid.*, p. 66; OV, VI, 510.    [228] Green, 'Family Matters', p. 157.

[229] *Gesta Stephani*, p. 82.    [230] *Ibid.*, p. 92.

and a cousin of William FitzAlan.[231] William in turn was said to have married a kinswoman of Robert of Gloucester.[232]

By the 1140s Reginald had established his power in Cornwall as had Baldwin in Devon, and the locally based families can be seen as moving into their orbit and sometimes witnessing their charters.[233] A daughter of Earl Reginald, Denise, married Baldwin's son and eventual successor, Richard. Even Okehampton, held in succession by two of the last surviving children of Baldwin FitzGilbert, as supporter of Stephen, passed to Robert FitzRoy, who has already been mentioned (see above, p. 306).[234] In north Devon, Stephen's principal and possibly only supporter was Henry de Tracy.[235] Stephen de Mandeville of Marshwood in Dorset was a close associate and tenant of Earl Baldwin, and in Wiltshire the Empress was supported by Patrick of Salisbury, Robert de Dunstanville, Humphrey de Bohun, and John FitzGilbert.[236] In other words, by reinforcing existing ties of neighbourhood and kinship, support for the Empress in the west was very much a family matter.

By 1140 King David held Cumbria, Northumberland, and probably both parts of Lancashire. For most of that year neither side appears to have made much headway, and attempts to reach a negotiated settlement failed. The trigger to the next phase of events was the revolt of Ranulf earl of Chester. To this point, little had been heard from Ranulf. He had performed homage to Stephen and, though his wife was a daughter of Robert

---

[231] There seems to have been some doubt in 1140 as to whose side John was on: cf. *Gesta Stephani*, p. 106; JW, p. 62; for Ludgershall see Winchester Annals, *Annales Monastici*, II, 51; for John's marriage see *L'Histoire de Guillaume le Maréchal* (ed. Meyer), I, 1. 363. [232] OV, VI, 520.

[233] Reginald's father-in-law William FitzRichard, lord of Cardinham and Bodardle, was the most powerful lord in Cornwall. The other important local lordship was Trematon, held by Roger de Vautorte.

[234] For the descent of Okehampton see *CP*, IV, 317; *Prs 2–4 Henry II*, p. 159; see also Green, 'Family Matters', p. 157.

[235] For Henry's activities see *Gesta Stephani*, pp. 82–4, 150, 210–12, 222; for his background, Green, 'Family Matters', pp. 159–60.

[236] *Charters of the Redvers Family*, pp. 66, 75, 76, 77, 78, 180; Stephen was a witness with Earls Reginald and Baldwin when the Empress granted Abergavenny to Miles of Hereford in 1141 or 1142; *RRAN*, III, no. 394; he also acted as a witness for Robert of Gloucester together with Earl Reginald in Robert's concord with the bishop of Bayeux: *RRAN*, III, no. 58. He died on the way to Jerusalem: *Two Cartularies of Bruton and Montacute*, Somerset Record Society, VIII (1894), no. 167. Walter of Salisbury is not known to have departed from his allegiance to Stephen, but his son William was addressed by the Empress with John FitzGilbert in 1141: *RRAN*, III, no. 791. Earl Patrick witnessed for Duke Henry, *ibid*., nos. 839, 795, 796, 704, 902. Robert de Dunstanville witnessed for both the Empress and Henry: *ibid*., nos. 64, 65, 111, 126, 128, 259, 309, 372, 438, 459, 492, 495, 496, 709, 796, 820, 821, 839. Humphrey de Bohun and John FitzGilbert each witnessed often for the Empress and Duke Henry.

of Gloucester, he did not immediately join the Empress when she arrived in England. What seems to have galvanized him into action was the peace treaty with the Scots. Ranulf had a claim to the lordship of Carlisle which his father had held, but Carlisle had been seized by David in 1136, and there was little hope by 1140 that Stephen could or would persuade David to hand it back. Ranulf plotted to ambush Prince Henry, presumably to use as a hostage to be exchanged for Carlisle, though this is nowhere spelled out in the sources, but he failed, thanks to the intervention of Queen Matilda.[237] Ranulf subsequently seized the royal castle at Lincoln, to the custody of which he had a claim through his mother, Countess Lucy. Stephen arrived at Lincoln in person and made an agreement with Ranulf and his brother.

The details of this agreement have to be reconstructed. Stephen issued a charter in favour of Ranulf – undated but now thought to have been issued later than 1140 – and some of the concessions recorded there were probably in fact confirmations of grants made on the earlier occasion. These included custody of the castle and city of Lincoln until such time as Ranulf recovered his Norman lands and castle, and permission to fortify one of his towers at Lincoln until he received the castle of Tickhill, after which the earl might keep his mother's tower, plus the constableship of 'Lincoln and Lincolnshire by hereditary right'. In addition the king granted him the castle of Belvoir, the soke of Grantham, Newcastle in Staffordshire, Rothwell and its soke in Leicestershire, Torksey, Derby, Mansfield, Stoneleigh, the wapentake of Oswaldbeck (Nottinghamshire), the land of Roger de Bully with the honour of Blyth, and all the land of Roger the Poitevin, the honour of Lancaster, the land between Ribble and Mersey, and land in the manor of Grimsby. Stephen also promised to restore to Adelaide de Condet all her land and her castle. The stipulations relating to Lincoln and the fortifications there were probably confirmations of the agreement between Stephen and the earl in 1140, and, as King has argued, this may also have been true of the grant of Belvoir.[238] Some of the other grants were of royal possessions, such as the soke of Grantham, Torksey and Grimsby in Lincolnshire, Derby (presumably the castle and borough), Rothwell in Leicestershire, Stoneleigh in Warwickshire, and Oswaldbeck in Nottinghamshire. The honour of Tickhill had been in the

[237] John of Hexham in SD, *Opera omnia*, II, 306.
[238] King, 'Foundation of Pipewell Abbey'; cf. Dalton, 'Armed Neutrality', p. 47, n. 34.

king's hands in 1130, though Stephen was said to have granted it to the count of Eu.[239] The two portions of Lancashire may already have been in Scots' hands and, if so, this was a licence to prospect for Ranulf. The grant of the other lands of Roger the Poitevin, however, was a more serious loss to the crown.

Soon after Christmas 1140, Stephen returned to Lincoln: evidently he was no longer prepared to acquiesce in the loss of the castle, and he laid siege to Ranulf and his brother. Ranulf escaped, joined forces with Robert of Gloucester, and the two defeated and captured the king.[240] The king's capture transformed the prospects of the Empress's party, and posed a fresh dilemma for the aristocracy. A number of leading magnates who were officers of the royal household changed sides at some point between 1139 and 1141: Humphrey de Bohun, Robert Malet, and Hugh Bigod, stewards; William de Pont de l'Arche and William Mauduit, chamberlains; Miles of Gloucester, Brian FitzCount, Robert d'Oilly, and William de Beauchamp, constables; and John FitzGilbert the marshal.[241] Other magnates followed suit, particularly those with large estates in Normandy, such as Waleran of Meulan. 1141 was the year when the Angevins managed to secure control over the whole of lower Normandy, though Rouen and some strongholds in upper Normandy continued to hold out.

The Empress now negotiated with those who held the keys of the kingdom. Bishop Henry was persuaded to admit her to Winchester and to summon another council in which the case was made for the recognition of her right to succeed her father. Archbishop Theobald and the other clergy did not automatically fall into line, however, but insisted on securing the king's permission for a change of allegiance, and the Londoners, who had been summoned to Winchester, refused to act as representatives for their fellows. This, as Davis pointed out, was a crucial failure because, if Matilda was to be crowned in Westminster Abbey as all previous Norman monarchs had been, she needed access to London.[242]

Stephen had been successful in building up his influence in London.[243] He probably conceded to the citizens the right to form a commune at the time of his accession, and confirmed the privilege of electing their own

[239] *Rotuli Curiae Regis*, ed. F. Palgrave for Record Commission, 2 vols. (London, 1835), II, 162.
[240] *Gesta Stephani*, pp. 110–14; WM, *Historia Novella*, pp. 46–50; OV, VI, 538–46.
[241] *RRAN*, III, xvii–xxi; xxx–xxxii.    [242] Davis, *King Stephen*, p. 55.
[243] Green, 'Financing Stephen's War', p. 109.

sheriffs and paying a reduced annual farm. His brother was dean of the college of St Martin le Grand, and his illegitimate son was abbot of Westminster. He and his queen were on particularly good terms with the community at Holy Trinity, Aldgate. The Empress, however, had an opportunity to strengthen her position by an ongoing dispute about a new appointment to the bishopric of London. This had reached a deadlock as one party supported the election of Abbot Anselm of Bury St Edmunds, while the other had appealed to the pope, who in 1138 quashed the election. Matilda's successful candidate was Robert de Sigillo, keeper of the seal under her father and a monk of Reading abbey. Yet apart from the new bishop, it is hard to see that she had many friends in London.[244] Hence the importance in her calculations of Geoffrey de Mandeville, who by 1141 held the Tower.[245]

The terms on which he was prepared to go over to the Empress were recorded in a famous charter, the first of two issued in his favour by the Empress, probably within weeks of each other, around midsummer 1141.[246] She confirmed Stephen's earlier grant of the earldom of Essex, added the hereditary custody of the Tower, the shrievalty and chief justiciarship of Essex, and made various supplementary grants, the most important of which were one hundred pounds of demesne land and the service of twenty knights. This in effect meant that Geoffrey held all the positions of authority in Essex as well as hereditary custody of the Tower. The second charter added the shrievalties of London and Hertfordshire, and the justiciarships of these counties plus that of Essex, confirmed the grants of £200 and £100 of land which Stephen and Matilda had given, and made a further string of grants and promises to Geoffrey and his allies. The problems of dating and interpretation of these charters were discussed by Round, who thought that the second charter dated from 1142 and was the price of Geoffrey's second desertion to the Empress. J. O. Prestwich agreed with Round's dating but a different view was expressed by R. H. C. Davis, who suggested that the second (M2) of the Empress's charters was issued within weeks of the first. The upshot was that Geoffrey did support her whilst she was in London, but her dramatic

---

[244] Osbert Huitdeniers, a sheriff and justice, was a tenant of Robert of Gloucester, but it is not certain when their relationship began: *Gloucester Charters*, nos. 6, 95; *RBE*, I, 189; Green, *English Sheriffs*, p. 58.

[245] See the debate between Davis and Prestwich on this point: 'Last Words on Geoffrey de Mandeville', *English Historical Review*, 105 (1990), 670–2.      [246] *RRAN*, III, nos. 274, 275.

flight when the Londoners rose up meant that Geoffrey was left stranded in a city whose citizens hated him. To effect an escape he took hostage the bishop of London, whom he found at his manor of Fulham.[247] Meanwhile the Empress had retreated to Winchester, but was in turn forced to leave in some disorder. Robert of Gloucester was captured, and both sides agreed to an exchange of prisoners. At the end of a dramatic year, Stephen and Robert were free once again.

The most decisive feature of the struggle between 1142 and 1148 was the final loss of Normandy to the forces of Duke Geoffrey; in England there was stalemate. Some of those who had gone over to the Empress in 1141 returned to the king after his release, for example Geoffrey de Mandeville. The king did not replace the officers of the royal household who had defected, nor did he rely on a bishop as a chief minister. Instead he chose to rely on a much narrower group of *familiares*, consisting of the steward William Martel, the constables Robert de Vere and Henry of Essex, and Richard de Lucy, Richard de Camville, and William de Chesney.[248] Stephen was reasonably secure in the east and south-east of England, but there was a hard core of support for the Empress in the south-west which he could not eradicate. The two individuals whose power represented the clearest challenge to his authority, however, were Geoffrey de Mandeville and Ranulf earl of Chester, and Stephen challenged each of them in turn.

Stephen had had little alternative when he was released but to confirm the grants which the Empress had made to Geoffrey de Mandeville. Were these to be allowed to endure, however, and would Earl Geoffrey stay loyal? Stephen decided to move against Geoffrey, possibly because he suspected the earl of planning to defect again. Stephen, however, waited until the autumn of 1143 to make his move, and then he used the same technique he had used against the three bishops in 1139, that of arresting potential or actual rebels at court and demanding surrender of their castles as the price for their release. If successful, as on this occasion, this ploy avoided the necessity of a siege. Stephen obtained Geoffrey's castles

---

[247] Trivet's Annals, p. 13; cited by Round, *Geoffrey de Mandeville*, p. 117.

[248] For William Martel, Green, 'Financing Stephen's War', pp. 110–13; for Robert de Vere see above, pp. 287–8; Henry of Essex was lord of Rayleigh: Sanders, *English Baronies*, p. 139; for Richard de Lucy, Amt, 'Richard de Lucy, Henry II's Justiciar'; for Richard de Camville and William de Chesney, Amt, *Accession of Henry II*, pp. 50–3.

of Pleshey and Walden, but Geoffrey himself retreated into the fens and based himself at Ramsey abbey, whence he was able to terrorize the surrounding countryside until his death from a wound that became infected.[249]

Meanwhile Ranulf of Chester had not been idle. In Lincolnshire he and his brother did all they could to consolidate their power in terms of lands, castles, local courts, and influence over lesser local lords and knightly families.[250] They did not have everything their own way. Ranulf met a formidable opponent in William count of Aumale, lord of Holderness in Yorkshire and Castle Bytham in Lincolnshire. At some point, possibly in 1144, Ranulf and Gilbert de Gant joined forces against William, possibly to assert a claim by Gilbert to William's honour of Holderness. Gilbert attacked the Aumale lands in Lincolnshire, captured Castle Bytham, and killed William's brother. In retaliation William destroyed Hunmanby castle with the help of Eustace FitzJohn and fortified Bridlington Priory.[251]

A few scattered references show how Ranulf was trying to exert influence in Yorkshire during the same period. He granted the constableship of Chester and its honour to Eustace FitzJohn, lord of Malton and Alnwick, and he granted land to Henry de Lacy lord of Pontefract.[252] His half-brother, William de Roumare, asserted a claim to the honour of Warter in Yorkshire: he issued a charter for Warter priory referring to the customs it had had in the time of his father, Roger FitzGerold.[253] Ranulf may himself have been asserting claims to the honour of Tickhill, on the basis of either William count of Eu's marriage to the sister of Earl Hugh I, or, more probably, the claim of his wife as a niece of Robert de Bellême.[254] Both Warter and Tickhill were granted by Stephen to Ranulf, who thus exercised considerable influence over parts of southern and eastern Yorkshire.

Ranulf also had important territorial interests in the midlands, extending southwards as far as Coventry. He tried to take over the honour of Belvoir which straddled the Lincolnshire–Leicestershire border and was held by William d'Aubigny the Breton. Although Stephen granted Ranulf the honour possibly as early as 1140, there is no evidence that he ever managed to dislodge William d'Aubigny, notwithstanding the charters

---

[249] *Chronicon Ramesiensis*, ed. W. Dunn Macray, RS (London, 1886), pp. 329–32.
[250] Dalton, 'Aiming at the Impossible'.     [251] John of Hexham, in SD, *Opera omnia*, II, 315.
[252] *Chester Charters*, nos. 73, 69.     [253] *Early Yorkshire Charters*, x, 114–116.
[254] I owe these suggestions to Mrs K. Thompson.

Ranulf issued for Belvoir priory.[255] In north Leicestershire the earl came up against a redoubtable rival in Robert earl of Leicester, and Edmund King has suggested that Ranulf was forced to recognize Robert's power in this county. Ranulf granted Robert the manor of Charley in the 1140s (which Robert may already have held); he also conceded Mountsorrel which he disputed with Robert. The two grants, it has been argued by King, were made at some point in the 1140s, though not necessarily in 1145 or 1146 as had previously been argued by Davis.[256] In a separate agreement, probably dating from some time between 1148 and 1153, the two earls concluded an agreement to limit as far as possible the circumstances in which they would fight each other.[257]

At Coventry the earl of Chester had succeeded to a manor held before the Conquest by Earl Leofric of Mercia. Here also there was a castle which in 1144 was held against the earl by Robert Marmion, lord of Tamworth, who was killed in the conflict.[258] Ranulf issued two charters for Robert Marmion, one granting him the fee of Osbert of Arden and the other, Coventry.[259] The latter, to which attention was drawn by Davis, referred to existing agreements between the earl and Robert Marmion.[260] The authenticity of the latter charter has been rejected, partly on the grounds of the text and the seal, and partly because it is at first sight hard to see why Ranulf would have wished to grant the manor to Robert shortly after he had recovered it. Ranulf, however, may simply have been recognizing that Robert Marmion was then in possession.

In Staffordshire Ranulf was more successful. He had large estates there and a castle at Newcastle under Lyme, and he also seems to have secured the allegiance of Robert of Stafford, the leading local magnate, who witnessed two of his charters.[261] Norman de Verdon of Alton, who was also a tenant of Ferrers, was a prominent member of Ranulf's entourage.[262] By the late 1140s, Ranulf also had the support of Robert de Ferrers of Tutbury. Robert had been a supporter of Stephen: he had been made an earl in 1138, and does not appear to have gone over to the Empress in 1141. He also witnessed Stephen's second charter to Geoffrey de Mandeville at Christmas

[255] King, 'Foundation of Pipewell Abbey', p. 171.

[256] King, 'Mountsorrel and its Region', pp. 1–10; cf. R. H. C. Davis, 'An Unknown Coventry Charter', *English Historical Review*, 86 (1971), 533–45; Davis, *King Stephen*, pp. 161–2. For the two texts, *Chester Charters*, nos. 82, 89.    [257] *Ibid.*, no. 110.    [258] William of Newburgh, *Chronicles*, I, 47.

[259] *Chester Charters*, nos. 74, 75.    [260] Davis, 'An Unknown Coventry Charter'.

[261] *Chester Charters*, nos. 62, 65.    [262] *Ibid.*, nos. 21, 22, 36, 55, 62, 63, 66, 67, 71, 73, 74, 80, 81, 88, 93.

1141, but cannot be tied down to Stephen's court again until a date between November 1153 and October 1154, which suggests that he may have kept a low profile from 1142.[263] Earl Ranulf must have made an uncomfortably powerful neighbour for Robert, who had his own agenda to pursue. Robert was married to a daughter of William Peverel of the Peak, and while William was in prison after the battle of Lincoln he appears to have styled himself earl of Nottingham.[264] In a treaty with the earl of Leicester, probably made between 1149 and 1153, Robert de Ferrers is mentioned as Ranulf's ally.[265]

Wherever we follow Ranulf, we find him consistently pursuing a policy of self-interest, defending his lands and castles, and bringing lesser men into his sphere of influence. His victory at the battle of Lincoln had placed him in a position to try to make effective many of the grants of lands and castles made him by the king, including the royal castle of Lincoln. Stephen besieged the castle in 1144 which suggests that Ranulf was still in possession, and this must have rankled with the king.[266] In 1146 Ranulf presented himself at Stephen's court and made his peace.[267] Later in the same year he reappeared at Stephen's court to ask for assistance in combatting the Welsh. On this occasion he was arrested and made to surrender his castles, after which he flew into revolt and tried to recover both Lincoln and Coventry.[268] Once again it appeared that Stephen had been able to remove a powerful enemy from a royal castle. There were limits to Stephen's success, however, because Ranulf remained the most powerful of all the magnates, and it was inevitable that the Angevins would seek to win his support after his alienation from the king.

Ranulf nevertheless sold his support at a high price. By the terms of an alliance with King David, Ranulf recognized David's right to Cumbria, and in return he was enfeoffed with the honour of Lancaster and the land between Ribble and Mersey.[269] Meanwhile Ranulf pursued his ambitions in the midlands, and more specifically sought to subdue William Peverel. William's son and wife had both died, and at some date after 1149 a second marriage was arranged for him by Earl Ranulf: Avice of Lancaster was the daughter of a leading tenant of the honour of Lancaster, by this

---

[263] *RRAN*, III, no. 864.    [264] Jones, 'Charters of Robert de Ferrers', pp. 17–18.
[265] Stenton, *First Century*, p. 288.    [266] HH, p. 277.
[267] *RRAN*, III, no. 178; for comment, Dalton, 'Armed Neutrality of Ranulf II', pp. 46–7.
[268] *Gesta Stephani*, pp. 192–8.    [269] John of Hexham in SD, *Opera omnia*, II, 322–3.

time in Ranulf's possession.[270] The marriage did not, however, foster more amicable relations between the two men.

As time went on the political stalemate continued, but the fortunes of Henry FitzEmpress on the continent were improving. When he arrived in England in 1153 he was already duke of Normandy and married to Eleanor, duchess of Aquitaine. But in England Stephen still showed no signs of giving ground. Henry needed allies, and most of all he needed the active support of Earl Ranulf, the most powerful of all the magnates. He issued a charter in the earl's favour restoring Ranulf's lands in Normandy, confirming many of the concessions made by Stephen (but not, significantly, custody of Lincoln castle), and making some new grants: the honour of Eye (currently held by Stephen), the county of Staffordshire, and the honour of William Peverel, with the castle and borough of Nottingham.[271] Ranulf was by now known to have been a mortal enemy of William, who tried to poison him in 1153. Refusing to answer when called to account by Henry, William took refuge in Lenton priory where he died.[272] In 1153 Robert de Ferrers was in a very difficult situation. So far as we know, he had remained loyal to the king, but he had his loyalty to his father-in-law (and his hope of succeeding to the Peverel honour) to con- sider, and his relationship with Ranulf. In 1153 Robert was besieged at Tutbury by Henry FitzEmpress, and when the castle surrendered Robert went over to Henry's side.[273] Although Robert transferred his allegiance, he did not receive the Peverel lands when these were confiscated by Henry II. Both he and William Peverel were in their different ways casualties of the war and of the ambitions of the earl of Chester. Ranulf himself died in 1153, and it is ironic that most of the items on what has aptly been described as 'Ranulf's shopping list' did not pass to his successor, who was a minor at the time of his father's death.[274]

The interests and ambitions of Earl Ranulf thus played a crucial role in shaping the course of politics in England between 1146 and 1153. Stephen could not, even if he had wished to, either win back his support or neutralize him. After Robert of Gloucester's death the Angevins lacked the leadership of a heavyweight political figure, but Ranulf was by no

---

[270] *RAN*, III, 441 refers to William's first wife Oddona and son Henry; Green, 'Earl Ranulf II and Lancashire', p. 107.     [271] *RRAN*, III, no. 180.

[272] Gervase of Canterbury, *Historical Works*, I, 155, 161; *Gesta Stephani*, p. 156; Robert of Torigny, *Chronicles*, IV, 183.     [273] *Gesta Stephani*, p. 234.     [274] King, 'Foundation of Pipewell Abbey', p. 175.

means willing and eager to take on the role except as and when it suited him. Ranulf's concerns were above all with his territorial interests, centred on Chester and until 1146 on Lincoln, and with building up a web of power and influence with tentacles across the midlands and south Yorkshire.[275] He was more successful in the west midlands than in the east where his ambitions clashed with those of Robert II earl of Leicester. Most of Ranulf's gains were lost because he was succeeded by a minor and Henry FitzEmpress did not feel obliged to make good the promises he had made in 1153. But the fact that his success was fleeting should not obscure the pivotal position he occupied in the later years of Stephen's reign, a period too often analysed from the standpoint of the king and Henry FitzEmpress.

The great men like Ranulf who were directly involved in military action must have had substantial military establishments, yet the latter are an aspect of the reign about which we know almost nothing because they rarely figure in the written sources. Whence were the knights recruited? How were they paid? Were some of them enfeoffed with land? The aristocracy had been accustomed to peace in England for more than three decades, though obviously some were active in Henry's campaigns in Normandy. It is likely that many had relatively few knights retained in their households, and if they answered a royal summons, or indeed were involved in local conflicts, we can only guess where their men came from.

Castles, too, had to be repaired, strengthened, and in some cases built from scratch. Many of the earthwork castles which traditionally were ascribed to the post-Conquest period may actually have been constructed at this time. The labour and resources had to be provided by the luckless peasantry, as the Anglo-Saxon Chronicle described in the well-known entry for 1137.[276] Robert of Torigny spoke of the destruction of over a thousand castles (which, if taken literally means approximately thirty per county) when peace was restored under Henry II.[277] Complaints about arbitrary levies recur in the chronicle accounts. Sometimes these were levies described as *tenserie*, which, Edmund King suggests, may have been taken from church estates.[278] Geoffrey de Mandeville is said to have gone

---

[275] J. H. Round, 'King Stephen and the Earl of Chester', *English Historical Review*, x (1895), 87.
[276] ASC 1137.        [277] Robert of Torigny, *Chronicles*, iv, 177.
[278] King, 'Anarchy of King Stephen's Reign', p. 137.

10 Coin issued at York and attributed to a northern magnate, Eustace FitzJohn. Reproduced by permission of the Ashmolean Museum, Oxford.

so far as to use spies who were sent out to try to discover who still had any resources, and to exact ransoms from them.[279] In 1143 the author of the *Gesta Stephani* reported that Robert of Gloucester was demanding knights or scutage for his campaigns.[280] For those in the thick of battle there was also the chance of capturing someone who could be ransomed. Miles of Gloucester took captives at Winchcombe in 1140, and prisoners were taken both at Lincoln and at Winchester in 1141.[281] Treasure was taken when the castle of 'Galclint' was captured in 1140, and in the same year it was the prospect of treasure which lured the besiegers to their deaths at Nottingham.[282] In 1144 royalist troops near Wareham relieved the bishop of Ely of the fighting fund he was taking to Rome.[283] A few magnates even went so far as to issue their own coins.[284]

We have no means of assessing whether the chief baronial protagonists could absorb the costs of war without strain. In a famous letter to Gilbert Foliot bishop of Hereford, Brian FitzCount claimed that he had impoverished himself in the Empress's service.[285] But was it necessarily the case that protagonists, whether great magnates or lesser men, suffered as a

---

[279] Dugdale, *Mon. Ang.*, iv, 142.  [280] *Gesta Stephani*, p. 151.

[281] JW, p. 50; Baldwin FitzGilbert and Richard FitzUrse were amongst those captured at Lincoln: HH, p. 274.  [282] John of Hexham in SD, *Opera omnia*, ii, 306; FW, Continuation, ii, 128.

[283] *Liber Eliensis*, pp. 324–5.

[284] For the most recent discussion of these issues see Blackburn, 'Coinage and Currency', pp. 147–8.

[285] Davis, 'Henry of Blois and Brian FitzCount', p. 302.

result of their involvement? We hear in the chronicles of freebooters who terrorized their neighbourhoods, but we are only usually told if they came to a bad end. One often-cited career is that of Warin of Walcote, described in proceedings before the royal justices in the early thirteenth century. Warin was by origin 'an honest itinerant knight' but in Stephen's reign he abducted Isabel of Shuckburgh against her will, and later with the coming of peace he turned to a life of crime and died in the pillory. Isabel returned to her father's house, married, and had a son, and it was a dispute over her land between the descendants of her sons by Warin and those by her husband William that brought the matter to court.[286]

One group which may well have benefited from the conflict were those honorial barons who were able to throw off their lords' demands for service. William de Launay ensconced himself in the castle of Ravenstone in Leicestershire, and his overlords, the earls of Chester and Leicester, were forced to take united action against him. Crouch has pointed out that the earl of Leicester used some of the land retrieved from William to endow the nunnery newly founded at Nuneaton.[287] At Biddlesden another of the earl's tenants, Robert of Meppershall, refused service. He was replaced and his successor used the manor for the foundation of an abbey.[288] If even a powerful earl like Robert had difficulty in securing service, how much more difficult was it for other lords?

The evidence about the impact of the war on those who fought is fragmentary and anecdotal. It is possible that many lords did not suffer unduly, and may have profited by usurping lands and privileges from the crown or from churches, and by exploiting the peasantry. Fighting was localized, and in many regions lasted for only a matter of months; only in the counties which formed a march between the Angevins and the royalists – Wiltshire, Gloucestershire, Oxfordshire, and Berkshire – must garrisons have been on constant alert.

There were, certainly, customs regulating and limiting the waging of war in aristocratic circles. The horror stories told by the northern chroniclers about the Scots invasion of 1138 reflect in part a sense of outrage at warfare which flouted the behaviour of civilized nations.[289] There were

---

[286] *Rolls of the Justices in Eyre Gloucestershire, Warwickshire, Staffordshire, 1221, 1222,* ed. D. M. Stenton, Selden Society, LIX (1959), pp. 167–9.      [287] Crouch, *Beaumont Twins,* pp. 80–1.      [288] *Ibid.,* p. 80.
[289] J. Gillingham, 'Conquering the Barbarians: War and Chivalry in Twelfth-Century Britain', *Haskins Society Journal,* 4 (1992), 67–84, at pp. 70–1.

conventions about sieges. Garrisons were not to be punished for the actions of their lords. At Exeter in 1136 the members of the garrison, having surrendered, were allowed not only to leave with their possessions but also to join any lord they wished.[290] Safe conducts, hostages, and pledges had to be given as guarantees of good faith. Safe conduct for the Empress was provided by Waleran of Meulan and Bishop Henry from Arundel to Bristol on the king's command 'which it is not the custom of honourable knights to refuse to anyone, even their bitterest enemy'.[291] One of the most famous hostages of the Civil War was the young William Marshal, delivered into Stephen's custody by his father who, when threatened with his son's death, defied the king saying that he had the wherewithal to make more sons.[292] Those who negotiated truces or treaties might well have to supply pledges, men who were prepared to vouch for the promises made. Indeed, the Empress's second charter for Geoffrey de Mandeville had two separate lists of pledges, one for herself, and one for her husband Geoffrey.[293]

Truces and treaties were manifold and, as King has pointed out, they were part and parcel of existing methods of conflict resolution.[294] Bilateral agreements were made covering quarrels over specific lands or castles, and these could be made while setting on one side the intractable issue of the succession. Thus, for instance, the earl of Chester could formally cede Mountsorrel in Leicestershire to the earl of Leicester in recognition of Earl Ranulf's problem in holding it. This was recorded in a charter of the usual kind.[295] Frequently bilateral arrangements were not enough; account had to be taken of third parties and contingency plans made. If these were recorded in writing, they might take the form of agreements variously described as *conventiones* or *confederationes*. The famous treaty between the earls of Chester and Leicester is a case in point. The earls strove to limit the circumstances in which they would go to war on each other, by making a final peace and concord before the bishop of Lincoln and before their own men. The arrangements about Mountsorrel were confirmed, and conditions were laid down to deal with the problem that might arise if the liege lord of either ordered an attack. In these cir-

[290] *Gesta Stephani*, p. 142.    [291] WM, *Historia Novella*, p. 35.

[292] *Histoire de Guillaume le Maréchal* (ed. Meyer), I, ll. 512–16.    [293] RRAN, III, no. 275.

[294] E. King, 'Dispute Settlement in Norman England', *Anglo-Norman Studies*, 14 (1992), 115–30.

[295] *Chester Charters*, no. 89.

cumstances no more than twenty knights were to be supplied to the liege lord. Each promised to help the other against all men except their liege lords and one other (named) ally; provision was made for dealing with the troublesome William de Launay; and no new castles were to be built within a defined area.[296] The elaborateness of the concord reflects the complexity of landed interests in the Leicestershire region, and of feudal relationships in general. William de Launay was as we have seen a tenant of both earls. Each earl nominated an ally. Simon de Senlis was nominated by Earl Robert; he was Robert's son-in-law and both men supported Stephen. Ranulf, who may not have seen himself as in breach of his allegiance to King Stephen, nominated Robert de Ferrers. The lack of any explicit reference to the king is very revealing.

Such treaties, which are rightly seen as one of the principal means by which attempts were being made by magnates to limit conflict, provide vivid insights into the parameters of action. Even where disputes were bilateral, men could not ignore their existing obligations to a superior lord. Agreements had to be made which took account of earlier promises. Homage had to be performed for land, but loyalty could not be exclusive. Somehow a means had to be found to reconcile conflicting loyalties. At a practical level the solution might be found in keeping a low profile so far as the courts of Stephen or of Henry were concerned: the number of committed royalists and Angevins by the final years was probably relatively small. If the worst came to the worst, the answer might be to promise to contribute only a limited force, like the twenty knights promised by the earls of Chester and Leicester.

Churchmen also lent their weight to peace negotiations, like Bishop Robert of Lincoln in the Chester–Leicester treaty.[297] The papal legate Alberic of Ostia took a leading part in the peace negotiations with the Scots in 1138.[298] Bishop Henry tried to broker a peace in 1140, but clearly the two sides were at that stage intransigent.[299] In 1152 Archbishop Theobald's efforts to unite the bishops in rejecting Stephen's plan for the succession of Eustace may have nudged forward peace negotiations.[300] Churchmen were obviously concerned not only about the iniquities of

---

[296] Stenton, *First Century*, pp. 250–3.

[297] On this subject see especially, C. Holdsworth, 'War and Peace in the Twelfth Century. The Reign of Stephen Reconsidered', *War and Peace in the Middle Ages*, ed. B. P. McGuire (Copenhagen, 1987), 67–93.

[298] Richard of Hexham, *Chronicles*, III, 167–76.     [299] WM, *Historia Novella*, pp. 44–5.     [300] HH, pp. 283–4.

warfare in general, including its effects on the weakest elements in society, but also about its impact on church lands and personnel in particular. On the other hand, it is too simplistic to see laymen as perpetuating the war and ecclesiastics working tirelessly for peace. Archbishop Thurstan and Bishops Henry of Winchester and Roger de Clinton of Coventry and Lichfield were all involved in military campaigns.

Why wars end when they do is as interesting (and debatable) as why they begin. Viewed in retrospect, the turning point always seems earlier and more inevitable than appeared at the time.[301] As time wore on some key figures left the scene. Robert of Gloucester died in 1147, and the Empress left England in the following year. Others such as Waleran of Meulan and William de Warenne left England for a time to join the crusade. Henry FitzEmpress had ventured to England in person in 1146 or 1147, but had been unable to achieve anything, even to pay the wages of his knights, a task performed for him by his uncle the king.[302] Two years later he returned. He was knighted by his uncle David, and the two, together with Earl Ranulf, planned an attack on York, though this was aborted. Henry was a promising outsider, but only a serious contender after his accession to the duchy of Normandy and his marriage to Eleanor. Stephen meanwhile continued to campaign indefatigably, and as White has shown, there were those who thought that he was on the point of final success in 1152, so much so that even leading Angevins like Roger earl of Hereford and William earl of Gloucester were rumoured to be on the point of going over to the king.[303] Stephen's ambitions were now focussed on securing the succession for his son Eustace. The king wished Archbishop Theobald to consecrate Eustace formally, but Theobald was consistent in his refusal, realizing only too well that such a consecration would severely reduce the chances of a negotiated settlement.

When a truce was achieved in 1153 it was basically because the magnates saw danger ahead if Stephen defeated Henry outright or vice versa. As we have already seen, Henry arrived in England with a substantial army, and he negotiated for support from Ranulf of Chester and Robert of Leicester.[304] In August 1153 when Henry's army faced that of the king at Wallingford they refused to fight.[305] A truce was established, and the

---

[301] As Graeme White has pointed out: 'The End of Stephen's Reign,' *History*, 75 (1990), 3–22.
[302] *Gesta Stephani*, pp. 204–6.     [303] White, 'End of Stephen's Reign', p. 5.
[304] *Gesta Stephani*, p. 230.     [305] *Ibid.*, pp. 234–40.

death of Eustace shortly afterwards cleared the way for a more lasting peace settlement. Other deaths in the same year altered the political landscape: King David died, as did Ranulf of Chester, Simon de Senlis, and Roger earl of Warwick.

The first issue to be settled was that of the succession to the throne. Stephen was to stay for the rest of his life, and was to be succeeded by Henry.[306] Whether this had been agreed in August is not clear, because Eustace was thereby disinherited; but Eustace died within a few weeks, and Stephen was content to negotiate a large landed endowment for his second son William, which comprised the Warenne lands in England and Normandy, a further grant of land and rights in Norfolk, the honour of Pevensey, and the service of Faramus of Boulogne. William and many others were to perform liege homage to Henry FitzEmpress, saving only their fealty to Stephen, and key castles were to be handed over to agreed castellans. The clergy were to swear allegiance to the duke, and to punish infringements of the peace.

A royal notification setting out these provisions was issued at November 1153 at Westminster, but certain highly sensitive subjects were omitted. From other sources, however, we can tell that these issues were confronted and principles laid down to deal with them. One was the issue of unlicensed castles: these were to be destroyed. Second there was the infinitely dificult question of a land settlement: lands were to be restored to their rightful owners.[307] What did this mean, however? Both Stephen and Henry had made grants to their followers, and there were many complaints of wrongs to be righted. Robert of Torigny's version of the peace terms referred to restoration to those who had held in the days of King Henry. But even this was not a total solution for, as Sir James Holt has pointed out, in some cases, like that of Robert III de Stuteville versus Roger de Mowbray, the disseisin complained of had occurred not under Stephen but under Henry I.[308] The whole question was a minefield, complicated by Henry FitzEmpress's need to win support and reward his followers, as well as to restore a degree of stability. The atmosphere in the weeks that followed was uneasy. According to Henry of Huntingdon, Henry FitzEmpress

[306] *RRAN*, III, no. 272.

[307] Robert of Torigny, *Chronicles*, IV, 177; *Gesta Stephani*, p. 240; for the suggestion that what was meant specifically was that inheritances, as opposed to acquisitions, were to be restored, see J. C. Holt, '1153: the Treaty of Winchester', *Anarchy of King Stephen's Reign* (ed. King), p. 297.    [308] *Ibid.*, p. 303.

complained that Stephen had not effected the destruction of all the castles.[309] Then there were rumours of an assassination attempt against Henry who, not surprisingly, decided to leave for Normandy. From his point of view it was fortunate that Stephen died when he did, leaving the way clear for a peaceful succession, for the peace could yet have unravelled.[310]

The more contentious issues were slowly sorted out. King David's grandson Malcolm was allowed to inherit Huntingdon, while Simon III de Senlis married the sister and heiress of Gilbert de Gant. He became earl of Northampton only after the war of 1173–4. Ranulf II had died leaving an under-age heir, so that Henry did not have to make good the extravagant promises he had made in 1153. He also ignored a grant he had made to Earl William of Gloucester of Eudo the steward's land.[311] The charge of attempted poisoning against William Peverel and the latter's flight meant that his lands escheated for felony, and this in turn meant that the king was not bound to recognize Robert de Ferrers's claim.

The difficult case of Berkeley, a large part of which had been granted to Robert FitzHarding, financier to the Angevin cause, had to be settled by a compromise. Berkeley was a large royal estate held in hereditary fee farm by the family of Roger of Berkeley. Maurice, a son of Robert FitzHarding, was to marry a daughter of Roger, and a son of Roger was to marry a daughter of Robert. Roger was to hold five knights' fees of Robert.[312] This was by no means a perfect solution. Roger was evidently not performing the service due for Dursley in 1166, but the new king was evidently not going to remove FitzHarding, and Roger had perforce to accept the situation.[313]

The new king's determination to recover lost rights brought him into conflict with William of Aumale and Hugh de Mortimer, neither of whom was prepared to surrender his gains without a fight. Henry was forced to allow the former to keep some of his acquisitions, but Hugh was compelled to surrender Bridgnorth. Henry was particularly concerned to make sure the aristocracy's castles were not in future more numerous or

---

[309] HH, pp. 289–91.   [310] Gervase of Canterbury, I, 158–9.

[311] D. Crouch, 'Earl William of Gloucester and the End of the Anarchy: New Evidence Relating to the Honor of Eudo Dapifer', *English Historical Review*, 103 (1988), 69–75.

[312] The marriage settlement is reproduced on plate 5 of R. B. Patterson, 'The Ducal and Royal *Acta* of Henry FitzEmpress in Berkeley Castle', *Transactions of the Bristol and Gloucestershire Archaeological Society*, 109 (1991), 117–31.   [313] RBE, I, 298.

stronger than those of the king. He therefore confiscated castles from those whose loyalty was suspect, like Hugh Bigod, levelled other castles, and strengthened and repaired his own.[314] He reduced the number and the independence of earldoms by allowing some to lapse and by making sure that there were royal justices and sheriffs in those counties where there were still earls. Cornwall alone, and that only until the death of Earl Reginald, escaped the reassertion of closer control.

In view of his recent troubles and his determination to enjoy his grandfather's rights, it is perhaps surprising that Henry II did not face a major revolt until 1173. When the documents issued in his name are collected and published, we shall have a much clearer idea of court politics from their content and witness lists. One point can be made at once, however: the lack of references in the pipe rolls of his reign to large proffers from magnates for lands and privileges is very striking. Unless payments were made but not recorded on the pipe rolls, it would appear that Henry did not make a practice of exacting large sums for the succession to land or for marriages or wardships, and that he was sparing with the ultimate weapon of disseisin. In political terms, as in the case of seisin and inheritance, he wanted to work within a framework that offered a chance of stability.

It is harder to assess the impact of the war on relations between lords and men, specifically on the tie created by homage. How successful were lords in retaining the loyalty of their vassals, or were middling and lesser tenants able generally to enjoy a greater measure of independence than they had before 1135? If so, were lords able to reassert control after 1154, or did the reinvigorated and expanding machinery of royal government prove to be a greater attraction for the upwardly mobile? It was suggested in chapter five above that from the start some honours were much more cohesive than others, and the former may have retained a corporate identity much longer. Until there are more published studies of honours in the middle and later twelfth century, we shall not know whether Stenton was right to apostrophize Stephen's reign as a period which saw 'the end of Norman feudalism'.[315]

It took years to sort out all the cases of disputed seisin and inheritance, and the development of new remedies generated new cases. Lost lands

---

[314] Brown, 'Royal Castlebuilding in England, 1154–1216'.
[315] Stenton, *First Century*, title to chapter seven.

were sought; lords pursued claims against tenants, and tenants against lords. Many sought the king's intervention in the form of royal writs, either writs of right, or writs of reseisin which aimed simply to put a plaintiff back in possession. Step by step royal justices moved to devise remedies to deal with the most common circumstances underlying disseisin: novel disseisin (disseisin without legal process) and mort d'ancestor (lords' refusal to accept the homage of an heir). The era of rapid growth in common-law writs was under way. The importance of Stephen's reign in this area may have been essentially negative. If, as has been suggested, hereditary succession to land was already relatively secure in the early twelfth century, the civil war was only an interruption in this process, but it was an interruption which had taught Henry II a political lesson. Whether his grandfather had acted within the limits of what was acceptable or had bent rules or acted despotically, the younger Henry appreciated that his survival depended on cautious pragmatism and the closer definition of procedures.

The ease with which Henry II turned back the clock to his grandfather's day is deceptive. In the early years he was absent from England for long periods, and when present he did not challenge too many magnates too directly. The repair and refurbishment of royal castles was necessary, and the fact that the balance of power was shifting away from the aristocracy to the crown was not immediately obvious. Similarly the full significance of the development of common law for seigneurial courts was probably not obvious at the time, and the new procedures were used by lords against tenants as well as tenants against lords.

The metaphor of the wheel of fortune used by contemporaries was one which aptly describes the politics of the century following the Conquest.[316] The vicissitudes of individual careers and the accidents of hereditary succession made for a high turnover at the top. In the welter of changing faces, however, two developments of longer-term significance stand out. The first was the way in which the growth of government, that of the king and of the great magnates, both lay and ecclesiastical, had started to provide a new range of opportunities for men whose expertise was not only or not even at all in the military sphere. The second was the gradual disengagement of many families from territorial interests in

---

[316] E. Mason, 'Magnates, Curiales and the Wheel of Fortune: 1066–1154', *Proceedings of the Battle Conference on Anglo-Norman Studies*, 2 (1979), 118–40, 190–5.

Normandy, a trend which the renewal of the link between England and Normandy under Henry II did not reverse. The trend was significant for a variety of social and cultural reasons, but in political terms it meant that only a rump of the aristocracy of Norman England conforms to the idea of a cross-Channel aristocracy: their sights were fixed on the nearer horizon. Their ambitions were as ever focussed on family and neighbourhood, and it is to the importance of family that we turn next.

# IV  Aristocratic society

# 10 Kinship, marriage, and family

The history of the aristocratic family in Norman England is sadly neglected in comparison with the massive scholarship devoted to kinship and family ties in continental aristocracies.[1] In part the reason lies in English historiography. Kinship has been treated as a powerful force in Anglo-Saxon society at a time when kingship was weak, but by the tenth and eleventh centuries kings were seeking to regulate and contain feud, and local groups were expected to regulate the behaviour of their number. In the brave new world after 1066 the Norman kings sustained a vigorous monarchical rule, and a different social bond, that of lordship, has been discussed at much greater length than ties of blood. In this world there has seemed to historians little need or scope for a prominent role for kinship. Ties of blood did matter, however. Kinsmen formed a solidarity, a group which co-operated for the benefit of its members, offering protec-

---

[1] For an early survey see Bloch, *Feudal Society*, I, chapter 10. A more recent survey can be found in D. Herlihy, *Medieval Households* (Cambridge, Mass., 1985), pp. 82–98; see also Herlihy's collected papers, *Women, Family and Society in Medieval Europe* (Providence and London, 1995); and *Famille et parenté dans l'occident médiéval*, ed. G. Duby et J. Le Goff, Collection de l'Ecole Française de Rome, xxx (1977). In France the work of Duby broke new ground in tracing the nobility in the Mâconnais in *La société au XIe et XIIe siècles dans la région mâconnaise*; his views may be conveniently consulted in English in *The Chivalrous Society*, especially 'Lineage, Nobility and Knighthood', 'The Structure of Kinship and Nobility', and 'French Genealogical Literature'. A series of studies of other French regions followed, see above, p. 5n; in addition see R. Hadju, 'Family and Feudal Ties in Poitou, 1100–1300', *Journal of Interdisciplinary History*, 8.1 (1977), 117–39. For Normandy, see Bates, *Normandy before 1066*, pp. 111–21; and Searle, *Predatory Kinship and the Making of Norman Power, passim*. For Germany, Karl Leyser's work provides a lucid introduction in English: 'German Aristocracy from the Ninth to the Twelfth Century'; and Leyser, 'Maternal Kin in Early Medieval Germany. A Reply', *Past and Present*, 44 (1970), 126–34, reprinted in *Communications and Power in Medieval Europe* (London, 1994), pp. 181–8. See also now B. Arnold, *Princes and Territories in Medieval Germany* (Cambridge, 1991), chapter eight. For Anglo-Saxon kinship see L. Lancaster, 'Kinship in Anglo-Saxon Society', *British Journal of Sociology*, 9 (1958), 230–51; 359–77; for a different view see T. Charles-Edwards, 'Kinship, Status and the Origins of the Hide', *Past and Present*, 56 (1972), 3–33. Exceptions to the neglect of kinship in Norman England include Painter, 'The Family and the Feudal System in Twelfth-Century England', *Feudalism and Liberty* (ed. Cazel), pp. 195–219; Holt, 'Feudal Society and the Family in Early Medieval England'; S. L. Mooers, 'Familial Clout and Financial Gain in Henry I's reign', *Albion*, 14 (1982), 267–92; Charlotte A. Newman, *The Anglo-Norman Nobility in the Reign of Henry I. The Second Generation* (Philadelphia, 1988), chapter two; K. S. B. Keats-Rohan, 'The Bretons and Normans of England 1066–1154: the Family, the Fief and the Feudal Monarchy', *Nottingham Medieval Studies*, 36 (1992), 42–78; Thomas, *Vassals, Heiresses, Crusaders, and Thugs*, chapter four.

tion and the redress of wrongs, a set of conventions by which land could be transmitted from one generation to the next, and a focus for affective relationships.

The problems for the historian of the Anglo-Norman family lie partly in the nature of the subject and partly in the sources. At first sight contemporary sources appear to have little explicitly to say about kinship groups as such but this impression is misleading. Clearly families in the Anglo-Norman aristocracy did not represent sharply defined autonomous and warring clans: ties to lords and ties to neighbours overlapped and intertwined with ties of blood. Moreover, the composition of the effective kin group differed according to circumstances. As we shall see, it was defined by the church as a group within which marriage was proscribed.

For much of the time the kindred was effectively a small group. The family household may well have been often a nuclear family, and in terms of personal relationships it was those between husbands and wives and parents and children that counted.[2] But ties of blood were often extended by spiritual and voluntary ties. In the first place, there were the ties of godchild to godparent, which were taken very seriously in the middle ages, as seen by the prohibition on marriage between godson and godmother or godmother's daughter.[3] An adroit choice of godparent could give a son an influential ally and strengthen ties between families. Yet only very rarely are godparents identified. We are told, for instance, that William of Alderi (? Audrieu), the cousin and steward of William of Eu and fellow rebel in 1095, had on one occasion acted as a godfather with the king.[4] In 1141 David Olifard, godson of King David of Scotland, saved his godfather from capture at the rout of Winchester.[5] In the *Chester Charters*, Ranulf, the son of Peter the clerk of Earl Ranulf III, is described as the earl's godson 'whom he had taken into his special custody and protection'.[6] Peter was the earl's chancellor and attested no fewer than fifty of the earl's charters, and his family was generously treated by the earl.[7]

Secondly, children were often brought up not with their parents but in other households. Sometimes this was because their father had died and

[2] For a recent review see J. S. Moore, 'The Anglo-Norman Family: Size and Structure', *Anglo-Norman Studies*, 14 (1992), 153–96.

[3] F. Pollock and F. W. Maitland, *The History of English Law*, reissue, 2 vols. (Cambridge, 1968), II, 389.

[4] WM, *De Gestis Regum*, II, 372.    [5] John of Hexham in SD, *Opera omnia*, II, 311.

[6] *Chester Charters*, no. 283.    [7] Crouch, 'Administration of the Norman Earldom', p. 88.

they became the wards of his lord. In other cases it was probably because of the advantages it was hoped they would gain, especially if they were boys, in the way of military training and advancement in royal or noble households. Great households thus probably had an element of a boarding school about them. We must remember, too, that the word used by contemporaries for such households was *familiae*, a word which was not limited to those related by blood and marriage.

Adult males sometimes formed associations, brotherhoods in arms, which may have been quite common. There was a tradition preserved at Oseney abbey that Robert d'Oilly and Roger d'Ivry were sworn brothers. The two were neighbours in Oxfordshire, probably worked closely as agents for the king in the land revolution, and collaborated in founding the collegiate church of St George within Oxford castle, so the tradition may be well founded.[8] Through godparenthood, fosterage, and blood brotherhood, therefore, the kin group was extended.

## Kinship

In a recent study of early ducal Normandy, Eleanor Searle has emphasized the role of powerful and predatory kinship groups in the creation of a cohesive society.[9] She has suggested that, instead of the previously accepted picture of a relatively cohesive principality taken over by the Normans, ducal Normandy was constructed from the bottom up as it were, by powerful and predatory kinship groups which worked in co-operation to safeguard and extend their interests. This interpretation of Norman history underestimates the contribution of the Carolingian legacy to the development of government in ducal Normandy.[10] Nevertheless its emphasis on kinship ties, and the strategies employed by the most powerful families in selecting heirs and brides is a salutary corrective to older views. Moreover, it raises the question of what happened to these ties in England after 1066. Historians of early English society have tended to confine their discussions of kinship to the pre-Conquest

---

[8] *Cartulary of Oseney Abbey*, ed. H. E. Salter, 6 vols., Oxford Historical Society, LXXXIX–XCI, XCVII–XCVIII, CI (1929–36), IV, 1. For a seventeenth-century reference to a brotherhood between Robert Marmion and Walter de Somerville, see Dugdale, *Mon, Ang.*, II, 366.

[9] Searle, *Predatory Kinship and the Formation of Norman Power*.

[10] For comment see D. Bates, 'The Rise and Fall of Normandy, *c*. 911–1204', *England and Normandy in the Middle Ages*, ed. D. Bates and A. Curry (London, 1994), p. 25.

period.[11] Are we to assume that strong familial ties suddenly became much weaker in England after 1066? A case could be made out along these lines: it could be argued that the men who came to England came as individuals or, at best, with only one or two close relatives with them, so that traditional ties were disrupted. The newcomers soon began to marry into other 'colonial' families, their neighbours and allies, or even into native families. They needed new alliances for they were a minority living in a conquered country. At that time their enemies were not so much each other as the vanquished English. The king instituted the murder fine, as described by the author of the *Dialogue*, because his followers were falling victim to murder by Anglo-Saxons, and they had no kin in England to take on the duty of vengeance. The Norman kings imposed a martial law in England which, whilst it did not preclude compensation for a killing, meant that homicide had become a royal plea by 1135 (see above, p. 243).

This line of argument is supported by the fact that the two major feuds we hear of in Norman England were in regions at the margins of royal control. The great Northumbrian feud which long predated the Conquest rumbled on and in 1080 claimed the life of the bishop of Durham, who was killed during tense negotiations to resolve an earlier killing.[12] A second feud in Cornwall in the late eleventh or early twelfth century is mentioned in both the 1130 pipe roll and the 'Prophecies of Merlin'.[13] Frewin the sheriff and other Cornishmen united to kill their enemies, the sons of Toki, who were probably Norman. The latter had earlier killed a Cornishman named Osulf, who could have been living in 1066. A later account into the lost rights of a minster church at Lanow mentioned that old people were reluctant to attend the church because of blood feuds arising from a murder, which may have been a reference to the same feud.[14]

Even if we hear nothing other than these two instances of bloodthirsty vendettas in Norman England, in a less dramatic and conspicuous way

---

[11]  e.g. Warren, *Governance of Norman and Angevin England*, chapter one.

[12]  SD, *Opera omnia*, II, 210, and see above, p. 109.

[13]  It has been discussed most recently by O. J. Padel, 'Geoffrey of Monmouth and Cornwall', *Cambridge Medieval Celtic Studies*, 8 (1984), appendix, 20–7.

[14]  W. M. M. Picken, 'The Manor of Tremaruustel and the Honour of St Keus', *Journal of the Royal Institute of Cornwell*, new series, 7 (1973–7), 226, cited by J. Blair, 'Introduction: from Minster to Parish Church', *Minsters and Parish Churches. The Local Church in Transition 950–1200*, ed. J. Blair, Oxford University Committee for Archaeology, Monograph no. 17 (1988), p. 18, n. 59.

family groups continued to co-operate to apply pressure to secure their own ends. According to his biographer, Bishop Wulfstan acted as a peacemaker reconciling local conflicts. In one case members of a family who refused to accept compensation for an accidental killing were told that their obduracy was the Devil's work. One of them was said to have emitted an evil smell which proved Wulfstan's point only too well, and the obdurate family came to terms.[15] The assumption in this story is evidently that accidental killings could be compensated for and were resolved outside the courts, in this case with a diocesan bishop acting as a peacemaker.

In a general way a man's kindred assisted him to secure justice for personal wrongs, for these affected the honour of his family as well as of himself. If such matters came to court – and in many instances they may not have done so – the kin assisted him by supporting his oath in court; if he was killed it was the responsibility of one of his kindred to bring an appeal of homicide. The kin also benefited from any compensation which could be negotiated for homicide. They may also have been able to apply pressure to secure a favourable judgement. It is hard to credit that a suitor whose cause was backed by powerful kinsmen would not prevail against a weaker party, and the same would be true of disputes resolved by negotiation where the success of a man's case might be rooted in the support he could command. Kinsmen were natural choices as pledges in commercial transactions, and as witnesses of charters; indeed, family gatherings were the obvious occasion for the ratification of land transactions.

Kinsmen could help in other ways, by helping to secure advantages, privileges, and patronage for each other. In her study of patterns of royal patronage in the 1130 pipe roll Stephanie Mooers concluded that 'familial clout' was much in evidence. She pointed out that many studies of Henry I's patronage have considered the recipients as individuals rather than as members of families, but that families who were loyal to the king can be seen to have benefited as a group.[16] There are several instances where men secured offices or patronage for their family, or where two or more sons did very well for themselves. Amongst the latter were the brothers Payn and Eustace FitzJohn, William d'Aubigny and Nigel, the sons of Walter FitzOter, and, most notably of all, the members of the Clare family.

---

[15] *Vita Wulfstani of William of Malmesbury*, ed. R. R. Darlington, Camden Society, new series, XI (1928), pp. 38–40, 45; cited P. Hyams, 'Feud in Medieval England', *Haskins Society Journal*, 3 (1991), 2–4.
[16] Mooers, 'Familial Clout and Financial Gain'.

Kinsmen who entered the church could be helped up the ladder of ecclesiastical preferment. In 1129 Roger de Clinton, a close relative (possibly a brother) of another royal chamberlain, Geoffrey de Clinton, is alleged to have paid a large sum to become bishop of Coventry.[17] Such a sum was presumably underwritten by Geoffrey. Humphrey Bigod, son of Roger Bigod the sheriff, became a royal chaplain and prebendary of St Paul's.[18] Jocelin de Bohun, a kinsman of Humphrey de Bohun lord of Trowbridge, became bishop of Salisbury, and Richard, Jocelin's brother, was dean of Bayeux and then bishop of Coutances.[19] Robert de Gant, son of Gilbert the Domesday tenant-in-chief, was Stephen's chancellor for a time and dean of York.[20] Robert of Gloucester's illegitimate son became bishop of Bayeux. Links between aristocratic families and the upper echelons of the church were thus not uncommon.

In a political context also ties of blood were important, more so than has often been allowed. Ties of kinship, lordship, and neighbourhood all went into the networks which made up political society.[21] In the earlier part of our period we usually can reconstruct the networks in a skeletal way, but under Stephen the protracted nature of political conflict and the growing volume of surviving charter evidence provide much more detail, so that we can see who was allied with whom, and what concerns they shared. One particularly striking demonstration of the role played by kinship already noted in the preceding chapter was in the formation of the Empress's party in south-western England. Here the locally important families tended to be essentially west-country landlords; they were already in some cases related to each other before 1135, and as support for the Empress coalesced further alliances were made through marriage. A second case was the way the war in the west in 1138 centred around different claimants to the offices and lands held by Payn FitzJohn (principally the Lacy inheritance). Again and again the aims of individual participants in the fighting can be seen to have been a particular lordship or a castle to which they believed they had an hereditary claim. Inheritance thus determined goals, and kinship determined alliances.

---

[17] SD, *Opera omnia*, II, 283.     [18] *RRAN*, II, x.

[19] A family tree may be found in *Vetus Registrum Sarisberiense alias dictum registrum S. Osmundi episcopi. The Register of St. Osmund*, ed. W. H. Rich Jones, 2 vols., RS (London, 1883-4), II, lv; for the family see also *Magni Rotuli Scaccarii Normanniae*, ed. T. Stapleton, 2 vols. (London, 1840-4), II, xxiii-xxvi.

[20] *Ibid.*, III, x.     [21] Holt, 'Patronage and Politics', p. 23.

## Kinship and succession to land

A major dimension of kinship was as a framework determining the orderly transmission of land from one generation to the next. Land was a family asset, to be conserved by inheritance strategies and extended by marriage into other kindreds. Custom prescribed who, all other things being equal, should inherit, what provision was to be made for younger sons, daughters, wives, and widows, but custom was not immutable: as circumstances changed so conventions were adapted to meet them. One noticeable trend in the eleventh and twelfth centuries was the preference for lineal over collateral descent. A second was a tendency to keep lands together for one son, to preserve the patrimony rather than disperse it by partible inheritance. The speed and progress of these developments are hard to assess because only rarely do we have a full picture of families' options. Moreover a distinction has to be made between norms, in the sense of what usually happened, and rules, what happened as a matter of prescriptive practice. Thus it is possible to see that, for instance, male primogeniture may have become the norm in Norman England, but the absolute right of a son to succeed to his father's fiefs took longer to establish.

The first issue here is the nature of succession customs in ducal Normandy, and on this, it must be admitted, nothing can be said for certain. Land passed from father to son; the problem lies in our incomplete knowledge of the number of children in families and the status of the lands concerned.[22] The volatility of Norman politics in the early eleventh century also makes it difficult to be sure what proportion of an individual's lands had been inherited compared with the proportion which he acquired during his lifetime, and of which he could freely dispose. Emily Zack Tabuteau, who made a detailed study of the material relating to transfers of property in eleventh-century Normandy, pointed out that lordship grew much stronger during the eleventh century. Was land which was held of lords less secure than that which was owned with no reference to any superior lord? One criterion of security was heritability, and Tabuteau demonstrated that the language of inheritance was being applied to fiefs as well as to land that was owned.[23] She drew attention to the point that lordship may well have extended rapidly during the

---

[22] *Ibid.*, pp. 118–20.    [23] Tabuteau, *Transfers of Property*, chapter five.

period of disorder in the early eleventh century. Presumably lords' recognition of claims to inheritance might have been the *quid pro quo* for an extension of lordship over land previously held in full ownership. At the level of practice, succession to fiefs as well as allodial lands was already strong by 1066. The next question is, who inherited?

Here, too, we are not on certain ground. In the pays de Caux, which was part of upper Normandy, at a later date the rule was primogeniture. Elsewhere the practice was partible inheritance in a form known as parage, whereby the younger brothers held their shares of the eldest, who held the principal estate and did homage.[24] It is difficult to know when and how these different practices developed. In some great families in the eleventh century there was a preference for keeping the core of the family lands together for one son, whom we must presume was usually the eldest, whilst younger sons and daughters were provided with a limited share. A distinction may already have been drawn between the patrimony, designated for one son, usually the eldest, and any acquisitions, which could be used by the lord to endow any younger sons. We should not too readily conclude that unigeniture or primogeniture had become the norm, however, for, as a recent analysis of successions in the ruling dynasty has shown, the dukes themselves did not find it easy to pass on an undivided inheritance.[25] The position of females was also delicate, especially where sons were lacking. One of the most important disputed successions of the mid-eleventh century in northern France was that to the lordship of Bellême, when eventually Mabel de Bellême's claim was given priority over that of her two brothers – and she just happened to be married to Roger of Montgomery (see below, pp. 372–3).

The evidence of the adoption of toponyms is useful here, but not entirely conclusive. Certainly leading men at the Conqueror's court had begun to identify themselves by reference to their chief castles: Roger of Montgomery, Roger de Beaumont, and Roger de Bully, for example. It is difficult to prove that these were already hereditary. One source that has been cited in this context, the record of Roger de Bully's sale of the tithe of Bully 'in so much as it belongs to him by hereditary right', is not strictly speaking contemporary.[26] For this reason it would be unwise to conclude

---

[24] Holt, 'Politics and Property', p. 10.     [25] Garnett, '"Ducal" Succession in Early Normandy', pp. 80–110.
[26] *Recueil des actes des ducs de Normandie*, ed. M. Fauroux, Mémoires de la Société des Antiquaires de Normandie, XXXVI (Caen, 1961), no. 200.

that the Normans' use of place names in the mid-eleventh century was indicative of their attachment to lineage, or, indeed, that it was fundamentally different from the situation in England where thegns sometimes identified themselves with reference to place names before 1066.[27]

After 1066 in England the tendencies towards both hereditary succession and male primogeniture grew stronger. The language of charters, the fact that grants for life were kept quite deliberately distinct from fiefs, and the way disputes over succession were conducted, all point to the same conclusion. Tenure was reasonably secure and the prospect of hereditary succession also reasonable for the loyal tenant who performed service. Stephen's reign may have witnessed a disruption in the trend towards strengthening inheritance, but it was resumed and developed further under Henry II.[28]

Primogeniture also prevailed, though this may not have occurred immediately or have been universal. The notion of parage seems to lie behind an account in the Abingdon chronicle of Gilbert Latimer and his family, who received 7½ hides by gift of the abbot. Each of his three daughters was provided with a marriage portion. There were three sons, and the abbot did not want to favour one over the others. Picot was made the abbot's man for one knight's fee, and the others were to assist him from their portions. If any died, their portion of land was not to be sold.[29] The *Leges Henrici Primi*, dating from the early twelfth century, awarded to the eldest son the *primum feodum*, the fief that was first in time or importance, which was contrasted with purchases or acquisitions which could be bequeathed at will.[30] Here we have the distinction between inheritance and acquisitions which was to be so important in family arrangements.

So far as the first generation after the Conquest was concerned, the patrimonial lands were those in Normandy or other regions of northern France. These in theory and often in practice formed the portion of the eldest son: William FitzOsbern's elder son William inherited Breteuil, and his second son Roger inherited the earldom of Hereford.[31] In later Norman custom it was possible, where acquisitions far outweighed the patrimony,

---

[27] It is often claimed that the Normans introduced surnames into England: J. C. Holt, 'What's in a Name?' *Family Nomenclature and the Norman Conquest*, Stenton Lecture 1981 (Reading, 1982), p. 11.

[28] Hudson, *Land, Law, and Lordship*, pp. 148–53, 275–81.    [29] *Chronicon Monasterii de Abingdon*, II, 34–5.

[30] *Leges Henrici Primi*, c. 70, 21. The phrase *primum feudum* also occurs in 48, 11.

[31] Holt, 'Politics and Property', p. 14; OV, II, 282, 284.

for the eldest son to choose the former rather than the latter, and Holt has suggested that this rule may well date back to the Conquest period.[32]

Other cases, more than is commonly thought, do not conform to division at the Channel, and Holt has suggested that a father probably had some latitude in the disposition of his lands.[33] He could if he wished arrange for one son to inherit both Norman and English estates, though we cannot always be certain that there was more than one son surviving, and so that the choice of heir was deliberate.[34] Another variant was for the Norman estate to be shared, as seems to have been the case with the fief held by the Lacy family of the bishopric of Bayeux. In 1133 the fief was held by Gilbert, representing the Lacy family of Hereford, and Henry, representing the Lacy family of Pontefract.[35] Alternatively a division might be made by which the Norman estates and some land in England were allotted to one son, leaving the bulk of the English estates to another, as occurred in the case of the sons of Robert of Meulan.[36] It was very rare for English baronies to be divided. The two clearest cases of this are the divisions of the estates of William de Raimes and Hardwin de Scales.[37] In the case of the latter the division persisted, and at the time of the inquest into knight service in 1166 the holder of each half of the barony returned a separate *carta*.[38] The reasons for division are not immediately apparent: possibly twins were involved.

What did not happen after 1066 was that fathers used their newly gained English wealth to provide for all their sons, although they could have done so, given that these were acquisitions. Once estates had passed as an entity to the next generation, they had become the patrimonial inheritance which could not be dismembered. That sense of a single holding may have been heightened by acts of homage like that at Salisbury in 1086, when men personally accepted both the lands and obligations on the land that had been granted to them. It was thus the

---

[32] Holt, 'Politics and Property', p. 16.     [33] *Ibid.*, pp. 15–16.

[34] William de Warenne, according to the (later) annals of Hyde, on the king's instructions left his English and Norman estates to William II whilst Rainald inherited those in Flanders: *Early Yorkshire Charters*, VIII, 6 citing *Liber Monasterii de Hyda*, ed. E. Edwards, RS (London, 1866), p. 299.

[35] Wightman, *Lacy Family*, pp. 218–19.

[36] Crouch, *Beaumont Twins*, pp. 8–9; a third son, Hugh, received rents in Paris.

[37] Holt, 'Politics and Property', p. 11 and n. discusses these and other cases of alleged division. In the case of William de Raimes the estates were subsequently reunited, then divided again: Sanders, *English Baronies*, p. 139.     [38] *Ibid.*, p. 30.

monarchy which had a vested interest in sustaining this idea, for kings did not wish to see lands on which military service was owed fragmented as generation succeeded generation. By taking homage from only one heir, they could ensure impartibility.

That heir was not always the eldest son. According to a tradition preserved in the Chancellor's Roll for 1208 in the case of the lordship of Geoffrey of Mandeville of Marshwood, King Henry I awarded the inheritance to Ralph, Geoffrey's son by a second marriage, over Robert, son of a first marriage, because the former was a better knight.[39] In fact this may be another case where the Norman lands went to one son, Robert, with only a small stake in England, answering for the service of one knight in 1166, whilst Ralph succeeded to the English estates, which passed to his daughter, Denise, and her husband, William FitzJohn, a royal servant.[40] A second case occurs in a charter which Stenton dated between 1162 and 1166.[41] This recorded a settlement by which an elder brother exchanged places with a younger and granted him the baronies of their father and uncle in return for lands, service, revenue, and rights over churches. The elder brother was called Henry, the younger Sewall, and the two baronies had belonged to their father Fulcher and uncle Henry. Stenton's interest in the document was as a record of the honorial court of Earl William de Ferrers, yet the family circumstances which had led to the exchange are also intriguing. Nothing is said of the provenance of the lands which Sewall had to offer, but they are not amongst those held of Ferrers by Sewall the elder, grandfather of the two brothers, in 1086. Nor do we know why Sewall was chosen to inherit, though it is clear from a later passage in the record that he had married Maud Ridel, possibly recently since no heir had yet been born. Perhaps her family had insisted that her future husband be well provided for.

Security of possession for the tenant and succession by his eldest son were signs of strengthening inheritance. Another was the tenant's freedom to dispose of his land without a challenge from his heir or other members of his family. In western France it was customary in this period to record the *laudatio parentum*, the agreement of kindred, in gifts to the

---

[39] *Ibid.*, p. 64; *PR 10 John*, p. 113 n.

[40] *Charters of the Redvers Family*, appendix I, nos. 2, 6; William FitzJohn was active in the king's service by 1130: *PR 31 Henry I*, p. 13. He held the castle of Harptree against Stephen in 1138: see *Gesta Stephani*, p. 66.    [41] Stenton, *First Century*, pp. 51–3.

church.[42] Such testimony was important at various levels: the donor's kin were associated with the aims and benefits of the gift, and it made a later challenge more difficult. In England the consent of the heir to a gift was usually recorded, but the consent of a wider group was less common, evidently because the position of the heir was regarded as being relatively strong.[43]

What therefore of younger sons, especially the third, fourth, and fifth in line? Acquisitions might well in practice be limited to their mother's marriage portion and, as we shall see, this might only consist of one or two manors. Some younger sons obviously did go off to Wales, or to Scotland, or on crusade. Marriage to an heiress or a rich widow was the most coveted avenue to wealth, but the competition for such women was great, and in the top levels of society such marriages were controlled by the crown. Even in the middling and lower ranks of the aristocracy, it cannot have been easy to persuade fathers to bestow their daughters on young men with few prospects of inheriting land.

One obvious solution to provision for younger sons was to enfeoff them as tenants. That this was commonly done in the early twelfth century can be seen from the returns to the inquest of 1166 when, as Painter pointed out, of the one hundred and forty tenants-in-chief who replied, no fewer than sixty-one had enfeoffed male relatives.[44] Such enfeoffments appear advantageous to both parties: younger sons could be provided for, but if they died without male heirs then the land reverted to the lord. By the time Glanvill was writing, however, a principle had been established that a man could not be both lord and heir: in other words, fathers would not be able to recover fiefs granted to younger sons.[45] In the early twelfth century, fathers do not seem to have been excluded in this way.[46] In Normandy, too, fathers were not excluded from the inheritance. It would otherwise be hard to account for the number of relatives in the 1166 Inquest who are reported as having been enfeoffed before 1135. If fathers did not grant fiefs to younger sons, the only alternative was either to give them land outright, or, if they themselves were

---

[42] S. D. White, *Custom, Kinship, and Gifts to Saints: the Laudatio Parentum in Western France, 1050–1150* (Chapel Hill, NC, 1988).      [43] Hudson, *Land, Law, and Lordship*, pp. 204–7.

[44] Painter, 'Family and the Feudal System', p. 209; for the suggestion that provision made for younger sons and daughters may have been particularly generous in Yorkshire gentry families, see Thomas, *Vassals, Heiresses, Crusaders, and Thugs*, pp. 119–30.      [45] *Glanvill*, VII, 1.      [46] *Leges Henrici Primi*, 70, 20.

tenants, to surrender a fief to their lords who then regranted it to the younger sons. In this way a father was still eligible to inherit should his son die before him.[47]

By the time that Glanvill was writing, it was established that lords should not alienate more than one-third of their inheritance. Occasionally, however, it is possible to find large enfeoffments. Three examples may be cited. First, there is the case of Reginald de Warenne, third son of William II de Warenne, who administered the honour while his elder brother was absent on crusade and did so again when the honour was held by William of Blois, King Stephen's son. Reginald became a leading tenant of the honour.[48] Secondly, Robert de Tosny of Belvoir, younger brother of William d'Aubigny, lord of Belvoir in 1166, held fifteen out of thirty-three 'old' fees of the honour. He also held four and half fees of the new enfeoffment, and of these there were three under-tenants whose names indicate that they also were relatives: Ywan d'Aubigny held one knight, Geoffrey d'Aubigny one knight, and Elias d'Aubigny one knight.[49] Robert evidently predeceased his brother.[50] Thirdly, there was the case of the barony of Weedon Pinkney in Northamptonshire. This had a relatively heavy quota of fifteen knights' fees which owed castleguard at Windsor. In 1166 the then lord, Gilbert de Pinkney, reported that he had nine and a half knights enfeoffed in the reign of King Henry, of which five and a half were held by Henry son of Robert de Pinkney and one by Ghilo de Pinkney; afterwards Gilbert said he had given one fee to his son Henry and a half to his son Gilbert, while the service of two knights was charged against his demesne.[51] In 1203 King John issued a writ to stop the then lord, Henry, disposing of any more of his land lest his son be disinherited.[52]

At the end of the first century after the Conquest we can see that inheritance and primogeniture of males were relatively strong, but the male line often failed, so that the position of women was crucially important.[53] How many daughters were to inherit, and whether those married at the

---

[47] For the case of William d'Anisy, see above, p. 199; Painter, 'Family and the Feudal System', p. 213; and *Sir Christopher Hatton's Book of Seals*, ed. L. C. Loyd and D. M. Stenton, Northamptonshire Record Society, xv (Oxford, 1950), no. 301.   [48] *Early Yorkshire Charters*, VIII, 26–8.

[49] *RBE*, I, 328; for the family relationships see Round, *Historical Manuscripts Commission. Rutland*, IV, 100, 106, 134.   [50] *Ibid.*, 159–60.   [51] *RBE*, I, 317–18; Painter, 'Family and the Feudal System', p. 210.

[52] *Rotuli Letterarum Patentium*, ed. T. D. Hardy, Record Commission (London, 1835), I part i, 31.

[53] For escheats, see above, p. 129–30.

time of their fathers' deaths were to inherit as well as those unmarried, are topics discussed in the following chapter, where it will be suggested that there may have been more flexibility than in the customs pertaining to succession by males.

How strongly rooted were notions of lineage in Anglo-Norman England? One source of evidence is naming patterns. By 1066 some Norman families were adopting toponyms derived from their chief castles, but by no means all. If toponyms had such powerful resonances of lineage, all landed families would surely have adopted them, whereas some used nicknames, such as Crispin (referring to sticking-up hair). Some of the greatest men simply described themselves as 'son of', such as William FitzOsbern, son of Osbern, the duke's steward, or used occupational names such as Haimo the steward or Gerold the steward. Thus toponyms, though a manifestation of the identification of family with place, had not as yet superseded alternatives, such as patronyms or nicknames.

In the upper echelons of the Domesday hierarchy of landed wealth, what can be seen most clearly is in fact the superiority of a comital title to any other description. Earl Hugh appears thus, rather than as Hugh son of Richard the *vicomte*, or Hugh d'Avranches; others appear as the count of Meulan, rather than Robert de Beaumont, or Robert FitzRoger, and so on. At these upper levels, toponyms, especially names of French places, were much more numerous than patronyms and occupational names. In group A of the Domesday magnates (see above, p. 36) there were eight laymen, four of whom were counts or earls (Robert of Mortain, Alan, Hugh, and Eustace of Boulogne), three had toponyms (Roger of Montgomery, William de Warenne, and Geoffrey de Mandeville) and only one, Richard FitzGilbert, was also known as Richard of Tonbridge or Richard of Clare (see below). In group B, there were ten laymen, plus one woman, Countess Judith. Of these five had toponyms, of which one was English (Henry de Ferrers, William de Briouze, Gilbert de Gant, William of Eu, and Edward of Salisbury), and five had cognomens (Robert Malet, Roger Bigod, Walter Giffard, Miles Crispin, and Ralph Baynard); there were no patronyms. In group C there were twenty-six men, of whom two were counts (Robert of Eu and Robert of Meulan), fifteen had toponyms, including two which were English (Walter de Lacy, Hugh de Montfort, Ralph de Mortimer, Aubrey de Vere, William de Mohun, Arnulf de Hesdin, Robert de Tosny, Hugh de Port, Robert d'Oilly, Roger d'Ivry, Hugh de Grandmesnil, Walter de Douai, Roger de Bully, and Alured of Marlborough and Robert of

Stafford). One had a patronym (William FitzAnsculf), five had cognomens (Ranulf Peverel, William Peverel, Robert Gernon, Roger the Poitevin, and Ivo Taillebois), and three had occupational names (Eudo the steward, Baldwin the sheriff who was also called Baldwin of Exeter, and Swein the sheriff, also called Swein of Essex). Finally, in group D there were thirty-one laymen plus the widow of Hugh FitzGrip, of whom twenty had toponyms, two or three of which were English (Geoffrey de la Guerche, Guy de Craon, Humphrey de Insula – presumably from the Channel Isles or the Isle of Wight, Ralph de Pomeroy, Ralph de Tosny, Walter de St Valery, Walter d'Aincourt, Hardwin de Scalers, Hugh de Beauchamp, Nigel d'Aubigny, Drogo de la Beuvrière, Roger de Courseulles, Ralph de Limesy, Peter de Valognes, Ralph de Belfou, Ilbert de Lacy, William d'Ecouis, Ralph Paynel, Picot of Cambridge, and Turchil of Warwick). Four had patronyms (Turstin FitzRou, Hugh FitzBaldric, Reginald FitzIvo, and Robert FitzGerold) and a fifth was described as Rannulf brother of Ilger, four had cognomens (Geoffrey Alselin, Roger Arundel, William Capra, and Walter the Fleming), and two had occupational names (Haimo the steward and Walter the Deacon).

What is even more interesting is the way a few men were described in more than one way. Richard and Baldwin were both sons of Count Gilbert of Brionne. Richard is usually described as son of Count Gilbert, but he also occurs as Richard of Clare and Richard of Tonbridge. His brother Baldwin is called Baldwin the sheriff or Baldwin of Exeter. Neither is called after their Norman estates, though Orderic writing in the twelfth century calls Richard 'de Bienfaite'. The early adoption of an English toponym by Baldwin is also noteworthy. Exeter was a royal borough with a castle, of which Baldwin was castellan, and it is likely that when individuals are called Edward of Salisbury or Robert of Stafford the association is as much with the castle as with the shrievalty. Hugh d'Ivry occurs in Domesday Book, as does his nephew Roger. Neither was lord of the town of Ivry, where the castle belonged to the duke, but their names associated them with this place. Roger was also castellan of Rouen for a time, yet we do not hear of him called 'of Rouen', or 'of Beckley', his chief English manor. Robert 'of Stafford' was an important landholder in that county. He had acquired all but one of Earl Edwin's manors, including Bradley by Stafford, and in Stafford he held thirteen dwellings which had belonged to Edwin, and thirteen others. He chose to associate himself with the chief town, rather than describing himself either as a member of the Tosny family, which he was, or as son of Roger. The choice may have been deliberate: as yet the tenacious hold of the crown on shrievalties and castles was not evident, and this was one way of asserting some kind of claim to custody, yet if we are looking for signs of self-perception it is intriguing. The evidence of names thus bears out the statement made earlier that although association with the chief castle of the lineage was reflected in many Norman names, other choices were possible.

Nevertheless the practice of using toponyms was increasingly widely adopted in the aristocracy of Norman England, and there is little reason to doubt that French toponyms were regarded as prestigious. C. P. Lewis has analysed naming patterns of the jurors identified in two of the Domesday satellites, the *Inquisitio Comitatus Cantabrigiensis* and the *Inquisitio Eliensis* and demonstrated that French toponyms were associated with higher social status. Nevertheless, as he also pointed out, more French jurors of lower status identified themselves with English placenames than their social superiors, whereas English jurors, not surprisingly, had the highest proportion of all of English toponyms.[54] We have very little to go on to understand why individuals chose English rather than French toponyms. Geoffrey de Clinton, for instance, took his name from Glympton in Oxfordshire, though he came from Saint-Pierre-de-Semilly. It might be argued that his family may have been lords of the former and not of the latter, but, as we have already seen, men did describe themselves as of places of which they were not lords.

The appearance of French toponyms in the aristocracy of Norman England was paralleled by the adoption of French Christian names, and the virtual disappearance of Anglo-Saxon names, especially for boys. Only English names like Alfred which had already passed into Breton usage by the mid-eleventh century continued to be employed. Those with names such as Godwin or Harding chose names like Robert or Henry for their sons. Thus Edgar Aetheling's companion on the first crusade was called Robert son of Godwin, and the great financier of Bristol in Stephen's reign was Robert son of Harding. Turchil of Arden's son was called Siward, but the latter's son was named Henry. Female names followed suit: names like Aelfgiva and Edith gave way to Emma and Matilda.

The adoption of personal emblems began to spread in the late eleventh century. They were probably first displayed on banners, of which those on

---

[54] C. P. Lewis, 'The Domesday Jurors', *Haskins Society Journal*, 5 (1993), 17–29; see especially table on p. 21.

the Bayeux Tapestry were very early examples.[55] The practice spread to shields, and then to surcoats, which were probably adopted during the first crusade, and had obvious utility as marks of identification in battle, on the tournament field, or, as the twelfth century wore on, on their seals.[56]

From being wholly personal emblems, designs were adopted by kinsmen, or allies. One famous early group of shields was the checkered shields adopted by the kinsmen of Ralph count of Vermandois, a descendant of the Emperor Charlemagne. These included the count of Meulan, the earl of Warwick, William de Warenne earl of Surrey, and the earl of Leicester.[57] Another was the chevrons of the Clare family and their allies, the families of Monmouth, FitzWalter, and Montfiquet.[58] A third was the quartered red and yellow shields which Round suggested may have been centred on Geoffrey II de Mandeville and were adopted by his allies and descendants: Say, Beauchamp of Bedford, the lords of Warkworth, and the earls of Oxford.[59] Gradually shields began to conform to conventions about colour and design. It has been argued that the shields in the illustration in John of Worcester's *Chronicle* which shows armed men threatening the slumbers of Henry I 'have a definite orderliness about them suggesting they were following new guidelines in composition and style'.[60] In the final stage in the development of heraldry, which seems to have begun in England in about the reign of Stephen, heraldic shields not only conformed to convention, but were passed on from generation to generation as a hallmark of lineage and also of title to lands and castles. In time the adoption of heraldic shields also began to spread downwards from the greatest families. Richard de Lucy, whose origins though aristocratic were relatively modest, became one of Henry II's chief justiciars, and adopted a shield showing a pike or *luz*, thus punning on his own name.[61]

A growing emphasis on lineage did not push maternal kin entirely out of the frame. Men related to women of higher and especially of royal

[55] A. Ailes, 'Heraldry in Twelfth-Century England: the Evidence', *England in the Twelfth Century*, ed. D. Williams (Woodbridge, 1990), p. 2 n.; Crouch, *Image of Aristocracy*, chapter seven, provides a survey.

[56] A. Ailes, 'The Knight, Heraldry and Armour: The Role of Recognition and the Origins of Heraldry', *Medieval Knighthood*, IV (Woodbridge, 1992), 1–21.       [57] Crouch, *Beaumont Twins*, pp. 211–12.

[58] J. H. Round, 'The Introduction of Armorial Bearings into England', *Archaeological Journal*, 51 (1894), 43–8; C. H. Hunter Blair, 'Armorials on English Seals from the Twelfth to the Sixteenth Centuries', *Archaeologia*, 89, second series, 39 (1943), 1–26.       [59] Round, *Geoffrey de Mandeville*, pp. 392–6.

[60] Ailes, 'Heraldry in Twelfth-Century England', p. 10.

[61] W. de G. Birch, *Catalogue of Seals in the Department of Manuscripts in the British Museum*, 6 vols. (London, 1887–1900), nos. 11439, 2245, cited Ailes, 'Heraldry in Twelfth-Century England', p. 5 n.

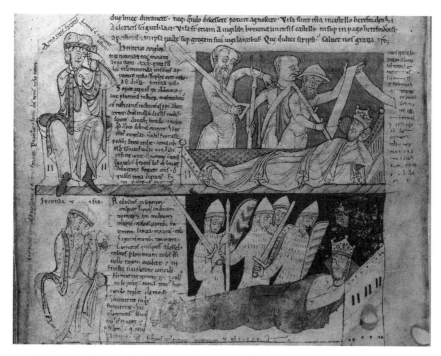

**11** Peasants and angry knights appear to the sleeping Henry I: Oxford, Corpus
Christi College, MS. 157 p. 382. The shields carried by the knights have heraldic or
proto-heraldic devices. Reproduced by permission of the President and Fellows of
Corpus Christi College, Oxford.

standing were named by reference to their relatives. The landless younger
brother of Queen Matilda styled himself David brother of the queen and
Queen Adeliza's brother Jocelin also sometimes similarly described
himself.[62] Descent from illustrious females was not forgotten. Robert of
Torigny writing in the mid-twelfth century traced the descendants of
sisters and nieces of Duchess Gunnor, wife of Duke Richard I of
Normandy.[63] A recent re-evaluation by Dr Elisabeth Van Houts has demonstrated that Robert's details, where verifiable, are often accurate.[64]

   The most usual reason for a son to adopt his mother's name rather than

---

[62] *RRAN*, III, no. 568; *Early Yorkshire Charters*, XI, nos. 68, 70, 71.

[63] *Gesta Normannorum Ducum* (ed. Van Houts), II, 264–75.

[64] E. M. C. Van Houts, 'Robert of Torigni as Genealogist', *Studies in Medieval History presented to R. Allen
      Brown*, ed. C. Harper-Bill, C. Holdsworth, and J. L. Nelson (Woodbridge, 1989), pp. 215–33. This super-
      sedes G. H. White, 'The Sisters and Nieces of Gunnor, Duchess of Normandy', *Genealogist*, 37 (1921),
      57–65, 128–32.

his father's was if he inherited her land. The son of Eustace FitzJohn by his first marriage to Beatrice de Vesci called himself William de Vesci, whereas the son of his second marriage was simply Robert FitzEustace. The latter married a niece of Ilbert de Lacy, and their grandson, who inherited the Lacy estates, adopted the Lacy name.[65] William son of Robert FitzWalter and Sybil de Chesney sometimes used his mother's name, sometimes his father's, and sometimes called himself William the sheriff or William of Norwich. His half-brother Simon son of Aveline also called himself after his mother.[66] Such examples do not jar with a preference for descent in the male line; they merely make the point that men were proud to associate themselves with powerful families, whether the link was on the male or the female side.

Aristocratic families must have preserved extensive and precise knowledge of their kindred.[67] None survives in a written record for Norman England, though the accounts of the lives of founders of religious houses, written down long afterwards, drew on family traditions. Because these sometimes contain mistakes, they have been neglected as a source and deserve more thorough and systematic investigation. Vercauteren and Duby have explored two of the earliest and best-known of family histories surviving from France, those composed for the lords of Ardres and for the counts of Anjou.[68] The verse history of William the Marshal, a unique biography of a layman, goes back to William's childhood in Stephen's reign, and this too preserved some information about William's family, though the author was not primarily concerned with genealogy.[69] Claims advanced in litigation were also often based on knowledge of family history reaching a long way back, reinforcing the point that in this era a knowledge of descent and kinship was not just a matter of family pride, but essential for advancing claims and making marriages.

---

[65] Holt, 'What's in a Name?', pp. 21–2, citing *CP* XII, pt. ii, 272–4; Wightman, *Lacy Family*, genealogical table.

[66] *Sibton Abbey Cartularies*, ed. P. Brown, Suffolk Records Society, VII, VIII, IX, X (1985–8), i, 13.

[67] See for example the knowledge displayed in a letter of Ivo of Chartres to King Henry I when a daughter of the king was betrothed to Hugh of Châteauneuf-en-Thimerais: Ivo of Chartres, letter no. 261, Migne, *Patrologia Latina*, CLXII, 265–6.

[68] F. Vercauteren, 'Une parenté dans la France du nord aux Xe et XIIe siècles', *Le Moyen Age*, 69 (1963), 223–45; G. Duby, 'Remarques sur la littérature généalogique en France au XIe et XIIe siècles', *Académie des Inscriptions et Belles Lettres, comptes rendus des séances de l'année 1967* (Paris, 1967) and 'French Genealogical Literature', in *The Chivalrous Society*; and see also Duby, *Medieval Marriage. Two Models from Twelfth-Century France*, trans. E. Foster (Baltimore and London, 1978), chapter three.

[69] D. Crouch, 'The Hidden History of the Twelfth Century', *Haskins Society Journal*, 5 (1993), 111–30.

## Marriage

Marriage in its social context was a means of allying with other families and possibly of bringing new wealth into the family. Two tendencies were at war here: on the one hand the desire to marry within a narrow circle and to keep land and property within the family, and on the other hand to marry out and thus to extend the family's interests. Marriage within too narrow a circle was condemned as incestuous, but in order to be able to know if marriages were incestuous, families had to have precise and detailed knowledge of their genealogies. The kinship group in the eleventh century could be reckoned in one of two ways. One was based on Roman law counting acts of generation to seven degrees, and allowed marriage between third cousins. An alternative system of reckoning was used in Germanic societies, however, which traced seven generations from a common ancestor. By this system marriage was only possible for sixth cousins and beyond – a much wider proscribed circle.[70]

The reformers in the eleventh-century church began to turn their attention to marriage, moved in part by the issues of clerical marriage and hereditary succession to benefices. A tract composed by Peter Damian in 1063, *De Parentelae Gradibus*, was particularly influential. He was especially concerned to promote Augustine's ideal of marriage as a means of promoting peace between clans or extended kinship groups.[71] In 1072 Pope Alexander II's canon proscribed marriage within seven degrees from a common ancestor, and from this point the papal view prevailed for a century.[72] The prohibition of marriage within seven degrees was extended to seven generations of one's deceased wife's relatives (one's affinity), and beyond, to the relatives of the wife's relatives.[73] The new rules were promulgated in England in church councils: in 1075 the Council of London prohibited marriage within seven degrees, and in 1125 the seven prohibited degrees were extended to include affinity. These rules, if strictly adhered to, would have caused major problems in royal and aristocratic families by drastically restricting the choice of partners. Although marriages were not commonly contracted within four degrees, those within

---

[70] J. Goody, *The Development of the Family and Marriage in Europe* (Cambridge, 1983), pp. 136–8.

[71] D. L. Davray, 'Peter Damian, Consanguinity and Church Property', *Intellectual Life in the Middle Ages. Studies presented to Margaret Gibson* (London, 1992), pp. 71–80.

[72] See especially Duby, *Medieval Marriage*.   [73] Pollock and Maitland, *History of English Law*, II, 307.

five or six degrees did occur. The problem was that such marriages (and the title of any children) were open to challenge. Sometimes it was convenient to use the new rules to prevent or challenge unions; an early instance was the way Henry I made sure that the marriage between his nephew William Clito and a daughter of the court of Anjou did not take place.[74] Sometimes husbands would use the grounds of their having married within the prohibited decrees to free themselves from wives who were no longer wanted, usually because they had failed to produce children. This is not to say that they contracted marriages with the escape route mapped out: simply that it provided an exit in a way that churchmen had probably not envisaged.[75]

In early medieval society, marriage ceremonies consisted of a formal betrothal or *desponsatio* in which the bride was solemnly handed over to her spouse with an exchange of gifts, and the arrangements in terms of land from her kindred and her husband's kindred were spelled out. The betrothal might take place in a domestic setting and the presence of a priest was not crucial. Religious ceremonies, blessing a ring, a nuptial mass, and blessing the marriage chamber, were desirable, but could take place at a later date. By the early twelfth century, however, the contractual and religious proceedings were brought together in a single ritual, conducted by a priest, and usually taking place at the church door.[76] Here the priest could make inquiry as to the eligibility of the partners to marry, and the free exchange of promises was made in public. In 1076 it was laid down at the council of Winchester that valid marriages required the presence of a priest. In 1094 it was further enacted that secret weddings subsequently denied by one partner were to be annulled, and those who knew about marriages within the prohibited degrees were to denounce them. Christopher Brooke has shown how these developments were reflected in the architecture of early twelfth-century churches in the provision of grand porches to provide a suitable setting for marriages.[77] Gradually churchmen's emphasis on the need for a religious ceremony took root, though marriage in church did not become a legal necessity until the Council of Trent. In the twelfth century, churchmen continued to develop and refine the criteria for valid marriages, emphasizing the centrality of

---

[74] OV, VI, 164–6.   [75] Duby, *Medieval Marriage*, pp. 25–81.

[76] J.-B. Molin and P. Mutembe, *Le rituel du mariage en France du XIIe au XVIe siècle* (Paris, 1973), pp. 35–6.

[77] Brooke, *Medieval Idea of Marriage*, chapter ten.

consent freely and legitimately given, even when consummation did not take place.[78]

A famous case where a daughter's right to inherit as the child of a legitimate union was at issue was that of Mabel of Francheville whose title was challenged by Richard of Anstey. The details of this case are known because of the survival, unique for this period, of Richard's account of his litigation expenses. William de Sackville, whose estates were in Essex, had contracted a marriage to Aubrey de Tresgoz. He then chose to marry Alice daughter of Amfrid the sheriff by a marriage involving a church ceremony. Several children including Mabel were born of the second marriage, but this broke up, and William had Alice ejected from the house. Alice took her case to the church, and it was heard first by Henry of Blois, bishop of Winchester and papal legate, and then in about 1140 by the Pope, Innocent II, who denounced the second marriage. Mabel, Alice's daughter, was for some years in possession of the estates until Richard, her cousin, decided to claim them. For five years the case lumbered on: Richard obtained royal writs to start it off, then it was heard in the archbishop's court, and finally referred to the pope, who once again proclaimed Mabel's illegitimacy.[79] The issue here was thus whether William de Sackville had been free to marry Alice, and whether his daughter Mabel was the product of a legitimate union and so his lawful successor.

The church's emphasis on the sacramental character of what had earlier been a much more secular affair could thus be circumvented on the score that the parties had not been free to marry or had not given their free consent: an unforeseen consequence of what had been intended by reformers as a tightening up of the rules of marriage. Nevertheless valid marriages were a life-long commitment and partners could not be shuffled off easily. Even if one partner entered the religious life, the other was expected to stay chaste. On the other hand, the legitimate wife was now accorded a measure of protection. From a husband's point of view, he was committed to serial monogamy in a way that protected both wife and children. Less official unions, and any children born to them, were henceforth downgraded, and, most significantly, the children of such unions did not have a claim on their father's inheritance. Hence the choice of a wife was of even greater importance than before. The most desirable

---

[78] Ibid., pp. 137–9; for a brief survey of canon law on marriage, see J. A. Brundage, Medieval Canon Law (London, 1995), pp. 70–5.   [79] Brooke, Medieval Idea of Marriage, pp. 148–52.

brides were those from more powerful and illustrious lineages, but their marriages were naturally the most strictly controlled, and such brides were few in number.

Kindred and affinity constituted one constraint on choice of marriage partner; in Anglo-Norman England the other was the lord's influence. We know most about the crown's influence over the marriages of female relatives of tenants-in-chief but the same considerations prevailed at the middling and lower levels. Marriage was, certainly, first and foremost a matter for kindreds, but the consent of the lord to something which so nearly affected his interests was also needed. This was made clear by Henry I's Charter of Liberties in 1100 when he stated that, although he would make no charge for his consent, he expected to be consulted about all marriages of his barons and tenants, and would not forbid them unless an enemy of his was involved.

In trying to identify the factors that determined marriage patterns, we are faced with very uneven evidence skewed towards identifying marriages which were important because of the illustrious lineage of the bride or her role in bringing wealth into the family. All too often charters and later genealogical material record only Christian names. This is especially true of families other than the greatest. It is also evident that the identities of sons and their wives are much more carefully recorded than daughters and their husbands, reflecting the fact that daughters were leaving the kindred. Only rarely, therefore, can we be reasonably sure that we have a full picture, as, for instance, when Orderic relates the history of the Giroie or Grandmesnil families about which he was certainly well informed.

The marriage strategies of the greatest families, unlike those of middling or lesser, included brides drawn from far afield as well as those from nearer his own estates. They paralleled the marriage strategies of the ducal house, and for much the same reasons: the hope of enhanced status for their own lineage and the possibility that their wives might inherit. In the top group of Domesday tenants-in-chief (see above, p. 36), the class A magnates, we find several instances of marriages outside the Anglo-Norman realm: Maine, Brittany, the Ile-de-France, Flanders, and even further afield. The value of such brides could barely be measured. Thus William FitzOsbern, whose first wife was a daughter of Roger de Tosny of Conches, married as his second wife Richilde, widow of Baldwin VI count of Flanders, whose son Arnulf was being challenged by his uncle Robert the Frisian. Flanders was already immensely wealthy, and a contested succession with himself married to the widow of the previous count must have seemed to William to offer the kind of opportunity that had faced the Conqueror in England. William de Warenne married a Flemish wife, the sister of Gherbod, first lord of Chester, who was probably related to the advocates of Ghent. This Flemish marriage may not have been like FitzOsbern's in that it was probably forged during the course of the Conquest.

The marriage strategy of the Montgomerys is also instructive. Roger of Montgomery's first wife was a great heiress, Mabel de Bellême, whose lands stretched beyond the southern frontiers of the duchy. His second was a daughter of Everard, lord of Le Puiset south of Paris.[80] Of his sons the eldest, Hugh, is not known to have married; his second son Robert married Agnes, heiress to Ponthieu; Arnulf married a daughter of Muirchertach O'Brien king of Leinster and high king of Ireland; and Roger the Poitevin married Almodis, daughter of Audebert II count of La Marche in Poitou. One of Roger's daughters, Matilda, married Robert count of Mortain, another married Hugh lord of Châteauneuf (-en-Thimerais), and a third daughter, Sybil, married Robert FitzHaimon. The sheer range of this opportunist strategy, from Maine southwards toward Poitou, and including both Wales and Ireland, is striking. Not every marriage brought territorial gains on the scale of Roger's own marriage, but Robert succeeded to the county of Ponthieu, whilst Arnulf's marriage, to a king's daughter, was possibly the most prestigious of all.

Other families in eleventh-century Normandy had similarly far-flung interests. The Grandmesnil family is one about which we are well informed thanks to Orderic Vitalis. Hugh de Grandmesnil, son of Hawise, daughter of Giroie, and of Robert of Grandmesnil, married a daughter of Ivo of Beaumont-sur-Oise and they had five sons and five daughters. Robert, the eldest, did not hold land in England. He married first a daughter of Ranulf of Bayeux, earl of Chester, secondly a daughter of Robert de Stuteville, and thirdly a daughter of Savaric son of Cana, from Maine. William de Grandmesnil married a daughter of Robert Guiscard, and Ivo married a daughter of Gilbert de Gant; Hugh died young, and Aubrey is

---

[80] For Louis VI's campaigns against Hugh of Le Puiset, son of Everard, see Sugar, *Life of Louis the Fat* (trans. Cusimano and Moorhead), pp. 84–90.

not mentioned as having a wife. Of the daughters, Adelina married Roger d'Ivry, Rohais married Robert de Courcy, Matilda married Hugh de Montpinçon, and Agnes married William de Sai, none of whom are themselves known to have had land in England, though their families did so at a later date. Hawise died unmarried.[81]

The Beaumonts also pursued marriage alliances outside Normandy. Roger de Beaumont married Adeline, daughter of the count of Meulan, his eldest son Robert married Isabel of Vermandois, and his younger son Henry married Margaret of Perche. Hugh earl of Chester and Gilbert FitzRichard both married daughters of Hugh count of Clermont-en-Beauvaisis. Like the marriage of Hugh de Grandmesnil to a daughter of Ivo de Beaumont-sur-Oise, these marriages showed the Normans' interest in the lands to the east of the river Epte, and also, in the case of the counts of Clermont, into a family descended from Charlemagne. The marriages of Hugh and Gilbert probably took place in Rufus's reign. Gilbert did not succeed to his father's estates until about 1088.[82] Hugh's son Richard was a minor at the time of his death, and Hugh's charters to St Evroul and Abingdon (dated respectively 1071/81 and 1089/90) do not mention his wife, but the charter of foundation of Chester abbey, not a contemporary text though purporting to date from 1093, does mention Countess Ermentrude.[83] Such marriages were a feature of the late eleventh century and of the greatest of the Anglo-Norman families, those which had large estates in Normandy as well as having received vast wealth in England. Fewer examples can be found in the first half of the twelfth century as families tended to split into Norman or English branches. This is not to say that the marriage strategies of individual families, particularly those in which strong cross-Channel ties persisted, did not involve marrying into Norman as well as Anglo-Norman families. The Beaumonts again provide one example; others are the Stutevilles and the Tancarvilles. But where the continental estates were few or had passed to cousins, the preference among the greater lords was to marry into other families settled in England.

In terms of rank the most prestigious brides of all were those of royal descent. The first wife of Eustace II count of Boulogne, who took part in the 1066 expedition, was Goda, a sister of King Edward the Confessor; his

[81] OV, IV, 230.    [82] CP, III, 243; Gesta Normannorum Ducum (ed. Van Houts), II, 270–1.
[83] Chester Charters, nos. 1–3.

second was Ida of Lorraine. Eustace III married Mary of Scotland, a daughter of Malcolm and Margaret. Count Alan the Red, lord of Richmond, wanted to marry Edith-Matilda, daughter of Malcolm and Margaret of Scotland. She united blood from the Anglo-Saxon and Scottish royal houses, but William Rufus refused to countenance the match which would have established a potentially dangerous alliance.[84] William of Warenne was another unsuccessful contender for Edith's hand in marriage; subsequently there was a scheme, also unsuccessful, for him to marry a daughter of Henry I.[85] It was not until 1118 that he was married, to Isabel de Vermandois, widow of Robert count of Meulan, daughter of the count of Vermandois and a descendant of Charlemagne.[86]

A marriage tie with the new ruling dynasty of Normandy and England was also highly sought after, as we have already seen in connection with the descendants of Duchess Gunnor. One of the Conqueror's daughters married Alan the Red, count of Brittany, and another married Stephen count of Blois. Henry I used the marriages of his daughters to extend his influence in Normandy and its southern marches. One daughter married Matthew of Montmorency, a second, Eustace of Breteuil, a third, Rotrou count of Perche, a fourth, William Gouet of Montmirail, a fifth, Roscelin of Beaumont-le-Vicomte in Maine, and a sixth, Conan III of Brittany.[87] Yet marriage to such highly born women was the purview only of the most distinguished families, the super-magnates, and was more common in the late eleventh century than subsequently. Again the tendency, increasingly obvious as time went on, was to arrange marriage with other families settled in England. The lower down the hierarchy of wealth and the more remote the region, the greater was the likelihood that a Norman bachelor would marry the girl next door.

It has been suggested that, in the first generation particularly, Normans may have married English women as a way of helping to legitimize their position.[88] Documented cases are few, though it is likely that they were not uncommon especially in the middling and lower ranks of the aristocracy and in northern England where Normans were thinner on the

---

[84] Barlow, *William Rufus*, pp. 310–14, and see below, p. 383.

[85] Anselm, Ep. 424, *S. Anselmi Opera Omnia*, ed. F. S. Schmitt, 6 vols., reprint (Edinburgh, 1946–61), V, 369–70.     [86] *Gesta Normannorum Ducum* (ed. Van Houts), II, 278–9.

[87] C. W. Hollister and T. K. Keefe, 'The Making of the Angevin Empire', *Monarchy, Magnates and Institutions*, p. 251.     [88] Searle, 'Women and the Legitimisation of Succession at the Norman Conquest'.

ground. By contrast very few men of native stock were permitted to marry Norman brides, at least in the early days after the Conquest. According to Orderic, Earl Edwin was estranged from the Conqueror in 1068 because the promised marriage to the king's daughter had not materialized.[89]

When a man had several daughters, it was not unknown – and may have been more common than we know – for at least one to marry into a tenant family. Such marriages brought no prestige, but they did have the useful function of strengthening links with tenant families. One of the sisters of Gilbert de Gant earl of Lincoln married William FitzWalter of Well, who in 1166 owed six knights' fees of the Gant honour.[90]

A few of the new men of Rufus and Henry I married women from high-ranking families, but cases of wide disparity of birth, such as the marriage of Geoffrey II de Clinton to Agnes, the earl of Warwick's daughter, were uncommon. The men who served as justices and sheriffs and were drawn from the middling or lower ranks of the aristocracy did not marry into top-ranking families. This is a point worth emphasizing because contemporaries were well aware of the role of marriage in enabling men to rise socially.

## Family relationships

Finally we turn to personal relationships within the family.[91] Here we have relatively little to go on: the private life of the aristocracy on the whole remains private.[92] Chroniclers, first of all, tend only to comment on family relationships when they are germane to the subject in hand. Secondly, there are the portrayals of relationships in literary sources, which, though fictional, were presumably designed to strike a chord with their audience. Finally, there are charters of donation to the church which sometimes contain requests for the souls not only for 'all our predecessors and successors' but those closest to the donor, usually his wife and children. These also await systematic study by historians of the family, and

---

[89] OV, II, 214, 216.     [90] RBE, I, 383; Rotuli de Dominabus, p. 9.

[91] A useful survey of the early twelfth-century evidence is to be found in Newman, Anglo-Norman Nobility in the Reign of Henry I, chapter two.

[92] See, however, A History of Private Life, ed. P. Ariès and G. Duby, II. Revelations of the Medieval World, ed. G. Duby, translated A. Goldhammer (Cambridge, Mass., and London, 1988), especially chapter two, 'The Aristocratic Households of Feudal France' by G. Duby and D. Barthélemy; and D. Herlihy, 'Family', Women, Family and Society in Medieval Europe, pp. 113–34.

only then will we know whether they reflect the concerns of the donor or possibly of the beneficiary of the gifts recorded.

So far as relations between husbands and wives are concerned, chroniclers certainly recognized the benefits of a happy marriage. Orderic Vitalis, for instance, describes the marriages of Walter of Auffay and Avice and of Ansold of Maule and Odeline, though in neither case, it must be said, was a rounded portrait drawn. Avice is praised chiefly for her devotion to good works; Odeline is said to have been married whilst young and unformed, and was schooled by her husband.[93] Arranged marriages did not preclude affection, of course, and Orderic's tale of Bricstan, accused unjustly of concealing the king's money, suggests he had a devoted wife who was prepared to suffer the ordeal by hot iron to back up her husband's word.[94] It has been suggested that the romantic literature of the twelfth century actually reflected a greater degree of romantic attachment between husband and wife than had existed hitherto because the new theology of marriage emphasized the binding character of marriage. A bond which was intended to last thus required a higher level of commitment and emotional engagement than before.[95]

References to marital difficulties occur occasionally, though this was not a topic to which monastic chroniclers were prepared to devote much space. Robert count of Mortain was said to have ill treated one of his wives and to have been brought to repentance for it by Vitalis of Mortain.[96] Nigel d'Aubigny married as his first wife Matilda de Laigle, the divorced wife of Robert de Mowbray, and was said to have so ill treated her as to arouse the wrath of her relatives. After the death of her brother, Gilbert de L'Aigle, Nigel divorced her on the grounds of consanguinity, and married Gundrada de Gournay instead.[97] Orderic is also the source of a comment about Robert de Bellême's cruelty to his wife, Agnes de Ponthieu.[98] Some wives may have given as good as they got. In this context the reference to the Countess Judith informing her uncle, King William, about the treachery of her husband Waltheof is worth noting.[99] Partners engaged in sexual

---

[93] M. Chibnall, 'Women in Orderic Vitalis', *Haskins Society Journal*, 2 (1990), 118; OV, III, 256–8; 180–2.

[94] OV, III, 352.     [95] Gillingham, 'Love, Marriage and Politics'.

[96] 'Vita Beati Vitalis', ed. E. P. Sauvage, *Analecta Bollandiana*, 1 (1882), 363.     [97] OV, IV, 282–4.

[98] *Ibid.*, IV, 300.

[99] *Ibid.*, II, 320. There does not seem to be any contemporary verification of the idea that Elstow nunnery was founded as an act of reparation, though this is not impossible: see Thompson, *Women Religious*, p. 167.

activity outside marriage, and illegitimate children crop up in the sources from time to time. We have no means of knowing how many were the result of liaisons which occurred before marriage, which for many had to be delayed literally until the right girl came along. Henry I's known mistresses included women of aristocratic birth such as Sybil Corbet, an unnamed member of the Gant family, Edith daughter of Forne (son of Sigulf, and himself a middling northern lord of native stock), and the Welshwoman Nest.[100] Occasionally we hear in written sources of adultery. At the time of the death of her husband, Robert count of Meulan, Isabel de Vermandois was said to have been having an affair with William de Warenne, whom she subsequently married.[101]

Marriages were likely to last for only a short period before being terminated by the death of one or other of the parties, and there was often a substantial discrepancy between the age of the partners. Men might well have to postpone marriage until they were in a position to support a wife; girls on the other hand were betrothed and married as children. Henry I was still unmarried at the time of his unexpected accession to the English throne at the age of just over thirty. His son was betrothed but not married at the time he died in the wreck of the White Ship, whereas his daughter Matilda (born in 1102) was dispatched to Germany at the age of eight for a formal betrothal, and was formally married in January 1114 just before her twelfth birthday. If women were able to survive childbirth, they might well outlive two or more husbands and die at a ripe old age: Matilda, for instance, did not die until 1167.

We know very little about the relationship between parents and children. The birth of an heir must have been an occasion for great rejoicing, and might well be marked by a gift to the church (see below, p. 423), though there was always the fear of infant mortality. Avice the wife of Walter of Auffay mentioned above had twelve children in fifteen years of marriage, most of whom died prematurely in infancy. If the heir did grow to manhood, problems could arise of the kind that bedevilled relations between the Conqueror and his eldest son Robert. Tensions were unsurprising: Robert was an adult, yet had no resources of his own to reward his followers, the members of his *familia*, and when he asked to be put in possession of Normandy, to which he was the designated heir, his father

---

[100] *CP*, xi, Appendix D.      [101] HH, p. 306.

refused.[102] The quarrel was patched up for a time, but broke out again in about 1079. Robert went into exile where his mother sent him money. When this was discovered by her irate husband, she was said by Orderic to have pleaded her affection for her first-born child and claimed that if he were dead she would give her own life if it would bring him back to life.[103]

Despite her attempts to mediate, William and Robert were not reconciled. Their difficult relationship can be paralleled in the twelfth century in the quarrels between Henry II and his sons, especially Richard. On the other hand Henry I doted on his heir, William.[104] His sorrow at the death of William and his half-sister in the wreck of the White Ship was the outcome of what was both a personal and a political tragedy. Stephen, too, was deeply moved by the deaths of his wife and eldest son. Some fathers may have had surprisingly little knowledge of their sons, if they themselves were frequently absent or their sons had been dispatched to other noble households for rearing while still relatively young. Thus, for instance, Simon III de Senlis seems to have spent some time in the household of Robert earl of Leicester, and the young William Marshal was sent to the household of his kinsman, the lord of Tancarville.[105]

If we hear little about the relationship between parents and sons, we hear even less about that between parents and daughters. They too may not have spent many years in the parental household. Agnes, daughter of Henry of Essex, was betrothed at the age of three to Geoffrey de Vere, brother of Aubrey earl of Oxford, spent three years in Aubrey's household, and then moved to that of her future husband. In 1162 or 1163, in a change of plan, the earl himself was betrothed to her, but soon afterwards her father was disgraced and the earl tried to renege. Eventually after lengthy legal proceedings the marriage was consummated, but in this context what concerns us is the period Agnes spent as a child in the households of Geoffrey and Aubrey.[106]

When widowed, women had their dower lands or bride-portions to support them until they remarried or, in a few cases, entered a religious house. Orderic noted approvingly that Ansold of Maule provided a home for his widowed mother in her husband's chamber for fifteen years, and a possible inference from this comment is that it was out of the ordinary for

[102] OV, III, 98–114.     [103] OV, III, 103–5.     [104] WM, De Gestis Regum Anglorum, II, 496.
[105] Crouch, Beaumont Twins, p. 84; Histoire de Guillaume le Maréchal (ed. Meyer), I, ll. 744–9.
[106] Brooke, Medieval Idea of Marriage, pp. 152–7.

a lengthy period of widowhood to be spent in what was now the heir's residence.[107] It will be suggested in the next chapter that long periods of widowhood were in themselves highly unusual.

Given the short duration of many marriages, step-relationships must have been very common, and fear of the evil designs of a second husband on the lands of his stepchildren led to children being removed from the custody of their mothers to that of their lords, who were held to have a more detached view of the interests of the children of their dead vassals. In 1100 Henry I laid it down that guardianship was to be given to the widow or someone else close to her, whichever was more just.[108] Simon II de Senlis was a minor at the time of his father's death and became the ward first of his stepfather David of Scotland until the latter became king of Scotland and then of his great-uncle, Stephen of Aumale.[109] In the 1130 pipe roll guardianship was in some cases accounted for by widows, in other cases by second husbands.[110] By the later twelfth century, however, seigneurial guardianship had become the norm.

We know all too little about personal relationships in aristocratic families in Norman England. One obvious contrast with those of late twentieth-century western societies is that in the middle ages illness or death was likely to end familial relationships after a relatively short space of time. These men and women did not need to be reminded that earthly joys were transitory. Relationships were also regulated much more by considerations of family and politics: which son or daughter could marry and the selection of partners were all thought about carefully and by the family as a whole. Freedom of personal choice was not an option. Kinship and marriage were both of crucial importance in the ordering of aristocratic society. Kinship constituted the basis of a solidarity able to protect and support its members and of a framework determining the transmission of land. The shift in emphasis towards lineage and primogeniture, in progress at the time of the Norman Conquest, had profound effects in increasing the importance of elder sons. It also made marriage strategies very complicated, in that calculations about successors were so easily overturned by mortality or lack of heirs. How many sons were enough to provide for the succession, and how many would constitute a strain on a

---

[107] OV, III, 180.    [108] Stubbs, *Select Charters*, p. 118.

[109] 'Vita et Passio Waldevi Comitis', *Vitae Quorumdum Anglo-Saxonum* (ed. Giles), p. 20.

[110] Green, *Government of England*, p. 85.

family's resources of land? The often-cited example here is that of Tancred de Hauteville who had twelve sons and several daughters. One son received the patrimony and the rest were advised to seek their living.[111] The male line in many families failed, however, and this raised the prospect of female succession. The marriage of daughters was thus crucially important, as we shall see in the following chapter.

[111] OV, II, 100.

# 11    Brides of men and brides of Christ[1]

The period between the mid-eleventh and the mid-twelfth centuries was of crucial importance in the history of Western women.[2] Changing views about land, power, and succession meant that as wives and heiresses women of high birth are conspicuous.[3] On occasion wives deputized for their husbands, and in rare circumstances they exercised power directly, as in the cases of Urraca queen of Castile and Melisende queen of Jerusalem.[4] Women even went to war, as in the cases of Sybil Bordet who defended Tarragona in Spain for a year and Isabel de Conches who went on campaign, both described by Orderic Vitalis.[5] At the same time, developments in theology and the church profoundly affected the way women were regarded. The cult of the Virgin presented an idealized view of womanhood and maternity, and a new view of marriage was advanced which stressed its nature as a sacramental and thus indissoluble union.[6] In the new literature of courtly love a different perspective on women emerges: women with the power to bestow or withhold affection.[7] Queens and noble ladies were prominent as patrons of the new literature.[8] As

---

[1] The material in this chapter formed the subject of papers delivered at Sheffield, Oxford, and Birmingham universities, and at the 1995 conference at La Bretesche in Brittany, published in *Anglo-Norman Political Culture and the Twelfth-Century Renaissance*, ed. C. Warren Hollister (Woodbridge, forthcoming), pp. 59–82. My thanks to all who offered comments and references on those occasions, and to Sir James Holt and Professor Pauline Stafford for reading and commenting on earlier drafts.

[2] For recent work on the subject see *A History of Women in the West. II. The Silences of the Middle Ages*, ed. C. Klapisch-Zuber (Cambridge, Mass., and London, 1992).

[3] J. Martindale, 'Succession and Politics in the Romance-speaking World, c. 1000–1140', *England and her Neighbours 1066–1453*, ed. M. Jones and M. Vale (London, 1989), pp. 19–41; for women and land see D. Herlihy, 'Land, Family and Women in Continental Europe, 701–1200', *Traditio*, 18 (1962), 89–120; and R. Hadju, 'The Position of Noblewomen in the Pays de Coutumes, 1100–1300', *Journal of Family History*, 5 (1980), 122–44.

[4] B. Hamilton, 'Women in the Crusader States: the Queens of Jerusalem', in *Medieval Women*, ed. D. Baker, Studies in Church History, Subsidia I (1978), pp. 148–57.

[5] Chibnall, 'Women in Orderic Vitalis'.

[6] Duby, *Medieval Marriage*; Duby, *The Knight, the Lady and the Priest. The Making of Modern Marriage in Medieval France*, trans. B. Bray (London, 1984); Duby, *Love and Marriage in the Middle Ages*, trans. J. Dunnett (Oxford, 1994).

[7] G. Duby, 'The Courtly Model', *History of Women in the West. II. The Silences of the Middle Ages* (ed. Klapisch-Zuber), pp. 250–66.

[8] M. D. Legge, 'L'influence littéraire de la cour d'Henri Beauclerc', *Mélanges offerts à Rita Lejeune* (Gembloux, 1969), pp. 682–3.

more is heard of women in the secular world, they were also prominent in
responding to the call to follow a life dedicated to Christ. The great wave
of evangelical fervour that swept through eleventh- and twelfth-century
Europe led many of both sexes to follow a life of evangelical poverty by
renouncing the world.

More is certainly heard about women than before, but this may be in
part a reflection of the greater documentation available, and it is by no
means clear whether their situation, or at least that of those royal and
aristocratic women on whose lives the surviving texts impinge, was in
general improving or deteriorating.[9] On the one hand, it has been argued
that feudal societies which stressed primogeniture amongst males tended
to downgrade the position of daughters, and their freedom to dispose of
such land as they were provided with was more strictly controlled.[10] On
the other hand, women could and did inherit land, and their prominence
as heiresses and widows is highly visible. The cult of the Virgin can be
interpreted as exalting women, but only in their role as mother. The
church's laws on marriage can also be seen as either protecting women,
or at least wives, or further subjecting them to rules devised by men. And
whilst there is no doubt that many religious houses for women were
founded, they were relatively poorly endowed, and women's religious
vocations were being organized and, to some extent, placed under male
control. Although the evidence presents problems of interpretation,
then, the question of the status of aristocratic women at this time is nevertheless important, and two aspects which are relatively well documented are the provision of land for them, and the foundation of
religious houses.

Despite a burgeoning literature on women's history, until recently relatively little had been written specifically about women in Norman
England. The second chapter of Lady Stenton's *English Woman in History*
had a few pages on women after the Conquest;[11] Victoria Chandler published an article on three great ladies, and Ragena DeAragon on marriage

---

[9] P. L'Hermite-Leclercq, 'The Feudal Order', *History of Women in the West. II. The Silences of the Middle Ages*
(ed. Klapisch-Zuber), pp. 202–3.

[10] For a clear summary of the reasons why the position of women might be thought to have deteriorated
in the middle ages see, for example, D. Herlihy, 'Did Women have a Renaissance?: a Reconsideration',
*Medievalia et Humanistica*, 13 (1985), 1–22, reprinted in *Women, Family and Society in Medieval Europe*
(Providence and London, 1995).

[11] D. M. Stenton, *The English Woman in History* (London and New York, 1957).

strategies;[12] and Pauline Stafford has discussed the questions of whether there was a golden age for women before 1066 and if the year 1066 was in any sense a turning point in the history of women.[13] On the subject of women and land the most important discussions are those by Sir James Holt, one of whose lectures to the Royal Historical Society was entitled 'The Heiress and the Alien', and S. F. C. Milsom's paper 'Inheritance by Women in the Twelfth and Early Thirteenth Centuries'.[14] On women religious, there are now two volumes by Sharon K. Elkins and Sally Thompson and a short survey of the Yorkshire nunneries by Janet Burton.[15]

Marriage or religion were usually the only options for aristocratic women in this period. If they married they were usually provided with land (as well, probably, as other forms of wealth), and it is in connection with their land that they crop up in charters. If they entered religion, they might well carry an endowment of land to the nunnery. The choice had to be determined as part of a family's strategy. Daughters were key pawns on the chess board, but marriage portions were a drain on family lands and the same considerations which were limiting the opportunities for sons to marry might also restrict the marriage prospects of daughters, especially in families of limited resources. Clearly the proliferation of nunneries in the twelfth century is primarily to be explained in religious terms: the desire of women to embrace a life of Christian endeavour, and in far greater numbers than could be provided for in existing houses. Women could have been prevented from entering religion, but their families were now permitting and even subsidizing them to do so. It is possible, though unprovable, that relatively more daughters than sons were being born into aristocratic families. Another possibility is that in those regions of England where new land was being taken into cultivation, families could

---

[12] V. Chandler, 'Intimations of Authority: Notes on Three Anglo-Norman Countesses', *Indiana Social Studies Quarterly*, 31 (1978), 5–17; R. DeAragon, 'In Pursuit of Aristocratic Women: a Key to Success in Norman England', *Albion*, 14 (1982), 258–67; DeAragon, 'Dowager Countesses, 1069–1230', *Anglo-Norman Studies*, 17 (1994), 87–100.

[13] P. Stafford, 'Women and the Norman Conquest', *Transactions of the Royal Historical Society*, 6th series, 4 (1994), 221–49. I am very grateful to Professor Stafford for sending me a copy of her paper in advance of publication and for commenting on an earlier version of the material in this chapter.

[14] Holt, 'Feudal Society and the Family in Early Medieval England: IV. The Heiress and the Alien'; S. F. C. Milsom, 'Inheritance by Women in the Twelfth and Early Thirteenth Centuries', *On the Laws and Customs of England. Essays in Honour of S. E. Thorne*, ed. M. S. Arnold, T. A. Green, S. A. Scully, and S. D. White (Chapel Hill, 1981), pp. 60–89.

[15] Elkins, *Holy Women of Twelfth-Century England*; Thompson, *Women Religious*; J. Burton, *The Yorkshire Nunneries in the Twelfth and Thirteenth Centuries*, Borthwick Paper no. 56 (York, 1979).

afford to allow women to enter the church. This might fit the situation in Yorkshire, for instance.[16]

## Land and marriage

The strengthening of inheritance, a slow transition from expectation to custom and eventually to right, and the narrowing of succession within families to downgrade collateral succession and strengthen lineage, had repercussions for the position of daughters. On the one hand, it is thought to have restricted the provision of land in the form of dowries for them, to conserve the patrimony for the eldest son. On the other, daughters had to be taken account of as potential heiresses if, as was not unlikely, there were no surviving sons. Nevertheless the whole issue of female succession was problematic and likely to be contested, and there were several issues to be resolved. Was one daughter to scoop the pool, or should she share equally with her sisters, married and unmarried at the time of their father's death? Were claims to offices, castles, and titles heritable by women? As Sir James Holt wrote two decades ago, it was not just a question of 'inheritance by whom?' but 'inheritance of what?'[17]

The evidence dealing with women and land falls into two broad categories: statements about existing or future practice such as the Charter of Liberties of Henry I and Glanvill; and contemporary charters, many of which remain unpublished. The principal problem of interpretation presented by charters is that of family reconstruction: in all too many cases we simply do not know how many marriages an individual contracted and how many children, especially female, these unions produced. There is a danger of trying to juggle the surviving pieces of the jigsaw to fit what is thought to have been custom, when an alternative explanation is that custom was less strictly defined than has been suggested. Hence Henry I was able to massage the marriage market using wealthy heiresses and widows for his own men on a scale that had not been possible before, and was not attempted in the later twelfth century. One development which has been identified as a key turning point in the final years of Henry I's reign, a shift from making one daughter sole heiress to dividing lands equally between all sisters when there were no surviving brothers, was

---

[16] Thomas, *Vassals. Heiresses, Crusaders, and Thugs*, pp. 119–30.    [17] Holt, 'Politics and Property', p. 25.

not as clear-cut and decisive as was suggested by Holt.[18] In other words, there were probably no hard and fast rules relating to female succession during the century following the Conquest.

According to custom a daughter could expect to be provided by her father with land as part of her marriage portion, though in circumstances where fathers did not wish to make inroads into family lands, valuables and property were given instead. By the early thirteenth century in Normandy, fathers were not to give away more than a third of their lands as marriage portions even if they wanted to.[19] Numerous daughters and limited resources were a constraint on generosity; another was the danger of establishing a little-known son-in-law in too large a share of one's lands. For although the marriage portion was intended to provide for the wife, in practice it passed into the husband's control. The corollary to the provision made for a bride by her family was the right she acquired in her husband's lands. Her husband could assign specific estates as dower at the time of the marriage; if he did not, what was her position? By the time *Glanvill* was written, after a husband's death a widow could claim from the heir up to a third of the husband's estates at the time of the marriage; but it is not known if this was the case in the Norman period.[20] Assigned dower, which is the subject of charter references, was usually much smaller than one-third of the whole. Widows who outlived their husbands kept their dower; in the early part of our period they also retained their marriage portions even if childless, although by the later twelfth century in such circumstances the marriage portions returned to their families.

Custom was a set of norms which were at once conservative and responsive to social change and political circumstances. Women were, as they always had been, counters to be used in political bargains, concluding alliances, and ending hostilities, but their importance in the transmission of claims to land was also growing, and custom evolved to accommodate this. In Norman England the power of the crown to intervene in the affairs of great families was marked, and its need to do so was heightened by the finite stock of land at its disposal for patronage. Rights over women figured prominently in the Charter of Liberties issued by Henry I in 1100 and were obviously a sensitive political issue at the time. Henry wished to be consulted over the marriages of all the female relatives of tenants-in-

---

[18] Holt, 'Heiress and the Alien'.

[19] *Coutumiers de Normandie*, ed. E. J. Tardif, 2 vols. (Rouen and Paris, 1903, 1896), I, 84.    [20] *Glanvill*, VI, 1.

chief and, as we have seen, promised not to prohibit them unless they were to an enemy of his; he promised to arrange the marriage of heiresses only after taking advice; to allow childless widows their dowers and marriage portions and not to marry them against their wills; and to grant the guardianship of under-age children to widows or next-of-kin, whichever was more appropriate.[21] Control of the marriage market was crucial to Henry's patronage as a means of preventing alliances between his enemies. By allowing childless widows to keep their marriage portions in addition to their dowers he made them an even more lucrative proposition than they would be later when marriage portions were returned to their paternal family. By using other people's daughters as heiresses he was able to reward his own men without further diminishing his own resources.

Royal control began to break down under Stephen. Some marriages were clearly negotiated without any reference to the king. Some of these have already been noted in the context of political events; here the emphasis is on the challenge to the king's rights of patronage. The marriage of William FitzDuncan, nephew of King David, to Alice de Rumilly, sister of Ranulf Meschin, which probably occurred between 1135 and 1140, gave William the lordships of Skipton in Yorkshire and Copeland in Cumbria, and thus helped to strengthen David's influence in northern England at a critical juncture.[22] David took control of Cumbria in 1136. William FitzDuncan is known to have been fighting at Clitheroe in 1138.[23] Within a short time William also succeeded his cousin Alan as lord of Papcastle in Cumbria, and thus became a force to be reckoned with in north-west England.[24] In 1140 Reginald, an illegitimate son of Henry I, married the daughter of William FitzRichard, the most powerful man in Cornwall, and was able to install himself in Cornwall. Equally as striking were the marriages arranged at the behest of Ranulf II earl of Chester. Two of these, the marriages of Hugh Wake and William II Peverel of Nottingham, have been discussed above (pp. 215, 314–15). In addition Gilbert de Gant, whom Ranulf captured at the battle of Lincoln, married Ranulf's niece, and her sister married a leading Gant tenant. Gilbert de Gant's own sister married Roger de Mowbray.[25] Finally, Nicholas of

---

[21] Stubbs, *Select Charters*, p. 118.　　[22] *Early Yorkshire Charters*, VII, 7.

[23] John of Hexham in SD, *Opera omnia*, II, 291; Dalton, *Conquest, Anarchy and Lordship*, pp. 211–18.

[24] Sanders, *English Baronies*, p. 134.　　[25] Abbott, 'Gant Family', pp. 38–9; *Mowbray Charters*, p. xxvii.

Stafford, a leading landholder in Staffordshire, another county where Ranulf had substantial estates, is said to have married a daughter of the earl of Chester.[26] It is likely that some if not all of these marriages were arranged without reference to, or the permission of, the king.

Marriage portions frequently consisted of just one or two manors, a small and preferably remote fraction of a family's wealth. There was no compulsion to treat all daughters equally, and much must have depended on the attractions of the parties to a marriage. Sir Charles Clay traced the marriage portions of the daughters of Count Stephen, lord of Richmond. Maud, who married Walter de Gant, was given four knights' fees in Swaledale; Tiffany, who married William de Tancarville, chamberlain of Normandy, received land at Coleby in Lincolnshire; and Olive, a third daughter, land at Long Benington in Lincolnshire.[27]

It was also a good idea to recycle the same piece of land as a marriage portion in successive generations. One example can be seen in a group of three early twelfth-century charters dealing with the marriages of a daughter and granddaughter of Walter of Gloucester, printed by Round in *Ancient Charters*.[28] Walter of Gloucester was granted Ullingswick and Little Hereford by the bishop of Hereford; Walter in turn used Ullingswick as the marriage portion of his daughter Maud, making the grant in free marriage. Little Hereford meanwhile was assigned in dower to his son's wife. Ullingswick was then used as a marriage portion for the daughter of Maud, who received another manor in exchange; and Maud's daughter finally granted it to St Peter's abbey, Gloucester in the mid-twelfth century. Marriage portions could be granted either with such obligations of knight service as lay upon the land or without; the latter clearly constituted a more generous grant.[29]

Dower was supposed to be assigned by husband to wife at the church door, at the time of the religious ceremony which the church was emphasizing as an essential component of a legitimate marriage.[30] An early reference to dower assigned at the church door occurs in a charter of William de Yspania to his wife Lucy of Willingale Spain, granting one knight's fee and a sokeman. The grant was 'made before the threshold of

---

[26] *CP*, XII, 1, 168 n.    [27] *Early Yorkshire Charters*, IV, 89.    [28] *Ancient Charters*, pp. 20–1.

[29] *Glanvill*, VII, 18.

[30] C. J. Moule, 'Entry into Marriage in the Late Eleventh and Twelfth Centuries *c.* 1090–1181', Cambridge PhD thesis, 1983.

the church door of St Mary at Shelford in Cambridgeshire when he married her'. The charter cannot be dated precisely, but William was living in the time of Count Alan of Richmond who died in 1146.[31]

It would seem to have been likely that husbands *did* assign dower, as assigned dower was generally less than the one-third share which the widow could later claim in common law. There was a potential disincentive to assignment if husbands were to lose control of dower land, but it is not clear that they did.[32] Husbands were supposed to ask their wives' permission to alienate dower land, but by the time *Glanvill* was written, women could not effectively withhold their consent.[33] Moreover there was the question of a widow's right to dower in any acquisitions which had been made in the course of the marriage. According to the *Leges Henrici Primi* a widow could claim a third of acquisitions, but *Glanvill* stated that if nothing had been said about acquisitions at the time of the marriage, the widow could not claim dower therein later.[34]

There is very little evidence to indicate what happened if dower was not assigned, specifically if a widow was able to secure as much as one-third of her husband's land. A possible instance of dower as a third share in the Norman period is provided by the descent of the lands held by Ivo Taillebois in 1086, one-third of which, twenty knights' fees, was held by the earl of Chester in 1166, and which, it may be suggested, was the share belonging to his grandmother, Countess Lucy. Two-thirds, forty fees, passed to William II de Roumare, Lucy's great-grandson by her second marriage.[35] The facts relating to the marriages and lands of Countess Lucy have been discussed on several occasions but the possibility that this is a case of a widow's third (possibly the earliest so far identified in the Norman period) has not been raised before.

---

[31] London, British Library, Additional Charter 28,347.

[32] See the discussions on this point by J. Senerowitz Loengard, '"Of the Gift of her Husband": English Dower and its Consequences in the Year 1200', *Women of the Medieval World. Essays in Honor of John H. Mundy*, ed. J. Kirshner and S. F. Wemple (Oxford, 1985), pp. 221–5; J. Biancalana, 'Widows at Common Law: the Development of Common Law Dower', *Irish Jurist*, new series, 33 (1988), 255–329, at p. 269.

[33] *Glanvill*, VI, 3; Emily Zack Tabuteau noted two cases in eleventh-century Normandy where wives successfully recovered dower land alienated by their deceased husbands against their will: *Transfers of Property in Eleventh-Century Norman Law*, p. 176.

[34] *Leges Henrici Primi*, 70, 22; *Glanvill*, VI, 2; Biancalana, 'Widows at Common Law', pp. 270–80.

[35] For the parentage of Lucy see *CP*, VII, Appendix J; the evidence has recently been reappraised by K. S. B. Keats-Rohan in 'Antecessor Noster: the Parentage of Countess Lucy made Plain', *Prosopon*, Newsletter of the Unit for Prosopographical Research, Linacre College Oxford, no. 2 (May 1995, not paginated).

Countess Lucy had married her first husband Ivo Taillebois (who may have been married before) before 1086.[36] After his death Lucy married Roger FitzGerold, who evidently held Ivo's lands, and by whom she had a son, William de Roumare. Roger died in about 1097 when his son was very young, and Lucy married, thirdly, Ranulf Meschin (Ranulf I earl of Chester), by whom she also had a son, Ranulf II. Ranulf I held all Ivo's lands, presumably during the minority of William de Roumare and, according to Orderic, handed them over to the king on becoming earl of Chester. William, who by this time was an adult, not surprisingly rebelled at this cavalier treatment, and the king was persuaded to restore most of his mother's lands.[37] This portion seems to have constituted two-thirds of the whole honour of Bolingbroke, as it came to be called, and was assessed at forty knights' fees. In 1165 the share of the honour in the possession of the then earl of Chester was assessed at twenty fees. These perhaps represented his grandmother's dower, used by her to endow her younger son by a third marriage.[38]

There are cases where the claim of childless widows to a share in their deceased husbands' lands was greater than one-third. One example occurs in an entry in the 1130 pipe roll where William Maltravers made a proffer to hold the land of Hugh de Laval for fifteen years, plus the dower and marriage portion of his widow after that; so by marrying the widow he acquired all her late husband's honour for the time being, and presumably hoped to have a son who would inherit. This was a special case, however, in that Hugh de Laval had been granted Pontefract by Henry I after the previous lord Robert de Lacy had lost his land for disloyalty.[39] A slightly different situation was that of the unfortunate Matilda de L'Aigle. She had been married to Robert de Mowbray who had lost his lands for rebellion in 1095. Having been divorced, she was then married to Nigel d'Aubigny who held the Norman lands of her first husband. When Nigel in

[36] *Early Yorkshire Charters*, v, 299; cf. H. C. FitzHerbert, 'An Original Charter of Tailbois and Neville', *Genealogist*, new series, 3 (1886), 31.    [37] OV, VI, 334.

[38] Sanders, *English Baronies*, p. 18 summarizes the evidence. In 1166 William de Roumare accounted for the whole honour: *RBE*, I, 376–8. The reconstruction sketched above must be regarded as tentative because it assumes that the only right Lucy enjoyed in the lands of Ivo Taillebois was first as his wife and then as his widow. Lucy however held land by inheritance, and in 1130 she accounted for £266 13s. 4d. for her *father's* land: *PR 31 Henry I*, p. 110. If her father had held all of the land held by Ivo Taillebois in 1086, then the one-third–two-thirds division was a disposition of her inheritance.

[39] Wightman, *Lucy Family*, p. 68. Another possible case where the second husband held the first husband's lands is that of Roger FitzGerold, mentioned above.

turn divorced Matilda because she was childless, he not only retained Montbrai but named the son of his second marriage Roger de Mowbray.[40]

Marriages in this period were often soon ended by the death of one or other of the partners, divorce being mentioned only rarely. The pressures on widows to remarry by this date were very great, because they took with them to a second or third marriage their marriage portions and dower in their deceased husbands' lands, always providing they did not disgrace themselves by having children outside marriage.[41] Here an important change took place at some point, whereby the marriage portions of childless widows returned to their kin. This was the state of affairs recorded by *Glanvill*, but in 1100 Henry had explicitly promised that widows could keep them. It would appear from the 1130 pipe roll that this was still the case, though for how much longer we do not know.[42] Perhaps it drew on an earlier tradition which allowed that the marriage portion belonged to the bride, and was not, as it were, a loan conditional on the fruitfulness of the marriage. When and how did the change occur? One possibility is that a change in custom was influenced by a contemporary debate among Roman lawyers on this very point.[43]

In 1130 Countess Lucy, whose marriages have just been discussed, had been recently widowed and had evidently decided to set her affairs in order. One of the agreements she made was to prevent her having to take a husband within five years.[44] Turold of Lincoln had given land at Spalding to St Nicholas, Angers before 1079, and, when Lucy made a grant to the priory in about 1135, in her charter the phrase was employed which became characteristic of widows' grants – 'in my free power'. The charter survives only in a later cartulary copy, but if the phrase was employed in the original charter, it is an early instance. On this occasion she made no reference to the consent of her sons, but she did so when she founded a

---

[40] *Mowbray Charters*, pp. xviii–xix.

[41] For Normandy see Tabuteau, *Transfers of Property*, pp. 25, 50; for England see Henry I's Charter of Liberties: Stubbs, *Select Charters*, p. 118.

[42] *Glanvill*, VII, 18. In most of the cases in 1130 where prospective husbands made a proffer for the marriage portions of widows, we cannot be certain that the latter were childless. This does however seem to have been the case for Hugh de Laval's widow, whose marriage was purchased by William Maltravers: Wightman, *Lacy Family*, p. 68; *PR 31 Henry I*, p. 34.

[43] E. Kantorowicz, *Studies in the Glossators of the Roman Law* (Cambridge, 1938), pp. 94–8. Martinus argued that *dos* could be kept if there were children, returned if not, unless in either case agreements had been made to the contrary. Dr C. Wickham kindly drew my attention to this debate.

[44] *PR 31 Henry I*, p. 110.

nunnery, which she probably entered herself, at Stixwould in Lincolnshire.[45] On the latter occasion she wrote to her two surviving sons, notifying them of her grant to the nunnery and asking her 'dearest sons' to uphold her gift because 'it will be most useful to them before the throne of God'.[46] So far as we know, Lucy was not compelled to remarry, and if, as seems likely, Stixwould was her chosen retirement home, we may surmise that she ended her days there.

Lengthy widowhoods were highly unusual. Countess Judith did not remarry after the execution of Waltheof. According to tradition she refused to marry Simon de Senlis, who married her daughter instead.[47] Margaret, wife of Henry I earl of Warwick, was widowed in 1119 and was still living in 1156.[48] Another woman who managed to remain in her widowed state for a surprisingly long period was Gundrada, whose husband, Nigel d'Aubigny, died in 1129, and who remained single until her death in about 1154. Gundrada's marriage portion in Normandy was probably lost when the Angevins moved in, as her son Roger de Mowbray supported King Stephen consistently; but her dower lands in England are mentioned in the Mowbray charters, and she was an attractive proposition for a husband. Instead of remarrying, however, she devoted herself to good works, and became a notable patron of religious houses in Yorkshire. A number of her charters survive. In every case, however, her own charter is paralleled by one from her son, underlining the point that widows did not have freedom to dispose of their dowers without the heir's consent.[49] Perhaps Henry I was in no rush to have Gundrada married off, and her marriage and the guardianship of her young son had not been settled at the time the king left England for what was to be the last time in 1133. Perhaps King Stephen did not want to press the issue, given his need for support. Presumably Roger had no objection since on remarriage Gundrada's dower lands would pass to another, and for personal reasons he may have desired his mother's continuing companionship.

In the case of the widow's claim to guardianship of under-age children,

---

[45] *Chester Charters*, nos. 15, 16; Thompson, *Women Religious*, p. 169.

[46] *Chester Charters*, no. 19, cf. no. 18.

[47] Ingulph, *Chronicle of the Abbey of Croyland*, ed. H. T. Riley (London, 1854), p. 146.

[48] D. Crouch, 'Oddities in the Early History of the Marcher Lordship of Gower, 1107–1166', *Bulletin of the Board of Celtic Studies*, 31 (1984), 133–41.

[49] *Mowbray Charters*, nos. 155, 156, 160, 232, 235, 236, 237, 300, 302, 47, 201. The exception was a gift to St Michael's, Whitby. Roger instead made a gift to Rievaulx: nos. 287, 243, 246, 249.

the period saw a shift to a strict application of the notion of wardship by the lord. Guardianship by the mother was perceived to present dangers in that her second husband might harm his stepchildren. The lord, it was thought, was less closely involved, and had a legitimate interest in protecting the children of his dead vassal.[50] The scanty evidence from eleventh-century Normandy by contrast seems to suggest that at that stage either the widow or the lord might act as guardian.[51] This can be interpreted in one of two ways: possibly there was more scope for providing for children of second marriages so stepfathers were perceived as less of a threat; or at that stage ducal power to regulate guardianship was less strong. There was still some scope for manoeuvre in 1130, as the *Leges Henrici Primi* and entries in the 1130 pipe roll show.[52] Later, however, guardianship, especially of the children of tenants-in-chief, was strictly controlled by the crown.[53]

When we come to the question of a woman's claim to inherit a larger share of the family lands than her marriage portion, we are in less well charted waters, both about the customs the Normans brought with them, and how these were applied in England to tenants-in-chief of the crown. It has been suggested that already by the time the Normans arrived in England the tendency towards lineal succession was gaining ground, and that a distinction was made between patrimony, which passed to one son, often the eldest, and acquisitions, which a father was free to bequeath as he wished. If this is broadly correct so far as males are concerned, it is hard to judge whether there was the same clarity about the position of women.

There is very little evidence about women and the succession to land in Normandy before 1066. The most famous instance of female succession from Duke William's time was that of Mabel to the lordship of Bellême, a lordship of composite origins including lands held of the duke of Normandy, the count of Maine, and the king of France (for this case see above, p. 336). The succession to Bellême after the death in 1027 of William de Bellême, who had at least six sons, is difficult to reconstruct. Ivo, bishop of Sées controlled part, and his brother William Talvas the

---

[50] J. Yver, 'Les caractères originaux de la coutume de Normandie', *Mémoires de l'Académie des Sciences, Arts, et Belles-Lettres de Caen*, new series, 12 (1952) 307–36.

[51] Tabuteau, *Transfers of Property*, p. 61.     [52] Green, *Government of England*, p. 85.

[53] For the thirteenth century see especially S. Waugh, *The Lordship of England. Royal Wardships and Marriages in English Society and Politics 1217–1327* (Princeton, NJ, and London, 1988).

remainder. William's daughter Mabel married a Norman, Roger of Montgomery, and eventually Mabel and Roger succeeded to the whole lordship after Bishop Ivo's death, irrespective of the fact that Mabel had a brother Oliver.[54] Perhaps Oliver's birth was not legitimate, or his claim was passed over, but in either case Mabel was the eventual heiress.

In the situation in post-Conquest England, another factor which has to be taken into account in assessing the role of women in transmitting claims to land was that of intermarriage between the newcomers and the natives. The Normans claimed to be the legitimate successors of Anglo-Saxon thegns by royal grant, yet by marrying English women it might have appeared as though the lands of their new wives' families were being channelled through the women at the expense of their male relatives. One example was the case of Wigod of Wallingford. He was probably the father of Toki who fought for the Conqueror at the battle of Gerberoi; and Alfred and Turold, who occur as minor landholders in Domesday Book, are described as *nepotes* of Wigod.[55] However Wigod's daughter married Robert d'Oilly and their daughter Matilda married Miles Crispin, who in 1086 was holding Wallingford and most of Wigod's lands.[56] When Miles died, his widow Matilda, or more probably a daughter and namesake, married Brian FitzCount, who in turn held the honour of Wallingford. Two charters survive issued by Matilda, Brian's wife, granting the two manors of Ogbourne to the abbey of Bec in Normandy; in the earlier, issued before 1147 she refers to the consent of her husband and says that she holds the manors *ex beneficio et hereditate* of her antecessors; in the later no reference is made to her husband and she says that the land is *de hereditate mea*. Both charters have surviving seals; on one she is styled Matilda the lady of Wallingford.[57] Despite the existence of male relatives, therefore, she (or her mother) had apparently inherited the bulk of Wigod's estates.

One surviving record of a marriage settlement is the royal confirmation in 1121 of the marriage of Miles of Gloucester to Sybil, daughter of

[54] K. Thompson, 'Family and Influence to the South of Normandy in the Eleventh Century: the Lordship of Bellême', *Journal of Medieval History*, 11 (1985), 215–26.

[55] ASC 1079; for Alfred and Turold, see DB, Oxfordshire, 43, and Gloucestershire 27,1; for other estates they may have held, see Williams, 'Vice-Comital Family', p. 290, n. 48.

[56] *Book of Fees*, I, 116; for a recent discussion of this account see K. S. B. Keats-Rohan, 'The Devolution of the Honour of Wallingford, 1066–1148', *Oxoniensia*, 54 (1989), 311–18.

[57] *Select Documents of the English Lands of the Abbey of Bec*, ed. M. Chibnall, Camden Society, 3rd series, LXXIII (1951), 24–5.

Bernard de Neufmarché, a marriage that was a crucial breakthrough in Miles's career. The terminology is suggestive, for the king gave the daughter as if he were making a grant of land (*dedit et firmiter concessisse*), with the land of her father and mother after their death, or before if they wished, with a specified marriage portion in their lifetime and the stipulation that all Bernard's tenants were to do liege homage to Miles. 'All this because of the payment Bernard made to me, and at the request of Bernard, his wife and their barons.' Bernard and his wife thus retained only a life interest in the land.[58] Sybil inherited her father's lands even though she had a brother, Mahel. His claim to inherit was passed over, according to Gerald of Wales writing much later, because his mother claimed untruthfully that he was not legitimate. According to Gerald, she was motivated by a desire for revenge on her son for attacking her lover.[59]

A second case where daughters were conspicuously well provided for is the succession to Roger Bigod, who died in 1107. Roger is thought to have been married twice, once to a woman known only as Adelidis (Adelaide), and then to Adelicia (Alice) de Tosny.[60] William Bigod, who succeeded Roger and died in the wreck of the White Ship, was probably a son of the first marriage.[61] Gunnora, who married Robert of Essex, also seems to have been a child of the first marriage, as she had no share in the Belvoir inheritance which came into the family later.[62] Roger Bigod's second wife Alice de Tosny ultimately inherited her father's honour of Belvoir, and these lands passed to their daughter Cecily, who married William d'Aubigny the Breton.[63] Hugh Bigod, who succeeded William in 1120, is likely to have

---

[58] *Ancient Charters*, pp. 8–10; *RRAN*, ii, no. 1280.

[59] Gerald of Wales, *Itinerarium Kambriae, Opera*, ed. J. S. Brewer, J. F. Dimock, and G. F. Warner, RS (London, 1861–91), vi, 29.     [60] *CP*, ix, 578.

[61] A charter issued by William Bigod for Thetford priory was issued for the souls of his father and his mother Adelidis, which suggests (though it does not prove) that his mother was dead by this time: London, British Library Lansdowne MS 229, f. 148. Alice de Tosny was still living after Stephen's accession: *RRAN*, iii, no. 82. Roger Bigod's charter for Rochester mentioned his wife and children thus: 'ego Rogerus Bigod et Adeliza uxor mea et filii et filie mee.' The witnesses included William 'our son', Humfrey Bigod, and Gunnora and Matilda 'our daughters': London, British Library MS Cotton Domitian A x ff. 199v–200. Gunnora described herself as daughter of Roger Bigod in a charter for Thetford, Dugdale, *Mon. Ang.*, v, 142. Hugh Bigod's charter for Norwich cathedral priory referred to his sister Gunnora: see *CP*, ix, 578. There may have been another sister, for Roger FitzRichard lord of Warkworth was said to have been a nephew of Hugh Bigod: C. T. Clay, 'The Ancestry of the Early Lords of Warkworth', *Archaeologia Aeliana*, 4th series, 32 (1954), 68.     [62] Dugdale, *Mon. Ang.*, v, 142.

[63] Robert de Tosny, Domesday lord of Belvoir, had at least three sons – Berenger, his father's under-tenant and a tenant in chief in 1086, William, and Geoffrey – and two daughters – Alice and Agnes. Berengar did not inherit any of the Belvoir lands and may have been the son of an earlier marriage.

been a son of Alice de Tosny, because although he did not inherit any of the Belvoir lands he did succeed to the lands which his uncle, Berengar de Tosny, had held in Yorkshire in 1086 as an under-tenant of Robert de Tosny, his father.[64] Finally, Matilda, who married William d'Aubigny, the king's butler, and was handsomely provided for with a marriage portion of ten knights' fees, could have been a child of either marriage. Although she did not share in the Belvoir inheritance, her son was created earl of Lincoln by Stephen and, as he did not have any other particular connection with the county, one possibility is that the choice of county reflected his descent from Robert de Tosny.[65] Clearly there are a number of missing pieces of the jigsaw in this complicated story, but the provisions made for Matilda Bigod and her sister or half-sister Cecily look notably generous. Hugh Bigod seems to have been a son of Alice de Tosny, yet his claim to his mother's land was passed over. Indeed, given the inroads into his father's lands and the fact that, unlike his father, he did not hold the shrievalty of Norfolk and Suffolk, Hugh looks like a man with frustrated ambitions.[66] The hope of reward from Stephen may have been one of the reasons why he was prepared to swear that Henry I on his deathbed had recognized Stephen as his successor to the throne.[67]

A third case where a daughter was conspicuously well provided for despite the fact that she had brothers is that of the daughter of Edward of Salisbury. It has been suggested above (p. 62) that he was probably an English survivor. He had a son, also called Edward of Salisbury, and it is very difficult to sort the two out in the sources. Lands held by the two Edwards passed in the male line to Walter of Salisbury and his son Patrick, the first earl, but a substantial amount passed to Matilda, daughter of Edward, probably Edward the younger, of Salisbury, who married Humphrey de Bohun.[68] One obvious possibility here is that Matilda inher-

---

The lands he held in chief passed via his widow to her second husband, Robert de Lisle. Robert was succeeded first by William de Todeni, and then by his daughter Alice, wife of Roger Bigod, and in turn by Cecily, daughter of Roger and Alice: Green, *Government of England*, p. 229. The help of Sir James Holt in elucidating this family's history is gratefully acknowledged.

[64] *Early Yorkshire Charters*, I, 466, 507–8.      [65] *RBE*, I, 397–8; Davis, *King Stephen*, p. 134.

[66] The sheriff of Norfolk and Suffolk in the latter part of Henry I's reign was Robert FitzWalter, a leading tenant of the honour of Eye in Suffolk: Green, *List of Sheriffs to 1154*, pp. 61, 77.

[67] HH, p. 270; *Historia Pontificalis of John of Salisbury*, ed. M. Chibnall (Edinburgh and London, 1956), p. 85; A. Wareham, 'The Motives and Politics of the Bigod Family, c. 1066–1177', *Anglo-Norman Studies*, 17 (1994), 233.

[68] Sanders, *English Baronies*, p. 91; Dugdale, *Mon. Ang.*, VI, 134 (benefactors of Llanthony priory).

ited her mother's lands and Walter of Salisbury inherited his father's lands, but there is no evidence on this point.

A fourth case where a daughter was given favourable treatment was that of Maud, who was a daughter of Arnulf de Hesdin and married Patrick de Chaworth.[69] Arnulf is known to have had two sons and two other daughters: Aveline, who married Alan FitzFlaad, and one who entered Shaftesbury Abbey.[70] A sizeable portion of Arnulf's lands passed to Patrick, and only part passed to Arnulf II. The latter was hanged in 1138 and his lands passed to William FitzAlan.[71] Again a possible explanation for the division of Arnulf I's lands was two marriages, though Barlow has suggested that this Arnulf may have been punished for complicity in the revolt of 1095 against Rufus.[72]

In other words, these cases show that whilst it is possible to fit the known facts into some kind of framework of custom, it may be that we are making the evidence fit preconceived ideas of what would have happened later when custom was more precisely defined, by suggesting, for example, that a son who was passed over must have been illegitimate, or that there may have been two marriages, or that daughters inherited all their mothers' lands. Nor can we be certain that contemporaries believed that daughters' share of their father's inheritance, that is their marriage portions, had of necessity to be small, especially if the king wished it otherwise.

Secondly, there was scope for different views about daughters as heiresses when their fathers had surviving brothers. This was the point at issue at the siege of Bedford in 1138. Simon de Beauchamp, castellan of Bedford, had no sons but a daughter whose marriage Stephen bestowed on Hugh de Beaumont, younger brother of the Beaumont twins, a man of high birth but few means.[73] However, Miles de Beauchamp, Simon's younger brother, held the castle against the king. Stephen demanded its surrender, and Miles replied that he would serve the king loyally providing he was not deprived of his inheritance, but he would never surrender the castle. The issue here, as Stenton pointed out, was the claim of a younger brother as opposed to a daughter, and though there was a clear

---

[69] See the comments of J. H. Round on the children of Arnulf, *CDF*, pp. xlvii–xlviii; Sanders, *English Baronies*, p. 125; Dugdale, *Mon. Ang.*, II, 220 (benefactors of St Albans abbey).

[70] Sanders, *English Baronies*, pp. 70–1; Dugdale, *Mon. Ang.*, II, 483.     [71] OV, VI, 520–2.

[72] Barlow, *William Rufus*, p. 358.     [73] *Gesta Stephani*, pp. 46–50; Stenton, *First Century*, pp. 237–8.

tendency in the early twelfth century to prefer the claim of a daughter, Miles evidently felt he had a reasonable case, and the possibility of collateral succession had not been ruled totally out of court. Also at issue was custody of a castle. The Beauchamp family had held this since the Conquest, and although the castle was technically the king's, was it reasonable to deprive the family of its custody?

A situation that was not uncommon was where there were no surviving sons, only daughters. Was one daughter to inherit everything apart from the marriage portions of her sisters? It was certainly the case that many inheritances did pass through one daughter as sole heiress in the Norman period; the difficulty is of knowing whether that daughter had surviving sisters. Only in one or two high-profile cases do we know that she had. One of these was the case of the honour of Huntingdon in about 1090. Waltheof and Judith had had two daughters, Matilda and Adeliza, but the bulk of the honour and the title of earl passed with Matilda to her husbands, Simon de Senlis and King David, and only a limited share to her sister Adeliza and her husband Ralph de Tosny in 1103.[74] Robert FitzHaimon and his wife had at least three daughters; two were put into nunneries and the third married the eldest illegitimate son of Henry I, Robert of Gloucester.[75] In both of these cases the inheritances were large and Rufus and Henry were directly involved. It is not clear whether, given a choice, kings would have preferred sole heiresses or partition: the former transferred lordships whole; the latter, as Holt has pointed out, increased the number of opportunities for the exercise of patronage.[76] Similarly it is hard to know if families preferred unigeniture or division. It might be assumed fathers would naturally wish to be able to provide for their younger daughters equitably. On the other hand, the prospect of complicated divisions might have been unwelcome.

Moreover, if the prevailing wind was blowing in the direction of primogeniture for daughters as well as sons, there were flurries in the other direction. There are at least two instances of division between daughters, and there may have been others. One possible form of division was at the Channel, as was often done in the case of sons. Thus William of Arques' Norman estates passed to one daughter, Maud, who married William de

---

[74] *CP*, vi, 639 n; Holt, 'Heiress and the Alien', pp. 8–9.
[75] *Ibid.*, p. 9; according to a tradition preserved at Tewkesbury abbey there was a fourth sister, Amice, who married a count of Brittany: Dugdale, *Mon. Ang.*, ii, 60–1. [76] *Ibid.*, p. 20.

Tancarville, whilst another, Emma, inherited the large estate of Folkestone.[77] The division of Robert de Rumilly's estates was slightly different: one daughter inherited the estates in Normandy and one estate in England, while the other inherited the other English estates.[78] Again, this can be paralleled in decisions taken about the division of estates between sons.[79] A third possible case is the lands of Richard de Sourdeval, a major tenant of Robert of Mortain in Yorkshire in 1086. We know that Richard's lands were subsequently divided between Ralph Paynel and Robert de Brus, and one possibility – for which, however, there is no evidence – is that the lands had passed via daughters.[80] It may be that a handful of cases of division between daughters should be regarded as exceptions to the rule, or that twins were involved, but we have no evidence on this point.

It has been suggested that uncertainty over the position where there were no sons but several daughters led to a decree that inheritances should be equally divided between co-heiresses. A reference to such a decree occurs in a charter discussed by Stenton and printed in *The First Century of English Feudalism*. This charter was issued by Roger de Valognes for Binham priory, confirming a gift made by his kinsman Walter, who was about to enter religion. The charter was probably issued in about 1141, slightly earlier than the date suggested by Stenton.[81] The gift was half of Barney, the inheritance of Walter's daughter Agnes, 'according to the decree that where there is no son the daughters divide their father's land by the spindles, nor can the elder take from the younger half of the inheritance by violence and injury'. The phraseology is unusual, perhaps reflecting ecclesiastical draftsmanship, and the circumstances are also out of the ordinary in that the father of Roger de Valognes, the overlord, had first granted Barney to Binham and had commanded Walter (possibly a younger son) that this should be done. Walter had evidently decided to enter religion and divided his lands between his two daughters, one of whom, Agnes, was at the time unmarried. Barney was to be hers – this is

[77] Douglas, *Domesday Monachorum*, pp. 42–4; Loyd, *Origins of Some Anglo-Norman Families*, p. 6.
[78] *Early Yorkshire Charters*, VII, 1–6; 31–2.     [79] Holt, 'Politics and Property', p. 14.
[80] *Early Yorkshire Charters*, VI, 4–5, 38–9, 58, no. 1. Dalton pointed out that there is no positive evidence as to the identity of Robert de Brus's wife: *Conquest, Anarchy and Lordship*, pp. 91–2.
[81] Stenton, *First Century*, p. 261; Roger de Valognes was living in 1141 when the Empress issued a charter in his favour: *RRAN*, III, no. 911. The case is re-examined in an appendix to my forthcoming paper, 'Aristocratic Women in Early Twelfth-Century England', as cited above, n. 1.

the slightly unusual feature of the situation as her marriage portion had already been given away – and so her consent to the confirmation was necessary. Agnes subsequently married, and both her husband and her sister's husband tried to withdraw the gift. It took the intervention of Archbishop Theobald and the threat of ecclesiastical sanctions to secure the confirmation of part of the gift, Agnes's half of Barney. The cartulary contains confirmations by both Agnes, her husband, and her daughter who succeeded her.

There is no reason to doubt the authenticity of the decree mentioned, but it is not immediately obvious whose it was. Stenton pointed out that the decision had evidently been taken before 1154, and Holt suggested more explicitly that the decision was Henry I's, that since there is no sign of partition in the 1130 pipe roll it may have been issued between 1130 and 1135, and that it was a decision which suited both the king and the barons.[82] More recently, Pauline Stafford has specifically related the decree to Henry I's plans in the last decade of his reign that his daughter should succeed him: (Henry) 'may well have been the first English king to put down in written form the right of a daughter to succeed him'.[83] In this context, however, a better case could be made for arguing that in making such a decision Henry was trying to be generally conciliatory to the magnates. The possibility of female inheritance was already recognized and what was at issue was how inheritance should be apportioned, by unigeniture or division.

It is also interesting that although there are more cases of co-heiresses after 1135, they did not become common until later. Between 1135 and 1140 at least two major inheritances were divided between heiresses, though the divisions were of different kinds. Ranulf Meschin died without male heirs leaving three sisters. His widow held Skipton, and each of his three sisters inherited part of his lands. However, the lion's share passed to one sister, Alice, the wife of William FitzDuncan.[84] Secondly, when Geoffrey Talbot died in 1140, leaving one lordship, it was divided between two nieces.[85] Later examples of divisions included William Peverel's honour of Bourn in 1147–8,[86] and Walter Espec's in 1155.

[82] Holt, 'Heiress and the Alien', p. 10.    [83] Stafford, 'Women and the Norman Conquest', pp. 226–7.

[84] *Early Yorkshire Charters*, VII, 4–8; Dalton, *Conquest, Anarchy and Lordship*, pp. 211–20, and above n. 22.

[85] Sanders, *English Baronies*, p. 144, citing *CP*, IX. 425.

[86] Sanders, *English Baronies*, p. 19, citing Farrer, *Feudal Cambridgeshire*, pp. 159–66.

The latter left three baronies: Wark in Northumberland, Helmsley in Yorkshire, and Old Warden in Bedfordshire, the first two of which had been granted to him by Henry I, and the third he had inherited from his uncle. In 1158 one of his sons-in-law Robert de Ros fined for a large amount to succeed to the whole inheritance, and the two other sons-in-law fined for a share. Robert succeeded to Wark, minus the castle which the king retained, Helmsley, and one knight's fee of Warden, whilst the other two brothers-in-law shared the remainder of Warden.[87]

Other divisions were far from equal. When the earl of Hereford died in 1165, he left three sisters. One took the Welsh estates and some of the English, while a second took the rest of the English estates and had to be persuaded over the next three decades to disgorge some of them to a third sister.[88] William de Chesney, a servant of Henry II, died leaving three daughters, one of whom was married to another royal servant, Hugh de Cressy, and inherited the bulk of her father's estates.[89] Only five other baronies passed to co-heiresses before 1180: Brattleby, Ellingham, Poorstock, Topcliffe, and Whalton.[90] To this list can be added Barnstaple and Totnes, where divisions were later made to recognise the claim of the Briouze family. In the case of Barnstaple, it appears that Alfred FitzJudhael, who was living in 1136, died leaving two sisters, of whom one was the wife of Philip de Briouze. Barnstaple passed to Henry de Tracy, possibly by marriage to the other sister, and in the mid-twelfth century it appears that the honour was divided between William de Briouze, son of Philip, and Oliver de Tracy, son of Henry.[91] Totnes had been held in 1086 by Judhael father of Alfred, but he was subsequently replaced by Roger de Nonant. Evidently the Briouze family nurtured a claim to this honour through the sister of Alfred FitzJudhael, and in 1206 the honour was divided between William de Briouze and Henry de Nonant.[92]

There is thus some variety in the way lands were parcelled out amongst daughters before the late twelfth century. Parceny in the form described by Glanvill, where the eldest sister's husband did homage to the king and was responsible for all the services of the lordship and the husbands of the younger sisters held of the eldest, was only one of the options being

---

[87] Holt, 'Heiress and the Alien', pp. 15–16.
[88] D. Walker, 'The "Honours" of the Earls of Hereford in the Twelfth Century', *Transactions of the Bristol and Gloucestershire Archaeological Society*, 69 (1960), 174–211.  [89] *Sibton Cartularies*, 21.
[90] Sanders, *English Baronies*, pp. 109, 41, 72, 148, 150.  [91] *Ibid.*, p. 104.  [92] *Ibid.*, p. 90.

employed. Holt has suggested that Glanvill may have been influenced by the prospect of his own lands passing to co-heiresses.[93] He was also clearly influenced by the Norman practice of parage, where sons divided an inheritance but homage was taken from the eldest.[94] It was only from about 1180 that the form of division described by Glanvill became more common.

The likelihood of sisters dividing up their father's lands was thus not entirely unknown before 1135. Divisions could take various forms, and this remained the case until the 1180s. Was the *statutum decretum* such a deliberate act of royal policy as has been suggested? It is possible that a few more divisions occurred under Stephen, and that the king was simply unable to prevent them happening. The succession to Ranulf Meschin's lands was clearly affected by the power of the Scots in northern England. It was obviously not in Stephen's interests, as already noted, that Ranulf's sister Alice, the heiress of Skipton, should marry the nephew of the king of Scots.[95] Geoffrey Talbot fought against Stephen in 1138 and William Peverel of Dover was a supporter of the Empress.[96] It is perhaps not a coincidence that William FitzDuncan, Geoffrey Talbot, and William Peverel of Dover represented the Angevin interest, and that, although their estates were probably partitioned without reference to Stephen, Henry II was not prepared to overturn these arrangements. Moreover, it is worth noting in this context that Stephen's decision in the case of the Lacy inheritance following the death of Payn FitzJohn in 1137 was in favour of one sister rather than partition (see above, p. 334). This was a difficult and sensitive problem, and Stephen's decision, in favour of the son of Miles of Gloucester, had the desired effect of keeping Miles on side until 1139, but it provoked a minor war in the west led by those who were disappointed.

What did not happen after 1154 was a resumption by Henry II of his grandfather's practice of exacting large sums in connection with marriage to widows and heiresses. If we assume for the moment that had such payments been made they would have been recorded on the pipe rolls, as they had been in 1130, the infrequency of such payments needs explain-

---

[93] Holt, 'Heiress and the Alien', p. 19.

[94] Pollock and Maitland, *History of English Law*, II, 276; Holt, 'Heiress and the Alien', p. 10.

[95] Dalton, *Conquest, Anarchy and Lordship*, pp. 211–20.

[96] JW, pp. 49–50; William Peverel of Dover was with Stephen in Normandy in 1137: *RRAN*, III, no. 598; he witnessed for the Empress as William of Dover, in 1141 and 1144 as constable: *RRAN*, III, nos. 393, 111.

ing.[97] Sole heiresses to great honours were few and far between, and it would appear (though this cannot be proved) that Henry II, perhaps for political reasons, was not prepared to intervene in succession in the way his grandfather had done to produce female inheritance. The sudden increase in cases of female inheritance in the form of parceny after about 1180 is perhaps best explained as a contemporary concern in the Angevin world about a potential loss of services if baronies were divided. In Brittany, Henry's son Duke Geoffrey issued a decree in 1185 prohibiting the division of baronies and knights' fees, which may have been an innovation or a restatement of existing practice.[98] In Normandy parage amongst sons developed as a way round the fragmentation of knights' fees, which may well have been larger there than in England.[99]

Women therefore represented a welcome window of opportunity for the Norman kings to channel lands in the direction of their own men. Henry I may have decided at the end of his reign to recognize the claims of younger sisters and their husbands when their fathers died without sons, or younger sisters and their husbands may simply have seized their chance when Stephen was not in a position to resist, and Henry II proved to be reluctant or unable to turn the clock back. In retrospect, therefore, the early twelfth century was a period when women's role in the transmission of land assumed greater importance than before, and at a time when the norms and procedures which regulated female succession had not yet been precisely established.

Some historians have contrasted the relative freedom of an English noble lady before and after 1066. Pauline Stafford, however, has demonstrated the difficulties in sustaining the idea of a contrast between a golden age for Anglo-Saxon women and their subsequent subordination. The evidence relating to families in the late Anglo-Saxon period is scanty and that of women's wills, which Stenton believed demonstrated their independence, may reflect the possibility that bequests by women would be challenged: it cannot be assumed that their provisions would be carried out. There is some evidence in late Anglo-Saxon England of royal intervention in the marriages of noble women; also women were not com-

[97] J. E. Lally, 'Secular Patronage at the Court of Henry II', *Bulletin of the Institute of Historical Research*, 49 (1976), 166, for the comment that Henry had the marriages of very few heiresses of the first rank at his disposal.        [98] *La très Ancienne Coutume de Bretagne*, ed. M. Planiol (Rennes, 1896), p. 321.

[99] *Coutumiers de Normandie*, I, 8–9; for comment, Holt, 'Politics and Property', p. 10; R. Généstal, *Le Parage normand* (Caen, 1911).

pletely free to dispose of their morning gifts (analogous to dower) and dowries.[100] The key factor, however, in the prominence of women was a recognition that daughters could inherit land in default of sons. This in turn was related to the rise of patrilineal descent, and of a desire to preserve inheritances intact rather than to partition them. Here we are hampered by a lack of evidence relating to inheritance of land in the pre-Conquest aristocracy. It is surely significant, however, that in the Romance-speaking world, as Jane Martindale has demonstrated, inheritance by women of great honours, especially those involving comital titles or even thrones, only became a practical proposition in the late eleventh century.[101] It could be argued that in Norman England, therefore, the possibility of female inheritance at the highest level was relatively new. It was combined, moreover, with vigorously enforced royal rights over the affairs of the great families, and it was this combination which made the whole subject of women and land so sensitive, as indicated in Henry I's Charter of Liberties in 1100. Henry I was prepared to make promises about his future good behaviour, but in practice he continued to exploit a lucrative marriage market, the conventions of which remained flexible.

## The religious life

The second important area of change affecting women was in the proliferation of religious houses. Although there were opportunities for women to dedicate themselves as hermits or anchoresses, or to live near houses for men, at the time of the Conquest there was only a handful of fully organized nunneries.[102] The more important of these were havens for royal and noble women. Christina, Edgar Aetheling's sister, became a nun, and was responsible for the education of her niece Edith, the future queen.[103] In 1093 the future of this girl became a matter of political importance, and William Rufus and her father King Malcolm visited her at Wilton. Malcolm, finding her wearing a veil allegedly for her own protection, tore it from her head, and said furthermore that he wanted her to marry Count Alan of Richmond. When the question of Edith's freedom to

---

[100] Stafford, 'Women and the Norman Conquest', pp. 223, 225–46.
[101] Martindale, 'Succession and Politics in the Romance-speaking World'.
[102] P. Halpin, 'Women Religious in Late Anglo-Saxon England', *Haskins Society Journal*, 6 (1994), 97–110.
[103] Searle, 'Women and the Legitimisation of Succession', pp. 166–9; Barlow, *William Rufus*, pp. 310–16; R. W. Southern, *Saint Anselm. A Portrait in a Landscape* (Cambridge, 1990), pp. 260–2.

marry recurred at the time of her marriage to Henry I in 1100, she claimed
that she only wore the veil in her aunt's presence because of the latter's
fear of the Normans.[104] Gunnhildr, a daughter of King Harold, was also a
member of the community at Wilton in the 1090s. She entered a union
with Count Alan and then with his brother.[105] These were two women
with the blood of kings in their veins, and thus highly valuable as brides,
but in this context their experiences provide illustration of the way
English women retreated to nunneries after 1066. We know from a surviving letter of Archbishop Lanfranc that those who had not been professed
or been presented at the altar were told to leave.[106] One interpretation of
the letter is that such girls were needed as brides of Normans, and could
not be allowed to withdraw themselves in this way; another is that they
were perhaps regarded by church leaders as disruptive influences if they
were not completely committed to a religious life.

The new aristocracy soon began to entrust its daughters to English
houses. Something can be discovered about those who entered
Shaftesbury abbey in Dorset in the Norman period. The abbey had been
founded by King Alfred and was relatively wealthy. It emerges that new
recruits whose families gave land were in almost every instance not from
the greatest Anglo-Norman families but from the second rank, some of
whom were associated with royal administration.[107] It has been pointed
out that, in some cases at least, daughters were probably put into the
nunnery as children; their parents had thus made a deliberate choice not
to arrange marriages for them, quite possibly in some instances for economic reasons.[108] A study of the location of family estates indicates that
Shaftesbury was selected, as opposed to other houses in the south-west or
elsewhere, for reasons of convenience. Only the greatest families of the
Anglo-Norman world were likely to have links with nunneries in northern
France. In any case, families presumably did not want to cut themselves
off altogether from their daughters.

The number of new foundations did not really begin to take off until
the fifth decade of the twelfth century, and even later in Yorkshire.[109]
There were always more obstacles to the foundation of houses for women

[104] Eadmer, *Historia Novorum*, pp. 121–2.

[105] WM, *Vita Wulfstani*, p. 34; Letters of Anselm, nos. 168, 169, *S. Anselmi Opera omnia* (ed. Schmitt), IV,
43–50.     [106] *Letters of Lanfranc*, no. 53.

[107] K. Cooke, 'Donors and Daughters: Shaftesbury Abbey's Benefactors, Endowments and Nuns c.
1086–1130', *Anglo-Norman Studies*, 12 (1990), 29–45.     [108] *Ibid.*, p. 37.

[109] Burton, *Yorkshire Nunneries in the Twelfth and Thirteenth Centuries*, pp. 5–11.

than there were for men, and the chronology of foundations is marked by fits and starts. One factor was that the prayers of women for the souls of the dead were not thought to be as efficacious as those of men. A second was that unease about the association of men and women in communities grew apace: the Cistercians in particular resolutely resisted the attempts of women to join their houses.[110]

In the years following 1066 it was the bishops who took the lead in promoting new foundations. Malling in Kent was established by Bishop Gundulf of Rochester, St Sepulchre's at Canterbury by Archbishop Anselm, and Stratford at Bow near London was founded on land given by a bishop of London. Archbishop Thurstan of York was sympathetic to female vocations. He was one of those who conducted Countess Adela of Blois to Marcigny where she took the veil. He counselled the recluse Christina of Markyate, and was responsible for the foundation of Clementhorpe nunnery in York.[111] Bishop Alexander of Lincoln was also prominent. He witnessed Christina's taking of vows, issued charters of confirmation for nunneries, was Gilbert of Sempringham's diocesan bishop, and was instrumental in the setting up of Haverholme.[112] The role of archbishops and bishops as founders may in some cases have been exaggerated, but their support was important. From their point of view, quite apart from a need to provide for female vocations, the new houses would be subject to their authority.

It may be the case, too, that the role of male lay founders has been exaggerated. We have few explicit statements about the impulses which directed the gifts to one type of community and, given that some contemporaries preferred to endow communities of male religious, it is likely that when houses for women were founded the wishes of wives and mothers lay behind them. Where there are charters, those issued by men did not necessarily have to make any reference to the fact that the land concerned was their wives' marriage portions, though conversely when women's charters were copied into cartularies they were usually accompanied by confirmations by their husbands or heirs, for religious houses were naturally concerned that benefactions might be challenged.

Elkins has pointed out that in some cases it is fairly clear that men did

---

[110] For a recent discussion of the context, see B. Golding, *Gilbert of Sempringham and the Gilbertine Order c. 1130–c. 1300* (Oxford, 1995), pp. 71–7.    [111] Nicholl, *Archbishop Thurstan*, pp. 194–200.

[112] A. G. Dyson, 'The Monastic Patronage of Bishop Alexander of Lincoln', *Journal of Ecclesiastical History*, 26 (1975), 17–24.

take the initiative. Clerkenwell priory near London was set up with the help of Jordan de Bricett, founder of the Hospital of St John of Jerusalem; Jordan gave Robert the chaplain the option of founding a house for monks or nuns, and Robert chose nuns.[113] Jordan's family continued as patrons, and some female members later joined as nuns, but, as Elkins points out, we must be cautious in assuming that nunneries were founded in order to provide for female relatives.[114] Sometimes male founders were providing endowments for women already *in situ*, although the point has to be made tentatively because of lack of evidence.[115]

It is significant that in a number of cases women were settled in or near towns and cities. Ranulf II earl of Chester is thought to have taken nuns from Clerkenwell to form a new community at Chester to which he gave land, crofts, and a boat for fishing on the Dee.[116] There were communities at or near Norwich, Cambridge, Northampton, York, London, Canterbury, Derby, Thetford, Stamford, Oxford, and Lincoln.[117] It may be that too much should not be read into this – after all, there were many religious foundations of different kinds in towns – but perhaps the type of endowments given to nuns, and the facility they offered for urban families, met a specific need for female vocation amongst townspeople, in the way that communities of Beguines later did in Flanders.

In a few cases we know that women were founders, for example, Countess Judith at Elstow and Countess Lucy at Stixwould. Although there is no direct evidence, it is tempting to believe that these great ladies themselves entered the communities. In each case neither subsequently remarried, and retirement to a religious house was a statement of disengagement from the marriage market, even if it was not always a conclusive statement. Occasionally, as the case of Edith-Matilda in 1100 shows, women were brought out of religious houses if they were needed as brides for men rather than brides of Christ. At the end of our period, Stephen's daughter Mary of Blois was removed from a nunnery to marry Matthew son of the count of Flanders. Mary had first been a nun at Stratford at Bow, then at Lillechurch, a community founded for her by her parents, King Stephen and Queen Matilda. She was abbess of Romsey at the time her marriage was arranged and, though the marriage took place, she later returned to Romsey.[118]

---

[113] Elkins, *Holy Women*, pp. 65–9.    [114] *Ibid.*, p. 70.    [115] e.g. at Oldbury: Elkins, *Holy Women*, pp. 71–2.
[116] *Chester Charters*, nos. 97–9, 117.    [117] See tables in Elkins, *Holy Women*, pp. 167–73.
[118] *Ibid.*, p. 189, n. 25 and references there cited.

By contrast with such women of very high social status, other founders came from middling or lesser families. Godstow priory was founded by the pious widow of a knight from Winchester. According to later tradition, she was instructed to go to Oxford in a vision where she chose a site and persuaded the lord to donate it. She herself entered the community and became its abbess.[119] The Arches family, honorial barons in Yorkshire, and those related to them by marriage, were instrumental in founding four houses for men and women, and they included two women founders: Agnes de Arches (Nunkeeling), and Alice de St Quintin, her daughter (Nunappleton). Agnes's brother William de Arches was the co-founder of Nunmonkton, and Alice's son-in-law was Simon of Kyme, founder of the Gilbertine priory of Bullington.[120] Here we see an interest in female vocations shown by both male and female members of a family of middling status. A remarkable number of other nunneries were founded in Yorkshire in the course of the twelfth century, and Burton has shown that their founders, like those of the Gilbertine houses, tended to be knightly families making very modest endowments, probably to provide for unmarried daughters.[121] Rather than sending them away to enter, say, Shaftesbury or Romsey, they established small houses for them much closer to home.

Another significant feature about the communities in which women participated was lack of clear definition – as far as the historian is concerned – of their status and even of their rules. Many women in the century following the Conquest seem literally to have camped on the doorstep of houses for men, a practice which, it has been suggested, was not new.[122] An early instance of this was the women of noble birth who associated themselves with the abbey of Bec in Normandy.[123] In England the great abbeys like St Albans under Abbot Paul (1077–93) attracted women. Paul was Lanfranc's nephew and one of the most dynamic abbots of the post-Conquest era (see below, pp. 396–7). He instructed the women to wear black habits and accommodated them in the almonry.[124] The association of women with houses for men in this era has been stressed by Thompson, though again the lack of documentation makes it difficult for

[119] *The English Register of Godstow Nunnery, near Oxford, written about 1450*, ed. A. Clark, Early English Text Society, old series, CXXIX, CXXX, CXLII (1905–11), CXXIX, 26–7.

[120] Elkins, *Holy Women*, pp. 96–7.     [121] Burton, *Yorkshire Nunneries*, pp. 17–27.

[122] Halpin, 'Women Religious', pp. 107–8.

[123] S. Vaughn, 'St Anselm and Women', *Haskins Society Journal*, 2 (1990), 88–9.

[124] *Gesta Abbatum S. Albani*, ed. H. T. Riley, 3 vols., RS (London, 1867–9), I, 59.

us to know how structured these communities of women were. The advantage for women in such communities was clear: access to the services of priests and to the abbey church as well as what might be described as a protected environment.

Some clearly preferred to lead a life that was oriented towards the eremetical rather than the communal. Christina of Markyate is the most famous example from Norman England because of the survival of her *Life*.[125] She was from an Anglo-Danish family in Huntingdon, and it was on a visit to St Albans abbey that she first made a private vow of dedication. Escaping with difficulty from the marriage her parents arranged for her, she took refuge at Flamstead not far from St Albans where she lived with an anchoress, moving after two years to Markyate, where her spiritual adviser was a hermit named Roger. In 1122 her betrothal and marriage vows were annulled by Archbishop Thurstan, who tried unsuccessfully to persuade her to be abbess of Clementhorpe nunnery in York; suggestions were also made that she might enter Fontevraud in Anjou or the great Cluniac nunnery of Marcigny-sur-Loire, but she remained at Markyate.[126] The life of Christina is an invaluable source for many aspects of the history of women. In this context we may note her difficulties in abjuring the world, her association with other recluses (the desire of twelfth-century hermits to get away from it all in the company of others is one of the more intriguing aspects of the popularity of eremitical religious life for the modern mind), the roles of Archbishop Thurstan, and also of Bishop Alexander and Abbot Geoffrey of St Albans, and the options available to her: she could have become an abbess, or crossed the Channel and entered Fontevraud, at this stage a community for men or women, or entered Marcigny as a Cluniac nun. Instead she was enclosed at Markyate, and played an important role as a spiritual counsellor. In the case of women, life as a hermit or anchoress (the two do not seem to have been clearly distinguished before the later twelfth century) was an outlet for their aspirations and a direct relationship with God not available in a male-dominated church, even though they were clearly dependent on the church for protection.[127]

Women answered the call to a life of prayer as enthusiastically as men; the problem, for the men, was rather how to keep women away because of

[125] *The Life of Christina of Markyate: a Twelfth-Century Recluse*, ed. and trans. C. H. Talbot (Oxford, 1959).
[126] *Ibid.*, p. 127.       [127] Mayr-Harting, 'Functions of a Twelfth-Century Recluse'.

the opportunities for sin they represented. The Arrouaisians and Premonstratensians were prepared to accept women at least for a period in their history (see below, p. 406), and there may have been women associated with the crusading order of the Knights of St John of Jerusalem. The Cistercians in particular were loath to accept female recruits, and St Bernard was deeply suspicious of the double houses set up by Robert of Arbrissel and Gilbert of Sempringham.[128] Gilbert began as a member of the household of the bishop of Lincoln, then became a parish priest in Lincolnshire. He attracted a following of women, and then built up a community of nuns with chaplains and lay sisters and brothers on the Cistercian model.[129] Gilbert tried to persuade the Cistercians to take on his houses, but they baulked at the idea.[130] Gilbertine houses not surprisingly proved to be very popular in Gilbert's own county, where seven houses were founded: Sempringham, Haverholme, Alvingham, Bullington, Catley, North Ormsby, and Sixhills. In addition a house at Lincoln was founded where there were canons only.[131] Outside Lincolnshire there were fewer foundations. In Yorkshire, for instance, though foundations for women were relatively numerous in the twelfth century, only two Gilbertine houses were founded, at Watton and Malton, by Eustace FitzJohn. In the case of Watton, the influence of Eustace's second wife, Agnes, may have been instrumental. She was a cousin of Gilbert de Gant, Gilbert of Sempringham's lord, and the vill of Watton was her marriage portion as her charter to the priory made clear.[132] Malton by contrast was a house for canons only, with responsibilities to care for the local poor and sick.[133]

Many of the girls who entered nunneries may have viewed a religious life with enthusiasm, or at least as a reasonable alternative to marriage: we should never underestimate the attractions of the religious life. Yet the proliferation of nunneries also reflected a willingness of their menfolk to allow women to withdraw from the marriage market. In other words, however enthusiastic women were, if their menfolk had wanted them to

---

[128] J. Smith, 'Robert of Arbrissel: *Procurator Mulierum*', in *Medieval Women* (ed. Baker), pp. 175–84; Thompson, *Women Religious*, chapter seven; for Gilbert see Golding, *Gilbert of Sempringham*.

[129] For Gilbert's life see *The Book of St Gilbert*, ed. and trans. R. Foreville and G. Keir (Oxford, 1987), and for discussion see Golding, *Gilbert of Sempringham*, chapters one and two.

[130] *Ibid.*, pp. 26–33.      [131] *Ibid.*, chapter four.      [132] *Ibid.*, pp. 216–17.

[133] *Ibid.*, pp. 220–1 (where the possibility is raised that Malton was founded on land which had accrued to Eustace by royal favour or by marriage); 229–30.

marry it would have been very difficult to escape. The fact is that men were prepared to allow them to do so, and even subsidized them, and their willingness can hardly be disassociated from the narrowing of inheritance and the channelling of family land through a single heir, preferably male. We have already seen one case in the early twelfth century where two of the daughters of Robert FitzHaimon entered the religious life so that a third, the bride of the king's son, became sole heiress of her father's land (above, p. 377).

Nuns had to be provided with dowries, but the size of these was probably smaller than marriage portions. Cooke drew attention to one instance at Shaftesbury where a daughter of Serlo de Burci entered the abbey with an endowment of £2, whereas Domesday Book mentions in passing that the marriage portion of another daughter, who married William of Falaise, was worth £5.[134] Nuns were cheaper than brides and in knightly families with limited resources this might well have been a critical factor. Does this perhaps explain the proliferation of modest foundations by knightly families? It is possible, though other factors such as family tradition and, in the north, lack of existing provision for women, either organized or more informal, also have to be taken into account. At all events, the two aspects of the lives of aristocratic women in our period about which most is known, the provision of land for them in marriage, and the foundation of nunneries, are likely to have been related.

For those who were destined for the religious life, the experience of aristocratic women in Norman England was comparable to that of noble women in other parts of Western Europe. There were more houses for women by the end of our period, and this was in part a response to female vocations and in part as a means by which families could dispose of surplus daughters into a controlled environment. With regard to land, however, the situation in Norman England was exceptional in that there was a unique combination of royal power of intervention, a growing acceptance of inheritance by daughters, and a lack of precisely defined custom.

[134] *DB*, I, 98, 97b, discussed by Cooke, 'Donors and Daughters', p. 38.

# 12    Founders and benefactors: the aristocracy and the church

The relationship between the aristocracy and the church provides invaluable insights into the thought world of the elite: its motives and priorities, its response to changing opportunities, and its identification with a new country. Here we see aristocrats' concerns about the wellbeing of themselves and their families in this world and the next, a mixture of spiritual and worldly considerations. Every aristocratic family had members who entered the church and whose careers were to be promoted. The foundation of churches and monasteries could help to buttress secular authority in a conquered land and provide chaplains for spiritual and secretarial services, while monks and canons prayed for the souls of benefactors. The vast majority of surviving aristocratic charters are in favour of religious houses, and so it is on the role of the aristocracy as founders and benefactors of religious houses that this chapter will concentrate, even though this means excluding the relationship between the aristocracy and secular cathedrals, and aristocratic involvement in the building of village churches. This was a century when a vast amount of land passed into the hands of the religious houses in Europe, when the monastic ideal met with its most positive response, and also a period when the options available proliferated. At the start of the period the Benedictine order was pre-eminent in England, but by the mid-twelfth century the choice available to benefactors had grown, and a much wider range of families were able to found their 'own' religious houses.

The Conquest was achieved by great men who had founded or patronized houses on the continent; one question that immediately arises is how far they retained those links, or sought to develop new ones with existing communities in England. A second question is how quickly they began to found English houses, of what type, and with what endowments. Here, as the century under review wore on, the range of opportunities not just for men but also for women, as discussed in the previous chapter, expanded. Finally, there is the question of the way in which individual families' patronage developed over time. Religious patronage was an area where individual choice could be exercised in response to changing opportunities; a balance between maintaining earlier foundations and following fashion had to be struck. Issues such as a change of lordship and tensions between lord and foundation are also important. An incoming lord might well have loyalties to other foundations; and relations with his predecessor's foundations could be difficult as a result. These and other shifts need to be considered.

There is both a geographical and a chronological aspect to this story. At the time the Normans invaded, there was an interest in reform in England, though as yet not with much reference to the papacy.[1] In the southern half of the country, the dioceses were relatively wealthy, minster churches were giving way to many local (later parish) churches, there were rich Benedictine monasteries and nunneries, and collegiate churches. In the northern half of the country, however, the picture was less rosy: the sees were poor, and monastic life, all but destroyed during the Viking era, had not recovered. The archbishopric of York was very large in size but only modestly endowed by comparison with Canterbury. The last four Anglo-Saxon archbishops of York were subsidized by the resources of the see of Worcester. In the north-east the community zealously guarding the relics of St Cuthbert had moved back to Durham in 995, and was sustaining a communal religious life. Bishop Edmund (1020–42) had tried to introduce Benedictine monks, but had been successfully resisted by the existing community. The north was therefore wide open for members of the new elite to found religious houses.

In the aftermath of Hastings, Normans were moved to give to the church for a variety of reasons: thankfulness for victory, penance for bloodshed, or, as time went on, the desire to provide for spiritual services near their principal castles. Their new wealth gave them a whole range of possible donations, including and especially churches and tithes. The message was coming through loud and clear from the reformers that lay possession of both was no longer acceptable, and thus churches and tithes were among the gifts most commonly made after the Conquest. It has also been suggested that tithes were becoming less profitable, and by giving them to monasteries lay lords were thus making spiritual gains without serious loss to themselves.[2] Land, mills, and rights and privileges of

---

[1] J. Barrow, 'English Cathedral Communities and Reform in the Late Tenth and the Eleventh Centuries', *Anglo-Norman Durham*, ed. D. Rollason, M. Harvey, and M. Prestwich (Woodbridge, 1994), pp. 25–39.

[2] B. R. Kemp, 'Monastic Possession of Parish Churches in England in the Twelfth Century', *Journal of Ecclesiastical History*, 31 (1980), 133–60.

various kinds were also given, but not, significantly, in abundance. We might have expected to see wealth pouring into the possession of churches, if not in England, then in Normandy, but this was not the case. In the later eleventh century there seems to have been a relative lull between the Norman reform of the early eleventh century and the great wave of religious foundations in early twelfth-century England. However, by the middle of the twelfth century this tide of new foundations was beginning to turn. One sign was the Cistercian general chapter's prohibition of new foundations in 1152. Also aristocratic families, some quicker than others, were beginning to experience a finite limit to their resources as other costs were rising. At the local level the proliferation of village churches slackened, as the process came to be more closely regulated. The mid-twelfth century in this, as in other respects, marked if not the end, then the beginning of the end, of an era.

## The Conquest generation

The greatest of the new men naturally tended to favour houses across the Channel with which they already had links. William FitzOsbern's donations all occurred within a relatively short period after 1066. He made donations to the two abbeys which he had founded in Normandy: Lire (founded about 1046) and Cormeilles (founded about 1060).[3] His gifts were principally of churches and tithes. Other benefactors included Roger of Montgomery, who made gifts to Almenêches, St Martin of Sées, and Troarn, and Robert of Mortain, gifts to Grestain.[4] Richard FitzGilbert and his brother Baldwin took the opportunity to strengthen their family's relationship with the abbey of Bec.[5] Sometimes, but not always, monks from the parent house were sent in sufficient numbers to form a priory. To take one example, Henry de Ferrers established a priory at Tutbury,

---

[3] S. F. Hockey, 'William FitzOsbern and the Endowment of his Abbey of Lyre', *Proceedings of the Battle Conference on Anglo-Norman Studies*, 3 (1980), 78–96; for Cormeilles see *DB*, I, 163, 166, 49, 52, 182b, 179b, 180, 180b, 184b, 174b.

[4] Almenêches: *DB*, I, 24b, 25; Sées: *DB*, I, 23, 24, 25, 25b; Troarn: *DB*, I, 166b, 44b, 25b; Grestain was granted ten estates in England by Robert, plus others in Northamptonshire granted by Robert or his wife, Matilda of Montgomery, plus land at Marsh Gibbon and Ickford, Buckinghamshire, two hides at Langborough (Gloucestershire) and 3½ hides at 'Tomestona' (unidentified): see D. Bates and V. Gazeau, 'L'abbaye de Grestain et la famille d'Herluin de Conteville', *Annales de Normandie*, 40 (1990) 20–1; *DB*, I, 193, 46b, 222b, 92b, 20b, 21b; II, 291b.

[5] J. Ward, 'Fashions in Monastic Endowment: the Foundations of the Clare Family, 1066–1314', *Journal of Ecclesiastical History*, 32 (1981), 428–37.

subordinate to the abbey of Saint-Pierre-sur-Dives. He gave to the priory the parish church of the castle, the vill of Marston-on-Dove (with certain exceptions), Doveridge and West Broughton, the tithe of tolls levied at Tutbury, the tithes of vineyards, hunting, pannage, free supplies of firewood and timber, free fishing and the tithe of honey, two-thirds of his demesne tithes in eleven vills, two churches with their tithes and a villein, and tithes in two further vills.[6] West Broughton does not appear in Domesday Book, Marston and Doveridge were each valued at £5, and the remainder of the original endowment was composed of churches and tithes. Henry's lands in Domesday Book were worth just under £500, so the endowment did not beggar him.

Of the non-Norman houses, Cluny was the most attractive to would-be benefactors in the late eleventh century.[7] The abbey had deeply influenced the development of Norman monasticism earlier in the eleventh century, it had a high reputation, and, from the point of view of founders, it was not English, that is, Anglo-Saxon. King William asked the abbot of Cluny to provide monks for the abbey he built at Battle in Sussex, but was refused.[8] William de Warenne and Gundrada his wife had visited the abbey, and had been deeply impressed by the religious life practised there. They wished to make the house they founded at Lewes near their chief castle a Cluniac priory. Four monks were eventually dispatched from Cluny, of whom Lanzo became the first prior.[9] Some thirty Cluniac houses were founded before 1154, and as Brian Golding has argued, they were especially important to their founders.[10] Patronage from the royal house continued to the end of our period. Rufus had a hand in the foundation of Bermondsey, though the real founder seems to have been an Englishman called Ailwin Child; Henry I turned to Cluny for monks for his own major foundation for black monks at Reading; and Stephen's foundation at Faversham was strongly influenced by Cluny.

Cluny, though the most prestigious, was not the only non-Norman house to attract benefactions from England. Marmoutier on the river Loire had a high reputation in the mid-eleventh century. The Conqueror

---

[6] *The Cartulary of Tutbury Priory*, ed. A. Saltman, Staffordshire Historical Collections, 4th series, IV (1962), Historical Manuscripts Commission JP2 (London, 1962), no. 51.

[7] For the following paragraph see B. Golding, 'The Coming of the Cluniacs', *Proceedings of the Battle Conference on Anglo-Norman Studies*, 3 (1980), 65–77.     [8] Barlow, *English Church 1066–1154*, p. 185.

[9] *Recueil des chartes de l'abbaye de Cluny*, A. Bernard and A. Bruel, IV (Paris, 1888), no. 3561, p. 689; Barlow, *English Church 1066–1154*, pp. 184–5.     [10] Golding, 'Coming of the Cluniacs', p. 67.

gave money for the building of the refectory there, and it was Marmoutier rather than Cluny which eventually supplied monks for his foundation at Battle.[11] The reputation of Charroux in Poitou was also at its height in the late eleventh century, both as a centre of worship and pilgrimage focussing on the Holy Saviour, and because of the discovery between 1077 and 1082 of a new relic called the Holy Virtue, which added to its prestige. Charroux had priories and property over much of southern and central France, and its reputation had reached Flanders, which led Gilbert de Gant to look to Charroux when refounding the monastery of Bardney in Lincolnshire by 1096. George Beech has also recently demonstrated that in the late eleventh century Charroux sent monks to Ham, La Beuvrière, Guînes, and Lillers.[12]

One problem for lords considering where to bestow their patronage was that the English Benedictine abbeys were filled with Englishmen, many of whom must have been of thegnly rank and had seen their families ruined by the Conquest. Some abbots actually fought against William: Aelfwig, abbot of the new Minster at Winchester was a brother of Earl Godwin and died at Hastings; Leofric of Peterborough was a nephew of Earl Leofric of Mercia and also fought at Hastings; Aethelnoth of Glastonbury was one of the hostages taken to Normandy in 1067, so his loyalty must have been suspect; Aethelsige of St Augustine's went abroad; Fritheric of St Albans, a relative of Cnut, joined the rebels on the Isle of Ely; and Godric of Winchcombe was first imprisoned and then entrusted to Aethelwig of Evesham; Sihtric of Tavistock was said to have taken to piracy; Ealdred of Abingdon to have conspired with the Danes; and Thurstan of Ely, nominated by Harold, to have been on terms of friendship with the Danish royal houses.[13] The list of actual or potential troublemakers – from the Norman point of view – was not inconsiderable. More than that, however, the whole culture of the monasteries might be said to have been rooted in the past; a present and future filled with Normans, must have seemed a dismaying prospect for the monks. As the Peterborough chronicler recorded in 1066, 'then the Golden City [of Peterborough] became a wretched city'.[14] It is easy to see why Normans did not wish to bestow some

[11] *The Chronicle of Battle Abbey*, ed. E. Searle (Oxford, 1980), p. 24.

[12] G. Beech, 'Aquitanians and Flemings in the Refoundation of Bardney Abbey (Lincolnshire) in the Later Eleventh Century', *Haskins Society Journal*, 1 (1989), 73–90.

[13] D. Knowles, *The Monastic Order in England*, 2nd edn (Cambridge, 1966), pp. 103–6.     [14] *ASC* 'E' 1066.

of their new wealth on existing English monasteries but instead often turned to houses across the Channel with which their families already had links.

Given the fact that many of the new lords already had ties to Norman houses, and possibly had ambivalent feelings about the richer Benedictine houses in England, it was hardly surprising that they were initially selective in their patronage of the existing Benedictine houses. Even Westminster Abbey, founded by the Conqueror's kinsman and kingly predecessor, which might have been thought to escape any taint of political unsoundness, did not attract much in the way of patronage from the new aristocracy. An exception was Geoffrey I de Mandeville, who gave the valuable manor of Ebury for the burial of his first wife, Adeliz.[15] He also founded a priory at Hurley in Surrey, but this gift was by way of restoration of land on which he had evidently encroached.[16]

A few existing houses did attract patronage. Abingdon abbey was not far from Windsor, and the Conqueror's son Henry paid a visit.[17] Henry de Ferrers gave tithes at West Lockinge to Abingdon.[18] Gilbert de Gant restored the abbey's house at Westminster.[19] In 1090 Earl Hugh conceded land at Shippon in Berkshire. This was not a one-sided gift as his charter makes clear, but in effect a gift in return for a cash payment and the privilege of confraternity.[20] Medical care provided by the abbey prompted some benefactions. For instance, Abingdon was given a large cash gift by Robert d'Oilly and his wife as a thank offering for Robert's recovery from an illness.[21] Aubrey de Vere gave the church of Kensington for the care of his son Geoffrey, who died and was buried at the abbey; Miles Crispin made a gift in return for the medical care he received from Abbot Faritius (1100–17), as did Robert FitzHaimon.[22] In some cases land given to Abingdon may have been restoration rather than a new gift: this certainly was the view of the author of the history of the deeds of the abbots.[23]

A few English abbeys provided monks for dependent priories. One of the most conspicuous in this area was St Albans under the dynamic leadership of Abbot Paul, Lanfranc's nephew, who was appointed in 1077.[24] St

[15] *Westminster Abbey Charters 1066–c. 1214*, ed. E. Mason, London Record Society, xxv (1988), no. 462.

[16] *Ibid.*, no. 436.    [17] *Chronicon Monasterii de Abingdon*, II, 12.    [18] *Ibid.*, II, 32.

[19] *Ibid.*, II, 15–16.    [20] *Chester Charters*, no. 2.    [21] *Chronicon Monasterii de Abingdon*, II, 12–15, 24–5; 204.

[22] *Ibid.*, II, 55, 97, 96.    [23] *Ibid.*, II, 288. Colne and Edwardstone are mentioned in this context.

[24] *Gesta Abbatum Monasterii S. Albani*, I, 51.

Albans had a lot going for it as the church of the protomartyr of Britain, and Paul was evidently an abbot of exceptional ability. He began to build a magnificent new church, and to develop the school and library. The community expanded, and women also were attracted by its reputation as we have seen (see above, p. 387). These projects were costly: Lanfranc subsidized the building costs.[25] Norman landholders in the region also made gifts. Tithes given at Hatfield Peverel by Ranulf Peverel were specifically assigned to pay for the copying of books.[26] Nigel d'Aubigny, lord of Cainhoe, gave the tithes of West Hendred in Berkshire, before 1086.[27] Nigel's brother Richard, a monk at Lessay, became abbot of St Albans in 1119. Anschetil de Rots gave – or rather restored – two hides in Shephall which he held of Lanfranc.[28]

As the reputation of St Albans grew, so its attractiveness to potential donors increased. The rapid expansion of the community meant that monks could be supplied to new cells. These included a priory at Wallingford, founded by Geoffrey the chamberlain of the Conqueror's daughter.[29] Robert de Tosny's foundation of Belvoir occurred before 1076. He may have chosen to make it a priory of St Albans because his predecessor Oswulf son of Fran had given land to St Albans.[30] Binham in Norfolk was founded by Peter de Valognes. His chief manor was at Long Benington in Hertfordshire, so he must have known the community at St Albans well. By contrast, Binham with nearby Wells next the Sea and Wood Dalling were Peter's only demesne manors in Norfolk, and he may have chosen to locate the new priory in Norfolk because he had relatively little land there, rather than giving land in a region where he perhaps wished to concentrate his demesne lands.[31] Ralph de Limesy's foundation charter for Hertford said that he was making the gift for his own soul and that of his wife, and for love of the abbot of St Albans. In return for the gift of land, a church at Pyrton, and tithes, the abbot was to provide six monks to say masses for the soul of Ralph, his wife, and all their descendants. The abbot was to receive Ralph as a brother and his wife as a sister, and both were to be buried at the priory.[32] Another case is that of Tynemouth in Northumberland which Robert de Mowbray gave to St Albans in 1092, though it had been given in 1065 to Jarrow by Edmund (a hermit who had

---

[25] *Ibid.*, I, 52.   [26] *Ibid.*, I, 58.   [27] *DB*, I, 59b.   [28] *Gesta Abbatum S. Albani*, I, 55.   [29] *Ibid.*, I, 56.
[30] Dugdale, *Mon. Ang.*, III, 288.   [31] *Gesta Abbatum S. Albani*, I, 56–7.   [32] Dugdale, *Mon. Ang.*, III, 299.

discovered St Oswin's body there) and had passed to Durham.[33] At first sight this was an odd and inevitably contentious decision, best explained perhaps by Robert's wish to be independent of the bishop of Durham and by some acquaintance with St Albans, possibly via the d'Aubigny family.[34]

Another house which prospered in the new regime was St Peter's, Gloucester under Abbot Serlo (1072–1104).[35] When Serlo arrived there from the abbey of Mont St Michel, there were said to be only two monks and eight novices; by his death there was a community of a hundred. Arnulf de Hesdin and Walter de Lacy were both early benefactors, but the real take off came in the 1090s, when gifts were made of land and property in distant parts of England and in Wales. Some benefactors were *curiales* like Hugh de Port and Roger Bigod, whose attachment to Gloucester abbey, as Bates has pointed out, was probably the result of visits there in the king's company, though they were also benefactors of other houses. The result was that the endowments of the abbey probably doubled.

Rochester cathedral priory was less conspicuously successful in attracting benefactions than Abingdon, St Albans, or Gloucester, but its experience in the new regime may have been more typical. Under Bishop Gundulf (1077–1108) the cathedral was rebuilt, the endowment of the see was increased, and the community grew from twenty-two monks to sixty.[36] Gundulf had most help from Archbishop Lanfranc, who had been responsible for bringing him to England. His most valuable gain, converting a lease on the manor of Heddenham to an outright grant from the king, was paid for by his construction of the royal castle at Rochester. The most significant lay benefactors to Rochester were Haimo the sheriff (the church of Tarenteford), Roger Bigod (the church of Walton in Suffolk), and William d'Aubigny.[37] Gilbert FitzRichard gave the church of Rotherfield, but this may have been an act of compensation.[38] The total is therefore not

---

[33] SD, *Opera omnia*, II, 177, 221.

[34] Nigel d'Aubigny is said to have marched against the Scots in a campaign described in the *Life and Miracles of St Oswi*; this could have occurred in 1094–5 or 1097: see Barlow, *William Rufus*, p. 291.

[35] D. Bates, 'The Building of a Great Church: the Abbey of St Peter's Gloucester and its Early Norman Benefactors', *Transactions of the Bristol and Gloucestershire Archaeological Society*, 102 (1984), 129–32; E. Cownie, 'Gloucester Abbey, 1066–1135: An Illustration of Religious Patronage in Anglo-Norman England', *England and Normandy in the Middle Ages*, ed. D. Bates and A. Curry (London, 1994), pp. 143–57.

[36] M. Ruud, 'Monks in the World: the Case of Gundulf of Rochester', *Anglo-Norman Studies*, 11 (1988), 245–60.     [37] Dugdale, *Mon. Ang.*, I, 164.

[38] *Ibid.*, I, 164; the lawsuit between Gundulf and Gilbert is described in the *Textus Roffensis*, f. 197r, facsimile edited by P. H. Sawyer, *Early English Manuscripts in Facsimile*, vii, ix (Copenhagen, 1957, 1962).

over-impressive, but when we turn to look at membership of the confraternity established there, probably by Gundulf, we find a mix of Normans and English, and among the Normans were Hugh de Port, possibly the first Norman sheriff of Kent, Walter Tirel, Rufus's friend, and William d'Aubigny, butler to Henry I.[39]

Only two of the new lords in the Conquest generation went so far as to found Benedictine abbeys from scratch in England: Roger of Montgomery at Shrewsbury, and Earl Hugh, evidently influenced by Roger, at Chester. Roger had the resources to found an abbey (though so did many others), and he also had had plenty of experience on the continent.[40] He had turned the collegiate church at Troarn into an abbey, refounded Saint Martin of Sées with monks from St Evroul, and had restored the nunnery at Almenêches. He was a benefactor of Cluny, providing money for the refectory and refounding the church of St Milburga as a Cluniac priory, and he made substantial gifts to St Stephen's, Caen.[41] He had also founded collegiate churches at his castles of Arundel, and probably also at Shrewsbury, and Quatford.[42]

The choice of Shrewsbury for the location of the new house rather than Sussex was deliberate in that this was a frontier county, and the abbey could help to provide a new focus of loyalty. Roger was urged to found a monastery there by Odelerius, father of Orderic Vitalis, according to Orderic's own account. Odelerius had charge of a small chapel dedicated to St Peter and St Paul and, whilst on a pilgrimage to Rome in 1082, swore to replace the wooden building with one of stone. Roger was thinking of founding his own monastery and Odelerius persuaded him to subscribe fifteen pounds and to take on the project.[43] Two monks from Sées were brought over to help construct the monastic buildings. In 1086 the abbey was in receipt, courtesy of Roger, of £12 from the burgesses and mills of Shrewsbury, from Eyton, paying £14, Emstrey, paying £11, and Boreton,

[39] H. Tsurushima, 'The Fraternity of Rochester Cathedral Priory about 1100', *Anglo-Norman Studies*, 14 (1991), 313–37.

[40] OV, II, 20 (Troarn); OV, II, 48 (Sées); OV, III, 142 (Almenêches; and see also L. Musset, *Les premiers temps de l'abbaye d'Almenêches-Argentan et Sainte-Opportune*, Paris, 1970).

[41] For Cluny, see R. S. Graham, 'The Monastery of Cluny, 910–1155', *Archaeologia*, 80 (1930), 155 and for Wenlock, *VCH Shropshire*, II, 39–40; for Caen, *Les actes de Guillaume le Conquérant et de la reine Mathilde pour les abbayes caennaises* (ed. Musset), nos. 1, 2.

[42] For Arundel see D. J. A. Matthew, *Norman Monasteries and their English Possessions* (Oxford, 1962), p. 55; *DB*, I, 252b (St Michael's), 254 (Quatford).    [43] OV, III, 142–40.

8s., plus the churches of Wrockwardine (with land, worth 5s.), Baschurch (£1 6s. 8d.), Hodnet, Morville (with land, worth £3 7s.), 'Corfham' (18s.), Ness, Stottesdon (with land, worth £1), Tugford (worth £2), and Lowe (10s.).[44] Some of these churches, including Morville, where there had been eight canons in King Edward's day, were minsters, and their bestowal on a monastery represented a further stage in the break-up of middle Saxon ecclesiastical organization. In all, the endowment totalled some £46 at that time, substantial by comparison with some £34 for Wenlock or only £13 for St Werburgh's, Chester, but only a fraction of Roger's wealth. Before he died Roger added the churches of six more manors.[45] Odelerius himself provided no less than two hundred pounds of silver, a massive sum for a household clerk.[46]

Roger's example was probably one of the factors which motivated Earl Hugh of Chester to turn a college of secular canons at Chester into a Benedictine abbey under the guidance of Anselm abbot of Bec. Hugh arranged that as the canons died their prebends should pass to the abbey, dedicated to St Werburgh, whose relics were at Chester. Hugh provided the buildings and a nucleus of monks, one of whom became the first abbot, came from Bec. The purported foundation charter of Chester abbey lists possessions in over a score of places, and property in Chester, two manors in Anglesey, one in Rhos, Irby in Wirral, ten bovates in Lindsey, Weston-on-Trent (after the death of Hugh's countess), the church and tithe of Aston-on-Trent, and tithes in a long list of manors, freedom from tolls and other services, the right to a court for tenants, and a three-day fair in Chester.[47]

In this first phase after the Conquest in the midlands and the south there are several distinctive features of ecclesiastical patronage. In the first place there is the choice of house, often a Norman house, as the recipient of gifts; English houses were patronized only selectively. Secondly, the gifts included lands, and also very commonly churches and tithes, of which the new elite found themselves in possession. The total amount given on the whole was not exceptional in money terms, though Earl Roger's Shrewsbury was well endowed by contemporary standards. The amount given was also related to expectations: some were evidently the basis from

---

[44] DB, I, 252b, 253, 253b, 254; see table in *Cartulary of Shrewsbury Abbey*, I, xviii–xix.

[45] *VCH Shropshire*, II, 30–1.     [46] OV, III, 143–50.     [47] *Chester Charters*, no. 3.

which spiritual services for the lord's principal castle could be provided;
others were given in the hope of commemorative prayers or confraternity.
The final point worth noticing is that the new lords, in the years of conquest and settlement, did not confine their gifts to one house, even if they
hoped that a particular community would become associated with their
family. Roger Bigod gave to Rochester and Gloucester, as we have seen, as
well as his main commitment, a priory at Thetford. Roger of Montgomery
was an active founder and benefactor wherever he went, and different
communities in different contexts fulfilled a variety of needs, but it was at
Shrewsbury that he donned a religious habit, and where he died.

The north of England presented a different kind of challenge. The
initial impulse came from three men: Aldwin prior of Winchcombe,
Aelfwig of Evesham, and Reinfrid, a Norman knight. Reinfrid was possibly
connected with the family of Arches and may have visited Whitby in the
early months of 1070 during the harrying of the north. The diocese of
Worcester had had close links with York as we have noticed, and the presence in Worcester of refugees from the harrying of the north must have
stirred up concern. The three men, fired by the ideal of seeking holy soli-
tude in that region which in the days of Bede had been a byword for its
monasteries, set off for the north. First they went to Monkchester but
could find no trace of the early monastery; next they visited Bede's own
monastery at Jarrow, the site of which was given to them by the bishop of
Durham, then Wearmouth, and Tynemouth, where they were given land
by Waltheof, then earl of Northumbria. Aldwin and Turgot, later prior of
Durham, also went to Melrose, but ran into difficulties because King
Malcolm demanded an oath of allegiance which they were not prepared
to give. Reinfrid, who may have been in the service of William de Percy,
went to Whitby, and settled on the site of St Hild's abbey, but was forced to
move because of pirates, first to Hackness, then to Lastingham, where
Saint Chad had been based, and finally to York, where St Mary's abbey was
founded in about 1088 under the patronage of William Rufus.[48] St Mary's
still awaits detailed study, yet it is clear that it soon became a focus for
benefactions by the new elite. William Rufus issued a confirmation

[48] L. G. D. Baker, 'The Desert in the North', *Northern History*, 5 (1970), 1–11; J. Burton, 'The Monastic Revival in Yorkshire: Whitby and St Mary's York', *Anglo-Norman Durham*, ed. D. Rollason, M. Harvey, and M. Prestwich (Woodbridge, 1994), pp. 41–51 offers a reappraisal of the foundation of these two houses.

charter listing his father's gifts and his own before those of Count Alan who was nevertheless described as 'inceptor et institutor' of the abbey. There then followed the gifts of Hugh FitzBaldric, earlier sheriff of Yorkshire, Osbern de Arches, Odo the crossbowman, Gilbert de Gant, William de Scohies, and Ilbert de Lacy.[49] The confirmation of Henry II lists other donations from the same period, by Gilbert Tison, Robert de Stuteville, Ralph Paynel, Ivo de Vesci, Geoffrey Bainard, Guy de Balliol, Nigel Fossard, and Ivo Taillebois, a list which reads like a roll call of the Normans in the north in the late eleventh century.[50]

Meanwhile Walcher bishop of Durham had been hopeful of founding a monastery at Durham but was murdered before his plan came to fruition. His successor Bishop William obtained the pope's permission for the monastery. The communities at Wearmouth and Jarrow were transferred, and that at Durham was given the option of its members becoming monks or being pensioned off: significantly only one of the clerks chose to enter the monastery.[51] Like Whitby and York, Durham prospered, and all three became wealthy from the gifts of local families.

Despite the attractions of monasticism for would-be founders, a number of great lords in the north and the south chose instead to establish colleges of canons. There was nothing intrinsically new about such colleges: a number already existed in pre-Conquest England and Normandy. Sometimes they consisted of only a handful of clerks, but they could serve the spiritual and secretarial needs of the lord's household by supplying chaplains and clerks who did not have to embrace monastic vows. Thus Robert de Beaumont founded the college of St Mary in Leicester castle, possibly in 1107, and the college of St Nicholas at Meulan possibly two years later.[52] His brother Henry, first earl of Warwick, founded two colleges at Warwick – St Mary's and St Sepulchre's.[53] But what was new from the closing years of the eleventh century was the foundation of communities associated with a rule believed to have been established by St Augustine, which emphasized poverty, simplicity, and practical good works.

---

[49] *Early Yorkshire Charters*, I, no. 350.     [50] *Ibid.*, I, no. 354.

[51] SD, *Opera omnia*, I, 122; for the suggestion that the clerks may have been implicated in the murder of Bishop Walcher, see D. Rollason, 'Symeon of Durham and the Community of Durham in the Eleventh Century', *England in the Eleventh Century*, ed. C. Hicks (Stamford, 1992), pp. 183–98.

[52] Crouch, *Beaumont Twins*, pp. 196–7.     [53] *VCH Warwickshire*, II, 124, 97.

## The changing landscape

The flexibility of the Augustinian rule meant that founders and benefactors with a variety of different needs were attracted to it. Existing communities of secular clerks could be reorganized into Augustinian priories, for instance, as could hermits, such as those at Nostell in Yorkshire or Llanthony in Monmouthshire. Some priories were combined with hospitals. Kealey demonstrated that there were a remarkable number of hospitals founded in Norman England, not through any great medical advances so much as an ideal of practical charity to care for the chronic sick and dying in institutions that combined elements of sheltered housing and hospices.[54] Some Augustinian houses specialized in dealing with that new scourge of western Europe – leprosy. Many churches were given to Augustinian canons and, though it is not clear if the donors generally expected the canons to provide parochial services themselves, it is clear that they believed the canons would at least supervise such provision.

Augustinian houses quickly became very popular in England, and in the twelfth century their houses came to outnumber those of Benedictine monks. They proved very popular with bishops, who had authority over them, unlike the new orders of the twelfth century. They were also popular with founders and benefactors because they were far less expensive to found than Benedictine abbeys, yet were dedicated to a rule which combined spiritual ideals with a bent for practical charity. The rule was introduced into England at the close of the eleventh century. The first house is said to have been St Botolph's, Colchester, though it is evident that several collegiate churches were adopting the Augustinian rule at about the same time. By 1107 they were sufficiently well organized to release brethren to form the nucleus of a house founded in London by Queen Matilda – Holy Trinity, Aldgate.[55] Henry I was responsible for St Denys, Southampton (1127), Dunstable (1131), Wellow by Grimsby, Carlisle (1122–3), and Cirencester (1133). Other members of the court followed the lead of the king and queen, and the founders included not only men from established baronial families but Henry's new men as well. Among the

---

[54] E. J. Kealey, *Medieval Medicus. A Social History of Anglo-Norman Medicine* (Baltimore and London, 1981).

[55] J. C. Dickinson, *The Origins of the Austin Canons and their Introduction into England* (London, 1950), pp. 97–103.

**12** Llanthony Priory, Monmouthshire, founded in the early twelfth century.
Photograph: Ian Green.

former were Ranulf II earl of Chester (Trentham), Robert de Ferrers
(Breedon), Gilbert de Gant (Bridlington), Robert earl of Leicester
(Leicester), Baldwin de Redvers (Breamore), William Meschin (Embsay),
and Robert d'Oilly (Oseney). Henry's new men were well represented by
Richard Basset (Launde), Bertram de Bulmer (Marton), Robert de Brus
(Guisborough), Walter Espec (Kirkham), Eustace FitzJohn (North Ferriby),
Gilbert the sheriff (Merton), Miles of Gloucester (Llanthony Secunda),
Rahere the king's jester (St Bartholomew, Smithfield), Geoffrey FitzPain
(Warter), and William de Pont de l'Arche (Southwick). The list of early
twelfth-century founders also includes bishops. An element of fashion
here is clear.[56]

---

[56] *Ibid.*, pp. 108–31.

**13** Doorway, probably from Kenilworth Priory, now at St Nicholas, Kenilworth. Photograph: Ian Green.

Thus the order was attractive to a wide band of men, ecclesiastical and lay, men from established families and new men, men from the very richest families and those of middling rank. The appeal was not something about the court of Henry I but about the nature of the new foundations, often incorporating older communities, and not as expensive to found as Benedictine houses in proportion to their founders' total wealth. Even where founders were generous, the amount they gave to found new priories was relatively modest in relation to their total wealth. Kenilworth priory was founded in 1124–5 by Geoffrey de Clinton, one of Henry I's new men, and on the eve of the Dissolution, when its lands were worth £539, the priory was one of the richer Augustinian houses.[57] Three charters of Geoffrey are recorded in the cartulary of the house. In the first he gave the flat land at Kenilworth, except what was needed for his castle, and three other manors which he held as a sub-tenant (in other words, they

[57] *Ibid.*, pp. 290–9.

belonged to others, one to a nun, 'Liuithe'), and three churches.[58] In the second charter he gave tithes, and in the third he gave the manor of Hughenden, which he had purchased; he also confirmed the church of Stone whose lord had been persuaded by Geoffrey to grant it to the priory.[59] Geoffrey was in fact using cash either to buy land to give, or to persuade others to give. Only the manor of Kenilworth, which he had received from the king, represented a direct loss from his estates.

Although the Augustinians were to be the most popular, the Arrouaisian and Premonstratensian canons also attracted patronage in England. The former were particularly austere. The order originated in about 1090 near Arras, and in the time of Abbot Gervase (1121–47) was strongly influenced by Cistercian practices, with the crucial difference that the Arrouaisians unlike the Cistercians were prepared to admit women as well as men. Two members of the original community at Arrouaise had been canons in England at the time of the Conqueror, and it has been suggested that they may have visited Waltham and that it was through this channel that the order attracted interest in England.[60] An alternative route, however, was via the household of Eustace III count of Boulogne where Gervase abbot of Arrouaise had been a clerk. Abbot Gervase was also a friend of Eustace's daughter Matilda, wife of King Stephen.

The first Arrouaisian house in England was founded at Missenden by William of Missenden. He was a tenant of Walter Giffard, who in turn was responsible for founding Nutley. The principal English house, however, was Harrold priory, founded between about 1136 and 1138 by Sampson le Fort, a vassal of the earl of Huntingdon, and a kinsman of Hilbert Pélice, a canon of Arrouaise.[61] Abbot Gervase seems to have visited England, possibly for the foundation of the priory, and may even have retired there.[62] A start may have been made before 1136 when King David was still earl of Huntingdon, and in about 1140 David himself made a grant to Arrouaise which resulted in the establishment of an abbey in Scotland at Cambuskenneth.[63] Barrow discussed the question of the means by which David came to know about the order and suggested that Adelulf bishop of

---

[58] London, British Library MS Harley 3650, ff. 1–2.    [59] Ibid., f. 2.
[60] Dickinson, Origin of the Austin Canons, p. 106.    [61] Thompson, Women Religious, p. 151.    [62] Ibid.
[63] Regesta Regum Scottorum. I The Acts of Malcolm IV, ed. G. W. S. Barrow (Edinburgh, 1960), no. 139; G. W. S. Barrow, 'The Royal House and the Religious Orders', The Kingdom of the Scots (London, 1973), pp. 181–3.

Carlisle and Malachy of Armagh were the likeliest contacts, but he does not discuss other possible routes, via Queen Matilda, or Sampson le Fort. Another early patron was Bishop Alexander of Lincoln, possibly because of the sympathy he seems to have had towards female vocations.[64]

The Premonstratensians, founded by St Norbert at Prémontré near Laon and following a rule heavily influenced by the Cistercians, were another order which attracted patronage in England. Henry I was a benefactor of the Premonstratensian house at Marienweerd, and Bishop Alexander of Lincoln was probably instrumental in encouraging the order in England.[65] The first English house was founded at Newhouse in or about 1143 by Peter of Goxhill, a minor Lincolnshire landholder, though it is not clear what prompted him to choose the Premonstratensian order rather than, say, the Gilbertines.[66] The new abbey was given land in Newhouse, the church of Habrough and one bovate of land, one-sixth of the church of Brocklesby and one bovate, plus 54 acres at Killingholme, and various other bits and pieces.[67]

A very strong tendency in contemporary religious feeling was that towards the eremetical life. Hermit-preachers drew crowds, deeply moved by the call to repentance and renunciation of sin. Hermits, either individually or more commonly in groups, retired to the wilderness to embrace a life of austerity. By degrees, they embraced a more structured and organized life and, inevitably, received gifts of lands and churches.[68] England had its own hermits, such as those on Goathland moor in Yorkshire in the early twelfth century, to whom Henry I granted land and pasture in the forests of Pickering, or those at Nostell who were replaced by Augustinian canons soon after 1120.[69] There were also hermits at Selby, Bridlington, and Kirkstall before the setting up of organized communities at those places.[70] In Lincolnshire there was a hermit at Kirkstead before the foundation of the abbey.[71] In Monmouthshire, Llanthony priory had originated in the desire of a former chaplain of the queen to devote himself to an eremetical life.[72] Before 1120 there were also hermits living in

---

[64] Dyson, 'Monastic Patronage of Bishop Alexander', pp. 10–12.   [65] *Ibid.*, p. 11.

[66] For a suggestion that Peter was trying to fend off William de Roumare's ambitions towards his lands, see Dalton, 'Ranulf II and Lincolnshire', p. 116.   [67] Dickinson, *Origins of the Austin Canons*, p. 121.

[68] H. Leyser, *Hermits and the New Monasticism* (London, 1984); C. Holdsworth, 'Hermits and the Power of the Frontier', *Reading Medieval Studies*, 16 (1990), 55–76.

[69] *RRAN*, II, no. 926; for Nostell see Nicholl, *Thurstan*, pp. 127–37.   [70] *Ibid.*, p. 46 and n.

[71] *Mowbray Charters*, no. 242.   [72] Dugdale, *Mon. Ang.*, VI, 128–34.

Whittlewood forest in Northamptonshire who were taken under the patronage of Earl Robert of Leicester.[73] Earl William of Gloucester made a grant to hermits living on an island whose identity has not been established but was probably situated off the coast of Glamorgan or Somerset.[74]

On the fringes of Normandy, groups under the leadership of Vitalis of Mortain, Bernard of Tiron, and Robert of Arbrissel, ended up forming new orders, respectively, the Savigniacs, the Tironensians, and the nuns of Fontevraud. Vitalis is known to have preached in England, and the first Savigniac house was set up there by Stephen as count of Mortain.[75] Other houses soon followed, including Basingwerk in Flint founded by Ranulf II of Chester in 1131, Quarr on the Isle of Wight founded by Baldwin de Redvers in 1132, and Stratford Langhorne in Essex by William de Montfiquet in 1135. The factors that directed the attention of these men to the order of Savigny rather than Cîteaux, with which it had close parallels and was soon to amalgamate, are not clear. After 1135, however, support for Savigny increasingly came to have political overtones because of its particular association with King Stephen. In 1147 when the Norman and French abbots of the Savigniac order voted for union with Cîteaux, whose leader Bernard of Clairvaux had been a strong critic of Stephen, the English houses initially refused to accept the decision, but were brought to compliance.

The Tironensians and order of Fontevraud made less impact on England. There were Tironensian priories and cells at Mapledurwell, Hamble, St Cross on the Isle of Wight, and Titley in Henry I's reign, but these were much less important than the abbey of St Dogmaels in Wales, founded by Robert FitzMartin.[76] Fontevraud originated as a double community for men and women, and had evolved into an abbey for women. It was the mother house of Nuneaton, founded in the mid-twelfth century by Robert earl of Leicester, or rather his countess, Amice, and of Westwood in Worcestershire founded by Eustacia de Say. The order had special ties with Henry II and Queen Eleanor, and when Henry II refounded the nunnery of Amesbury in Wiltshire it was as a Fontevraudine house.[77]

---

[73] Crouch, *Beaumont Twins*, p. 198.    [74] *Gloucester Charters*, no. 170.

[75] Knowles, *Monastic Order*, pp. 227–8, 249–52; B. D. Hill, *English Cistercian Monasteries and their Patrons in the Twelfth Century* (Urbana, 1968), pp. 80–115; B. Poulle, 'Savigny and England', *Normandy and England* (ed. Bates and Curry), pp. 159–68; J. Burton, 'The Abbeys of Byland and Jervaulx, and the Problems of the English Savigniacs, 1134–1156', *Monastic Studies*, 2 (1991), 119–31.

[76] Barlow, *English Church 1066–1154*, p. 206.    [77] Thompson, *Women Religious*, chapter seven.

The Cistercians proved to be the most successful of the new orders in England. To recruits and patrons alike they epitomized the highest ideals of the monastic life. They only accepted adult entrants who had to undergo a full year's novitiate, and rejected wealth in the form of ecclesiastical ornament and economic gain. In the early days they refused gifts of churches and tithes, for instance, and they would not accept mills and bakeries. The earliest house in England was founded by William Giffard, bishop of Winchester, at Waverley in Surrey in about 1128. Bishop William was catholic in his support for different orders: he promoted Augustinian houses, was the founder of a small Tironensian house at Hamble, and evidently became interested in the Cistercians too.[78]

It was, however, in northern England that the Cistercians made their greatest impact. Bernard himself planned the enterprise like a military campaign, as the letter he addressed to Henry I made clear.[79] The first northern house was set up at Rievaulx through the concerted efforts of Walter Espec and Archbishop Thurstan; they were soon followed by secessionists from St Mary's, York, whom the archbishop established at Fountains.[80] The order then rapidly threw out colonies, especially during Stephen's reign, until the Cistercian general chapter in 1152 forbade any further foundations.

The attractions for founders and benefactors were self-evident. Unlike the Benedictines, Cistercians were directly involved in the physical labour of land clearance and farming, so that benefactors could give relatively small amounts of land which was as yet unproductive. Walter Espec originally seems only to have given nine ploughlands at Helmsley to the monks of Rievaulx. Those whom Thurstan settled at Fountains had a very tough time for the first two years until more recruits with funds arrived. Yet the north offered almost ideal conditions for the spread of the order, as there were still relatively few monastic communities there, and plenty of land ripe for cultivation.

Was there any special connection between the spread of the order and the conditions of Stephen's reign? Bennett Hill argued that there was, in

---

[78] M. J. Franklin, 'The Bishops of Winchester and the Monastic Revolution', *Anglo-Norman Studies*, 12 (1989), 47–65.

[79] *The Letters of St Bernard of Clairvaux*, ed. B. S. James (London, 1953), pp. 141–2.

[80] Nicholl, *Thurstan*, pp. 151–91; D. Bethell, 'The Foundation of Fountains Abbey and the State of St Mary's of York, in 1132', *Journal of Ecclesiastical History*, 17 (1966), 11–27; D. Baker, 'The Foundation of Fountains abbey', *Northern History*, 4 (1969), 29–43.

the sense that the nobles deliberately chose to found Cistercian houses as a means of buttressing their own power in a way that Benedictine houses could not. The latter, it is argued, were linked very closely to the governmental structures of church and state, whereas the Cistercians were independent of both, not owing knight service or tithe, and in practice free from episcopal intervention. It is natural, Hill argued, that the Cistercians should have expanded at a time when royal authority was weak, and their founders, far from being disinterestedly benevolent, gave little and expected returns.[81]

This line of argument, however, fails to set the expansion of the Cistercians in the wider context of the overall expansion of religious houses during the period, especially the comparable rise in Augustinian foundations. Moreover, the ending of the period of rapid expansion of this order came about mainly because of the prohibition of 1152, and, it has been suggested, donors then simply switched their patronage towards the Premonstratensians. Much wealth also passed into the hands of the crusading orders, which began to recruit wealth in England at the end of Henry I's reign, as we shall see shortly.

The conflict of Stephen's reign did lead indirectly to some foundations, in that one obvious way of neutralizing disputed land was to give it to the church. Bordesley abbey in Worcestershire was founded by Waleran of Meulan, on land which had been royal demesne prior to Waleran's creation as earl, and which the Empress evidently regarded as still royal land.[82] A few years later Waleran's twin, Earl Robert, founded Biddlesden abbey on land which Robert de Meppershall claimed was his, but which his overlord, the earl of Leicester, had granted to his steward Ernald de Bosco claiming that no service had been performed. Robert of Meppershall had to be ejected after a siege, Ernald founded an abbey there, and persuaded Robert of Meppershall to give his consent.[83] There was nothing new about the practice of giving land of which the title was contested in some way to the church, but circumstances in Stephen's reign provided ample opportunities for doing so.

The last new category of religious community that needs to be consid-

[81] Hill, *English Cistercian Monasteries*, pp. 36–41, and chapter two passim.
[82] Crouch, *Beaumont Twins*, p. 51; cf. Chibnall, *Empress Matilda*, pp. 134–5.
[83] Crouch, *Beaumont Twins*, pp. 80–2.

ered here as a potential source of gifts are the crusading orders. Here the
secular values of the knightly class intermingled with the call to a religious life, an amalgam which was to prove immensely attractive from the
early twelfth century. In 1128 Hugh de Payens, master of the order of the
Temple, visited the court of Henry I, and probably established a headquarters in London at the Old Temple. However, it was the patronage of Queen
Matilda and King Stephen which marked the real breakthrough. The
queen, as the niece of Godfrey de Bouillon and Baldwin, kings of
Jerusalem, evidently felt a special attachment to the crusading order. She
gave Cressing from the lands of the honour of Boulogne, followed by land
in Uphall in Great Tey, the manor and half-hundred of Witham (all in
Essex), and Cowley in Oxfordshire.[84] Stephen's father had taken a prominent if not altogether successful role in the first crusade, and, as Emilie
Amt has pointed out, Hugh de Payens came from Champagne, which was
ruled by Stephen's brother, while Godfrey of St Omer, the other founder of
the order, was a vassal of the count of Boulogne.[85]

The lead given by the king and queen was followed by members of their
court. Benefactors included William Martel, Turgis of Avranches, Bernard
de Balliol, Robert de Ferrers, and Simon of Odell.[86] Although links with
Stephen's court were strong, the appeal of the order was not restricted to
the royalist party: benefactors on the Angevin side included Robert and
Miles of Gloucester and Robert II d'Oilly.[87] Between 1140 and 1150 interest
in the crusading ideal in England was growing stronger. Those who stayed
at home could support the cause by making gifts to the Templars, or to
the other great crusading order, the Hospitallers, founded in the late
eleventh century to provide a hostel and hospital service for pilgrims. The
crusading orders, especially the Templars, did receive valuable gifts of
land, such as Cressing and Cowley mentioned above, but they also
received many small parcels of rent-paying land from benefactors of a
lesser social rank. This reflected the nature of their operations, in that revenues were raised in the west and dispatched to the near east.[88]

By the end of our period, the range of possibilities for would-be donors

---

[84] *RRAN*, III, nos. 843, 844, 845, 850.      [85] Amt, *Accession of Henry II*, p. 103.
[86] *RRAN*, III, nos. 849, 855, 859–864.      [87] Amt, *Accession of Henry II*, pp. 104–5.
[88] *The Cartulary of the Knights of St John of Jerusalem in England*, ed. M. Gervers, British Academy Records of
Social and Economic History, new series, VI (London, 1982), pp. xxxvii, xxxviii.

was thus very much greater than it had been at the start. The landscape offered many variant forms of the religious life for men or women or both, in which precise distinctions between monks and canons, or between one order and another, must have been as hard for contemporaries to make as they are for historians. At one level, donors simply recognized the virtues of those seeking to live the life of Christ, and there must also have been an awareness that there were different and evolving forms of trying to achieve this.

Nevertheless we can identify changing trends. At the start of our period the new elite ranged over a wide geographical area in the hunt for holiness. The Conqueror turned to monks from Marmoutier for Battle, William de Briouze to St Florent de Saumur, and William de Warenne to Cluny.[89] Flemings and other non-Normans who came over with the Conqueror also naturally looked further afield, and as we have seen the high reputation of Charroux led to Gilbert I de Gant's decision to give land to the house at Bardney in Lincolnshire. Even Normans did not necessarily feel that they had to turn to the duchy for monks.

The cost of establishing religious communities in the mid-eleventh century meant that only two members of the new elite contemplated the foundation of fully fledged abbeys: priories of monks or colleges of clerks situated close to a new lord's chief castle were the more usual pattern. Gifts were made to existing monasteries, but not usually in the form of land, whilst houses for women were fewer in number and less well endowed than those for men. Less than forty years after the Conquest, the Augustinians were spreading rapidly. They were popular because they met such a variety of needs: they were austere, they could take over existing communities of clerks or canons, they were up-to-date in providing hospitals, and it took much less landed wealth to found an Augustinian priory than a Benedictine abbey, so that families of middling landed wealth could found their 'own' religious house with which they and their descendants could have a special relationship. By the 1140s the Cistercians seemed to many to be the acme of perfection in their austere simplicity, while for those with an interest in the crusades there were the Templars and Hospitallers.

Personal or family contacts were obviously important in influencing

---

[89] For Saint-Florent, see J. Martindale, 'Monasteries and Castles: the Priories of Saint Florent de Saumur in England after 1066', *England in the Eleventh Century*, ed. C. Hicks (Stamford, 1992), pp. 135–56.

the decision as to who should receive patronage.[90] The Cistercian mission to Yorkshire, for instance, was planned with particular care. There were Yorkshiremen at Clairvaux, including Henry Murdac, the future archbishop, and Walter Espec must have indicated that he was prepared to give the monks land at Rievaulx. The *Life of Ailred* relates how Ailred later called at Walter's castle when travelling south, and Walter took him to the fledgling monastery.[91] Stephen of Blois as count of Mortain must have known Vitalis of Mortain, who died in about 1122, and this presumably directed Stephen's thoughts towards the Savigniacs when he founded a community at Tulketh in Lancashire. Roger de Mowbray and his mother Gundrada, patrons par excellence of many of the religious houses of Yorkshire, chose to found not a Cistercian house but one affiliated to Savigny, because Gundrada herself had seen the refugees from Calder outside the Mowbray castle of Thirsk, and was persuaded to help them.[92] The chronicle of Walden describes how Geoffrey II de Mandeville was personally involved in the choice of the site.[93] It was said that the count of Aumale founded a Cistercian abbey (his second) at Meaux in Yorkshire because he was persuaded by Adam, a Cistercian monk, that by this means he could be free from the vow he had taken to go to the Holy Land.[94]

The influences shaping magnates' decisions are more likely to be mentioned in the sources than those of lesser men. The greater lords were in turn often influential in persuading their tenants to make donations to houses they endowed, as in the case of the tenants of Roger of Montgomery to Shrewsbury abbey and the tenants of Earl Hugh of Chester to St Werburgh's at Chester. Such patterns of benefactions were obviously important in binding lords and men to each other, to the religious house, and to the local community, a network of mutual obligations which helped the newcomers to root themselves in local society. Yet by the twelfth century it was proving to be possible for lesser families themselves to take the initiative in founding religious houses, for the material investment required was now less costly. In Yorkshire the fashion in knightly

[90] See for instance the comments made by C. Holdsworth, 'The Cistercians in Devon', *Studies in Medieval History presented to R. Allen Brown*, ed. C. Harper-Bill, C. Holdsworth, and J. L. Nelson (London, 1989), pp. 179–91.

[91] *The Life of Ailred of Rievaulx by Walter Daniel*, ed. F. M. Powicke (Edinburgh 1950, reprinted Oxford, 1978), p. 14.      [92] Dugdale, *Mon. Ang.*, v, 349.

[93] H. Collar, 'Book of the Foundation of Walden Abbey', *Essex Review*, 45 (1936), 78.

[94] *Chronicon Monasterii de Melsa*, ed. E. A. Bond, 3 vols., RS (London, 1866–8), I, 76–82.

families was for nunneries, as we saw in the previous chapter, and in some cases at least the aim was to provide a home for widows and daughters of the founding family. Gilbert of Sempringham's reputation was obviously a decisive factor in the concentration of Gilbertine houses in his native Lincolnshire. Here Golding has drawn attention to the factors which shaped patterns of endowment, the timing, the tenurial context, and the status of founders. Most houses were founded between 1148 and 1160, at a time when there was increasing competition for endowments, and in a county where, rather than one magnate family, there were several locally important knightly families, often related by kinship or marriage. It was from families such as these, including Gilbert's own, that most early endowments came.[95] Yet although such knightly families seem to have taken the initiative in foundations, the success of fledgling houses might well depend on the co-operation of the overlord, as Golding also points out.[96]

## Gifts and givers

In the foregoing pages we have already seen something of the range of gifts that might be made to religious houses. First, there was land which could support the nascent community either by direct exploitation in the case of the Cistercians, or by rents in the case of the other orders. The original grants were often not very large, and the intention obviously was to make a start. Sometimes the land was not the founder's: William de Roumare's foundation charter for the Cistercian abbey of Revesby stated explicitly that the land was not of his own demesne, and that he had accordingly given an exchange to Lambert Bristica's nephew.[97]

References to gifts of churches in the first century following the Conquest often do not make clear what was being bestowed; in earlier charters the donor simply gave the church, without spelling out the implications of the gift. Sometimes the advowson was included, sometimes only a financial interest was being conveyed. If the former, either the beneficiary could choose to take the tithe and appoint a vicar at a fixed stipend, or he could appoint a rector, who then paid a fixed pension. Because arrangements only slowly clarified in the twelfth century and

---

[95] Golding, *Gilbert of Sempringham*, chapter five.    [96] *Ibid.*, p. 211.    [97] Dugdale, *Mon. Ang.*, v, 454.

were often the subject of dispute, donors gradually came to be more precise in the phrasing of charters. Even so, we cannot be sure what the implications of such gifts were for the parishioners, though this was not a consideration which weighed with donors.

The religious were deemed to be Christ's poor, and as such were worthy to receive the tithe. Only Cistercians for a time refused to accept churches.[98] The new lords believed that as one-third of the tithe of a vill was reserved for the parish church, they had the right freely to dispose of the remaining two-thirds.[99] Their tenants often followed their lords' example by granting tithes of their demesne manors. Thus, for instance, Robert II de Ferrers's confirmation charter to Tutbury priory listed the donations of kinsmen and tenants: Nigel d'Aubigny and his wife Amicia, daughter of Henry de Ferrers, had given the church of Catton with its tithes and appurtenances, and 'Wibaldeston' near Didcot with two virgates and appurtenances; Sewal gave two parts of his demesne of Hoon and four acres of Marston; Ralph de Bagpuize two parts of his demesne of Ashden and 'Urlestona'; and so on.[100] Founders also often exempted the new house from the tools collected by lords, as did Earl Hugh for Chester abbey, for instance, and William de Warenne for Lewes priory.[101] Earl Roger endowed Shrewsbury abbey with a set sum from the profits of his burgesses and mills in Shrewsbury.[102] This was a privilege founders might also accord to other religious houses, because it was one that could be easily given. They also made grants of fishing rights or pasturage. As an example of the range of lands and rights of various kinds which could be given, we may cite Roger de Bully's foundation charter for Blyth priory (1088). This gave the priory the church and the whole vill with its appurtenances and such customs as the men of the vill used to render him, namely, ploughing, carrying, mowing, reaping, haymaking, paying merchet, and making the millpond. In addition he granted toll and passage from Radford to 'Thornewad' and from 'Frodestan' as far as the river Idle, and market and fair in Blyth and all his privileges there, namely, sake and soke, toll and team, infangthief, iron and pit, and

[98] B. R. Kemp, 'Monastic Possession of Parish Churches in England in the Twelfth Century', *Journal of Ecclesiastical History*, 31 (1980), 133–59; J. Burton, 'Monasteries and Parish Churches in Eleventh- and Twelfth-Century Yorkshire, *Northern History*, 23 (1987), 39–50.

[99] M. Brett, *The English Church under Henry I*, (Oxford, 1975), p. 225.

[100] *The Cartulary of Tutbury Priory*, no. 52.     [101] *Chester Charters*, no. 3; *Early Yorkshire Charters*, VIII, no. 32.

[102] *DB*, I, 252b.

gallows. He also granted land in three other vills, the tithes of twenty-three ploughlands, two-thirds of the tithes of eleven places in all, and the tithe of one ploughland in a twelfth place. The benefits were given on condition that forty shillings were paid each year to the church of Holy Trinity, Rouen.[103]

In the century following the conquest when donors gave land their charters often included the statement that the gift was made 'freely', or 'in free and perpetual alms'. The implication was evidently that gifts were not to be subject to lay services; quite what that meant in practice in our period is not easy to establish.[104] Joan Wardrop suggested from her study of the Fountains charters that when gifts were made in alms, unless otherwise stated, donors had made arrangements to discharge any services owing.[105] Where services were specified, this might have been because the donor either did not wish, or could not afford, to give them up.[106]

The Cistercians established the privilege of exemption of their lands from the payment of tithe. It appears that they also managed to secure exemption from danegeld, at least after a struggle.[107] But if they accepted land owing knight service, they did not have the right to exemption from that service. It is not necessary to go as far as Hill in suggesting that the magnates in Stephen's reign deliberately gave land owing knight service as a way of avoiding service; it is more likely that this occurred accidentally, since the amount of service involved was not usually large.[108] Magnates could use their influence with the king to secure further privileges for monastic houses, such as the grants of fairs or markets, or jurisdictional privileges. And kings might well have been happy to make such grants; not only did they thus share in the spiritual benefits, but, in the case of northern England particularly, flourishing abbeys and priories helped to strengthen the Norman regime there.

---

[103] *The Cartulary of Blyth Priory*, ed. R. T. Timson, Thoroton Society, xxvi, Historical Manuscripts Commission JP 17 (1973), no. 325.

[104] For a valuable discussion of free alms tenure see B. Thompson, 'Free Alms Tenure in the Twelfth Century', *Anglo-Norman Studies*, 16 (1993), 221–43; Thompson, 'From Alms to Spiritual Services: The Function and Status of Monastic Property in Medieval England', *Monastic Studies*, ed. J. Loades, II (Bangor, 1991), 227–62, especially pp. 242–9. Earlier studies include E. G. Kimball, 'Tenure in Frank Almoign and Secular Services', *English Historical Review*, 43 (1928), 341–53; Kimball, 'The Judicial Aspects of Frank Almoign Tenure', *English Historical Review*, 47 (1932), 1–11.

[105] J. Wardrop, *Fountains Abbey and its Benefactors 1132–1300* (Kalamazoo, Michigan, 1987), p. 35.

[106] *Ibid.*, pp. 37–8.      [107] Green, 'Last Century of Danegeld', pp. 251–2.

[108] Hill, *English Cistercian Monasteries*, pp. 57–60.

Gifts could also take the form of precious objects – manuscripts, fur-nishings, and vestments – which had symbolic as well as material value. Each new lord would at the very least be expected to grant a charter confirming the endowments made by his predecessors; it would be a bonus if he could at the same time be persuaded to augment them, espe-cially as there were so many rival possibilities opening up for donors. Thus Earl Hugh of Chester's heir, Richard, who succeeded as a minor, does not appear to have been much interested in St Werburgh's, and only added a small piece of land, a mill, and a court to its endowments. The next earl, Ranulf I, gave the manor of Upton when the founder's body was moved from the abbey's graveyard to the chapter house. Ranulf II, despite being a benefactor of a number of religious houses, did not show a great deal of interest in the abbey until the end of his life. He gave the tithe of his mills, a tenth of his rents from Chester, and of the fish taken at Chester bridge, but the major gifts came when he gave the valuable manors of Eastham and Bromborough in recompense for alleged wrongs against the abbey.[109]

Gifts made in the first flush of enthusiasm to continental houses tended to be vulnerable to changes of heart by later generations. One case high-lighted by Emma Mason was the church and tithes of Walthamstow which were given by the Tosny family to the abbey of Conches in Normandy, close to their chief castle. After the burial of Hugh de Tosny at Holy Trinity, Aldgate, however, his mother Alice granted to this house the church of Walthamstow with its lands and tithes, reserving to Conches only two-thirds from the demesne of Walthamstow.[110] A different case of second thoughts was the way the Beaumont twins altered the colleges of canons founded by earlier generations on their lands. Robert earl of Leicester changed the college of St Mary which his father had established at Leicester into an Augustinian house and gave Wareham to the abbey of Lire in Normandy. Waleran gave the college of St Nicholas founded by his father at Meulan to the priory of St Nicaise, and Holy Trinity at Beaumont-le-Roger to the abbey of Bec. The twins clearly felt that collegiate churches were following a rule which was not sufficiently ascetic.[111] Walter Espec evidently also thought he could change his mind about the rule to be

---

[109] *Chester Charters*, nos. 8, 13, 25, 26, 34.

[110] E. Mason, 'English Tithe Income of Norman Religious Houses', *Bulletin of the Institute of Historical Research*, 48 (1975), 91–4.    [111] Crouch, *Beaumont Twins*, p. 200.

observed by a house he had founded. He had established an Augustinian priory at Kirkham in about 1122, and when the Cistercians arrived the canons were persuaded to agree to give up the location to the white monks in return for a new site elsewhere. The plan to move the canons seems to have failed, however, and Kirkham stayed where it was, possibly because other benefactors for Rievaulx materialized.[112]

Jennifer Ward has analysed the changing ecclesiastical patronage of another great family – the Clares.[113] Since Richard and Baldwin were the sons of Count Gilbert, a man who was the overlord of Herluin, founder and first abbot of Bec, it was not surprising that the brothers each gave land in England to that abbey. Richard was instrumental in the foundation of a cell of Bec at St Neots and his son Gilbert for the priory of Stoke by Clare. Soon various members of the family made gifts to other houses in England and subsequently shared in their contemporaries' enthusiasm for houses of canons, for Cistercian abbeys, and for the crusading orders. Loyalty to the family's earliest foundations, especially Stoke by Clare, persisted, but as new lordships came into the family these too attracted their share of patronage.

Studies of other families throw further light on the interplay of personal choice, the strength of family ties, and the attractions of new forms of monasticism. Geoffrey I de Mandeville was a benefactor of Westminster abbey, but his successor William I is not known to have made any gifts to that house. Geoffrey II founded a Cistercian house at Walden in about 1136,[114] but neither of his successors, Geoffrey III and William II, were founders. The latter stands out for his patronage of Norman houses, at a time, in the late twelfth century, when this was not typical of magnates, even those with lands on both sides of the Channel.

The charters of the earls of Chester also indicate the changing interests of successive lords of, in this case, one of the greatest lordships in England. As we have seen above (p. 400), Hugh I, in addition to founding Chester abbey, refounded the abbey of St Sever in Normandy, and made

---

[112] D. Baker, 'Patronage in the Early Twelfth Century: Walter Espec, Kirkham and Rievaulx', *Traditio – Krisis – Renovatio aus Theologischer Sicht. Festschrift Winifred Zeller* (Marburg, 1976), pp. 92–9.

[113] Ward, 'Fashions in Monastic Endowment'.

[114] *The Heads of Religious Houses England and Wales 940–1216*, ed. D. Knowles, C. N. L. Brooke, and V. London (Cambridge, 1972), p. 75.

gifts to the abbeys of St Evroul, Abingdon, Bec, and Whitby.[115] His son
Richard, evidently under the influence of his guardian, Henry I, endowed
a cell in Normandy dependent on Troarn. He also was a benefactor of St
Evroul and probably founded Calke, an Augustinian priory.[116] Ranulf I,
Richard's cousin, is known to have made only one gift to Chester abbey,
that of the manor of Upton. His widow Lucy was a benefactor of Spalding
priory, and we have met her in the previous chapter (above, p. 370–1) as
the founder of a nunnery at Stixwould.[117] The interests of Ranulf II were
much more catholic, however, reflecting his lengthy tenure of the
earldom, the wider range of possibilities available, his territorial ambitions, and, at the end of his life, a desire for reparation and repentance.
Ranulf founded either three or four houses: a Cistercian abbey at
Basingwerk in Flint, a nunnery at Chester, and an Augustinian priory at
Trentham in Staffordshire, and he may also have founded a leper hospital
outside Chester.[118] He made gifts to a number of other communities:
Chester abbey, Garendon, Louth, Shrewsbury, Hartsholme, the leper hospital and the hospital of Holy Sepulchre at Lincoln, Norton priory,
Leicester abbey, Lenton priory, Bordesley, Wenlock, Gloucester, Coventry
(possibly), and the Templars, and in Normandy to the abbey of
Montebourg. In addition he made grants in compensation to the church
of Lincoln and the abbeys of Bardney and Burton as well as St Werburgh's;
he took under his protection the priories of Belvoir and Radmore and
Pipewell abbey, as part of his attempts to strengthen his authority in their
vicinity; and his widow Matilda was a benefactor of Calke (Repton).[119] His
son Hugh II, earl between 1153 and 1181, was by contrast benefactor of a
much smaller number of houses, and founded none. Once again, the wave
of enthusiasm faded away in the later twelfth century. The range and
scale of Ranulf II's patronage was exceptional, but it was not unique.
Roger de Mowbray was even more remarkable in this respect. He founded
an Augustinian priory at Newburgh; he and his mother resited the

---

[115] *Chester Charters*, nos. 1, 2, 4, 5; for the tradition that Hugh refounded St Sever, see no. 181.

[116] *Ibid.*, nos. 9–11, 45.  [117] *Ibid.*, nos. 14, 16, 17, 18, 19.

[118] *Ibid.*, nos. 36 (Basingwerk), 97–9 (nunnery), 118 (Trentham), 198 (leper hospital).

[119] *Ibid.*, nos. 26, 29–34 (St Werburgh's), 41 (Garendon), 48 (Louth Park), 61–5 (Shrewsbury), 76–8
(Hartsholme), 79 (leper hospital at Lincoln), 107–8 (Holy Sepulchre, Lincoln), 81 (Norton priory), 83
(Leicester abbey), 84 (Lenton priory), 100–1 (Bordesley), 109 (Wenlock), 116 (Gloucester abbey), 113–114
(Coventry), 66 (Templars), 183 (Montebourg); 104, 96, 115, 50–4, 94, 57–8, 95, 119–122.

refugees from Calder first at Hood and then at Byland, and in addition he made grants (as opposed to confirmations) to some twenty-two houses, and to the Hospitallers and the Templars.[120]

Can a profile be drawn of the 'typical' pattern of patronage of the leading baronial families? It was clearly very common for the first holder to found or reorganize a community close to his chief estate and castle, sometimes opting for monks, sometimes for clerks. Many of the latter were subsumed into Augustinian priories from the very end of the eleventh century. Those whose wealth was newly acquired or enlarged in the reign of Henry I might well opt for a relatively rich endowment for an Augustinian house, like Kenilworth, Guisborough, or Bridlington. In the 1140s the tide was running very strongly in favour of the Cistercians, and families with sufficient resources not infrequently at this time set up a Cistercian house. Within these broad trends, however, personal tastes, resources, and timing all had a part to play.

So far we have been considering how the range of religious foundations greatly increased during our period, and the types of benefactions that were made. The emphasis has been on gifts of lands and rights, which have been considered in a straightforward way, as if they were one-way transactions, whereas the reality was often more complicated. A gift was rarely entirely one-sided; it was to be expected that some kind of counter-gift, however small, would be made.[121] Often the counter-gift was not small, and a transaction which purported to be a gift was nothing of the kind, the language of the document concealing what was in fact a sale. The Cistercians were supposed only to accept unsolicited freewill gifts, but, as we have seen, gifts made to them in free and perpetual alms often still carried a burden of service. The language of documents is often deceptive in other respects, too, in that a grantor often said he was 'giving' lands and rights which in reality he was only confirming. A charter of confirma-

---

[120] *Mowbray Charters*, nos. 194–5, 197–206, 208–211 (Newburgh); 32–46, 48–56, 58–69 (Byland). Roger was a benefactor of Bridlington, Burton Lazars, Combe, Fountains, Furness, S. André-en-Gouffern, Hirst, Jervaulx, Malton, Newstead, Nostell, North Ormsby, Pipewell, Rievaulx, Selby, Welford, Whitby, Vaudey, Villers-Canivet, St Leonard's, York, St Mary's, York and St Peter's, York; for his gifts to these and to the crusading orders see *Mowbray Charters, passim*.

[121] On this whole subject see B. Rosenwein, *To be the Neighbour of St Peter. The Social Meaning of Cluny's Property 909–1049* (Ithaca, NY, 1989).

**14** Robert FitzHaimon and Sybil, commemorated as founders of Tewkesbury Abbey in a sixteenth-century manuscript, Oxford, Bodleian Library, MS. Top. Glouc. d. 2. f. 13r. Reproduced by permission of the Bodleian Library, Oxford.

tion was nevertheless crucial to the beneficiary in our period, because a new lord might try to take back his predecessor's gifts. The occasion on which a confirmation was granted provided an opportunity for a renewal of the relationship between his family and the religious house.

Donors hoped for a whole range of benefits, both spiritual and material, in return for their gifts.[122] Overriding all was the belief that those who had renounced the world were living their lives in the fullest accord with the precepts of the gospel. Many answered that call in person. Herluin,

[122] For useful discussions of motives, see C. Harper-Bill, 'The Piety of the Anglo-Norman Knightly Class', *Proceedings of the Battle Conference*, 2 (1979), 63–77; Thomas, *Vassals, Heiresses, Crusaders, and Thugs*, chapter five; and Golding, *Gilbert of Sempringham*, chapter six.

the founder of Bec, had been a knight in the household of Count Gilbert of Brionne.[123] Earl Hugh's chaplain, Gerold, preached with such persuasiveness that three of the knights of the household were converted.[124] Several knights in Roger de Mowbray's household entered the fledgling Savigniac house at Hood.[125] Penitence led many to make gifts, especially if death seemed close. A well-known letter of Nigel d'Aubigny to his brother when he believed he was soon to die listed the reparations he wished to make to various churches, and to his men.[126] It was not uncommon for men to enter religious houses in their final illness, and to die in the habit of a monk or canon. Roger of Montgomery died at Shrewsbury, Earl Hugh at Chester, and Ralph Basset, Henry I's justice, at Abingdon abbey.[127] Waleran of Meulan, twenty days before his death, became a monk at the family house of St Peter, Préaux, and his twin – at least according to a much later source – took the habit of the Augustinians.[128]

For those who remained outside, what the religious could offer were prayers for the souls of their benefactors. Charters issued by benefactors spell this out in different ways: grants are made for the donor's soul, for those of his wife and son, and all their predecessors and successors. Sometimes charters also mention the soul of the king, and possibly the queen as well. Thus William de Percy's charter for Whitby, issued between 1091 and 1096, listed the souls of King William, Queen Matilda, William Rufus, Earl Hugh of Chester, himself, his wife Emma de Port, and Alan de Percy his son.[129] Roger Bigod's foundation charter for Thetford mentioned that in setting up the priory he had acted with the counsel and advice of King Henry, Queen Matilda, and Bishop Herbert of Norwich, and of his wife Adeliza and his men, 'for the common salvation and remedy of our souls, for the living and the dead, and especially for the soul of the lord king William the elder, his wife Matilda, and their son William'.[130] In his charter granting Felixstowe to Rochester cathedral priory, Roger made his grant 'for the soul of King William who gave me that land and of my wife and specifically for King Henry and for us and our sons and daughters and for Norman the sheriff whose land it was and for our predecessors and

---

[123] 'Life of Herluin', for translated extract relating to Herluin's conversion see R. Allen Brown, *The Norman Conquest*, Documents of Medieval History, no. 5 (London, 1984), pp. 43–4.    [124] OV, III, 226–8.

[125] 'Historia Fundationis' of Byland: Dugdale, *Mon. Ang.*, v, 350.    [126] *Mowbray Charters*, no. 3.

[127] OV, v, 314; OV, III, 148; *Chronicon Monasterii de Abingdon*, II, 170–1.

[128] Crouch, *Beaumont Twins*, pp. 79, 95.    [129] *Early Yorkshire Charters*, XI, 1.

[130] Dugdale, *Mon. Ang.*, v, 148.

successors'.[131] William d'Aubigny's charter for Rochester, issued probably not long after Henry I's accession, mentioned Kings William and Henry, his own soul, and those of his father, mother, wife, brother Nigel, and nephew Humphrey.[132] Robert II d'Oilly, in the foundation charter for Oseney of 1129, made his grant 'for the salvation of the king and the well-being of the whole realm'.[133] The foundation charter of Horkesley priory issued by Robert son of Godebold and his wife Beatrice had a particularly specific list of names to be prayed for: 'for the lord King Henry, our lord Robert, for myself, for Beatrice my wife and Severia her mother and Robert and Richard our sons and Gunnora our daughter and our other infants and for Osbert son of Hugh and Hadewis my sister and for the souls of Robert son of Wymarc and Swein his son and my father Godebold and Raginild my mother, Richard my brother and William my son and for the souls of William [an incomplete name] and Turold his brother'.[134] Sometimes the reference was to the donor's lord. Ralph son of Thorald, a benefactor of Binham Priory in Norfolk, made his gift 'for the soul of Peter de Valognes who enfeoffed my grandfather and founded the church of Binham'.[135]

On some occasions new houses were founded as a substitute for a vow to go on pilgrimage, as in the case already mentioned (see above, p. 413) of William count of Aumale's foundation of the abbey of Meaux, because he had not carried out a vow to go to the Holy Land.[136] A vow of a different kind was Waleran of Meulan's promise during a storm at sea to found a Cistercian abbey if he were spared. This led to the foundation of the abbey of Le Valasse in Normandy.[137]

Personal problems sometimes provided the context in which major gifts were made, whether or not charters referred directly to them. Lack of a male heir or fear of losing one was not infrequently a spur to conscience. William earl of Gloucester made a gift to St Nicholas Exeter for the health of his only son.[138] Conversely, joy at the birth of an heir might lead to a thank offering. Robert of Essex and his wife made a gift to Thetford priory for this reason after the birth of their son Henry.[139]

---

[131] *Textus Roffensis* (ed. Sawyer), ff. 199v–200.     [132] Dugdale, *Mon. Ang.*, I, 164.

[133] *Cartulary of Oseney Abbey*, I, 1.     [134] Dugdale, *Mon. Ang.*, V, 156.

[135] Douglas, *Feudal Documents of the Abbey of Bury St Edmunds*, p. lxxxv, n.

[136] *Chron. Mon. de Melsa*, I, 76–82.     [137] Crouch, *Beaumont Twins*, pp. 68–71.

[138] *Gloucester Charters*, no. 69.     [139] Dugdale, *Mon. Ang.*, V, 142.

The scale of William count of Mortain's foundation of a Cluniac priory at Montacute in Somerset arouses suspicions that this was in some way motivated by personal crisis. Montacute or Bishopton was the place where, shortly before the Conquest, Tofig the Proud had discovered a fragment of the true cross. This he dispatched to a new foundation at Waltham, Essex, while the site of the find was given to Athelney abbey. In 1086 Robert of Mortain was holding the manor, having granted Athelney the manor of Purse Caundle in exchange, and he built a castle there. In about 1100 his son William gave the manor, castle, borough, parish church, and appurtenances to a new priory which was also generously endowed with other lands. Count William had in effect dismantled his Somerset demesne. Was he concerned about the violation of a place with sacred associations?[140]

The names of benefactors were inscribed in gospel books. These were used in the solemn ceremonies by which benefactors were received into confraternity, and, each day when mass was celebrated, names from the relevant pages were read out.[141] Earl Hugh of Chester, in making a grant to Abingdon abbey, received £30 in return, the privilege that he would be treated as one of the brethren, that his wife and father and mother would be remembered in their prayers and their names inscribed in the book of remembrance, and that they should receive the obsequies of brethren when they died.[142] Hugh's charter seems to have antedated his foundation of an abbey at Chester, but we should not assume that magnates necessarily put all their eggs in one basket. Robert of Mortain was a generous benefactor of Grestain, where he was buried, but he nevertheless is known to have entered into a confraternity agreement with the collegiate church of St Martin le Grand.[143] In some cases, the names of husbands, wives, fathers, children, were all inscribed in 'books of life'. Moreover, a recent study of the fraternity at Rochester in about 1100 has pointed out that fraternity not only established a tie between individuals and perhaps their immediate families and the monks, but also with other donors. At Rochester lords and their men are found seeking the privilege of confraternity in groups. The names of Norman lords and both Norman and

---

[140] Golding, 'Coming of the Cluniacs', pp. 174–5.
[141] C. Clark, 'British Library Additional MS 40,000', *Anglo-Norman Studies*, 7 (1985), 55–6; H. E. J. Cowdrey, 'Unions and Confraternities with Cluny', *Journal of Ecclesiastical History*, 16 (1965), 152–62.
[142] *Chester Charters*, no. 2.      [143] London, Westminster Abbey Muniments, 13, 280.

English under-tenants are found and the importance of such group decisions in helping to build solidarity between lords and men, natives and newcomers, in the first critical decades after Hastings should not be underestimated.[144]

As Earl Hugh's charter indicates, one of the most commonly desired privileges was burial within the precincts of a house, to place one's mortal remains within the community in death as well as in life, to await the Last Judgement. Ralph de Limesy's foundation charter of Hertford priory similarly requested that he and his wife should be recognized as brother and sister, and be buried there.[145] The knights of Peterborough abbey expected to give two-thirds of the tithes of their lands to Peterborough, and to be buried there.[146] Places of burial were of concern to religious communities, who wished to preserve ties with the founder's family, and they give clues about an individual's sense of identity.[147] The very greatest lords, who were already associated with houses in Normandy before they arrived in England, might well be buried there. Roger de Beaumont was buried beside his father at Préaux, for instance, and Robert count of Mortain beside his father at Grestain.[148] Hugh de Grandmesnil died in England, but his body was taken back to be buried at St Evroul with which he was particularly associated and where his brother was abbot.[149] Those who founded abbeys or priories in England, however, were often buried there. Thus Earl Hugh was buried at Chester and Roger of Montgomery at Shrewsbury.[150] According to the house history of Belvoir priory, Robert de Tosny was buried there, as were his successors as lords of Belvoir.[151] Eudo the steward founded Colchester abbey and, though he died at Préaux in Normandy, his body was brought back for burial at Colchester.[152] The right to bury a prominent lord was sometimes disputed, as in the case of Roger Bigod who was buried at Norwich though the monks of Thetford claimed him.[153] There was a similar dispute between Llanthony and Gloucester over the body of Miles of Gloucester.[154] The chronicle of Walden abbey relates how the knights of Geoffrey III de Mandeville escorted his corpse to

---

[144] Tsurushima, 'Fraternity of Rochester Cathedral Priory', pp. 336–7.     [145] Dugdale, *Mon. Ang.*, III, 299.

[146] *The Peterborough Chronicle of Hugh Candidus*, ed. W. T. Mellows (Oxford, 1949), pp. 90–1.

[147] On this subject see B. Golding, 'Anglo-Norman Knightly Burials', *The Ideals and Practice of Medieval Knighthood*, I (Woodbridge, 1986), pp. 35–48.     [148] Crouch, *Beaumont Twins*, p. 79.     [149] OV, IV, 336.

[150] *Ibid.*, V, 314; III, 148.     [151] Dugdale, *Mon. Ang.*, III, 289.     [152] *Ibid.*, IV, 608.

[153] Dugdale, *Mon. Ang.*, V, 152–3.

[154] *Historia et Cartularium Monasterii Sancti Petri Gloucestriae*, I, lxxv–lxxvii.

Walden and had to prevent his mother from hijacking it and having it buried at Chicksands, a house she particularly favoured.[155]

As time went on there were choices to be made between the burial place of previous generations of a family, and one's own foundation. The Conqueror was buried at Caen, but Rufus at Winchester, the major church closest to the place of his death in the New Forest. Henry I died in Normandy but his body was transported back to the abbey he had founded at Reading, and Stephen was buried at his foundation at Faversham in Kent. Even in the ruling house, therefore, there was no clear precedent. Moreover, the Cistercians were reluctant to allow the burial of laymen within the monastic precincts. Place of burial was thus a matter where personal choice and circumstance played a part. Relatively soon after 1066 the odds were that the location would be in England not in Normandy, but within the same family the place might change from generation to generation. Thus Gilbert de Gant was buried at Bardney as was his son Walter, but Gilbert II was buried at Bridlington, where he had been brought up and of which he was especially fond.[156] Richard de Redvers was buried at Montebourg in Normandy, a house to which he was a generous benefactor, but his son Baldwin was buried at the (Cistercian) abbey of Quarr on the Isle of Wight.[157]

In addition to assistance in the afterlife, religious houses also provided an invaluable range of social services for their benefactors. Much the most common, and potentially open to abuse, was hospitality. Religious houses, especially the larger and more commodious abbeys conveniently situated on major throughfares, such as St Albans, might well find themselves invaded frequently by large and disruptive aristocratic retinues. Mabel of Bellême's frequent descents on St Evroul were evidently resented, and Orderic relates with evident relish how they were brought to a stop when that redoubtable lady was punished for them by illness because she refused to moderate her demands.[158] Noble boys and girls could also be sent there for education, like Gilbert de Gant at Bridlington. By the twelfth century the trend was moving away from accepting child oblates, the Cistercians laying down a minimum age of eighteen for their recruits. Religious houses were also places of retirement, the equivalent of sheltered housing today. Some had reputations for their medical care, most famously perhaps Abingdon.

---

[155] Collar, 'Book of the Foundation of Walden Abbey', *Essex Review*, 45 (1936), 152–6.
[156] *Early Yorkshire Charters*, II, no. 1138.     [157] OV, VI, 146; Dugdale, *Mon. Ang.*, V, 381.     [158] OV, II, 56.

Cistercian houses enjoyed autonomy from influence by founders; not so Benedictine and Augustinian monks, canons, and nuns. Founders of these had considerable influence over the appointment of ecclesiastical heads, and they also enjoyed the right to the revenues of the houses during vacancies.[159] In addition to these more formal areas of influence, there were others, less formal. First, when communities were being set up founders obviously had the last word in the choice of a site. They may even have taken an interest in the building work: Walter de Lacy met his death by falling off a scaffold at St Guthlac's priory whilst inspecting the building work in 1085.[160] Secondly, religious houses were sources of wealth, and as such founders who fell on hard times, or were contemplating expensive activities like participation in the crusade, might reasonably expect to raise a loan, or if necessary, to raise money by selling land to the house.

Points of tension arose as, with the passage of time, later generations sometimes regretted the generosity of their predecessors. On occasion the objection was to the size of a gift, as for instance in King John's reign when a notable quarrel blew up between the monks of Walden and Geoffrey FitzPeter, who had successfully prosecuted his claim to the Mandeville lands. Geoffrey made an initial inspection, vividly described in the house history, and complained that he had been disinherited. He evidently objected to Earl William's deathbed bequest of half his demesne in Walden, and to the elevation of the priory to an abbey. Eventually the quarrel was patched up and Geoffrey was persuaded to restore some of the land he had seized, but the whole episode shows what could happen.[161] Frequently tensions arose over services: as mentioned above, the objection to making gifts entirely free was the loss of any kind of control over them afterwards, and specifically the difficulty of securing the performance of services. Grants of churches and tithes were frequent sources of dispute. So far as the former were concerned, beneficiaries sometimes had difficulty in holding on to the churches, or establishing exactly what had been given. In the first generations after the Conquest lords had been so generous that their descendants might find themselves with very few livings with which to reward the clerks in their service, and the beneficiaries

[159] E. Mason, 'Timeo Barones et Dona Ferentes', *Religious Motivation: Biological and Sociological Problems for the Church Historian*, Studies in Church History, xv (1978), 61–75; S. Wood, *English Monasteries and their Patrons in the Thirteenth Century* (Oxford, 1955) is also useful.

[160] *Historia et Cartularium Monasterii de Gloucestriae*, I, 73.

[161] Collar, 'Book of the Foundation of Walden Abbey', *Essex Review*, 46 (1937), 88–98, 164–170, 227–234; 47 (1938), 36–41, 94–9, 150–5, 216–220.

might well have to come to some kind of compromise. In the later twelfth century, for instance, Earl William de Mandeville complained that his father had given all the churches on his land to Walden, and he did not have a single one to bestow on his clerks. The abbey evidently found it advisable to accept the earl's candidates in seven churches.[162] Ongoing points of friction could well come to a head if there was a change of lordship, as in Walden's tribulations. It has been pointed out that Shrewsbury's situation seems to have been somewhat precarious after the downfall of Robert de Bellême in 1102 until Henry I formally confirmed all the abbey's rights and possessions.[163]

Serious quarrels were rare, however, and the abiding impression is of the importance of the connection to founder and community alike. The century following the Conquest saw a great transfer of land into the hands of religious houses. Much would probably have been given anyway as men, moved by the new ideal of the Christian life, sought to share in its aims, albeit by proxy. But as an elite taking over a foreign country, the experience of conquest accelerated change. The new lords believed they had the right to dispose of churches and tithes on their lands, and gave them away to religious houses. In the north of England they found a desert ideal for colonization by the religious orders, and all the more suitable because it had been in an earlier age such a flourishing centre of monasticism. The values of the religious were a reproach to the ethos of the military elite, yet the two were indissolubly intermingled.

[162] *Ibid.*, 45 (1936), 225, 227.     [163] *Shrewsbury Cartulary*, I, xii.

# Conclusion

## 'Nobles of England, Norman by birth'

Thus Ralph, bishop of the Orkneys, was said by the chronicler Henry of Huntingdon to have begun his address to the army which had assembled in 1138 at Northallerton in Yorkshire to face the invading Scots. He went on to recite the great victories of their predecessors in France, England, and Apulia and at Jerusalem and Antioch.[1] The self-perception of the aristocracy of Norman England is an important issue in its own right, and also because the Norman kings and their Angevin successors were committed to keeping Normandy at all costs. To what extent was this commitment shared by the ruling elite in England, through whom resources of men and money had to be raised? Among historians the issue of identification has long been discussed because of the perceived importance of 1066 in national history as the last foreign invasion: at what point thereafter did England cease to be under 'foreign' rule?[2] Nationalist preoccupations in historical writing on the Conquest waned in the twentieth century, and a further sign of its decline came when in 1976 John Le Patourel pointed out that to view the Conquest as something which happened to England was not how the Normans themselves would have viewed the conjuncture of England and Normandy.[3] The Norman dominions, he argued, were controlled by an itinerant ruler, whose household provided a central apparatus of government, and there was also a unitary aristocracy whose estates and interests spanned the Channel.

There are at least two levels on which the issue of relations with continental origins may be perceived, material, and emotional, and the former is obviously easier to document than the latter. On a material level it is

---

[1] HH, pp. 262–3; in Ailred of Rievaulx's account of the battle, the army was addressed by Walter Espec. He is not made to employ precisely the same phrase as Henry, but he too extols the inspiration of past Norman victories: 'Relatio de Standardo', *Chronicles*, III, 185–9.

[2] Relations between Normans and English were discussed by E. A. Freeman, *The History of the Norman Conquest of England*, 5 vols. and index (Oxford, 1870–79), v, appendix W; a recent discussion is to be found in M. T. Clanchy, *England and Its Rulers, 1066–1272* (London, 1983); Williams, *The English and the Norman Conquest* considers the fate of the English.     [3] Le Patourel, *Norman Empire*, chapter 9.

clear that a substantial section of aristocracy, often amongst its richest members, retained estates on both sides of the Channel, sometimes as a result of inheritance, sometimes of a deliberate decision to keep estates together.[4] In addition, new cross-Channel complexes were created in the twelfth century such as those for Richard de Redvers and for Robert son of Henry I, so that any view that the Normans-in-England viewed Normandy as 'over there' must take such interests into account. In addition to lands, there were kinsfolk in northern France, and the fact that as a youth William Marshal was dispatched for his military training to his kinsman the lord of Tancarville (to whom he was not particularly closely related) shows that such links were kept up.[5] Perhaps there were special circumstances for those who wanted the 'best' military training in tournaments, but William can hardly have been the only youth to have been so sent. Those who served the Norman kings crossed the Channel frequently, at least until 1137, and had the opportunity to renew links with the land of their ancestors. When Baldwin de Redvers had to leave England after the failure of his revolt against Stephen, and took refuge in the Cotentin, he recruited into his entourage men whose ties to the Redvers family probably went back to his father's lifetime.[6] There were contacts, too, through churchmen who crossed to England to attend to their land and property.

On the other hand, there were also some very obvious factors which rooted the newcomers in their country of adoption. For the first generation, there were lands to defend, and possibilities of further gains in the north or the west. Particularly between 1087 and 1106, when disputes within the ruling house suggested the advisability, family lands were divided at the Channel, and henceforth one branch of the family concentrated on their English estates.[7] In such cases marriage alliances, except for the very greatest families, were usually sought relatively close to home. Although in the first generations patronage of Norman houses was kept up by those families which had pre-existing links, fraternity might also be sought with English houses. From the late eleventh century the foundation of 'family' religious houses in England created a focus for

---

[4] E. J. R. Boston, 'The Territorial Interests of the Anglo-Norman Aristocracy, c. 1086–c. 1135', University of Cambridge PhD thesis, 1979; W. B. Stevenson, 'England and Normandy 1204–1259', University of Leeds PhD thesis 1974.    [5] *Histoire de Guillaume le Maréchal* (ed. Meyer), l. 744 ff.

[6] Bearman, 'Baldwin de Redvers', p. 38.    [7] Holt, 'Politics and Property', pp. 14–15.

loyalty and a place of burial for the founder and his kin, as we have seen in the previous chapter.

Even whilst retaining cross-Channel estates, some evidently chose to live mainly or wholly in England or Normandy. Presence on the witness lists of royal documents has to be used with caution, but should not be totally discounted as evidence of presence at court. Walter Giffard III who died in 1164 seems to have visited England only rarely. He may have been in England and was probably still a minor when he was addressed in two royal documents of 1111. He is also said to have been present at the consecration of the abbey church at St Albans in 1115, and was possibly in England in 1121–2, but otherwise he attests only for Henry I in Normandy. Again he is said to have been in England in 1136, but not otherwise for the rest of Stephen's reign.[8] In the case of the Beaumont twins, the elder, Waleran, had estates in France and Normandy to which he retired after 1141. Waleran went on pilgrimage to St James of Compostella in 1144, and on crusade in 1146–7. He failed to win the confidence of Henry FitzEmpress and in due course lost the earldom of Worcester granted to him by Stephen and almost all his gains in Normandy. When he died he was buried in the abbey of Préaux in Normandy with his ancestors. By contrast, his twin Robert remained in England in the service of Stephen, and did not go on crusade. He successfully managed the transition to Henry II's service and became chief justiciar in England. He also recovered his wife's honour of Breteuil in Normandy, lost during the 1140s. He chose not to be buried in Normandy: his body was buried at Leicester abbey, and his heart at the hospital at Brackley in Northamptonshire.[9] For many families there were important and continuing links with Normandy which co-existed with concerns centred on their estates.

So far as perceptions of identity are concerned, such evidence as there is may be interpreted in different ways.[10] One source of evidence is the address clauses in royal charters which distinguish between 'French' and 'English'.[11] Significantly the 'Normans' tended to be subsumed into the wider category of 'French', a usage which is paralleled by the regulations about procedure laid down by William the Conqueror. King William

---

[8] *RRAN*, II, nos. 974, 979, 1102, 1204, 1205, 1285, 1547, 1693, 1908; see also no. 911 (dubious); III, nos. 284, 600, 653, 734, 909.     [9] These details are taken from Crouch, *Beaumont Twins*, chapter three.
[10] Similar ground, though with a different emphasis, is covered by Williams, *The English and the Norman Conquest*, chapter eight.     [11] Stenton, *First Century*, p. 29.

promised to maintain peace between the two peoples, and he placed the
lives of Frenchmen under his special protection. Regulations were prescribed for legal procedures: the English were to have access to the new
procedure of trial by battle in appropriate cases if they wished (though
they were not compelled to use it), but were not allowed to clear themselves of serious charges by using oath-helpers, on the grounds, presumably, that it would be all too easy for them to escape justice by perjuring
themselves for fellow Englishmen.[12] Law was seen as the custom of a
people, or *gens*.[13] Yet, unlike the situation in Wales or Ireland, the legal distinction between French and English faded, and faded remarkably
quickly.[14] It has been pointed out that in 1100 the murder fine was not
explicitly confirmed by Henry as one of his father's innovations. He pardoned all fines incurred before the day of his coronation, and stated that
those incurred in the future were to be amended according to the law of
King Edward.[15] What determined where cases were dealt with and the procedures used was not determined by nationality. From the late twelfth
century, it was the division between free and unfree status which was the
chief determinant.

The early twelfth century witnessed a great revival of historical writing
in England which has been quarried by historians interested in examining
the process of acculturation.[16] Only one writer (the Hyde chronicler), uses
the term widely used by modern historians of the Normans in England,
'Anglo-Normans', and the phrase should not be interpreted as 'an inspired
terminology invented to describe a cross-Channel realm', but rather as an
adaptation of a term sometimes used before 1066 for kings of the 'Anglo-
Saxons'.[17] Some of the key writers were Benedictine monks with a particular concern to preserve a knowledge of their own past in an unfriendly

---

[12] W1 Lad: Liebermann, *Die Gesetze der Angelsachsen*, i, 483–4.

[13] For the situation in England see Garnett, 'Franci et Angli', *passim*.

[14] R. Bartlett, *The Making of Europe. Conquest, Colonization and Cultural Change 950–1350* (London, 1993), chapter eight.     [15] Stubbs, *Select Charters*, p. 119.

[16] R. W. Southern, 'Aspects of the European Tradition of Historical Writing. IV. The Sense of the Past', *Transactions of the Royal Historical Society*, 5th series, 23 (1973), 246–9; the question was raised by J. Campbell, 'Some Twelfth-Century Views of the Anglo-Saxon Past', reprinted in *Essays in Anglo-Saxon History* (London, 1986), p. 227; Williams, *The English and the Norman Conquest*, pp. 164–86.

[17] Bates, 'Normandy and England after 1066', p. 862 (discussing the view of C. Warren Hollister, 'Normandy, France, and the Anglo-Norman Regnum', *Monarchy, Magnates and Institutions*, pp. 46–7); and see most recently Gillingham, 'Henry of Huntingdon and the Twelfth-Century Revival of the English Nation, Appendix', pp. 90–1.

world and to record the histories of English saints and shrines, and the lands and privileges given to their communities. In other words, it was in their interests to see the history of the English and their kings as a continuum which the intrusion of alien kings and their followers did not breach. Such comments as they made about the ethnicity of the ruling class tend to occur in their accounts of the Conqueror's reign. Eadmer, for instance, in his account of William's rule in his *History of Recent Events*, said that there was not much point in describing the king's treatment of the English, and concentrated on his main aim which was to set the scene for Anselm's archiepiscopate.[18] William of Malmesbury and Symeon of Durham were writing histories of the kings of the English, and, in William's case, his patron was Matilda, wife of Henry I. William, a man of mixed race, treated the Normans and English as different peoples. In a famous passage dealing with the Conquest he wrote of the English as a people punished for their sins, and the Normans as the instrument of moral and religious regeneration.[19] When it came to the political history of the Norman period, William abandoned a narrative approach and provided instead pen portraits of the Conqueror, Rufus, and Henry I, one solution to the difficulty he evidently felt in dealing with a sensitive subject. When he wrote of the exclusion of the English from high office in the church in his own day, however, his feelings clearly got the better of him.[20]

John (Florence) of Worcester and Symeon of Durham also have little to say on the question of ethnic identity after dealing with the Conqueror's reign. John described the ravages of the Normans in the north in 1069, and the ferocity which had forced Liulf (the Northumbrian thegn killed in 1080) to take refuge in Durham.[21] Symeon echoed this account, but he suggested that Bishop Aethelwine's decision to resign his bishopric in 1070 was due to his 'dreading the rule of a foreign nation whose language and customs he knew not', and he also described how at the ecclesiastical council at Winchester the king made it his business to deprive as many Englishmen as possible so that he could replace them with his compatriots.[22]

Orderic Vitalis's perspective was rather different for, although he had been born in England of mixed parentage, he spent most of his life in a Norman monastery and set out to write not the history of the English but

---

[18] Eadmer, *Historia Novorum*, p. 9.   [19] WM, *De Gestis Regum Anglorum*, II, 304–6.   [20] *Ibid.*, I, 278.
[21] FW, II, 4.   [22] SD, 'Historia Regum', *Opera omnia*, II, 190, 193.

an ecclesiastical history. His treatment of the Conquest, probably composed in the second decade of the twelfth century, is illuminating for its
discussion of the morality of the Conquest and the treatment meted out
to Earl Waltheof. Like others, he describes the new elite as Normans. In
the deathbed speech he attributed to William, he included a famous
description of the Norman race which both reflected and helped to foster
the self-image of the Normans. By the time he came to describe political
events in the early twelfth century, however, the Normans are evidently
those who inhabited Normandy, and the aristocracy of England is rarely
alluded to as a group.[23] One occasion when he did refer to the latter
occurred when he described how after the death of Henry I the 'Normans',
who met at Neufbourg, wanted Theobald to rule them, but when they
heard that the 'English' had accepted Stephen, they decided to serve one
lord.[24] These monastic historians were in a very difficult position in
writing of the recent past. While still deeply attached to the past, they had
to face the reality of what had happened and come to terms with the
present. The perspective of monastic historians, although providing
invaluable insights, should not be taken as indicative of a general
rapprochement between Normans and English.

Henry of Huntingdon's aim and perspective as an historian were different again from those discussed above. He wrote a history of the English
from the invasion of Caesar to his own time, composed over a period and
dedicated to Alexander bishop of Lincoln (1123–48). Unlike William of
Malmesbury or Symeon, he was not a Benedictine monk but archdeacon
of Huntingdon; if he had English blood in his veins he did not mention
the fact.[25] In the 1130s he inserted into his chronicle a speech for Duke
William at Hastings in which the deeds of Rollo and his successors were
recalled and compared with those of the English, 'a people accustomed to
be conquered'.[26] In his retrospective summing up of the Conqueror's
reign he wrote of the Normans as having accomplished the righteous will
of God on the English nation, so that it was a disgrace even to be called an
Englishman. The Normans were fiercer than any other people and when
foreign wars ceased they turned their hostility against their own people,
in Normandy and England, Apulia, Calabria, Sicily, and Antioch.[27] At the

---

[23] OV, VI, 282,450, 456,470.      [24] OV, VI, 454.

[25] HH, pp. xxx–xxxvi; D. Greenway, 'Henry of Huntingdon and the Manuscripts of his *Historia Anglorum*',
*Anglo-Norman Studies*, 9 (1986), 103–21.      [26] HH, pp. 201–2.      [27] *Ibid.*, p. 208.

beginning of book VII dealing with the period 1087 to 1135, he related how God alienated favour and rank from the English people and caused it to cease to be a people, but then described how the Normans themselves were afflicted with various calamities.[28]

John Gillingham has suggested that Henry's references to the 'Normans' in the early years of Stephen's reign were to the dominant faction at Stephen's court led by the Beaumont twins, men who still had substantial interests in Normandy, as opposed to the 'English' magnates whose lands were wholly or primarily in England.[29] Yet Henry also used the term 'Norman' of some of Stephen's opponents whose estates were mainly or wholly in England, such as Hugh Bigod and Robert of Bampton. He also described Baldwin de Redvers, who had very considerable estates on *both* sides of the Channel, as a 'Norman'.[30] It is true that in his description of the battle of the Standard, Henry began to refer directly to the army which faced King David as 'English', but in the speech attributed to Bishop Ralph, who addressed the royalist army drawn up to face the Scots at Northallerton, the bishop described its leaders as 'nobles of England, Norman by birth', and recalled the heroic exploits of the Normans. Was Henry confused about the identity of the aristocracy? It is more likely that in this passage he was tapping a vein of contemporary material composed in celebration of a great victory against the Scots.[31] If so, it is revealing that the victory was presented not as a victory of the English people, but of the Normans. The tangle in Henry of Huntingdon's treatment of the battle of the Standard shows something of the difficulty of using ethnicity alone as a definition of aristocracy: although 'English', those who fought for Stephen were exhorted to look to a glorious Norman past. The rival army, as Henry himself knew, included men described as English and Normans, under the command of King David's son, who was himself Norman, Scots, and English by descent.

The tone of Geoffrey Gaimar's history prompts similar conclusions. He was asked to write a history of the English in French, by a lady named

---

[28] *Ibid.*, p. 214.

[29] J. Gillingham, 'Henry of Huntingdon and the English Nation', *Concepts of National Identity in the Middle Ages*, ed. S. Forde, L. Johnson and A. V. Murray, Leeds Texts and Monographs, New Series, XIV (1995) 80–5.      [30] Gillingham, 'Henry of Huntingdon', pp. 81–5; HH, p. 259.

[31] In addition to Ailred of Rievaulx's account of the battle (see above, n. 1), see also Richard of Hexham *Chronicles*, III, 181–99; 139–78; Hugh the Chanter wrote a poem about the battle mentioned by Richard of Hexham, *Chronicles*, III, 163.

Constance, wife of Ralph FitzGilbert. This in itself is suggestive that members of the new French-speaking aristocracy were interested in the history of England and the English.[32] For much of the period before 1066 Gaimar simply reworks the Anglo-Saxon Chronicle. When he comes to the eleventh century, however, he has a great deal to say about Cnut, Havelock the Dane, and Hereward, and little about the Norman Conquest as such. Gaimar is thought to have been writing in 1136 and 1137, and his patroness lived in Lincolnshire. His choice of subject matter suggests that in this part of England remembrance of the past was directed towards the Danes, and that the exploits of an English resistance hero had more audience appeal than the story of the Norman Conquest.

The popularity of the work of Gaimar's contemporary, Geoffrey of Monmouth, again indicates an interest in a past peopled with heroes, but they are not Norman heroes, or even 'English': here the subject was the history of the kings of Britain.[33] What mattered were tales of valour, not the ethnic identity of the protagonists or the locality in which the tales were played out. In Geoffrey's case an added factor, it has been suggested, was a determination to combat a view gaining ground at the time that the English, unlike the other inhabitants of Britain, were a 'civilized' people in contrast to the lesser breeds without the law in Wales, Scotland, and Ireland.[34]

In Norman England some incomers may have seen themselves as Norman (or Flemish, or Breton), whilst putting down roots in their country of adoption. The foundation of religious houses and the burial there of successive generations, or the associations built up with older houses where English saints were venerated, can only have helped this process. However, a distinction must be made between identification and assimilation, and between different levels of the aristocracy. The likelihood of marriage into English families in the middling and lower levels of the aristocracy has been mentioned above (p. 97). In this context the

---

[32] Gaimar, *L'Estoire des Engleis*, ed. A. Bell (Oxford, 1960); on the date of composition see I. Short, 'Gaimar's Epilogue and Geoffrey of Monmouth's *Liber vetustissimus*', *Speculum*, 69 (1994), 323–43.

[33] J. Gillingham, 'The Context and Purposes of Geoffrey of Monmouth's *History of the Kings of Britain*', *Anglo-Norman Studies*, 13 (1990), 99–118.

[34] *Ibid.*, p. 106; Gillingham, 'The Beginnings of English Imperialism', *Journal of Historical Sociology*, 5 (1992), 392–409; 'Conquering the Barbarians: War and Chivalry in Twelfth-Century Britain', *Haskins Society Journal*, 4 (1993), 69–86.

comment of the *Dialogue of the Exchequer* on the difficulty of distinguishing between Normans and English by the late twelfth century because of intermarriage is often cited.[35] Marriage between Normans and English at the highest social levels was, however, relatively rare. In the aristocratic world French remained the language of speech and literature and it would appear that those who could not speak French were looked down on (see above, p. 14). The nicknames of Henry I and his first wife Matilda, 'Godric' and 'Godgifu', were not intended to be complimentary.[36] The incidental comments of William of Malmesbury, Eadmer, and Symeon of Durham, about the lack of promotion prospects for Englishmen in the English church tell their own story. Aelnoth of Canterbury, in exile in Denmark in the early twelfth century, wrote of the English race, killed, scattered, or reduced to servitude.[37] The feelings of the conquered towards the conquerors are buried, but can we conclude that the mood was one of acceptance rather than tension? Orderic Vitalis living in a Norman monastery reported a rumour in 1137 of an intention to murder all the Normans in England and hand the country over to the Scots, and again this is surely suggestive that he had heard of some animosity.[38]

Finally, perceptions of identity have to be viewed in a wider cultural context. Members of the aristocracy could identify themselves by ancestry and kinship, by reference to place or people, but by the mid-twelfth century there were wider, one might say, international horizons – the world of crusades and of chivalry. The preaching of the second crusade particularly made an impact in England, and several members of the aristocracy took the cross. The aristocracy of Norman England also shared with their continental counterparts the values of the code of chivalry, and were early patrons of the literature produced for princely and noble courts. William Rufus's was an early example of such a court, and a

---

[35] *Dialogus de Scaccario*, p. 52.

[36] WM, *De Gestis Regum Anglorum*, II, 471. Walter Map attributed to Henry I a policy of encouraging intermarriage: *De Nugis Curialium. Courtiers' Trifles*, ed. and trans. M. R. James, revised C. N. L. Brooke and R. A. B. Mynors (Oxford, 1983), p. 436. This may be taken at face value, or was the author perhaps making a humorous reference to Henry's own marriage?

[37] Aelnoth of Canterbury in *Scriptorum Rerum Danicorum*, ed. Jacob Langebek (Copenhagen, 1774), III, 346–7, as cited by Williams, *The English and the Norman Conquest*, p. 81.

[38] OV, VI, 494. Gillingham, 'Henry of Huntingdon and the English Nation', p. 84 suggests that this report should not be interpreted as racial animosity but as language reflecting opposition to the court faction identified as 'the Normans'.

magnificent setting was created for it by his new hall at Westminster.[39] Members of the aristocracy of Norman England were early patrons of a literature produced in and for these courts. The glittering world of courtly love and of tournaments was the outward manifestation of wider shared values in western aristocracies. In sum, therefore, the aristocracy of Norman England identified itself in different, co-existent, and sometimes conflicting, ways depending on circumstance, by reference to ancestry, country of origin or adoption, by a sense of distinction from other races, and by values shared with other aristocracies.

At this point it is time to pull together the threads of certain recurring themes. The first is the very real power of the greatest families, who dominated their own localities by their landed wealth and castles, their power over lesser families, and their influence over command structures. We have seen a number of great lordships were territorially compact, created as bulwarks for self-protection and bases for forward advance. Individuals like Peverel in Nottinghamshire and Ferrers in Derbyshire dominated their counties. The Norman kings did not usually seek to challenge the power of such men, but worked through them. Loyalist magnates could be commissioned as justices; they might be the sheriff's overlord; and they might well have the hundred courts attached to their demesne manors. The creation of additional earldoms by Stephen and Matilda gave scope to those appointed to extend their local influence even further. Aristocratic power in Norman England was achieved notwithstanding – and partly as a result of – the relatively developed structures of royal government and the vigorous rule of the Norman kings.

Secondly, the new elite was above all a military elite, established by conquest. We have seen how revolts were triggered by disputed royal successions, and how the trend was away from capital punishment. The threat or deployment of armed force against the king was thus a tactic which had a fair chance of success.

Thirdly, the circumstances of the conquest meant that the giving of land was in a very immediate way at the heart of political relationships. The idea that all land was held of the king, so directly conveyed in the lists

---

[39] Gillingham has showed how Geoffrey Gaimar's work was permeated with these values: 'English Chivalry in French', *Anglo-Norman Political Culture and the Twelfth Century Renaissance*, ed. C. Warren Hollister, forthcoming (Woodbridge, 1997).

of landholders in each county in Domesday Book, gave a sharpness and clarity to relations between the king and the great men which it is not possible to detect before 1066. The Norman kings were *domini* as well as *reges*, and dealt with the great men as lords with their vassals, taking aids and reliefs, and arranging marriages and the custody of minors. The conventions and language employed were those of feudalism, informed by the rights inherited from English kings and shaped by the pressing military and fiscal needs of their Norman successors. Those conventions in turn formed the basis of relations between tenants-in-chief and *their* men, and of the customs governing tenure by knight service. The issue of feudalism and its origins in England is perennially contentious, and it is a moot point whether the relations between Norman kings and the magnates were based on 'feudal' rights or on a straightforward exercise of political will. It is clear that the Norman kings retained pre-Conquest obligations of military service, and that the old English aristocracy had been a military elite with retinues of armed followers. Yet while recognizing the contribution of earlier precedents, there are other factors which indicate cumulatively that fundamental change had occurred: the pervasiveness of dependent tenure after 1066, the adoption of the conventions of lord and vassal between king and aristocracy, the language of charters, and the concomitant changes in military technique and the proliferation of castles.

Fourthly, kinship was a thread weaving in and out of the political and social fabric of aristocratic life. Not only was kinship the bedrock of personal affections, but also it proved a framework for the distribution of land within families, and, through marriage alliances, for the transmitting of land between families. It was instrumental in shaping political allegiances, as in the formation of a party to support the Angevin cause after 1135. At the local level, kinship united with lordship and neighbourhood to forge networks of influence encompassing other families, religious houses, and perhaps wealthy townsfolk.

Fifthly, political society in Norman England was multi-faceted, and, while the royal court exercised a powerful draw, the importance of understanding politics from the standpoint of aristocratic families whose interests extended beyond the court has been emphasized here. The distribution of wealth and power varied from region to region. In Kent, for instance, the wealth of the archbishop of Canterbury gave him a dominant role locally. The perspective of families in Wales or the borders, or along the border with Scotland, was different from those whose lives centred on the court. Further studies are needed of individual magnate families, based on their charters, to put flesh and blood on the bones of the body politic.

Finally, how far was this aristocracy comparable with, and how far different from, continental aristocracies, and particularly that of France, in the same period? In some respects there are obvious similarities: the role of castles, the retinues of knights, and the importance attached to lineage. Knights were crucial to the regime in England, yet there is little indication in our period that knighthood in itself conferred high social status. On the other hand, we do not hear of knights who were legally unfree, as in Germany. The king's power was obviously a force to be reckoned with in Norman England, more so than in most parts of France or Germany. In Norman England before 1135 we hear little of armed disputes *between* magnates, or of freebooters. Instead most magnate revolts occurred when disputed successions provided opportunities to exercise pressure on the claimants for lands or castles.

After 1135 the parallels between the aristocracies of England and those of France and Germany become closer. The war in England can itself be interpreted not only as a civil war but also as an episode in noble aggrandizement, as an extension of the ongoing contest for power in France between the comital houses of Blois and Anjou. In England more is heard than before of violent clashes between magnates and of the building of castles from which 'castlemen' terrorized the local countryside exacting services, food, and protection money. Lands and rights belonging to churches were taken over, though some churchmen, far from being victims of war, were involved in building castles and hiring knights. The attempts to record consent of neighbours to land grants has been interpreted as indicative of a rise of affinities; more probably they represent the extra care needed to make sure that grants or settlements were carried out by securing the support of those who might otherwise have challenged or overthrown them. Private treaties, or *conventiones*, proliferated, as participants tried to stabilize the situation in their localities by defining areas of influence and setting limits to their participation. Little is heard of effective royal justice in the localities.

Most strikingly we hear at this time of the activities of men of lower standing who oppressed their neighbours, such as William de Launay who based himself at Ravenstone in Leicestershire (see above, p. 318), and Robert FitzHubert who took the castle of Devizes by stealth and boasted of his ill-treatment of prisoners.[40] The depredations of men such as these were symptomatic of a wider problem – the weakening of discipline exercised by the great men over the knights. Some seem to have acquired lands and property from different lords, sometimes by playing off one against another, and again this could be interpreted as a sign of weakening ties between magnates and knights.

The conquest of England by a French-speaking aristocracy was part of a wider phenomenon of conquest, colonization, and evangelization expanding the frontiers of Latin Christendom. The 'long' eleventh and twelfth centuries are in many ways an age of aristocracy, when the possibility of greater profits to be made from lordship of the land combined with greater opportunities to acquire land especially in frontier zones. The conquest of England was one of the most successful and relatively speedy of its type, but it was not unique. An interesting comparison could be made with contemporary Norman activity in Sicily, which was proceeding much more slowly and in a different context. Moreover, England proved to be a stepping stone to further conquests in Wales, Scotland, and Ireland. Thus whilst the establishment of the new elite had profound effects on England and Normandy, it also led to a realignment of political relationships in the British Isles. More generally it marked a shift in north-western Europe. The fortunes of England moved out of a Scandinavian orbit and towards those of northern France, a re-orientation which both determined the political priorities of her rulers and helped to fashion her future cultural development.

---

[40] WM, *Historia Novella*, pp. 43–4.

# Select bibliography

## 1 Manuscript sources

London, British Library
  Additional Charter 28, 347.
  Cotton Manuscripts:
    Domitian A x
      Vespasian A XVIII.
      Vespasian E XVIII.
    Harley MS 3650.
    Lansdowne MS 229.
London, Public Record Office, Chancery Miscellanea C 47/9/5.
London, Westminster Abbey Muniments, 13, 280.

*Unpublished dissertations*

Abbott, M. 'The Gant Family in England, 1066–1191', PhD thesis, University of Cambridge (1973).

Atkin, S. A. J. 'The Bigod Family: an Investigation into their Lands and Activities, 1066–1306', PhD thesis, University of Reading (1979).

Boston, E. J. R. 'The Territorial Interests of the Anglo-Norman Aristocracy, *c.* 1086–*c.* 1135', PhD thesis, University of Cambridge (1979).

Charlton, A. 'A Study of the Mandeville Family and its Estates', PhD thesis, University of Reading (1977).

Golob, P. E. 'The Ferrers Earls of Derby: A Study of the Honour of Tutbury', PhD thesis, University of Cambridge (1985).

Mason, J. F. A. 'Aspects of Subinfeudation on some Domesday Fiefs', DPhil thesis, University of Oxford (1952).

Moule, C. J. 'Entry into Marriage in the late eleventh and twelfth centuries *c.* 1090–1181', PhD thesis, University of Cambridge (1983).

Stalley, R. A. 'The Patronage of Roger of Salisbury', MA report, Courtauld Institute of Art (1969).

Stevenson, W. B. 'England and Normandy 1204–1259', PhD thesis, University of Leeds (1974).

Thompson, K. 'The Cross-Channel Estates of the Montgomery-Bellême Family, *c.* 1050–1112', MA thesis, University of Wales (1983).

## 2 Printed primary sources

*Les actes de Guillaume le Conquérant et de la Reine Mathilde pour les abbayes caennaises*, ed. L. Musset, Mémoires de la Société des Antiquaires de Normandie, XXXVII (Caen, 1967).

*Ancient Charters*, ed. J. H. Round, Pipe Roll Society, X (1888).

*The Anglo-Saxon Chronicle: a Revised Translation*, ed. D. Whitelock, D. C. Douglas, and S. I. Tucker (London, 1961).

*Annales Monastici*, ed. H. R. Luard, 5 vols., RS (London, 1864–9).

*The Beauchamp Cartulary Charters 1100–1268*, ed. E. Mason, Pipe Roll Society, New Series, XLIII (1980).

*Book of Fees: Liber Feodorum. The Book of Fees commonly called Testa de Nevill, reformed from the earliest MSS, by the Deputy Keeper of the Records*, 3 vols. (London, 1920–31).

Brown, R. Allen (ed.) *The Norman Conquest*, Documents of Medieval History, no. 5 (London, 1984).

*Calendar of Documents preserved in France, illustrative of the History of Great Britain and Ireland*, Volume I, A. D. 918–1216, ed. J. H. Round (London, 1899).

*Calendar of Inquisitions Post Mortem*.

*Carmen de Hastingae Proelio of Guy bishop of Amiens*, ed. C. Morton and H. Muntz, Oxford Medieval Texts (Oxford, 1972).

*Cartulaire de Saint-Martin de Pontoise*, ed. J. Depoin (Pontoise, 1899).

*Cartularium Monasterii de Ramesia*, ed. W. H. Hart and P. A. Lyons, 3 vols., RS (London, 1884–93).

*The Cartulary of Blyth Priory*, ed. R. T. Timson, Thoroton Society, XXVI, Historical Manuscripts Commission JP 17 (1973).

*The Cartulary of the Knights of St John of Jerusalem in England*, ed. M. Gervers, British Academy Records of Social and Economic History, new series, VI (London, 1982).

*The Cartulary of Oseney Abbey*, ed. H. E. Salter, 6 vols., Oxford Historical Society, LXXXIX–XCI, XCVII–XCVIII, CI (1929–36).

*The Cartulary of Shrewsbury Abbey*, ed. U. Rees, 2 vols. (Aberystwyth, 1975).

*The Cartulary of St Michael's Mount*, ed. P. L. Hull, Devon and Cornwall Record Society, new series, V (1962).

*The Cartulary of Tutbury Priory*, ed. A. Saltman, Staffordshire Historical Collections, 4th series, IV (1962), Historical Manuscripts Commission JP2 (London, 1962).

*Charters of the Honour of Mowbray 1107–1191*, ed. D. E. Greenway, British Academy Records of Social and Economic History, New Series, I (London, 1972).

*Charters of the Redvers Family and the Earldom of Devon 1090–1217*, ed. R. Bearman, Devon and Cornwall Record Society, new series, XXXVII (1994).

*The Chartulary of the Priory of St Pancras of Lewes*, ed. L. F. Salzman, 2 vols., Sussex Record Society, XXXVIII, XL (1933–5).

*The Chartulary of St John of Pontefract*, ed. R. Holmes, Yorkshire Archaeological Society, 2 vols. (1899, 1902).

*The Chronicle of Battle Abbey*, ed. E. Searle, Oxford Medieval Texts (Oxford, 1980).

*The Chronicle of John of Worcester*, ed. J. R. H. Weaver, Anecdota Oxoniensia, Mediaeval and Modern Series, XIII (Oxford, 1908).

*Chronicles of the Reigns of Stephen, Henry II and Richard I*, ed. R. Howlett, 4 vols., RS (London, 1884–9).

*Chronicon Abbatiae Ramesiensis*, ed. W. Dunn Macray, RS (London, 1886).

*Chronicon Monasterii de Abingdon*, ed. J. Stevenson, 2 vols., RS (London, 1858).

*Chronicon Monasterii de Melsa*, ed. E. A. Bond, 3 vols., RS (London, 1866–8).

*Chronicon Ramesiensis*, ed. W. Dunn Macray, RS (London, 1886).

*Chroniques des comtes d'Anjou et des seigneurs d'Amboise*, ed. L. Halphen and R. Poupardin (Paris, 1913).

*The Coucher Book of Selby*, ed. J. T. Selby, 2 vols., Yorkshire Archaeological Society Record Series, X, XIII (1891–3).

*Councils and Synods, with other documents relating to the English church*, I part ii *1066–1154*, ed. D. Whitelock, M. Brett, and C. N. L. Brooke (Oxford, 1981).

*Court Rolls of the Manor of Wakefield*, I, II, ed. William Paley Baildon, III, IV, ed. John Lister, V, ed. J. W. Walker, Yorkshire Archaeological Society Record Series XXIX, XXXVI, LVII, LXXVIII, CIX (1900, 1906, 1917, 1930, 1945 for 1944).

*Coutumiers de Normandie*, ed. E. J. Tardif, 2 vols. (Rouen and Paris, 1903, 1896).

*Curia Regis Rolls.*

Douglas, D. C. (ed.) *The Domesday Monachorum of Christ Church, Canterbury* (London, 1944).

*Dialogus de Scaccario*, ed. and trans. C. Johnson with corrections by F. E. L. Carter and D. E. Greenway, Oxford Medieval Texts (Oxford, 1983).

*Diplomatic Documents preserved in the Public Record Office*, ed. P. Chaplais (London, 1964).

*Documents Illustrative of the Northern Danelaw*, ed. F. M. Stenton (London, 1920).

*Domesday Book*, ed. A. Farley for Record Commission, 4 vols. (London, 1783–1816).

*Domesday Book*, ed. J. Morris, 35 vols. in 40 (Chichester; Puillimore, 1975–86)

Dugdale, W. *Monasticon Anglicanum*, new edn, 6 vols. in 8 (London, 1817–30).

*Durham Episcopal Charters 1071–1152*, ed. H. S. Offler, Surtees Society, CLXXIX (1968).

Eadmer, *Historia Novorum*, ed. M. Rule (RS, 1884).

Eadmer, *Vita Anselmi*, ed. R. W. Southern, Oxford Medieval Texts (Oxford, 1962).

*Earldom of Gloucester Charters*, ed. R. B. Patterson (Oxford, 1973).

*Early Scottish Charters prior to A. D. 1153*, ed. A. C. Lawrie (Glasgow, 1905).

*Early Yorkshire Charters*, I–III, ed. W. Farrer (Edinburgh, 1914–16); IV–XII, ed. C. T. Clay, Yorkshire Archaeological Society, Record Series, Extra Series, I–III, V–X,

1935–65. Extra Series vol. IV is Index to first three vols., C. T. Clay and E. M. Clay (eds.), 1942.

*English Lawsuits from William I to Richard I*, I, *William I to Stephen*, ed. R. C. Van Caenegem, Selden Society, CVI (1990).

*The English Register of Godstow Nunnery, near Oxford, written about 1450*, ed. A. Clark, Early English Text Society, Old Series, 3 vols., CXXIX, CXXX, CXLII (1905–11).

*Eye Priory Cartulary and Charters*, II, ed. V. Brown, Suffolk Record Society, XIII (1994).

Eyton, R. W. *The Staffordshire Cartulary*, Collections for a History of Staffordshire, II (1881).

*Feodarium prioratus Dunelmensis*, ed. W. Greenwell, Surtees Society, LVIII (1872).

*Feudal Documents from the Abbey of Bury St Edmunds*, ed. D. C. Douglas (London, 1932).

Florence of Worcester, *Chronicon ex Chronicis*, ed. B. Thorpe, 2 vols. (London, 1848, 1849).

Gaimar, *L'Estoire des Engleis*, ed. A. Bell (Oxford, 1960).

Galbert of Bruges, *The Murder of Charles the Good Count of Flanders*, trs. J. B. Ross, reprint (New York, 1967).

*Gallia Christiana in Provincias Ecclesiasticas Distributa*, ed. P. Piolin, 16 vols. (Paris, 1715–65).

Garnier de Pont Saint-Maxence, *La Vie de Thomas Becket*, ed. E. Walberg (Lund, 1922).

Gerald of Wales, *Itinerarium Kambriae, Opera*, 8 vols., I–IV, ed. J. S. Brewer, V–VII, ed. J. F. Dimock and VIII, ed. G. F. Warner, RS (London, 1861–91).

*Gesta Abbatum S. Albani*, ed. H. T. Riley, 3 vols., RS (London, 1867–9), I, 59.

*The Gesta Normannorum Ducum of William of Jumièges, Orderic Vitalis, and Robert of Torigni*, ed. E. M. C. Van Houts, 2 vols., Oxford Medieval Texts (Oxford, 1992, 1995).

*Gesta Stephani*, ed. K. R. Potter and R. H. C. Davis, Oxford Medieval Texts (Oxford, 1976).

*Gilbertine Charters: Transcripts of Charters relating to the Gilbertine Houses of Sixle, Ormsby, Catley, Bullington and Alvingham*, ed. F. M. Stenton, Lincoln Record Society, XVIII (1922).

Giles, J. A. (ed.) 'Vita et Passio Waldevi comitis', *Vitae Quorundum Anglo-Saxonum*, Caxton Society (1854).

Harmer, F. E. (ed.) *Anglo-Saxon Writs* (Manchester, 1952, reissued Stamford, 1989).

*Hemingi Chartularium Ecclesiae Wigorniensis*, 2 vols., ed. T. Hearne (Oxford, 1723).

Henry of Huntingdon, *Historia Anglorum*, ed. T. Arnold, RS (London, 1879).

*Histoire de Guillaume le Maréchal*, ed. P. Meyer, 3 vols., Société de l'Histoire de France (Paris, 1891–1901).

*Historia et Cartularium Monasterii Sancti Petri Gloucestriae*, ed. W. H. Hart, 3 vols., RS (London, 1863–7).

*Historia Pontificalis of John of Salisbury*, ed. M. Chibnall (Edinburgh and London, 1956).

*The Historical Works of Gervase of Canterbury*, ed. W. Stubbs, 2 vols., RS (London, 1879, 1880).

Ingulph, *Chronicle of the Abbey of Croyland*, ed. H. T. Riley (London, 1854).

Jocelin of Brakelond, *Chronica*, ed. H. E. Butler (Edinburgh and London, 1949).

Jocelin of Furness, 'Vita Waldevi', *Acta Sanctorum*, August, 1, 242–78.

John of Ford, *The Life of Wulfric of Haselbury*, ed. M. Bell, Somerset Record Society (1933).

*Leges Henrici Primi*, ed. L. J. Downer (Oxford, 1972).

*Letters of Lanfranc*, ed. H. Clover and M. Gibson (Oxford, 1979).

*The Letters of St Bernard of Clairvaux*, ed. B. S. James (London, 1953).

*Liber Eliensis*, ed. E. O. Blake, Camden Society, 3rd series, XCII (1962).

*Liber Memorandum de Bernewelle*, ed. J. W. Clark (Cambridge, 1907).

*Liber Monasterii de Hyda*, ed. E. Edwards, RS (London, 1866).

*Liber Vitae Ecclesiae Dunelmensis*, ed. J. Stevenson, Surtees Society, XIII (1841).

Liebermann, F. (ed.) *Die Gesetze der Angelsachsen*, 3 vols. (Halle, 1903–16).

*The Life of Ailred of Rievaulx by Walter Daniel*, ed. F. M. Powicke (Edinburgh and London, 1950, reprinted Oxford, 1978).

*The Life of Christina of Markyate: a Twelfth-Century Recluse*, ed. and trans. C. H. Talbot (Oxford, 1959).

*Magni Rotuli Scaccarii Normanniae*, ed. T. Stapleton, 2 vols. (London, 1840–4).

*Materials for the History of Thomas Becket*, 7 vols., I–VI, ed. J. C. Robertson and VII ed. by J. C. Robertson and J. B. Sheppard, RS (London, 1875–85).

Orderic Vitalis, *The Ecclesiastical History*, ed. M. Chibnall, 6 vols., Oxford Medieval Texts (Oxford, 1969–80).

*Patrologia Latina*, ed. J.-P. Migne, 221 vols. (Paris, 1844–64).

*The Peterborough Chronicle of Hugh Candidus*, ed. W. T. Mellows (Oxford, 1949).

*Pipe Roll 31 Henry I*, ed. J. Hunter for Record Commission (London, 1833). *Pipe Rolls 2–4 Henry II* were also edited for the Record Commission; subsequent rolls by the Pipe Roll Society.

*Radulfi Diceto Lundoniensis Opera Historica*, ed. W. Stubbs, 2 vols., RS (London, 1876).

*Records relating to the Barony of Kendale by W. Farrer*, I (Kendal, 1923).

*Recueil des actes des ducs de Normandie*, ed. M. Fauroux, Mémoires de la Société des Antiquaires de Normandie, XXXVI (Caen, 1961).

*Recueil des chartes de l'abbaye de Cluny*, A. Bernard and A. Bruel, 6 vols. (Paris, 1876–1903).

*Recueil des historiens des Gaules et de la France*, ed. M. Bouquet and others, 24 vols. (Paris, 1869–1904).

*Red Book of the Exchequer*, ed. H. Hall, 3 vols., RS (London, 1896).

*Regesta Regum Anglo-Normannorum 1066–1154*, 4 vols., vol. I ed. H. W. C. Davis, vol. II ed. C. Johnson and H. A. Cronne, vols. III and IV ed. H. A. Cronne and R. H. C. Davis (Oxford, 1913–69).

*Regesta Regum Scottorum.* I. *The Acts of Malcolm IV,* ed. G. W. S. Barrow (Edinburgh, 1960).

Reginald of Durham, *Libellus de Vita et Miraculis S. Godrici, Heremitae de Finchale, Auctore Reginaldo Monacho Dunelmensis,* ed. J. Stevenson, Surtees Society, xx (1847).

*The Register of the priory of St Bees,* ed. J. Wilson, Cumberland and Westmorland Antiquarian and Archaeological Society, Chartulary series, no. III (Kendal, 1915).

*The Register of Wetheral,* ed. J. E. Prescott, Cumberland and Westmorland Antiquarian and Archaeological Society (1897).

Robertson, A. J. (ed.) *Anglo-Saxon Charters* (Cambridge, 1939).

*Rolls of the Justices in Eyre Gloucestershire, Warwickshire, Staffordshire, 1221, 1222,* ed. D. M. Stenton, Selden Society, LIX (1959).

*Roman de Rou de Wace,* ed. A. J. Holden, 3 vols. (Paris, 1970–3).

*Rotuli Curiae Regis,* ed. F. Palgrave for Record Commission, 2 vols. (London, 1835).

*Rotuli de Dominabus et Pueris et Puellis de Donatione Regis in XII Comitatibus 31 Henry II, 1185,* ed. J. H. Round, Pipe Roll Society, xxxv (1913).

*Rotuli Litterarum Patentium,* ed. T. D. Hardy, Record Commission I part i (London, 1835).

*S. Anselmi Opera Omnia,* ed. F. S. Schmitt, 6 vols., reprint (Edinburgh, 1946–61).

Sauvage, E. P. (ed.) 'Vita Beati Vitalis', *Analecta Bollandiana,* 1 (1882), 355–410.

*Select Documents of the English Lands of the Abbey of Bec,* ed. M. Chibnall, Camden Society, 3rd series, LXXIII (1951).

*Sibton Abbey Cartularies,* ed. P. Brown, Suffolk Records Society, VII, VIII, IX, X (1985–8).

*Sir Christopher Hatton's Book of Seals,* ed. L. C. Loyd and D. M. Stenton, Northamptonshire Record Society, xv (Oxford, 1950), no. 301.

Stenton, F. M. *Free Peasants of the Northern Danelaw* (Oxford, 1969).

Stubbs, W. *Select Charters,* 9th edn, ed. H. W. C. Davis (Oxford, 1913).

Suger, *Vie de Louis VI le Gros,* ed. H. Waquet (Paris, 1929), translated by R. C. Cusimano and J. Moorhead (Washington, 1992).

Symeon of Durham, *Opera omnia,* ed. T. Arnold, 2 vols., RS (London, 1882–5).

*Textus Roffensis,* ed. P. H. Sawyer, Early English Manuscripts in Facsimile, VII, IX (Copenhagen, 1957, 1962).

*The Treatise on the Laws and Customs of the Realm of England Commonly Called Glanvill,* ed. and trans. G. D. G. Hall, Oxford Medieval Texts, reprint (Oxford, 1993).

*La Très Ancienne Coutume de Bretagne,* ed. M. Planiol (Rennes, 1896).

*Two Cartularies of Bruton and Montacute,* Somerset Record Society, VIII (1894).

*Vetus Registrum Sarisberiense alias dictum registrum S. Osmundi episcopi. The Register of St. Osmund*, ed. W. H. Rich Jones, 2 vols., RS (London, 1883–4).

*Victoria History of the Counties of England* (London, 1900, in progress).

*Vita Wulfstani of William of Malmesbury*, ed. R. R. Darlington, Camden Society, New Series, XI (1928).

Walter Map, *De Nugis Curialium. Courtiers' Trifles*, ed. and trans. M. R. James, revised C. N. L. Brooke and R. A. B. Mynors (Oxford, 1983).

*Westminster Abbey Charters 1066–c. 1214*, ed. E. Mason, London Record Society, XXV (1988).

William of Malmesbury, *De Gestis Regum Anglorum libri quinque, historiae novellae libri tres*, ed. W. Stubbs, 2 vols., RS (London, 1887–9).

*Gesta Pontificum*, ed. N. E. S. A. Hamilton (RS 1870).

*Historia Novella*, ed. K. R. Potter (Nelson's Medieval Texts), (London, 1955).

William of Poitiers, *Gesta Guillelmi*, ed. R. Foreville (Paris, 1952).

## 3 Secondary sources

Abels, R. P. *Lordship and Military Obligation in Anglo-Saxon England* (Berkeley, Los Angeles, and London, 1988).

Ailes, A. 'Heraldry in Twelfth-Century England: the Evidence', *England in the Twelfth Century*, ed. D. Williams (Woodbridge, 1990).

'The Knights, Heraldry and Armour: the Role of Recognition and the Origins of Heraldry', *Medieval Knighthood*, IV (Woodbridge, 1992), 1–21.

Aird, W. M. 'An Absent Friend: The Career of Bishop William of St Calais', *Anglo-Norman Durham*, ed. D. Rollason, M. Harvey, M. Prestwich (Woodbridge, 1994), pp. 283–97.

Amt, E. M. 'Richard de Lucy, Henry II's Justiciar', *Medieval Prosopography*, 9 (1988), 61–87.

'The Forest Regard of 1155', *Haskins Society Journal*, 2 (1990), 189–95.

'The Meaning of Waste in the Early Pipe Rolls of Henry II', *Economic History Review*, 44 (1991), 240–8.

*The Accession of Henry II in England. Royal Government Restored 1149–1159* (Woodbridge, 1993).

Ariès, P. and Duby, G. *A History of Private Life*, II, *Revelations of the Medieval World*, ed. G. Duby, translated A. Goldhammer (Cambridge Mass., and London, 1988).

Armitage, E. S. *Early Norman Castles of the British Isles* (London, 1912).

Arnold, B. *German Knighthood 1050–1300* (Oxford, 1985).

*Princes and Territories in Medieval Germany* (Cambridge, 1991).

'Instruments of Power: The Profile and Profession of *Ministeriales* within German

Aristocratic Society, 1050–1225', *Cultures of Power. Lordship, Status, and Process in Twelfth-Century-Europe*, ed. T. N. Bisson (Philadelphia, 1995), pp. 36–55.

Baker, D. 'The Foundation of Fountains Abbey', *Northern History*, 4 (1969), 29–43.

'The Desert in the North', *Northern History*, 5 (1970), 1–11.

'Patronage in the Early Twelfth Century: Walter Espec, Kirkham and Rievaulx', *Traditio – Krisis – Renovatio aus theologischer Sicht. Festschrift Winifred Zeller* (Marburg, 1976), pp. 92–9.

Barlow, F. *Edward the Confessor* (London, 1970).

*The English Church 1066–1154* (London, 1979).

*William Rufus* (London, 1983).

Barlow, F., Biddle, M., Von Feilitzen, O., Keene, D. J. *Winchester in the Early Middle Ages. Winchester Studies*, I (Oxford, 1976).

Barrow, G. W. S. *The Kingdom of the Scots* (London, 1973).

'The Pattern of Lordship and Feudal Settlement in Cumbria', *Journal of Medieval History*, 1 (1975), 117–38.

*The Anglo-Norman Era in Scottish History* (Oxford, 1980).

Barrow, J. 'English Cathedral Communities and Reform in the Late Tenth and the Eleventh Centuries', *Anglo-Norman Durham*, ed. D. Rollason, M. Harvey, and M. Prestwich (Woodbridge, 1994), pp. 25–39.

Barthélemy, D. *Les deux âges de la seigneurie banale. Coucy (XIe–XIIIe siècles)* (Paris, 1984).

'La mutation féodale a-t-elle eu lieu?', *Annales*, 47 (1992), 767–75.

*La société dans le comté de Vendôme, de l'an mil au XIVe siècle* (Paris, 1993).

'Qu'est-ce que la chevalerie, en France aux Xe et XI siècles?', *Revue historique*, 290 (1993), 15–74.

'Castles, Barons and Vavassors in the Vendômois and Neighboring Regions in the Eleventh and Twelfth Centuries', *Cultures of Power. Lordship, Status, and Process in Twelfth-Century Europe*, ed. T. N. Bisson (Philadelphia, 1995), pp. 56–68.

Bartlett, R. *The Making of Europe. Conquest, Colonization and Cultural Change 950–1350* (London, 1993).

Bates, D. 'Notes sur l'aristocratie normande. II. Herluin de Conteville et sa famille', *Annales de Normandie*, 23 (1973), 21–38.

'The Character and Career of Odo, bishop of Bayeux (1049/50–1097)', *Speculum*, 50 (1975), 1–20.

'The Land Pleas of William I's Reign: Penenden Heath Revisited', *Bulletin of the Institute of Historical Research*, 51 (1978), 1–19.

'The Origins of the Justiciarship', *Proceedings of the Battle Conference*, 4 (1981), 1–12.

*Normandy before 1066* (London, 1982).

'The Building of a Great Church: the Abbey of St Peter's Gloucester, and its Early

Norman Benefactors', *Transactions of the Bristol and Gloucestershire Archaeological Society*, 102 (1984), 129–32.

'Lord Sudeley's Ancestors: the Family of the Counts of Amiens, Valois and the Vexin in France and England during the Eleventh Century', *The Sudeleys – Lords of Toddington*, The Manorial Society of Great Britain (1987).

'Normandy and England after 1066', *English Historical Review*, 104 (1989), 851–80.

*William the Conqueror* (London, 1989).

'Two Ramsey Writs and the Domesday Survey', *Historical Research*, 63 (1990), 337–9.

*Bishop Remigius of Lincoln 1067–1092* (Lincoln, 1993).

'The Rise and Fall of Normandy, *c.* 911–1204', *England and Normandy in the Middle Ages*, ed. D. Bates and A. Curry (London, 1994), pp. 19–35.

'The Prosopographical Study of Anglo-Norman Royal Charters: some Problems and Perspectives', *Family Trees and the Roots of Power. The Prosopography of Britain and France from the Tenth to the Twelfth Century*, ed. K. S. B. Keats-Rohan (Woodbridge, forthcoming).

Bates, D. and Gazeau, V. 'L'Abbaye de Grestain et la famille d'Herluin de Conteville', *Annales de Normandie*, 40 (1990), 5–30.

Bearman, R. 'Baldwin de Redvers: Some Aspects of a Baronial Career in the Reign of King Stephen', *Anglo-Norman Studies*, 18 (1995), 19–46.

Beckerman, J. S. 'Adding Insult to *Iniuria*: Affronts to Honor and the Origins of Trespass', *On the Laws and Customs of England. Essays in Honor of Samuel E. Thorne*, ed. M. S. Arnold, T. A. Green, S. A. Scully, S. D. White (Chapel Hill NC, 1981), pp. 159–81.

Beech, G. 'Aimeri of Thouars and the Poitevin Connection', *Anglo-Norman Studies*, 7 (1985), 224–45.

'The Participation of Aquitainians in the Conquest of England 1066–1100', *Anglo-Norman Studies*, 9 (1987), 1–24.

'Aquitainians and Flemings in the Refoundation of Bardney Abbey (Lincolnshire) in the Later Eleventh Century', *Haskins Society Journal*, 1 (1989), 73–90.

Beeler, J. 'Castles and Strategy in Norman and Early Angevin England', *Speculum*, 31 (1956), 581–601.

*Warfare in England 1066–1189* (Ithaca, New York, 1966).

Beresford, G. *Goltho. The Development of an Early Medieval Manor c. 850–1150* (London, 1987).

Beresford, M. *New Towns of the Middle Ages. Town Plantations in England, Wales, and Gascony* (London, 1967).

Bethell, D. 'The Foundation of Fountains Abbey and the State of St Mary's of York, in 1132', *Journal of Ecclesiastical History*, 17 (1966), 11–27.

Bettey, J. H. *Wessex from AD 1000* (London, 1986).

Biancalana, J. 'For Want of Justice: the Legal Reforms of Henry II', *Columbia Law Review*, 88 (1988), 433–536.

'Widows at Common Law: the Development of Common Law Dower', *Irish Jurist*, new series, 33 (1988), 255–329.

Birch, W. de G. *Catalogue of Seals in the Department of Manuscripts in the British Museum*, 6 vols. (London, 1887–1900).

Bishop, M. W. 'Multiple Estates in late Anglo-Saxon Nottinghamshire', *Transactions of the Thoroton Society*, 85 (1982 for 1981), 37–47.

Bishop, T. A. M. 'The Norman Settlement of Yorkshire', *Studies in Medieval History Presented to Frederick Maurice Powicke*, ed. R. W. Hunt and others (Oxford, 1948), pp. 1–14.

Bisson, T. N. 'Nobility and Family in Medieval France: a Review Essay', *French Historical Studies*, 16 (1990), 597–613.

'The "Feudal Revolution"', *Past and Present*, 142 (1994), 6–42.

'Medieval Lordship', *Speculum*, 70 (1995), 743–59.

Blackburn, M. 'Coinage and Currency', *The Anarchy of King Stephen's Reign*, ed. E. King (Oxford, 1994), pp. 145–205.

Blair, C. H. Hunter 'Armorials on English Seals from the Twelfth to the Sixteenth Centuries', *Archaeologia*, 89, second series, 39 (1943), 1–26.

Blair, J. 'William FitzAnsculf and the Abinger Motte', *Archaeological Journal*, 138 (1981), 146–8.

Blair, J. (ed.) *Minsters and Parish Churches. The Local Church in Transition 950–1200*, Oxford University Committee for Archaeology, Monograph no. 17 (1988).

'Frithuwold's Kingdom and the Origins of Surrey', *The Origins of Anglo-Saxon Kingdoms*, ed. S. Bassett (Leicester, 1989), pp. 97–107, 231–6.

*Early Medieval Surrey. Landholding, Church and Settlement*, Surrey Archaeological Society (1991).

Bloch, M. *Feudal Society*, translated L. A. Manyon, 2 vols., 2nd edn (London, 1962).

Bonassie, P. *La Catalogne, du milieu du Xe au fin du XIe siècle* (Paris, 1975).

Boon, G. C. *Coins of the Anarchy 1135–54*, National Museum of Wales (Cardiff, 1988).

Bosl, K. *Die Reichsministerialität der Salier und Staufer: Ein Betrag zur Geschichte des Hochsmittelalterlichen Deutschen Volkes, Staates und Reiches*, Schriften der Monumenta Germaniae Historica (Stuttgart, 1950–1).

Bouchard, C. B. 'The Origins of the French Nobility: a Reassessment', *American Historical Review*, 86 (1981), 501–32.

'Family Structure and Family Consciousness among the Aristocracy in the Ninth to Eleventh Centuries', *Francia*, 14 (1987), 39–58.

Bournazel, E. *Le gouvernement capétien au XIIe siècle, 1108–1180* (Limoges, 1975).

Boussard, J. 'Le comté de Mortain au XIe siècle', *Le Moyen Age*, 58 (1952), 253–79.

Bradbury, J. 'The Early Years of Stephen', *England in the Twelfth Century*, ed. D. Williams (Woodbridge, 1990), pp. 17–30.

*Stephen and Matilda. The Civil War of 1139–1153* (Stroud, 1996).

Brett, M. *The English Church under Henry I* (Oxford, 1975).

Britnell, R. H. *The Commercialisation of English Society 1100–1500* (Cambridge, 1993).

Brooke, C. N. L. and Keir, G. *London 800–1216: The Shaping of a City* (Berkeley, Los Angeles, and London, 1975).

Brooke, C. N. L., Keir, G., and Reynolds, S. 'Henry I's Charter for the City of London', *Journal of the Society of Archivists*, 4 (1972), 558–78.

Brooke, G. C. *A Catalogue of English Coins in the British Museum. The Norman Kings*, 2 vols. (London, 1916).

Brown, R. Allen 'Royal Castlebuilding in England, 1154–1216', *English Historical Review*, 70 (1955), 353–98.

*The Origins of English Feudalism* (London, 1973).

'The Status of the Norman Knight', *War and Government in the Middle Ages. Essays in Honour of J. O. Prestwich*, ed. J. Gillingham and J. C. Holt (Woodbridge, 1984), pp. 18–32.

*Castles from the Air* (Cambridge, 1989).

*The Normans*, 2nd edn (Woodbridge, 1994).

Brown, R. Allen, Colvin, H. M., Taylor, A. J. *The History of the King's Works*. I, II, *The Middle Ages* (London, 1963).

Brown, S. A. 'The Bayeux Tapestry: Why Eustace, Odo and William?', *Anglo-Norman Studies*, 12 (1990), 7–28.

Brundage, J. A. *Medieval Canon Law* (London, 1995).

Bur, M. *La formation du comté de Champagne v. 950–v. 1150* (Nancy, 1977).

Burton, J. *The Yorkshire Nunneries in the Twelfth and Thirteenth Centuries*, Borthwick Paper no. 56 (York, 1979).

'Monasteries and Parish Churches in Eleventh- and Twelfth-Century Yorkshire', *Northern History*, 23 (1987), 39–50.

'The Abbeys of Byland and Jervaulx, and the Problems of the English Savigniacs, 1134–1156', *Monastic Studies*, 2 (1991), 119–31.

*Monastic and Religious Orders in Britain, 1000–1300* (Cambridge, 1994).

'The Monastic Revival in Yorkshire: Whitby and St Mary's York', *Anglo-Norman Durham*, ed. D. Rollason, M. Harvey, and M. Prestwich (Woodbridge, 1994), pp. 41–51.

Cam, H. 'The Evolution of the Medieval English Franchise', *Speculum*, 32 (1957), 427–42.

Campbell, J. 'Some Twelfth-Century Views of the Anglo-Saxon Past', *Peritia*, 3 (1984), 131–50, reprinted in *Essays in Anglo-Saxon History* (London, 1986), pp. 209–28.

Chandler, V. 'Intimations of Authority: Notes on three Anglo-Norman Countesses', *Indiana Social Studies Quarterly*, 31 (1978), 5–17.

Charles-Edwards, T. 'Kinship, Status and the Origins of the Hide', *Past and Present*, 56 (1972), 3–33.

Chibnall, M. 'Robert of Bellême and Castle of Tickhill', *Droit privé et institutions régionales. Etudes historiques offerts à Jean Yver* (Paris, 1976), pp. 151–6.

*Anglo-Norman England 1066–1166* (Oxford, 1986).

'The Empress Matilda and Church Reform', *Transactions of the Royal Historical Society*, 5th series, 38 (1988), 107–33.

'Women in Orderic Vitalis', *Haskins Society Journal*, 2 (1990), 105–21.

*The Empress Matilda* (Oxford, 1991).

'The Charters of the Empress Matilda', *Law and Government in the Middle Ages*, ed. G. Garnett and J. Hudson (Cambridge, 1994), pp. 276–98.

Clanchy, M. T. *England and Its Rulers, 1066–1272* (London, 1983).

Clark, C. 'British Library Additional MS 40,000', *Anglo-Norman Studies*, 7 (1985), 50–68.

Clarke, P. A. *The English Nobility under Edward the Confessor* (Oxford, 1994).

Clay, C. T. 'The Family of Amundeville', *Lincolnshire Architectural and Archaeological Society Reports and Papers*, new series, 3 (1949), 109–36.

'The Ancestry of the Early Lords of Warkworth', *Archaeologia Aeliana*, 4th series, 32 (1954), 65–71.

'Hugh Bardolf the Justice and his Family', *Lincolnshire History and Archaeology*, 50 (1966), 5–28.

Clay C. T. and Greenway, D. *Early Yorkshire Families*, Yorkshire Archaeological Society (Wakefield, 1973).

Coad, J. G. *Castle Acre Castle* (English Heritage, London, 1984).

Coad, J. G. and Streeten, A. D. F. 'Excavations at Castle Acre Castle, Norfolk', *Archaeological Journal*, 139 (1982), 138–201.

Collar, H. 'Book of the Foundation of Walden Abbey', *Essex Review*, 45 (1936), 73–85, 147–56, 224–36; 46 (1937), 12–16, 86–98, 164–70, 227–35; 47 (1938), 36–41, 94–9, 150–5, 216–20.

Cooke, K. 'Donors and Daughters: Shaftesbury Abbey's Benefactors, Endowments and Nuns c. 1086–1130', *Anglo-Norman Studies*, 12 (1990), 29–45.

Corbett, W. J. 'The Development of the Duchy of Normandy and the Norman Conquest of England', *Cambridge Medieval History*, v, ed. J. R. Tanner and others (Cambridge, 1926), 507–20.

Coss, P. R. 'Bastard Feudalism Revisited', *Past and Present*, 125 (November, 1989), 27–64.

*The Knight in Medieval England 1000–1400* (Stroud, 1993).

Coulson, C. 'The Castles of the Anarchy' in *The Anarchy of King Stephen's Reign*, ed. E. King (Oxford, 1994), pp. 67–92.

Cowdrey, H. E. J. 'Unions and Confraternities with Cluny', *Journal of Ecclesiastical History*, 16 (1965), 152–62.

Cownie, E. 'Gloucester Abbey, 1066–1135: An Illustration of Religious Patronage in Anglo-Norman England', *England and Normandy in the Middle Ages*, ed. D. Bates and A. Curry (London, 1994), pp. 143–57.

Crispin, M. J. and Macary, L. *Falaise Roll Recording Prominent Companions of William Duke of Normandy at the Conquest of England* (London, 1938).

Cronne, H. A. 'Ranulf de Gernons, Earl of Chester', *Transactions of the Royal Historical Society*, 4th series, 20 (1937), 103–34.

Crook, D. 'The Establishment of the Derbyshire County Court 1256', *Derbyshire Archaeological Journal*, 103 (1983), 98–106.

Crosby, E. U. *Bishop and Chapter in Twelfth Century England*, Cambridge Studies in Medieval Life and Thought, 4th series, xxiii (Cambridge, 1994).

Crouch, D. 'Geoffrey de Clinton and Roger Earl of Warwick: New Men and Magnates in the Reign of Henry I', *Bulletin of the Institute of Historical Research*, 55 (1982), 113–24.

'Oddities in the Early History of the Marcher Lordship of Gower, 1107–1166', *Bulletin of the Board of Celtic Studies*, 31 (1984), 133–41.

'Robert, earl of Gloucester, and the Daughter of Zelophehad', *Journal of Medieval History*, 11 (1985), 227–43.

*The Beaumont Twins*, Cambridge Studies in Medieval Life and Thought, 4th series, i (Cambridge, 1986).

'Earl William of Gloucester and the End of the Anarchy: New Evidence Relating to the Honor of Eudo Dapifer', *English Historical Review*, 103 (1988), 69–75.

*William Marshal* (London, 1990).

'The Administration of the Norman Earldom,' *The Earldom of Chester and Its Charters*, Chester Archaeological Society, 71 (1991), pp. 69–95.

'Debate. Bastard Feudalism Revised', *Past and Present*, 131 (1991), 165–77.

*The Image of Aristocracy in Britain 1000–1300* (London, 1992).

'Earls and Bishops in Twelfth-century Leicestershire', *Nottingham Medieval Studies*, 37 (1993), 9–20.

'The Hidden History of the Twelfth Century', *Haskins Society Journal*, 5 (1993), 111–30.

'Normans and Anglo-Normans: a Divided Aristocracy', *Normandy and England in the Middle Ages*, ed. D. Bates and A. Curry (London, 1994), pp. 51–67.

'The Local Influence of the Earls of Warwick, 1088–1242: A Study in Decline and Resourcefulness', *Midland History*, 21 (1996), 1–22.

Dalton, P. 'William Earl of York and Royal Authority in Yorkshire in the Reign of Stephen', *Haskins Society Journal*, 2 (1990), 155–65.

'Aiming at the Impossible: Ranulf II earl of Chester and Lincolnshire in the Reign of King Stephen', *Earldom of Chester and its Charters*, Chester Archaeological Society, lxxi (1991), pp. 109–34.

'*In Neutro Latere*: the Armed Neutrality of Ranulf II Earl of Chester in King Stephen's Reign', *Anglo-Norman Studies*, 14 (1992), 39–59.

*Conquest, Anarchy and Lordship. Yorkshire 1066–1154*, Cambridge Studies in Medieval Life and Thought, 4th series, xxvii (Cambridge, 1994).

'The Kings of Scotland and Durham', *Anglo-Norman Durham*, ed. D. Rollason, M. Harvey, M. Prestwich (Woodbridge, 1994), pp. 311–23.

Darby, H. C. *Domesday England* (Cambridge, 1977).

David, C. W. *Robert Curthose* (Cambridge, Mass., 1920).

Davis, H. W. C. 'The Anarchy of Stephen's Reign', *English Historical Review*, 8 (1903), 630–41.

'Henry of Blois and Brian FitzCount', *English Historical Review*, 24 (1910), 297–303.

Davis, R. H. C. 'King Stephen and the Earl of Chester Revised', *English Historical Review*, 75 (1960), 654–60.

'Geoffrey de Mandeville Reconsidered', *English Historical Review*, 79 (1964), 299–37.

'What Happened in Stephen's Reign', *History*, 49 (1964), 1–12.

'The Norman Conquest', *History*, 51 (1966), 279–88.

'An Unknown Coventry Charter', *English Historical Review*, 86 (1971), 533–45.

*The Normans and their Myth* (London, 1976).

'Domesday Book: Continental Parallels', *Domesday Studies*, ed. J. C. Holt (Woodbridge, 1987), pp. 15–39.

Comments appended to an article by J. O. Prestwich, 'The Treason of Geoffrey de Mandeville,' *English Historical Review*, 103 (1988), 313–17.

'Last Words on Geoffrey de Mandeville', *English Historical Review*, 105 (1990), 671–2.

*King Stephen*, 3rd edn (London, 1990).

Davison, B. 'Sulgrave', *Medieval Archaeology*, 5 (1961), 328; 6–7 (1962–3), 333.

'Early Earthwork Castles: a new model', *Château Gaillard*, 3, (1966), 37–47.

'The Origins of the Castle in England: the Institute's Research Project', *Archaeological Journal*, 120 (1967), 202–11.

Davray, D. L. 'Peter Damian, Consanguinity and Church Property', *Intellectual Life in the Middle Ages. Studies presented to Margaret Gibson* (London, 1992), pp. 71–80.

DeAragon, R. 'In Pursuit of Aristocratic Women: a Key to Success in Norman England', *Albion*, 14 (1982), 258–67.

Debord, A. *La société laïque dans les pays de la Charente Xe–XIIe siècles* (Paris, 1984).

De Boüard, M. 'Les petites enceintes circulaires d'origine médiévale en Normandie', *Châtau Gaillard*, 1 (1964), 21–36.

Devailly, G. *Le Berry du Xe siècle au milieu du XIIIe siècle* (Paris, 1973).

Dickinson, J. C. 'The Origins of Carlisle Cathedral', *Cumberland and Westmorland Antiquarian and Archaeological Society*, 45 (1946), 136–46.

*The Origins of the Austin Canons and their Introduction into England* (London, 1950).

'Walter the Priest and St Mary Carlisle', *Cumberland and Westmorland Antiquarian and Archaeological Society*, 69 (1969), 102–14.

Dodwell, B. 'East Anglian Commendation,' *English Historical Review*, 63 (1948), 289–306.

Douglas, D. C. 'Companions of the Conqueror', *History*, 28 (1943), 129–47.

*William the Conqueror* (London, 1964).

Duby, G. *La société au XIe et XIIe siècles dans la région mâconnaise* (Paris, 1953).

'Remarques sur la littérature généalogique en France au XIe et XIIe siècles', *Académie des Inscriptions et Belles Lettres, comptes rendus des séances de l'année 1967* (Paris, 1967).

*The Chivalrous Society* (London, 1977).

*Medieval Marriage. Two Models from Twelfth-Century France*, trans. Elborg Forster (Baltimore, 1978).

*The Knight, The Lady and the Priest. The Making of Modern Marriage in Medieval France*, trans. B. Bray (London, 1984).

*Love and Marriage in the Middle Ages*, trans. J. Dunnett (Oxford, 1994).

*Famille et parenté dans l'Occident médiéval* (ed., with Jacques Le Goff) Collection de l'Ecole Française de Rome, xxx (1977).

Dugdale, W. *The Baronage of England*, 3 vols. in 1 (London, 1675–6).

Dumbreck, W. V. 'The Lowy of Tonbridge', *Archaeologia Cantiana*, 72 (1955), 138–47.

Dyson, A. G. 'The Monastic Patronage of Bishop Alexander of Lincoln', *Journal of Ecclesiastical History*, 26 (1975), 1–24.

Eales, R. 'Local Loyalties in Norman England: Kent in Stephen's Reign', *Anglo-Norman Studies*, 7 (1985), 88–108.

'Royal Power and Castles in Norman England', *The Ideals and Practice of Medieval Knighthood*, iii, ed. Christopher Harper-Bill and Ruth Harvey (Woodbridge, 1990), 49–78.

Elkins, S. K. *Holy Women of Twelfth-Century England* (Chapel Hill, 1988).

Ellis, A. S. 'Biographical Notes on Yorkshire Tenants named in Domesday Book', *Yorkshire Archaeological Journal*, 4 (1877), 114–57, 215–48, 384–415.

Ellis, H. *An Introduction to Domesday Book*, 2 vols. (London, 1833).

English, B. *The Lords of Holderness 1086–1260* (Oxford, 1979).

'William the Conqueror and the Anglo-Norman Succession', *Historical Research*, 64 (1991), 221–36.

Evergates, T. 'Nobles and Knights in Twelfth-Century France', *Cultures of Power. Lordship, Status and Process in Twelfth-Century Europe* (Philadelphia, 1995), pp. 11–35.

Farrer, W. *Feudal Cambridgeshire* (Cambridge, 1920).

*Honors and Knights' Fees*, 3 vols. (London and Manchester, 1923–5).

Feuchère, P. 'Une tentative manquée de concentration territoriale entre Somme et Seine: la principauté d'Amiens-Valois au XIe siècle', *Le Moyen Age*, 60 (1954), 1-37.

Finberg, H. P. R. 'Uffculme', *Lucerna* (London, 1964), pp. 204-21.

Finn, R. Welldon, *The Norman Conquest and its Effects on the Economy 1066-1086* (London, 1971).

FitzHerbert, H. C. 'An Original Charter of Tailbois and Neville', *Genealogist*, new series, 3 (1886), 31-5.

Fleming, D. 'Landholding by *Milites* in Domesday Book: a Revision', *Anglo-Norman Studies*, 13 (1991), 83-98.

Fleming, R. 'Domesday Book and the Tenurial Revolution, *Anglo-Norman Studies*, 9 (1986), 87-102.

*Kings and Lords in Conquest England*, Cambridge Studies in Medieval Life and Thought, 4th series, xv (Cambridge, 1991).

'Rural Elites and Urban Communities in late Saxon England', *Past and Present*, 141 (1993), 3-27.

'Oral Testimony and the Domesday Inquest', *Anglo-Norman Studies*, 17 (1995), 101-22.

Flori, J. *L'essor de la chevalerie XIe-XII siècles* (Paris, 1986).

'Encore l'usage de la lance . . . La technique du combat chevaleresque vers l'an 1100', *Cahiers de Civilisation Médiévale*, 31 (1988), 213-40.

Fossier, R. *La terre et les hommes en Picardie jusqu'au milieu du XIIIe siècle*, 2 vols. (Paris, 1968).

*Enfance de l'Europe Xe-XIIe siècles*, 2 vols. (Paris, 1982).

Fox, C. *The Personality of Britain* (Cardiff, 1959).

Franklin, M. J. 'The Bishops of Winchester and the Monastic Revolution', *Anglo-Norman Studies*, 12 (1989), 47-65.

Freed, J. B. 'The Origins of the European Nobility: the Problem of the Ministerials', *Viator*, 11 (1976), 211-41.

'Reflections on the Medieval German Nobility', *American Historical Review*, 91 (1986), 553-75.

Freeman, E. A. *The History of the Norman Conquest of England*, 5 vols. and index (Oxford, 1870-79).

Galbraith, V. H. *The Making of Domesday Book* (Oxford, 1961).

*Domesday Book: its Place in Administrative History* (Oxford, 1974).

Garnett, G. '"Franci et Angli": the Legal Distinctions between Peoples after the Conquest', *Anglo-Norman Studies*, 8 (1985), 116-28.

'Coronation and Propaganda: Some Implications of the Norman Claim to the Throne of England', *Transactions of the Royal Historical Society*, 5th series, 36 (1986), 91-116.

'"Ducal" Succession in Early Normandy', *Law and Government in Medieval England and Normandy*, ed. G. Garnett and J. Hudson (Cambridge, 1994), pp. 80–110.

Généstal, R. *Le parage normand* (Caen, 1911).

Génicot, L. *L'économie namuroise au bas moyen age. II. Les Hommes, la Noblesse* (Louvain, 1960).

George, R. H. 'The Contribution of Flanders to the Conquest of England, 1065–1086', *Revue Belge de Philologie et d'Histoire*, 5 (1926), 81–99.

Gillingham, J. 'The Introduction of Knight Service into England', *Proceedings of the Battle Conference on Anglo-Norman Studies*, 4 (1981), 53–64.

'Love, Marriage and Politics in the Twelfth Century', *Forum for Modern Language Studies*, 25 (1989), 292–303.

'"The Most Precious Jewel in the English Crown": Levels of Danegeld and Heregeld in the Early Eleventh Century', *English Historical Review*, 104 (1989), 373–84.

'The Context and Purposes of Geoffrey of Monmouth's *History of the Kings of Britain*', *Anglo-Norman Studies*, 13 (1990), 99–118.

'The Beginnings of English Imperialism', *Journal of Historical Sociology*, 5 (1992), 392–409.

'Conquering the Barbarians: War and Chivalry in Twelfth-Century Britain', *Haskins Society Journal*, 4 (1992), 67–84.

'1066 and the Introduction of Chivalry into England', *Law and Government in the Middle Ages. Essays in Honour of Sir James Holt*, ed. G. Garnett and J. Hudson (Cambridge, 1994), pp. 31–55.

'Henry of Huntingdon and the English Nation', *Concepts of National Identity in the Middle Ages*, ed. S. Forde, L. Johnson, and A. V. Murray, Leeds Texts and Monographs, New Series, 14 (1995) 75–101.

'English Chivalry in French', *Anglo-Norman Political Culture and the Twelfth-Century Renaissance*, ed. C. Warren Hollister (Woodbridge, forthcoming).

Goebel, J. *Felony and Misdemeanour* (New York, 1937).

Golding, B. 'The Coming of the Cluniacs', *Proceedings of the Battle Conference on Anglo-Norman Studies*, 3 (1980), 65–77.

'Simon of Kyme: the Making of a Rebel', *Nottingham Medieval Studies*, 27 (1983), 23–36.

'Anglo-Norman Knightly Burials', *The Ideals and Practice of Medieval Knighthood*, i (Woodbridge, 1986), pp. 35–48.

'Robert of Mortain', *Anglo-Norman Studies*, 13 (1991), 119–44.

*Gilbert of Sempringham and the Gilbertine Order c. 1130–c. 1300* (Oxford, 1995).

Goody, J. *The Development of the Family and Marriage in Europe* (Cambridge, 1983).

Gover, J. E. B., Mawer, A., Stenton, F. M., and Houghton, F. T. S. *Warwickshire, English Place-Name Society* (Cambridge, 1936).

Graham, R. S. 'The Monastery of Cluny, 910–1155', *Archaeologia*, 80 (1930), 143–78.

Graham, T. H. B. 'Turgis Brundos', *Cumberland and Westmorland Antiquarian and Archaeologicul Society*, new series, 29 (1929), 49–56.

Green, J. A. 'William Rufus, Henry I and the Royal Demesne', *History*, 64 (1979), 337–52.

'The Last Century of Danegeld', *English Historical Review*, 96 (1981), 241–58.

'The Sheriffs of William the Conqueror', *Proceedings of the Battle Conference*, 5 (1982), 129–45.

'Lords of the Norman Vexin', *War and Government in the Middle Ages. Essays in Honour of J. O. Prestwich*, ed. J. Gillingham and J. C. Holt (Woodbridge, 1984), pp. 47–61.

*The Government of England under Henry I*, Cambridge Studies in Medieval Life and Thought, 4th series, II (Cambridge, 1986).

'Henry I and the Aristocracy of Normandy', *La France Anglaise au Moyen Age, Actes du 111e Congrès National des Sociétés Savantes* (Paris, 1988), pp. 161–73.

'Anglo-Scottish Relations, 1066–1174', *England and Her Neighbours 1066–1453. Essays in Honour of Pierre Chaplais*, ed. M. Jones and M. Vale (London, 1989), pp. 53–73.

'Unity and Disunity in the Anglo-Norman State', *Historical Research*, 62 (1989), 114–34.

*English Sheriffs to 1154*, Public Record Office Handbooks no. 24 (1990).

'Earl Ranulf II and Lancashire', *Earldom of Chester and its Charters*, Chester Archaeological Society, 71 (1991), pp. 97–109.

'Financing Stephen's War', *Anglo-Norman Studies*, 14 (1992), 91–114.

'Henry I and David I, *Scottish Historical Review*, 75 (1996), 1–19.

'Aristocratic Women in Early Twelfth-Century England', *Anglo-Norman Political Culture and the Twelfth-Century Renaissance*, ed. C. Warren Hollister (Woodbridge, forthcoming), pp. 59–82.

'Family Matters: Family and the Formation of the Empress's Party in South-West England', *Family Trees and the Roots of Politics. The Prosopography of Britain and France from the Tenth to the Twelfth Century*, ed. K. S. B. Keats-Rohan (Woodbridge, forthcoming).

Green, T. A. 'Societal Concepts of Criminal Liability for Homicide in Medieval England', *Speculum*, 47 (1972), 669–94.

Greenway, D. 'Henry of Huntingdon and the Manuscript of his *Historia Anglorum*', *Anglo-Norman Studies*, 9 (1986), 103–21.

Gregson, N. 'The Multiple Estate Model: some Critical Questions', *Journal of Historical Geography*, 11 (1985), 339–51.

Guillot, O. *Le comté d'Anjou et son entourage au XIe siècle* (Paris, 1972).

Hadju, R. 'Family and Feudal Ties in Poitou, 1100–1300', *Journal of Interdisciplinary History*, 8.1 (1977), 117–39.

'The Position of Noblewomen in the Pays de Coutumes, 1100–1300', *Journal of Family History*, 5 (1980), 122–44.

Hallam, H. E. *Rural England 1066–1348* (London, 1981).

Halpin, P. 'Women Religious in Late Anglo-Saxon England', *Haskins Society Journal*, 6 (1994), 97–110.

Hamilton, B. 'Women in the Crusader States: the Queens of Jerusalem', in *Medieval Women*, ed. D. Baker, Studies in Church History, Subsidia I (Oxford, 1978), pp. 143–74.

Harfield, G. 'A Handlist of Castles recorded in the Domesday Book', *English Historical Review*, 106 (1991), 371–92.

Harper-Bill, C. 'The Piety of the Anglo-Norman Knightly Class', *Proceedings of the Battle Conference*, 2 (1979), 63–77.

Hart, C. *The Hidation of Northamptonshire*, Department of English Local History Occasional Papers, second series no. 3 (Leicester, 1970).

Harvey, M. 'Open Field Agriculture and Landholding Arrangements in Eastern Yorkshire', *Transactions of the Institute of British Geographers*, new series, 9 (1984), 60–74.
'The Development of Open Fields in the Central Vale of York: a Reconsideration', *Geografiska Annaler*, 67 ser. B (1985), 35–44.

Harvey, P. D. A. 'The Pipe Rolls and the Adoption of Demesne Farming in England', *Economic History Review*, 27 (1974), 345–59.

Harvey, S. 'The Knight and the Knight's Fee in England', *Past and Present*, 49 (1970), 1–43.
'Domesday Book and Anglo-Norman Governance', *Transactions of the Royal Historical Society*, 5th series, 25 (1975), 175–93.
'The Extent and Profitability of Demesne Agriculture in England in the Later Eleventh Century', *Social Relations and Ideas. Essays in Honour of R. H. Hilton*, ed. T.H. Aston, P. R. Coss, Dyer, J. Thirsk (Cambridge, 1983), pp. 45–72.
'Taxation and the Economy', in *Domesday Studies*, ed. J. C. Holt (Woodbridge, 1987), pp. 249–65.
'Domesday England', *The Agrarian History of England and Wales*, II, ed. H. E. Hallam (Cambridge, 1988), 45–136.

Haskins, C. H. *Norman Institutions* (Cambridge, Mass., 1988).

Hayward, J. 'Hereward the Outlaw', *Journal of Medieval History*, 14 (1988), 293–304.

Hedley, W. Percy *Northumberland Families*, 2 vols. (Newcastle upon Tyne, 1968, 1970).

Helmerichs, Robert 'King Stephen's Norman Itinerary, 1137', *Haskins Society Journal*, 5 (1993), 89–97.

Herlihy, D. 'Land, Family and Women in Continental Europe, 701–1200', *Traditio*, 18 (1962), 89–120.
'Did Women have a Renaissance?: A Reconsideration,' *Medievalia et Humanistica* 13 (1985), 1–22, reprinted in *Women, Family and Society in Medieval Europe* (Providence and London, 1995), pp. 33–56.

*Medieval Households* (Cambridge, Mass., 1985).

*Women, Family and Society in Medieval Europe* (Providence and London, 1995).

Hicks, M. *Bastard Feudalism* (London, 1995).

Hicks, S. B. 'The Impact of William Clito on the Continental Policies of Henry I of England', *Viator*, 10 (1979), 1–21.

'England's Henry I and the Flemish Succession Crisis of 1127–1128', *Journal of the Rocky Mountain Medieval and Renaissance Association*, 2 (1981), 41–9.

Higham, N. J. *The Kingdom of Northumbria AD 350–1100* (Stroud, 1993).

'The Domesday Survey: Context and Purpose', *History*, 78 (1993), 7–21.

Hill, B. D. *English Cistercian Monasteries and their Patrons in the Twelfth Century* (Urbana, 1968).

Hill, J. W. F. *Medieval Lincoln* (Cambridge, 1949).

Hockey, S. F. 'William FitzOsbern and the Endowment of his Abbey of Lyre', *Proceedings of the Battle Conference on Anglo-Norman Studies*, 3 (1980), 78–96.

Holdsworth, C. 'War and Peace in the Twelfth Century. The Reign of Stephen Reconsidered', *War and Peace in the Middle Ages*, ed. B. P. McGuire (Copenhagen, 1987), pp. 67–93.

'Hermits and the Power of the Frontier', *Reading Medieval Studies*, 16 (1990), 55–76.

'The Church', in *The Anarchy of Stephen's Reign* (ed. King), pp. 207–30.

Hollister, C. Warren, *The Military Organization of Norman England* (Oxford, 1965).

'1066: "The Feudal Revolution"', *American Historical Review*, 62 (1968), 708–23, reprinted in *Monarchy, Magnates and Institutions*, pp. 1–16.

'The Strange Death of William Rufus', *Speculum*, 48 (1973), 637–53, reprinted in *Monarchy, Magnates and Institutions*, pp. 59–77.

'The Anglo-Norman Civil War: 1101', *English Historical Review*, 88 (1973), 315–34, reprinted in *Monarchy, Magnates and Institutions*, pp. 77–96.

'Magnates and "Curiales" in Early Norman England', *Viator*, 4 (1973), 115–22, reprinted in *Monarchy, Magnates and Institutions*, pp. 97–115.

'The Misfortunes of the Mandevilles', *History*, 58 (1973), 18–28, reprinted in *Monarchy, Magnates and Institutions*, pp. 117–27.

'The Anglo-Norman Succession Debate of 1126', *Journal of Medieval History*, 1 (1975), 19–39, reprinted in *Monarchy, Magnates and Institutions*, pp. 145–69.

'The Taming of a Turbulent Earl: Henry I and William de Warenne', *Réflexions Historiques*, 3 (1976), 83–91, reprinted in *Monarchy, Magnates and Institutions*, pp. 137–44.

'Normandy, France, and the Anglo-Norman Regnum', *Speculum*, 51 (1976), 202–42, reprinted in *Monarchy, Magnates and Institutions*, pp. 17–57.

'Henry I and Robert Malet', *Viator*, 8 (1977), 63–81, reprinted in *Monarchy, Magnates and Institutions*, pp. 129–36.

'Royal Acts of Mutilation', *Albion*, 10 (1978), 330–40, reprinted in *Monarchy, Magnates and Institutions*, pp. 291–301.

'Henry I and the Anglo-Norman Magnates', *Proceedings of the Battle Conference*, 2 (1979), 93–107.

'London's first Charter of Liberties: is it genuine?', *Journal of Medieval History*, 6 (1980), 289–306, reprinted in *Monarchy, Magnates and Institutions*, pp. 191–208.

*Monarchy, Magnates and Institutions in the Anglo-Norman World* (London, 1986).

'The Greater Domesday Tenants-in-Chief', *Domesday Studies*, ed. J. C. Holt (Woodbridge, 1987), pp. 219–48.

'The Campaign of 1102 against Robert of Bellême', *Studies in Medieval History presented to R. Allen Brown*, ed. C. Harper-Bill, C. Holdsworth, and J. L. Nelson (Woodbridge, 1989), pp. 193–202.

'The Vice-Regal Court of Henry I', *Law, Custom, and the Social Fabric. Essays in Honour of Bryce Lyon*, ed. B. S. Bachrach and D. Nicholas (Kalamazoo, 1990), pp. 131–44.

'The Aristocracy', *The Anarchy of Stephen's Reign*, (ed. King), pp. 37–66.

Hollister, C. Warren and Keefe, T. K., 'The Making of the Angevin Empire', *Journal of British Studies*, 12 (1973), 1–25 reprinted in *Monarchy, Magnates and Institutions*, pp. 247–71.

Holt, J. C. 'Politics and Property in Early Medieval England', *Past and Present*, 57 (1972), 3–52.

'The End of the Anglo-Norman realm', *Proceedings of the British Academy*, 61 (1975), 223–65.

'*What's in a Name?' Family Nomenclature and the Norman Conquest*, Stenton Lecture 1981 (Reading, 1982).

'Feudal Society and the Family in Early Medieval England', Presidential addresses to the Royal Historical Society, I, 'The Revolution of 1066', *Transactions of the Royal Historical Society*, 5th Series, 32 (1982), 193–212; II, 'Notions of Patrimony', *ibid.*, 33 (1983), 193–220; III, 'Patronage and Politics', *ibid.*, 34 (1984), 1–25; IV, 'The Heiress and the Alien', *ibid.*, 35 (1985), 1–28.

'The Introduction of Knight Service into England', *Anglo-Norman Studies*, 6 (1983), 89–106.

'The Loss of Normandy and Royal Finance', *War and Government in the Middle Ages. Essays in Honour of J. O. Prestwich*, ed. J. Gillingham and J. C. Holt (Woodbridge, 1984), pp. 92–105.

'1086' in *Domesday Studies*, ed. J. C. Holt (Woodbridge, 1987), pp. 41–64.

*Magna Carta*, 2nd edn (Cambridge, 1992).

'1153: the Treaty of Winchester', *The anarchy of King Stephen's Reign* (ed. King), pp. 291–316.

Hooper, N. 'Anglo-Saxon Warfare on the Eve of the Conquest: a Brief Survey', *Proceedings of the Battle Conference*, 1 (1978), 84–93.

'Some Observations on the Navy in Late Anglo-Saxon England', *Studies in Medieval History presented to R. Allen Brown*, ed. C. Harper-Bill, C. Holdsworth, and J. L. Nelson (Woodbridge, 1989), pp. 201–13.

Hoyt, R. S. *The Royal Demesne in English Constitutional History* (Cornell, 1950).

Hudson, J. *Land, Law and Lordship in Anglo-Norman England* (Oxford, 1994).

Hurnard, N. D. 'The Anglo-Norman Franchises', *English Historical Review*, 64 (1949), 289–327, 433–60.

*The King's Pardon for Homicide before AD 1307* (Oxford, 1969).

Hyams, P. R. *Kings, Lords, and Peasants in Medieval England* (Oxford, 1980).

'"No Register of Title": the Domesday Inquest and Land Adjudication', *Anglo-Norman Studies*, 9 (1986), 127–41.

'Feud in Medieval England', *Haskins Society Journal*, 3 (1991), 1–21.

Ivens, R. J. 'Deddington Castle, Oxfordshire, and the English Honour of Odo of Bayeux', *Oxoniensia*, 49 (1984), 101–19.

Jewell, H. M. *The North–South Divide. The Origins of Northern Consciousness in England* (Manchester, 1994).

Jolliffe, J. E. A. 'Northumbrian Institutions', *English Historical Review*, 41 (1926), 1–42.

Jones, G. R. J. 'Multiple Estates Perceived', *Journal of Historical Geography*, 11 (1953), 352–63.

'Multiple Estates and Early Settlement', *Medieval Settlement*, ed. P. H. Sawyer (London, 1976), pp. 11–40.

Jones, M. 'The Charters of Robert II de Ferrers, Earl of Nottingham, Derby and Ferrers', *Nottingham Medieval Studies*, 24 (1980), 7–26.

'Notes sur quelques familles bretonnes en Angleterre après la conquête normande', *Mémoires de la Société d'Histoire et d'Archéologie de Bretagne*, 58 (1981), 73–97.

Jope, E. M. and Threlfall, R. I. 'The Twelfth-Century Castle at Ascot Doilly, Oxfordshire: Its History and Excavation', *Archaeological Journal*, 39 (1959), 219–73.

Kantorowicz, E. *Studies in the Glossators of the Roman Law* (Cambridge, 1938).

Kapelle, W. E. *The Norman Conquest of the North* (London, 1979).

Kealey, E. J. *Roger of Salisbury* (Berkeley, Los Angeles, and London, 1972).

*Medieval Medicus. A Social History of Anglo-Norman Medicine* (Baltimore and London, 1981).

Keats-Rohan, K. S. B. 'The Devolution of the Honour of Wallingford, 1066–1148', *Oxoniensia*, 54 (1989), 311–18.

'The Bretons and Normans of England 1066–1154: the Family, the Fief and the Feudal Monarchy', *Nottingham Medieval Studies*, 36 (1992), 42–78.

'The Prosopography of Post-Conquest England: Four Case Studies', *Medieval Prosopography*, 14 (1993), 1–50.

'Antecessor Noster: the Parentage of Countess Lucy made Plain', *Prosopon*, Newsletter of the Unit for Prosopographical Research, Linacre College Oxford, no. 2 (May 1995, not paginated).

Keats-Rohan, K. S. B. and Thornton, D. E. 'COEL (the Continental Origins of English

Landholders) and the Computer: towards a Prosopographical Key to Anglo-Norman documents, 1066–1166', *Medieval Prosopography*, 17 (1996), 223–62.

Keefe, T. K. *Feudal Assessments and the Political Community under Henry II and his Sons* (Berkeley, 1983).

Keen, L. 'The Umfravilles, the Castle, and the Barony of Prudhoe, Northumberland', *Anglo-Norman Studies*, 5 (1982), 165–84.

Kemp, B. R. 'Monastic Possession of Parish Churches in England in the Twelfth Century', *Journal of Ecclesiastical History*, 31 (1980), 133–60.

Kent, J. P. C. 'South Mimms, Middlesex', *Medieval Archaeology*, 8 (1964), 255.

Kimball, Elizabeth G. 'Tenure in Frank Almoign and Secular Services', *English Historical Review*, 43 (1928), 341–53.

'The Judicial Aspects of Frank Almoign Tenure', *English Historical Review*, 47 (1932), 1–11.

King, D. J. Cathcart 'The Field Archaeology of Mottes in England and Wales: eine Kurze Übersicht', *Château Gaillard*, 5 (1970), 101–12.

*Castellarium Anglicanum*, 2 vols. (London, 1983).

*The Castle in England and Wales* (London, 1988).

King, D. J. Cathcart and Alcock, Leslie 'Ringworks of England and Wales', *Château Gaillard*, 3 (1966), 90–127.

King, E. 'King Stephen and the Anglo-Norman Aristocracy', *History*, 59 (1974), 180–94.

'The Origins of the Wake Family. The Early History of the Barony of Bourne in Lincolnshire', *Northamptonshire Past and Present*, 5 (1975), 167–73.

'The Parish of Warter and the Castle of Galchlin', *Yorkshire Archaeological Journal*, 52 (1980), 40–51.

'Mountsorrel and its Region in King Stephen's Reign', *Huntington Library Quarterly*, 64 (1980), 1–10.

'The Anarchy of King Stephen's Reign,' *Transactions of the Royal Historical Society*, 5th series, 34 (1984), 133–53.

'The Foundation of Pipewell Abbey', *Haskins Society Journal*, 2 (1990), 167–77.

'Dispute Settlement in Norman England', *Anglo-Norman Studies*, 14 (1992), 115–30.

(ed.) *The Anarchy of King Stephen's Reign* (Oxford, 1994).

Knowles, D. 'The Case of St William of York', *Cambridge Historical Journal*, 5 (1936), 162–77, reprinted in *The Historian and Character* (Cambridge, 1963).

*The Monastic Order in England*, 2nd edn (Cambridge, 1966).

Knowles, D., Brooke, C. N. L., and London, V. (eds.) *The Heads of Religious Houses England and Wales 940–1216* (Cambridge, 1972).

Lally, J. E. 'Secular Patronage at the Court of Henry II', *Bulletin of the Institute of Historical Research*, 49 (1976), 159–84.

Lancaster, L. 'Kinship in Anglo-Saxon Society', *British Journal of Sociology*, 9 (1958), 230–51, 359–77.

Latimer, P. 'Grants of "Totus Comitatus" in Twelfth-Century England: their Origins and Meaning', *Bulletin of the Institute of Historical Research*, 59 (1986), 137–45.

Lawson, M. K. 'The Collection of Danegeld and Heregeld in the reigns of Aethelred II and Cnut', *English Historical Review*, 94 (1984), 721–38.

'"Those Stories look true": Levels of Taxation in the Reigns of Aethelred II and Cnut', *English Historical Review*, 104 (1989), 385–406.

*Cnut. The Danes in England in the Early Eleventh Century* (London, 1993).

Leedom, J. W. 'William of Malmesbury and Robert of Gloucester Reconsidered', *Albion*, 6 (1974), 251–63.

Legge, M. D. 'L'influence littéraire de la cour d'Henri Beauclerc', *Mélanges offerts à Rita Lejeune* (Gembloux, 1969).

*Anglo-Norman Literature and Its Background* (Oxford, 1971).

'Anglo-Norman as a Spoken Language,' *Proceedings of the Battle Conference*, 2 (1980), 108–17.

L'Hermite-Leclercq, P. 'The Feudal Order', *A History of Women in the West. II. The Silences of the Middle Ages*, ed. C. Klapisch-Zuber (Cambridge, Mass., and London, 1992), pp. 202–49.

Le Maho, J. 'L'apparition des seigneuries châtelaines dans le Grand-Caux à l'époque ducale', *Archéologie Médiévale*, 6 (1976), 5–148.

'Note sur l'histoire d'un habitat seigneurial des XIe et XIIe siècles en Normandie: Mirville', *Anglo-Norman Studies*, 7 (1984), 214–23.

Lennard, R. L. *Rural England. 1086–1135* (Oxford, 1959).

Le Patourel, J. 'Geoffrey of Montbray, Bishop of Coutances, 1049–1093', *English Historical Review*, 59 (1944), 129–61.

*The Norman Empire* (Oxford, 1976).

Lewis, C. P. 'The Norman Settlement of Herefordshire under William I', *Anglo-Norman Studies*, 7 (1985), 195–213.

'The Earldom of Surrey and the Date of Domesday Book', *Historical Research*, 63 (1990), 329–36.

'The Early Earls of Norman England', *Anglo-Norman Studies*, 13 (1991), 207–23.

'The Formation of the Honor of Chester, 1066–1100', *The Earldom of Chester and Its Charters*, ed. A. T. Thacker, Journal of the Chester Archaeological Society, 71 (1991), pp. 37–68.

'The Domesday Jurors', *Haskins Society Journal*, 5 (1993), 17–29.

Leyser, H. *Hermits and the New Monasticism* (London, 1984).

Leyser, K. 'The German Aristocracy from the Ninth to the Early Twelfth Century', *Past and Present*, 41 (1968) reprinted in *Germany and Its Neighbours, 900–1250* (London, 1982), pp. 161–89.

'Maternal Kin in Early Medieval Germany. A Reply', *Past and Present*, 44 (1970), 126–34, reprinted in *Communications and Power in Medieval Europe* (London, 1994), pp. 181–8.

'The Anglo-Norman Succession 1120–1125', *Anglo-Norman Studies*, 13 (1990), 225–41.

Loengard, J. S. '"Of the Gift of her Husband": English Dower and its Consequences in the Year 1200', *Women of the Medieval World. Essays in Honor of John H. Mundy*, ed. J. Kirshner and S. F. Wemple (Oxford, 1985), pp. 215–55.

Louise, G. *La seigneurie de Bellême Xe–XIIe siècles*, Le Pays Bas-Normand, nos. 199 and 200 (1990).

Loyd, L. C. 'The Origins of the Family of Warenne', *Yorkshire Archaeological Journal*, 31 (1934), 97–113.

*The Origins of Some Anglo-Norman Families*, ed. C. T. Clay and D. C. Douglas, Harleian Society, CIII (Leeds, 1951).

Loyn, H. R. 'The Hundred in England in the Tenth and Early Eleventh Centuries', *British Government and Administration*, ed. H. Hearder and H. R. Loyn (Cardiff, 1974), pp. 1–15.

Maillefer, J.-M. 'Une famille aristocratique aux confins de la Normandie: les Géré au XIe siècle', *Autour de pouvoir ducal normand Xe–XIIe siècles*, Cahiers des Annales de Normandie, no. XVII (Caen, 1985), pp. 175–206.

Maitland, F. W. *Domesday Book and Beyond*, reissue (Cambridge, 1987).

Martindale, J. 'The French Aristocracy in the Early Middle Ages: a Reappraisal', *Past and Present*, 75 (1977), 5–45.

'Succession and Politics in the Romance-speaking World c. 1000–1140', *England and Her Neighbours 1066–1453. Essays in Honour of Pierre Chaplais*, ed. M. Jones and M. Vale (London, 1989), pp. 19–41.

'Monasteries and Castles: the Priories of Saint Florent de Saumur in England after 1066', *England in the Eleventh Century*, ed. C. Hicks (Stamford, 1992), pp. 135–56.

Mason, E. 'English Tithe Income of Norman Religious Houses', *Bulletin of the Institute of Historical Research*, 48 (1975), 91–4.

'Timeo Barones et Dona Ferentes', *Religious Motivation: Biological and Sociological Problems for the Church Historian*, Studies in Church History, 15 (1978), 61–75.

'Magnates, Curiales and the Wheel of Fortune: 1066–1154', *Proceedings of the Battle Conference on Anglo-Norman Studies*, 2 (1979), 118–40, 190–5.

'The King, the Chamberlain and Southwick Priory', *Bulletin of the Institute of Historical Research*, 53 (1980), 1–10.

'William Rufus and the Historians', *Medieval History*, 1, no. 1 (1991), 6–22.

Mason, J. F. A. 'The Date of the Geld Rolls', *English Historical Review*, 69 (1954), 283–6.

'The Companions of the Conqueror: an Additional Name', *English Historical Review*, 66 (1956), 61–9.

'The Officers and Clerks of the Norman Earls of Shropshire', *Transactions of the Shropshire Archaeological Society*, 57 (1957–60), 244–57.

'Roger of Montgomery and his Sons', *Transactions of the Royal Historical Society*, 5th series, 13 (1963), 1–28.

*William I and the Sussex Rapes*, Historical Association 1066 Commemoration Series, Hastings and Bexhill Branch (St Leonard's, 1966).

'Barons and their Officials in the Later Eleventh Century', *Anglo-Norman Studies*, 13 (1991), 243–62.

Matthew, D. J. A. *Norman Monasteries and their English Possessions* (Oxford, 1962).

Mayr-Harting, H. 'Functions of a Twelfth-Century Recluse', *History*, 60 (1975), 337–52.

Miller, E. and Hatcher, J. *Medieval England. Rural Society and Economic Change 1086–1348* (London, 1978).

Milsom, S. F. C. *The Legal Framework of English Feudalism* (Cambridge, 1976).

'Inheritance by Women in the Twelfth and Early Thirteenth Centuries', *On the Laws and Customs of England. Essays in Honour of S. E. Thorne*, ed. M. S. Arnold, T. A. Green, S. A. Scully, and S. D. White (Chapel Hill, 1981), pp. 60–89.

Mitchell, S. K. *Taxation in Medieval England* (New Haven, 1951).

Molin J.-B. and Mutembe, P. *Le rituel du mariage en France du XIIe au XVIe siècle* (Paris, 1973).

Mooers, S. L. 'Familial Clout and Financial Gain in Henry I's reign', *Albion*, 14 (1982), 267–92.

'Patronage in the Pipe Roll of 1130', *Speculum*, 59 (1984), 284–307.

Moore, J. S. 'The Anglo-Norman Family: Size and Structure', *Anglo-Norman Studies*, 14 (1992), 153–96.

Moriarty, G. A. 'The Balliols in Picardy, England and Scotland', *New England Historical and Genealogical Register*, 106 (1952), 273–90.

Morillo, S. *Warfare under the Anglo-Norman Kings 1066–1135* (Woodbridge, 1994).

Morris, W. A. *The Frankpledge System* (Cambridge, Mass., 1910).

*The Mediaeval English Sheriff to 1300* (Manchester, 1927).

Mortimer, R. 'The Beginnings of the Honour of Clare', *Anglo-Norman Studies*, 3 (1981), 119–41.

'Land and Service: the Tenants of the Honour of Clare', *Anglo-Norman Studies*, 8 (1985), 177–98.

'The Baynards of Baynard's Castle', *Studies in Medieval History presented to R. Allen Brown*, ed. C. Harper-Bill, C. Holdsworth, and J. L. Nelson (Woodbridge, 1989), pp. 241–53.

Musset, L. 'Actes inédits du XIe siècle. V. Autour des origines de Saint-Etienne de Fontenay', *Bulletin de la Société des Antiquaires de Normandie*, 56 (1961–2), 11–41.

'Les fiefs de deux familles vicomtales de l'Hiémois au XIe siècle, Les Goz et les Montgommery', *Revue Historique de droit français et étranger*, 48 (1970), 431–3.

*Les premiers temps de l'abbaye d'Almenêches-Argentan et Sainte-Opportune* (Paris, 1970).

'Aux origines d'une classe dirigeante: Les Tosnys, grands barons normands du Xe au XIIIe siècles', *Francia*, 5 (1977), 45–80.

Navel, H. 'L'enquête de 1133 sur les fiefs de l'évêché de Bayeux', *Bulletin de la Société des Antiquaires de Normandie*, 42 (1934), 5–80.

Newman, C. A. *The Anglo-Norman Nobility in the Reign of Henry I. The Second Generation* (Philadelphia, 1988).

Nicholas, D. *Medieval Flanders* (London, 1992).

Nicholl, A. J. *Archbishop Thurstan* (York, 1964).

O'Brien, B. R. 'From *Mordor* to *Murdrum*: the Pre-Conquest Origin and Norman Revival of the Murder Fine', *Speculum*, 71 (1996), 74–110.

Offler, H. S. 'William of St Calais, First Norman Bishop of Durham', *Transactions of the Architectural and Archaeological Society of Durham and Northumberland*, 10 (1950), 258–79.

'The Tractate De Iniusta Uexacione Willelmi Episcopi Primi', *English Historical Review*, 66 (1951), 321–41.

'Rannulf Flambard as Bishop of Durham (1099–1128)', *Durham University Journal*, 64 (1971), 14–25.

Owen, D. 'Bishop's Lynn: the First Century of a New Town', *Anglo-Norman Studies*, 2 (1979), 141–53.

'The Beginnings of the Port of Boston', *A Prospect of Lincolnshire*, ed. N. Field and A. White (Lincoln, 1984), pp. 42–5.

Padel, O. 'Geoffrey of Monmouth and Cornwall', *Cambridge Medieval Celtic Studies*, 8 (1984), 1–28.

Painter, S. 'English Castles in the Early Middle Ages: their Number, Location and Legal Position', *Speculum*, 10 (1935), 321–32, reprinted in *Feudalism and Liberty* (Baltimore, 1961), pp. 125–43.

*Studies in the History of the English Feudal Barony* (Baltimore, 1943).

'The Family and the Feudal System in Twelfth-Century England', *Speculum*, 35 (1960), 1–16 reprinted in *Feudalism and Liberty*, ed. F. A. Cazel (Baltimore, 1961), pp. 195–219.

Palliser, D. *Domesday York*, University of York Borthwick Paper no. 78 (1990).

'Domesday Book and the "Harrying of the North"', *Northern History*, 29 (1993), 1–23.

Palmer, J. J. N. 'The Domesday Manor', *Domesday Studies* (ed. Holt), pp. 139–53.

Parisse, M. *Noblesse et chevalerie en Lorraine médiévale* (Nancy, 1982).

Parker, M. S. 'The Province of Hatfield', *Northern History*, 28 (1992), 42–69.

Patterson, R. B. 'William of Malmesbury's Robert of Gloucester: a Re-Evaluation of the *Historia Novella*', *American Historical Review*, 70 (1965), 983–97.

'Robert Fitz Harding of Bristol: Profile of an Early Angevin Burgess-Baron

Patrician and his Family's Urban Involvement', *Haskins Society Journal*, 1 (1989), 109–22.

'The Ducal and Royal *Acta* of Henry FitzEmpress in Berkeley Castle', *Transactions of the Bristol and Gloucestershire Archaeological Society*, 109 (1991), 117–31.

Percival, J. 'The Precursors of Domesday Book', *Domesday Book: a Reassessment*, ed. P. H. Sawyer (London, 1985), pp. 5–27.

Philpott, M. 'The De Iniusta Uexacione Willelmi Episcopi Primi and Canon Law in Anglo-Norman Durham', *Anglo-Norman Durham*, ed. D. Rollason, M. Harvey, M. Prestwich (Woodbridge, 1994), pp. 125–37.

Pollock, F. and Maitland, F. W. *The History of English Law*, 2 vols. reissue (Cambridge, 1968).

Poly, J.-P. *La Provence et la société féodale (879–1166)* (Paris, 1976).

Poly, J.-P. and Bournazel, E. *La mutation féodale Xe–XIIe siècles*, translated by C. Higgitt as *The Feudal Transformation 900–1200* (New York and London, 1991).

Postles, D. 'Choosing Witnesses in Twelfth-Century England', *Irish Jurist*, new series, 23 (1988), 330–46.

Poulle, B. 'Savigny and England', *Normandy and England*, ed. D. Bates and A. Curry (London, 1994), pp. 159–68.

Prestwich, J. O. 'The Treason of Geoffrey de Mandeville', *English Historical Review*, 103 (1988), 283–312, 961–66.

'Last Words on Geoffrey de Mandeville', *English Historical Review*, 105 (1990), 670–1.

'The Career of Ranulf Flambard', in *Anglo-Norman Durham*, ed. D. Rollason, M. Harvey, M. Prestwich (Woodbridge, 1994), pp. 299–310.

'Military Intelligence under the Norman and Angevin Kings', *Law and Government in England and Normandy*, ed. G. Garnett and J. Hudson (Cambridge, 1994), pp. 1–30.

Reedy, W. T. 'The First Two Bassets of Weldon', *Northamptonshire Past and Present*, 4 (1966–72), 241–5, 295–8.

Reid, R. 'Barony and Thanage', *English Historical Review*, 35 (1920), 161–99.

Renn, D. *Norman Castles in Britain* (London, 1968).

Reuter, T. (ed.) *The Medieval Nobility: Studies on the Ruling Classes of France and Germany from the Sixth to the Twelfth Century* (Amsterdam, 1978).

Reynolds, S. 'Bookland, Folkland and Fiefs', *Anglo-Norman Studies*, 14 (1992), 211–27. *Fiefs and Vassals* (Oxford, 1994).

Roberts, B. K. 'Norman Village Plantations and Long Strip Fields in Northern England', *Geografiska Annaler*, 70 ser. B (1988), 169–77.

Roffe, D. 'The Origins of Derbyshire', *Derbyshire Archaeological Journal*, 106 (1986), 102–22.

'Domesday Book and Northern Society: a Reassessment', *English Historical Review*, 105 (1990), 310–36.

'From Thegnage to Barony: Sake and Soke, Title and Tenants-in-Chief', *Anglo-Norman Studies*, 12 (1990), 157–76.

'Hereward "the Wake" and the barony of Bourne: a Reassessment of a Fenland Legend', *Lincolnshire History and Archaeology*, 29 (1994), 7–10.

'The Making of Domesday Book Reconsidered', *Haskins Society Journal*, 6 (1994), 153–66.

Rollason, D. 'Symeon of Durham and the Community of Durham in the Eleventh Century', *England in the Eleventh Century*, ed. C. Hicks (Stamford, 1992), pp. 183–98.

Rosenwein, B. *To be the Neighbour of St Peter. The Social Meaning of Cluny's Property 909–1049* (Ithaca, NY, 1989).

Round, J. H. 'The Introduction of Knight Service into England', *English Historical Review*, 6 (1891), 417–23, 625–45; 7 (1892), 11–24, reprinted in *Feudal England*, reset edn (London, 1964), pp. 182–245.

*Geoffrey de Mandeville* (London, 1892).

'The Introduction of Armorial Bearings into England', *Archaeological Journal*, 51 (1894), 43–8.

'King Stephen and the Earl of Chester', *English Historical Review*, 10 (1895), 87–91.

*The Commune of London* (London, 1899).

'Odard the Sheriff', *Genealogist*, 5 (1899), 25–8.

'The Counts of Boulogne as English Lords', *Studies in Peerage and Family History* (London, 1901), pp. 147–80.

'Notes on the Sussex Domesday', *Sussex Archaeological Collections*, 44 (1901), 140–3.

'Castleguard', *Archaeological Journal*, 59 (1902), 144–59.

'Tregoz of Tolleshunt Tregoz', *Essex Archaeological Society Transactions*, New Series, 8 (1903), 330–2.

*Family Origins and Other Studies*, ed. W. Page (London, 1930).

Rowlands, I. W. 'The Making of the March: Aspects of the Norman Settlement in Dyfed', *Proceedings of the Battle Conference on Anglo-Norman Studies*, 3 (1980), 142–57, 221–5.

Ruud, M. 'Monks in the World: the Case of Gundulf of Rochester', *Anglo-Norman Studies*, 11 (1988), 245–60.

Sanders, I. J. *English Baronies* (Oxford, 1960).

Sauvage, R. N. *L'abbaye de Saint Martin de Troarn au diocèse de Bayeux des origines au seizième siècle*, Mémoires de la Société des Antiquaires de Normandie, 4th series, IV (1911).

Sawyer, P. H. '1066–1086: a Tenurial Revolution', *Domesday Book. A Reassessment*, ed. P. H. Sawyer (London, 1985), pp. 75–85.

Scammell, J. 'The Formation of the English Social Structure: Freedom, Knights, and Gentry, 1066–1300', *Speculum*, 68 (1993), 591–618.

Schmid, K. 'Zur Problematik von Familie, Sippe und Geschlecht, Haus und

Dynastie beim Mittelalterlichen Adel', *Zeitung für die Geschichte des Oberrheins*, 105 (1957), 1–62.

'The Structure of the Nobility in the Earlier Middle Ages', *The Medieval Nobility*, ed. T. Reuter (Amsterdam, 1978), pp. 39–49.

Scott, J. R. 'Charters of Monks Horton Priory', *Archaeologia Cantiana*, 10 (1876), 169–281.

Searle, E. 'Women and the Legitimisation of Succession at the Norman Conquest', *Proceedings of the Battle Conference on Anglo-Norman Studies*, 3 (1981), 159–70.

*Predatory Kinship and the Creation of Norman Power, 840–1066* (Berkeley, Los Angeles, and London, 1988).

Sheppard, J. 'Pre-enclosure Field and Settlement Patterns in an English Township', *Geografiska Annaler*, 48 ser. B (1966), 59–77.

'Metrological Analysis of Regular Village Plans in Yorkshire', *Agricultural History Review*, 22 (1974), 118–35.

Short, I. 'On Bilingualism in Anglo-Norman England', *Romance Philology*, 33 (1980), 467–79.

'Patrons and Polyglots: French Literature in Twelfth-Century England', *Anglo-Norman Studies*, 14 (1992), 229–49.

'Gaimar's Epilogue and Geoffrey of Monmouth's *Liber vetustissimus*', *Speculum*, 69 (1994), 323–43.

Simpson, G. 'The Familia of Roger de Quincy Earl of Winchester and Constable of Scotland', *Studies in the Nobility of Medieval Scotland*, ed. K. J. Stringer (Edinburgh, 1985), pp. 102–30.

Skinner, P. *Family Power in Southern Italy. The Duchy of Gaeta and its neighbours 850–1139*, Cambridge Studies in Medieval Life and Thought, 4th series, XXIX (1995).

Slade, C. F. *The Leicestershire Survey*, University of Leicester Department of English Local History Occasional Papers no. 7 (Welwyn, 1956).

Smith, J. 'Robert of Arbrissel: *Procurator Mulierum*', *Medieval Women*, ed. D. Baker, Studies in Church History, Subsidia I (1978), pp. 175–84.

Soulsby, I. N. 'Richard FitzTurold, lord of Penhallam, Cornwall', *Medieval Archaeology*, 20 (1976), 146–8.

Southern, R. W. 'Ranulf Flambard', *Transactions of the Royal Historical Society*, 4th series, 16 (1933), 95–128 reprinted in *Medieval Humanism and other studies* (Oxford, 1970), pp. 183–205.

'The Place of Henry I in English History', first published *Proceedings of the British Academy*, 47 (1962), 127–70, reprinted in *Medieval Humanism and Other Studies* (Oxford, 1970), 206–33.

'Aspects of the European Tradition of Historical Writing. IV. The Sense of the Past', *Transactions of the Royal Historical Society*, 5th series, 23 (1973), 243–63.

*Saint Anselm. A Portrait in a Landscape* (Cambridge, 1990).

Stafford, P. *The East Midlands in the Early Middle Ages* (Leicester, 1985).

'Women and the Norman Conquest', *Transactions of the Royal Historical Society*, 6th series, 4 (1994), 221–49.

Stenton, D. M. *The English Woman in History* (London and New York, 1957).

Stenton, F. M. *William the Conqueror and the Rule of the Normans* (London, 1908).

*The First Century of English Feudalism 1066–1166*, Ford Lectures 1929, 2nd edn (Oxford, 1961).

*Anglo-Saxon England*, 3rd edn (Oxford, 1971).

Stephenson, C. 'The Origin and Nature of the Taille', *Revue Belge de Philologie et d'Histoire*, 5 (1926), 801–70.

'The Seignorial Tallage in England', *Mélanges d'histoire offerts à Henri Pirenne par ses anciens élèves et ses amis*, 2 vols. (Brussels, 1926), II, 465–74.

Stone, L. and J. Fawtier Stone, *An Open Elite? England 1540–1680* (Oxford, 1984).

Strickland, M. 'Securing the North: Invasion and the Strategy of Defence in Twelfth-Century Anglo-Scottish Warfare', *Anglo-Norman Studies*, 12 (1989), 177–98.

Stringer, K. J. *Earl David of Huntingdon 1152–1219* (Edinburgh, 1985).

*The Reign of Stephen* (London, 1993).

Summerson, H. *Medieval Carlisle: the City and the Borders from the Late Eleventh to the Mid-Sixteenth Centuries*, 2 vols., Cumberland and Westmorland Antiquarian and Archaeological Society, Extra Series, XXV (1993).

Suppe, F. *Military Institutions on the Welsh Marches AD 1066–1300* (Woodbridge, 1994).

Tabuteau, E. Z. 'Definitions of Feudal Military Obligations in Eleventh-Century Normandy', *On the Laws and Customs of England. Essays in Honour of S. E. Thorne*, ed. M. S. Arnold, T. A. Green, S. A. Scully and S. D. White (Chapel Hill, 1981), pp. 18–59.

*Transfers of Property in Eleventh Century Norman Law* (Chapel Hill, London, 1988).

'The Role of Law in the Succession to Normandy and England, 1087', *Haskins Society Journal*, 3 (1991), 141–69.

Tanner, H. J. 'The Expansion of the Power and Influence of the Counts of Boulogne under Eustace II', *Anglo-Norman Studies*, 14 (1992), 251–86.

Taylor, B. H. 'The Excavation of a Motte at Abinger in Surrey', *Archaeological Journal*, 107 (1952), 15–43.

Tellenbach, G. *Königtum und Stämme in der Werdezeit des Deutschen Reiches* (Weimar, 1939).

'Vom karolingischen Reichsadel zum deutschen Reichsfürstenstand', *Adel und Bauern im deutschen Staat des Mittelalters*, ed. Theodor Mayer (Leipzig, 1943), translated in *The Medieval Nobility: Studies on the Ruling Classes of France and Germany from the Sixth to the Twelfth Century*, ed. T. Reuter (Amsterdam, 1978), pp. 39–49.

Tengvik, G. *Old English Bynames* (Uppsala, 1938).

Thomas, H. M. 'A Yorkshire Thegn and his Descendants after the Conquest', *Medieval Prosopography*, 8 (1987), 1–22.

*Vassals, Heiresses, Crusaders, and Thugs: Yorkshire 1154–1216* (Philadelphia, 1993).

Thompson, B. 'From Alms to Spiritual Services: The Function and Status of Monastic Property in Medieval England', *Monastic Studies*, ed. J. Loades, II (Bangor, 1991), 227–62.

'Free Alms Tenure in the Twelfth Century', *Anglo-Norman Studies*, 16 (1993), 221–43.

Thompson, K. 'Family and Influence to the South of Normandy in the Eleventh Century: the Lordship of Bellême', *Journal of Medieval History*, 11 (1985), 215–26.

'Monasteries and Settlement in Norman Lancashire: Unpublished Charters of Roger the Poitevin', *Transactions of the Historic Society of Lancashire and Cheshire*, 140 (1990), 201–25.

Thompson, S. *Women Religious* (Oxford, 1991).

Tsurushima, H. 'The Fraternity of Rochester Cathedral Priory about 1100', *Anglo-Norman Studies*, 14 (1992), 313–37.

Tyerman, C. *England and the Crusades* (Chicago and London, 1988).

Van Houts, E. M. C. 'The Ship List of William the Conqueror', *Anglo-Norman Studies*, 10 (1987), 159–83.

'Robert of Torigni as Genealogist', *Studies in Medieval History presented to R. Allen Brown*, ed. C. Harper-Bill, C. Holdsworth, and J. L. Nelson (Woodbridge, 1989), pp. 215–33.

'Wace as Historian and Genealogist', *Family Trees and the Roots of Politics. The Prosopography of Britain and France from the Tenth to the Twelfth Century*, ed. K. S. B. Keats-Rohan (Woodbridge, forthcoming).

Vaughn, S. *Anselm of Bec and Robert of Meulan. The Innocence of the Dove and the Wisdom of the Serpent* (Berkeley, Los Angeles, and London, 1987).

'St Anselm and Women', *Haskins Society Journal*, 2 (1990), 83–93.

Vercauteren, F. 'Une parenté dans la France du nord aux Xe et XIIe siècles, *Le Moyen Age*, 69 (1963), 223–45.

Walker, D. 'The "Honours" of the Earls of Hereford in the Twelfth Century', *Transactions of the Bristol and Gloucestershire Archaeological Society*, 69 (1960), 174–211.

Ward, J. 'Fashions in Monastic Endowment: the Foundations of the Clare Family, 1066–1314', *Journal of Ecclesiastical History*, 32 (1981), 428–37.

Wardrop, J. *Fountains Abbey and its Benefactors 1132–1300* (Kalamazoo, Michigan, 1987).

Wareham, A. 'The Motives and Politics of the Bigod Family, c. 1066–1177', *Anglo-Norman Studies*, 17 (1994), 223–42.

Warlop, E. *The Flemish Nobility before 1300*, 4 vols. (Kortrijk, 1975–6).

Warren, W. L. 'The Myth of Norman Administrative Efficiency', *Transactions of the Royal Historical Society*, 5th series, 34 (1984), 113–32.

*The Governance of Norman and Angevin England* (London, 1987).

Waugh, S. *The Lordship of England. Royal Wardships and Marriages in English Society and Politics 1217–1327* (Princeton, NJ, and London, 1988).

Welby, A. C. E. 'Bytham Castle and Coleville Family', *Lincolnshire Notes and Queries*, 15 (1919), 18–26.

Werner, K. F. 'Bedeutende Adelsfamilien im Reich Karls des Grossen', *Karl der Grosse: Lebenswerk und Nachleben*, ed. H. Beumann, 4 vols. (Düsseldorf, 1965), I, 83–142.

White, G. 'King Stephen, Duke Henry and Ranulf de Gernons Earl of Chester', *English Historical Review*, 91 (1976), 555–65.

'Were the Midlands "Wasted" during Stephen's Reign?', *Midland History*, 10 (1985), 26–46.

'The End of Stephen's Reign,' *History*, 75 (1990), 3–22.

'Continuity in Government' in *The Anarchy of Stephen's Reign*, ed. E. King (Oxford, 1994), pp. 117–43.

White, G. H. 'The Sisters and Nieces of Gunnor, Duchess of Normandy', *Genealogist*, 37 (1921), 57–65, 128–32.

'Constables under the Norman Kings', *Genealogist*, new series, 38 (1922), 113–27.

White, S. D. *Custom, Kinship, and Gifts to Saints: the Laudatio Parentum in Western France, 1050–1150* (Chapel Hill, 1988).

Whitney, K. P. *The Jutish Forest* (London, 1976).

Wightman, W. E. 'The Palatine Earldom of William FitzOsbern in Gloucestershire and Worcestershire (1066–1071)', *English Historical Review*, 77 (1962), 6–17.

*The Lacy Family in England and Normandy 1066–1194* (Oxford, 1966).

'The Significance of "Waste" in the Yorkshire Domesday', *Northern History*, 10 (1975), 55–71.

Williams, A. 'The King's Nephew: the Family, Career and Connections of Ralph, earl of Hereford', *Studies in Medieval History presented to R. Allen Brown*, ed. C. Harper-Bill, C. Holdsworth, and J. L. Nelson (Woodbridge, 1989), pp. 327–43.

'A Vice-Comital Family in Pre-Conquest Warwickshire', *Anglo-Norman Studies*, 11 (1989), 279–95.

'A Bell-house and a Burh-geat: Lordly Residences in England before the Norman Conquest', *Medieval Knighthood*, IV, ed. C. Harper-Bill and R. Harvey (Woodbridge, 1992), pp. 221–40.

*The English and the Norman Conquest* (Woodbridge, 1995).

Williamson, T. *The Origins of Norfolk* (Manchester, 1993).

Wilson, D. *Moated Sites* (Aylesbury, 1985).

Wilson, R. M. 'English and French in England, 1100–1300', *History*, 28 (1943), 37–60.

Winchester, A. J. L. *Landscape and Society in Medieval Cumbria* (Edinburgh, 1987).

Wood, M. *The Medieval English House* (London, 1965).

Wood, S. *English Monasteries and their Patrons in the Thirteenth Century* (Oxford, 1955).

Wormald, P. 'Domesday Lawsuits: a Provisional List and Preliminary Comment', *England in the Eleventh Century: Proceedings of the 1990 Harlaxton Symposium*, ed. C. Hicks (Stamford, 1992), pp. 61–102.

'Lordship and Justice in the early English Kingdom: Oswaldslow revisited', *Property and Power in the Early Middle Ages*, ed. W. Davies and P. Fouracre (Cambridge, 1995), pp. 114–36.

'Oswaldslow: an "Immunity"?', *St Oswald of Worcester. Life and Influence*, ed. N. Brooks and C. Cubitt (Leicester, 1996), pp. 116–28.

Yoshitake, K. 'The Arrest of the Bishops in 1139 and its Consequences', *Journal of Medieval History*, 14 (1988), 97–114.

Young, A. *William Cumin: Border Politics and the Bishopric of Durham 1141–1144*, University of York, Borthwick Paper no. 54 (1979).

Yver, J. 'Les caractères originaux de la coutume de Normandie', *Mémoires de l'Académie des Sciences, Arts, et Belles-Lettres de Caen*, new series, 12 (1952), 307–36.

Zadora-Rio, E. 'L'enceinte fortifiée du Plessis-Grimoult, résidence seigneuriale de XIe siècle', *Château Gaillard*, 5 (1970), 227–39.

# Index